MW01093174

YOUR ESTATE MATTERS

Gifts, Estates, Wills, Trusts, Taxes and Other Estate Planning Issues

PATTI S. SPENCER, ESQ.

AuthorHouse™
1663 Liberty Drive
Bloomington, IN 47403
www.authorhouse.com
Phone: 1-800-839-8640

Published by AuthorHouse 01/08/2015

ISBN: 978-1-4969-3529-8 (sc)

Library of Congress Control Number: 2014921716

CONTENTS

ABOUT THIS EDITION

This book came into being because I wrote a weekly column for Lancaster's New Era/Intelligencer Journal called "Taxing Matters." The column appeared every week from October 1999 through December 2013.

You can still read the column every Monday by signing up for the e-mail edition at www.spencerlawfirm.com. Enter your e-mail address under "Sign up for our Newsletter" on the right hand side of the home page.

This is the second edition of "Your Estate Matters" because taxes and state law, like the weather, change by the minute. Or at least by the day. We estate planners feel like we have been through the mill. Congress' legislation, and failure to legislate, has left us not knowing what to recommend to clients. There was no estate tax at all in 2010, although this was at the cost of no step-up in basis. Later that year, Congress changed the rules again and said you could elect to be subject to estate tax if you wanted to. Now we have the estate tax back with a $5.34 million exemption in 2014. What's next?

ACKNOWLEDGMENTS

Writing a column every week for 14 years is no mean feat. I could not have done it without the help and support of many people. Over those years, my co-workers from time to time, Adam Clark, Yvonne Crouse, Deb Williard, Miriam McLeod, Kathryn Wanner, Fen Alankus, Lisa Hubbell, Nicole Peters, Doug Smith, Brielle Valle, and others have helped to edit the column every week and make sure it meets deadline (and have been known to write a column or two or three, like when I had pneumonia.). My husband, Don Feldman, in addition to being my better half, is also a CPA and one of my best critics. My kids, Samantha and Benjamin, put up with their eccentric mother and all the people who stop us and interrupt their outings with comments about the column.

I take full responsibility for all the errors. See if you can find them.

DISCLAIMER

Given the unpredictability of the actions of the U.S. Congress, no representation can be made about the accuracy of any information presented in this book. You can fully expect the law to change, and change often. The information contained in these materials is based upon sources believed to be accurate and reliable. Reasonable care has been exercised to assure the accuracy of the information. However, no representation or warranty is made as to such accuracy. Readers and their advisors should check primary sources where appropriate and use the traditional legal research techniques to make sure that the information has not been affected or changed by recent developments. Get professional advice. Estate Planning, Trust and Estate Administration, and Income Tax are not areas where a do-it-yourself approach will work.

INTRODUCTION

The ancient Egyptians built elaborate fortresses and tunnels and even posted guards at tombs to stop grave robbers. In today's America, we call that estate planning.

Bill Archer, Chairman of the House Ways and Means Committee

Kick the bucket, meet my maker, get hit by a truck, push up daisies, pass on – all the ways we avoid saying "it."

When meeting with new clients I never say "it" until they do and I see what euphemism they use. Then we refer to "it" by that phrase for the rest of the meeting. Most people don't respond well if asked bluntly "who will inherit your property when you *die*." So we resort to who will receive your property when you are "called home."

After getting over the suggestion of mortality, my next job is debunking myths. Thanks to the living trusts mills, many people think probate is worse than death. Probate is not worse than death, a revocable living trust is not a panacea. Find out what probate is. Read this book and find out why it is that settling an estate takes so long and how much it costs.

What happens if you die without a will? No, your property doesn't go to the state. State law, however, does have a will for you in the form of the intestacy statute. Do you know who gets your property? If your spouse dies without a will, do you get everything he or she had? Probably not. Now that's a reason to have a will, or at least for your spouse to have one.

How can you avoid paying inheritance and estate taxes? You can't. But read on for ways to reduce them. Many techniques are available, but all of these techniques run up against the eternal truth of estate planning: you can't keep control of all of your assets and also pay no death taxes. All techniques to reduce death taxes involve some loss of control, and in some cases, complete loss of control. You can't both own the property and not pay death tax on it. That's a corollary of "you can't take it with you." The estate planner's art is in designing a plan where the client keeps as much control and benefit for his or her purposes as possible while also reducing the tax burden.

Children and grandchildren feel entitled to inherit an ancestor's property. When their rich, bachelor Uncle Scrooge dies, Huey, Dewey and Louie assume they are next to own the millions. When Uncle Scrooge's will leaves all of his money to his former housekeeper, the nephews are outraged and talk of "breaking" the will. That is an emotional statement, nothing more. There is no "right" of inheritance. The nephews can be passed over completely with a validly executed will. This is a tough concept for many to grasp. When Dad dies some kids are ready to clear out the house and empty the bank accounts before the funeral, but they have no legal right to any of their Father's property if he has willed it to someone else – like his girl-friend whom you hate and to whom you give the ice treatment. Do you think she'll give some of it to you? Nahhhhh.

You think prenuptial agreements are unromantic? Every marriage is a contract. It's just a question of whether or not you accept the one-size-fits-all contract that the state legislature has written for you or whether you make your own contract. The state legislature has a marriage contract for you that tells you what are your rights of inheritance, your rights on divorce, and your rights to support. Do you know what your legal rights as a married person are? Why is it unromantic to state your own wishes instead of accepting the state legislature's standard marriage form?

Lots of people threaten to contest wills. In fact, it is difficult to overturn a will unless it can be shown that the person making the will lacked capacity or was under the undue influence of someone. Wills are not easily "broken." That doesn't mean that the process can't be delayed, drawn out, and made expensive. Litigation only enriches lawyers. Read on to learn what is required for a valid will and under what circumstances a will may not be valid.

Taxes, taxes, taxes. Estate taxes, inheritance taxes, income taxes, excise taxes. When you die (excuse me, when you "pass on") the tax man is there with his hand out. Reducing the impact of taxes is big part of estate planning. As Justice Learned Hand of the U.S. Supreme Court put it, "[t]here are two systems of taxation in our country: one for the informed, and one for he uninformed." Make sure you are one of the informed.

Your Estate Matters covers these areas and more. None of us know how many days we are given. Take care of your estate now.

DURING LIFE

WILLS

Of Sound and Disposing Mind and Memory

Any person 18 or more years of age who is of sound mind may make a will.
Pennsylvania Probate,
Estates and Fiduciaries Code §2501

What is a sound mind? Would that I knew.

In Pennsylvania, a person is considered to have testamentary capacity, that is, having the soundness of mind required to make a will, if he "appreciates, in a general way knows who his relations are and what property he possesses, and indicates an intelligent understanding of the disposition he desires to make of it." *In re Olshefski's Estate* 337 Pa. 420 (1940). An executed will is presumed to be signed by a person with capacity. The burden of proving incapacity is on the contestant of the will.

It is the best practice for the attorney who draws a will to meet in person with the testator, privately, and also for the attorney to supervise the signing of the will. The attorney who prepares a will for someone he or she's never met, at the request of a beneficiary of the will, and does not supervise the signing of the will, is serving the beneficiary, not the testator.

An attorney should meet with the person wanting to make a will so that the attorney has a chance to formulate an opinion about the capacity of her client and whether or not the client is under undue influence. The attorney should also supervise the execution of the will so that the opinion about capacity can be revisited based on the client's capacity at that time. If a contest is suspected, the attorney should have the witnesses and notary take notes of conversation at the signing.

Old age and its various infirmities do not give rise to incapacity. A person can have memory lapses, be unable to recognize acquaintances, and have trouble speaking and still have testamentary capacity. Rambling or repetitive speech may not signal incapacity. The person making the will can be blind, with impaired hearing, or paralyzed. None of these things constitute lack of testamentary capacity. The statute of wills makes express provision for signing a will by a mark, and if even a mark cannot be made, for another person to sign the will for the testator at the testator's direction.

Even a person who has been adjudicated an incompetent could execute a valid will during a lucid period. Elderly persons with senile dementia or Alzheimer's disease may have testamentary capacity, or may have testamentary capacity during a lucid interval. There are many factors to consider and the testator lacks capacity to make a will only when there is a profound general mental incapacity.

The testimony of the testator's physician may or may not be useful. The testimony of the physician will not overcome positive statements of witnesses who were present when the will was executed. Also, sometimes a physician's opinion of mental capacity is formed without regard to the legal definition of what level of mental acuity is required to constitute testamentary capacity.

In addition to lack of capacity, undue influence is another ground on which a will can be contested. Undue influence involves acts by a person attempting to influence a will which does not represent the testator's true wishes. Undue influence sufficient to void a will must be "imprisonment of the body or mind, fraud, or threats or misrepresentations or circumvention, or inordinate flattery or physical or moral coercion, to such a degree as to prejudice the mind of the testator, to destroy his free agency and to operate as a present restraint upon him in the making of the will" *Koons' Estate*, 293 Pa. 465 (1928). If the client seems to say, "I don't want to do this, but I must," undue influence might be involved.

Family members and social contacts naturally influence a person. We all try to persuade each other to do all sorts of things. This is not undue influence. Care and attention do not constitute undue influence. If the testator is in a weakened physical or weakened mental condition, he may be more susceptible to influence but the weakened state itself is not enough to show undue influence.

This is an oft repeated tale. An elderly testator makes a will favoring a caregiver or friend instead of blood relations. Even blood relations who have not seen or communicated with a deceased for decades feel a strong sense of entitlement to the decedent's property and will be quick to cry that the caregiver or friend unduly influenced the testator. Sometimes, this is the case, of course. Other times, it is a perfectly natural disposition of the testator's property.

What is this claim of blood? Surely property is an individual right. What is yours is not owned collectively by all your blood kin. But when you die, your blood relations feel an overwhelming sense of entitlement. The daughter who has not spoken to her mother in years stands ready to clear out the house after the funeral (or before). It is ever so.

Wholly reprehensible is the practice of contesting a will in hopes of getting a settlement! It is easy to contest a will, that is, to start the wheels of a contest in motion and bring the distribution of an estate to a halt. Unfortunately, due to the nature of litigation in the United States today, a will contest suit, even if completely unsuccessful, can delay the settlement and distribution of an estate for years. Knowing this, a challenger can "put a stick in the spokes" in the hope of getting a nice settlement just for withdrawing the contest action. "Give me some money and I will go away." This repugnant practice can be combated only with actions against the contestant for abuse of the legal system.

Don't Let Your Heir Down: Draw Up a Will or You May End Up "Intestate"

What happens to your property when you die if you don't have a will? Some folks think that if they don't have a will "it all goes to the state." Not so. Some folks say "it all goes to pay taxes." Not so.

What does happen? When a person dies without a will, we say that he or she is "intestate." The property is then distributed in accordance with Pennsylvania's intestacy statute. The Pennsylvania intestacy statute for a decedent domiciled in Pennsylvania determines how all his or her personal property — that includes bank accounts, securities, and tangible property — gets distributed. Real estate passes according to the intestacy laws of the state in which it is located.

The short answer is that the decedent's family will inherit. Whether that means immediate family or extended family depends on who is still living.

The statute first makes provision for a surviving spouse, if there is one. A divorced former spouse is not a "surviving spouse." The portion of the estate the surviving spouse receives depends on whether or not the decedent leaves living issue or living parents.

If the decedent leaves no living issue (issue are children, grandchildren, etc.) and also no living parent, then the surviving spouse receives the whole estate.

If the decedent leaves no living issue, but leaves a living parent or parents, then the spouse gets the first $30,000 plus one-half of the balance of the estate. The parents receive the balance.

If the decedent leaves living issue all of whom are also issue of the surviving spouse (in other words, the surviving spouse is the mother or father by birth or adoption of all of the decedent's children), then the surviving spouse gets $30,000 plus one-half of the balance of the estate.

If there are surviving issue of the decedent, one or more of whom are not issue of the surviving spouse, then the surviving spouse receives one-half of the estate.

After determining the share of the surviving spouse, the statute determines the heirs of the decedent. The heirs are, in order, issue (descendants of all generations), parents, brothers and sisters or their issue, grandparents, uncles, aunts and their children or grandchildren, and finally the Commonwealth of Pennsylvania.

Shares of an estate pass to living issue of the decedent according to the generation level of the issue. Different generations are referred to as different degrees. When shares pass to issue of different degrees, for example to two children and three grandchildren who are the children of a deceased child, you go to the first degree closest to the decedent where there is issue living and divided into equal shares at that level. In our example, that would be a one-third share for each of the two living children and the remaining one-third share to be divided equally among the three grandchildren whose parent was the deceased child; each grandchild taking one-ninth.

Persons of the same degree receive equally. For example, if the heirs are brothers and sisters of the decedent, each receives an equal share. Brothers and sisters of the decedent receive equally whether or not they are half-brothers or half-sisters or whole brothers or sisters. If they share the decedent as a parent, they receive an equal share.

For children born to unmarried parents, the child is always an heir of the mother. The child is an heir of the father only if (1) the parents subsequently married, (2) the father openly holds out the child to be his and receives the child into his home, (3) the father openly holds out the child to be his and provides support for the child, or (4) there is clear and convincing evidence that the man was the father of the child, which may include a prior court determination of paternity.

Adopted persons are treated the same as natural children of the adopting parents. An adopted child is not an heir of her natural parents. However, if natural kin other than the birth parents maintained a family relationship with the adopted person, then the adopted person will be considered a child of his natural parents for purposes of the distribution of the natural kin's intestate estate. For example, if the natural grandparents of the adopted child maintain a family relationship with the grandchild, even though the grandchild was adopted by another family, that adopted child could be an heir of the natural grandparents, but not of the birth parents.

The intestacy statute of Pennsylvania is designed to locate heirs and to distribute the estate of an intestate decedent as the Commonwealth believes is equitable. The statute requires that the decedent's grandparents and their issue be considered before determining that the estate reverts to the Commonwealth. Only in unusual circumstances does "it all go to the State."

The State of Your Will: Where You Live Does Make a Difference

You've just moved to Pennsylvania. Or maybe you're planning to retire in the Sun Belt. Do you have to change your will? It depends.

Often your will is fine in the new jurisdiction. But sometimes it isn't. Often it's valid, but the results might be different than you intended. Only your lawyer knows for sure.

The common law rule is that a will is valid if it is valid in the jurisdiction where it was executed or if it is valid in the jurisdiction where it is offered for probate.

Usually the jurisdiction for probate is the state in which you are domiciled. Domicile is a legal term which means that place to which you always intend to return — what the law considers your "home." But since the rule is that a will is valid anywhere if it is valid in the jurisdiction in which it is executed, then if you have a valid will when you sign, as a general rule, it is valid anywhere in the U.S. But you might be surprised by the way it is interpreted in the state where it is offered for probate.

The difficulty springs from the federal system we enjoy here in the United States, causing a whole field of legal study called conflicts of laws. Each state has its own laws which govern property located within that state. The question of which state's law governs can be extremely complex. Just imagine this: a will signed in New York, but probated in Pennsylvania, which includes real estate located in Alaska, Arizona, and Florida, beneficiaries in various states, and with many jurisdictions trying to tax the estate, not to mention the federal government. Because of these complexities, it is very important to have your estate plan reviewed when you move to another state. Maybe it will require revisions; maybe not.

For example, states differ in how much of the estate the surviving spouse is entitled to. A will that gives the spouse one-third may be valid and enforceable in the state where it is signed. When this will is probated in another state, the spouse may be able to elect against the will and take a bigger share.

Similarly some states provide that children cannot be disinherited unless the will specifically states that they are to be omitted. Pennsylvania is not like that. If a will leaves everything to the surviving spouse, this disposition will be carried out in a Pennsylvania probate even if no mention is made of the children. However, if the same will is offered for probate in Massachusetts, the children have a right to get a share of the estate. That is why Massachusetts wills say something like, "I specifically make no provision for my issue in the event my spouse survives me."

Perhaps most importantly, those who are considered to be your children and issue can vary from state to state. How are adopted children treated? How are children born of unwed parents treated? How are stepchildren treated?

In some states divorce revokes a will in its entirety. In others, only the provisions for the divorced spouse are revoked. The standards for enforcing prenuptial and postnuptial agreements vary from state to state.

In some states marriage revokes a will. In others, the will remains in effect and the new spouse may be given some rights to receive a share.

The interpretation of a bequest when a beneficiary dies before the testator also varies from state to state. In some states the beneficiary's children receive the bequest. In some states, it goes to the residuary beneficiaries.

Tax apportionment is another big area of divergence. Do the residuary beneficiaries have to pay all the estate and inheritance taxes, or do all sharers bear a pro rata portion of the taxes?

In the United States, all fifty states require at least two witnesses for a will. Vermont requires three, but Vermont also specifically allows a will that is valid where it is signed, so a will signed in another state with two witnesses is acceptable. Some practitioners use three witnesses just to be on the safe side, but this isn't necessary.

Louisiana is an exception (it almost always is). The other 49 states model their state laws on English common law. Louisiana is the only state whose laws follow the "civil law" modeled from the French and the Napoleonic Code. As Thomas Atkinson, the great scholar of the law of wills puts it: "Attorneys unskilled in the civil law should not attempt to execute wills for use in Louisiana or other civil law jurisdictions." If you move to Louisiana, there is no question. Go to a lawyer and make a new will.

When you move to a different state or when you acquire real estate in a different state, this is a good time to have your plan reviewed. A trust and estate lawyer in the new jurisdiction would review your documents and your financial situation to determine if your plan is still appropriate and whether or not you should have new documents. This lawyer also would advise you on how the will would be interpreted in the new jurisdiction and determine whether this is consistent with your wishes.

Naming a Guardian to Care for Your Children

Do you have minor children? Who will take care of the children if you die? This is the number one reason for you to make a will. You do everything you can to be a good parent. Make sure you make a will and have plans for your children's care if you are no longer around to do it.

Pennsylvania permits a parent to appoint a guardian of his or her minor children in a will. The appointment must be made in a valid will. A letter or memorandum written by a parent requesting the appointment of a guardian in the event of his or her death is not binding. If there is no will and the parents are deceased, the court will select and appoint a guardian.

A guardian is a sort of substitute parent. For so long as the ward (the minor child is called a ward of the guardian) is under the age of majority, age 18, the guardian has the same rights and duties as a parent. As parents, you and your spouse are the so-called "natural guardians" of your minor children. Natural guardianship is a personal right to the custody of a child until the child reaches the age of majority. Where the parents are unmarried, the mother is considered the "natural guardian."

There are really two offices and responsibilities: (1) Guardian of the person, which is physical custody of the minor, and (2) Guardian of the minor's estate, which is the care and management of the minor's property. It is not necessary that the same person hold both offices. You can split the responsibilities.

When you name guardians for your children in your will, it is customary, but not legally required, that you ask the guardians if they would be willing to serve. You should also name successors in case when the time comes, your first choice guardians are also deceased, or are ill, or have other life situations which will make it impossible for them to raise your children. If you choose a couple, a husband and wife, to be the substitute parents for your children, you should address the possible divorce of the couple. Should one of them be the sole guardian in that case?

Another option is to provide a mechanism in the will for the selection of a guardian. For example, instead of naming the proposed guardian, you may provide for a committee who will be charged with selecting your children's guardian. Perhaps, you might say that a group consisting of your parents, your spouse's parents, and your siblings and your spouse's siblings would decide, by majority vote, who will be chosen as a guardian.

Since the age of majority is 18, many parents who make wills name a guardian of the person for minor children, but direct their property to be held by a trustee. By doing this they can instruct the trustee exactly what to do with the money, for what purposes it should be made available to the child, and at what age it should ultimately be distributed. For example, the trustee may be directed to use the income and principal for the child's health, education and support, as the trustee deems appropriate, and distribute the principal of the trust in thirds at ages 21, 25 and 30. Again, sometimes it is appropriate to have the same person who is guardian of the person of the minor as trustee, and sometimes it is not.

If the trustee is someone other than the person who has physical custody of your children, make sure that the guardian with physical custody is paid appropriately, and is compensated if, for example, he or she has to stop working to take care of your kids. Also consider — will the home be big enough to accommodate their kids and yours? Will they have to move? Should your will provide for that expense? Nothing is simple.

If you are divorced with minor children, and you die, custody of your children automatically passes to the other parent as natural guardian, unless proven unfit. A natural guardian, however, does not have any authority to exercise control over the minor child's property, except in limited circumstances where the court has approved an award to the parent. In fact, Pennsylvania law provides that the court shall NOT appoint as guardian of the estate of a minor the parent of the minor, except that a parent can be appointed as a co-guardian with another co-guardian.

Actually, Pennsylvania law permits anyone who gives property to a minor in his will to name a guardian of that property. For example, if grandparents leave their estate to a minor grandchild, the grandparents in their will may name a guardian to manage such funds for the benefit of the minor grandchild even if the parents are living and even if the parents do not agree with the choice.

State law, by the way, also provides that no parent, who for one year or more prior to his death, shall have willfully neglected or refused to provide for his or her child, or who, for one year or more prior to death have deserted the child or willfully failed to perform parental duties has the right to appoint a guardian for such child in his will.

There's Nothing Simple About Writing a Simple Will

> *For every human problem, there is a neat, simple solution and it is always wrong.*
>
> H. L. Mencken

"I want a simple will." Estate planning attorneys often hear this from clients. What do they mean? Simple to them means short and inexpensive.

Short is not always better. If you need open heart surgery do you tell the surgeon you want a short operation? If your car's brakes must be replaced do you tell the mechanic you want him to do the job in 10 minutes? Of course, no one wants surplus verbiage and unnecessary repetition. But short can mean incomplete — leaving unanswered questions creating problems of construction and interpretation — or short can mean that all contingencies are not covered.

As to the cost, of course, no one wants to pay an excessive price for the value received on any purchase. If you're buying a car seat for your new baby, do you ask for the cheapest one? If you need a root canal, do you look for the cheapest dentist?

As Abraham Lincoln said, "a lawyer's time and advice are his only stock in trade." Your documents must be drafted correctly for your wishes to be fulfilled at your death. Any lawyer worth his or her salt will need time to get to know you, your financial situation, and your family picture.

Contrary to popular belief, a lawyer can't just "press a button" and a will comes out of the word processor. Very, very seldom do I see a client who does not need some customized provisions in his or her estate plan.

What leads to these customizations? Do you have minor children? Whom are you going to name as guardian to have physical custody of your children? Will you name a successor guardian? Will the same person control the child's money or will there be a separate trustee. What are appropriate expenditures? Can the trustee pay for college? Buy a car for the child? At what age should the child be given control of his or her own inheritance? Does the person you name as guardian get paid? What if he or she has to quit work or enlarge the house to take care of your kids?

Here are some more questions that you may need to address in your will. Who are your children? Does the word "children" include stepchildren? If it's a second marriage, are your children treated the same as your wife's children? Are the children you have with your first wife treated equally with the children you have with your second wife? Does your second wife agree? Working out how to treat children who are yours, mine, and ours can be complicated.

What about grandchildren? Are adopted grandchildren treated the same as natural grandchildren? Are your son's wife's children treated as your grandchildren? Is your son's out-of-wedlock daughter treated as a grandchild in your will, even if you've never seen her? If a child predeceases you, do your grandchildren take that child's share? Or does it go to his or her spouse?

Does your spouse or a child have a disability? Do any of your children have bad marriage or creditor problems? Does a child or grandchild have an addiction? Does anyone participate in a government entitlement program?

Should you create a trust for your surviving spouse? Do you have a prenuptial agreement? Should you make a postnuptial agreement? Do you want to protect assets for your children in the event of your spouse's remarriage after your death?

Have you loaned money to one of your kids? Does the loan get forgiven when you die or is it subtracted from his or her share of your estate?

In addition to drafting documents that address your personal situations and wishes, the work involved in will preparation also includes review and possible revision of beneficiary designations and asset ownership. Different sorts of problems are created by different sorts of assets. Keep in mind that the purpose of the will is to dispose of your assets according to your wishes, at the time of your death. But not all your assets are governed by the terms of your will.

Wills, for instance, do not govern the disposition of assets that are paid according to beneficiary designations like 401(k) plans, life insurance, and IRAs. However, these beneficiary designations have many complex income tax considerations. Your beneficiary designations must be coordinated with your will or estate plan. This is a very complex matter and may require as much time and effort as preparation of a will.

Bank accounts or brokerage accounts in joint names or in transfer on death registration are another example. These need coordination with the will to prevent equalization challenges. What does it mean when the client says “my daughter’s name is on the account?” Is it a joint account? Does the daughter hold a power of attorney?

And, finally, of course, time is required to make sure the will is properly executed, witnessed, and self-proving affidavits notarized.

All of these questions and more arise even before any estate tax issues present themselves. Life is complicated, but with competent legal advice you can accomplish your goals. You don’t want a simple will; you want one that accomplishes your objectives.

> *Everything should be made as simple as possible, but not simpler.*
>
> Albert Einstein

Make Sure What You Can’t Take With You Gets to the Right Place

When we think about what we would like our descendants to have, we often focus on money in one form or another — cash or securities, for example — and real estate. But we may have personal possessions like jewelry, china, and collectibles which, valuable or not, are meaningful in our lives and which we would like to pass along to those who are special to us.

A person may leave personal possessions to particular individuals in a will. However, Pennsylvania law also permits the use of a separate document for this purpose, a writing usually called a Memorandum. There are two approaches. One is to have a legally binding Memorandum which must be referred to in the will and must be in existence at the time the will is executed. This kind of Memorandum is “incorporated by reference” and becomes part of the will. The second approach is to leave a Memorandum with your will that is created after the will is executed, which is an expression of your wishes to your family members and executor. While such a

Memorandum is not legally binding, usually the wishes expressed in such a Memorandum are respected.

Writing peoples' names on tags attached to furniture or labeling envelopes containing coins or jewelry with beneficiaries' names are not legally binding ways of disposing of personal property. In a harmonious family situation, such methods may work because everyone agrees to respect the wishes of the decedent. However, you need to know that such arrangements are not legally binding, and if a family member is not in agreement, persons identified as beneficiaries in this way have no legal rights to the property.

Why is a Memorandum a useful tool? Usually, a will is somewhat general in terms of the disposition of such items as jewelry, collectibles, and similar possessions. Lawyers don't like to spend time and their client's money enumerating who gets a teacup and who gets the pearl earrings. There is also a common misunderstanding that if the property is mentioned in a will "you have to pay inheritance tax on it." Inheritance tax must be paid on personal property whether or not it is specifically enumerated in the will.

In my twenty years of trust and estates practice, some of the most wrenching family disputes have been over the tangible personal property. These personal items are highly valued for sentimental reasons and often become battlefields for siblings. If, however, the client gives thought to preparing a Memorandum, these problems can be avoided. If the Memorandum is incorporated by reference into the will, the executor has a legally binding and specific listing of the desired disposition of personal tangible property. Even if the Memorandum is not legally binding, most families will not haggle if Mom wrote down the names of those people she wanted to receive certain items.

The Memorandum is a legally binding document only when it exists prior to the execution of the will and it is referred to in the will. But in this instance "legally binding" doesn't imply that preparing and signing it are complicated. Few requirements apply. The will must specifically state that tangible personal property is disposed of in a separate Memorandum which is incorporated by reference in the will. The Memorandum itself may be handwritten or typed, and it should be signed and dated; it is preferable, though not mandatory, to have the signature witnessed. The items cited need to be described clearly to avoid ambiguity, and the beneficiary of each item must be identified by his or her proper name and relationship to the signatory. It is also helpful if the beneficiary's address is given. And, as is the case with many legal documents, citing an alternate is advisable; if the first beneficiary does not survive to take possession of the property, then a successor is already named.

The occasion might arise for one or more changes in a Memorandum. A beneficiary may predecease the testator; a piece of tangible personal property may be destroyed or stolen; the items or beneficiaries may change for any number of reasons. It must be stressed that, should alterations be made on a signed Memorandum that is incorporated by reference in the will, the Memorandum's legal validity is negated. In order for changes to be made and for the Memorandum to be legally binding, the individual should consult with his or her lawyer to prepare either a new will or a codicil. On the other hand, if you are using the Memorandum in a non-binding fashion just to express your wishes to your family, you can make changes to it as frequently as you like and no formalities of execution need be observed.

If you feel strongly about who will inherit your cranberry glass, your squadron leader's sword, or your scorecard autographed by Richie Ashburn, you might want to consider working on a Memorandum on one of these cold, snowy winter nights.

But Grandma Said I Was to Have Her Diamond Ring

Since before Jacob tricked Esau out of his birthright and his father Isaac's blessing, families have argued, fought, and become embittered over inheritances. Some of the most bitter disputes are over things — cars, silver, guns, china, clocks, and in one case I know of, a ceramic cookie jar. Why do possessions create such misery?

Grandpa's gun collection and Grandma's china trigger a myriad of memories and emotions. The chipped china bowl that Grandma used to serve you homemade chicken soup in when you were sick is esteemed well beyond its five-cent value. The .22 that Grandpa taught you to shoot has more sentiment attached to it than its market value could ever match. But when these things are put up for auction they may be considered as just "stuff" or "junk."

The best gift you can give your loved ones is to work out these issues of "who gets what" while you are alive and well. Giving this matter thought shows your love and caring — to make sure that your family stays a family.

Yes, I know. You're thinking to yourself; "my children won't fight like that." Keep in mind that the parents of most of the children in those situations where terrible feuds have developed all thought the same thing. These are the same children who can't agree on what to watch on TV and who can recite, in detail, the things that their siblings were allowed to do that they weren't. Some things never change.

Let's say you've accepted the responsibility and are prepared to deal with the issue of who gets what tangible personal property. A car is tangible, household furnishings and collections are tangible. A bank account is not tangible, although it is personal property.

Often I suggest that clients write a letter or Memorandum to place with the will detailing who should get tangible personal property. Personal property means property other than real estate. Tangible personal property means property you can touch, pick-up, and carry. Again, this is not legally binding but most families will respect wishes expressed in this way.

Myths about how to handle tangible personal property abound. Here are a few.

1. *If you mention it in the will it gets taxed.* Wrong. If you own it when you die, it is part of your estate and subject to inheritance tax. It makes no difference whether it is mentioned in the will or not. The only thing not mentioning it in the will does is make it easier to get away with lying and saying Grandma didn't have any silver. If that's what you have in mind, don't. It's tax fraud. Often it is the best course to specifically mention important pieces of tangible personal property in the will. Who gets the grand piano and who gets the 1957 Chevy should be spelled out.
2. *Grandma put tags on everything showing who should receive each item.* This is not legally binding. If everyone involved agrees to go along, it may work; but there is absolutely no way of legally enforcing Grandma's wishes when they are expressed this way. Besides, tags can be moved.

3. *I gave it to him so I get it back.* It's very common for family members to try to reclaim gifts that they made to the deceased. Again, there is absolutely no legal basis for this. If you bought a TV for Dad and gave it to him, when he passes it goes under his will — not back to you because you gave it to him. If that's what he wants, it better be made clear in his will.
4. *He told me I was to have it.* This causes tremendous bad feeling. Mom tells Suzy that she will get the grand piano and puts nothing in her will. Imagine Suzy's chagrin when the piano is sold by the executor. Worse, Mom tells Suzy she gets the piano and 15 years later forgetting that she already promised it to Suzy, she tells Kathy that she gets the piano. In any event, none of these oral promises are enforceable.
5. *Get it out of the house so it won't be in the estate.* You've heard the stories of the truck pulled up to the house the day before the funeral. Until the appointment of an executor or administrator, no one has any authority whatsoever to take possession of any of the decedent's belongings. And then the executor becomes the title holder and is bound to secure the items, have the items appraised, pay any tax due, and distribute them in accordance with the terms of the will or the intestacy statute.
6. *Tell the appraiser it's for "estate purposes."* We all know that appraising is not an exact science and that most appraisers will give a range of value. Of course, if you have to pay an excise tax on value you want to use a value in the low end of the range. Fine. But "for estate purposes" should not be used as code for appraise at 50% or 25% of actual value. It's not only taxes that are affected by the appraisal; it's also how the property is divided among beneficiaries and equalization of shares.
7. *I already gave everything to my kids.* Some folks claim that they gave all their jewelry, artwork, and furniture to the kids, it's just "staying in the house for me to use." Sorry, that won't work. Even if you really did intend to make gifts of these items and if you have retained the use of them, the full value of the property is included in your estate and subject to estate and inheritance taxes.

No method for distributing tangible personal property is right for all families. Discuss with your family how items should be distributed. Talk to your kids individually and in private; talk to them in a group. Address the "touchy" issues now. Discussions that are slightly awkward or uncomfortable now can prevent family disintegration later.

You Can Disinherit Your Children, Not Your Spouse

At common law, the surviving spouse was not an heir, but was entitled to dower. Remember those Trollope novels where the widow goes to live in the dower house, while the eldest son succeeds to the manor? At common law the widow was entitled to a life estate in one-third of the deceased husband's property. On the other hand, when the husband survived, he got a life estate in *all* of the wife's estate. This was called courtesy.

The husband's right of courtesy also kept the wife from making any conveyance of the property since the husband's right of courtesy began at the time of the marriage. Interestingly enough, an unmarried woman had the same rights with regard to conveying and controlling her property as a man. But marriage was considered to create a disability in the woman, so that a married woman could make no conveyance without the consent of her husband. A woman's gender did not create her legal disability, it was her marriage!

Through a long series of statutory changes, the law in Pennsylvania finally has evolved to make the rights of husbands and wives the same, and to guarantee those rights by means of a surviving spouse's elective share of the deceased spouse's estate.

If you leave a will that makes little or no provision for your surviving spouse, or if you have arranged title of assets so that assets pass by joint title or beneficiary designation to beneficiaries other than your spouse, your surviving spouse is entitled to elect a statutory forced share equal to one-third of certain property interests.

It is the policy of the law to make sure that a surviving spouse does not become impoverished because of the loss of the support of the deceased spouse as well as to reward the spouse's contribution to the financial success of the marriage. The survivor is entitled to what our legislature has determined to be a "reasonable" share, that is, one-third.

Whether the marriage lasts for one day or 50 years, the elective share is and remains one-third. The share is not limited to property acquired after the marriage, but applies to all of the decedent's property interests including gifts and inheritances. Whether the current spouse is the first, second, third, or later spouse, the current spouse is still entitled to the one-third share.

The surviving spouse is entitled to the one-third share even if divorce proceedings are pending. However, it is possible to forfeit this right. A spouse who, for one year or more before the death of the deceased spouse has "willfully neglected or refused to perform the duty to support the other spouse," or who, for one year or more has "willfully and maliciously deserted the other spouse," shall have no right of election, or even of receiving an intestate share.

The share is not paid automatically. There are specific procedural requirements. To claim the share the surviving spouse must "elect" to take the share. Presumably a spouse will not make the election if he or she is satisfied with what she receives under the will. The spouse has six months from the later of the date of death or the date of probate to make this election. The election is made by filing a claim with the Clerk of the Orphan's Court in the county of the decedent's domicile. Note that if the spouses entered into a prenuptial agreement, usually the right to make this election is waived as part of the agreement.

It is easy to see that if you give away all your property during life, or create trusts or joint tenancies, that you may leave no estate against which a surviving spouse can make a claim. In order to treat the surviving spouse fairly, many of these contrivances are ignored for purpose of determining the one-third share.

When the election is made, the surviving spouse is entitled to one-third of the following items: (1) the decedent's probate property, that is, property that passes under the decedent's will; (2) property from which the decedent was entitled to receive the income if that property was transferred by the decedent during the marriage; (3) property transferred by the decedent during life where the decedent could revoke the transfer and get the property back, or could withdraw or invade the principal of the property for the decedent's own benefit; (4)

joint property owned with another to the extent the decedent could have conveyed or revoked the joint account; (5) annuity payments to the extent the annuity was purchased during the marriage and the decedent was receiving payments; and (6) gifts made within one year of death to the extent they exceed $3,000 per beneficiary.

The following property interests are *not* subject to the election: (1) any transfer made with the consent of the surviving spouse; (2) life insurance on the decedent's life; and (3) retirement plans (although many retirement plans other than IRAs must be paid to the surviving spouse unless the surviving spouse consents to a different beneficiary designation).

If the surviving spouse makes the election to take the one-third share, then he or she gives up any other provisions that were made for him or her. Making the election is considered to be a disclaimer of all benefits passing to the surviving spouse under the will.

In other words, you can't keep what the deceased spouse gave you *and* get a one-third share. You have a choice. You can keep what you got, or you can give up what you got and elect a one-third share.

This provision of the law is complex. If you think you need to claim an elective share, you should seek professional advice as soon as possible.

In Wills, Trusts, Your Choice of Boilerplate Is Crucial

"Boilerplate" provisions in a contract, will, or other legal documents are sections of apparently routine, standard language. The term comes from an old method of printing. Today, "boilerplate" is commonly stored in computer memory to be retrieved and copied when needed. A layperson should be aware that the party supplying the boilerplate form usually has developed supposedly "standard" terms (some of which may not apply to every situation) to favor and/or protect the provider of the form.

In the late 1800s and early 1900s, "boilerplate" or ready-to-print material was supplied to newspapers. Advertisements or syndicated columns were supplied to newspapers in ready-to-use forms as heavy iron, prefabricated printing plates that were not (and, indeed, could not) be modified before printing. These never-changed plates came to be known in the late 19th century as "boilerplates" from their resemblance to the plates used to construct boilers. Eventually, any part of the paper that rarely changed (such as the masthead) came to be called "boilerplate." If you were the linotype machine operator, you loved boilerplate; instead of setting type for an article, you could just drop the big square piece of lead in the page setup. Maybe you could fill up a whole page that way!

The term "boilerplate" was later adopted by lawyers to describe those parts of a legal document that are considered "standard language," although any good lawyer will tell you to always read the "boilerplate" in any document you plan to sign.

In a will or trust, the choice of boilerplate is crucial. Let me give you a few examples.

Wills should contain a tax clause. A tax clause is a provision that says where the executor should get the money to pay federal and state death taxes. A common boilerplate provision could provide that all taxes are to be paid from the residue of the probate estate. Maybe your will says that.

What if some of the decedent's property was jointly held or payable pursuant to beneficiary designations and passed outside the will? Let's say that a decedent held bank accounts jointly with a son and that the decedent has a will that leaves the remaining property to a daughter. On decedent's death, the son (as surviving joint owner) becomes sole owner of the bank accounts. The will, when probated, gives the rest of decedent's property (if any) to the daughter. But, the will says (in the boilerplate) that all death taxes are to be paid by the executor from the estate. This means that the estate and inheritance taxes payable on the bank accounts passing to the son are paid out of the property that passes to the daughter. Son pays no inheritance tax, but daughter pays the tax on his share as well as on her own. Is that what was intended? Probably not. But that result is mandated by the "boilerplate" provision that was used in the will.

Boilerplate often is used in a will or trust to provide definitions. For example, the will may refer to children, grandchildren, descendants or issue. Who is included? Is a stepchild included in the class? Is an adopted child included in the class? Are children born of unmarried parents included? If there is a definition in the boilerplate, it may exclude stepchildren as beneficiaries. Is this intended? Perhaps. Then again, perhaps not. This is a case where the definition in the boilerplate goes to the heart of the matter — who is a beneficiary and who gets a share of the estate.

If you name a bank or trust company as executor or trustee, do you want them to be able to invest your money in their own stock? If they invest your money in mutual funds, can they have a fee from the mutual funds as well as from your trust? Often boilerplate provisions provide that the answer is yes. Is that what you want?

If you name an individual or a bank or trust company as a trustee, can the beneficiaries ever remove that trustee? Thirty years later when the trustee's fees are high, investment performance is poor, and there is inadequate customer service, can the trust be moved? It depends on what it says in the boilerplate.

All boilerplate is not equal. The choice of the boilerplate that is appropriate to the circumstances and is in accordance with the intentions of the parties is very important. There is no standard, across-the-board language for anything. It is all written by someone, the words have meaning, and they are binding. The quality of the attorney is often reflected in the quality of the boilerplate. Never skip over something saying "it's just boilerplate."

Why Do You Lawyers Always Have to Speak Latin?

Clients often ask, "Why do you use Latin words?" Contrary to popular belief, it's not to protect the lawyer's franchise. Lawyers would be perfectly happy to use two English words instead of two Latin words if the two English words would do the job. Unfortunately, that is not the case in this example. Take the phrase "*per stirpes*." This appears in many wills and has been interpreted by courts for centuries. Its meaning is well-settled and these two words incorporate a multitude of concepts that if you were to explain in plain English would take many paragraphs.

Per stirpes is the method of dividing an estate where a group of beneficiaries take the share which their deceased ancestor would have been entitled to, had he or she lived. The group of beneficiaries take by their right of representing the ancestor and not because they are owed anything as individuals. Example: Grandmother had two sons; one of them had one child, and the other had three. Both of the sons predeceased Grandmother. A *per stirpes* distribution of her estate would be that the grandchild who is the only child of a deceased son gets one-half of the estate and the other three grandchildren share the other deceased son's one-half share, each receiving one-sixth.

Per stirpes is to be contrasted with *per capita. Per capita* means by the head or by the polls, according to the number of individuals, share and share alike. Let's take the same example where Grandmother had two sons, one of them had one child, the other had three. If both sons predeceased Grandmother a *per capita* distribution of her estate would be that each of the four grandchildren would receive equal one-fourth shares of her estate — equally near, equally dear.

If one son survives Grandmother and the other son predeceases, then the distribution is the same under *per capita* and *per stirpes.* In either case, the division into equal shares occurs at the child level; the grandchildren take, by representation, the share that would have been their father's.

In the vast majority of the estate plans, distribution after the death of both parents is "to issue, *per stirpes.*" Issue means children, grandchildren, great-grandchildren and so forth. Issue is all persons who have descended from a common ancestor.

Many lawyers include a definition in estate planning documents that defines *per stirpes* by reference to the Pennsylvania intestacy law. This is a little confusing because the scheme provided in the Pennsylvania intestacy law is actually per capita with representation. Pennsylvania law provides that the estate "shall be divided into as many equal shares as there shall be persons in the nearest degree of consanguinity to the decedent living and taking shares therein and persons in that degree who have died before the decedent and have left issue surviving who take shares therein. One equal share to pass to each such living person in the nearest degree and one equal share shall pass by representation to the issue of each such deceased person." You look for the first generation where there is a descendant living. Equal shares *per capita* are made at that generation, and further distribution to descendants is by representation.

Pennsylvania law provides further that persons take in equal shares without distinction between those of the whole blood and those of the half blood. Stepbrothers and stepsisters inherit in shares equal to brothers and sisters of the full blood. Any person who fails to survive by five days is deemed to have predeceased the decedent.

There is a presumption that any child born in wedlock is entitled to inherit from both the husband and the wife. If other parentage is proved, this presumption can be overcome. A child born out of wedlock is treated as a child of the mother for purposes of inheritance.

A child born out of wedlock is treated as a child of the father for purposes of inheritance if (1) the parents of a child born out of wedlock shall have married each other, (2) if during the lifetime of the child, the father openly holds out the child to be his and receives the child into his home, or openly holds out the child to be his and provides support for the child which shall be determined by clear and convincing evidence, or (3) if there is clear and convincing evidence that the man was the father of the child, which may include a prior court determination of paternity.

For purposes of inheritance by, from, or through an adopted person, the adopted person shall be considered to be the issue of his adopting parent or parents. An adopted person is not considered as continuing to be the child of his natural parents for purposes of inheritance except when distributing the estate of a natural kin, other than the natural parent, who has maintained a family relationship with the adopted person.

All of these concepts, and more, are embodied in those two Latin words, *per stirpes.*

The Self-Proving Will

Is your will notarized? Wills do not have to be notarized. So why are wills written by lawyers almost always notarized? It is not the will itself that is notarized but rather the "self-proving affidavit" that is attached to the will.

When a person's will is presented for probate after the person's death, the will must be "proved." Proving a will means that a witness to the will gives testimony to the Register of Wills that he witnessed the signing of the will. Obviously, if a will was signed many years ago, it may be difficult or impossible to locate the witnesses. They may be deceased, they may have moved away; they may be incapacitated and not able to give testimony. If the witnesses are not available, the will can be "proved" by the testimony of two persons who did not witness the will, but who can identify the decedent's signature on the will.

These witnesses are called "non-subscribing witnesses." They were not present when the will was signed and they did not subscribe their names to the will as witnesses.

Looking for witnesses and getting them to the Register's office can be difficult and burdensome to those involved. The need for external proof requires sworn testimony by knowledgeable parties familiar with the signature in question. Remember, because most folks die when they are old, people who can credibly verify signatures may be incapacitated, dead, or "living in Florida."

Since 1976, this procedure of requiring witness testimony to prove a will can be avoided by the addition of a "self-proving affidavit" to the will. This law allows the person making the will and the witnesses to take an oath before a notary public at the time the will is signed. If this is done, then no witnesses must "prove" the will after death. The will is simply filed, the Register of Wills notes that self-proving affidavit, and no witness testimony is required. Isn't that much easier?

If a notary is unavailable and a Pennsylvania admitted attorney is present, the attorney can take the oaths and then the attorney can subsequently make the certification to a notary. If this is the case, it is important for the form of affidavit to make it clear that the oath was taken by the attorney and that the attorney later appeared before a notary.

While a will is still valid without the self-proving affidavit, it is now the standard practice to make wills self-proving. Sometimes it is difficult to arrange for the presence of a notary at the time the will is signed, but a little extra effort at this point can save your beneficiaries much more trouble and expense later.

If your will was made before 1976, it cannot be self-proving. (And regardless of whether it's self-proving or not, it's time to have a will that old reviewed!) If your will was executed after that date, it may or may not be self-proving depending on the practice of the attorney who drafted it.

Is lack of self-proof grounds for creating a new will? No, there is no need to go to the expense of creating a new will just to add a self-proving affidavit. However, if you are making a new will, it is highly recommended that it be self-proving. It is possible to make an old will self-proving by adding a codicil. Since the codicil makes changes to a will and reaffirms the parts that aren't changed, the will is "republished" by the codicil. Thus, the self-proving codicil also proves the will. I have found as a practical matter that the Registers of Wills in all counties do not view this matter in the same way. For example, the view of the Allegheny County Register is that both the Will and the Codicil must be self-proving in order to avoid testimony. Thus, to be safe, instead of adding a codicil, do a new will with a self-proving affidavit attached.

A little front-end work on your will can make a world of difference to the executor in getting the will accepted as genuine by the court system. Most of us are fond of the executor we named, so do that person a small favor in return for the significant effort that will be expended in settling your estate. Have a notary eliminate the signature problem before it occurs.

Who Is an Heir? The Answer Is Changing With the Times

Who is the heir? This is an age-old question. Simply, an heir is the person who inherits a decedent's property if the decedent left no will. (If the decedent left a will, those who inherit are typically called beneficiaries, not heirs.)

Throughout history the answer to who is an heir has changed many times. Keep in mind that statute determines who the heir is. There is no "right" of inheritance. The law has long dealt with family relationships and procreation. Legislatures have passed laws to determine who inherits a decedent's property based on what most people would want. Doctrines have evolved to cover all sorts of situations.

Now, due to new medical technologies and changing mores, "times, they are a-changing." New situations are arising.

It used to be that only the firstborn male inherited under English primogeniture. In the Torah, sons were the primary inheritors with the eldest receiving a double portion. In all of the United States today, children of both sexes inherit and share equally.

Under the common law, any child born in wedlock (even a day after the marriage) is presumed to be legitimate. Legitimate for these purposes means entitled to the support of the father and to be an heir of the father. A child born after the death of his father was also presumed legitimate if the child was "en ventre sa mere" (in the womb of his mother) when his father died. So if birth occurred within nine months of death, the child was deemed an heir of the father even though born posthumously.

In all of the states, without a will, all of Dad's children are his equal heirs. However, Dad's stepchildren get nothing, even if Dad has raised them since infancy.

By statute, adopted children came to be considered heirs of the adoptive parents. Similarly, by statute, adopted children are not considered to be heirs of the birth parents.

Today, however, infertile couples don't always adopt children to have a family. Sometimes, there are children born from donated sperm or eggs. Is the baby an heir of the sperm donor? Babies are born to surrogate mothers into whose womb a fertilized egg has been implanted. Is the baby an heir of the surrogate mother? Is the baby an heir of the woman who produced the egg?

Spouses have not always been entitled to inherit any of their deceased husband or wife's property. In the United States today, all fifty states consider a surviving spouse an heir, entitled to a portion of the estate.

Common law marriage is a legal concept that evolved to give support and inheritance rights to men and women who live together, holding themselves out as husband and wife, but never having been legally married. In Pennsylvania, doing this for six years gives you the status of a husband or wife at common law, if established prior to January 1, 2005. (There are also similar doctrines for adoption where a child is taken in by a family and held out as a son or daughter even though there is no legal adoption.)

In addition, society is now looking to answer a new question: what's a spouse? Laws are being shaped that may define spouses to include others than a couple consisting of a man and a woman, either legally married or in a common-law arrangement.

In Vermont, civil union status is given to same-sex couples who have had their union certified by a judge, justice of the peace or clergy member and offers the same-sex couple the same rights as a traditional married couple. Vermont law allows a partner in a same-sex union a spouse's inheritance rights and rights to own property by entirety. The federal government does not recognize these unions, and the federal Defense of Marriage Act denies these couples federal benefits and protections that are given to spouses. This act also exempts other states from having to recognize a civil union performed elsewhere and thirty states have similar defense of marriage laws in place.

In Kansas, as reported in the March 4, 2002, issue of *Time Magazine*, a son is disputing his father's second wife's right to half of the father's estate. Dad's second wife, Mrs. Gardiner, was born a man and had undergone sex reassignment surgery and then married Dad. Is she (or he) a wife? Entitled to inherit? Or does the son get everything? Dad could have done anything he wanted in a will. But like so many, he died without a will. His heirs are determined by the Kansas intestacy statute which gives half of his property to his surviving spouse. Kansas law prohibits same-sex marriages. Is this a same-sex marriage? Or does someone who undergoes sexual reassignment surgery have a new gender? What is gender?

In May 2002, an appellate panel considering a similar case overturned a February 2000 Federal District Court ruling that sex is determined at birth and can never be changed. The panel, considering statistics that showed that 275,000 to 2.5 million people in the United States were born with a mix of chromosomes, genitalia, and hormones that made them neither clearly male nor female, outlined a formula for determining sex based on a mix of psychological and physiological factors. At their core, these cases revolve around the question of what makes a man a man and a woman a woman.

If you'd rather not have your estate subject to changing intestate laws, make a will. Your will, which takes precedence over the intestate laws discussed above, will assure that your property will be distributed according to your wishes.

Hey! What Happened to My Inheritance?

Grandpa told Sally he was going to leave her $40,000 for college in his will. Now Grandpa has passed away, and the executor tells Sally she doesn't get the $40,000 that she was expecting. What happened?

Chances are that Sally's $40,000 bequest was attacked, not by the killer bees, but by the killer "A"s: age, ademption, abatement, and advancement.

Age may be a barrier to taking the principal of a bequest if the beneficiary is not *sui juris*. "Sui juris" is a Latin phrase used not for show but for clarity of legal meaning. Sui juris means "in their own right," and it refers to beneficiaries who enjoy full rights under the law and do not share them with a guardian. Beneficiaries who have not attained the age of majority (age 18 in Pennsylvania) are not *sui juris*; they cannot make contracts or transfer land. If Sally is under age 18, she won't receive the $40,000. It may be paid to a court appointed guardian for her. Perhaps the will authorizes payment of the $40,000 to a custodian for Sally under the Uniform Transfer to Minors Act. Also, adults who are incompetent are not *sui juris*. Again, a guardian may be required to receive a bequest directed to an incompetent beneficiary.

The word "adeem" means to take away. A legacy in a will is adeemed if the property that is the subject of the legacy no longer exists. Let's suppose Grandpa left Sally his IBM stock in his will. At the time he made the will, the IBM stock was worth $40,000. After he signed the will, Grandpa sold the stock to pay for medical bills. Then he passed away, not having changed his will. What happens? It depends.

If the bequest of IBM stock was a specific bequest, which means that Grandpa's will specified, "I leave *my* shares of IBM stock to Sally," then Sally gets nothing. Grandpa, by selling the stock, is adeeming the bequest to Sally.

On the other hand, if Grandpa's will simply says, "I give $40,000 worth of IBM stock to Sally," this is considered a general legacy, not a specific one. His intention is that the executor buys the stock if it is not owned at his death. Sally is entitled to receive either IBM stock purchased by the executor or its equivalent value in cash.

What is the difference? A specific legacy or bequest includes words of ownership or identification. A bequest of "my IBM stock" refers to specific shares. A bequest of "IBM stock" does not. Much turns on the little word "my." If Grandpa had made a specific bequest of the stock, then Sally gets nothing. If he had made a general legacy of it, then Sally gets the $40,000.

What if Grandpa became incompetent before he died, and his attorney-in-fact, acting under a power of attorney, sold the IBM stock? Then, Sally is entitled to receive the equivalent value from the estate; the legacy is not adeemed even if it was a specific bequest.

These rules and interpretations are very difficult and confusing. For obvious reasons, they often result in litigation. It's hard for Sally to understand that the difference between her getting $40,000 and getting zero may be the word "my" in Grandpa's will. For this reason, it is a bad idea to leave specific stocks, bonds, or bank accounts to a beneficiary. It is recommended that you leave your beneficiaries either dollar amounts, or fractions or percentages of your total estate. Cash is never adeemed since it is just part of the cash holding of a person, and one $50,000 chunk of it cannot be distinguished from another $50,000 chunk.

Abatement is the reduction or elimination of bequests to pay debts, expense of administration, and taxes. Payment of the decedent's debts, the expenses of administration of the estate and taxes of all types are required to be paid before any beneficiaries receive assets from the estate. Usually, a will specifies which fund or funds bear the burden of these payments. If the will does not provide, state law determines where the payments come from. Usually, all of these costs are paid from the residue of the estate which is often the biggest portion of the estate's assets. If the residue is insufficient, specific bequests of money or property to beneficiaries abate — that is, they are reduced by the payment of expenses and taxes.

Let's assume Grandpa left $40,000 to Sally and the residue of his estate to George. His total estate was $100,000, but he and his estate owed debts and taxes amounting to $80,000. Before the executor pays the debts and taxes, it looks as if Sally gets $40,000, and George gets the $60,000 residue. The executor first uses the residue to pay the debts and taxes. The entire $60,000 that would have gone to George is taken for these payments; the entire bequest of the residue to George is abated. Then, there is still $20,000 worth of debts and taxes due. This comes out of Sally's $40,000 bequest. Her bequest is abated to the extent of $20,000, and she still receives the remaining $20,000.

Advancements are like an advance on your salary. If a parent has given $10,000 to one child and not to others, the $10,000 is assumed to be an "advance" on the child's intestate share of the estate only if it is declared to be an advance, in writing. Where there is a will, a similar analysis applies. If Grandpa leaves a $40,000 bequest to Sally and, before he dies he gives her $30,000 for college tuition, she may only receive $10,000 under the will. The $30,000 is treated as an advance if it can be shown that this was Grandpa's intention. The bequest is said to be partially satisfied by the lifetime gift.

If someone says they will leave you $40,000 and give you $30,000 as an advance on that gift, then only $10,000 is left of the original pledge. If Grandpa states in his will that the gift was or was not an advance, then his word is what governs. If he is silent on such gifts, then another beneficiary may know about the gift and petition the court to consider the lifetime gift as an advancement or partial satisfaction of the bequest. Whether or not the $40,000 bequest is reduced will depend on what can be proven to be Grandpa's intention.

So, here's a word to the wise. Wait until that inheritance check is in your hands before going on a shopping spree or taking that dream vacation.

How to Write a Will That Will Stand Up to a Challenge

When you make a will, how do you know it will stand up to challenge by a disgruntled heir?

First, the will must be in correct form. A holographic will is one type of correct form. A holographic will is a will written entirely in the testator's handwriting and signed by the testator. No witnesses are required. A holographic will is legal in Pennsylvania and a few other states. If parts of the will are on a preprinted form and parts are filled in by the testator in writing and then signed by the testator, the will may survive as a holographic will if, and only if, the handwritten portions make sense by themselves without looking at the preprinted portions of the form.

If the will is written or printed by someone other than the testator, the will must be signed by the testator at the very end, and two witnesses must see him do it. The two witnesses must sign the will as witnesses in each other's presence and in the presence of the testator. The signature of any witness that is a beneficiary is without effect. If the testator has become physically incapacitated and cannot sign his name, a mark will suffice. If the testator cannot even make a mark, another person can sign the will for the testator at the testator's express direction.

The testator must declare, before the witnesses, that this is his will; this declaration is called a publication of the will. At the time of the signing of the will, the testator must be of sound mind, under no undue influence, and over the age of 18.

Wills, otherwise valid in form, can be challenged, based on defects in the form or ceremony as described above; wills can be challenged based on lack of testamentary capacity, the presence of undue influence, or by fraud.

Testamentary capacity demands that the testator be of majority age, which is 18 in Pennsylvania. It also requires that the testator know what he was doing when he made the will. In order to have testamentary capacity, the testator needs to know what his assets are, who his beneficiaries would be if he died intestate (the law refers to these people as the "natural objects of your bounty"), and thus, how he is changing his testamentary distribution by making a will. Testamentary capacity can exist even though a person's capacity has been diminished. For example, a person who has had a stroke, or is diagnosed with Alzheimer's disease, may still have sufficient capacity to make a will even though there is some impairment of speech, some impairment of thought processes, and/or some physical impairment.

A person can behave in strange ways and still have testamentary capacity. All that is needed is to know (generally) what your assets are, who are the "natural objects of your bounty," and what you are doing when you make a will. It's a lower hurdle than most people realize, but a real one nonetheless.

Undue influence is the use of coercion to force a testator to make a will. Undue influence is the replacement of the testator's desires with the desires of another by pressure or threat. The testator is left to say, "I don't want to do this, but I must." Holding a gun to the testator's head is clear undue influence. Telling Grandpa that you'd love to have him stay in your house but only if he leaves you a certain something (like everything) in his will could be coercion. Influencing a person to disinherit one person in favor of the person exerting influence is a classic case. A person can have testamentary capacity but be subject to undue influence. Many people in their terminal illnesses are unduly influenced to make wills in favor of their caregiver.

Finally, we have the matter of fraud. Fraud can come in the inducement to make a will. For instance, Son tells Grandpa (who is in the retirement home) that the nice lady who used to live next door to him has died, knowing that Grandpa will then give the share he was going to give to the nice lady to Son instead. Fraud can come in the commission as well. We could put a document in front of Grandpa and say it is the will he asked us to have made for him which leaves everything to charity. It is really a will containing quite different provisions, giving his property to us, the children, but we don't tell him that. He can't read so well anymore and trusts us, so he signs it. Remember, no one has a right to inherit. Grandpa is entirely free to leave all his wealth to charity, or even to a stranger, so long as he has testamentary capacity and is not under undue influence.

Wills made as a result of fraud are invalid, but the fraud must be proven. The elements to be proven are: means, motive, opportunity and result. Someone must be proven to be in a position to be able to deceive the testator, have the opportunity to deceive the testator, the testator must have been deceived, and the deceiver or his benefactor must benefit from the will that was made, or not made, as a result of the deception.

Employing a lawyer in the preparation of a will can go a long way in ensuring that it can withstand the assaults of a challenge. No one can guarantee that a will won't be challenged; the key is whether or not the challenge will be successful. A lawyer will make sure the will is in correct form, will provide witnesses and testimony regarding testamentary capacity, and will be on the lookout for undue influence. If you are trying to avoid lawyers by making your own will, in all likelihood, you're making more work for lawyers when that will is submitted to probate!

Disinheritance and In Terrorem Clauses

We usually think of a person's will as a financial document used to make sure his or her estate is distributed according to his or her wishes. The will can also be used as a constructive tool or a destructive weapon to reach other goals, which often do not involve money.

Eddy M. Elmer, in his article, "The Psychological Motives of the Last Will and Testament" describes the use of wills. Used positively, a will can be used to foster a sense of continuity for the survivors and to preserve family relationships. Used negatively, through imposed conditions, disinheritance, unequal treatment, and attaching "strings," a will can be used to control from the grave and continue dysfunction in a family.

With the power to make a will, comes the right to disinherit. By the common law, anyone may give his estate to a stranger, and thereby disinherit his heir apparent. In the words of Mr. Elmer, "Disinheritance is one of the more vengeful goals of will-writing."

Most states include protections for a surviving spouse so that the spouse cannot be completely disinherited, although in Pennsylvania, the spouse has a right to receive only one-third of the deceased spouse's estate. In all the states except Louisiana, children can be disinherited.

When it is the intention of the person making the will to disinherit a child or someone who is an heir at law, it is important to make it clear that the omission of the person from the will is not a mistake or oversight. For this reason, sometimes wills provide "I give my son John $1.00." Leaving someone a dollar is not intended to be a gift to them. It is a formal statement of disinheritance. Similarly, a will could provide "I leave nothing to my son John," or "I am leaving nothing to my son John, for reasons known to both of us."

Questions can arise about these provisions. If John predeceases the parent who made the will, do John's children inherit? Is the disinheritance of John to be assumed a disinheritance of his children also? The will must be drafted to make the answer to this question clear.

It is best not to give a reason for the disinheritance. If a reason is given, and it is proven to be a mistake of fact, then there could be a dispute about the validity of the disinheritance. For example, a will could provide "I give nothing to my son John because he is a convicted felon." If John is not a convicted felon, is he still disinherited?

A writer of a will can also disinherit anyone who challenges the validity of the will in what is called an "in terrorem" clause. "I leave anyone who challenges this will or any part of it one dollar." Sometimes these clauses are called "no contest clauses."

An in terrorem clause (pronounced (in TEHR-ROAR-EM) is from Latin for "in fear." It is any provision in a will which threatens that if anyone challenges the legality of the will or any part of it, then that person will be disinherited or given $1.00, instead of receiving his or her stated bequest in the will.

An in terrorem clause is intended to discourage beneficiaries from legal battles after the testator is deceased. However, if the will is challenged and found to be invalid (perhaps because of lack of capacity or undue influence), then the in terrorem clause which was part of the failed will fails as well. Whether or not to challenge the will then becomes a calculated risk.

An in terrorem clause is not much help to disinherit a child or other beneficiary entirely. It is most useful when the child or other beneficiary receives something meaningful under the will, but just less than what he or she might feel entitled. If you completely disinherit someone, and include an in terrorem clause in the will, there is not much of a threat. If the person you are concerned about challenging the will is not a beneficiary, he or she has nothing to forfeit (and nothing to "fear"). So an in terrorem clause would have no effect on him or her. For the clause to work, you have to leave enough to the disfavored beneficiary so that the beneficiary has too much to lose if the challenge fails.

In Pennsylvania, under the 1994 changes to the Probate Estates and Fiduciaries Code, "[a] provision in a will or trust purporting to penalize an interested person for contesting the will or trust or instituting other proceedings relating to the estate or trust is unenforceable if probable cause exists for instituting proceedings." Probable cause, in general, is when a reasonable person, properly advised, would conclude that there is a substantial likelihood that the will contest will be successful. The policy behind allowing this probable cause exception is to ensure that a person is not intimidated into remaining silent out of fear of losing a bequest where there is a good faith belief that the will is invalid.

An (in terrorem) clause may be viewed favorably as a means of discouraging frivolous litigation. On the other hand, courts tend to construe the clauses strictly because their enforcement causes a complete forfeiture of the claimant's interest, a harsh result. There are many court cases on what should be the fair boundaries of the power to condition a gift on not contesting a disposition. The law frowns on a provision which seeks to repress a search for the facts surrounding a disposition in a will. Florida and Indiana have statutes that completely void the use of in terrorem clauses.

It is unhealthy for the living, as well as the dead, if we use our death as an occasion to get even and settle petty accounts — with our own children, no less.

Where to Turn When Beneficiaries Die Before You

What happens when a beneficiary of your will dies before you die? The typical lawyer's answer applies. It depends.

Consider how a will is typically drafted. First are bequests of tangible personal property such as jewelry, furniture and cars — things you can touch. Then there are bequests of sums of money or property. Next there is the residuary clause, disposing of everything that wasn't disposed of above. Despite its name, the residuary clause usually disposes of the bulk of the estate. If the recipient of a bequest is deceased and the bequest lapses, it falls to the residue, the last provision of the will.

If I leave $1,000 to my friend, Mary Jones, and she fails to survive me, her bequest lapses. Mary Jones is deceased, and her estate has no right to receive the bequest on her behalf. Instead, the bequest is not paid, and the $1,000 that would have been distributed to Mary Jones, if she had survived me, is added to the residue and distributed to the beneficiaries specified there.

Pennsylvania has an anti-lapse statute that modifies this rule for some categories of beneficiaries. If a testator leaves a bequest to a child, or other descendants such as a brother, a sister, or a child of a brother or sister, the bequest does not lapse if the named beneficiary predeceased and left issue surviving. Instead, the bequest is paid to the deceased beneficiary's issue.

To illustrate the application of the anti-lapse statute, let's look at an example. If I bequeath $30,000 to my daughter, and she predeceases me but leaves three children surviving, each of my three grandchildren would receive $10,000. Note that this happens because of state law even though the will does not specifically include this provision. If I didn't want that result, I would have had to condition the bequest of the $30,000 on my daughter's survival. If my will had said "I give $30,000 to my daughter if she survives me," then, the anti-lapse statute would not be applicable, the bequest would lapse, and the $30,000 would pass as part of the residue of my estate. Note that the words "if she survives me" make the difference between the grandchildren receiving the $30,000 or not. Large sums of money can hinge on a very few words.

Pennsylvania's anti-lapse statute provides further that it does not apply to a bequest to a brother, sister, or child of a brother or sister if the lapsed bequest would go to the testator's spouse or issue. (Nothing is simple.) Suppose I leave a bequest of $10,000 to my sister and the rest, residue, and remainder of my estate to my children. Now, let's assume my sister predeceases me. Do her children get the $10,000? In Pennsylvania, the answer is no. Even though as a sister she is in the class protected by the anti-lapse statute, if the $10,000 lapses, it would pass to my children. In that case, the anti-lapse statute doesn't apply. The $10,000 that would have gone to my sister (had she lived) goes to my own children, not hers.

If my will provided $10,000 to my sister and the rest, residue, and remainder of my estate to XYZ charity, then, if my sister predeceased, the $10,000 would go to her issue.

When a bequest lapses it falls to the residue. What happens if the provision in the residue fails? For example, what if the will states: "I give the rest, residue, and remainder of my estate to my son." When you die, your son has predeceased you leaving no issue. Who gets the property? If there is a lapse of the residue, then the assets pass by intestacy. The state intestacy statute applies and looks first for other living descendants, then parents, etc.

Suppose there are two or more beneficiaries mentioned in a bequest. Whether or not issue of a deceased beneficiary may depend on whether the bequest is a gift to a class or to separate individuals. For example, if the will provides: "I give $30,000 to my cousins Vicki, June, and Mary, each to receive one-third." These are gifts to individuals rather than gifts to a class of individuals. This would be interpreted as $10,000 to Vicki, $10,000 to June, and $10,000 to Mary. If Mary predeceased me, the $10,000 bequest to her would lapse and pass as part of the residue of my estate. Vicki and June would each receive $10,000.

On the other hand, what if the will provides: "I give $30,000 to my cousins Vicki, June, and Mary, in equal shares." This is a class gift. The members of the class are determined on my death. If Mary predeceased me, then there are two members of the class and the $30,000 is distributed in two $15,000 shares to Vicki and June.

The difference between the two formulations is that the law interprets the first one as specifying in advance what each beneficiary is to receive. In a class gift, the members of the class and the number of shares to be distributed aren't determined until my death.

Pennsylvania's anti-lapse statute applies to class gifts only if the members of the class are issue of the testator, brothers, sisters, or children of brothers and sisters.

As you can guess, there have been many cases of arguing whether a gift was to a group or to individuals. Much is riding on that determination. Consider a gift to Vicki and to the surviving children of June. The children of June are a class, but Vicki is an individual. Is Vicki lumped in with the children of June as a group or not?

Answers vary, and the experts are in disagreement on this mixed example as well. In most jurisdictions, the answer would be that the gift to Vicki falls to the residuary if she predeceases the testator. The best approach is to state in the bequest that the testator intends Vicki and the children of June to be considered as a class of beneficiaries. The individual and class rules are default rules. They are overridden by clear statements to the contrary in the will.

Be sure your will has enough words to take care of the possibility of a beneficiary not surviving you. These rules are extremely complex and confusing. It is best to avoid them altogether by spelling out plainly in the will what your intentions are if a beneficiary predeceases you.

Writing a Will Is Great — Now, Store It Properly

Please don't keep your will at home. A couple of recent cases have prompted me to revisit the answer to the question of where you should keep your will.

A client died unexpectedly, only a few months after making his will. He had gone to great pains to make a will to protect his only child and his son's children. Because of the son's history and circumstances, the will created trusts for the child and for the grandchildren. In the client's judgment, the child could not handle receiving large sums of money all at once. When provided with a copy of the father's will the day following his father's death, the son became angry and abusive. He threatened that if he did find the will, he would tear it up. The son immediately moved into the father's home and reputedly began searching through all the decedent's belongings. The original will was never found.

Another client, a businessman, also died shortly after making his will. This will also was a disappointment to some family members, distributing the assets of the business in a way that displeased some of his children. After signing the will at the lawyer's office, he took the original will with him saying he would put it in his safe deposit box. In fact, the client did follow through and put the will in his safe deposit box. Had he not, or if he died before he made it to the box, this will would have been available to disgruntled heirs as well.

Even if your will won't disappoint your heirs and all your family members are very trustworthy, it is still not a good idea to keep your will at home. Sometimes, if clients do not have a safe deposit box and do not wish to rent one, they choose to keep their will wherever they keep other important papers at home. Most folks in this category have a safe, strong-box, or "fireproof" box. I always caution folks that there is no such thing as "fireproof." These boxes are fire-rated to withstand high temperatures for a given period of time, say one or two hours, and this is often inadequate for a fire which stays hot long after it appears to be "out." These boxes are nice little ovens.

There are other options to the safe in the spare bedroom or den. Keeping your will in your safe deposit box at your bank is the option I usually recommend, so long as no one who could benefit by the destruction of the will has access to the box. I recommend that you drive immediately from the lawyer's office to the bank to put your freshly signed will into your safe deposit box.

In Pennsylvania, a decedent's safe deposit box can be searched, in the presence of two bank officers, for a will, and a will and cemetery deed can be removed. This is so even if no one else's name is "on the box," meaning that no one is designated as deputy or attorney-in-fact on the card maintained by the bank. Also, when the box is searched after death, an original will can only be turned over to the named executor, which provides some additional safeguards.

If the will names a bank or trust company as executor and/or trustee, often the bank will offer safekeeping services and hold the original document. This is also a good solution to the problem of where to keep the original will.

Some folks let the lawyer who wrote the will hold it in "safekeeping" for them. This is usually a service provided by law firms at no charge. Sometimes the law firm's motivation for offering the safekeeping service is to make sure that the family has to come to that law firm to retrieve the original will and thus, that firm gets first crack at the business of settling the estate. In fact, some lawyers just assume that is the case, taking over the estate settlement, and the executor and family members don't even realize that they have a choice.

Despite the law firm's motivation for offering to hold your will, this could provide the needed safety. It is a good option so long as the executor and family members understand that the will is being held in safekeeping and that the executor is free to interview other law firms and make an informed decision about what lawyer or law firm is going to be attorney for the estate. This gives the executor the opportunity to compare fees and the expertise of other lawyers before making a decision.

Notaries and Wills

Many of us have dealt with a notary public in our lifetime, most often when we transfer title to a car. But what does a notary do in return for that modest fee?

A notary is a representative of the state. The notary watches a person sign a document, verifies the person is who the person claims to be, either through recognizing the person or by identity check of some sort. Having matched the identification requirement with the signature witnessing requirement, the notary uses a metal clamp to emboss the paper to indicate it is an original that was signed in person, and that the two requirements were met.

If the document's authenticity is challenged in court, the notary may be called to testify that he or she indeed witnessed the signing of the document and that the person claiming to have signed the document actually did sign it. A notary is required to keep a log of all documents witnessed, noting the time and date when the signature took place. This is to aid in affirmatively testifying about the event the notary witnessed.

An application to become a notary requires that an elected official and a judge vouch for and affirm the person's appointment. The requirements are not nearly as stringent as those for becoming a lawyer (law degree, bar examination, and state Supreme Court approval) but certification is not just handed out on the street corner either.

Do wills have to be notarized? No, they do not. So why are wills written by lawyers almost always notarized? The answer lies in the degree of difficulty in proving to the Orphan's Court that the will is genuine. If a notary verified the signature of the testator and of two witnesses, the degree of difficulty is nearly zero. Of all the grounds for contesting a will, the state felt that legitimacy of the signature should be a rarity. To make it a rare occurrence, the state set a simple standard which, if met, would eliminate the signature as a point of contention. Notarization of all signatures on a will is that standard. When all signatures on a will are notarized, the will is said to be self-proving.

Absent full notarization, not only the signature of the testator must be verified by currently living and available individuals, but those of any witnesses must be similarly verified. If a will is not self-proving, it must be proven externally meaning proof outside the will must be offered to verify its authenticity, proof such as personal testimony of people familiar with the signature(s) in the will.

If you have a will that is several decades old, it is probably not self-proving, since the concept is fairly new. Even if you have a relatively new will, it may not be notarized. Maybe there was no notary available at the time of signing, or maybe it was self-written and usefulness of notarization was unknown to the testator.

The need for external proof requires sworn testimony to the Clerk of Orphans Court by knowledgeable parties familiar with the signatures in question. Remember, most people die when they are old. People who credibly can verify signatures may be incapacitated, dead, or living in Florida.

Is lack of self-proof grounds for creating a new will? No, there is no need to go to the expense of creating a new will just to bring the signatures up to the current level standards of proof. But, if you want to do something about the documentation, just add a codicil (addition) to your will, and have it notarized and witnessed. Different localities have different policies about codicils, but if you add a self-proving codicil to an otherwise non-self-proving will, the entire will usually will be self-proving. Even if the codicil simply states, "I reaffirm my will," that will normally be enough to convert it to a self-proving will.

Speaking of grounds for a new will, anyone who gets married or divorced invalidates their will. The only exception is if the will specifically states that it is to survive marriage or divorce. It makes sense when you think about it. When either of these events occurs, the person you want to receive the bulk of your estate changes. Rather than dealing with foreseeable will contests in the case of death after these events, the state simply automatically voids all previous wills and codicils. The person then either makes a new will or dies intestate, allowing the state's intestacy laws determine the distribution of wealth.

Revocation of Wills: Have Caution When Handling

A will can be revoked by operation of law, by some physical act performed on the will with intent to revoke, or by a subsequent written instrument, meeting the statutory requirements.

Revocation or modification by operation of law refers to statutory provisions that modify or revoke will provisions in the event of marriage, divorce, birth or adoption of children, and the like.

In some states, marriage revokes a will. In Pennsylvania, marriage does not revoke a will. However, if marriage occurs after the will is made, unless the will is made in contemplation of the marriage, the surviving spouse is entitled to receive the share of the estate to which the surviving spouse would have been entitled if the deceased spouse had died intestate (unless the will gave the surviving spouse a greater share).

In Pennsylvania, divorce modifies a will. If a person becomes divorced, after making a will; any provisions in the will for the former spouse are void and without effect.

A child born to or adopted by a testator after the execution of the will is entitled to receive an intestate share of all property not passing to the surviving spouse.

The law makes these "modifications" to wills because of the presumed change in the testator's intentions resulting from a fundamental change in the testator's situation. All of these provisions can be overcome by specific direction in a will. The law attempts to salvage the situation when the testator has neglected to change his or her will after a fundamental change in his or her circumstances.

A will can be revoked by physical act — by being burnt, torn, canceled, obliterated, or destroyed with the intention of revocation. The act must be done by the testator himself or by another person in his presence and by his express direction. If the act of revocation is done by any person other than the testator, it must be proved by the oaths of two witnesses.

Unfortunately, laypersons seem to have a propensity to perform physical acts on their wills. Numerous questions arise as to whether the intention to revoke was present and whether the act was done by the testator. Often, it is the import of the act itself that is questioned. If there is a large cross mark or "X" on one of the pages, or on the cover of the will, is this considered a revocation? Is a will "burned" if its edges are singed? What if some of the dispositive provisions are lined out? Was the intention to revoke the whole will or only the mutilated provisions? The cases are numerous and the results vary widely. You should ***never*** write on your will. If you want to change your will, it must be done by making a new will or by an amendment to your will called a codicil. The new will or codicil must be signed with the same formalities as the original will. If you write on your will, or cross out provisions, you will either revoke it or you will do nothing. The one thing you will not do by writing on your will is modify it. Courts have held that the interlineation of one provision operates as a revocation of the entire will. I cannot stress this strongly enough. Do not attempt to change your will by writing on it or drawing lines through any of its provisions. Initialing the change does nothing.

If an original will cannot be found when a person dies, the question arises as to whether or not the will is simply misplaced or if it was destroyed with the intention to revoke it. The law in most states provides that there is a strong presumption that if the will cannot be found, it has been destroyed with the intention to revoke. If this presumption of revocation is successfully rebutted by testimony, then a copy of the will may be submitted for probate, or the will's provisions can be proved by testimony.

A will can be revoked by a subsequent will or codicil. Making a new will that revokes all prior wills is the method most often used to revoke prior wills. But suppose the new will is invalid. There is a principal called dependent relative revocation which holds that the old will is revoked only if the new will is valid. If a will is denied probate for any reason, such as incompetence, undue influence, fraud, or a deficiency in form or attestation, then the court must decide how to distribute the decedent's property. The choices of disposition are the next-to-last will, or the state's intestacy statute. The law presumes that the testator would prefer the provisions of the previous will. That presumption is open to rebuttal by an interested party, but the burden of proof is on that party. Thus, revocation by a new will only works if the new will survives.

I recommend that clients keep their old wills with the new ones they execute. One never knows what challenges may be made successfully to any will in the future. Usually, a testator would rather have his next to last will probated rather than relying on the state intestacy statute. Also, having the old wills is useful to show the pattern of disposition. This can be very important in cases of undue influence or incompetency.

Revocation by other writing means that the testator does not make a new will, but does make another document which revokes all prior wills and codicils. The writing must have all the formality of a will including witnesses. A handwritten document signed by the testator alone (called a holographic document) is another form of revocation accepted in some states, including Pennsylvania and New Jersey, but not any of our other neighbors. The entire document must be in the testator's handwriting, and the signature must come at the end of the document.

In the case of *Thompson v. Royall*, Mrs. Kroll of Virginia told her lawyer she wanted to revoke her will. Her lawyer said she should keep the will as a basis for making a new one, so he (not Mrs. Kroll) made the following notation on the back of the document: "This will null and void and to be only held by H. P. Brittain instead of being destroyed as a memorandum for another will if I desire to make same.

This 19 Sept., 1932." Mrs. Kroll then signed the statement. The same procedure was performed on the codicil to that will.

Mrs. Kroll died before a new will was executed. The court held that since the handwritten note did not obliterate any writing of the will (it was on the cover), and that it was not a holographic disposition (remember, she did not write the entire note, she only signed it), neither the will nor the codicil was revoked.

Suing the Writer of a Will: Some Can, Some Can't

> *LITIGATION, n. A machine which you go into as a pig and come out of as a sausage.*
>
> Ambrose Bierce, *The Devil's Dictionary*

When people you love die, you think you'll need a long time to get over it. Reading the will may change your mind. If your stepmother gives all of your deceased father's assets to her kids instead of to you, you may shift from sad to mad in a heartbeat. But they were her assets and it was her choice to make.

Where was the lawyer? He drafted a will for Dad in which Dad gave everything to your stepmother. Didn't your Dad want to make sure you got something? What did the lawyer do to protect you? Can you sue the lawyer for doing a lousy job?

Usually, only parties to a contract may sue for breach of contract or for negligence. These parties are said to have "privity" and be in such a relationship that obligations and duties are owed to one another. The parties to the contract to draft a will are the lawyer and the testator. The testator engages the lawyer to prepare the will in exchange for payment of the lawyer's fee. Usually if an error is discovered, the testator is dead; so the testator isn't around to sue the lawyer when things go wrong. Can the beneficiaries of the will, third parties to the contract, sue the lawyer who drafted the will? Maybe. Surely there must be some redress. Otherwise lawyers would never be responsible for errors made in wills if the lawyer's only duty is to the deceased.

Third party beneficiary rights were first established in Pennsylvania in an 1897 case, *Lawall v. Groman*. Mrs. Lawall sold real estate to her brother in return for a promissory note and a lien on the property. The brother's lawyer wrote the papers. Mrs. Lawall asked for a first lien, and her brother's lawyer assured her she would have a first lien. As it turned out, Mrs. Lawall had a third lien which was practically useless. She sued her brother's lawyer and the court was asked to determine if she had standing to sue since the lawyer only had a contract to represent her brother.

She won the lawsuit because the court said that "one who undertakes to perform a service for another, even without reward, is bound to exercise reasonable care and can be held responsible for misfeasance, though not for nonfeasance." (Misfeasance means doing something poorly. Nonfeasance means not doing it at all.) *Lawall* requires a specific undertaking on the attorney's part to perform a specific service for a third party, coupled with the reliance of the third party and the attorney's knowledge of that reliance in order for the third party to bring suit. In the case of wills, beneficiaries don't usually have a conversation with the lawyer as Mrs. Lawall had with the brother's real estate lawyer, and therefore, will beneficiaries were not able to sue using the theory of that case. The lawyer escapes liability.

A refinement was added in 1950 in *Spires v. Hanover Fire Insurance Co.* This case held that for a third party beneficiary to have standing to recover on a contract, both parties (attorney and testator) must express an intention that the third party be a beneficiary to whom the attorney's obligation runs in the contract itself. In other words, the obligation to the third party must be created, and must affirmatively appear in the contract between the lawyer and the client.

Under the *Spires* analysis, a beneficiary of a will would be a third party beneficiary with standing only if the testator and the attorney had a written contract to write a will, and the contract indicated the intention of both parties to benefit the legatee. The fact that the beneficiary is named in the will is not relevant to third party status. Thus, it is very unlikely that a beneficiary could ever bring suit under the *Spires* requirements. The lawyer still escapes liability.

The *Spires* rule was overturned in 1983 in *Guy v. Leiderbach* and *Guy* remains the rule today. In *Guy*, the Pennsylvania Supreme Court decided to adopt the policy in the Second Restatement of Contracts where intended beneficiaries are given the right to sue. "The beneficiary of a promise is an intended beneficiary if recognition of a right to performance in the beneficiary is appropriate to effectuate the intention of the parties and either (a) the performance of the promise will satisfy an obligation of the promisee to pay money to the beneficiary; or (b) the circumstances indicate that the promisee intends to give the beneficiary the benefit of the promised performance." (How's that for legalese?)

The result is that beneficiaries named in the will are given standing to sue the drafting attorney as third party beneficiaries. As for unnamed beneficiaries, it is up to a court to decide if they are intended beneficiaries or not. Unintended beneficiaries may not bring suit. The lawyer may or may not escape liability.

The theory of the court in the Leiderbach case was that justice balances the needs of the individual and of society. On the one hand, beneficiaries who receive less than a fair inheritance due to the actions of the attorney deserve redress. On the other hand, the public needs affordable legal assistance. If a drafting attorney could be sued by anyone and everyone who thinks the testator intended to leave him something in the will, the lawyer's job becomes almost impossible. The amount of paperwork, contracts, and necessary protections would make getting a will drafted prohibitively expensive. Legal assistance gets to be unaffordable when the ability to sue the lawyer becomes the right of every being on earth for every will ever written.

The court opined that strict privity favors the public too much, while allowing every person on earth to sue the writer of a will favors the individual too much. Limiting the ability to sue the lawyer to those with privity and to intended third party beneficiaries is the court's latest attempt to balance the scales. Do you think they are balanced?

Preparing For the Worst: Do-It-Yourself Wills

> *If you want anything done well, do it yourself. This is why most people laugh at their own jokes.*
>
> Bob Edwards

Wall Street Journal, on January 20, 2004, carried a column by Hannah Kate Kinnersley entitled "Testing the Do-It-Yourself

Will." The author dutifully reviews five of the more popular software packages. She tested all programs writing a will which disinherits a child. Not surprisingly some were better than others, and according to the law professor who reviewed the finished products, some left open the possibility that the disinherited child could successfully challenge the will. The problem is — how do you, the user, know which ones?

Maybe you want to make a will that provides a trust for a child in a bad marriage. How will you know which software does a good job, and which software fails?

There is do-it-yourself home repair, do-it-yourself hair color, do-it-yourself film developing, and do-it-yourself tattooing. On the other hand, you never hear about do-it-yourself brain surgery, do-it-yourself tooth extraction, or even do-it-yourself personal injury litigation. Why do some (too many) people seem to think that writing a will is more like the activities in the first group than in the second group?

Here are things to consider and questions you should be able to answer if you want to write your own will.

1. What is the difference between *per stirpes* and *per capita*?
2. In your state, what bequests are protected by the anti-lapse statute?
3. Who are your intestate heirs and in what proportions would they take your property?
4. In your state, what is the maximum permissible duration of a trust?
5. What effect does divorce have on a will and when does it take effect?
6. What happens if a beneficiary is a witness to the will?
7. What are the inheritance rights of adopted children? Of stepchildren?
8. What rights does your spouse have in your estate?
9. What property is subject to the Pennsylvania inheritance tax and at what rates?
10. What property is subject to the federal estate tax and at what rates?

My theory is that people continue to write their own wills because the problems are not discovered until after death. Think about it. Your will causes absolutely no problems at all until you die. You're dead and the will is ambiguous, wrong, incomplete, and improperly executed. Guess what — you don't even know! And your beneficiaries? They are so frustrated and disgusted with the length of time, expense, and number of lawyers involved in settling your estate that they think lawyers are to be avoided like the plague. It's a classic case of penny-wise and pound-foolish — saving money by writing your own will only to forfeit thousands of dollars because of mistakes.

Whatever we may think about homemade estate plans, we can agree that most people have already made the worst estate planning choice by default. About 53% of U.S. adults have not created wills or estate plans of any kind, according to a survey by Thompson Corp., a publisher of legal and business services information. Other sources estimate that the total may be as high as 70%.

People without a will have no say in how their property will be divided after their death or who will care for minor children who survive them. Nor will they select an executor to settle their estates. All of these decisions will be made by probate court judges who follow the rigid rules that vary from state to state — rules which you probably would not choose if you gave the matter any thought at all.

I'll bet you're thinking I don't want people to write their own wills so there will be more work for attorneys like me. You know what? There is much more money to be made in straightening out poorly written do-it-yourself estate plans. If my financial gain was the motivator, I would be encouraging you to do it yourself.

If you insist on doing it yourself, don't just use a form. At least do some background research to become familiar with the terms and concepts used in estate planning. And please, ask an attorney to review the documents before you sign them — always.

Wills of the First Three Presidents

Barring fill-in-the-blank type wills; no two are alike. The family situations of our first three presidents, the value of their estates, and their insistence on writing their own wills produced three quite diverse estate plans.

In Washington's case, Martha entered the marriage a widow with two children and a large inheritance from her parents. George and Martha had no children of their own, but George did have several nephews he was fond of, not to mention Martha's children and grandchildren, whom the couple adopted. It was a classic case of yours, mine and ours, including the 300 slaves they owned. Given this blended family composition, the Washington's could truly have benefitted from a prenuptial agreement. But, with one exception, their wills were honored and both branches of the family were treated in proportion to the assets of both parties.

George wrote his will himself, taking 30 pages to do so. Upon his death (several years before Martha's), he made many bequests of money, land (about 10,000 acres), and tangible personal property.

He left the majority of his estate in a life estate for Martha, with the remainder to his nephews, mostly Bushrod Washington. The residue of his estate after many bequests was divided into 23 parts to be divided up among his and Martha's family.

To fulfill his promise to Marquis de Lafayette, Washington wrote a clause in his will to free all of his slaves upon the death of the survivor of himself and Martha. Freeing them earlier would have been problematic for everyone, since some were his, some were dowery slaves of Martha and some were a result of intermarriages of the slaves. Before her death, Martha freed George's slaves because she feared they would hasten her end to gain freedom sooner. Martha's executors did not free the rest of the slaves, a situation that could have been overcome by a prenuptial contract.

Washington named his wife along with six other relatives as co-Executors. In spite of all branches of the family being represented in the Executor position, he foresaw disputes. With this in mind, he created a dispute resolution mechanism whereby each disputing party would name an agent to settle the dispute, and those agents would agree on another agent to join them in settling the dispute.

John and Abigail Adams struggled to live within their means for most of their lives. Public service drained their personal resources because the President was not paid enough in salary and expenses to cover all the receptions that the Adams' hosted in Philadelphia or Washington while he was President. However, they did purchase lots adjoining their farm in Quincy, Massachusetts, from estates when available, and John accumulated a considerable library during his envoy duties in France and England.

Preceded in death by his wife, he left his residence, 103 acres of land, his French writing desk, all his public and private papers and his library to his son, John Quincy Adams, under the condition that his son pay his other son, Thomas, an amount equal to half the value of the library. This kept his library intact and still treated his son Thomas fairly.

The residue was given to his two surviving sons, his grandchildren, and Abigail's niece, Louisa Smith. His gross estate was about $100,000.

Thomas Jefferson was a widower most of his life. He spent more than he made, constantly borrowing against future crops, as did many Virginia farmers, but Jefferson spent these advances on rare European books and furniture and building materials from Italy and France for his master work, Monticello.

In the end, he devised some real estate to a grandson, Francis Eppes, directed the payment of his debts, and then directed many bequests and devices, none of which could be fulfilled because his debts at his death (about $100,000) exceeded the worth of his assets. Monticello, in disrepair at the time, was sold at a price much lower than its cost. His slaves were sold, and there were still insufficient funds to fulfill fanciful bequests such as purchasing a gold watch for each grandchild upon turning 21 (16 for the girls).

He did free five slaves in his will, none of them being Sally Hemming, the rumored mother of several offspring. His daughter, Martha Randolph, rescued Sally by purchasing her and setting her free.

Jefferson, author of our Declaration of Independence, could have used help in drafting his will, but even more he could have used a tough accountant most of his life. Or a wife.

Ethical Wills: You Don't Have to Be Wealthy to Leave a Legacy

What, in the end, do we leave behind? Money? A house? Investments? All these are but fleeting and will come to naught. The only thing that lasts is the wisdom of a life — values, beliefs, lessons learned from life, dreams, and hopes for future generations. These things should be left to your children too — in an ethical will.

We all want to be remembered. And surely we will be, whether we leave a writing behind or not. Yet what will be remembered and for how long? How often do you search your memory for some saying of your grandfather's? Or try to remember how your uncle described his experience in the coal mines? Or in World War II? Don't you wish you could read their words and tell their stories to your own children and grandchildren?

Psychologists point out that writing down your values also helps you to clarify them. It helps you to focus on what you value the most, how to cultivate it and preserve it for future generations. You learn a lot about yourself when you write an ethical will. You must subject your life to self-examination and face up to failures as well as successes. As Rabbi Rammer, editor of *So That Your Values Live On* puts it: "I have learned that ethical wills have the power to make people confront the ultimate choices that they must make in their lives. They can make people who are usually too preoccupied with earning a living stop and consider what they are living for."

While ethical wills have gained wide popularity in recent years, they were originally a Jewish tradition, with roots in early Biblical times. Recall Moses' address to the people before he died; Joseph's blessings of his sons where he described their respective characters and their futures, and King David's prayers for his son. Perhaps the most famous of ancient ethical wills is Moshe Nachmanides' (Ramban's) letter to his son, *Letter for the Ages*. There is also the letter of the Vilna Gaon written at age 27 giving his wife and mother instructions for the education of the children.

How do you go about writing an ethical will yourself? There are many useful books on the subject. One of the best known volumes is *Ethical Wills: Putting Your Values on Paper* by Barry K. Baines. The author is a physician and hospice director. Baines defines an ethical will as "a vehicle for clarifying and communicating the meaning in our lives to our families and communities." Baines discusses the history of the practice of leaving an ethical will, its enormous benefits to the dying and to their families, and how to make them.

Other resources are *So That Your Values Live on: Ethical Wills and How to Prepare Them* by Rabbi Jack Rammer and Nathaniel Stampfer, and *Women's Lives, Women's Legacies: Passing Your Beliefs and Blessings to Future Generations: Creating Your Own Spiritual-Ethical Will*, by Rachael Freed.

Some legal scholars have objected to calling such a personal statement a "will" lest it confuse people and they think they do not need to write a real will which disposes of their property. Instead, some refer to it as a "Personal Legacy Statement," but the term "Ethical Will" seems to have stuck.

Here's a partial list of common themes seen in more modern ethical wills which are listed at *www.ethicalwill.com*: important personal values and beliefs, important spiritual values, hopes and blessings for future generations, life's lessons, love, forgiving others, and asking for forgiveness.

Humorist, Sam Levenson wrote, "Ethical Will and Testament to His Grandchildren and to Children Everywhere" in 1976. I encourage you to read it (found on Santa Clara University's website) and share it with your family; an ethical will may be the most cherished and meaningful gift you can give to your family, after all.

TRUSTS

What Is a Trust?

A trust is a creature of English common law, originally devised to avoid the reversion of lands to the crown and the strictures of primogeniture. Legal scholars have struggled to give a definition. There is a famous definition from a law book that describes a trust negatively by listing all the things it is not. A trust is not a bailment, a trust is not an executorship, a trust is not an agency …

A trust is a relationship with respect to property. The grantor (or settlor) creates the trust either by declaring himself trustee or making a transfer to a trustee. Legal title to the property is held by the trustee, but the property is held by the trustee for the benefit of the beneficiaries on the terms specified by the grantor. At common law, there had to be some property, no matter how small, in order to create the trust. That is why many trust documents recite that $1 is being transferred to the trustee. At common law, "a mere peppercorn will do." The statutory law of most states (including Pennsylvania), now permits the creation of "empty" trusts — vehicles awaiting funding on some future date.

There are more types of trusts than you can shake a stick at. Some of the categories are (1) revocable vs. irrevocable, (2) *intervivos* vs. testamentary, and (3) grantor vs. simple or complex.

A revocable trust can be revoked, amended, changed in any way. An irrevocable trust can't. I once was supervising a client's execution of an irrevocable trust. I explained, "This trust is irrevocable — you can't amend it and you can't revoke it." The client looked at me searchingly and said, "Then how do you change it?" That is precisely the point — it can't be changed. However, a good estate planner knows how to include flexibility in even an irrevocable trust.

An *intervivos* trust is one that is created during life. A testamentary trust is created in a will and does not come into existence until after the death of the person who wrote the will. A testamentary trust is always irrevocable — by definition the creator of the trust is deceased and can exercise no power over the trust. An *intervivos* trust may be revocable or irrevocable. A good example of an irrevocable *intervivos* trust is an Irrevocable Life Insurance Trust. By contrast, many people use a revocable *intervivos* trust to manage their affairs. This is sometimes called a Living Trust. Assets titled to a revocable *intervivos* trust avoid probate.

Trusts are treated variously for income tax purposes. A revocable trust, for example, is ignored for income tax purposes. All of its income and deductions simply pass through to the grantor. In income tax nomenclature, this is a "grantor" trust. Some trusts are treated as separate entities for income tax purposes. There can be trusts that distribute all their income; they are called "simple" trusts. On the other hand, the trustee may choose to accumulate income or to distribute principal; in such cases, the trusts are "complex." These trusts require careful accounting, and the Internal Revenue Code provides complicated rules for the allocation of income and deductions between the trust and the beneficiaries.

For centuries, only an individual could be a trustee. In the 19th century in the United States, state legislatures began authorizing banks and trust companies to act as trustees. To this day, banks and trust companies are the only corporate entities who are permitted to be trustees. However, there remain many firms of private individual trustees, especially in Boston and Philadelphia, many of them lawyers who manage billions — in large part what you and I would call "old money."

Trusts fulfill a myriad of purposes and intentions. Some are to protect minors, providing for management and distribution of the funds during a child's tender years. Some are for the benefit of incapacitated persons who cannot handle their own financial affairs. Some are used as vehicles to provide investment management advice. Some are used for tax planning strategies; an important part of estate planning is to minimize the impact of estate and gift taxes.

The dispositive provisions of a trust are those that dictate when and to whom the trustee is to distribute the property. These provisions are tailored to each case, depending on the intentions of the person creating the trust and the needs of the beneficiaries. The trustee is bound to carry out the terms of the trust. The trustee has a duty to manage the trust for the benefit of the beneficiaries. This fiduciary duty is the highest duty known to the law and requires impartiality, loyalty, prudence, and fairness. A trustee is personally liable for any breach of the duty.

Consumers Beware: Trust Mills Aren't to Be Trusted

Fear mongers have used the *intervivos* trust, also called revocable living trust, to sell books, trust kits, trust documents, and other products and services. They often do this without regard to the individual's tax and personal objectives. They scare the client by telling them that probate is a dreadfully complicated and horrendously expensive process. Then, they offer to "save" the client. If you buy our estate plan, which gives you a revocable living trust for $2,000 (or more), you will avoid all of this.

There is nothing wrong with a living trust. A living trust is a part of many appropriate estate plans. Living trusts can be beneficial depending on the type of assets you own, such as real estate located in several states. In addition, if you want someone else to manage your financial affairs, perhaps because you travel frequently, having a trustee of a living trust may offer fewer problems than relying on a Power of Attorney document.

But for other people, it can be a waste of money and time, or worse, it can actually defeat their intentions. In their attempt to save their heirs the perceived expense, time, and loss of privacy caused by probate, other problems arise.

In fact, probate fees, themselves, are quite modest. For example, in Lancaster County, Pennsylvania, a will for a decedent with a $1 million probate estate can be admitted to probate in 2013 for less than $1000. Notice must be published in two newspapers, each costing about $60 in addition to the filing fee.

Avoiding probate by using a trust does offer some privacy. A will when probated becomes a public record which can be viewed by anyone. However, even where there is no probate property, the inheritance tax return is filed with the Register of Wills, so much of the financial information may be available to the public. In Lancaster County, inheritance tax returns are available for public inspection, whether or not the estate was probated.

Living trusts are sometimes promoted as a way to avoid excessive court supervision. However, with a living trust, you eliminate protections given to heirs in probate proceedings. A successor trustee of a trust may find it easier to succeed in illegally misdirecting your assets than would a will's executor. Some states, Pennsylvania being one, subject wills to very little court supervision, therefore avoiding probate for this reason may be risky.

A living trust does not always eliminate the need for probate. If you don't transfer all your assets to the trust (and some assets — such as your everyday checking account or car don't work well inside a trust) your estate will still need to be probated.

The main problem with living trusts is that they are marketed as an estate planning cure-all when they are not. Unscrupulous profiteers have discovered that preying upon fears, especially of the elderly, in regards to the estate planning process has led to the creation of estate mills.

What is a trust mill? As described by the American College of Trusts and Estates Counsel, trust mills are organizations which promote the indiscriminate marketing of *intervivos* trusts by non-lawyers; often with the assistance of local counsel. Typically trust mill organizations consist of insurance agents, financial planners, stockbrokers, and other individuals who are not lawyers, but who prepare estate planning documents from various forms. Sometimes these documents are sent to local counsel for "attorney review."

A trust mill promotes its product door-to-door, on TV, radio, in seminars, workshops, and through the mail. Prices can range from $25 for a do-it-yourself kit to $5,000. The trust mill advertises with slogans like "Protect your assets," "Leave more to your heirs," and "Avoid the agony of probate." The trust mill makes exaggerated claims of reduced taxes, exaggerates the cost of probate and the need for privacy. The prices for these living trust packages often far exceed the legal fees that would be paid to a lawyer for a true estate plan.

"Don't trust trust kits," says the Michigan Bar Association. Their web site, *www.michbar.org*, lists some warning signs to make consumers beware of a living trust scam:

1. An ad or salesperson promising the consumer will "save on legal fees."
2. The use of a salesperson: the ethics rules of governing attorneys do not permit the use of salespersons.

3. Encouragement to purchase other products such as investments or insurance.
4. A "first step" in the program that is anything other than a one-on-one meeting with a licensed attorney.
5. An offer to purchase the fill-in-the blank forms or an estate planning kit.
6. No permanent local office.

Many states have taken action against trust mills on grounds of consumer fraud and the unauthorized practice of law. Preparing a trust in Pennsylvania requires a lawyer. Pennsylvania Attorney General issued a Consumer Advisory in 2005 about Living Trust Scams, *http://www.attorneygeneral.gov/consumers.aspx?id=304*. If you have any questions, or want to file a complaint, call the Pennsylvania Attorney General's Bureau of Consumer Protection hotline: 1-800-441-2555, or visit their website at *www.attorneygeneral.gov.*

The Federal Trade Commission has issued warnings about living trust promoters, see *http://www.ftc.gov/opa/2000/07/livingtrust.shtm* as has AARP,*http://www.aarp.org/money/estate-planning/info-04-2009/truth_about_living_trusts.html.*

We haven't even touched on abusive trust schemes that claim to save income taxes. If you hear words like "Pure," "Pure Equity" or "Constitutional" Trust — these schemes are even worse than the living trust scams. Don't be taken in. These trusts are tickets to the federal penitentiary. If you are approached by anyone selling a "Pure Trust" or a "Constitutional Trust" or similar vehicle with a pitch that the trust is exempt from income taxes, notify the F.B.I. or the Criminal Investigative Division of the Internal Revenue Service.

As Steve Leimberg says in his book, *The New Book of Trusts*, "The revocable trust (or, more accurately, the lack of an estate planning process that leads to the revocable trust) did not make matters better, but worse, just like the wrong surgery, the wrong drugs, or the right drugs in the wrong dosage, can make a patient worse, not better."

The Federal Trade Commission recommends that before you sign any papers to create a will, a living trust, or any other kind of trust, to follow six guidelines as seen in the FTC's article, found here: http://www.nextavenue.org/article/2011-03/keep-control-assets-after-death

Remember, the best estate planning tool in the business is a competent legal advisor whom you can trust. Before you buy services and sign documents regarding your estate, take the time to seek out *independent* advice about the full range of options that might be best for you. Also, be on guard when doing business with someone who contacts you first. You will often be better served if you do your homework and then select and contact the professional of your choice.

Beware Trustee's Fees: Some Are Worth It, Some Not

Trustees almost always charge a fee based on the market value of the trust's assets. Investment managers, too, often charge a fee based on a percentage of the account's value. The theory is that the larger the account, the greater the responsibility shouldered by the trustee or manager; hence, the larger the fee.

Let's examine that premise. Account No. 1 holds $300,000 invested equally in three mutual funds. Account No. 2 holds $600,000 invested equally in the same three mutual funds. Charging a 1% annual fee, the trustee's or investment manager's fee for Account No. 1 is $3,000 annually. The trustee's or investment manager's fee for Account No. 2 is $6,000 annually. What additional work must be performed by the trustee or investment manager of Account No. 2 to earn the additional $3,000? Nothing I can think of.

I feel like I'm telling the story of the Emperor's New Clothes. The emperor walks down the street naked in front of his subjects and every bystander is afraid to say the truth. So the Emperor continues to strut down the avenue in his new (nonexistent) finery until a child cries out that "He doesn't have anything on!" Isn't it intuitively obvious to the casual observer that the market value of the account does not bear a proportional relationship to the amount of work involved in managing it? In other words, the emperor doesn't have anything on!

Nonetheless, it is the industry standard to charge fees based on market value. You will be hard-pressed to find trust services charged on any other basis. Money managers charge so-called "wrap" fees, which are market value fees and transaction fees. One can get money management on a commission basis, but the amount of the fee here is also dependent on the value of the transaction. Trustees and managers never charge by their results. The value of the assets under management is what drives the fee.

Among financial planners there is a move to charge investors on a fee-only basis. Fee-only planners do not accept commissions or any payments from anyone other than the client. This is good in that the built-in conflict that is present when a planner is compensated by commission is absent. However, the amount of assets invested in the product or managed by the planner still drives the fee.

A further refinement is the hourly fee-only financial planner. Now we're getting somewhere. The success of a financial planner should not be based on the number of products a client purchases, but on the success of his or her client's investments. This is why no referral fees, commissions, or other reimbursements from the implementation of recommendations are accepted by fee-only planners, and why the fee of an hourly fee-only planner is not dependent on your net worth, but rather on the time and value of the advice given. Being compensated by a predetermined client fee rather than commissions assures that the advice clients receive is unbiased and always in their best interest.

Despite innovations in fee structures, the industry standard for trustees and many money managers continues to be a market value fee. What is a reasonable fee? Well, first, let's try to discover what fees are being charged.

Take your typical bank or trust company. First, it is likely there will be a market value fee charged annually. This can range anywhere from 0.5% to 3.0%. Often the fee will vary depending on whether the account is invested in mutual funds, or whether the trustee is investing the account in individual stocks and bonds (mutual fund accounts are cheaper).

There is a myriad of other fees not included in the market value fee. Here are some examples. Some trustees charge a percentage fee on income collected. Sometimes there are commissions to be paid on purchases and sales of securities. If trust assets are invested in mutual funds or money market funds, what are the fees in those funds? (It is a rude awakening to find you are paying fees for management of the mutual fund and then another 2.5% of the fund's value to a trustee.) Do the mutual funds or money market fund share fees with the bank? In other words, does the bank receive part of the fee collected by the mutual funds or money market fund? Does the bank reduce its fees to the trust by the amount kicked back by the fund companies?

Some trustees charge extra if they must serve with an individual co-trustee. The extra charge is to compensate them for the need to consult with a co-trustee. The co-trustee's fees, if any, are additional.

Does the trustee charge special fees for holding real estate, selling real estate, holding insurance policies, and annuities? Is there a charge per check issued by the trustee? Does the trustee charge extra for providing tax information or for sending statements more frequently than quarterly? If the trustee does an accounting, is there an additional charge?

Is there a transaction charge when the trustee invests cash in a money market (sometimes called a "sweep" fee)?

Is there a minimum fee? In other words, if the trustee charges 1% but a minimum of $5,000 per year, your $250,000 account would actually be paying 2% if the minimum fee applied.

Is there a termination fee? That is, if you close the account, or move to another trustee is there an additional charge? And if so, how much?

Has the trustee disclosed all the fees to you? In many states, every corporate trustee must have a published fee schedule that is publicly available. That is not required in Pennsylvania, although there are other disclosure requirements if you are an actual trust customer. When fee schedules are publicly available, comparison shopping is much easier.

Trustee services are important and valuable. Trustees should be compensated fairly. Just make sure you know how much and for what you are paying.

With a Name Like Crummey, These Trusts Have to Be Good

"Crummey" trusts get their name from Mr. Crummey who had a great tax planning idea in the 1960s. He was the plaintiff in a well-known U.S. Tax Court case. A "Crummey" trust is definitely not crummy. It's a great estate tax planning technique.

There is a $14,000 per donee annual exclusion from the application of the gift tax. The exclusion applies only to *present interest gifts*. You can write a check to your donee, register stock in the donee's name, transfer a real estate title to your donee. The problem with all these present interest gifts is that the donee has the gift. The donee, who might be age 16 (or even a babe in arms), will have access to the money to buy cars, drugs, Pokemon cards, trips to Europe, you name it.

What you really want is to get the annual exclusion while *not* giving the property to the donee. Am I right? That's what Mr. Crummey wanted, too. His idea was that he would transfer assets to a trust. Usually a transfer to a trust doesn't qualify for the annual exclusion because the trust provides for the beneficiary to receive trust assets at some time in the future — to pay for college, or at age 35, for example. A Crummey trust includes a provision that for a period of 30 days after a transfer to the trust the beneficiaries have an opportunity to withdraw the gift from the trust. After the 30-day window closes, the property stays in the trust and the usual trust provisions take over. The trust might provide for education distributions and ultimate distribution one-half at age 30 and the balance at age 35. The fact that the beneficiary *could* have withdrawn the gift makes the gift a present interest — thus spoke the Tax Court.

The Crummey trust has been used since 1968 and is a well-known, low risk technique. It is not "aggressive" tax planning. The IRS has issued a number of rulings giving guidance on how to administer and design the trust in order to assure the availability of the annual exclusion.

There are various requirements. The beneficiaries must be notified of the withdrawal right. It may not be desirable for the entire withdrawal right to lapse in a single year. However, there can be as many beneficiaries with withdrawal rights as you like, and the gifts can be made every year.

If Mom and Dad have four kids, each of whom has a spouse, and each kid has produced two grandchildren, that's a potential group of 16 Crummey beneficiaries. So Mom and Dad could give 448,000 per year to this trust with no gift or estate tax consequences. Mom can give $224,000 and Dad can give $224,000. Obviously, significant sums can be removed from Mom's and Dad's estates with a program of annual giving. $448,000 per year soon adds up to real money.

This technique is frequently encountered as a means of funding Irrevocable Life Insurance Trusts. It works fine for that. Gifts are made to the trust, qualifying for the annual exclusion because the trust has Crummey powers. The trustee then uses the funds to pay life insurance premiums on policies owned by the trust. The missed opportunity is using Crummey powers to fund a trust that invests in marketable securities, or other trust investments.

If you already have an insurance trust, and are not contributing as much as you can, you may be able to use the same vehicle and make additional gifts for investment.

These QTIPs Help Take Care of Surviving Spouses

You don't find a QTIP Trust in the medicine cabinet. "QTIP" is an acronym for Qualified Terminable Interest in Property.

QTIP trusts were authorized by the ERTA (Economic Recovery Tax Act of 1981). We are going to learn about QTIPs ASAP.

Marital deduction is the provision in the federal estate and gift tax that gives a 100% deduction for the value of property passing to a surviving spouse. To qualify for the marital deduction, the first spouse to die can pass property (1) directly to the surviving spouse, (2) to a general power of appointment trust where the surviving spouse gets the income and has the power to make withdrawals or appoint the property in her will on her death, or (3) to a QTIP trust.

The minimum requirement for a QTIP trust is that the surviving spouse must be given the income from the trust for her life. This right can never be taken away. The right to income can't be conditioned on not remarrying or anything else. The trust must produce income. The surviving spouse's rights to income can't be defeated by a trustee who invests in something that doesn't produce any interest or dividends. If the minimum income requirement is met, then the trust is a "Qualified Terminable Interest in Property" or QTIP.

When the first spouse dies and a QTIP trust is created, the first spouse's executor has a choice. The executor can choose to elect marital deduction treatment for the QTIP, or not. This choice is made on the federal estate tax return for the first spouse and is called the "QTIP election."

If the executor elects QTIP treatment, then the transfer of property to the QTIP qualifies for the marital deduction, and the property in the QTIP trust is not subject to federal estate tax in the first spouse's estate. The consequence of making the election and obtaining the deduction in the first spouse's estate is that the QTIP property *will* be subject to estate tax in the surviving spouse's estate.

If the executor of the estate of the first spouse to die does not elect QTIP treatment, then the property in the QTIP trust is subject to estate tax in the first spouse's estate and is *not* subject to estate tax in the surviving spouse's estate.

The QTIP election gives the executor the choice of what time to subject the trust assets to estate tax. Should they be taxed in the estate of the first spouse to die, or should they be taxed in the surviving spouse's estate?

Most executors choose to make the QTIP election and, thus, defer the federal estate tax until the death of the surviving spouse. This is psychologically appealing because neither spouse is alive to see the check for estate tax written to the Internal Revenue Service. However, it may result in an overall higher tax before the property passes to the children or other intended beneficiaries. This is because the property may be taxed at higher brackets in the survivor's estate. The executor should carefully analyze the alternatives with the advice of competent professionals before deciding whether or not to make the QTIP election. Once the election is made, it is irrevocable.

The minimum requirement for a QTIP trust is that it provides for payment of the income to the surviving spouse for life. Unfortunately, many lawyers stop there. Much more flexibility can be added. The surviving spouse can be the trustee of the QTIP trust. The surviving spouse can be given principal from the trust. If there is an independent trustee acting with the spouse, the surviving spouse can be given principal in any amount, for any purpose. If the surviving spouse is the sole trustee of the QTIP, then principal distribution must be limited to amounts for health, maintenance, and support.

The surviving spouse can be given the annual right to withdraw an amount of principal equal to the greater of (1) $5,000 or (2) 5% of the value of the trust principal. This is called a "5 and 5 power."

The surviving spouse can be given a special power of appointment over the QTIP trust property exercisable by will. The terms of the power can be very broad or can be limited. The broadest possible power would give the surviving spouse the authority to direct the distribution of the QTIP trust property to any person(s) or any organization(s) in the world except her own estate or her creditors. That is a very broad power.

There is one remaining feature of a QTIP that must be mentioned. It has a special status under the Generation-skipping Transfer Tax. There are some circumstances where a QTIP trust must be used for part of the marital deduction in order to take full advantage of the exemption from the application of the Generation-skipping Transfer Tax.

If your estate planner recommends a QTIP trust, make sure you and the planner are clear on what the other choices are and their respective pros and cons. If a QTIP is decided upon, make sure you review what features will be included over and above the required minimum distribution of income.

When the Surviving Spouse Acts as Trustee

The object of estate tax planning is to minimize taxation of assets at death. The basic tool for a married couple with assets more than $5,250,000 is to arrange ownership of assets so that each spouse has sufficient, separately titled assets to fund a credit shelter bypass trust, sometimes called a credit shelter trust.

True, there is a marital deduction that exempts all property passing to a surviving spouse, but that is actually a deferral, not an exemption. The property will be taxed when the surviving spouse dies. Taxation is avoided (not just deferred) by placing assets up to the exclusion amount ($5,250,000 in 2013) into a bypass trust. The trust income can be paid to the spouse, and some trust principal can be paid to the spouse even with the spouse acting as trustee.

In general, if a person can direct the payment of trust assets to herself, her creditors, her estate, or the creditors of her estate, she has a "general power of appointment" and is taxed for estate and gift tax purposes as if she were the owner of the trust's assets.

For the bypass trust to work, the surviving spouse cannot be treated as the owner. The surviving spouse cannot have a general power of appointment over the assets in the credit shelter trust. You don't want the surviving spouse to own the bypass trust assets because then they will be taxed in her estate. (When you see the words "in general," you know there are exceptions to come.)

Let's assume Husband dies leaving a will which creates a bypass trust for the benefit of his Wife. Wife is the Trustee of the bypass trust. The trust document says that the Trustee can distribute any amount of income and principal to the Wife. Remember that the Trustee is the Wife. That means Wife can take as much of the trust property for herself as she wants. The law rightly treats this as tantamount to outright ownership and Wife is taxed as if she were the owner of the property. If Wife dies, the assets in this trust would be included in her estate and the bypass trust strategy would have failed.

An exception to this tax treatment is where Wife's power to distribute trust property to herself is limited by an ascertainable standard.

What is an "ascertainable standard?" The Internal Revenue Code provides that "[a] power to consume, invade, or appropriate property for the benefit of the decedent which is limited by an ascertainable standard relating to the health, education, support, or maintenance of the decedent shall not be deemed a general power of appointment." Examples of phrases using these four magic words that the regulations specifically endorse are "support in reasonable comfort," "maintenance in health and reasonable comfort," "support in his accustomed manner of living," "education, including college and professional education," and the health care costs of "medical, dental, hospital and nursing expenses and expenses of invalidism."

The regulations implementing the code further state that, "[a] power to use property for the comfort, welfare, or happiness of the holder of the power is not limited by the requisite standard."

The penalty for going over the line is that the bypass trust strategy fails and the assets in the bypass trust are subject to estate tax.

The theory is that if trust distributions must be in accordance with a "standard," then there is an objective criterion for distribution. A judge could review the trustee's actions and determine if they were in accordance with the standard. Since the trustee's discretion is limited by an enforceable standard, the power to make trust distributions is not treated as a general power of appointment for estate tax purposes.

Here are three examples to clarify what is allowed as far as invasion of principal is concerned.

Example 1. Husband creates a trust under his will for the benefit of his wife for her lifetime. She is the Trustee and is to receive all of the income. Invasion of principal is allowed for the health maintenance and support of both her and their children. The remainder, on her death, is to be distributed to their children. The principal invasion is allowed without a penalty because it is limited by an ascertainable standard, and the recipients of that principal are current income beneficiaries and remainder beneficiaries, and no one else.

Example 2. Same facts as above except that the husband states in his trust that the standard for invasion of principal is for the health, maintenance, support, and happiness of his wife and children. "Happiness" is not an ascertainable standard. The wife has a general power of appointment and the principal of the trust will be included in her estate.

Example 3. Husband creates a trust under his will for his wife for her lifetime. He provides for invasion of principal for his wife according to ascertainable standards. He names his two children as remainder beneficiaries, each to receive half of the principal and accumulated income on the death of his wife. He provides for an unrestricted invasion of principal for the benefit of his children for any reason at the discretion of his Trustee (his wife) provided that any such invasion will proportionately reduce subsequent income and principal payments made to the child receiving the principal. Thus, if one-half of the corpus is paid to one child, all of the income from the remaining half is, thereafter, payable to the other child. The wife is not treated as an owner by reason of this power even though there is no ascertainable standard. She can change only the time of a child's receipt of the property, not the amount ultimately distributed to the child.

One last wrinkle — the trustee may, if allowed in the document, add after-born children and after-adopted children to the group of beneficiaries. Now does the case of a widow adopting the youthful gardener make sense?

How Long Can the Dead Hand Rule the Living?

Much of estate planning is concerned with maintaining control over assets. Through trusts, individuals can maintain control of assets for long periods of time even after they are dead. Family fortunes can be held by trustees and doled out to beneficiaries in accordance with a decedent's instructions for generations. Often, significant tax advantages can also be secured in these arrangements.

Exactly how long can these trusts last? Purely charitable trusts can last forever. But the duration of trusts that benefit individuals is limited by something called the Rule Against Perpetuities.

If you already have a trust, it probably includes a provision stating that regardless of any other provisions in the trust, the trust must come to an end 21 years after the death of the last survivor of a group of people, usually your issue. This is called a savings clause. Its purpose is to cut off a trust so that it cannot violate the Rule. If a trust violates the Rule Against Perpetuities, it is void. None of its provision has any effect, and the property is distributed outright to the person who created the trust or his or her heirs.

The Rule Against Perpetuities puts a limit on how long a trust can tie up property. In round numbers, the maximum permissible duration of a trust usually turns out to be around 100 years, as we will explain, but first, let's talk about how this common law rule came into being.

The Rule developed in the 15th century. Courts in medieval England opposed the use of trusts to tie up the title to land for indefinite periods. Wealth, at that time, was almost entirely in land. There were no stock markets and no banks as we know them. Judges feared that perpetual trusts would eventually own all the land in the world and commerce would come to a halt. Courts differed on when a trust lasted "too long" until the Duke of Norfolk's case came along in 1682. At the beginning of the case, he was the Earl of Arundel, but his son later restored the dukedom (the most senior of all dukedoms) to the family, and so it is by the name of the Duke of Norfolk that this case is known.

Those were the days of primogeniture. The Earl of Arundel had eight sons, but the eldest was infirm in mind and body. The Earl enlisted the aid of Sir Otto Bridgemen in planning his estate (Sir Otto was an esteemed counsel and the premier estate planner of his day). The plan was essentially this: eldest son, Thomas, would inherit all of the Earl's property except the barony of Grostock, which would go to the number two son, Henry. But, if Thomas died without children and Henry survived him (which was likely), Henry would inherit all, and the barony would go to the number three son, Charles.

In 1652, the Earl died. Although Thomas, the eldest (and infirm), was living, Henry, the number two son, wasted no time in taking control of Thomas's kingdom. He sent older brother Thomas off to Padua, Italy, where he was incarcerated (good old prison therapy for the insane was the norm in those days). In 1660, Henry restored the coveted dukedom of Norfolk to the family. In 1677, Thomas died without issue, leaving Henry in possession of all but the small barony. Under the terms of the will, the number three son, Charles should now get the barony of Grostock. Henry was a greedy sort though, and he sued in court to gain the barony as well, claiming it was an illegal gift because it was a perpetuity. (Some people never have enough.)

The Chancellor, an equity judge called the "keeper of the king's conscience," was sympathetic with the reasonable plans of a father with land and a mentally infirm first son. He decreed that the interest of the third son, Charles, would "wear itself out" in his lifetime, and that no perpetuity existed. His rule, therefore, was that if a future interest must vest by the end of a life in being, it is good and not void as a perpetuity. Later judges kept adding years to the "life in being" concept, until in 1699 the rule became lives in being plus 21 years. Furthermore, in 1805, the court decreed that there was no limit on the number of lives to be used as a measuring life, only that they be traceable by the courts.

The classic statement of the Rule Against Perpetuities was given by legal scholar and Harvard professor of property law, John Chipman Gray, who wrote an entire book on the subject of the rule: "No interest [in real or personal property] is good unless it must vest, if at all, not later than twenty-one years after some life in being at the creation of the interest." That is still the common law rule but some states, including Pennsylvania, have prospectively repealed the rule. The rule no longer applies in Pennsylvania to interests created after January 1, 2007.

Estate Planning for Pets

> *Near this spot are deposited the remains of one who possessed Beauty without Vanity, Strength without Insolence, Courage without Ferocity, and all the Virtues of Man, without his Vices. This Praise, which would be unmeaning Flattery if inscribed over human ashes, is but a just tribute to the Memory of Boatswain, a Dog.*
>
> Lord Byron

According to the Humane Society of the United States, sixty-two percent of U.S. households have a pet. Many pet owners treat these pets as true members of their families. They buy them special clothing, get them professionally groomed at day spas, buy gourmet pet food, and take their animals for frequent check-ups at the vet. As put by Henry David Thoreau, "It often happens that a man is more humanely related to a cat or dog than to any human being."

Small wonder, then, that these pet owners want to make sure these pets are cared for after the owner dies. Traditionally, the pets themselves could not be beneficiaries of the owner's will. The pet itself could be bequeathed to someone since the pet is tangible property, but any money for the pet's care had to be given to the new owner with the hope that it would be used to take care of the pet.

One solution was for the pet owner to set up a trust with the pet's caregiver as the beneficiary. The caregiver received trust distributions so long as the pet was living and the caregiver was taking adequate care of the pet. Another party acted as trustee to enforce the terms of the trust by managing the funds and by having the power to move the pet from one caregiver to another.

The Uniform Trust Code (UTC), adopted by Pennsylvania on November 4, 2006, introduces a new concept and makes it possible to make a trust for the benefit of a pet where the pet is treated as the beneficiary. Under the terms of the UTC, a trust may be created to provide for the care of an animal alive during the settlor's lifetime. The trust terminates upon the death of the animal or, if the trust was created to provide for the care of more than one animal alive during the settlor's lifetime, upon the death of the last surviving animal. The law provides that the trust property is to be applied only for the care of the animal. It is very important to make a gift of the remainder to some other person or charity. If the trust terms do not provide for remaindermen, the remainder interest will be distributed through a resulting trust to the settlor, if living, or the settlor's estate. There won't be any millionaire kitties eating out of crystal on silver trays. According to Marilou Gervacio, writing for UTC Notes, the average amount put into such trusts has been said to be about $25,000 per animal.

Who pays the income taxes on the trust's investments? If the caregiver is considered a beneficiary of the trust (which is the case for common law trusts, not pet trusts under the UTC) then the caregiver reports distributions from the trust as income on his or her personal 1040 to the extent they carryout trust income. Revenue Ruling 76-486 provides that if the pet is considered the beneficiary of the trust (which is the case in a pet trust under the UTC), the trust gets no deduction for amounts distributed for the pet's care and the trust must pay income taxes on earnings. Note that the trust does not qualify as a charitable trust even if the remainder beneficiary after the death of the pet is a charity.

Your pet needs care if you become incapacitated, too. The principal's power of attorney can include language directing the agent to care for your pet and expend amounts necessary to provide such care. This could be important if the agent's actions are challenged as violating the duty of the agent to expend sums only for the benefit of the principal.

Professor Gary Beyer, of the Texas Tech University School of Law wrote an article called "Estate Planning for Non-human Family Members" in which he advises that in addition to setting aside funds for the care of your pet, you need to make sure the relevant people know what should be done with your pets if something happens to you suddenly.

Professor Beyer next recommends that the owner should prepare an "animal document." This document should contain information about the animals, their care needs, who will take care of them, and perhaps additional details as well. This document is intended to be kept in the same location where the pet owner keeps his or her estate planning documents.

Finally, the owner can provide signage regarding the pets on entrances to the owner's home to alert individuals entering the home that pets are inside. The signage is also important during the owner's life to warn others who may enter the dwelling (e.g., police, fire fighters, inspectors, meter readers, friends) about the pets. The Humane Society of the United States supplies cards and signage alerting others of the existence of pets and information regarding their care.

How do you know the pet that is the trust beneficiary is still alive? Certainly, the pet needs to be identified. Beyer cites a report that "[a] trust was established for a black cat to be cared for by its deceased owner's maid. Inconsistencies in the reported age of the pet tipped off authorities to the fact that the maid was on her third black cat, the original long since having died." Veterinary records and photographs are helpful. It has been suggested that the pet could be tattooed. Although this could later "cause problems" for the pet because a pet thief could mutilate the pet to remove the tattoo, such as cutting off an ear or leg, if the pet's primary function is breeding. (Indeed!)

A microchip can be implanted in the animal and the trustee can then have the animal scanned to verify that the animal the caregiver is minding is the same animal. But, an enterprising caregiver could surgically remove the microchip and have it implanted in another physically similar animal.

How far can this go? It is suggested that the best, albeit expensive, method to assure identification is for the trustee to retain a sample of the animal's DNA before turning the animal over to the caregiver and then to run periodic comparisons between the retained sample and new samples from the animal. (Whew!)

North to Alaska!

The common law limits the maximum duration of trusts to an arcane formula: "lives in being plus twenty-one years." Most states follow this Rule. Pennsylvania follows it only for interest created before January 1, 2007, but adopts a "wait and see" approach. In Pennsylvania, a trust that may violate the Rule is not declared void at the outset; rather, the specified period of time is waited out, and if a violation occurs, then the interest that violates the Rule is voided.

Several states have changed the Rule. Some have just adopted a fixed number of years, ranging from 80 to 120 years. Some states have repealed the Rule altogether! Delaware has repealed the Rule so that trusts can exist in perpetuity, although the Delaware statute does still limit trust periods for real estate to 120 years. In the east, Maine, Pennsylvania, and New Jersey have followed Delaware's lead. Rhode Island has abolished the Rule completely. In the Midwest, Illinois followed Delaware's lead. South Dakota and Wisconsin abolished the Rule some years ago. The Rule has been repealed in Alaska.

As you can see, the Rule varies widely from state to state. Any trust should specify which state's law governs. Usually there is a provision included near the end of a well-drafted will or trust that specifies which state's laws shall apply. Even more important is the savings clause which forces termination within the allowable period for the trust's existence.

Let's look at some examples of how a trust can violate the Rule.

The Fertile Octogenarian. Ann bequeaths a fund in trust for her 80-year-old sister for life, then for her sister's children for their lives, then to distribute the principal at the death of her sister to her sister's issue then living. This trust violates the Rule. How? Ann could die today. The conclusive (meaning irrebuttable) presumption is that Ann could have more children and the measuring life has not yet been born. This violates the Rule. If you think this is unfair, consider a gift to Ann's 80-year-old brother instead of her sister. Is parenthood so unbelievable then? Suppose Ann's sister adopts a child? Does that change your thinking?

The Unborn Widow. Ann creates a trust in her will to continue until the death of both of her sons and of her sons' widows, if any. The widows are not identified. Ann dies. Two years later a girl is born. Eighteen years later the girl marries one of Ann's sons. The girl could easily live more than 21 more years, and the sons could be dead by then. The trust would easily outlast any lives mentioned specifically in the will plus 21 years. The bequest fails.

The Unborn Sibling. Suppose Ann bequeaths property in trust for her sister for life, then to her sister's children until the youngest reaches age 25, then to distribute the property to her sister's issue, *per stirpes.* That age, 25, should be sounding alarm bells in your head already. Suppose at Ann's death, her sister has a son, age 10. Suppose that she later has another child. There is a possibility that before that child reaches age 4, both Ann and the older child would die. It would be more than 21 years before the second child reaches age 25. Since the younger child might meet the condition precedent more than 21 years after the death of all measuring lives, the trust fails. Unless there is a clause in the document that has a backup time limit that satisfies the Rule (a perpetuities saving clause), gifts to a younger generation should vest by age 21.

In those states that have repealed the Rule Against Perpetuities, trusts can last forever. That means you can put your assets in the hands of a trustee and no one can ever have them! That appeals to some people.

On a more serious note, it allows assets to stay in trust, generation after generation, and escape transfer tax. Since the estate and gift tax operates at a maximum rate of 40% and applies, on average, every 25 to 30 years, which is the length of a generation, a trust that can escape this tax will grow astronomically. This kind of trust is often called a "dynasty trust."

Why are perpetual trusts so popular? Simple. They're the next best thing to taking it with you. The law has always been opposed to control of property by a "dead hand" but in some states, the dead hand is preferred to the IRS's hand.

You don't have to be a resident of a state to use the law of that state to govern your trust. For example, you can use the Alaska or Delaware law that has no perpetuities period for investment assets just by using a Trustee in that state. The planning techniques afforded by the repeal of the Rule are thus available to everyone.

Both Delaware and Alaska have made other changes to their law of trust to attract more trust business to their states. They have provided in their statutes that a person can create a trust for himself, and that his creditors cannot reach the trust assets. This is a very dramatic change in the law. The law has always held that if a person creates a trust for someone else, and includes language limiting the rights of creditors, that the creditors of a beneficiary cannot reach trust assets. These are often called "spendthrift" trusts. In fact, the reason the trust was created was to protect the beneficiary and make sure he did not squander the trust assets.

Until these statutory changes in Delaware and Alaska, it has never been the law in the United States that a person can create this protection for himself. Many folks used the technique in foreign jurisdictions. This is one of the purposes served by offshore trusts. One can make a trust for oneself in the Cook Islands, for example, and creditors cannot reach the assets of the trust.

Many folks feel uncomfortable with all their assets on an island 1500 miles off the coast of New Zealand. If they can get the same treatment closer to home, that is very appealing.

The laws in Alaska and Delaware that provide this protection have not been tested. Many commentators are concerned that the laws will not be upheld and will be found to be unconstitutional because they result in one state not giving "full faith and credit" to the laws of other states. This remains to be seen.

In the meantime, with no Rule Against Perpetuities and the possibility of protection from creditors, many assets are finding their way to Delaware and Alaska.

Encouraging Some Behavior through Incentive Trusts

The older your children get the harder it is to control their behavior. Nevertheless, many people try to use the purse strings to control the kids. How many children, teenagers, and even mature adults, have been threatened with disinheritance? While occasionally a child is cut completely out of the will, most parents are reluctant to take that extreme step.

The use of an "incentive trust" has become a popular topic for discussion among estate planning professionals and their clients. Incentive provisions in a trust are designed to encourage particular behaviors, address specific problems, or promote a general philosophy of life. The incentive offered is financial. If the trust beneficiary exhibits the desired behavior, then he or she receives more money from the trust.

Sometimes the trust includes a general statement of the philosophy of the parents. The Trustee is then directed to be guided by this statement of philosophy in exercising its discretion. For example, the Trustee may be directed not to make any trust distributions that would remove the incentive for a beneficiary to be self-supporting. Sometimes there are objective standards for the Trustee to monitor that will govern distributions. Someone has suggested that trust distributions should equal earned income. The more you earn, the more you get from the trust.

Many wealthy clients express concern that leaving too much to children as an inheritance will "spoil" the children. They are concerned that a child will not work and achieve, that having too much money will keep the child from being a productive member of society. In fact, there are many such children who are "professional heirs" and who do nothing but live lavishly on their inherited wealth.

The simplest solution to this is not to leave the children everything. As Warren Buffet said, the perfect inheritance is "enough money so that they feel they could do anything, but not so much that they could do nothing." Anything over the "perfect inheritance" would be given to charity, or other beneficiaries.

For many clients, the most important thing is that a child be involved in productive employment. This is simple to say, but not so easy to draft into a trust document. What if the child is in school? What if the child is disabled because of injuries or illness? What if the child is staying home to raise a family? What if the child is performing volunteer services? What if a child is the caregiver for an elderly parent? What if there is an economic recession and the number of jobs available is severely reduced? All of these possibilities and more must be addressed in the document.

It is impossible to predict what the future will bring and what special circumstances may involve a trust beneficiary. These types of trusts are very difficult to draft, but even more difficult to administer. The Trustee is given a much more difficult task than usual. In order to monitor objective criteria, the Trustee must obtain and analyze income tax returns, medical reports, economic circumstances, and much more. The Trustee will need broad power to investigate the beneficiary's circumstances and request objective proof that beneficiaries are entitled.

Who can be the Trustee? The parents may have siblings or friends who can be a Trustee for a while, but the lives of the children and grandchildren will be longer than the lives of these individuals. It seems that a corporate fiduciary must be considered, at least as a successor to named individuals. Any Trustee who accepts this type of responsibility will want to make sure that the trust instrument provides lots of liability protection. Any Trustee would be concerned about a trust beneficiary who is a homeless person because the conditions for trust distributions for the trust haven't been met.

Many other objectives could be sought with an incentive trust. The possibilities are as endless as the imagination. It is not hard to imagine clients who would like to condition inheritances on a child not marrying a certain individual. Or on a child not divorcing.

Inheritance could be conditioned on becoming a doctor, becoming a lawyer, or not becoming a lawyer, as the case may be. The incentive could relate to religion, place of residence, number of children, length of hair, color of clothes — what would be the limit?

The real question is, "Does an incentive trust work?" The answer is "maybe." A beneficiary who is troubled is unlikely to be helped. Telling a drug addict he won't get his inheritance unless he stops taking drugs is not likely to get him off heroin. Telling a beneficiary that he can't have trust funds unless he graduates from college and is making $50,000 a year may work. But query whether the inheritance is really what motivated the child to reach that level of achievement. Chances are this child didn't need an incentive to act responsibly.

Total Return Unitrusts in Pennsylvania

Pennsylvania legislation, passed by the General Assembly and signed by Governor Mark Schweiker on May 16, 2002, extensively revised Pennsylvania law provisions on trust principal and income and made many other changes as well.

Trust income beneficiaries and remaindermen have historically been at odds. Income beneficiaries are entitled to receive dividends and interest. Remaindermen get the principal remaining when the income beneficiary dies. Thus, income beneficiaries want trustees to invest in high income yielding investments; remainderman want trustees to invest in highly appreciating assets. Trustees have for years tried to take a middle course — and have succeeded only in making both sets of beneficiaries very disappointed and angry.

The 2002 Pennsylvania statute permits trustees to take one of two approaches: (1) to make adjustments between principal and income, or (2) to convert to a unitrust.

The law gives the trustee power to adjust between income and principal by allocating an amount of income to principal or an amount of principal to income to the extent the trustee considers it appropriate if the governing instrument permits. For example, a trustee could allocate interest to principal, or a capital gain to income. While on the surface, this seems appealing, it puts the trustee in a tough spot. Is the trustee going to treat all trusts under its management the same? How is the trustee going to decide whether and to what extent to make adjustments? The statute lists factors to be taken into account — the size of the trust, the estimated duration of the trust, the liquidity and distribution requirements of the trust, the needs for regular distributions and preservation and appreciation of capital, the expected tax consequences of an adjustment, the assets held in the trust and the extent to which they consist of financial assets, closely held businesses, tangible and intangible personal property, real property — the list goes on and on.

The implementation of such discretionary power on a broad scale by a professional trustee is obviously problematic. The evaluation of all these considerations takes considerable time and skill and would have to be done for every single trust on an ongoing basis. Every allocation decision would be open to criticism by trust beneficiaries. Trustees are going to be reluctant to use this power.

The second alternative is much more sensible — the trustee has the power to convert to a unitrust. A unitrust establishes a specific payout rate to the "income" beneficiary so that the trustee is not pulled in opposite directions for investment. It is the trustee's obligation to invest for the trust's best total return, thus benefiting both sets of beneficiaries.

In order to convert to a unitrust, the trustee must give written notice to all beneficiaries, and if no beneficiary objections are made, the trust is converted. As simple as that! Informed beneficiaries are unlikely to object as the conversion quite clearly will benefit both income beneficiaries and remaindermen. Alternatively, the conversion to a unitrust can be made with court approval if a beneficiary objects, or if beneficiaries are not capable, within the meaning of the statute, of consenting or objecting.

The most significant change to a beneficiary's position is that a beneficiary may request a trustee to convert to a unitrust. If the trustee does not convert, the beneficiary may petition the court to order the conversion. Never has a beneficiary had such power.

The court shall approve or direct the conversion to a unitrust if the court concludes that the conversion will enable the trustee to better carry out the intent of the settlor or testator and the purposes of the trust. If the trust is converted to a unitrust, then the trustee shall follow total return investment policy, seeking the best total return whether from appreciation of capital, or from earnings or distributions from capital.

After conversion to a unitrust, the term "income" as it is used in the trust shall mean an annual distribution (the unitrust distribution) equal to 4% of the net fair market value of the trust's assets, averaged over the lesser of the 3 preceding years, or the period during which the trust has been in existence. The 4% rate is an attempt to state a payout that will preserve the real value of the principal after inflation over long periods of time. This is reasonable if trust investments are mostly equities and turnover and trustee fees are not too high. The trustee or a beneficiary may petition the court to select a payout percentage other than 4%. Under IRS proposed regulations, a payout rate of 3% to 5% is considered an equitable apportionment between principal and income.

Expenses which would be deducted from income if the trust were not a unitrust may not be deducted from the unitrust distribution. Conversion doesn't take away a trustee's discretion to distribute principal.

Note that either approach requires that both income beneficiaries and remaindermen be given notice and on the one hand, not object, or on the other hand, be interested parties in a court proceeding. In Pennsylvania, there is an oddity in the administration of trusts. Many corporate trustees in Pennsylvania routinely give no information to remaindermen until the income interest terminates. There are thousands of trusts in Pennsylvania, currently being administered by corporate trustees, with remaindermen who have no idea that they are, in fact, remaindermen. These trusts go on for years and years with no accounting given. This is an anomaly of Pennsylvania trustee practice, and in my view, not supported by law (or even prudent business practice). In any event, the remaindermen will have to be brought into the picture for a unitrust conversion — as they should.

This legislation improved the lives of many trust beneficiaries, but its benefits require proactive steps on the part of the trustees or beneficiaries. Make sure you use it to your advantage.

Rules Define Trust Income

On February 15, 2001 the U.S. Treasury issued new proposed regulations that change the way trust income is defined. Sounds pretty boring, doesn't it? Not according to Steve Leimberg, noted estate planning expert. He says these regulations "may be the single most important regulatory change of the decade." Indeed, the long-term implications of the regulations are astounding.

Regulations paved the way for the Total Return Unitrust. Many trusts and estates lawyers are drafting Total Return Unitrusts. With these federal regulations and 2002 Pennsylvania legislation, such trusts are becoming the norm. However, it took old fashioned lawyers some time to adjust to the twenty-first century. Any person who is creating a split interest trust now should definitely consider a Total Return Unitrust instead of a traditional income rule trust. (A split interest trust provides income for one beneficiary with the remainder to another.)

Traditionally, trusts have been written directing income to be paid out to one person (the income beneficiary), and on that person's death, the remainder is distributed to another person or group of persons (the remaindermen). There is an inherent conflict in a trust like this. The income beneficiaries want the trust's money invested in bonds to maximize income. The remaindermen want the trust's money invested in equities to maximize the growth of the principal. As the stock market has soared, the problem of conflicting interests has intensified. Lifetime income beneficiaries measure the performance of a trust in terms of the size of their monthly check, and they won't be satisfied with stock dividends. The dividend yield on the Standard & Poors 500 is about 2% and about 9.4% is in appreciation. Remaindermen measure the performance of a trust against the current Standard & Poors appreciation performance, and they don't want to hear about higher income-yielding bonds that do not appreciate like stocks.

The trust document, rather than sound investing principles, determines the trust's return. None of the beneficiaries can be satisfied because of the inherent conflict created by the document. Many states, including Pennsylvania, have adopted the prudent investor rule. This law changes the standards by which a trustee's investment performance is measured and encourages trustees to adopt a total return approach. Under this investment strategy, trust assets should be invested for total positive return, that is, ordinary income plus appreciation, in order to maximize the value of the trust. Thus, under certain economic circumstances, equities, rather than bonds, would constitute a greater portion of the trust assets than they would under traditional investment standards. Even with passage of this law, trustees are still torn between the demands of income beneficiaries and remaindermen.

In a Total Return Unitrust, a percentage of the entire trust balance is paid annually to the lifetime beneficiary. For example, the trustee might be directed to pay out 4.5% of the market value of the trust annually. The trust is invested for maximum total return, i.e., appreciation plus income, and it is diversified for safety. The 4.5% unitrust payment is made by selling some shares of stock as necessary.

The Total Return Unitrust is a modernization of the dispositive provisions of a trust so that the trustee can invest using modern portfolio theory to maximize return. The trustee's difficulty of impartiality is removed, and the lifetime beneficiary's expectations can be met at no detriment to the long-term prospects of the remaindermen.

Traditionally, trust income was determined under the terms of the governing instrument and applicable local law and almost always was interest and dividends. Capital gains were not income and were allocated to principal. Some states have passed legislation, like the Uniform Principal and Income Act of 1997, that permits "equitable adjustments" between income and principal. A trustee could pay out capital gains to income beneficiaries using this provision, or hold back income for remaindermen. This approach has the disadvantage that trustees are often reluctant to exercise discretion when that exercise is likely to be challenged by unhappy beneficiaries. Most fiduciaries want a rule that allows them to invest for total return but does not expose them to liability for their exercise of discretion. Some states, including Pennsylvania, permit a unitrust amount, a fixed percentage of the trust's fair market value determined annually to be defined as trust accounting income.

The IRS recognizes that the current Internal Revenue code definition of income has not kept pace with changes in the way money is currently invested and income is currently defined under state law. The preamble to the regulations acknowledges that "changes in the types of available investments and in investment philosophies have caused states to revise, or to consider revising, the traditional concepts of income and principal."

Under the new proposed regulation issued by the Treasury, trust income is defined a new way. A state law or language in a trust document that provides for the income beneficiary to receive an annual unitrust amount between 3% and 5% of the annual fair market value of the trust assets is a reasonable apportionment of the total return of the trust. Also, a state law or language in the trust document that permits the trustee to make equitable adjustments between income and principal to fulfill the trustee's duty of impartiality between income and remainder beneficiaries is a reasonable apportionment of the total return of the trust, even an allocation of capital gains if permitted by the instrument and applicable local law.

The proposed regulations go on to provide that a unitrust amount or equitably apportioned income will satisfy the income requirement for obtaining the marital deduction for a trust. Similarly, this type of distribution is also allowed for Qualified Domestic Trusts, which are important for noncitizen surviving spouses.

Trusts irrevocable on September 25, 1985 which are exempt from the application of the generation-skipping tax will still be exempt, even if modified by state law to permit a unitrust payout.

Pure Trusts: Scams in the Purest Sense of the Word

"The Internal Revenue Service wants to confiscate wealth that rightfully belongs to you." What do you think of a statement like this? Part of you might feel drawn to agree. After all, few of us really like paying taxes. But seriously, folks, do you really believe that the federal income tax is illegal and unconstitutional? Do you really believe that you have no legal obligation to pay taxes and you are the victim of a monumental fraud and deception imposed on you by the federal government?

That is what the proponents of trust scams would have you believe. The schemes they sell go by many names: Pure Trusts, Constitutional Trusts, Freedom Trusts, Patriot Trusts, Contract Trusts, Final Trust, Common Law Trusts, and more. Part of the sales pitch is that the government and all the lawyers and accountants are in cahoots to defraud the citizenry (or are simply stupid) and that any lawyer or accountant who tells you one of these schemes won't work is either lying to you or completely taken in by the fraud.

It's sort of like telling someone they don't have cancer and if a doctor tells them they do, that doctor is either lying, or just telling them that so they can make money. How do you argue with that short of dying to prove the point?

In the case of these trusts scams, for some, the only proof is conviction of tax evasion and sentencing to a federal penitentiary.

In the words of Robert L. Sommers, the scam artists who push these schemes "advertise on business talk radio. They run infomercials on public access television. They infiltrate your local church. They are the modern version of the "snake oil" salesmen, and they're out to steal you blind. The worst part is that you'll never know it until the IRS comes knocking at your door and by then, the rip-off artist is long gone."

Here is how the best antifraud site on the web, *www.quatloos.com*, defines them: "Constitutional Trusts and Pure Trusts: Worthless entities created by the tax protester crowd which won't get you anything except an extended stay at Club Fed."

Another sales pitch of these trust scams is that they provide protection of assets from liability lawsuits. Proponents claim that the complex construction of interlocking trust and partnerships will let you keep and enjoy your assets but protect them from the claims of any creditors, whether legitimate or not. Hogwash.

Fees paid to hawkers of these trust scams can range from several hundred dollars to thousands. If you follow their advice and stop paying income taxes you face interest, penalties, fines, and criminal prosecution. This hoax has proliferated on the internet.

The IRS issued a notice in 1997 that talks about these abusive trust schemes in detail. It is IRS Notice 97-24. It can be viewed at *http://www.unclefed.com/Tax-Bulls/1997/Not97-24.pdf.* Basically, the IRS position is that the attempts to create so-called Pure or Constitutional Trusts (whatever you want to call them) are simply futile exercises and that no new entity exists. The original taxpayer remains the owner of all assets, and the original taxpayer is liable for all back taxes.

The con artists who sell these schemes tell you that the Pure Trust does not owe any taxes. And you know what? They're right.

Since the attempt to create an entity fails, you, the original owner and taxpayer remain the owner and taxpayer. The tax liability you are flouting is yours, not the so-called trust's.

A typical scam website opens with the statement: "Lawfully Stop Paying Taxes." The argument cites Article 1, Section 10 of the Constitution of the United States which provides (in pertinent part): "No state shall . . . pass . . . any law impairing the Obligation of Contracts. . . ." These scam artists say that since the Constitution is the highest law of the land, this means you can *contract to do anything you want*, including not pay income tax. Following this argument you could also contract to deal heroin, or contract for the murder of your spouse.

If someone tells you not to consult with the IRS or a licensed tax attorney or CPA prior to implementing a trust, there is something seriously wrong. Don't engage in such planning.

Quatloos has a better name for these trusts: "Con Trusts" — that's what they are — a pure con for the misguided and naive. If you are approached about setting up one of these, report the scam to your local FBI office and the Criminal Investigative Division of the IRS.

If you have been victimized by one of these schemers, get in touch with a tax attorney immediately. If you have stopped paying income taxes using one of these trusts, you have probably committed criminal tax fraud. You should not contact an accountant. A good accountant will stop you as soon as you mentioned one of these trusts and refer you to a lawyer to tell the rest of your story. There is no accountant-client privilege, but there is an attorney-client privilege.

The best way to avoid prosecution is to recognize these trusts for what they are — scams. Avoid them altogether.

Estate Planning for Special Needs Kids

Many parents of special needs children do not expect their special child to ever be financially independent. These parents also know full well that they are likely to die before their child. Yet many of these parents have not made a will or done any other planning for their child's future without them. Where will the child live when the parents die? Who will take care of the child? Where will the money come from?

Special needs can range from disabilities readily identified such as physical challenges, through various mental, social, and emotional disorders. The parent with a special needs child lies awake at night wondering who will care for the child when the parent dies. These parents face many challenges - they research and seek out medical care, advocate for the best educational setting, search for financial assistance for the many expenses they face, and deal with their other children, spouses and family members - not to mention holding down a job. Planning for care options if they predecease the child often falls to the bottom of the list.

In some families, the parents arrange for the siblings of the child to take over the responsibility. Sometimes the siblings simply can't take over or don't want to. It can be a huge responsibility and financial burden to someone who has a family of his or her own to care for. Even for parents who think their other children will take care of their special child, they must make a will, create a trust for the benefit of the special child, and set funds aside. Funds intended for the special needs child's care should not be given to siblings.

While the services available through government benefit programs are substantial, especially with regard to medical care, actual cash benefits are generally quite small. The special needs child lives below the poverty level and does not have enough funds for many basic needs. For an individual with a disability to live comfortably and respectably, family members or charitable organizations have to help.

One of the key factors in planning for the care of a special needs child is to make sure that government benefits remain available to the child, while supplemental needs can be provided for. Future columns will address special needs trusts - a kind of trust to preserve access to government benefits while funding additional needs for the child. These trusts are the cornerstone of a plan for a special needs child.

You need to have the basics taken care of. Make a will that appoints a guardian for the child if he or she is a minor and that includes a trust for the child that will allow the child to continue to receive government benefits. Select a person to manage the funds you set aside for the child. Make sure there is a back-up in case the person you selected cannot serve.

Also make sure you have a power of attorney for financial matters and a medical directive. If your special needs child is 18 or over and has the capacity, you should make sure the child also has a power of attorney and medical directive.

Having this basic plan in place will go a long way to making sure your child is cared for. The basic plan can be improved and refined, but it is the foundation for everything you do to plan your child's future.

Special Needs Trusts

A special needs trust, sometimes called a supplemental needs trust, is a trust designed to hold assets for the benefit of a person with disabilities or special needs. The trust is designed so that the beneficiary can retain eligibility for government benefits such as Medicaid and SSI, while still allowing the trust assets to be used for the beneficiary's supplemental needs.

There are two kinds of special needs trusts: One is created and funded with assets belong to the beneficiary. This is called a self-settled trust. The second type is created by someone else for the benefit of the child or disabled person, usually by a parent or grandparent.

The first type of trust — a self-settled special needs trust — is often used when damages are to be paid to an injured person. Sometimes the personal injury settlement or verdict arose out of the incident that created the disability, but this is not necessarily so. Holding the settlement or judgment in a special needs trust permits the beneficiary to live with more dignity and comfort, being able to buy things beyond the bare necessities.

The funds in the trust can be used to supplement benefits received from various governmental assistance programs including SSI and Medicaid. The beneficiary has no direct control or access to funds in the Trust. It is managed by a Trustee who has broad discretion to make distributions on behalf of the beneficiary to provide for superior care options and opportunities for treatment and rehabilitation, housing, electronic equipment, computers, job training, vacations, and so on.

In order for a self-settled special needs trust to be deemed a non-countable asset for benefits qualification, it must provide that the government is paid back for services it provided if there is anything left in the trust when the beneficiary with a disability or special needs dies.

The second type of special needs trust is one that is created for the beneficiary by others. If you are a parent of a child with special needs, how you leave your child's inheritance to him can greatly affect the child's quality of life after your death. An outright inheritance will immediately cause all government benefits to stop. Your child will have to pay for 100% of his medical care, medicines, personal care attendants, therapy, doctor's visits, room and board or residency fees wherever he is living. This will continue until the entire inheritance is exhausted. Then your disabled child will re-qualify for benefits.

If the inheritance is exhausted because it had to be spent down to re-qualify for benefits, there will no longer be no additional funds to pay for education, over-the-counter medicines, dental care beyond what is covered by government benefits, trips to see family members, reading materials and supplies such as razors, soap, toothpaste and shampoo. There will be no money available for telephone bills, ball game or movie tickets, meals out, snacks, materials for a hobby, videos or other favorite entertainment. Government benefits do not cover these types of expenses.

Rather than giving the inheritance outright (or even worse, disinheriting the child with special needs) these parents should include special needs trusts in their estate plans. The special needs trust does not provide for basic food, clothing or shelter. However, the wide variety of supplemental needs can be paid for. The trust might be able to buy a house for your disabled child to live in or could pay for an advocate to make sure the child receives the services he needs.

Grandparents and other relatives can add to the trust. When the child with special needs dies, the balance remaining in the trust can be distributed to other family members. This type of trust requires advance planning. Make it a part of your estate plan now.

Tax Relief and the Child with Special Needs

The cost of raising and educating a child with special needs can put a severe financial strain on parents. The tax code provides some relief for these parents.

The costs of a "special" school for a child with special needs is deductible as a medical expense. Managing or correcting the disability must be the principal reason for attending the school, and any ordinary education received must be incidental to the special education provided.

A regular school can be a "special" school. The deductibility of tuition depends on what the school provides to an individual student. A school can have a regular education program for most students, and a special education program for those who need it. A school can be "special" for one student but not for another. When an individual attends a "special" school for the physically or mentally disabled, the cost of deductible medical care includes the cost of meals and lodging, if supplied, and the cost of ordinary education furnished which is incidental to the special services furnished by the school. All the costs of transportation, supervision, care, treatment, and training are also deductible as medical expenses.

If the school is a regular school but the child receives special services from the school related to a physical or mental disability, the extra cost for the special services may be claimed as a medical expense. Another possible medical expense deduction is private tutoring by a specially trained teacher to provide therapeutic and behavioral support services.

If the parents travel to and attend a medical conference in order to make informed decisions about the child's treatment, the costs of the conference and transportation costs are deductible as medical expenses. There is no deduction for lodging costs.

If parents have to make modifications or improvements to their home to accommodate a child with special needs, part of these costs may be deductible. To the extent the costs of modification or improvement exceed any increase in the home's fair market value they may be deducted.

Medical expenses are deductible only to the extent that they exceed 7.5% of adjusted gross income. A better result can be obtained if the parents' employer provides a medical flexible spending account (FSA). The parents' salary reductions to fund the FSA are completely excluded from their gross income. Using funds from the FSA will make the expenses, in effect, 100% deductible without reference to the 7.5% limitation.

If special education qualifies as a medical expense, it can also be used to justify a "hardship" withdrawal from a 401(k) retirement plan.

Parents can generally claim a dependent care credit for the costs incurred to care for dependents under age 13 so that the parents can be gainfully employed. If a child is physically or mentally incapable of caring for himself or herself, the costs are eligible for the dependent care credit regardless of the child's age.

A child is no longer a "qualifying child" for the dependency exemption when he or she reaches the age 19, or age 24 if a student. If a child is over 24 and his or her gross income does not exceed the amount of the exemption, the child can still be claimed as a dependent. Gross income for this purpose does not include income earned by a "permanently and totally disabled" dependent in a sheltered workshop as long as the availability of medical care is the principal reason for the dependent being there.

If you adopt a child with special needs, there is an $11,390 per child tax credit available. An eligible child is also a child with special needs if he or she is a United States citizen or resident and a state determines that the child cannot or should not be returned to his or her parents' home and probably will not be adopted unless assistance is provided. The full amount of the credit can be taken regardless of the actual expenses.

Does Your Special-Needs Child Need a Guardian?

A guardianship is a legal mechanism that grants an adult legal power to make decisions for another person, called the "ward," who is incapable of making decisions himself or herself. A ward can be a minor child (under 18 in Pennsylvania) or an adult who has some physical and/or mental incapacity.

In the case of a minor child, guardianship terminates when the child turns 18. It surprises many people to know that a parent is not automatically the legal guardian of a minor child. The parent, by virtue of his or her relationship, is natural guardian having custody of minor children, but a parent is not automatically the financial guardian in charge of a minor's money or property, known as the ward's estate. Only a court can appoint a financial guardian.

The law treats the minor as a separate person in his or her own right and the control of the minor's property is governed by laws to protect the minor. There are several mechanisms for legal supervision and protection of a minor's property.

One option is for the court to order establishment of a "sequestered" bank account. Any amount payable in cash to a minor may, by order of the court, be deposited in one or more savings accounts in the name of the minor. This type of court order provides that no withdrawals can be made until the minor reaches age 18, except as authorized.

Another option for small amounts, defined by the statute as when the entire estate of the minor is $25,000 or less, is that all or part of the property may be received or held and deposited by the minor, or the parent, or another person maintaining the minor without the appointment of a guardian if (1) it is an award from a decedent's estate or trust and the court so directs, or (2) when the court having jurisdiction to sell or mortgage real estate in which a minor has an interest shall so direct, or (3) other circumstance in which the court so directs.

The court, upon petition, can appoint a guardian of the minor's estate. If the court appoints a guardian of a minor's estate, the guardian must either be a corporation authorized to act as a fiduciary in Pennsylvania or an adult who is not the parent of the minor, except that a parent may be appointed a co-guardian with another fiduciary or fiduciaries. The statute directs the court to give preference to a person of the same religious persuasion as the parents. Preference is also given to a person nominated as guardian by a minor over the age of fourteen (14).

Persons who transfer property to a minor can make use for the Uniform Transfer to Minors Act and name a custodian to hold and control the minor's property. UTMA custodianships last until age 21 in Pennsylvania (and in some circumstances for assets passing under wills, trust and beneficiary designations to age 25).

When a minor turns 18, if he or she is unable to take care of his or her own affairs because of incapacity, the court will appoint a guardian for the incapacitated person. This requires another court proceeding to appoint a guardian for an incapacitated person, even if a guardian for the minor has already been appointed.

Pennsylvania law permits a parent to appoint a guardian for a minor child in their will. This is very important for every parent to do and, obviously, very important for the parent of a child with special needs.

It is also important to write a "letter of intent" to provide direction to the person who will care for your child with special needs. This letter is not legally binding, but is an important resource for the caregiver. The letter should set out the child's medical history and daily care needs, as well as set out your plans and wishes for the child's future. Make sure you identify those who love your child, who will visit, take him or her home for the holidays, ask what he or she needs, and advocate for his or her care.

POWERS OF ATTORNEY AND MEDICAL DIRECTIVES

New Power of Attorney Law in Pennsylvania

Pennsylvania has made broad changes to the law governing powers of attorney. H.B. 1429, which makes a number of changes to powers of attorney, was unanimously passed by the Pennsylvania House and Senate and signed by the Governor on July 2, becoming Act 95 of 2014.

The only parts that take effect before the end of 2014 are the sections requiring honoring of the POA by third parties, recognizing POAs made in other states, and the legislative intent of overturning the case of *Vine v. Commonwealth State Employees' Retirement Board.*

Most of the new law's provisions are effective January 1, 2015.

We have until the end of the year to incorporate the new longer warning, and to figure out how to let the client elect to grant the "hot powers". Also, the gift-making provision probably needs to be spelled out to meet the new law's intent.

Third Party Reliance

One of the biggest practical problems faced by agents trying to use their authority under POA's is a third party, such as a bank, brokerage house, or other third party refusing to accept the POA.

This problem was exacerbated by the PA Supreme Court's holding in the case of *Vine v. Commonwealth State Employees' Retirement Board*, 9 A.3d 1150 (Pa. 2010). That case involved the statutory immunity afforded to third parties and held, much to the consternation of the bar, that a third party that relies on a power of attorney is not immune from liability if the power of attorney is not valid. The Vine decision called into question third parties' acceptance of powers of attorney.

The new law legislatively reverses the *Vine* court's holding. Broad protection is given to banks and other third parties who in good faith accept a POA.

In addition to reversing *Vine,* the new law provides third parties who are asked to accept a POA the right to request additional information and documentation such as an agent's certification of facts, a translation of the document if it is not in English, and an opinion of counsel that the agent is acting within the scope of the authority granted. Reversing Vine was good news. I'm not so sure being asked as an attorney to opine that an agent is acting within the scope of granted authority is such good news. Now we have to be guarantors for the agent?

Signatures

Under current law, powers of attorney just have to be signed and dated by the principal. Only powers of attorney signed by mark or signed by someone at the direction of the principal required two witnesses. Beginning January 1, 2015, all POAs must be witnessed by two individuals neither of whom is the agent, or an individual who signed the POA on behalf of and at the direction of the principal, or the notary before whom the POA is acknowledged.

Also, beginning January 1, 2015, the signature or mark of the principal must be acknowledged before a notary public. This requirement for notarization does not apply to a POA which exclusively provides for making health care decisions or mental health care decisions

Notice

There is new language provided for the Notice to the principal which is required to appear in ALL CAPITALS at the very beginning of the POA. The new language warns that the POA may grant the agent the power to give away the principal's property or to change how the property is distributed at the principal's death.

Also, the new notice advises the principal to seek the advice of an attorney at law before signing the POA.

Agent's Acknowledgment

The acknowledgment form that the agent must sign has been changed to say that the agent must act in accordance with the principal's reasonable expectations to the extent that the agent actually knows them and, otherwise, in the principal's best interest. As if signing such a statement will make it true, the new acknowledgment states that the agent must act in good faith and within the scope of authority granted in the POA.

"Hot" Powers

An agent is prohibited from some actions unless the authority is expressly granted in the POA. These "hot" powers are:

(1) Create, amend, revoke or terminate an inter vivos trust (unless permitted under the statute language that permits the agent "To create a trust for my benefit." or to "To make additions to an existing trust for my benefit."
(2) Make a gift.
(3) Create or change rights of survivorship.
(4) Create or change a beneficiary designation.
(5) Delegate authority granted under the power of attorney.
(6) Waive the principal's right to be a beneficiary of a joint and survivor annuity, including a survivor benefit under a retirement plan.
(7) Exercise fiduciary powers that the principal has authority to delegate.
(8) Disclaim property, including a power of appointment.

Limited Gifts

Under the new law an agent may make limited gifts only under certain circumstances. It is specifically stated that gifts must be in the principal's best interest which may include "eligibility for a benefit, program or assistance under a statute or regulation. Limited gifts are double if the principals spouse will consent to gift split. Limited gifts can be made to a trust, and UTMA account or a 529 plan and don't have to qualify for the gift tax annual exclusion, although the amount of limited gifts is determined by reference to that exclusion amount.

Don't Wait 'Til You're Run Down to Check Out a Power of Attorney

Most folks acknowledge that they need a will in case they are hit by a truck and killed. They don't much like the idea but they accept it. But what if the truck doesn't kill them but leaves them completely incapacitated? Then what?

As unpleasant as this is to contemplate, everyone should name someone to handle his financial affairs in the event of incapacity, whether it is temporary or permanent. This is done by signing a document called a "Power of Attorney" in which an agent is designated to act on the person's behalf. The agent is called the "attorney-in-fact."

Incapacity comes in many guises. Alzheimer's disease strikes and leaves an elderly person incapable of managing even the simplest of financial matters. A stroke leaves its victim incapable of handling financial affairs. A head injury sustained in an accident wreaks devastation. Severe injuries leave their victim incapacitated for a period of time even though there is eventual recovery. In the meantime, who takes care of paying the bills, handling the investments, filing the tax returns, filing the medical insurance claims, depositing checks?

You may be surprised to know that a spouse does not automatically have these powers by virtue of being married to the incapacitated person. For property held in joint names, the spouse may be able to deal with most transactions; but the spouse has no authority over assets in the incapacitated spouse's name alone.

The law's answer to the problem is the court appointment of a guardian. A guardian of the estate (that is, property) of the incapacitated person is appointed by the county judge. As guardian, this person becomes a fiduciary responsible for all of the incapacitated person's property, financial obligations, and responsibilities. In some cases, the guardian is given physical control over the incapacitated person. This is referred to as "guardian of the person." It is not uncommon for two persons to be named, one as guardian of the person and one as guardian of the estate. In many counties, a judge will only appoint a financial institution as guardian of the estate.

Appointment of a guardian is an expensive and laborious procedure. The guardian is required to make extensive reports to the court and may not spend principal without the court's permission. In short, the need for the court appointment of a guardian should be avoided by the execution of a Power of Attorney.

A Power of Attorney is the appointment of an agent. According to common law, the authority of an agent terminates on the incapacity of the principal. The principal is the person on whose behalf the agent acts. In the situations we have been discussing, this is exactly the time when the power is most needed. The statutes of all the states now provide for a *Durable* Power of Attorney. A Durable Power is one that remains in effect even if the principal is incapacitated, which is exactly what is needed in order to avoid the court appointment of a guardian. In Pennsylvania, any Power of Attorney is deemed to be durable. Nevertheless, most documents granting the power contain words indicating that the grant of the power is intended to be "durable." For example, "The authority granted in this document continues without regard to the incapacity of the principal."

Most folks intend that the agent use the Power of Attorney only if there is incapacity of the principal. This is problematic. If the document itself provides that it is effective only on the principal's incapacity, this presents an evidentiary problem for a third party relying on the power. For example, let's say Jack is named as attorney-in-fact in a durable Power of Attorney signed by Jill, but the document provides that Jack only has the power if Jill is incapacitated. Jack takes the Power of Attorney to the bank to make a withdrawal from Jill's bank account. How does the bank know whether or not Jill is incapacitated? The obvious answer is, they don't. How is incapacity to be proved? A letter from a doctor? Which doctor? A court determination? That would defeat the purpose. For this reason, I usually recommend against powers of attorney that "spring" into life only on the occurrence of incapacity.

For those who are uncomfortable with a Power of Attorney which grants a current agency to the attorney-in-fact, I suggest an escrow agreement. The documents will be held in escrow by an attorney or some other person who is trusted to make the determination about the appropriateness of their use, and the powers are not released to the attorney-in-fact unless the escrow agent is satisfied that the principal is incapacitated and it is appropriate for the agent to act.

There are various forms available to make a "do-it-yourself" Power of Attorney. None are recommended. Some provisions are appropriate for some folks, and some are not. Special attention must be given to powers that permit the making of gifts, the creation of trusts, and other matters. Some Powers of Attorney are "general," meaning that they authorize the agent to do all things which the principal could do. Other Powers of Attorney are "limited," authorizing only certain actions on the part of the attorney-in-fact. See a lawyer. Check it out.

Benefits of Guardianship Versus Power of Attorney

What do you do when your mother can no longer take care of herself or her finances? If Mom has signed a Power of Attorney and named someone to act as her attorney-in-fact, this will probably take care of all the issues. If not, perhaps Mom still has sufficient capacity to sign a Power of Attorney. Get her to a lawyer!

Failing that, sometimes there are sufficient funds in a joint account to "take care of" Mom for a while. The joint owner can write checks or withdraw funds to pay Mom's bills. If that source of funds runs out or is not available, the only choice is to commence a court proceeding to have a guardian appointed for Mom.

Pennsylvania law authorizes the appointment of guardians for incapacitated persons. The Pennsylvania statute was amended in 1992 to define an "incapacitated person" as "an adult whose ability to receive and evaluate information effectively and communicate decisions in any way is impaired to such a significant extent that he is partially or totally unable to manage his financial resources or to meet essential requirements for his physical health and safety."

The prior wording provided for guardians for "incompetents." The new definition was intended to enlarge the meaning and reduce the supposed stigma attached to the designation and, also, to include those who are mentally sound but, nevertheless, lack the capacity to take care of their person, regardless of the reason.

When a guardian is appointed for an incapacitated person, the incapacitated person is referred to as the "ward." The guardian of the ward has the duty to take care of the physical needs of the ward. The guardian of the estate of the ward has the duty to manage the financial affairs of the ward. The guardian of the person and the guardian of the estate may or may not be the same person or institution. Also, it may be the case that the proposed ward needs a guardian of the estate but not of the person.

A guardian is appointed by the court upon petition and after a hearing. Any person or institution interested in the welfare of a person may be the petitioner. Notice must be given to the alleged incapacitated person by personal service — someone actually has to hand deliver the notice to the alleged incapacitated person. Notice also must be given to those persons residing in Pennsylvania who would be entitled to share in the estate of the alleged incapacitated person if he or she dies intestate at that time and to the person or institution providing residential services to the alleged incapacitated person. The alleged incapacitated person shall be present at the hearing unless the court is satisfied, upon the testimony or statement of a physician or licensed psychologist that this proposed ward's physical or mental condition would be harmed by his or her presence at the hearing. Counsel should be appointed to represent the incapacitated person in appropriate circumstances.

If appropriate, the court will give preference to a nominee of the incapacitated person. The law specifically states that it is the duty of the guardian of the person to assert the rights and best interests of the incapacitated person. "Expressed wishes and preferences of the incapacitated person shall be respected to the greatest possible extent."

All income received by a guardian of the estate of an incapacitated person including all funds received from the Veteran's Administration, Social Security Administration, and other periodic retirement or disability payments under private or governmental plans may be expended by the guardian for the care and maintenance of the incapacitated person without court approval. The court may authorize payments from principal. The statute also authorizes the court to do estate planning for the incapacitated person. The authority for planning is quite broad and can include gifts, creation of trusts (both revocable and irrevocable), contracts, disclaimers, and other techniques to minimize current or prospective taxes.

A guardian can engage in more sophisticated estate planning than can be done under a Power of Attorney. Sometimes, a guardian is appointed for this purpose even though a very broad Power of Attorney is in existence.

Who can be a guardian? An individual, corporate fiduciary, nonprofit organization, or guardianship support agency. Pennsylvania's statute also contemplated the appointment of limited guardians, giving a guardian authority over some things and allowing the ward to retain authority over others.

Appointment of a guardian requires a court proceeding, attorney fees, physician's testimony, and reporting requirements. The expense and inconvenience of a guardianship proceeding can be avoided, if a Power of Attorney is in place. Review your personal situation to make sure that you have a Power of Attorney.

Power of Attorney: How Much Power Does It Have?

A prominent national brokerage firm refused to accept the instructions of one of my clients as an agent under a Power of Attorney drafted in accordance with Pennsylvania law. In fact, the brokerage firm asked for some specific words to be removed from the document — words that were required to be included on the first page of the Power of Attorney in all capital letters by Pennsylvania state law. Upon having this explained to the brokerage firm, that the words had to stay because they were required by law and after seeing a copy of the state law which required the words, they responded that they were still unsatisfied and were "not willing to incur the legal cost necessary to have the matter researched." The brokerage firm instead invited their customer to move her account elsewhere. So much for customer service. Interestingly enough, the firm was willing to accept the agent's instructions to move the account. Go figure.

This is not the first time powers of attorney have not been honored. Some financial institutions — banks, brokerage houses, insurance companies, mutual funds — flat out refuse to honor a Power of Attorney unless the power is on their own form.

Here is another situation. Mom is in a nursing home and her son needs to make withdrawals from her IRA to pay her bills. The Mutual Fund company which holds that IRA refuses to accept the son's authority under the Power of Attorney.

Even though powers of attorney are very common and the notion of a durable power has become very popular, agents bearing Power of Attorney documents are not always treated as if they stand in the principal's shoes. It is frustrating for an agent to find his powers refused or disregarded in transactions on a principal's behalf. Although an agent can get a court to enforce his powers, the prospect of having to litigate transactions that should take place in the ordinary course of business is not welcomed. Litigation is expensive and time-consuming.

Commerce requires the general acceptance of orders that are valid on their face. Can you imagine what would happen if your bank refused to pay your checks? Or what would happen if your stockbroker refused to accept your instructions to buy or sell, no matter how relayed? Chaos would result.

All of us, lawyers and laypersons alike, have viewed the durable general Power of Attorney as the panacea to incompetency. It is part of a complete estate plan — always recommended to make sure that in the event of incapacity, your financial affairs can be taken care of without resorting to the appointment of a guardian through the Orphan's Court.

Can a bank or other institution refuse to honor a valid Power of Attorney? Sure. Can they be held liable for refusing? Yes. The law provides that "[a]ny person who is given instructions by an agent in accordance with the terms of a Power of Attorney shall comply with the instructions. Any person who without reasonable cause fails to comply with those instructions shall be subject to civil liability for any damages resulting from non-compliance. . . ." Further, the law provides that "[a]ny person who acts in good faith reliance on a Power of Attorney shall incur no liability as a result of acting in accordance with the instructions of the agent."

The Pennsylvania statute sounds more powerful than it is. Take the case of my client whose brokerage house would not accept her Power of Attorney, for example. Showing this statute to the back office of the brokerage house had no effect whatsoever. I could sue them. But how much would that cost? And what are my client's damages? It is much cheaper and more effective to simply move the account to another brokerage house that will honor the Power of Attorney.

But what if you can't move the account? What do you do if the brokerage house won't let you move the account? Or what if the next brokerage house won't accept the Power of Attorney either? Then you have to go to court to force compliance or as a last resort, seek the appointment of a guardian of the principal's estate. This means a court hearing, expert testimony from a physician, an attorney for the proposed guardian, and another attorney for the proposed ward. Notice, hearing, time, and money. And, some things that are authorized under a Power of Attorney for an agent's actions may not be permissible acts of a guardian, even with court approval.

Of course, it is understood that no financial institution wants to be a party to fraud. We count on them to safeguard our money and investments. If someone cleaned out my bank account using a fraudulent Power of Attorney, I would be fit to be tied and I would certainly hold the bank responsible. We must allow the financial institution to protect itself and also to continue to safeguard its customer funds. What is the answer?

The best answer would be enforcement of the law that we have and insisting that third party financial institutions accept agents' authority and hold them liable for damages for failing to obey instructions. Concomitantly, the financial institution must not be held liable for accepting a Power of Attorney valid on its face. If this law is not enforced, and enforced soon, powers of attorney will become worthless.

Until that happens, the best answer to the question is to avoid the problem by being prepared. Principals should be certain to contact any financial institution where they have accounts, safe deposit boxes, securities and the like, as soon as the Power of Attorney is executed. Copies should be provided, and any form that any of the institutions require of the principal or attorney-in-fact, such as authorizations or signature cards, should be executed.

Some institutions will only accept a Power of Attorney on their own form. Ask for the form. Take it to your attorney for completion as part of your estate plan. A nuisance? Yes. But the alternative is a court appointed guardian.

Advance Directive for Health Care

The question of when to withhold or terminate life support for an unconscious or terminally ill individual is one that is hotly debated. There are a host of medical, ethical, religious, and legal issues. Before legislation was passed, these decisions were usually made by family members in conjunction with physicians and, if disputes arose, the issue was ultimately brought to the courts. You may remember the Cruzan case in Missouri where the court held that a permanently unconscious patient could refuse medical treatment, but her wishes had to be expressed by clear and convincing evidence before the onset of the unconsciousness. This rule has generally been followed in Pennsylvania as well.

Since it became of crucial importance that a person set forth their wishes about so-called "heroic measures," it became the common practice for a person to make a "Living Will." A "Living Will" is a document in which you express your wishes about medical treatment in the event that you are unable to make decisions about your own care. The Living Will specifies the medical treatments you wish to accept or refuse and the circumstances under which your wishes will be carried out.

Many people make the mistake of thinking that a Living Will gives the order to "pull the plug." While some people want that and include it in their Living Will, a Living Will can contain any instructions, including using all life-saving and life-supporting measures possible. A Living Will can be personalized and gives you the opportunity to say what you want.

If you've been admitted to the hospital in the last 10 years, and you may qualify for Medicare or Medicaid benefits, you know that you will be asked if you have a Living Will. You will be asked to provide a copy of it, and if you don't have one, one will be offered to you. You do not have to sign one in order to be admitted, but information about a Living Will and the opportunity to sign one must be provided to you. This is required by the Patient Self-Determination Act of 1990, a federal law passed by Congress.

The Pennsylvania legislature enacted the Advance Directive for Health Care Act in 1992 to establish rules for the effectiveness of Living Wills and how they should be utilized. Pennsylvania law refers to a Living Will as an "Advance Directive for Health Care." Any person who is over age 18 or has graduated from high school may execute an Advance Directive. It must be signed by the individual and have two witnesses. The form may be notarized, but this is not required. The statute refers to the person who makes the Living Will as the "declarant."

The Pennsylvania statute also provides for the designation of another person to make the treatment decisions if the declarant is incompetent, is in a terminal condition, or is permanently unconscious. "Terminal condition" is defined as an "incurable and irreversible medical condition in an advanced state caused by injury, disease or physical illness which will, in the opinion of the attending physician, to a reasonable degree of medical certainty, result in death regardless of the continued application of life-sustaining treatment." A "permanently unconscious" person is defined as an individual diagnosed "in accordance with currently accepted medical standards and with reasonable medical certainty" as having a "total and irreversible loss of consciousness and capacity for interaction with the environment." The term includes a persistent vegetative state or irreversible coma.

The declarant's physician must make the directive a part of the declarant's medical record. Once the declaration is operative because the attending physician has determined the patient to be incompetent, in a terminal condition, or in a state of permanent unconsciousness, the medical provider must either comply with its directions or make every reasonable effort for the transfer of the patient to another provider who will comply with the directive.

The statute includes a suggested form of Declaration, but this form need not be used. The statutory form lists seven specific areas regarding treatment decisions. The declarant is asked to check off whether he or she *does* or *does not* want (1) cardiac resuscitation, (2) mechanical respiration, (3) tube feeding or any other artificial or invasive form of nutrition (food) or hydration (water), (4) blood or blood products, (5) surgery or invasive diagnostic tests, (6) kidney dialysis, and (7) antibiotics.

It is very helpful to family members for the declarant to name a surrogate to make decisions. The surrogate is similar to the attorney-in-fact you would appoint in a Power of Attorney for financial matters; you may appoint one person only, one person backed up by a successor, or two surrogates who must agree. Whatever option you go with, you will want to be sure that the surrogate understands your wishes, is willing to take on the responsibility, and is ethically and emotionally prepared to carry out your Directive. Fairly recent technological advances now allow for prolongation of life far beyond what was "normal" in the past; controversial areas are addressed in this sort of document, and it is critical for you to name as your surrogate an individual who agrees with your directions.

Generally speaking, a person names a relative, a close friend, or religious advisor as the surrogate and sees to it that the person has a copy of the Advance Directive. It is also important to give your Directive to your physician and to family members and friends as you deem appropriate.

An Advance Directive is legally binding, but when you sign it you need not feel you are making irrevocable choices. While it is important to think through the decisions called for and then to execute the document, you can make revisions or even revoke the Directive at any time. No judgment is called for regarding your mental or physical condition at the time of revocation. You can implement these changes in writing, orally, or even by an action such as a wink or a shake of the head that says "No way!" Your revisions or revocation is effective upon communication to a witness, the attending physician, or another health care provider.

What is the process for preparing a Health Care Directive? Many attorneys prepare Advance Directives at the same time they prepare wills and Powers of Attorney. The form suggested in the statute is readily available. For example, the Allegheny County Medical Society and Bar Association make available a form and explanatory booklet. See *http://www.acms.org/lw.html* or contact them at 713 Ridge Avenue, Pittsburgh, PA 15212, telephone: 412-321-5030; FAX 412-321-5323. The Pennsylvania Medical Society provides a model Living Will. See *http://www.kepro.org/Bene_LivingWillForm.html.* LegalDocs provides a form of Living Will. See *http://legaldocs.com/docs/living_will.d/pa-livw1.mv.*

For Living Wills in accordance with Jewish Halachic Law, see *http://jlaw.com/Forms/hlw_pa_inst.html.* Here is a directory of state specific information: *http://www.mindspring.com/~scottr/will.html.*

State specific living will forms are available from the legal counsel for the elderly at AARP, PO Box 96474, Washington, D.C. 20090-6474 for $5.

Out-of-Hospital Do-Not-Resuscitate Orders

> *Life is pleasant. Death is peaceful. It's the transition that's troublesome.*
>
> Isaac Asimov

Emergency medical personnel who come to your assistance when 911 is called will not change their response based on a living will or an advanced directive for health care. They are not doctors. Their job is to stabilize the patient and transport him or her to a hospital where decisions about treatment can be made. They are, however, authorized to follow a doctor's written "Do Not Resuscitate" order.

The General Assembly of the Commonwealth of Pennsylvania enacted The Do-Not-Resuscitate Act ("DNR Act") to empower terminally ill patients to make personal decisions regarding resuscitation including CPR in the out-of-hospital setting. The first section of the law states: "Although cardiopulmonary resuscitation has saved the lives of individuals about to experience sudden, unexpected death, present medical data indicates that cardiopulmonary resuscitation rarely leads to prolonged survival in individuals with terminal illnesses in whom death is expected. In many circumstances, the performance of cardiopulmonary resuscitation may cause infliction of unwanted and unnecessary pain and suffering. Existing emergency medical services protocols may require emergency medical services personnel to proceed to cardiopulmonary resuscitation when an individual is found in a cardiac or respiratory arrest even if the individual has completed a living will or advance directive indicating that the individual does not wish to receive cardiopulmonary resuscitation."

Under the statute, cardiopulmonary resuscitation (CPR) is defined as cardiac compression, invasive airway techniques, artificial ventilation, fibrillation and other related procedures. When a person is seriously ill, CPR may not work or may work only partially, leaving the patient brain-damaged, with broken bones, dependent on a ventilator, or otherwise in a worse medical state than before the heart stopped.

Because of this, some people prefer to be cared for without aggressive efforts at resuscitation. Also, some persons with terminal conditions perceive death by cardiac or respiratory arrest to be a natural conclusion of their life and do not wish to receive CPR to prolong it.

The law permits a terminally ill person or that person's surrogate named in a medical directive to obtain an out-of-hospital do-not-resuscitate order, bracelet or necklace that directs emergency medical services (EMS) personnel in the out-of-hospital setting not to provide the person with CPR. An out-of-hospital do-not-resuscitate order is a written order that is issued by an attending physician that directs EMS providers to withhold CPR from the person in the event of cardiac or respiratory arrest. In addition to issuing the order, the attending physician also may secure and issue a bracelet or necklace for the person. The physician purchases the bracelets and necklaces from a vendor designated by the Department of Health.

If an ambulance is called and the ambulance crew is shown a copy of the out-of-hospital DNR order with original signatures, or observes that the person is wearing an out-of-hospital DNR bracelet or necklace, the ambulance crew will not attempt CPR.

An out-of-hospital DNR order may be revoked by the patient without the physician's approval or knowledge by destroying or not displaying the order, bracelet or necklace, or by conveying the decision to revoke the out-of-hospital DNR order verbally or otherwise at the time or immediately preceding the time the person experiences cardiac or respiratory arrest.

For a DNR order to be effective, it must be obvious to EMS providers that the DNR order exists. Patients who leave their approved bracelets or necklaces on a dresser or in a pocket may be resuscitated by emergency personnel because the emergency personnel may believe that the person has changed his or her mind about the DNR order.

An out-of-hospital DNR order is only an order to an EMS provider not to provide CPR. It does not relate to any other treatment. An EMS provider may offer care that is intended to provide comfort and alleviate pain.

If the attending physician is not willing to issue an out-of-hospital DNR order for a person who qualifies for the order, the physician must explain the reason to the patient or the surrogate. Since the order may be issued only by a physician who has primary responsibility for the treatment and care of the patient, the physician must make every reasonable effort to help the patient or surrogate to obtain the services of another physician who is willing to issue an order for the patient, and who will undertake primary responsibility for the treatment and care of the patient.

A person qualified to receive an out-of-hospital do-not-resuscitate order is one who has a terminal condition which is defined for this purpose as "an incurable and irreversible medical condition in an advanced state caused by injury, disease or physical illness which will in the opinion of the attending physician, to a reasonable degree of medical certainty, result in death regardless of the continued application of life-sustaining treatment."

The order may be requested by the patient. The surrogate of the patient may also request an out-of-hospital DNR order for a person who is in a terminal condition. If the patient has executed a declaration under the Advance Directive for Health Care Act that states that no CPR or no life-sustaining procedure shall be provided to the person should the person become permanently unconscious and experience cardiac or respiratory arrest, or if the declaration designates a surrogate to make medical care decisions should the person become permanently unconscious and experience cardiac or respiratory arrest, the person's surrogate may request an out-of-hospital DNR order for the person if that person becomes permanently unconscious.

HIPAA and Your Medical Power of Attorney

> *... Silly doctors, to be so spooked by the prospect of $10,000 fines for overstepping hundreds of pages of guidelines.*
>
> Meg Kissinger, *Milwaukee Journal Sentinel*

> *What do you call someone who complains incessantly about HIPAA?*
>
> A HIPAAchondriac

We've lived with HIPAA, the federal Health Insurance Portability and Accountability Act, since it became effective April

14, 2003. (Some say HIPAA stands for Highly Intricate Paperwork in Abundant Amounts.)

HIPAA makes sweeping changes to how health care providers are allowed to transmit and disseminate your medical information. Now, more than ever, it is very important for you to make a Medical Directive or Health Care Power of Attorney. Further, many lawyers are recommending that existing Medical Directives and Health Care Powers of Attorney be updated to add language referring specifically to the new HIPAA rules.

Medical Directives or Health Care Powers of Attorney have become a standard part of a complete estate plan. A Medical Directive is a document whereby you designate a surrogate to make medical decisions for you in the event you are unable to do so. Often it is combined with a living will in which you express your wishes about your care in the event of terminal illness and permanent unconsciousness.

Under HIPAA, medical providers must take great care not to disseminate "Protected Health Information" which is broadly defined to include any information that identifies a patient and relates to a past, present, or future physical or mental condition, provision of health care or payment for health care (in other words, just about everything). The penalties to health care providers for noncompliance with the HIPAA privacy rules are severe. Fines can be from $100 per violation to criminal penalties of up to a $50,000 fine and one year in prison. If the information is used for commercial advantage, personal gain or malicious harm, then the criminal penalties increase to a $250,000 fine and ten years in jail.

HIPAA permits disclosure of information to a "Personal Representative." A Personal Representative is someone who has the legal authority to make medical decisions for the patient. Parents who have authority to make health care decisions on the child's behalf are generally the Personal Representative. Spouses are not automatically, by marriage, each other's Personal Representative. A Surrogate appointed in a valid Medical Directive or Health Care Power of Attorney *is* a Personal Representative.

Therefore, as a legal matter, a well-drafted Medical Directive or Health Care Power of Attorney is sufficient so that Protected Health Information can be given to your surrogate. The problem is that the medical providers are so afraid of breaking the law and incurring stiff penalties that they are very cautious and may not *know* whether or not your Medical Directive has sufficient authority for them to release information. They will look for a reference to HIPAA and if they see none, they may be afraid that your document is not good enough.

For this practical reason, many lawyers are recommending that Medical Directives and Health Care Powers of Attorney contain a specific reference to HIPAA.

Here is some language recommended by Thomas J. Murphy writing for the *Arizona Lawyer* December 2003 issue:

"HIPAA Release Authority. I intend for my agent to be treated as I would be with respect to my rights regarding the use and disclosure of my individually identifiable health information or other medical records. This release authority applies to any information governed by the Health Insurance Portability and Accountability Act of 1996 (aka HIPAA), 42 U.S.C. § 1320d and 45 C.F.R. §§ 160-164. I authorize:

1. any physician, health care professional, dentist, health plan, hospital, clinic, laboratory, pharmacy or other covered health care provider, any insurance company and the Medical Information Bureau Inc. or other health care clearinghouse that has provided treatment or services to me or that has paid for or is seeking payment from me for such services,
2. to give, disclose and release to my agent, without restriction,
3. all of my individually identifiable health information and medical records regarding any past, present or future medical or mental health condition, to include all information relating to the diagnosis and treatment of HIV/AIDS, sexually transmitted diseases, mental illness and drug or alcohol abuse.

The authority given my agent shall supersede any prior agreement that I may have made with my health care providers to restrict access to or disclosure of my individually identifiable health information. The authority given my agent has no expiration date and shall expire only in the event that I revoke the authority in writing and deliver it to my health care provider."

Here is another good example from the well-known legal drafting software, Virtu-will, which authorizes the agent:

"To have full access to my medical and hospital records and all information regarding my physical or mental health, to review my medical records and medical bills, to execute releases of confidential information from medical providers and insurers or other third party payers, and to consult with my physicians and other health care personnel and providers. My Agent shall be considered to be my personal representative for health care disclosure purposes under applicable Federal HIPAA regulations, including without limitation, designation of my agent as my personal representative as defined in 45 C.F.R §164.502. This authorization and consent to disclosure shall apply whether or not I continue to have the capacity to give informed consent. I consent to and direct covered entities to provide my protected health information to my Agent."

Sometimes being legally correct is not enough. In an emergency situation, you don't want a legal argument; you want the document to be accepted and to be effective.

Accountability of Your Agents

Your brother was given Power of Attorney by your Mom many years ago. She has had a debilitating stroke and is now in a nursing home. Your brother is paying her bills using the Power of Attorney as her agent. He just bought a new car and is going on a cruise. You suspect he is inappropriately using Mom's money. What can you do?

First, you can ask him if he's using Mom's money for himself. Let's assume he denies using Mom's money for his personal benefit. Second, you can ask him to prove it. He may show you his records, or he may not. He would be within his rights to refuse to share any records with you.

To whom is he accountable? Tough question. A grant of Power of Attorney is the creation of a principal/agent relationship. The person holding the Power of Attorney is the agent. The person granting the power is the principal. At common law, the agent is accountable to the principal.

We now have legislation that creates "durable" powers of attorney. That is, powers of attorney that continue in effect even though the principal has been incapacitated and is no longer able to oversee the activity of the agent and make the agent accountable.

If you suspect the agent is breaching his or her fiduciary duty by improperly administering the principal's funds, you don't have many options. If you ask for proof of proper administration and are rebuffed, you are left with little recourse.

One alternative would be to petition the local orphan's court for the appointment of a guardian. If you or some other person or institution is appointed guardian, then you have the legal authority to act on the principal's behalf and can demand an accounting from the attorney-in-fact. If the guardian meets with a refusal for an accounting from the agent, the guardian has the legal standing to ask the court to compel an accounting. Most people want to avoid the appointment of a guardian and the court supervised administration of their affairs and the expense it involves. Only an agent appointed by the principal or a court appointed guardian has the legal authority to act on the principal's behalf.

In egregious cases, a criminal investigation may be appropriate. Inappropriately taking another person's funds for your own benefit is stealing. Many times this kind of activity goes uninvestigated or undiscovered until the death of the principal. Other family members who are beneficiaries of the deceased principal's estate are surprised to find that the principal's assets have been depleted or have disappeared. The executor of the will or administrator of the estate has the legal authority to request the court to compel an accounting by the agent. The executor has the authority to get bank records and statements of activity in accounts so that a full investigation can be made.

Many times, the agent is also the executor. As a matter of fact, when the agent acts properly, this arrangement makes a lot of sense. If that is the case, then if you are a beneficiary of your mom's will or are an heir, you can require the executor to give an accounting and to thus require an accounting of activities of the agent.

Let's assume that by one of the avenues above, you are able to get the facts to see that, in fact, your brother has been using Mom's money. That's not the end of the story. What does the document which grants him Power of Attorney authorize him to do? It may be that his actions are appropriate given the terms of the document. Often a Power of Attorney gives the agent authority to make gifts. This would include making gifts to himself. An agent is also entitled to reasonable compensation for services rendered. Sometimes the principal approves or ratifies the actions of the agent.

Ever since powers of attorney became "durable," that is, the agent's authority continued even though the principal is incapacitated, many questions have arisen about the accountability of the agent. There is no established, simple mechanism in the law for reviewing the actions of the agent.

As a matter of public policy, perhaps the need for administration of an incapacitated person's assets outweighs the safeguards present in more formal fiduciary appointments. But anyone who has watched an agent take advantage of the principal will not agree. This is an area that needs further legislation. Wouldn't it be a better idea if any heir could insist on an accounting?

Some Guidelines for Springing Powers of Attorney

A Power of Attorney is a document in which you appoint an agent to transact business on your behalf. The agent is called your attorney-in-fact. You, the person appointing the agent, are called the principal. You are free to give the attorney-in-fact whatever powers you choose. The grant of authority can be very broad or the authority can be limited to a single act or transaction.

In most powers of attorney, the grant of authority to the attorney-in-fact is effective immediately. That is, as soon as the document is signed, the attorney-in-fact could exercise the powers given in the document. Usually the principal intends that the powers not be exercised by the attorney-in-fact until the principal (that's you) needs help. But legally, the authority is granted and effective immediately.

Many clients are uncomfortable with this. When they are hale and healthy, they don't like the idea of a spouse or child visiting the bank and cleaning out their accounts using the Power of Attorney. Most people would like it if the Power of Attorney became effective only when they became incapacitated. This kind of Power of Attorney is called a "springing" Power of Attorney because it springs into life when needed. This sounds good, but is fraught with difficulties.

The key to a springing power is what event triggers the power's effectiveness. Some attorneys include language in the Power of Attorney providing that it only becomes effective if two physicians sign a document in which they say that the principal is incapable of managing his or her own affairs. Imagine that you are a physician. The child of one of your patients comes to you and asks you to sign a document so that the child can have complete control of your patient's finances. Are you going to sign it? You probably shouldn't. If the patient is in an irreversible coma maybe you would feel comfortable signing such a document. But that's the easy case. What about the patient who is going downhill, having good days and bad days, periods of lucidity, times of confusion? Do you, the medical doctor, give control of the finances to the child? Or the next-door neighbor who is named in the Power of Attorney? It is easy to see that there might be uncertainty, disagreement, or squabbling among doctors and/or family over the degree of the principal's incapacity.

Even if you get two physicians to sign, and you take the Power of Attorney and two physician's certifications to the bank, would you as the banker accept the attorney-in-fact's authority? How do you know if the signatures of the physicians are genuine? For that matter, how do you know that the individuals who sign are, in fact, physicians? How do you know that the physicians have made the correct determination?

To take the medical profession off the hook, we sometimes recommend that another person or family member make the determination of whether or not the Power of Attorney should be activated. A friend or family member may be more willing to stick his or her neck out, but the problem of third party reliance remains. The Pennsylvania statute protects a bank or other third party that relies on a Power of Attorney. The statute does not stretch so far as to protect the bank or third party from relying on another person's, even a physician's, certification that the principal has become incapacitated.

Similarly, sometimes the drafting attorney will hold the Power of Attorney under an escrow agreement, only releasing the document to the attorney-in-fact when the attorney believes the principal is incapacitated. This shifts the burden of liability to the lawyer. (Which pleases the physicians, but is not so good for the lawyer.)

Remember, you are making a Power of Attorney to simplify matters if you become disabled or unable to act. By putting in conditions on the attorney-in-fact's authority, you are creating issues that may need to be resolved by a court, for example, whether you are disabled, thereby defeating the purpose of simplicity in dealing with issues that may arise.

All powers of attorney end when the principal dies, unless the document specifies an earlier date. The principal also can change or revoke a Power of Attorney at any time. If a spouse is the agent, the Power of Attorney ends when divorce papers are filed.

The bottom line is that if you can't trust the person not to use the power until you are incapacitated, then you can't trust the person (period). Someone whom you cannot trust should not be named as your attorney-in-fact. When there is no family member who would be a suitable attorney-in-fact, other choices include banks and trust companies who provide Power of Attorney services for a fee. This is often the best alternative.

Another word to the wise about powers of attorney. We have found that many financial institutions are refusing to accept powers of attorney unless they are on the financial institution's own forms. Again, this defeats the purpose of having a Power of Attorney. However, options are limited if a financial institution refuses to accept the attorney-in-fact's authority. They can be sued, of course, and we know how much time and money that takes. Alternatively, a guardian can be appointed in court — the very thing the Power of Attorney was intended to avoid.

IRAS AND QUALIFIED PLANS

Navigating the Maze of Qualified Retirement Plans

Once upon a time, Uncle Sam created a program to prevent older citizens from living in poverty. It was a good plan, called Social Security, and the idea of helping out those who would be in need, grew. But the need grew faster than funding could keep up.

In addition, Congress saw a surplus in this program, while the rest of the federal budget was in the red. Instead of looking at Social Security as a trust fund, Congress saw ways of making up for deficit spending by raiding the Social Security fund, as long as the income and outgo matched. The problem, of course, is that instead of a contributor getting out what he or she paid in, he or she is getting only what today's workers are putting in. The ratio of depositors to claimants has dwindled, producing the current mess.

This mess was anticipated long ago. Because Congress couldn't discipline itself to repair the program, it attacked the problem by enacting tax incentives to get workers to do what Congress could no longer do: save for retirement without raiding those savings. In 1974, the Economic Retirement Income Security Act (ERISA) was enacted. It essentially said that if money is put away for retirement, the income tax would be deferred until it was taken as income. Further, the interest on the income would not be taxed until the funds were withdrawn.

Not only would funds contributed by the employee be tax deferred, but if the employer wanted to kick in some matching funds, he could deduct them as a business expense. For employees, this leveraged their savings through tax deferral and avoidance, and for employers, this provided a tax deductible way to attract and retain employees.

Now this turned out to be such a good thing, employees began to use it not just to save for retirement, but to avoid paying taxes. And employers began to use it to offer key employees and executives the perk of a retirement vehicle that wasn't offered to the rank, and, file employees.

Neither of these uses met the original intention of preventing older citizens from living in poverty. Therefore, Congress decided to put some qualifications on the program. Refinements came through the following series of subsequent laws: TEFRA '82, DEFRA '84, TRA '86, SEPPRA '86, PPA '87, OBRA '93, TRA '97, and our current masterpiece, EGTRAA '01. The latest laws make so many changes in so many years, that many employers are struggling to keep their Plan legally up-to-date. Failure to navigate the maze results in full taxation and penalties due to the government.

Despite all the confusing twists and turns of the program, there are some basic elements of the Qualified Plans of which taxpayers and plan participants should be aware. A Plan has four elements, a sponsor, a Plan, an administrator, and participants. The Plan must be raid-proof (Congress' way of saying, "Do as I say, not as I do.") There are minimum reporting and disclosure requirements to fulfill. Also there are minimum participation, funding, and vesting requirements.

The Plan must be for all employees, not just the key employees. There must be minimum participation: 50 employees or 40% of the work force, whichever is less, must be participants every day of the year. New hires must be eligible to participate after one year of service or on their twenty-first birthday, whichever is later.

Early or late withdrawals are penalized. To be sure it would be used as a retirement vehicle and not a tax avoidance vehicle, Congress insisted on withdrawals around retirement age, which historically has meant 65 (however, beginning with people born in 1938 or later, that age gradually increases until it reaches 67 for people born after 1959). "Around" had to be defined. Plus or minus five years sounded good. But when do you turn 60? Congress says you're 60 the day you become closer to 60 than to 59, hence the early limit of 59 and a half. The same idea holds for exceeding 70 years of age, hence the 70 and a half limit. Take anything too soon, or not take enough every year while past the retirement window, and excise taxes kick in.

There are exceptions here and there. For instance, if you separate from service after your 55th birthday, you may take the money without penalty, since Congress figures no one gives up a job at that age just to get at their qualified plan funds, when society's age bias makes getting another job very difficult. And surviving younger spouses can use their own age instead as a trigger for mandatory withdrawals. But in general, Congress frowns on raiding qualified plans early or letting them continue to compound interest tax-free too long.

Now, some folks get upset when they realize that withdrawals from the plan are taxed. Remember, this is a tax *deferral* plan, designed to allow taxpayers to pay tax on earned income at a time when their income is less than during their peak earning years. This really is quite a benefit. Not only does it encourage saving, and therefore financial security, for retirement, but it reduces the taxes owed during a taxpayer's working years. It may even allow the taxpayer to remain in a lower tax bracket prior to retirement.

Ten Stupid Things People Do to Mess up Their IRAs

1. <u>Not getting professional advice</u>. The complexity of the rules governing IRA distribution and beneficiary designations is incredible. Especially where substantial amounts of money are involved, don't try to "do-it-yourself." Who to name as beneficiary? When to take distributions? How much to take out? Should you use a trust? Is it best to name your spouse? These are complicated issues. Lawyers, accountants, and other financial professionals spend hours learning the complex rules that govern these areas. Don't try this at home.
2. <u>Not naming beneficiaries</u>. When you set up an IRA or become a participant in a retirement plan, you don't have to name a beneficiary and many people don't. Sometimes an IRA owner may designate one beneficiary, the spouse, and leave it at that. Usually plan documents provide that if no beneficiary or contingent beneficiary is named, the IRA is payable to the owner's estate. This may be the worst possible result from an income tax point of view.
3. <u>Naming the wrong beneficiaries</u>. Don't name your minor kids as beneficiaries. See the next topic, naming a minor as your IRA beneficiary. If your seven-year-old is the beneficiary of your retirement plan, the company will not pay it to him. It will be necessary to go to the expense and inconvenience of having a court appointed guardian for the minor who will get custody of the minor's estate, including the retirement plan assets. In your will, you wouldn't give your property to your seven-year-old. Why would you give your retirement plan to him? You need to name a custodian or a trustee.

Even if your kids are adults, fashioning the beneficiary designation is complicated. If a child predeceases you, does his share go to his children? Are they minors? Or does the retirement plan provide that if a beneficiary is deceased, his or her share is divided among other named living beneficiaries? Don't automatically name your spouse. The best tax deal may be to name your adult children, or even adult grandchildren, or a trust for grandchildren, because they will be able to maintain the tax deferment provided by the IRA or retirement plan for a much longer time.

4. Not beginning the required distributions on time. You are required to begin taking the minimum required distribution (MRD) by April 1 of the year following the year in which you attain the age of 70½. Making this withdrawal is your responsibility. It is not the responsibility of the broker or mutual fund or investment advisor who holds the IRA assets. They may remind you as a courtesy but it is your responsibility to handle this. It is also your responsibility to determine the correct MRD. If you have multiple IRAs you may take the entire MRD from only one of them if you chose.

   If you wait until the last permissible time, that is, before April 1 of the year following the year in which you attain age 70½ to begin withdrawals, you will have to take two withdrawals in that year. It may be wise to take the first withdrawal in the year in which you attain age 70½. That way, it may be taxed at a lower rate. Deferral is not always the best policy.

5. Being a prisoner of the form. Preprinted beneficiary designation forms often give you a three inch single line to name your beneficiary. Don't feel constrained by this. Don't decide who gets all of the assets in your retirement plan based on what can fit on the line. You can always attach a sheet of paper spelling out exactly how the benefit should be distributed. If your IRA administrator doesn't like it, there are plenty of other ones who will. Move the account.

6. Not knowing what forms of distribution the plan permits. Planning for a stretch-out of IRA payments to your kids or grandchildren is useless if the IRA custodian's account agreement provides for a lump sum payout on your death. Not all IRAs include all the options permitted under the law. Do you know what yours allows?

7. Not keeping copies of your account agreement and beneficiary designations. These documents should be given the same care and safekeeping as your will and power of attorney. These are the documents that will determine your rights and your beneficiaries' rights to receive the assets in these accounts. Many people don't even know who their beneficiaries are. Your will has no effect on who gets these plans if you've designated a beneficiary.

   You can't rely on the financial institution's records. Do you know how many mergers and takeovers there have been in this industry? Stories abound of whole truckloads of records carted away and discarded. With personnel changes every few months, your records are easily "lost." Keep your own records.

8. Putting the wrong investments in the IRA. Don't put municipal bonds in your IRA. The IRA pays no income tax; it does not need to take a reduced rate to receive tax-free income. Don't buy an annuity in your IRA. The IRA is already tax deferred, you don't need to buy a product for tax deferral — the IRA already gives you tax deferral.

9. Rolling all your retirement plans and IRAs into one IRA because it is "neater," or easier to invest. It can be very beneficial to have multiple IRAs with different beneficiaries. That way, each beneficiary can use his or her own life expectancy for withdrawals. Also, some IRAs and retirement plans may have grandfathered estate planning advantages that would be destroyed by moving them to another plan with different beneficiary designations. Drawing out 401(k)s and profit sharing plans to put in an IRA is not always advisable.

10. Making charitable bequests out of other assets and giving IRA assets to your children and grandchildren. If you want to make charitable gifts when you die, and you have an IRA or retirement plan, the gifts should be made from the IRA or retirement plan. But beware, the beneficiary designation should not be a group or class gift including the charity as one of a group of beneficiaries.

This is an excellent place for a separate IRA for the amount to be paid to the charity on your death. The charity, unlike your heirs, can receive the IRA benefit free of estate tax and free of income tax. Because of the special tax breaks given to the charity, the IRA assets are worth far more to the charity than they are to your heirs. If you use the IRA assets for the charitable gift, instead of other assets, both the charity and your heirs get more. Under the Taxpayer Relief Act, passed in early January 2013, the ability to make tax-free distributions from individual retirement plans directly to qualifying charities has been extended through 2013 and made retroactive for 2012.

Naming a Minor as Your IRA Beneficiary

IRAs and qualified plans are great vehicles for saving for retirement. Contributions to the plans are not taxed, and the assets inside the plan enjoy tax free reinvestment and accumulation. The income tax is payable only when the assets are withdrawn from the plan.

Unfortunately, while IRAs and other retirement plans are great for retirement savings, they are not so great for passing wealth on to your beneficiaries. The assets in the plan are subject to federal estate tax (if your gross estate exceeds $5.25 million for 2013) and they are also subject to income tax when received by the beneficiary. If the beneficiary is a person two or more generations below that of the owner of the plan, it is possible for these plans to also be subject to generation-skipping tax. The net effect of all this taxation is that in the hands of the beneficiary, the IRA or retirement plan may be worth only a fraction (possibly one-fourth) of what it was to the original account owner.

Since the IRA beneficiary can make withdrawals over his or her life expectancy, naming a very young person or persons as beneficiaries can be very attractive. When the beneficiary inherits the IRA, he or she can stretch the required minimum distributions over his or her own life expectancy, deferring taxes until withdrawals are made. The younger the beneficiary, the longer the life expectancy, the less that has to be withdrawn each year, and the more time the assets can grow inside the plan, tax-deferred.

Here is an example. You leave a $100,000 IRA to a grandson Jack born the year you die. Jack's life expectancy at age 1, according to the IRS life-expectancy table for inherited IRAs is 81.6 years. Jack could stretch the minimum required distribution over 82 years! The first year distribution would be only $1,323. If the IRA has an average growth rate of 8% during his life expectancy, the account would wind up worth a cumulative $8.8 million in total withdrawals by the time he has to empty it at age 83. That is not a misprint — a $100,000 IRA results in over $8.8 million in withdrawals by Jack!

The $8.8 million in withdrawals depends on the assumed rate of return of 8%. Look at what happens at other rates of return. At an assumed 7% return, total withdrawals are $4.6 million, for 6% total withdrawals are $2.4 million, 5% - $1.3 million, 4% - $750,000. (Don't forget that the average return numbers are net of fees.) At the other extreme, a return of 10% results in a total of $32 million in withdrawals.

To get these kinds of returns, it is important that the beneficiary designations on the IRA are done correctly. One of the most common estate planning disasters I have seen in my years of experience is naming minors individually, i.e., as outright beneficiaries. Minors are not allowed to make property transactions in Pennsylvania until they attain the age of majority. Naming a minor can result in costly, time-consuming court proceedings, legal disputes, or holding estates open for years which ultimately dwindles the benefit of the accumulated IRA.

The significant returns illustrated also depend on the beneficiaries' discipline to withdraw only the minimum required distributions over their lifetimes. Beneficiaries are often tempted to simply withdraw the IRA and pay the tax in one lump sum shortly after attaining the age of majority. Fortunately, both pitfalls are easily avoided with proper estate planning and the full benefit of the IRA can be realized by your beneficiaries. Furthermore, only you are in the position to assure that the structure is in place to have your intent carried out.

You really shouldn't name baby Jack as the IRA beneficiary. Why, because Jack, the babe-in-arms, can't make the required withdrawals. He lacks legal capacity. In fact, he won't have legal capacity until he attains the age of 18. The IRS doesn't care; baby or no, the minimum distribution rules still apply. When the minimum required distribution is not withdrawn, a very stiff 50% penalty applies.

There are three choices for properly designating a minor beneficiary of your IRA: (1) a legal guardian can be appointed for Jack (This is expensive and unwieldy — not a good choice.); (2) you can create a trust for the benefit of Jack that meets the IRS requirements for stretching out payments over Jack's, the beneficiary, life expectancy; (3) you can name a custodian under the Uniform Transfers to Minors Act (UTMA) for the benefit of Jack to receive the IRA on his behalf until he is 21.

A trust specifically to receive the benefit is probably the best choice. It provides the most flexibility and will cover all possible contingencies. This alternative is the most expensive because of the need to create a trust before death, but it gives you the most control over making sure your wishes are carried out.

The most common type of trust used as an IRA beneficiary is a conduit trust. This type of trust requires the trustee to distribute the required distributions each year from the trust to the child so that the child pays the tax rather than the trust, which would generally owe more. The distributions can be made to a UTMA custodian for the minor.

Another type, called an accumulation trust, allows the trustee to stretch-out the IRA withdrawals over the child's life expectancy but the trustee could keep all, or part, of those withdrawals in the trust. Withdrawals kept in the trust would be taxed as income at the trust's income tax rate, and any amounts distributed to or for the benefit of the child would be taxed at his or her personal income tax rate. An accumulation trust has the added benefit of giving you control of deciding when your beneficiaries actually receive money from the IRA withdrawals. There is no requirement that the funds be distributed to the child upon attaining the age of majority.

The third option is a viable, low-cost option of naming a minor as a beneficiary of an IRA. In the beneficiary designation of your IRA account you may designate a custodian, and even a successor custodian, under the Uniform Transfer to Minors Act, for the benefit of Jack (much like should be done in your will for any property passing to a minor). This named custodian receives the minimum required distribution annually, invests it in an account titled "Custodian's Name, Custodian for Jack under PA UTMA" until Jack turns 21. The short-coming of this low-cost option is that Jack inherits both the accumulated funds and the IRA outright when he turns 21.

If the IRA you leave to Jack is a Roth IRA, then you have really hit the ball out of the park. If we assume an 8% return, the entire $8.8 million in distributions to Jack will be federal income tax free.

When using any of these techniques, always get written acknowledgment from the plan custodian that they have accepted the beneficiary designation you have made. Keep a copy with your will and other important papers. If your custodian won't cooperate, move your account to a custodian who will. This is much too important to let slide.

Final Regulations for Retirement Plan Distributions

In January 2001, the IRS published proposed regulations to simplify and improve IRA and Qualified Plan withdrawal requirements. On April 17, 2002, the IRS published the final regulations which took effect in January 2003. The final regulations made some significant changes to the proposed regulations but the distribution rules are even better now than before. There are some new provisions that will allow mistakes to be corrected and allow more IRA owners and plan participants to take advantage of the new rules.

The IRS allows you to defer income tax on money you sock away for retirement until you actually take it out of the retirement account. In addition, earnings on the funds in the retirement account compound over the years tax-free. The IRS only demands two things when you take the money out. First, pay the income tax that you didn't pay before. Second, make minimum withdrawals at a steady rate when you reach retirement age and at a rate that will deplete the account by the time you die. The policy behind the tax-favored treatment of retirement accounts is to help workers save for retirement, not to give them a way to compound their estate for their children without paying income tax.

Under the new regulations, there are three tables that are to be used for determining required minimum distributions from the plans. The three choices are the Uniform Lifetime Distribution Table, The Single Life Table, and The Joint Life Table. New life expectancy data were used in the tables so life expectancy is extended about one year compared to the table issued with the proposed regulations. Most IRA owners and plan participants will use the Uniform Lifetime Distribution Table. If the primary beneficiary is a spouse who is more than ten years younger, then the Joint Life Table is used. The Single Life Table is for use by designated beneficiaries on inherited accounts. See your financial advisor for the current table.

Under the new final regulations, the date for determining the designated beneficiary after the owner's death is moved up from December 31 of the year following the year of death to September 30 following the year of death. Because the first annual withdrawal must be made by December 31 of the year following the year of death, there is no sense in having these deadlines coincide. This change helps plan administrators, and gives three months to determine who gets the withdrawals, and how much needs to be withdrawn. The beneficiary or beneficiaries still have to be named before death, but after death disclaimers can be made and accounts can be split.

The so-called gap period has now been addressed. Suppose the beneficiary dies between the death of the plan owner and the September 30 deadline. The question is how to determine the life expectancy in this case. The new regulations say the life expectancy of the deceased beneficiary is to be used, calculating as though he or she were still alive. Using the deceased beneficiary's life expectancy is a much better result for the taxpayer.

If there are multiple beneficiaries to an IRA account, the life of the oldest is used for determining minimum distributions. However, the account may be split up as one account for each of the beneficiaries, and then each account would require a distribution based on the age of the individual beneficiary. This is a break for all but the oldest beneficiary.

What if a couple encounters divorce and death in the same year? The answer is that marital status is determined as of January 1 of the distribution year. This means the spousal exception described above can be used for the first year, but not following years.

What if a trust is named as beneficiary? The IRS requires that (1) the trustee provide information to the plan administrator regarding the beneficiaries, and (2) that this information be provided by October 31 of the year following the year of death. Old trusts were grandfathered, but only if they provided the information by October 31, 2003.

S-t-r-e-t-c-h-i-n-g I-t O-u-t: Plan IRA Distributions

> *Man fools himself. He prays for a long life, and he fears an old age.*
>
> Chinese proverb

IRAs are one of the best tax shelters available. You can defer the income tax on money contributed to the IRA (or rolled over to an IRA from another retirement plan) until you withdraw the funds during retirement. During that time you get tax-free accumulation inside the IRA account and get the earnings. One of the catches is — you have to start drawing the money out at age 70½ and pay income tax on the withdrawn amounts. A table shows how much you have to withdraw each year. (See your financial advisor for the current table.) What happens if the account owner dies? It depends on who is the beneficiary and what actions are taken post death.

One of the best planning techniques is to make the IRA a "stretch IRA." That means to plan a beneficiary designation so that on the death of the account owner, the balance in the IRA can be paid out over the longest time period possible. This continues the highly desirable tax-free buildup inside the IRA account and defers the payment of income tax over a longer period of time.

Here are some provisions of the "stretch" IRA regulations.

Beneficiaries of an IRA are determined as of the date of death of the participant. Beneficiaries can be removed up until September 30 of the year after the year of death by having their share distributed in a lump sum or by qualified disclaimer. No beneficiaries can be added after the participant's death. The age of the oldest of a group of beneficiaries is used to determine the portion of the account that must be withdrawn each year. But, if the account is broken down into separate accounts for each beneficiary before December 31 of the year following death, then each account may be distributed according to the age of each individual beneficiary. The account can be broken down years later as well, but once the December 31 of the year following death has passed, all accounts must be distributed using only the age of the oldest beneficiary of the group at the date of death.

December 31 of the year after the year of participant's death is also the deadline for establishing a separate account payable solely to the surviving spouse for purposes of the special distribution rules applicable to the surviving spouse of a participant who died before age 70½. This means that the account can be rolled over and be considered the spouse's own account. In other words, the survivor can avoid withdrawals until age 70½ and then use his or her own age as the withdrawal requirement factor.

When accounts are split up, the capital gains and losses must be split up proportionately. The longer the delay in splitting up: the bigger the headache of splitting.

If an IRA is payable to a trust, the life expectancy of the trust beneficiary can be used to stretch out the IRA payments if the trust meets certain criteria. There used to be a before-death deadline for supplying a copy of a trust that is named as a beneficiary of IRA benefits to the plan administrator that caused a lot of attempted "stretch IRAs" to fail. Now there is a new deadline for supplying a copy of a trust which is a beneficiary to the plan administrator — October 31 of the year after the year of the participant's death. In the October 31 certification, the trustee certifies who were the beneficiaries of the trust on the September 30 Designation Date.

Death of a beneficiary prior to Designation Date does not cause loss of Designated Beneficiary status. Under the regulations, a person who is a beneficiary as of the date of death, but then dies prior to the Designation Date, does *not* lose his status as a "designated beneficiary." This is good, because if death eliminated the last beneficiary, withdrawal rates would accelerate considerably.

Beneficiaries used to have to choose between a five-year payout period or a life expectancy payout schedule. The five-year option only required the account to be empty by the end of the fifth full year after death. Some fiduciaries simply withdrew nothing in hopes of better treatment. For a limited time, those forced to have a five-year period under prior regulations can switch to the lifetime payout period. When switching to the lifetime payout period, payments that have not been taken under the five-year period, but would have been taken under the lifetime payout period must be taken. These payments must equal those that would have been made under the lifetime payout period had it been an option.

Finally, those using the old joint and survivor table can switch to the new Joint and Last Survivor Table to take advantage of the longer life expectancy in the new table.

As Balthazar Gracian said, "Always leave something to wish for, otherwise you will be miserable from your very happiness." The new life expectancy at age 114 is 2.1 years.

Our thanks to Natalie Choate and her web site at *www.ataxplan.com*.

Designate Your Beneficiaries or Someone Else Will

How much of your estate is in life insurance and retirement plans? Do you realize that your will does not govern who receives these benefits? Life insurance death benefits, survivor's benefits from qualified plans and IRAs, annuities, and other contracts are payable to those persons designated as beneficiaries. Do you recall whom you have designated as beneficiaries? Have your circumstances changed since you set up these plans?

Here is a common and practical example. You could have a will leaving everything to your spouse, but if you own a life insurance policy you bought before you were married, you may have named your parents as beneficiaries. If you make no change in beneficiary designation, your parents would get the death benefit, not your spouse.

It is just as important to review and perhaps change beneficiary designations as it is to review your will. When you apply for insurance, or buy an annuity, or get coverage under an insurance or retirement plan because of employment, you are asked to fill out a beneficiary designation form. This beneficiary designation governs who gets that asset when you die.

When you started work, were you married? Maybe you named your mother as beneficiary of group life insurance provided by your employer. How many children did you have when you bought an annuity? Did you name the children individually? If you did, children born after that date would not be beneficiaries. Do you really want minor children to be named as beneficiaries so that a court-appointed guardian has to be named to accept the money for them? All of these questions should be addressed as part of your estate planning process.

Changes of beneficiary are easy to make. You must request a change of beneficiary form from the contracting company and fill it out in accordance with their directions. Most of these forms provide a few blank spaces to write a designation, but don't be a prisoner of the form! If your designation is more complicated, attach a sheet. You are not limited in the disposition of your $500,000 IRA just because the blank on the form isn't big enough.

Most lawyers who do estate planning ask clients to bring beneficiary designations in for review as part of the estate planning process. If changes are necessary, explicit instructions are given for how the new beneficiaries should be named, and, in some cases, the lawyer prepares the change requests as part of the legal services provided. Think about it. The lawyer drafts the will. If there is a large asset that passes outside the will, don't you want the same care, tax planning, and advice for its disposition?

In the area of retirement plans and IRAs, the questions are even more serious. Who the beneficiary is determines how the benefits can be paid and how long the tax-free inside buildup provided by the plan can be maintained. You also need to be aware that in some rare instances changing a qualified plan beneficiary designation can be very detrimental. This is because some plan benefits may be exempt from the estate tax only so long as the designation remains unchanged. As these points illustrate, it is important that you be knowledgeable about the tax consequences of your designated beneficiaries.

Beneficiary designations for retirement plans are almost a science unto themselves. First, the payout options provided by the particular plan must be determined. Then the income tax and estate tax repercussions must be taken into account. So, if qualified plan benefits are a substantial part of your estate, you need to have the help of a financial professional who is familiar with these matters.

Pension and IRA Penalties for Early Withdrawals

Many people are tapping into their retirement accounts before they reach age 59½. This can be very expensive — not only are the withdrawals subject to income tax but there is also a penalty for withdrawals before age 59½. The purpose of the penalty on early withdrawals, is to discourage use of the funds for purposes other than retirement.

"Substantial penalty for early withdrawal," states the advertisement.

What's substantial, what's early, and is there an exception?

In general, the penalty for an early withdrawal is 10%. For early withdrawals from a Simple Pension Plan (for companies with fewer than 100 employees earning more than $5,000 a year) the penalty is even greater — 25%. So much for what "substantial penalty" means. "Early" means before age 59½.

If you need continued early access to your pension plan, section 12(t) of the Internal Revenue Code offers a few exceptions from the application of the penalty. What exceptions are available depends on what kind of plan you are withdrawing from. The types of plans are IRAs and qualified plans such as 401(k)s, pension and profit sharing plans, and annuity plans.

If distributions from either an IRA or a qualified plan are made early because you are totally and permanently disabled, there will be no penalty. An individual is considered disabled if "he is unable to engage in any substantial gainful activity by reason of any medically determinable physical or mental impairment which can be expected to result in death or to be of long-continued and infinite duration."

Distributions up to the amount of deductible medical expenses, that is, the amount of your medical expenses that are more than 7.5% of your adjusted gross income, can be withdrawn early with no penalty. This applies even if you don't itemize deductions on your income tax return.

For both IRAs and qualified plans, the 10% penalty does not apply to distributions which are part of a series of substantially equal periodic payments (SOSEPP). Such payments are made at least annually for the life or life expectancy of the individual or the joint lives or joint life expectancy of the individual and his designated beneficiary. SOSEPPs are frequently used since you do not need a reason for the withdrawals, they can begin at any age, and they can begin whether or not you continue to be employed. More on SOSEPPs later.

There are two exceptions to the early withdrawal penalty that apply to qualified plans, but not IRAs. They are distributions made to you after you separated from service with your employer, if the separation occurred after you reached age 55, and distributions made under qualified domestic relations orders (QDROs). Qualified domestic relations orders are used for marital property settlements when a qualified plan needs to be divided between divorcing spouses.

There are two exceptions to the penalty that apply only to IRAs — distributions made to pay for certain qualified higher education expenses and distributions up to $10,000 made to pay for first-time home buyers. Get this — a first-time home buyer means that neither the taxpayer nor the taxpayer's spouse has owned a home in the past two years. (Essentially, a first-time home buyer for this purpose is not necessarily a first-time home buyer.)

If you are making withdrawals from your IRA using a series of substantially equal periodic payments, a SOSEPP, you need to be aware of guidelines issued by the IRS in early October 2002. This ruling allows a once-in-a-lifetime change in payout methods. The ruling was spurred by the dramatic decline in value of many persons' accounts. Under the old SOSEPP rules, once a method of withdrawal was established, it had to be continued, or else there was a retroactive application of the 10% penalty. With accounts declining markedly in value, many participants who were already in a SOSEPP were being forced to withdraw too much. Accounts could be exhausted prematurely. Once started, SOSEPP payments must continue for five years or until age 59½, whichever is longer.

Once you've met the five-year or age 59½ point, you can change the distribution pattern, and even stop distributions. An IRS ruling will allow participants receiving SOSEPPs to reduce the payments, but they may cause the participant to receive too little. Now you have an overview as to what plans are subject to what penalties and under what circumstances. Don't try this at home. Consult a financial advisor before making an early withdrawal from any IRA or qualified plan. Mistakes can be extremely costly.

IRA Misinformation: There's No Shortage of It

The Supreme Court issued a decision in *Rousey v. Jacoway* on April 4, 2005. It's not often we estate planners get a Supreme Court case on our topics. This is big news.

> Here is what the headlines said:
>
> *Wall Street Journal Online:* High Court Rules IRAs Untouchable
>
> *New York Times:* Supreme Court Ruling Bars Creditors from IRA Assets
>
> *Washington Post:* Bankruptcy Shield for IRAs Upheld
>
> *USA Today:* Supreme Court rules IRAs exempt from bankruptcy
>
> proceedings
>
> *Los Angeles Times: Justices:* Creditors Can't Seize IRAs

There is only one problem. Those headlines are not what the Court held. The holding does not mean that IRAs are generally exempt from the claims of creditors. The issue will most often be decided by reference to state law which varies widely. Did any of these reporters actually read the court's opinion?

Richard and Betty Jo Rousey of Berryville, Arkansas, declared Chapter 7 bankruptcy. They claimed exemption for their IRAs under the bankruptcy exemptions for stock bonus, pensions, profit sharing, annuity or similar plans and because the funds were reasonably necessary for their support. The Bankruptcy Court denied the exemption, claiming that IRAs are not included in the exempt class. The Court of Appeals for the Eighth Circuit upheld the Bankruptcy Court saying IRAs were "readily accessible savings accounts of which debtors may easily avail themselves (albeit with some discouraging tax consequences) at any time for any purpose." Because there was conflict on this issue among the circuits, the Supreme Court took the case.

The Supreme Court set up a three-prong test for the exemption of IRAs:

1. The right to receive a payment must be from a "stock bonus pension, profit sharing, annuity, or similar plan or contract." The Supreme Court says IRAs are "similar plans."
2. The right to receive the payment must be "on account of illness, disability, death, age, or length of service." The Supreme Court says that the IRAs are subject to a 10% early withdrawal penalty for withdrawals before age 59½ so that this makes them "a right to payment on account of age."
3. The right to receive payment may be exempted only "to the extent" that it is "reasonably necessary to support" the account holder or his dependants. The Supreme Court made no ruling on this because the issue was not before them. This issue is yet to be decided. *We don't even know if the Rouseys' IRAs are going to be exempted.*

The federal bankruptcy law has a list of exemptions. Most states have their own list of assets that are exempt from the claims of creditors. The person who declares bankruptcy must choose either the federal exemptions or the state exemptions. Further, states are permitted to "opt out" of the federal exemptions and require that the state exemptions be used. Thirty-five states have chosen to opt out — Alabama, Alaska, Arizona, California, Colorado, Delaware, Florida, Georgia, Idaho, Illinois, Indiana, Iowa, Kansas, Kentucky, Louisiana, Maine, Maryland, Mississippi, Missouri, Montana, Nebraska, Nevada, New York, North Carolina, North Dakota, Ohio, Oklahoma, Oregon, South Carolina, South Dakota, Tennessee, Utah, Virginia, West Virginia and Wyoming. In these 35 states, the Supreme Court holding in *Rousey* is irrelevant because *Rousey* dealt with a situation where the debtor claimed the federal exemptions. Some of these states have state laws that exempt IRAs but that will be determined under the state law, not the federal bankruptcy law. In the other 15 states, including Pennsylvania, the holding in *Rousey* is applicable but only if the debtor chose the federal exemptions.

If the federal exemptions apply because the bankruptcy is in one of the 15 states that didn't opt out and the debtor chose the federal exemptions, the Court's holding only protects IRAs if the IRA is necessary to support the bankrupt or his or her dependents. Bankruptcy decisions on support are generally only for providing support at a subsistence level. This is not going to be useful to shelter multi-million dollar IRAs.

Natalie Choate points out that it is unlikely the ruling will apply to Roth IRAs. When the 10% premature withdrawal penalty doesn't apply to Roth IRAs, the Roth will fail the second prong of the test — the Roth IRA will not be "a right to payment on account of age."

Pennsylvania law (42 Pa. C.S.A. §8124(b)) exempts IRAs from creditors' claims with two exceptions: (1) amounts contributed to the IRA within one year of bankruptcy, and (2) those amounts contributed by the debtor that exceed $15,000 in any one year period. The law was amended in 1998 to provide that neither exception applies to a rollover from a qualified plan or other exempt IRA. Generally, a creditor cannot reach a rollover IRA since the statute was amended in 1998. It is unknown whether rollovers that occur before that date are protected. Further the statute refers to amounts "directly rolled over" which seems to imply that only a trustee to trustee transfer will be protected. If the debtor received a distribution and then opened an IRA, the statute might not exempt the rollover and the $15,000 per year and within one year of bankruptcy rules apply.

Under Pennsylvania law, IRAs are treated as marital property for the purposes of equitable distribution in divorce but IRAs are not subject to claims for child support.

The best protection still is to have all retirement plan assets in a qualified plan subject to ERISA, that is a pension, profit sharing plan, 401(k), or stock bonus plan, because no assets can be seized by any creditor. Next best protection is to live in a state where the IRA is 100% protected under state law from creditors' claims. I understand that New Jersey is such a state.

Buying an Annuity in Your IRA: It's Still a Bad Idea

> *Urgent message for life and annuity agents: Now you can get immediate and exclusive leads from highly qualified prospects who WANT you to call! XXXXXXXX Annuity Exchange delivers the hottest most reliable annuity leads anywhere: real prospects looking for annuities.*
>
> Web advertisement

Previously listed as one of the "Ten Stupid Things People Do To Mess Up Their IRAs," is: "don't buy an annuity in your IRA. The IRA is already tax deferred, you don't need to buy a product for tax deferral — the IRA already gives you tax deferral."

What is a variable annuity? A variable annuity is a contract with an insurance company that offers investment features that are similar in many respects to investments in mutual funds. A variable annuity has some features that are not available in mutual funds: tax-deferred treatment of earnings, a death benefit, and annuity payout options that can provide guaranteed income for life. On the down side, assets in the variable annuity do not get a step-up in basis when the owner dies and growth on the initial investment is eventually taxed at ordinary income rates, not capital gains rates.

Variable annuities have two phases. In the accumulation phase the investor pays premiums (or makes contributions) and these are allocated among various investments. In the distribution phase the investor withdraws money, either as a lump sum or through various annuity payment options. The investment return inside the annuity *varies* with the mutual fund investments made inside the annuity — hence the name *variable* annuity. There is no guarantee that you will have earnings on your investment, and there is a risk that you will lose money.

Variable annuities are long-term investments. If within a specified period which can be as long as seven years you need to get your money out, you can expect to pay surrender charges. (I have heard of contracts with 12 years of surrender charges.) A variable annuity that locks you in with surrender charges for seven years typically pays the broker as much as 7% of your investment in an up-front commission. (Let me do the math for you. If you buy a $100,000 annuity the broker's commission could be $7,000.) There are annuities available now with no surrender charges — this is very important to know. Variable annuities without surrender charges may provide the selling broker with a commission as little as 1%. Most withdrawals before 59½ are subject to a 10% penalty in addition to the income tax. Most variable annuities have sales charges. There are also mortality and expense risk charges, administrative fees, fund expenses for the mutual funds and additional charges for special features. Fees can be 2% or more of the annuity's value annually *in addition* to the surrender charge and sales charges.

If your annuity is in an IRA you must begin withdrawing the minimum required distribution at age 70½ regardless of any surrender charge that may be imposed on the withdrawals.

As always, each investor must weigh the cost-benefit of investment alternatives, including annuities. The question always is, are the features worth the fees?

You can pay for special features including specific guarantees. For example, a death benefit may be guaranteed. Variable annuity salespeople often claim that the annuity product is good if you are worried about losing principal by saying that your initial investment is guaranteed. What they don't point out is the fee you are paying for this guarantee (which is actually a small amount of life insurance), and the fact that the guarantee does *you* absolutely no good at all. The guarantee only applies if you're dead. If you die, your beneficiary is guaranteed to receive at least as much as your initial investment.

Annuities are also touted as providing income for life. If you annuitize (and the vast majority of annuities are never annuitized) you can get a specified monthly payment for life. The flip side of guaranteed income for life — meaning that you annuitize your contract, agreeing to receive a monthly payment for your lifetime, is that if you die prematurely, your entire remaining account balance is forfeited to the insurance company. It is possible to get a guaranteed term, say life or ten years, whichever is longer — but, of course, there is an additional charge for that.

Some annuities guarantee a minimum rate of return per year (a feature for which you pay.) There can be a catch -- as little as 60% of the invested funds may be eligible for this guaranteed return. The percentage of your investment subject to the guaranteed return is called the participation rate.

In these years of market volatility and declining markets, the idea of a guaranteed return is very appealing to many investors — inside or outside an IRA. However, what is the guaranteed rate of return and how much does this feature cost? A typical guaranteed rate of return could be 4 to 5% per year. Ask how much this additional feature costs and ask what the other costs of the annuity are. How much are you ahead? If this is your primary goal — no principal loss and guaranteed rate of return — compare it to other principal secure options like long-term CDs and treasury bonds. Remember that you have to pay for the guaranteed rate option, even if your investment inside the annuity outperforms the guaranteed rate, thus reducing your returns.

It is also possible to buy a feature that will guarantee market value over a specific period of time even if the markets lose value. Typically the period is seven to ten years. The option may only be available if you annuitize.

As one commentator put it, "variable annuities have more moving parts than a 747." If they are ever appropriate, it is when they are long-term investments and the investor expects her income tax bracket when withdrawals are made to be lower. (Which is anybody's guess.) Then, one hopes that the tax deferral and tax-free accumulation of earnings can overcome the additional costs of the annuity and the annuity's conversion of capital gains income to ordinary income. For those who have crunched the numbers, this proposition is dubious at best. If you already have tax deferral in an IRA vehicle, there is no way the numbers will put you ahead over the long term when compared to another investment in the IRA.

The National Association of Securities Dealers, NASD, published an Investor Alert on May 27, 2003, entitled *Variable Annuities: Beyond the Hard Sell* which includes the following: "Investing in a variable annuity within a tax-deferred account, such as an individual retirement account (IRA) may not be a good idea. Since IRAs are already tax-advantaged, a variable annuity will provide no additional tax savings. It will, however, increase the expense of the IRA, while generating fees and commissions for the broker or salesperson."

Check out the SEC's website and read its guide, *Variable Annuities: What You Should Know*.

Inheriting a Roth IRA

An inherited Roth IRA is truly a "gift that keeps on giving." It is an exceptional estate planning tool.

When deciding whether or not to convert your traditional IRA to a Roth IRA, most people (or their advisors) "run the numbers." The cost and benefits of a Roth conversion is compared to the status quo — maintaining the traditional IRA. Assumptions are made about investment returns, future income tax rates, life expectancy, etc.

In most cases, using reasonable assumptions, the Roth IRA conversion usually looks like the better choice, although the psychological hurdle of paying a big income tax bill now still prevents many IRA owners from doing the conversion. (Maybe it's not just psychological — I suppose income taxes could be lower in the future, although that seems to conflict with the reality principle.)

But don't stop there. Comparing the traditional IRA against the Roth IRA for the lifetime of the owner and his/her spouse is not enough. Transferring a Roth IRA to your beneficiaries on your death is a VERY valuable opportunity. To understand what it means to a beneficiary inheriting a Roth IRA, the projections have to keep going.

If the beneficiaries intend to liquidate the IRA right away and spend it, never mind — there is no additional advantage.

A person who inherits a Roth — unlike the original owner of the account — is required to take a minimum required distribution. The beneficiary must withdraw a percentage of the funds annually, based on his/her age. If the beneficiaries, instead of withdrawing the Roth IRA immediately, maintain the Roth IRA as an inherited IRA and take the minimum required distributions over their life expectancies, then they are getting a terrific benefit. They have an asset which will grow at a compounded tax-free rate for their lifetimes and any withdrawals they make will be completely tax free. There is simply nothing else like it. No other investment will give this kind of tax-free return. The younger the beneficiary is when the IRA is inherited, the longer the beneficiary can stretch out withdrawals, giving more time for tax-free compounded growth of the investments inside the Roth. The beneficiaries' inheritance could get bigger as he or she gets older.

That makes inheriting a Roth IRA much more valuable than inheriting any other asset. Any other asset, whether it be stocks and bonds, real estate or cash, will be subject to income tax on its income and growth. Traditional IRA distributions will be subject to income tax.

Younger beneficiaries with a longer opportunity for stretching out distributions get the most benefit. Consider naming grandchildren as your Roth IRA beneficiaries. If you are concerned about leaving a substantial sum to young children, there are solutions. You can name Custodian under the Uniform Transfer to Minors Act (UTMA) to receive distribution and then the custodian can accumulate the withdrawals and use them as needed for the child until the child is 21. If you set up a trust as a beneficiary for the benefit of the minor child, the trustee can hold the accumulated distributions until the beneficiary reaches a more mature age--30, 35 or any other age you would like to specify. For a trust to be able to be used with the stretch-out of distribution, the trust must be carefully drafted to comply with complex IRS rules.

If you cannot bring yourself to pay the current income tax required to convert your traditional IRA to a Roth, if you know your life expectancy is limited (I'm trying to put this delicately. If you think you may be passing on soon. . . . . . .) then do the Roth conversion before you pass away. The income tax due as a result of the conversion will be paid by your executor as a debt of your estate and will be deductible for inheritance and estate tax purposes. Your beneficiaries will get the benefit of inheriting a Roth IRA--the best asset to inherit.

The inherited Roth IRA has a "hidden" value in the estate. The value of an estate should be measured in the hands of your heirs. If the heirs spend or withdraw the Roth IRA money immediately upon inheritance, the strategic value of passing on the Roth IRA is lost. If the heirs are interested in providing for their future, they will choose to let the Roth IRA continue to grow, income tax free, perhaps only depleting the Roth IRA funds by their required minimum distributions based on the heir's life expectancy. The dollar value of the inheritance at the time of death is paltry compared to its potential worth when it is kept in the tax free environment for as long as possible. So, how do you measure the potential value of a Roth IRA?

The point is that even in the case where the conversion results in a breakeven for the original IRA owner, when the child or grandchild beneficiary elects to take only minimum required distributions from the Roth IRA, the Roth IRA's value is substantially greater than the value of the same amount of after-tax funds. However, the challenge of turning the inherited Roth IRA into a gold mine will fall to your heirs. It is essential that your beneficiaries understand that the value is achieved over time, and that the Roth IRA should be preserved in its tax-free environment as long as possible.

Having Roth Regrets? Re-characterize

If you converted a traditional IRA to a Roth IRA, you have until October 15 of the year following the conversion to change your mind.

If your Roth IRA is now worth less than it was when you made the switch, you may be able to save a lot of money by switching the Roth back to a traditional IRA, getting back the tax you paid, then re-converting to a Roth when you're allowed to, not fewer than 30 days after the October re-characterization. Your tax bill for the conversion may be much smaller than it had been in the prior year.

Here's an example. You converted a traditional IRA to a Roth in March 2002 when it was worth $40,000. You paid 2002 income tax of $11,000 based on the $40,000 account value. If the account is worth only $20,000 now, you can re-characterize the Roth back to a traditional IRA and get back the $11,000 you paid in taxes. In January 2004, if you wanted to convert to a Roth then, you could. Let's say it's still worth $20,000. You can convert, pay income tax on that, maybe only $5,500 and go from there.

It's not an all or nothing thing. You can re-characterize any part of your Roth conversion; it doesn't have to be the whole thing. For example, if you converted two IRAs to Roths and the investment in one went like gangbusters, it would be best to leave that one alone. If the investment in the other one tanked, that one could be re-characterized. However, if all the investments are in a single Roth IRA account, you cannot "cherry-pick" the investments you want to re-characterize.

How do you re-characterize? You must do two things: (1) Contact the financial institution that administers your IRA and have them make a direct transfer from the Roth back to a traditional IRA. Because so many taxpayers are choosing to re-characterize, many financial institutions make their re-characterization request forms easily available on their Web sites. The transfer to the traditional IRA is treated as if it were the original recipient of the rollover, so the tax consequences of the initial conversion to the Roth IRA are avoided (i.e., the taxpayer does not recognize the income that would have been recognized with the initial Roth conversion). Note that the transfer must include the earnings allocable to the converted amount. You cannot withdraw funds from a Roth and redeposit them to a traditional IRA — that won't work. The transfer has to be trustee to trustee. (2) For example, you already filed your 2012 return and you file an amended return on a Form 1040X to claim a refund for the tax you paid on the conversion. The sooner you file the amended return the sooner you get your refund. You have three years from the due date of your 2012 return to amend, but only until October 15, 2013 to actually go through the steps necessary to re-characterize your 2012 Roth if that's what you want to do.

If you haven't already, consider converting IRAs to Roth IRAs if you qualify. Contributions to a Roth IRA are not deductible, however all earnings are income tax free when you or your beneficiary withdraw them. Also, you don't have to comply with the minimum distribution requirements by beginning withdrawals at age 70½ as you do in a traditional IRA. When you convert, you have to pay all of the income tax on the IRA. This can be a big percentage of the IRA. Not everyone can do this. There are limits on your modified adjusted gross income. The phase-out limits are $80,000-$90,000 for single filers and $160,000-$180,000 for married filing jointly.

The theory is that it is better to pay tax now (hopefully at a relatively low rate) and get tax-free availability of appreciated funds in the future.

That works great as long as the funds appreciate in value. It is a bad move, if you pay taxes on the whole IRA, convert to a Roth and the value of the Roth sinks. Then you've paid tax on something you don't have anymore. Many people re-characterize because the value of the account on which they paid tax has plummeted. Some people just get "sticker shock" at the amount of tax due and change their minds about doing a Roth at all.

October 15 is also the deadline for re-characterizing your traditional IRA contributions, as well as Roth contributions. If you contributed $3,000 to your traditional IRA in 2011 and now realize you don't qualify, you can re-characterize that contribution to a Roth. Or, the reverse: you contributed $3,000 to a Roth and made too much money, failing to qualify. Now you can convert to a traditional IRA.

Remember, Pennsylvania treats IRAs completely different than the federal IRS. There is no Pennsylvania deduction for contributions to a traditional IRA. Earnings in an IRA account are not subject to tax if withdrawals are taken from the IRA as retirement benefits. If premature withdrawals are taken from an IRA, Pennsylvania taxes the withdrawals to the extent they were not previously taxed (e.g., on account earnings since contributions were previously taxed.) No Pennsylvania tax is due on a Roth re-characterization.

ESTATE PLANNING

The Portable Estate Tax Exemption

The American Taxpayer Relief Act of 2012 (ATRA), which tried to keep us from going over the "fiscal cliff," raised the federal estate tax exemption to $5.25 million ($5.34 in 2014) and made permanent an estate tax concept called "portability." How long the exemption will stay at $5.25 million (ignoring annual inflation adjustments) is anybody's guess.

"Portable" means easily carried or transferred, like a portable typewriter (remember those?). In this case, "portable" means easily transferred to a surviving spouse.

The federal estate and gift tax gives one exemption per person, so with planning, a married couple can potentially use two exemptions. For years, the classic estate plan for a married couple with assets over the exemption amount has been to divide assets between the spouses and for each spouse to have an estate plan which creates a trust on the first spouse's death, or at least the possibility of funding a trust with a disclaimer. The first spouse to die's exemption is applied to the trust, by-passing the tax. The surviving spouse is the beneficiary of the trust during his or her period of survivorship. When the surviving spouse dies, he or she gets another exemption, and the assets in the by-pass trust are not taxed again. Thus, the couple has used two exemptions.

Critics of the estate tax point out that the practical effect of this is to create two systems of estate tax: one for those who consult lawyers and make estate plans with by-pass trusts, and a second system of taxation for those who don't.

The idea for portability of the exemption is that it is a way for both spouses' exemptions to be used without separating title to assets and creating a by-pass trust.

In order to "port" a deceased spouse's exemption to the surviving spouse, the executor of the first deceased spouse's estate must file a federal estate tax return and make an election to allocate the unused exemption to the surviving spouse. That means that for estates of decedents for which a federal estate tax return would normally not be filed, a federal estate tax return will now have to be filed just to "port" the exemption. Where there are separate families because of second marriages, there will be situations where the fiduciary who is responsible for the first dying spouse's estate will not cooperate to make the election. Some commentators have suggested that wills (or codicils) include language to permit the surviving spouse to require the filing of an estate tax return and the filing of the election, and may require the surviving spouse to pay expenses attributable thereto.

The deceased spouse's unused exemption amount is the "DSUEA." Only the last deceased spouse counts. A surviving spouse does not lose the first deceased spouse's DSUEA by remarrying (or remarrying and divorcing). Only when the subsequent spouse predeceases the survivor during marriage does he or she replace the prior spouse for purposes of determining the DSUEA available to the surviving spouse.

Even with portability, we recommend that married couples continue to structure their estate plans to take full advantage of their estate and gift tax exemptions by using by-pass trusts and splitting up ownership of their assets. There are several reasons for this:

- There is no guarantee that there will be a DSUEA in the future.
- Appreciation of assets placed in the by-pass trust will escape estate taxation in the survivor's estate.
- Creditor protection for by-pass trust beneficiaries is achieved.
- Funding of the trust helps ensure that the children of the first dying spouse have a good chance to receive an inheritance, especially if the surviving spouse remarries and is inclined to share assets with the next spouse and his or her family.
- The generation-skipping transfer (GST) tax exemption is not portable so without a by-pass trust to which the first dying spouse's GST tax exemption could be allocated, the first spouse's GST tax exemption could be lost.

The disadvantages of a by-pass trust are:

- There would be no further stepped-up basis on death of surviving spouse (although perhaps an unrelated trust protector could dissolve the trust for distribution to surviving spouse).

- The first estate may consist in large part of property that it is desirable to leave to the surviving spouse rather than to be put in a by-pass trust (for example, an IRA, which can be rolled over by the spouse but not by the trustee of a by-pass trust).
- If the estate tax is repealed (for real), then administrative costs are wasted (accounting, income tax returns, etc.).
- Some clients think it's too complicated to have a trust.

Emotional Blocks to Estate Planning

Q: What is the difference between death and taxes?
A: Congress does not meet every year to make death worse.

Death and taxes — two subjects that are highly emotionally charged. Nobody really wants to talk about either one of them — together they are, well, taxing and deadly.

Do you break out in a cold sweat when discussing your will? Can you bear to think whether there will be enough money to live on if your spouse dies? Can you even think about which kid will run the business when Dad dies? Let alone talk about it in a family meeting?

The first hurdle to be overcome is facing your own mortality. Whenever I meet a client I try to wait until they use their own euphemism for death, then I use that expression for the rest of the conference. There's a wide selection of substitutions for the "D" word — "pass on," "kick the bucket," "meet my maker," "when something happens to me," "get hit by a truck," "pushing up daisies," "six feet under" — just to name a few. People will say anything rather than "When I die." (I had one client who said "When I croak" — I like that!)

Some folks hold to the superstition that making a will brings on death. Superstitious, yes, but nevertheless, it is a real impediment to many people.

The next hurdle is the fear of giving up control. Estate planning doesn't mean giving your assets away. Many people know they must do something to reduce taxes, but fear giving control of assets to children. They have heard too many horror stories about ungrateful children who spend the family savings and turn their backs on their parents. Most people want it both ways — they want to retain complete unfettered control over all their assets and also pay no estate taxes. There are techniques that permit transfer of value while retaining significant control and there are ways to protect funds. Learning about these approaches is part of the estate planning process.

Fear of dealing with an attorney is another big hurdle. (Now who could be afraid of a lawyer?) You might be afraid the lawyer will think you are uninformed, unsophisticated. Do you feel uninformed because you have to call the repairman to fix the air conditioner? Of course not. In the same way that you don't know how to fix an air conditioner, you don't know how to do an estate plan. This is no reflection on your intelligence or character.

You might be afraid of being gouged by fees, or be afraid the attorney isn't going to listen to you, but just forge ahead with a standard plan you don't want. The key to overcoming these fears is finding the right lawyer. Most estate planning lawyers will talk to you on the phone briefly so that you can get a sense of their approach and how you will relate to him or her. You don't have to stick with the first lawyer you talk to. Like anything else, a referral from a satisfied client is often the best approach. Ask your friends who they use for an estate lawyer. Like any other important decision, it is good to do research and talk to a few lawyers before making the hiring decision. If you are married, perhaps you and your spouse shouldn't have the same attorney — especially if it's not a first marriage and there are children from a prior marriage. Don't forget — you are the boss, you are paying the bill.

What does it cost? Fear of the expense is another thing that keeps people from estate planning. Let's face it. Estate planning is not for you — it's for those you leave behind. You aren't going to be hurt by estate taxes. You will be "long gone." You aren't going to have to negotiate who gets the grandfather clock — the kids are going to have to slug that out. So how much money (not to mention time and emotional energy) are you willing to spend on an estate plan for your family? Estate planning is truly a gift to your family. Recognize it for what it is — caring for others. Leaving a well designed plan behind is the best gift you can give your family. Arrange your affairs to do the most good for your family, friends, and charities.

Don't be afraid to ask how the attorney charges. Most attorneys will charge an hourly rate and you can expect to pay a high rate for a specialist. (Heart surgeons charge more than nurse practitioners.) Some estate planning is done on a flat fee basis, but an estimate can't be given until the attorney knows what will be involved. Almost no one gets a "simple will." More is involved than a will and every family situation is different. As Zoe Hicks says in her book *The Women's Estate Planning Guide*, "[b]e especially wary of attorneys who write themselves into your will as the estate's legal counsel. Sometimes these attorneys may charge very little (even nothing) for preparing the will, only to take a huge fee, in the form of a percentage of the estate, for acting as the estate's legal counsel later."

Tough family decisions are another emotional stumbling block. Is there a divorce looming for one of your children? Is one of the grandchildren handicapped? Will you or your spouse remarry? Who is going to control the family business after the parents are dead? Are any of the children capable of running it? Facing these issues can be so painful that they are avoided indefinitely. Then a real mess is left behind. Avoiding the problem doesn't make it go away.

What if one of the children is in and out of drug rehab; or one of the kids is a successful professional and the other is a struggling single parent with small kids and a minimum wage job? Do these children get treated equally in the estate plan?

What about blended families — the children are yours, mine, and ours. Do all of them share equally in both Mom's and Dad's estates? Facing tough decisions like these is hard. The estate planning attorney can give you options and choices, but ultimately the tough decisions are yours to make. Do you really want to have someone else make these decisions for you after you are dead? Worse, do you want your family to be torn apart with the fighting over your estate?

> *"You gain strength, courage and confidence by every experience in which you really stop to look fear in the face. . . . You must do the thing which you think you cannot do".*

Eleanor Roosevelt

The Top Ten Common Estate Planning Mistakes

1. Procrastinating. Maybe you won't die today, or next week, even next year. But rest assured, someday you will. When are you going to make an estate plan? Let me guess. You call your lawyer on Monday when you're leaving for Switzerland on Saturday (a trip planned months ago) and need a will before you go. Or, worse, you wait until you are in hospice, in the end stages of your battle for life, and decide perhaps you'd best make a will. Give yourself the gift of time and due consideration. Make your estate plan now, when you are not rushed, when you are not ill, when you are not desperate.
2. Trying to take it with you. There is no money in heaven (or the other place). It stays here. But you are empowered to determine who gets it, if you choose to exercise the power. One of the biggest choices is how much the federal and state governments will get in death taxes. This is very much under your control. Almost anything you can do to reduce the impact of death taxes requires some loss of control on your part — making lifetime gifts, setting up trusts, changing the title to property. Remember, just because you don't make an estate plan doesn't mean you don't have one. The government has one for you. Only problem is, you may not like it.
3. Taking advice from the wrong people. A lot of people know something about estate planning, but very few know enough to give you competent advice. Estate planning covers many areas — wills and trusts, taxes, real estate, business law, family corporations, partnerships, debtor/creditor law, valuation, and so on. Many financial professionals have training in estate planning and can raise issues with you, make suggestions, or point out problems. These include accountants, financial planners, brokers, insurance agents, bankers, many of whom do an excellent job. On the other hand, while you can legally write your own will, the law provides that only lawyers can draft wills, trusts, and other estate planning documents for other persons. However, just because a person is a lawyer, doesn't mean he has expertise in this type of work. That leaves you, the layperson, in a tough position. Where do you turn for advice? Often input is needed from all of these

advisors and many estate plans are put together by a team of financial advisors and a lawyer.

4. Not telling the whole story. This applies to both personal and financial information. Estate planning involves both taxes, and personal planning for the distribution of your assets on your death. Neither one of these tasks can be well done if the lawyer does not know what your assets and liabilities are. This information must and will be held in the strictest confidence. Depending on the nature and size of your assets, various techniques will be recommended to you to reduce taxes and accomplish your objectives. It is important that your attorney knows the facts. If there are divorces, adopted children, children born outside of the marriage, mental illness, substance abuse, financial irresponsibility — these facts can be crucial for your attorney to know. Otherwise, the words used in your documents may have unintended results. Your attorney is bound to keep all information in the strictest confidence and it is only with full knowledge of the facts that the attorney can protect you and make sure that your intentions are carried out.
5. Not reading the drafts. I know this may come as a shock, but lawyers make mistakes. Don't assume that your documents say what you told the lawyer to put in there. Lawyers are people too and have bad days. It is your responsibility to *read* your will, trust, power of attorney, before signing them.
6. Pretending "legalese" is a foreign language. Your documents are written in English. If you run across a word you don't understand, the lawyer will be happy to explain it to you. Or you can look it up in the dictionary. Of course, the documents are strange to read — you don't read wills, trusts, deeds, and contracts every day. That does not mean you can't read them. Remember that particular words are often used because these words have been interpreted by the courts and their meaning is well-established. I always figure that the client will find the documents to be boring. That's a reason not to read them?
7. Not wanting to pay for quality work. Contrary to popular belief, almost no client gets a plan that is "just a form." Sure, some sections are standard, but you would be surprised at

the broad diversity of estate plans. We have a saying in my office: "There is no such thing as a simple will." The plan that disposes of a lifetime's accumulation of assets and protects the interests of your beneficiaries, while keeping administration costs and death taxes to the minimum, is a skilled piece of work. Don't be penny-wise and pound-foolish. Saving money on a will may mean thousands of dollars in taxes and costs later.

8. Refusing to consider unpleasant possibilities. Making an estate plan means facing up to a lot of unpleasant possibilities. The first is your own demise. Then there is the demise of your loved ones. All of the possible orders of death must be considered. Most of these contingencies are remote, but they are possibilities nevertheless. What will happen to your estate if your children predecease you? Who will hold your power of attorney if your children predecease you? Who will be the guardians of your children if your first choice can't do it? Who will pay your bills and handle your investments if you are in a nursing home? Many folks refuse to plan for these contingencies, saying that if it happens, then they'll change their will. Maybe they will. Maybe they won't be able to because they are incapacitated, or too grief-stricken to deal with it. It is far, far better to make a plan that covers all possibilities, however unpleasant to contemplate.
9. Not updating the plan when there are changes in the family or changes in the law. The will you made when your first child was born is not going to be appropriate when you have grandchildren. The estate plan you made when the federal estate tax exemption was $600,000 may not be appropriate when the exemption is $5.25 million (as of 2013). The estate plan you had during your first marriage is not going to work when you are in your second or third marriage. Make sure your plan is up-to-date.
10. Not following through. Did you tell the lawyer you were going to write a memorandum to put with your will detailing who would get what items of jewelry and furniture? Did you change the title to your bank and brokerage accounts as instructed? Did you change the beneficiary designations

on retirement plans, IRAs, and life insurance as instructed? Doing these things is just as important as having a will. Your plan may not be carried out if you don't follow through with all of the necessary actions.

To avoid these mistakes and have an effective estate plan requires forethought, deliberate action, careful selection of estate planning professionals, honesty, review and comprehension of your plan, updating from time to time, and a commitment to prepare for the inevitable.

Domicile: Your State of Affairs

Domicile is "the place where a man has his true, fixed and permanent home and principal establishment, to which, whenever he is absent, he has the intention of returning." A person can have only one domicile, no matter how many residences he owns.

Your state of domicile determines: (1) to which state you pay state income taxes; (2) where your will is probated and where your estate will be administered; (3) to which state your estate pays inheritance and estate taxes; and (4) which state's laws govern the enforcement of judicial orders.

The state of domicile also determines spousal rights in property. Most of the states, like Pennsylvania, are common law states. Arizona, California, Idaho, Louisiana, Nevada, New Mexico, Texas, Washington and Wisconsin are community property states. A move to any of these states requires special planning.

It is very possible for more than one state to claim that you are a domiciliary. When this happens, all of the states that have claims can assess income tax and inheritance or estate tax. Some states are parties to agreements to resolve these issues as they affect death taxes, but many are not. The battle over Howard Hughes' estate went on for years, with Texas, Nevada and California all claiming him as a domiciliary. In perhaps the most famous estate tax domicile case, the estate of Mr. Dorrance, the founder of Campbell's Soup Company, was taxed by both Pennsylvania and New Jersey, in each case as if he was domiciled there. Each of Pennsylvania and New Jersey collected about $17 million. The U.S. Supreme Court upheld this result.

Since domicile depends on where you intend to return, it is a subjective concept. Nevertheless, many objective actions can give indications of your intention. There are lists available for actions that should be taken to give evidence of your intention to change your domicile. You don't have to do everything on the list. None of these things, except the requirement for physical presence in the new domicile, are absolute requirements. However, you have to do enough of them, especially the more significant ones, to convince the tax authorities that you have truly moved your domicile. Here are some actions that show intention to change domicile:

- Buy or lease property in the new domicile state, furnish it as a permanent residence, not a vacation place.
- Spend more than 183 days per year in the new state — this is the most important requirement. In some states this is an ironclad rule for tax purposes. For example, if you maintain a residence in New York and spend more than 183 days per year there, New York considers you a resident for tax purposes regardless of your intentions.
- Obtain a driver's license in the new state.
- Register your cars in the new state.
- Register to vote in the new state, and vote.
- Go to doctors, dentists, lawyers and other professionals in the new state and have your records moved from the old state to professionals in the new state.
- File your federal income tax return with the appropriate IRS service center and show your new state as your address.
- File a Declaration of Domicile if your new state has such a procedure.
- Move bank accounts and safe deposit boxes to the new state.
- Send notifications of a change of address to family, friends, business associates, professional organizations, credit card companies, brokers, and insurance companies.
- Use the new state as a home base. When you travel, leave from and return to the new state.
- Keep your family heirlooms, furniture and keepsakes in the new state.
- Change legal documents to reflect residency in the new state.

- Update your estate plan and have your estate planning documents identify you as a resident of the new state.
- Join organizations, such as clubs, religious groups and become active with local charities in the new state.
- Apply for a homestead in the new state if applicable.

Not only must you adopt a new domicile, but your old domicile must be abandoned. In your former state of domicile:

- Have your name removed from the voter registration list.
- Turn in your driver's license.
- Pay income tax as a non-resident if applicable.
- Mark your last state income tax return "FINAL" and use the new state's address.
- Spend as little time in the old state as possible.
- Close accounts in the old state.
- Change all club membership, religious and social affiliations to "non-resident" status.

Timing of the change in domicile can be important. If you sell your business or your home in the old state, where you are domiciled at the time of the sale can impact how the gains are taxed. If you are creating trusts, the "resident state" of the trust will often depend on your domicile at the time you create the trust. This means a trust could remain taxable in the old state even though you move your domicile to the new state.

If you stop filing taxes in your old state, this doesn't mean that they have no claim on you. Remember that if you don't file a return for a year, the statute of limitations never starts running. There is no limit to the number of years they can go back and assess tax. Consider filing a non-resident return.

Be consistent. If you want to be a Floridian to escape Pennsylvania income tax, don't register your car in Pennsylvania to get lower insurance rates. Use common sense. Does your neighbor who has lived in Florida all her life have her car registered in Pennsylvania? Of course not. Does she belong to a church or synagogue in Pennsylvania? No. Just imagine yourself explaining that to a tax auditor.

Marital Deduction Planning

Since 1981, transfers between spouses have been estate and gift tax free, if, and only if, the transfer to the spouse qualifies for the marital deduction. Before 1981, the estate and gift tax applied to inter-spousal transfers. There was a 50% deduction, so that half of the value transferred to the spouse was subject to either gift tax or estate tax.

With the passage of the 2012 Taxpayer Relief Act, the federal estate tax exemption is retained at $5.25 million for 2013. For many people, no federal tax planning is needed. For those with assets near $10.5 million, the standard estate planning technique for a married couple is to use both spouses' exemptions and defer all estate taxes until the death of the survivor. How do you do this?

Step 1. Divide title to assets so that each spouse owns at least $5 million in separately titled assets. (Preferably assets other than IRAs or qualified retirement plans.)

Step 2. Make an estate plan that provides for the first spouse to die to use his or her exemption. This can be done by creating a "bypass" or "credit shelter" trust. Leaving $5.25 million in assets to the children, with no trust involved, also works.

Step 3. Make sure the balance of the first deceased spouse's assets (assets over the $5.25 million exemption amount) pass to the surviving spouse in a form that qualifies for the marital deduction.

Many estate planners assume that these steps must be satisfied by creation of a so-called "A-B Trust." That works, but it is not the only way. And furthermore, it is probably not the best way. Many a surviving spouse has been shocked and surprised to find that all of her husband's assets went into trust for her benefit instead of to her directly.

A trust is often the best solution to accomplish the use of the first spouse's exemption. The first spouse to die could give the $5.25 million exemption amount to the children and/or grandchildren and accomplish the tax objective. However, use of the bypass trust accomplishes the tax objective *and* keeps the assets available for the surviving spouse during the period of survivorship. If the trust document so provides, the surviving spouse can get the income from the assets in the bypass trust, can get principal if needed, and can withdraw the greater of $5,000 or 5% of the principal annually. If principal distribution is limited to distributions for health, maintenance, and support, the surviving spouse can even be the sole trustee. (Was that option offered to you when you did your estate plan?)

To avoid estate tax on the death of the first spouse, the balance of the deceased spouse's assets over the $5.25 million exemption amount should qualify for the marital deduction. How can one qualify for the marital deduction? The easiest way is an outright transfer to a spouse. That's right, just give it to the surviving spouse. This eliminates the need for the "A" Trust in the "A-B Trust." The estate plan can consist of a will that creates a bypass trust on the first death, with the balance of assets distributed directly to the surviving spouse.

An alternative to giving the property directly to the surviving spouse is to put it in a trust for the benefit of the surviving spouse. If a trust is used instead of outright distribution, this is the "A" Trust in an "A-B Trust." There are three types of trusts that can qualify for the marital deduction. They are: (1) a general power of appointment trust, (2) a Qualified Terminable Interest in Property trust ("QTIP" trust), and (3) an estate trust.

A general power of appointment marital deduction trust must provide that the surviving spouse gets the income for life and the principal of the trust is either subject to the surviving spouse's unrestricted withdrawal during his or her life, or subject to the surviving spouse's general power of appointment to direct who should be the next owner of the trust principal on his or her death.

Obviously, a general power of appointment trust permits the surviving spouse to change the beneficiaries of the trust property. Because this was unacceptable to many couples, especially in second marriages where the objective was to provide for the surviving spouse but ensure that the principal ultimately passed to children from a first marriage, in 1981, Congress enacted legislation that authorizes QTIP trusts.

A QTIP marital deduction trust must provide only that the surviving spouse is given the income from the trust for his or her life.

The surviving spouse need not be given any access to principal at all. The trust may be more generous in its provisions for the spouse, but it need not be.

Finally, an estate trust qualifies for the marital deduction. An estate trust is one that needs to make no provision whatsoever for the surviving spouse except that it is payable to the surviving spouse's estate on his or her death. (This type of marital deduction trust is rarely seen.)

Again, the marital deduction trust is not needed to get the marital deduction. The marital deduction can be easily obtained by simply giving assets directly to the surviving spouse. Use of a marital trust instead of an outright distribution provides a way for the first spouse to retain control over the assets during the surviving spouse's lifetime. Do you know which type you have and why?

Some Tips for Couples on Estate Planning

For a married couple, the first step in estate planning is to make sure that each spouse uses the available federal exemption. The federal estate tax exemption recently increased to $5.25 million per person for 2013

Let's assume Mom and Dad have $10,500,000 in assets, all jointly held, and Dad dies first. There is no federal estate tax because property passing to the surviving spouse, Mom, in our example, qualified for the unlimited marital deduction. When Mom dies, her estate is worth $10,500,000; she has one $5,250,000 exemption. Her estate must pay ? in federal estate tax (this is in addition to any state inheritance or estate taxes due). If Mom and Dad had done estate planning, they would have been advised to divide the joint assets so that each owned $5,250,000 in assets in his or her name alone. They would execute wills and trusts which provide that on the first spouse's death, his or her $5,250,000 of assets pass into a bypass trust instead of outright to the surviving spouse.

There is no magic about the trust. There doesn't even have to be a trust. The point is that the first spouse to die leaves his or her assets to beneficiaries other than the surviving spouse. A bypass trust is often suggested so that the surviving spouse can still have the benefit of the assets, but not have them taxed in her estate. For tax purposes, it would work just as well for the first spouse to die to leave his $5,250,000 of assets to the children. We don't want the tax tail to wag the dog, so we often see the first spouse's $5,250,000 going into a liberal trust for the benefit of the surviving spouse.

If the first spouse to die has more than the available exemption amount in assets, the excess should pass to the surviving spouse. The assets over the exemption will thus qualify for the unlimited marital deduction and no federal estate tax will be payable.

I want to debunk a myth. There is no need for an A-B Trust. An A-B Trust is a traditional estate plan where the B Trust is the bypass trust and the A Trust is a *trust* for the benefit of the surviving spouse that qualifies for the unlimited marital deduction. There is no need for a marital deduction trust — an outright bequest to the surviving spouse works just as well.

If you are doing generation-skipping tax planning there may be a reason to have part of the marital deduction property in trust, but that is the only circumstance when tax planning requires it.

A lot of folks sign estate planning documents that establish the credit shelter trust and then don't follow through with dividing the assets. Reasons for this include simply not getting around to it, a failure to understand the importance of separate titling, or a mistaken belief that title determines who gets assets on divorce. If all assets are held by Mom and Dad jointly, no matter what the will says, all assets pass by operation of law to the surviving spouse and the first spouse's exemption is wasted *unless* the surviving spouse *disclaims* part of the assets.

A surviving spouse can refuse to accept assets passing to her from the deceased. This is called a disclaimer. If the disclaimer is made within nine months of the decedent's death and the surviving spouse has accepted no benefits from the disclaimed property, the disclaimer is considered "qualified" for estate tax purposes. This means it is not taxed as a gift by the surviving spouse, but rather, the property is deemed to have passed directly from the deceased spouse to the next beneficiary, determined as if the surviving spouse had predeceased. If the will provides for the first $5,250,000 to pass to a bypass trust, any joint property disclaimed by the surviving spouse will be used to fund this trust. Thus, the estate plan can be rescued, even though Mom and Dad didn't follow through with the instructions to retitle assets.

To effectively use a disclaimer you should consult a lawyer as soon as possible after death. Postmortem estate planning can be very effective.

The Gift of Information and Explanation

A while back I wrote a column called "A Guide for the Surviving Spouse" — which had advice and a list of steps of what to do when you are widowed. (E-mail me if you would like a copy.) That can be a bit like shutting the barn door after the horse is out. Before the horse escapes, you need to make sure that the widow or widower has access to all of the information he or she will need.

I would like to encourage everyone to make sure that he or she compiles all of the information necessary for his or her survivors so that, in addition to grief and loneliness, widows and widowers will not be faced with financial emergencies and overwhelming questions.

It is common for there to be a division of labor in a marriage. Each spouse has his or her own talents and responsibilities. After the death of one spouse, however, the survivor needs to have the tools and information necessary to cope with all of the jobs.

I met with a couple, this week, to review their estate plan, and the husband brought along a 3-ring binder he had prepared for his wife. In this marriage, the husband was the spouse who took responsibility for financial matters. The notebook was a very complete and well organized collection of the information his wife would need if she found herself to be a widow. It was a truly loving and thoughtful gift — not only of the information, but of his time for the preparation of this book. Whether you make a notebook, or organize the information some other way, here are the things you should have available to your spouse:

1. Persons and organizations to contact regarding the death. Make a list of friends, family, business associates, organizations who should be notified.
2. Location of your safe deposit box, location of the keys to the safe deposit box and a list of its contents.
3. Where to find birth certificates, social security cards, passports, military discharges, marriage certificates and other identification documents.

4. Computer usernames and passwords for all internet services and accounts, or the place where this confidential information can be obtained.
5. How to get money. In other words, where are the checks and ATM cards? What accounts should be used for cash needs, which financial institutions hold your accounts?
6. How to pay bills. Where are billing records, including paid bills, kept? If bills are paid by phone, instructions for this. If bills are paid online, instructions for this.
7. What retirement benefits is the survivor entitled to and how are they to be claimed?
8. Medical insurance policies. How to pay medical bills, file claims and review charges.
9. Prescription drugs. Is there insurance coverage? How to order by mail.
10. Information on investments, where accounts are held and how they are titled. Contact person and phone number at each institution.
11. Information about insurance--life, auto, homeowners, renters, liability, etc. Where are the policies, who is the agent, and when and how are premiums paid?
12. Information about automobiles. Where are the titles, where are the service records, what are scheduled inspections, etc.
13. Location of (and copies of) any will, trusts, power of attorney and medical directive and other legal documents.
14. Location of (and copies of) any deeds, leases, sales agreements or other information regarding real estate owned.
15. Location of (and copies of) any notes, mortgages, or other indebtedness, how to find balance due and terms of repayment.
16. Location of copies of income tax returns.
17. Information about any collections or particularly valuable or unusual items of tangible personal property.
18. List of professional advisors including all contact information for attorney, accountant or tax preparer, insurance agent, physicians, dentists, investment advisors, and so on.
19. Pre-arranged (and/or pre-paid) funeral arrangements.
20. Location of cemetery deed.
21. Draft of your obituary.

Compiling all of this may not be fun, but it is a true labor of love. It is a gift to your spouse or your children and will save them not only many hours of work, but also save them the stress and anxiety of searching, wondering, and worrying.

Disclaimer Plan to Fund Bypass Trust

The tax legislation has been touted as simplification. In fact, for married couples with more than $5.25 million in assets, it presents a horrendous planning problem. This includes "regular" people as well as the wealthy. Real estate, property, retirement investments, etc., can quickly boost the value of one's estate to beyond $5.25 million. Many married couples with assets in excess of $5.25 million have divided the title of their assets between them and then created estate plans that set up "A-B Trusts," or at least a credit shelter trust. These are plans which were designed to make sure that both spouses' $5.25 million exemptions from the federal estate tax are fully utilized. These plans consist of a will and at least one trust, sometimes in the will, sometimes as a living trust. Most of these plans should be changed if they were made before 2012.

Existing plans typically provide for the $5.25 million exemption amount to pass to a trust instead of passing to the surviving spouse. This is what was good planning when the exemption was $1.5 million. The new law changes the exemption but it's quite a moving target. The exemption rose to $2 million in 2006 and $3.5 million in 2009. In 2010 there was no estate tax at all so an unlimited number of assets could pass free of tax. Then the exemption fell back to $1 million in 2011 (this is because of the so-called sunset of the new tax law.) In 2013, the exemption has been retained at the level of $5.25 million. Your estate plan needs to be designed to work with all of these exemption amounts, no matter what year you die.

If you are married and have a credit shelter trust plan, you really must have the plan reviewed and revised if needed. Now.

If you don't, the surviving spouse is going to find himself or herself in a very uncomfortable position. Why? Most of these plans say that the exempt amount goes into a trust and the balance over the exemption goes to the spouse. As the exemption rises, a larger and larger share of assets will go into the trust instead of to the surviving spouse. Many surviving spouses will receive no inheritance from the deceased spouse and will have to deal with a trustee to receive money from the trust set up under the deceased spouse's will.

This is *not* what most people intended. Most people only set up the credit shelter trust to reduce estate taxes. Under the new law, many people will not need a trust to save taxes, but their estate plans, drafted under the old law will set up the trusts anyway. No one wants to be a surviving spouse with too little money and dependent on a trustee for distributions.

On the other hand, some folks in this situation have children by a prior marriage and it was their intention that part of the estate be set aside for the surviving spouse and part given to the children. The new law may wreak havoc with this plan, too. The increase in the credit from, $1.5 million to $5.25 million, from 2004 to 2013, means that any formula division of the estate will have a wide variation. Most people will need to set a dollar or percentage limit on the division of the estate in order to care for two sets of beneficiaries.

Estate planning professionals are currently wrestling with how to draft estate plans under the new law and what makes the most sense for recommendations to clients.

I intend to recommend to many clients one plan that works: have the credit shelter trust set up under the will or revocable trust, but not to direct any funding to it. The will or trust would provide that all of the property of the first spouse to die passes to the surviving spouse.

Then, at the death of the first spouse, the surviving spouse disclaims (that is, refuses to accept) part or all of the inheritance, and the disclaimed portion passes to the credit shelter trust. A surviving spouse has nine months in which to make such a disclaimer and during that nine-month period may have accepted none of the benefits of the disclaimed property. This approach allows the surviving spouse, with the help of her advisors, to assess the tax law and the size of the estate at the time of the decedent's death and decide what would be the best funding amount. The surviving spouse can then disclaim the amount of inheritance that should pass into the bypass trust.

The downside of this approach is that it requires a decision on the part of the surviving spouse within nine months of the decedent's death — which may not be a good time to expect a grieving spouse to make a major financial decision. However, with proper education and explanation at the time the plans were drafted, the decision becomes one of many the spouse will make with the help of his or her advisors.

Until there is more certainty about what the estate tax exemption will be, I think this is a good method to preserve as much value as possible for the family, and keep the estate taxes to the bare minimum.

Estate Planning for Women: Wills, Taxes, and Family

> *In my experience, the single most common mistake women make around their wealth is ignoring it. The second most common mistake I've seen is women abdicating responsibility for investment decisions to someone else . . . a spouse, family member or advisor — because it is easier not to have to take responsibility for your decisions. Remember — no one cares about your wealth as much as you do.*
>
> Jane N. Alibanta

According to the United States Bureau of the Census, at some point in their lives, an overwhelming majority of American women — fully 90% — will have to bear responsibility for their own financial security by virtue of widowhood, divorce, or choosing to remain single.

How many wives have attended meetings with their husbands on their estate plan — but were not interested, and left it to the husband to understand the issues and make the decisions? Then, when these women find themselves to be a surviving spouse, they are shocked, disappointed, and angry about the provisions for them.

How many widows and single women have refused to make a plan for death, disability, and incapacity? Of course these things are not pleasant to contemplate, but part of being a grown-up is to be responsible for yourself.

This is emphasized by Suze Orman in her book, *9 Steps to Financial Freedom*: "The fourth step to financial freedom is being responsible, which starts with being responsible to those you love. It is not okay when you get sick, or when you die, to leave financial chaos behind you for everyone else to clean up. It will be hard enough for those around you to bear the grief of your terrible illness or death;

imagine, for a minute, their pain. Please don't force them to deal as well with all the matters you could have taken care of while you were healthy or alive

Do you have a will? Does your husband have a will? Do your parents have a will? Do you know who will receive your assets if you die? Do you know how much of your husband's estate you will inherit if he dies? Do you assume it will be everything? Think again.

If your husband does not have a will, you are entitled to joint property as the surviving joint owner. You may (or may not) be named as beneficiary on insurance policies and retirement plans. For property in your husband's sole name, including his business, his investments, his vehicles, you are entitled only to the first $30,000 and one-half of the balance if there are children. You are entitled to only one-half if he has children who are not yours. If there are no children, but he has a parent or parents surviving, you get the first $30,000 plus one-half of the balance while the parents get the other half.

If your husband has a will and chooses not to leave his estate to you, you may be limited to an election against his will netting you only one-third of his estate.

"When a husband or parent dies, a woman stands to gain (or lose) a great deal, depending on the adequacy of her husband's or parents' estate planning documents. Being involved in the planning stage is vitally important. If trusts are used . . . the selection of trustees and the terms of a trust can make your life either miserable or enjoyable. A good estate plan can dramatically reduce — and in most cases eliminate — estate taxes, professional fees, and other costs associated with the administration of an estate."

"There can be no better investment of a woman's time than good estate planning. . . . The thought of a drain of that magnitude on the value of a parents' estate should motivate any daughter to encourage both parents to seek competent estate planning counsel. A married woman should make sure that her husband's estate plan takes full advantage of the deferral of estate taxes available through the federal estate tax marital deduction and the federal exemption available. That way, at his death, she will not have to turn over any of his assets to Uncle Sam, and taxes will be minimized or eliminated for her children at the time of her death." Zoe M. Hicks, Esq., *The Women's Estate Planning Guide*, Contemporary Books, 1998, pp. 4–5.

Do you have a durable power of attorney? It is very likely that you will have at least one period of disability in your life. Who will take care of your financial affairs? A spouse, just by being a spouse, does not have authority over your finances. A child, just by being a child, does not have authority over your finances. A joint bank account may carry you for a little while. You have to *give* someone the *authority* to handle your affairs by naming an agent to have power of attorney over your affairs.

Do you have a living will and medical directive? Who will make medical decisions for you when you are unable to? What are your wishes about treatment of a terminal illness or permanent unconsciousness?

Do you have adequate life insurance? Do you have long-term care insurance or the means to pay for long-term care? If you can comfortably afford $6,000 a month (that's a low figure) for nursing care, maybe you do not need to plan. But how many people can do that? If you're a couple — can you spend $6,000 for one of you and the other stay at home with all of the usual house and living expenses?

Do you have a Prenuptial Agreement? If not, do you regret not having one? Should you make a Postnuptial Agreement? How do you know your children with your former husband will be provided for if your second husband survives you?

Take care of yourself and your family. You don't have to be an expert in these matters but you do have to find and use competent help. Making a good estate plan is a wonderful gift to your loved ones. Do it now.

Estate Planning For Men: Wills, Taxes, and Machismo

All men think all men mortal, but themselves.

Edward Young

Any married man should forget his mistakes.
There's no use in two people remembering the same thing.

Duane Dewel

Men and women are different. Statistics show that women outlive men and more women are in nursing homes than men. The final responsibility for estate planning will fall on the shoulders of more women than men. So here is a message for all the men — don't keep telling your wife not to worry about all this estate planning stuff because she probably will. She would much rather deal with some of these issues while you are around to help!

While the majority of affluent Americans (58%) age 45 and older agree that it's important to them to leave an inheritance to their children or beneficiaries, 25% have not yet made any plans for their estates, according to a survey commissioned by Charles Schwab & Co. Further, seven in ten of those individuals planning to leave a financial legacy cite the impact of estate taxes as their biggest concern in leaving an inheritance, yet less than a third (28%) have taken advantage of the annual gift tax provision, and only one in ten say they are very likely to leave money to charity.

The number one reason given for not having an estate plan — including a simple will — is a familiar one: procrastination. Most men spend thousands of hours during their lifetime trying to build an estate, but just a couple hours determining what will be done with it. It is indeed a sad commentary to deal with a surviving spouse — most often the wife — where the man adamantly refused to do any proper planning for his family.

Let me ask you some questions. You consider yourself a responsible husband and father, right? If you died next week, do you have any questions about what would become of your surviving spouse, your children, your assets? If you became incapacitated or disabled would that cause difficulties for your spouse and children? Do you know the beneficiaries of your life insurance and your retirement plans? Who are the beneficiaries if there is no surviving spouse?

When you neglect to make an estate plan, some of the most important financial decisions concerning where you want your assets to go could be determined by others, or your beneficiaries could find themselves faced with legal obstacles and unnecessary tax burdens — not to mention family strife.

Some folks hold on to superstitions about making wills — they think that if they make a will they will die. I've been doing this work for over 25 years and I can assure you — people don't die from making wills. Others don't want to pay for estate planning. This is difficult to understand — you would prefer that your beneficiaries pay unnecessary taxes, and fees rather than paying a lawyer now? A good estate plan without sophisticated tax planning should cost in the hundreds of dollars. Paying less is like representing yourself in court. Paying more is unnecessary in most cases.

Of course it's not fun to plan for your death or incapacity. But it's part of being a responsible grown-up. Estate planning isn't just about death taxes, it's also about family relationships and responsibilities. Unhappily married couples, as well as happily married couples, may be reluctant to bring up sensitive topics. Multiple marriages bring other complexities. How are you going to balance the interests of your children from your first marriage with those of your current wife? Black sheep and fragile relationships are more comfortably not spoken about. Avoiding conflict by ignoring difficult issues is a favorite delaying tactic. Many families gloss over sensitive areas to preserve ostensible harmony. Unfortunately, glossing over a problem today makes a bigger problem tomorrow.

Are there others depending on you for financial support? Are you caring for elderly parents? Are your kids through school? If you die will your surviving spouse have enough income to live?

What if you win the actuarial contest and you are the surviving spouse, or if you are a single man? What is your plan for incapacity? I know — you're never going to a nursing home. Well, when you find yourself there, how is your care going to be paid for? Who is going to pay your bills, sell your house, file your taxes, or make medical insurance claims for you? Do you have a durable power of attorney?

We know no one can do it as good as you can. We know you've always done it yourself. You are only one accident away from being unable to take care of your affairs. Look at Christopher Reeve. You have to get beyond your own comfort level and make a plan for your survivors and for your caregivers. When you make a well-considered estate plan you're really being a responsible man.

An Estate Attorney Goes to the Theater

> *"Big Daddy... What is it that makes him so big? His big heart, his big belly, or his big money?"*
>
> Brick Pollitt, character in the play

My husband and I saw Tennessee William's play "Cat on a Hot Tin Roof" at the Fulton Theatre. The theme of truth vs. mendacity runs through the play as a dysfunctional family fights over an inheritance in the Mississippi Delta.

Plantation owner Big Daddy has come home from the clinic on his 65th birthday. In addition to Big Mama, his sons and their families are there to welcome him and to tell him he is dying of cancer! Big Daddy favors his tormented, alcoholic, former-football-hero son Brick, married to Maggie the cat. Their marriage is childless and on-the-rocks. Brick has quit his job and taken to drinking after the death of his friend Skipper, with whom he is intimated he had a homosexual relationship. Gooper, the less-loved son, and his over-bearing wife Mae are there with their 5 children (no-neck monsters) and another on the way.

Everyone except Big Daddy knows that he does, in fact, have terminal cancer. The maneuvering begins for the inheritance. What does Big Daddy own? "Close on ten million in cash an' blue-chip stocks, outside, mind you, of twenty-eight thousand acres of the richest land this side of the valley Nile!"

As the family quarrels and postures, trying to gain control of Big Daddy's estate, we are given lessons in human nature, family dynamics and estate planning:

1. Make your will now. Big Daddy couldn't decide whether to leave the plantation to older son Gooper, whom he hates, or younger son Brick, whom he loves but knows is an alcoholic. "I didn't make up my mind at all on that question and still to this day I ain't made no will! — Well, now I don't have to. The pressure is gone. I can just wait and see if you pull yourself together or if you don't." The audience knows he is in fact dying — so it looks as though he will die without a will. Don't wait until there is a crisis situation to make a will. If drafted in response to a crisis, the disposition of your estate may not be the result of thoughtful, careful consideration, but a knee-jerk reaction influenced by the situation.
2. Is blood thicker than water? Should it be? Big Daddy's hesitation over leaving the plantation to Brick is two-fold: (1)

he is an alcoholic and Big Daddy doesn't want to "subsidize a [@#$%&*] fool on the bottle;" and (2) Brick has no children so that Big Daddy's legacy will not continue past Brick's generation. An estate plan can address questions such as: (1) do I need to control distributions to a beneficiary who is incapable of handling money; (2) do I want to provide for future generations or; (3) are there beneficiaries other than family members I want to consider.

3. Even with an estate plan, don't think there won't be sibling rivalry. Even if your kids get along with each other and you, they may have spouses. Gooper and Mae pretend to be the dutiful, attentive son and daughter-in-law, when in truth they are driven solely by the desire for material gain. Children who keep their animosity damped down while you are around lose that inhibition when you are gone. No matter what Big Daddy does, it appears that the sequel to "Cat on a Hot Tin Roof" will be Cat and the Will Contest.
4. Don't try to use your money to control people. They may be nice to your face, but behind your back they will hate you. Who could expect Big Daddy's statement to Brick as to who will inherit the plantation, "I can just wait and see if you pull yourself together or if you don't," to produce anything but Brick's disdain for his father.
5. Provide for your spouse. What about Big Mama? It becomes clear that Big Daddy hates her, although he puts on a show of caring for her. What does she get when Big Daddy dies? No one seems to think she will inherit — it's only the two sons. If you are married, make sure your spouse is providing for you adequately. If your spouse dies without a will in Pennsylvania, you do not inherit the whole estate. If there are children, you get the first $30,000 and one half of the remaining amount with the kids getting the other half.
6. Bring out the skeletons. There are repressed ideas in "Cat on a Hot Tin Roof" that are finally revealed at the climax of the play. But in many lives, hidden secrets are never exposed. Don't assume you know and understand everyone in your family. If there are difficult situations or problems, your attorney needs to know.

The biggest lesson of all? In Big Daddy's words, "You can't buy back your life when it's finished."

Life Estates: What Are They and How Are They Taxed?

A life estate is an interest in real or personal property that is limited in duration to the lifetime of its owner or some other designated person or persons. The person who has the right to use and occupy the property for his or her life is referred to as the life tenant. The person or persons who will own the property when the life tenant dies are called the remaindermen.

A life estate can be created for the life tenant and remaindermen by another party either by deed, trust, agreement, or will. For example, Grandfather could deed the farm to Grandmother for her life, and on her death to her children. Grandmother is the life tenant and the children are the remaindermen. Or a life estate can be reserved by the original owner; Mother is the owner of the property and she deeds the remainder interest to her three children, but reserves a life estate for herself.

The life tenant may sell or lease her interest but may not disregard the rights of those who are the owners of the remainder, that is, those who become the owners on the death of the life tenant. Under Pennsylvania law, a life tenant is responsible for repairs and maintenance to the property, real estate taxes, municipal assessments such as sidewalk construction, and mortgage interest. The life tenant does not have to maintain insurance to protect the property for the remaindermen, but it is obviously prudent to do so as it protects the life tenant's interest as well.

What are the tax consequences? First, the income tax. If the property in which the life estate exists is sold, what is the tax consequence? The sale proceeds are divided between the life tenants and the remaindermen. The income tax cost basis of the property must be allocated between the life tenant and the remaindermen. This is done based on the respective values of the two property interests. The value of the life estate depends in part on the age and consequent life expectancy of the life tenant and partly on the interest rate required to be used for the valuation of term interests. Under current IRS tables, a life estate for a person who is age 70 is worth about 40% of the value of the whole property, the remainder interest is worth about 60%. The income tax basis would get allocated between the life tenants and the remaindermen in the same proportion.

In general, Internal Revenue §121(a) currently provides that gross income does not include gain from the sale or exchange of property if, during the five-year period ending on the date of the sale or exchange, such property has been owned and used by the taxpayer as the taxpayer's principal residence for periods aggregating two years or more. The amount of gain that can be excluded is $250,000 ($500,000 for a married couple filing a joint return.)

If the life tenant uses the property as his principal residence, can he get the exclusion of gain on the sale of a principal residence when the property is sold? Under the current law, the answer is "no." The statute makes a special provision for the sale of a remainder interest, saying that the owner of a residence can sell a remainder interest, keeping a life estate and will be able to take the exclusion of gain for the sale of the remainder interest. The exclusion is not available for the sale of any other partial interest, so the sale of a life estate does not qualify for the exclusion of gain on a principal residence.

For gift tax purposes, if Grandfather transfers an income interest to Daughter and a remainder interest to Granddaughter, obviously, Grandfather has made a gift of the entire value of the property, part to Daughter and part to Granddaughter. A gift tax return must be filed and the gift uses up part of Grandfather's estate tax exemption and no value is included in his estate at his death.

If, on the other hand, Daughter is the owner of the property and transfers the remainder interest to Granddaughter, retaining a life estate for herself, then Daughter has made a gift of the remainder interest. The gift is the actuarial value of the remainder interest and does not qualify for the $14,000 annual exclusion because it is a gift of a future interest. Daughter is required by law to file a gift tax return. The gift will use up some of Daughter's available exemption.

What happens for estate tax purposes in Daughter's estate? If Grandfather had given Daughter the life estate at the same time he gave Granddaughter the remainder interest, then on Daughter's death, there is no estate tax. Daughter's interest in the property expired and no part of the value of the property is included in her estate for estate tax purposes.

However, if Daughter had been the owner of the property and transferred the remainder interest to Granddaughter while reserving a life estate for herself, then on Daughter's death, the *entire value* of the property is included in Daughter's estate for estate tax purposes. The entire value of the property is also subject to Pennsylvania inheritance tax. But, you say, how can that be? Daughter was already taxed for giving a gift of the remainder interest to Granddaughter!

Quite simply, the estate and gift tax do not fit together as well as they might. It is true that this transfer is subject to *both* the gift tax and the estate tax. As an equitable measure, when this happens and the full value of the property is included in the estate even though part of it was subject to gift tax, the amount of credit "spent" on the gift tax is restored to the estate. Thus, there is no double taxation.

The taxation of life estates is complex. Before you make one, make sure you understand all of the ramifications.

Who Controls a Minor's Property?

A parent does not have control over a minor child's money. The law treats the minor as a separate person in his own right and the control of the minor's property is governed by laws to protect the minor. In Pennsylvania, anyone under the age of 18 is a minor, and there are several mechanisms for legal supervision and protection of a minor's property.

One option is for the court to order establishment of a "sequestered" bank account. Any amount payable in cash to a resident or nonresident minor may, by order of the court, be deposited in one or more savings accounts in the name of the minor in banks, building and loan associations, or savings and loan associations insured by a governmental agency. The amount deposited in any one such savings institution shall not exceed the amount to which accounts are thus insured. Every such court order shall contain a provision that no withdrawals can be made from any such account until the minor attains his majority, except as authorized by a prior order of the court. Notably, this does not permit investment of the minor's funds in anything other than bank accounts.

A second option for small amounts, defined by the statute is when the entire estate of the minor is $25,000 or less, all or part of the property may be received or held and deposited by the minor, or the parent, or another person maintaining the minor without the appointment of a guardian if (1) it is an award from a decedent's estate or trust *and* the court so directs, or (2) when the court having jurisdiction to sell or mortgage real estate in which a minor has an interest shall so direct, or (3) other circumstance in which the court so directs.

As a third option, the court, upon petition, can appoint a guardian of the minor's estate. If the court appoints a guardian of a minor's estate, the guardian must either be a corporation authorized to act as a fiduciary in Pennsylvania or an adult who is not the parent of the minor, except that a parent may be appointed a co-guardian with another fiduciary or fiduciaries. The statute directs the court to give preference to a person of the same religious persuasion as the parents. Preference is also given to a person nominated as guardian by a minor over the age of 14.

Any person who makes a will or trust, deed, or gift, or designates a beneficiary of an insurance policy or annuity, may nominate a guardian of the estate for any minor so named. The nomination is usually followed by the court unless evidence shows that the nominated guardian is unfit or incapable. While the law grants the power to name a guardian of the estate, it is by far preferable to appoint a custodian under the Uniform Transfers to Minors Act (UTMA) of the appropriate state.

Similarly, any person making a will or trust, or designating a beneficiary of a life insurance policy, annuity, IRA, or other qualified plan, or any other property transferred on the occurrence of some future event, can nominate a Custodian under the Pennsylvania Uniform Transfers to Minors Act to receive the property of a minor. The nomination may be made in a will, trust, deed, or other instrument. If the document does not authorize distribution to a UTMA custodian, the executor or trustee may still distribute funds not exceeding $10,000 to a custodian. Amounts more than $10,000 require court approval.

A Custodianship does not require court involvement nor the time and expense associated with the court proceedings. The custodian is given broad powers to use the minor's property for the minor's benefit without court approval. The custodian may be the parent, and the custodianship lasts until age 21 as compared to age 18 for a guardianship.

Even with authorization for distribution of a minor's property to a custodian, it is still important to name a guardian for the minor. A person competent to make a will who is the sole surviving parent or surviving parent of an unmarried minor child may appoint, in his or her will, a guardian for such minor. However, no person who for one year or more prior to his or her death shall have willfully neglected or refused to provide for his or her child shall have the right to appoint a guardian.

All estate planning instruments, wills, trusts, beneficiary designations, or any other documents should avoid the outright transfer of property to a minor. If the minor's assets are less than $25,000, a court order will be required to have the property held for the minor by the parent. If the assets are more than $25,000, a guardianship will be required and a parent cannot be sole guardian. The court requires close supervision of a guardianship. This can involve considerable time and administrative expense to comply with the court's accounting requirements. The law requires an individual guardian to post bond unless the bond requirement is excused by the court. Further, the guardian is limited in his or her ability to expend funds for the minor's benefit. Principal can be spent only with court approval. A guardianship ends at age 18 and, thus, places the funds in the hands of the minor beneficiary at a time when he or she may not have the maturity to handle them. Whenever there is a minor beneficiary or contingent beneficiary, the estate plan should include either a trust or authority to deliver a minor's property to a custodian under the Uniform Transfers to Minors Act.

Inheritance By Adopted Persons

> *It is not flesh and blood but the heart which makes us fathers and sons.*
>
> Schiller

When a person dies intestate, that is, without a will; the law determines who are that person's heirs. The general rule for an adopted child is that the adoption severs the parent-child relationship between the adopted child and his or her natural parents including severance of all inheritance rights.

Thus, under Pennsylvania law, for purposes of inheritance by, from and through an adopted person, the adopted person is considered as a natural child of his or her adopting parents; and an adopted child is not considered to be a child of his or her natural parents. Pennsylvania provides a limited exception to this rule. A child who has been adopted may inherit from his or her natural kin (but not natural parents) when the natural kin has maintained a family relationship with the adopted person. The comment to the statute when it was enacted says that "[t]he exception recognizes that family relationships frequently continue for grandparents and others where an adoption may have occurred after the death or divorce of a parent."

Here is an example: John and Katie are married and have a son, Buddy. John dies. Katie remarries. Her new husband, George, adopts Buddy. John's parents, Buddy's natural grandparents, are very much involved in his life, are frequent visitors and maintain a family relationship with Buddy. Under the Pennsylvania statute, if John's parents die intestate, Buddy, even though adopted, would inherit from them.

What about step children? If they are not adopted, they do not inherit from their parent's spouse. This can create some unfortunate results. Let's say Amy has a child, Josh. Amy marries David who is not Josh's natural father. They live together as a family for years, but David never adopts Josh. That means that Josh is not David's heir. If David dies without a will, Josh has no rights to David's estate as an heir.

In these days of blended families, where the children can be yours, mine, and ours, it is extremely important that parents make wills that spell out the rights of their children. It can completely destroy a family if only some of the children in a household inherit and others are cut out because of these rules of inheritance.

What if a will or trust directs distribution to a person's children. Does that include adopted children? In construing a will, making a devise or bequest to a person described by relationship and not by name (e.g., "my children" or "John's issue"), any adopted person shall be considered the child of his adopting parent or parents. In construing the will of a testator who is not the adopting parent, an adopted person shall be considered the child of his adopting parent or parents only if the adoption occurred during the adopted person's minority or if an earlier parent-child relationship existed during the child's minority.

Why the age limit? You can adopt and be adopted at any age. Mrs. Dowager left a will providing for distribution to her children and grandchildren. Mrs. Dowager's 65- year-old son, Libertine, is unmarried and has no children. However, he has a lady friend, Floozy age 45. Libertine adopts Floozy. If Libertine dies, Floozy is Mrs. Dowager's grandchild by adoption. However, since the statutory rule of interpretation provides that in interpreting Mrs. Dowager's will, an adoption has to occur during a person's minority (under age 18) to be given effect, Floozy would not inherit any part of Mrs. Dowager's estate. (And that's probably the way Mrs. Dowager would have wanted it.)

Choosing Your Executor

Before you can select an executor, you need to know what an executor does. The executor is the person responsible for carrying out the terms of your will. The duties are many and varied. When you die, your executor must first probate your will and be appointed as executor by the local Register of Wills. Then the work begins. The executor collects all your assets and values them, which may require hiring qualified appraisers. The executor opens a bank account in the name of the estate and transfers all financial assets into the name of the estate. The executor pays any bills you left behind and the costs of your last illness and funeral expenses.

It is the executor's responsibility to file and pay all taxes. The tax responsibilities include your final federal and state income tax returns, federal estate taxes, state inheritance or estate taxes, and federal and state income tax returns for the estate. If there is property that is included in the taxable estate but does not pass under the will (such as life insurance, pension benefits, or joint property), the executor must also value these assets, report them to the tax authorities and pay the tax attributable to them. In some cases the executor must collect taxes due from the recipients of this property.

There are various tax elections and planning techniques which may benefit the estate. Some of these are disclaimers, choice of a fiscal year for the estate, elections for the deductibility of administration expenses, elections regarding the taxation of Series E Bond interest, election of marital deduction treatment, valuing real estate as "special use" property, and installment payment of estate taxes. Obviously, a lay person acting as an executor cannot be expected to know about all these choices and will need competent advice to make the appropriate decisions.

It is the executor's duty to preserve the value of the estate and administer it for the benefit of the beneficiaries. The executor collects income from investments, business interests, and real estate. The collected assets must be invested prudently and, in many cases, estate assets must be sold and these sales are handled by the executor. The executor accounts for all transactions and when all creditors have been satisfied and all taxes paid, distributes the estate in accordance with the terms of the will.

An executor is entitled to be compensated for the very substantial work and responsibility involved. The amount of the fee will depend on the amount of work performed. Sometimes an individual executor will do a tremendous amount of work and sometimes he will hire professionals who will do almost all of the work. And of course, in some cases, the work is shared.

Usually the executor engages the services of a lawyer and possibly an accountant to advise the executor of his or her duties, the due dates for various actions, assist with preparing tax returns, resolve disputes, make tax elections, and so forth. The taxation of trusts and estates is a very complex matter and a trained professional can often save the estate substantial dollars in taxes with good postmortem tax planning.

You may have an estate which, for one reason or another, is complex. The estate may hold real estate, closely held stock, or a variety of business interests, and postmortem tax planning and liquidation of business interests may be part of your executor's "job description." In such cases, you might consider naming a professional executor such as a bank or trust company, or a private professional executor. A professional and family member, of course, may serve as co-executors.

There are some practical considerations. Does the person you prefer live so far away that carrying out the duties of an executor will be inconvenient and excessively costly? Is the individual who seems most competent also abrasive and impatient? Is he or she likely to alienate the beneficiaries or be seen as biased because of ancient family feuds? Since an executor has a number of responsibilities, some of which are time consuming and demanding, it makes good sense to discuss with a person whether he or she is willing to be your executor. Both you and the potential executor need to realize that an executor can be held personally liable by the estate beneficiaries if errors are made or the estate is negligently handled. Beneficiaries may sue an executor to recover these losses. In most cases, individuals name capable and honest executors who fulfill their responsibilities with integrity and conscientiousness; nevertheless, we have all heard horror stories of situations where an executor and beneficiaries are at odds with each other.

The executor should be in a position to expend time and energy in this role, to handle considerable detail, to keep good records, and to expect the bureaucratic wheels to turn slowly at times. He or she may often need to exercise patience and to explain to beneficiaries what steps are required to administer the estate. If the executor has a realistic outlook and realizes that sometimes settling an estate is neither quick nor simple, the process will be considerably more tolerable!

This is the main point. View the executor's position as a *job*, one for which certain skills and characteristics are essential. Think carefully about who the right person is for that job, let that person know that he or she is your choice, and hope that the answer is "Yes"!

Selling Your House for $1 Might Prove an Expensive Option

"Can I sell my house to my kids for a dollar?" Clients have posed that question to me time after time. The answer is that if you own your house, you can sell it to anyone at any price. *But*, if you sell a $100,000 house to a child for $1, you are really making a $99,999 gift at the same time you sell 1/100,000 of the property for $1. The IRS reasons that you would not sell the house to a stranger for a dollar.

The price is only $1 because the buyer is a child. Therefore, it is not an arm's length sale but is part sale and part gift.

Most folks who pose the question think that such a sale is a way to avoid estate and inheritance taxes. The estate and inheritance tax result depends on whether or not the seller/donor continues to use and occupy the property.

Let's take the easy case first. The original owner, who "sells" the house for $1, no longer uses or occupies the property. The $99,999 gift does not escape federal transfer taxes because the $99,999 is treated as a gift. The $14,000 gift tax annual exclusion is available and the gift in excess of the $14,000 starts to use up the giver's $1,000,000 federal gift exemption equivalent. For Pennsylvania inheritance tax purposes, if the person who makes the gift (the donor) survives the transfer by one year, there will be no Pennsylvania inheritance tax. On a gift to children, this saves the 4.5% inheritance tax on the value of the house when the owner dies. This may sound like good tax planning, but if the property is sold, there will be a capital gains tax on any gain at a 20% rate. When property is transferred by gift, the recipient takes over the donor's income tax cost or basis. If the giver had held onto the property and it was included in his or her estate, there would have been a 4.5% Pennsylvania inheritance tax, but the recipient who gets the house gets a "stepped-up" income tax cost basis to the date-of-death value. If the property is sold for the date-of-death value, there is no capital gain to be taxed. So you see, some people avoid a 4.5% tax just so the recipient can pay a 20% tax — not smart.

If the estate is big enough to be subject to estate tax, that is, larger than $650,000, maybe this strategy makes sense. Then the beneficiaries pay a 20% capital gains tax instead of estate tax which starts at a 45% rate.

Now for the harder case. If the original owner of the house continues to use and occupy the house after having made the sale for $1 and $99,999 gift, then we get a different result. For both federal and Pennsylvania death taxes, the continued occupancy of the residence causes the whole value of the property to be included in the gross estate and subject to tax. The tax authorities take the position that the continued occupancy of the property was part of the deal. In other words, there was an understanding between the parties that went something like this: "I will sell you my house for one dollar, but you will let me stay in it as long as I want." Even if this understanding is not in writing, the tax authorities have successfully maintained that the agreement existed because, in fact, that is what happened. Therefore, no tax savings has been accomplished; the value of the house is subject to federal estate tax and Pennsylvania inheritance tax. (Remember there is a $5,250,000 exemption from the federal estate tax.)

Some folks think that paying rent is the answer. That won't help either. The general rule is that when any property is transferred during life, and the person who transferred the property retains the income from the property or the use and occupancy of the property, then the *full value* of the transferred property is included in the transferor's estate. There is an exception: If the transfer of the property was for full value, that is, the transfer was a sale and the transferor received other property or cash equal to the fair market value of the property. Paying rent is not full value for the *transfer*. It may be fair value for the use and occupancy, but that doesn't help the estate tax question.

There are some estate planning techniques that involve changing the title to personal residences. Make sure you get good advice before attempting any do-it-yourself estate planning.

Preplanned Funerals

In 1963, journalist Jessica Mitford wrote a book called *The American Way of Death*. The book was an investigation of this country's funeral business. Claiming that there was gross overspending on funerals, she pilloried undertakers as high pressure salesmen who pressured families into agreeing to their excessive standards for burial. Mitford is credited with being the catalyst for many reforms in the funeral industry.

Mitford died in 1996, and her own funeral, which was a direct cremation, cost $548. According to the National Funeral Directors' Association, the average cost of an adult funeral in 2001 was $5,180. Cemetery expenses can be another $3,000. As more and more family-owned funeral homes are acquired by large corporations, competition will disappear and prices may climb ever higher.

Cremation

An increasing proportion of the U.S. population, about 21%, is choosing cremation. Cremation can be quite economical. However, in many cases the funeral costs are the same, just changed to "memorialization" from "funeral services." And, of course, there is an active market in cremation urns and even cremation jewelry — keepsake pendants that allow several family members to share and wear a relative's ashes. With all these add-ons, cremation may be anything but cheap.

Preplanning

As an extension of their estate planning, many people are now preplanning their funerals. There are many advantages. It gives you the opportunity to control the content and the cost of your own funeral services. For your loved ones, it is truly a gift. They are relieved of the stress, confusion, and emotional pressure of making purchasing decisions when they are bereaved. Preplanning your funeral places no financial obligations on you, and you can change your mind about the arrangements at any time. When family and friends are far away, or cannot be involved, preplanning can make sure that your wishes are carried out.

Preplanning a funeral does not require that the funeral be paid for in advance. AARP advises consumers to preplan but not to prepay, largely because pre-need agreements can leave so many important questions unanswered.

Prepaying

A pre-need agreement is a prepaid contract between the individual and the funeral director. It is funded through a trust or escrow account, or possibly with the purchase of life insurance. The individual loses access to the funds upon signing the agreement, and can regain access to the funds only through the termination of the agreement. Upon the individual's death, the funds are used by the representative of the funeral home or cemetery to provide the designated goods and services.

In Pennsylvania, the funeral director is required by law to deposit 100% of the monies he receives on a pre-need contract into an escrow account or trust account at a bank. Most funeral directors comply with the law, but there have been cases where the funds have been embezzled.

While the law requires the deposit, there are no good mechanisms in place to protect the consumer to make sure the deposit is made.

FTC rules: There is no federal legislation regarding pre-need agreements. The Federal Trade Commission does have a "Funeral Rule" which provides that consumers are entitled to price information about funeral goods and services, whether they are inquiring by telephone or in person. Funeral homes are required to give individuals a general price list that can be used for comparative shopping. The FTC's Funeral Rule does not cover trust funds established through the sale of pre-need funeral and burial agreements. There are no federal standards for pre-need agreements and there is no federal requirement for full disclosure of pre-need agreement terms and conditions and of the risks consumers bear if they cancel a contract. The FTC publishes a *Consumer Guide on Funerals*. It is available for download at *http://www.ftc.gov/bcp/conline/pubs/services/funeral.htm* or call 1-877-FTC-HELP (1-877-382-4357).

Disadvantages: The main disadvantage of prepaid funeral plans is the potential for fraud. Make sure you check the contract for provisions to cancel the contract in the event of a move to another place or to cancel for other reasons. Individuals who relocate, decide they prefer another funeral home or cemetery, or want to cancel their agreement may not be able to transfer or cancel without a penalty. In some cases, individuals could lose significant amounts of money.

What if . . .: What items in the contract are provided for a guaranteed price? Are there some items which will cost additional when the funeral is held? How much of the contract price can the funeral director keep if you cancel the contract? In Pennsylvania, if the purchaser defaults, for example, by failing to make all of the required installment payments, the funeral director may keep 30% of the contract price as damages. If the purchaser moves out of state, the purchaser can cancel the contract and the purchaser is entitled to get the principal amount of deposit back from the bank, and the funeral director is allowed to keep the interest.

Alternative: Instead of prepaying, it is possible to set up a burial trust account in a bank for the purpose of covering burial or funeral costs. It is not necessary to designate a particular funeral director or cemetery. That decision may be left to the discretion of an executor or other representative. In the event there is a surplus in the account after expenses are paid, the surplus is payable to the estate. The burial trust account eliminates the potential for fraud; however, the individual does not "lock in" the costs (as in a pre-need agreement).

Make sure your family knows about the plans you've made and where the documents are kept. If your family isn't aware that you've made plans, your wishes may not be carried out, and they could end up paying for the same arrangements.

Anatomical Gifts

> *One who saves a single life—it is as if he has saved an entire world.*
>
> Pirke D'Rav Eliezer, Chapter 48

Many people die each year or go through painful and expensive medical procedures while waiting for organ donations. An anatomical gift is a donation of organs and tissues. Advancements in medicine have now made it possible to transplant many different human organs and tissues, including corneas, heart, liver, kidney, lungs, pancreas, bone and skin. Donations may also be used for research related to diseases, disabilities and injuries, and are used for teaching courses in human anatomy to medical and dental students.

If you are considering making an anatomical gift, discuss it with your family and with your clergy. Most of the major religions support organ donation and transplantation. However, within each religion there are different schools of thought, which means views may differ. It is important that you check with your spiritual leader so that no conflict arises.

In Pennsylvania, competent individuals over eighteen (18) years of age may authorize the donation of their organs and tissue. This can be done by agreeing to be a donor when getting a driver's license. The words "ORGAN DONOR" are put on the license. The Department of Transportation is required to ask individuals when they are applying for or renewing their licenses, "Do you wish to have the organ donor designation printed on your driver's license?"

Alternatively, a person over eighteen (18) can give the authorization for organ and tissue donation by obtaining an organ donor card from the Center for Organ Recovery & Education (CORE). Call 1-800-DONORS-7 or go to *www.core.org* to get a donor's card. The card must be signed by the donor in the presence of two (2) witnesses who sign in the presence of the donor.

Pennsylvania law also allows agents under Powers of Attorney to make anatomical gifts. An agent under a Power of Attorney can be given the power "to make an anatomical gift of all or part of my body." The agent is allowed to "arrange and consent, either before or after the death of the principal, to procedures to make an anatomical gift."

A person can give directions about organ donation in an Advance Directive for Health Care Declaration. Care must be taken so that language in the Advance Directive stating that the individual does not want certain procedures, such as being placed on a respirator, will not prevent the individual from being an organ or tissue donor. A donor may need to be placed on a respirator while waiting for the gift to be made. Consider adding language to the Advance Directive to allow the use of certain procedures to allow for organ and tissue donation.

In addition, the following individuals (listed in order of priority) may make gifts on behalf of a decedent, provided that the deceased individual did not express a contrary intent: 1) spouse, 2) adult brother or sister, 3) adult son or daughter, 4) guardian of the person, 5) either parent, 6) any other person who has the authority or obligation to dispose of the body. The agreement of any of these people may be in writing, by a telegram, or by a recorded telephonic or other type of recorded message.

Note that if a donor card, driver's license, living will, durable power of attorney or other document evidencing the donor's intention to make a gift of organs or tissue has been signed, then the consent of any person listed above is not required.

An anatomical gift can be authorized in a person's Last Will and Testament. This gift made in a will becomes effective once the testator dies without the need for probate. If the law required that the gift not be made until after a will was probated, it might be too late to use the organs or tissue. Nevertheless, it is not recommended to make your anatomical gift in the will because often the will is not even read or found until it is too late to take organs or tissue from the body. If the will authorizes an anatomical gift, that portion of the will is valid even if the will is subsequently declared invalid.

Organ and tissue donation is considered only after all efforts to save your life have been exhausted and does not occur until death is certified.

Some people add to their consent by any of the above means donor card and additional restriction that organs and tissue not be removed if the donor is on life support. On the other hand, some donors, realizing that it is more likely for organs to be useful, specify that life support may continue even after brain death in order to preserve the utility of their organs and tissues for transplant. Different strokes.

Some people wish to donate their entire body for medical research. These arrangements should be made with a medical school while you are alive. Most medical schools have very strict requirements and conditions that must be met and require pre-planning with your family, physician, and funeral director. Some schools will reject a donation if any organs have been removed from the body. On the other hand, Anatomy Gifts Registry, a national organization supplying research centers and schools, gives a priority to organ donation with the remaining body distributed to institutions for study and research. You can get more information about them at *http://www.anatomicgift.com*.

While an individual may decide to make an anatomical gift at any point prior to death, a gift of the whole body must be made in writing at least fifteen (15) days before the date of death. Those family members or guardians with the ability to make a gift may do so immediately before or after the death.

For people living in Pennsylvania, The Humanity Gifts Registry receives and distributes bodies to medical schools and physicians in Pennsylvania for scientific study or teaching to promote medical science. The Humanity Gifts Registry may be contacted at P.O. Box 835, Philadelphia, PA 19105-0835, (215) 922-4440.

Organ Donation Myths and Harmful Urban Legends

Unfortunately, rumors and myths about organ transplantation are widespread. Grisly stories have appeared in the tabloids and have circulated on the internet. Urban legends about organ transplants are especially damaging since organ transplantation cannot succeed without the participation and support of the majority of the population. An example of a false urban legend is the "kidney harvest" chain letter describing drugged travelers awakening in ice-filled bathtubs only to discover one of their kidneys has been harvested by organ thieves.

According to the Urban Legends Archive, any rumor regarding a black market in stolen organs needs to be evaluated in light of the necessity of matching the organ and recipient in order to avoid rejection by the recipient's immune system. "One cannot take any old organ and just put it anywhere you please. A rather complex system has been set up in the U.S. to handle matching and distribution. It's unlikely that any number of evil people in the U.S. or abroad will be able to duplicate such a system in secret. Adding these simple facts with the necessity of having many highly skilled medical professionals involved, along with modern medical facilities and support, makes it plain why rumors of the involvement of murder, violence and organized crime in organ procurement cannot be given any credence." There has never been a documented case of kidney theft.

The buying and selling of organs and tissues is illegal, as part of The National Organ Transplant Act. Violators are subject to fines and imprisonment. There are many public policy reasons behind this prohibition, not the least of which is that the buying and selling of organs might lead to inequitable access to donor organs with the wealthy having an unfair advantage.

Sales of organs in foreign countries do happen. National Geographic has reported illegal organ transplant rings operating in South America and India, calling one village in India "Kidney Village" because so many of its residents had sold a kidney. The going rate is $800 for a kidney — approximately one year's wages. Such practices have led to "transplant tourism." Patients travel to countries where they can obtain the transplant they need on the black market.

Another thing that people fear is the "harvesting" of organs before they are legally dead. The longer a body has been dead, the less likely it is that the organs will be of use to anyone. Usually, doctors pronounce a patient dead when all brain activity ceases. On occasion, that means that organs can be taken from a body that is still on life-support. As one writer put it: "Doctors are sometimes willing to remove organs from a body that undertakers would be unwilling to bury." I have heard some clients say that they will not become organ donors because they fear the grisly possibility of organs being taken from donors who are not totally dead.

According to the production, Gift of a Lifetime, which you can view at *www.organtransplants.org*, brain death is a legal determination of death and involves the complete and irreversible loss of brain function including the brain stem, which controls breathing and heart rate. Brain death can occur in patients who have sustained injuries to the brain resulting from traumatic causes — auto accidents, gunshot wounds, falls, blows to the head — and non-traumatic causes such as strokes, aneurysms, drowning, and heart attacks during which time the brain is deprived of blood and oxygen. Brain dead patients are patients who are in the hospital in an intensive care unit on total artificial life support. Brain death should not be confused with coma or persistent vegetative state. These are conditions under which patients still have some brain function and may be breathing on their own.

Note that physicians who certify the death of the donor or who become donees are prohibited from participating in the procedure of removing or transplanting the organ.

The following facts dispel other myths you may have heard:

1. There are no age limits on organ donation. Don't think that you are too old for any organs to be useful. Donation depends on the condition of the organs. The general age limit for tissue donation is age 70.
2. Organ donation does not mutilate the body. Organs are removed surgically in a routine operation similar to gallbladder or appendix removal. The body is not disfigured, and there is no change in the way it looks in a casket.
3. Even if you have a serious health problem, you may still be able to donate organs or tissue. Your potential to donate will be determined at the time of death. Even if you have had a serious health problem like diabetes, high blood pressure, heart disease, certain types of cancer, or even hepatitis, you may still be able to donate at the time of death.

4. Organ donation costs nothing to the donor's family or estate. Your family does not have to pay for the removal surgery.
5. If you are in an accident and the hospital knows that you want to be a donor, that will have no effect on the doctors' attempts to save your life. Organ and tissue recovery takes place only after all efforts to save your life have been exhausted and you have been declared legally dead. The transplant team is not notified until your family has consented to donation.
6. Most major religions in the U.S. approve of organ and tissue donation and consider it an act of charity. Be sure to consult your clergy for special restrictions and conditions.
7. Organs that can be transplanted include the heart, kidneys, pancreas, lungs, liver and intestines as well as bone marrow. Tissue that can be donated include the eyes, skin, bone, heart valves and tendons.
8. You don't have to consent to the donation of all of your organs. You may specify what organs may be donated.

How to Handle Your Estate's Home Away From Home

Everybody knows a little place like Kokomo ... if you wanna go and get away from it all ...

The Beach Boys, 1988
Mike Love and Terry Melcher

How many states are involved in your estate plan? Do you have a condo in Florida? Summer house at the shore? Time-share in Arizona?

Every state in which you own real estate will be involved in the settlement of your estate, unless you arrange your estate plan to avoid this complication.

Real estate law is state law. Only the courts of a particular state have authority to resolve issues about title and ownership of real property located in that state. If you are a resident of Pennsylvania when you die and own a condo in Florida, settlement of your estate will require a principal probate in your county of residence in Pennsylvania and something called an "ancillary probate" in Florida.

In fact an ancillary probate is required in each state where property is owned in the name of the decedent.

Not only are there probate proceedings required in the other states, but there can be inheritance and estate tax due to those other states as well.

This is an area in which I strongly advise you to avoid probate. It should be a goal of your estate planning to minimize the cost and effort of having multiple probate in numerous states. There are various solutions. The simplest is titling property in other states in joint names — first with a spouse, and then with intended beneficiaries such as children. This simple device means that the property will pass to the surviving joint owners on your death and no probate proceeding is required.

Another common technique is to transfer title of the out-of-Pennsylvania real estate to a revocable trust. The title to the shore home is then held by a Trustee, not by the individual. When the individual dies, the trust continues and there is no need for a probate since no title question has arisen. This technique has the added benefit of retaining complete control of the property in the hands of the creator of the trust.

Sometimes these properties are transferred to entities like corporations, limited liability companies, and partnerships. Again, since the decedent did not hold the title to the real estate, but rather, the entity which has a continuing existence held the real estate, there is no need for an ancillary probate.

Most of these techniques do not remove the property from the taxing jurisdiction of the state where the real estate is located so your executor can expect to file state death tax returns and perhaps pay tax in these other states.

A frequent objective of families with vacation homes is to maintain the home for the use of all family members even after Mom and Dad die. The house at the lake where the children spent every summer holds many fond memories and Mom and Dad like to imagine the grandchildren (and great-grandchildren) enjoying it for many years into the future. A partnership or trust may be able to provide this sort of arrangement. A mechanism is required to "moderate" which kid gets which week. The arrangement must also be funded so that real estate taxes, insurance, utilities, repairs, and maintenance can be paid. You can count on the children having different financial resources, different family situations, and different priorities. You cannot expect them all to devote the same amount of time, interest, and their own resources to maintain the family vacation home.

A partnership agreement or trust could address all these variables. Design options include buyout provisions for the child or grandchild who doesn't want to or can't participate. The agreement should establish procedures to allocate time slots, and a management structure for repairs, maintenance, and so forth. A trust or partnership to manage the vacation property for the extended family can also solve the problem of the ancillary probate.

There is a special technique available for residences which can be used for the primary residence and/or a secondary residence. It is a Qualified Personal Residence Trust (QPRT). In addition to solving the ancillary probate problem, and possibly addressing the sharing of the residence by the family after Mom and Dad are gone, this technique also offers substantial estate tax savings. A QPRT is an irrevocable trust that provides for the occupancy of the residence by Mom or Dad for a period of years. At the end of the term, Mom and Dad's right of occupancy ends and the beneficiaries become the new owners. When the trust is created, a gift is made, but the value of the gift is steeply discounted — hence the estate tax savings.

What if your getaway place is an island villa in Kokomo, Antigua, or a home in another foreign locale? You'll need to consider the foreign country's probate and estate tax systems in your estate plan. Instruct your lawyer to research the laws in that country and draft accordingly.

Inter-Vivos QTIP (No, It's Not in the Medicine Chest)

When I was in law school, I remember being absolutely shocked to discover that when a person transferred property to his or her spouse, the transferor was making a gift. If the value of the transfer was large enough, a gift tax was due. Imagine that — paying gift tax for transferring property to your spouse!

Those days are over, at least, in most cases. There is now an unlimited marital deduction. That means that while making a transfer of property to your spouse is still a gift, such gifts are 100% deductible and do not generate a gift tax. There are a couple of catches, though, and a big one is that such gifts must not be terminable interests. A terminable interest is one that terminates on the lapse of time or on the occurrence or non-occurrence of a future event.

It is a very common estate planning recommendation to a married couple that they divide assets between them. These inter-spousal gifts are commonly made in order to take full advantage of each spouse's federal estate tax exemption. The current federal exemption is $5.25 million.

Spouses divide assets between them so that each holds separately titled assets equal to the amount of the exemption and they have the appropriate estate planning documents with by-pass trusts in place, the exemption can be effectively doubled for a married couple.

One can't let the tax tail wag the dog. Sometimes these transfers cannot be made because of non-tax considerations. Sometimes significant assets are in restricted stock, or qualified plans, or partnerships with restrictions on transfers. Sometimes the family situation makes such transfers inappropriate. For example, when it's a second marriage and each spouse has children from the first marriage, asset transfers like this will disrupt the planned distribution of inheritances.

When the estate planning consideration to reduce estate tax would militate toward a division of assets but other circumstances make an outright transfer inappropriate, there is a solution: the Inter-vivos QTIP trust. QTIP is an acronym for Qualified Terminable Interest in Property. Inter-vivos means that the trust is made during the donor's life, not at his death.

A QTIP trust is an irrevocable trust. The minimum requirement for a QTIP trust is that the spouse be given the income from the trust for his or her life. This right can never be taken away. The right to income cannot be conditioned on not remarrying. If the trust is elected to be a QTIP trust on the gift tax return, it is treated as if it were owned by the spouse who received the income for estate tax purposes, thus fulfilling the need to transfer assets to the spouse to use his or her exemption.

The significance of a QTIP is that a transfer to a trust like this qualifies for the marital deduction even though it is a terminable interest. That means that the donor spouse can have his cake and eat it too. Both spouses' exemptions can be utilized, but since the property is transferred to a trust, not to the spouse directly, the donor spouse retains control of the ultimate disposition of the property.

The minimum requirement for a QTIP trust is that it provides for payment of the income to the surviving spouse for life. Unfortunately, many lawyers stop there. Keep in mind that this trust will continue for the life of the spouse, even after the donor spouse dies. Much more flexibility can be added if appropriate to the situation. The spouse can be given principal from the trust in the trustee's discretion or in accordance with a standard for health, maintenance and support. The spouse can be given the annual right to withdraw an amount of principal equal to the greater of (1) $5,000 or (2) five percent of the value of the trust principal. (Don't include this power if the surviving spouse is the trustee.) Also, the spouse can be given a power to designate who should receive the trust property after his or her death by will.

An inter-vivos QTIP trust is one of a myriad that can be used creatively in estate plans.

A "Defective Trust" Can Actually Be Good Planning

A "defective trust" can be a very effective estate planning tool. It has an unfortunate label. It sounds like there is something wrong with it. How would you like it if your lawyer gave you a "defective" trust? Despite the label, in many situations it allows a person to provide tax-free income for their beneficiaries.

In a Defective Grantor Trust, the Grantor is taxed on income that he or she does not receive (the income is received by the Trust's beneficiaries). At first that sounds like a bad idea. But what it means is that the Grantor is reducing his or her estate by the amount of the income tax, and the beneficiary who received the gift is relieved from paying income tax. The payment of income tax by the Grantor on trust income is really a tax-free gift to the beneficiaries. This is a great way to get additional dollars transferred from the Grantor to the beneficiary without paying estate or gift tax.

Making gifts to trusts is a very common estate planning technique and its importance cannot be underestimated. Gifts use exclusions from tax and remove future appreciation on the transferred property from the Grantor's estate. Making gifts to a trust provides for management of the property and control over the beneficiary's use of the gift.

Transfers to trusts usually fall into one of two categories for estate and gift tax purposes. Either the transfer to the trust is a gift and the trust property is not included in the Grantor's estate, or the transfer to the trust is not a gift and the trust property is includable in the Grantor's estate when the Grantor dies.

One would think that if a transfer of property to a trust is a completed gift and the trust property is not subject to estate tax in the Grantor's estate, that the Grantor shouldn't have to pay income tax on the trust's income. It ain't necessarily so.

Because the income tax system, is separate and distinct from the estate and gift tax system, there are some situations where the tax treatment of a particular transaction may appear to be inconsistent. One example is in the taxation of trusts.

There is a section of the Internal Revenue Code called the Grantor Trust Rules. These rules describe circumstances where the Grantor is treated as the owner of all or a portion of a trust for income tax purposes *only*. When the Grantor trust rules apply, even if a transfer to a trust is a completed gift, the Grantor must still pay the income tax on the trust's income.

The fact that the trust's income is taxable to the Grantor does not make the trust includable in the Grantor's estate for estate tax purposes. Grantor trust rules apply *only* for income tax, not estate and gift tax. Hence, the anomaly — the gift is complete, but the Grantor still has to pay the income tax generated by the property that was the subject of the gift.

When the trust is defective, it is drafted to result in income tax inclusion but not estate tax inclusion. How do you know if you have a defective trust? It's not so easy. You can't go by the title on the document. A trust can be named anything — that doesn't control how it is taxed. A tax professional must read and analyze the document. Here is a list of provisions, any one of which can make a trust a Grantor trust for income tax purposes. (The list is a sampling and doesn't include everything that might apply.)

1. The Grantor has the power, in a non-fiduciary capacity, to reacquire the trust corpus by substituting property of equivalent value.

2. The Grantor retains the right, in a non-fiduciary capacity, to either sell trust assets or change the nature of trust assets.
3. A non-adverse party has the power to add beneficiaries, other than after-born and after-adopted children.
4. The income may be used to pay insurance premiums on the Grantor's life, provided the trust actually holds such insurance. (Thus, almost all irrevocable life insurance trusts are Grantor trusts.)
5. Trust income may be paid to the Grantor's spouse.
6. The Grantor retains the power to borrow trust assets without adequate security.

The Operation of Qualified Personal Residence Trusts

> *I don't know exactly why the notion of home ownership has such a grasp on the American imagination. Perhaps as descendants of landless immigrants we turn our plots into symbols of stability.*
>
> Ellen Goodman

> *A man builds a fine house; and now he has a master, and a task for life; he is to furnish, watch, show it, and keep it in repair, the rest of his days.*
>
> Ralph Waldo Emerson

For many people, their principal residence is their single most valuable and coveted asset. The home is often a measure of its occupant's success. What to do with it in the estate plan?

A valuable residence, or vacation home, is subject to estate tax when it passes to the owner's beneficiaries. The value is determined by appraisal to be the fair market value at the date of death; and if the estate is over the $5.25 million exemption, there will be state and federal death taxes amounting to about one-half of its value.

Fortunately, there is a special estate planning technique, especially for residences, that provides death tax savings opportunities. This technique is the Qualified Personal Residence Trust or "QPRT."

A Qualified Personal Residence Trust is an irrevocable trust that is a vehicle for transferring a principal residence to beneficiaries at a significantly reduced gift tax cost. You (the "Grantor") establish and set the terms of the trust, specify the remainder beneficiary(ies), and transfer your residence to the trust. You retain the right to occupy the residence for a stated term of your choosing. Upon termination, the remainder beneficiary(ies) receives the remaining trust assets. The residence could then be rented by you from the remainder beneficiary(ies).

During the term of the trust you will have the unlimited right to use the property. Rights include the right to occupy the property, receive rentals if the property is rented, and sell the property and purchase other substitute property. You are responsible for paying all expenses related to the property. Once in the trust, the Trustee may sell the residence, and may purchase another one, or just reinvest the proceeds and pay you an annuity.

If the term of the trust expires during your life, the property will pass to the trust remainder beneficiary(ies), which could include your spouse and children. The trust can provide that you, the Grantor, may have a right to rent the residence from the remainder beneficiary(ies) at fair market value or to purchase the property from the remainder beneficiary(ies) at fair market value. Rent payments transfer more wealth to beneficiary(ies) without using gift or estate tax exemption — a good thing.

During the term of the QPRT all income and deductions are reported by you as the Grantor of the trust. Separate income tax filings for the QPRT are only required if the Grantor is not a trustee. The Grantor remains eligible for the exclusion from gain on sale of a principal residence if the occupancy requirements are met.

If you fail to survive the trust term, the trust will end. The value of the house will be included in the Grantor's gross estate for federal estate tax purposes.

Here is an example. If you are 60 and have a house worth $500,000, you can transfer it to a 10-year QPRT and the value of the gift that you make will be about $242,000; you will use some of your $5.25 million exemption. If you survive the ten-year term, no part of the value of the house will be included in your estate. If the house appreciated at the modest rate of 5% per year over the ten-year term, it would be worth $814,447 and you would have made a gift of only $242,000.

What happens if you do nothing? You die owning the appreciated asset, say at $814,447 and your estate pays estate tax on the full $814,447. Making the $242,000 gift is clearly preferable.

If a husband and wife own a residence jointly, each can contribute his or her one-half interest to a QPRT. This is even better. The value of each one-half interest can be discounted because of the lack of marketability of fractional interest in real estate. This reduces the transfer tax even further.

What is the downside? First, if you die during the term (ten years in our example, but any term that you chose) the technique does not work and your estate pays estate tax on the date-of-death value of the house. That is the same thing that would happen if you did nothing; so the only risk is the legal and accounting fees for setting up and maintaining the QPRT.

The second downside is that if you survive the term and succeed in getting the estate tax benefit, your beneficiaries receive the property with a carry-over basis, not a basis stepped up to date-of-death value. If the home in the QPRT is a vacation home intended to stay in the family, this is not an issue at all. If the residence will be sold by the beneficiaries, the advantage of the stepped up basis must be weighed against the advantage of reducing estate tax.

Using a QPRT is a very low-risk technique. It is specifically authorized by the Internal Revenue Code and is not aggressive at all. If you follow the directions, you are entitled to the benefit. The QPRT provides an opportunity to significantly reduce estate and gift taxes on a residence. In fact, each single taxpayer is permitted to transfer two residences to separate QPRTs. A married couple could transfer three residences.

GRITs Are Good for You When Estate Planning

If your intended beneficiaries are nieces and nephews, there is an estate planning technique available to you that is not available to anyone else. The technique is called a Grantor Retained Income Trust (GRIT).

GRITs used to be available to anyone, but Congress changed the law so that GRITs are not available if your beneficiaries are family members. As the term "family member" is defined for this purpose, it includes children, parents, and brothers and sisters. Notably, nieces and nephews are *not* included in the definition of family members. Thus, GRITs are still available to use if your beneficiaries are nieces and nephews.

What is a GRIT? It is an irrevocable trust. The Grantor transfers assets to a Trustee (who may be the Grantor). The terms of the trust provide that the income generated by the trust assets is to be paid to the Grantor for a term of years. The term is selected by the Grantor when the trust is created. At the end of the term, the Grantor's income interest terminates and the trust assets are either paid out to the intended beneficiaries or held in continuing trust for the benefit of the beneficiaries. If the Grantor dies during the term, the trust assets are returned to the Grantor's estate.

When the trust is created, the Grantor is making a gift. Since the Grantor reserved the right to receive income for a term of years, this portion of the trust property is not a gift. (You can't make a gift to yourself.) The remainder interest, which is the right of future beneficiaries or trusts to receive the trust property at the end of the term of years if the Grantor survives the term, is a gift. The value of the gift is determined under IRS regulations to be the present value determined by using the interest rate prescribed monthly by the IRS. For November 2013, the rate was 2.0%. Also included is the actuarial probability that the Grantor will survive the selected term of years. The older the Grantor, and the longer the term of years, the smaller is the value of the gift.

To get the most leverage, the Trustee invests the trust assets in something that does not produce much, if any, income. A good example is growth stocks that pay little or no dividends. All growth in the trust assets is then in principal. This can produce very dramatic tax savings. Let us assume a 70-year-old Grantor creates a GRIT for nieces and nephews and selects a term of seven years. Transferred to the trust is $200,000 in marketable securities. The value of the gift on the date of creation of the GRIT is $61,546. That much of the Grantor's unified credit is expended. Let's assume the trust assets are invested in growth stocks that pay little or no dividends. Any dividends received are paid to the Grantor but will be very small amounts. If the trust assets appreciate in value at a rate of 12% per year, at the end of the seven-year term the trust assets will be worth $442,000. This $442,000 will pass to the beneficiaries or trust for them, completely gift and estate tax free.

What has the Grantor accomplished? The Grantor used $92,940 of his $5,250,000 applicable exclusion amount and transferred $442,000 to the intended beneficiaries. This is tremendous leverage.

An Outline of Qualified Domestic Trusts, or QDOTs

Is your spouse a citizen of the United States? If not, your estate will not be entitled to the unlimited marital deduction if you predecease your spouse. Any estate planner should ask if you and your spouse are both citizens of the U.S. If one or both of you are not citizens, a very different estate plan is required.

Let's say your husband died, leaving all property to you, and you, the surviving wife, are a British citizen. Instead of paying no federal estate tax, all property passing to you is taxed, after the application of the $525,000,000 federal exemption. The tax rate starts at an effective rate of about 40%. If you were a U.S. citizen, your husband's entire estate could have passed to you tax free.

Why does the law make this distinction? The theory of the marital deduction is that the estate tax on assets owned by a husband and wife can be deferred until the death of the survivor of them. The government is assured of collecting a tax only if the surviving spouse remains subject to U.S. estate and gift tax laws. Apparently, the legislators thought that there was a high risk of a surviving noncitizen spouse leaving the U.S. If the surviving spouse is not a U.S. resident or citizen on his or her death, the U.S. would not receive any estate tax on that family's assets except for tax on real estate located in the U.S.

To make sure that U.S. estate tax is paid in this situation, no marital deduction is permitted for property passing to a surviving spouse who is not a U.S. citizen. The rule applies whether or not the surviving noncitizen spouse is a resident or nonresident of the U.S. This can be a nasty shock. The surviving spouse may be expecting to have the full value of the marital assets available to provide income during the survivorship period and be shocked to find that a significant estate tax is due on the first spouse's death, reducing the available assets by as much as 50%. The first $5,250,000,000 representing the federal exemption equivalent, can pass tax free to the spouse, even if he or she is not a citizen. Anything over that amount is subject to the regular estate tax.

Most planners recommend a Qualified Domestic Trust (QDOT) for the benefit of a surviving noncitizen spouse. This is a trust which provides for the payment of income and principal on certain conditions to the surviving spouse. If principal is distributed from the trust to the surviving noncitizen spouse, a special tax is paid by the Trustee at the time of the distribution. Income can be paid to the surviving noncitizen spouse without any estate or gift tax payable. (It remains subject to income taxation under the usual rules.)

If death occurs and a QDOT is not in place, the surviving spouse can remedy the situation by creating the QDOT herself or himself. This must be done before the estate tax return is due. Alternatively, the surviving spouse can become a citizen of the U.S. before the estate tax return is due. If QDOT treatment is chosen, the executor must make the appropriate election on the estate tax return.

A QDOT must have at least one trustee that is a U.S. citizen or U.S. domestic corporation. If the trust exceeds $2 million, one of the trustees must be a bank, or the individual trustee must post a bond equal to 65% of the trust value. The trust must provide that if the trustee makes any principal distribution, the trustee will withhold the special tax due on the QDOT distribution.

Complex rules are also in place to make sure that a surviving noncitizen spouse pays estate tax on qualified plans and IRAs. The surviving noncitizen spouse can sign an agreement to remit part of the special estate tax annually as distributions are received, or to distribute the principal portion of each payment or withdrawal to a QDOT established before the filing of the estate tax returns. This means that not only must the surviving spouse pay income tax on the distribution, but, also, the special estate tax as distributions are received. This may leave only a small fraction of the distribution actually available to the surviving spouse.

For jointly owned property, the whole value of the property is subject to estate tax (not just one-half) unless the executor can show financial contribution to the acquisition of the joint property by the surviving noncitizen spouse.

Obviously, these rules are complex, and, where circumstances allow, spouses in this situation are advised to pursue citizenship.

The gift tax marital deduction, also, is not available to a noncitizen spouse. The annual exclusion for gifts to a noncitizen spouse is raised from the usual $14,000 to $136,000 in 2011, $139,000 in 2012 and $143,000 in 2013. Gifts to a noncitizen spouse in excess of $110,000 per year are subject to the gift tax. Gifts more than $110,000 per year start using up the $1,000,000 exemption and then generate gift taxes payable.

To avoid this result, you and your spouse need to plan now. There are a few choices available. (1) Become a U.S. citizen. For some, this is intellectually or emotionally unacceptable although it is a quick and certain fix of the estate tax problem. (2) When the first spouse dies, your estate plan could provide that the property passing to the surviving noncitizen spouse goes into a Qualified Domestic Trust, or "QDOT." (3) Plan to have your surviving spouse create and fund a QDOT before the estate tax return is due, nine months from the first death.

Don't assume that your advisor knows your citizenship status. I have been surprised again and again to learn the diverse citizenship of my clients. If you or your spouse is not a United States citizen, you would be well advised to have your plan reviewed to make sure these issues are addressed.

The Latest Word on Family Limited Partnerships

> *Over and over again, courts have said that there is nothing sinister in so arranging one's affairs as to keep taxes as low as possible. Everybody does so, rich or poor; and all do right, for nobody owes any public duty to pay more than the law demands; taxes are enforced exactions, not voluntary contributions.*
>
> Judge Learned Hand

What is the controversy over Family Limited Partnerships? First, an explanation of what a family limited partnership is.

The biggest challenge for estate planners is how to reduce estate taxes, but allow the client to retain control over his assets. Family limited partnerships provide a solution to this problem.

When you place investments, a business, or real estate holdings in a family limited partnership, you retain control of the assets while at the same time making gifts of limited partnership interests to your beneficiaries so that they own part of the equity. Because the limited partnership interests that are given to the beneficiaries are not marketable, they are valued at a discount, which maximizes the amount of the underlying assets that can be transferred free of gift taxes. The family limited partnership also provides other benefits for asset protection from creditors and providing for centralized control and management.

The older generation member ("Dad") forms a partnership (I will spare you the technical details of how this is accomplished). Dad contributes $1 million assets to the partnership. The contributed assets now belong to the partnership. Dad is the general partner and in control of the partnership. Dad is in charge of all decisions regarding whether partnership assets are sold, purchased, distributed, or held.

Next, Dad makes gifts of the limited partnership interests to children, grandchildren, trusts for grandchildren, whomever he chooses. What can a child or grandchild do with the limited partnership interest? Nothing. The interest can't be transferred, can't be sold, can't vote, and can't exercise any control over the partnership assets. It is a piece of paper representing an interest in the partnership, which entitles the owner to partnership distributions *if* they are made and to liquidation proceeds *if* the partnership is liquidated. The terms of the partnership agreement restrict the limited partners' ability to transfer, or otherwise enjoy the asset.

This gives us a twofold benefit as follows: (1) Dad stays in control even though he has made gifts, and (2) because of the restrictions placed on the limited partnership interest by the partnership agreement, the value of the gifts is much less than a pro rata value of the underlying assets. Thus, Dad can transfer more property by making gifts of limited partnership interest than by making outright gifts of the assets. Both the psychological goal of retained control and the estate planning goal of a reduced taxable estate are reached.

There are considerable nontax advantages as well. The partnership can protect property against the claims of future creditors. Creditors and others that may sue the partnership cannot reach the personal assets of the limited partners and the general partner (if the general partnership is a limited liability company or corporation). Creditors of the partners themselves may be more willing to settle than be saddled with limited partnership interests and non-controlling general partnership interests that will cause them to have income tax liability but no guarantee of distributions with which to pay the taxes.

The partnership property can be managed through one account, thus consolidating and simplifying the management of the family's investments. The partnership would simplify the manner in which you make gifts to your beneficiaries in the future. Instead of being required to select and gift several securities, you simply could transfer limited partnership units.

The Internal Revenue Service has devoted increased scrutiny to transfers of interests in family limited partnerships and, in the course of gift or estate tax audits, has sought to challenge the basis upon which the taxpayer has reported the combined valuation discount claimed in respect of the limited partnership interests. The taxpayer can expect to have to defend the amount of the discount, so an excellent appraisal from a qualified appraiser is an absolute necessity if you would like to pursue this planning technique.

The IRS continues to apply various theories to disallow the discounts the tax planners are obtaining. One of the theories being pushed lately is that because of the retained control of the general partner, all of the partnership assets should be included in the Dad's estate. In order to combat this theory extra care must be taken in the administration of the partnership and consideration must be given to Dad giving up some of the control.

The IRS's position on a disputed issue is not the law. The law is enacted by Congress and interpreted by the Courts. When a tax issue is litigated, the IRS is one party before the court and the taxpayer is the other. The IRS is *not* a neutral party. Some clients have such a fear of the IRS that they do not wish to do anything other than toe the line as perceived by the IRS. Others go too far, stepping way over the line — not because they are challenging the IRS, but because they are not following the law. As long as you are following the law, it has long been the view of U.S. courts that the taxpayer is free to reduce his tax by any legal means.

The family limited partnership is a valuable technique, but it is somewhat controversial. Let's say you form one and claim a 45% discount. The IRS objects and rather than go to litigation you agree on a 25% discount. What do you call that? I call that Victory. You won a 25% discount. If you think that losing the whole 45% is failure, a family limited partnership is not for you.

The technique is not suitable for everyone and every situation. It is not simple, and it is not cheap. But the possible benefits are huge.

Sorting Out Who's in Charge of Your Assets

An estate plan names multiple fiduciaries. An Agent is appointed in the power of attorney to manage the client's affairs when the client is unable to do it herself or himself. A Surrogate is named in a medical directive to make medical decisions when the client is unable to. An Executor is appointed in the will to settle the estate, marshal the assets, value them, file tax returns and pay taxes, settle debts and claims, and carry out the terms of the will. A Trustee may be named to administer part or all of the estate for a long period of time for the benefit of beneficiaries.

Who are all these people? Should you name a different person for each office? Or should they all be held by the same person?

The Agent, Executor, and Trustee are given principally financial powers. The medical surrogate makes decisions of a more personal nature. Often clients will chose a different person to make the medical decision than they choose to put in charge of financial matters. Skill and understanding in one area does not necessarily transfer easily to the other — it makes sense to choose different individuals for these types of functions.

The duties of an Agent under a power of attorney are to take care of a Principal's financial matters during the Principal's lifetime. Sometimes the Principal is incapacitated, sometimes merely unavailable. Some Agents restrict their activities to writing and signing checks to pay bills. Others take full responsibility for investment decisions, property sales and transfers, tax planning and preparation of tax returns, and estate planning.

An Agent's authority under a power of attorney terminates absolutely at the moment of the Principal's death. From then on, the Executor (or the Administrator if the decedent died intestate) takes over the care, custody, and management of the decedent's assets. In many cases the person who handled the client's affairs as an Agent before death is the logical person to be named the Executor and continue to manage the affairs of the estate as the Executor after the decedent's death.

Some professionals think that a different person or entity should be Executor. That way, another objective person will be able to review the actions of the Agent. Unfortunately, there are quite a few instances where Agents under powers of attorney have abused their powers, many times exercising the powers in favor of themselves in ways that are not permitted. If the Agent continues on as Executor, these things may never be discovered as no one else is reviewing the situation with a view to determine whether the Agent's actions were proper.

Both the Agent and the Executor may need professional advice. One can't expect trusted family members to be investment advisors, estate attorneys, and accountants all rolled into one. It is expected that professional help will be needed and the Agent and/or the Executor are free to engage professionals and pay for them from the Principal's funds or from the estate.

The Executor's job will have an end. The estate will close. It may take a year, two years, sometimes even more depending on the issues presented by the estate. If there is a trust under the will, the Executor will turn over assets to the Trustee to begin the administration of the trust.

A Trustee may serve for years. The Trustee's primary duties are care and management of the trust assets and making payouts from the trust in accordance with the directions given by the creator of the trust. Trusts are wonderfully flexible vehicles. Frequently, the creator of the trust gives a Trustee discretion to make trust distributions to the trust beneficiaries for certain purposes or in accordance with defined standards set forth in the document. The creator of the trust gives the best possible instructions and chooses a Trustee who will carry out those intentions for the beneficiaries. This is a matter requiring personal knowledge of the beneficiaries and their circumstances and personal knowledge of the wishes of the creator of the trust. Often a family member or trusted professional advisor is perfect for this role. However, the Trustee with the family relationship or family knowledge may not have the investment, accounting, and tax skills required for proper administration. A good solution to this is to have a professional Trustee serve as co-Trustee with the family member or other trusted personal advisor.

It is always important to provide for successor Trustees. If all else fails, the beneficiaries should be able to choose a successor. If there is a corporate fiduciary, a bank or trust company, I always recommend that someone — either an independent third party or the trust beneficiaries, be able to remove the corporate Trustee and replace it with another one.

Sometimes there is a revocable living trust that is funded during lifetime accompanied by a pour-over will. When that is the case, it almost always makes sense for the Executor of the will and the Trustee of the revocable trust to be identical. Although many or even most of the decedent's assets may be in the trust, it is the Executor who has the responsibility for reporting the value of the assets and coordinating the payment of debts and claims and, of course, paying death taxes. Often the Executor must use trust assets to meet these obligations. The job of the fiduciaries is much easier when one person wears both hats — Executor and Trustee.

Who's Going to Take Care of Fluffy When You're Gone?

How many kittens and puppies did Santa Claus bring? Aren't they cute? What wonderful gifts provide love and companionship for years? Pets snuggle and nuzzle a child through many a sadness and many a hurt. Pets are good therapy for older folks too. The same affection is even more beneficial for folks who are separated from family and find themselves outliving their friends. The trouble is, in the end, the pet often outlives its master. Many pet owners want to make sure their dear animal friends are taken care of and want to so provide in their wills.

Providing for the welfare of a pet in the owner's will is not the easiest thing to do. We tend to anthropomorphize our pets; that is, we tend to think of our pets as people, and we attribute human characteristics to them. The law, however, is not so kind. As far as the law is concerned, the dog or cat is property that can be left to someone, but nothing can be left to the dog or cat.

Realizing that we can't leave money to an animal, what's to be done to be sure our pet is taken care of? The answer is to bequeath the pet to someone we trust and who has agreed to care for the animal and, also, to make a bequest of money to that person. While we cannot make a trust and make the obligation legally binding, we can express our hope and wish that the person will use the money to support the pet.

Other ways have been tried. In California, in 1968, a woman wrote her will on two sides of a three by five card. On one side, she left gold and diamonds to a niece; on the other side, she left everything else to a friend and Roxy Russell. She then signed her name. The part that was not clear from reading the will was that Roxy Russell was her pet dog. We surmise that the decedent's intent was that the friend use part of the inheritance to care for the dog after she died. The niece argued that California law lists eligible beneficiaries under a will and that dogs are not on that list. Therefore, the niece argued, half of the bequest, the half that was earmarked for Roxy Russell, was void and should pass to her as the intestate heir. The friend claimed that the entire bequest to him and the dog was really a bequest to him and that he was to use some of the assets to care for the dog.

The trial court agreed with the friend, but the State Supreme Court (yes, it went that far) disagreed, saying that nothing in the will indicated that the bequest was anything other than a gift to be divided equally between two parties, the friend and Roxy Russell, the dog. One party, Roxy, was ineligible to receive; therefore, Roxy's half fell to the residue and to the niece according to intestacy laws.

Had the woman given the bequest to the friend and included precatory language expressing her wish that the bequest be used in part to care for her dog, that would have been upheld. Precatory language is language that expresses a hope or wish but is not intended to be legally binding or impose any trust.

In a 1950 Ohio case, a gentleman created a testamentary trust for the care of his dog, naming as trustee a friend who had volunteered to care for the dog. The trust was funded with $1,000 and was to be disbursed at the rate of 75 cents per day for the care of the dog. The problem with a trust for benefit of a dog is that in order for a trust to be honored, there must be a trustee and a beneficiary, and the beneficiary must be able to hold the trustee accountable in carrying out the terms of the trust. A dog, regardless of how intelligent and talented, cannot sue in court. Therefore, an enforceable trust was not created. The law does recognize something called an honorary trust. Courts have held that if the trustee is willing and ready to carry out the purpose of a trust with no human beneficiary, he will be allowed to do so. But, if the so-called honorary trustee retains the property for his own benefit or neglects the purpose of the trust, the bequest fails and reverts to the decedent's other beneficiaries or heirs.

The Ohio Court of Appeals upheld the Probate Court which stated that an honorary trust existed and would be honored as long as the decedent's friend honored the purpose of the trust.

The best that one can do in providing for a pet after death is to give the pet to a trusted friend in the will, and make a pecuniary bequest to the same friend, and impose a moral obligation (but not legally binding) by requesting, or expressing the hope and wish that the money be spent for the care of the pet. An honorary trust may be set up, but if one relative finds the pet ignored in any way, the assets can be sent to the residuary beneficiaries by a judge in a heartbeat.

Here is another approach. Sidney Altman of Beverly Hills left a six million dollar estate, complete with $350,000 for the upkeep of his 15-year-old dog. His girlfriend was to have the use of the house and an income of $60,000 a year during the *dog's* life. She thought she would be taken care of for life, but didn't reckon on that being a dog's life (Los Angeles Times, September 28, 1998).

The Final Word: Who's Responsible For Estate Plans?

When there is a problem with a decedent's estate plan, who is responsible? There are many aspects to a plan — the documents themselves (including wills and trusts), the titling of assets, the wording of beneficiary designations, and the nature and amount of transfers made during life. There are many opportunities for error.

Often beneficiaries are disappointed. Some beneficiaries are shocked at the amount of taxes due. Some beneficiaries feel unfairly treated. Sometimes the way assets are titled makes the will and trust irrelevant. As is human nature, these beneficiaries want to know who is at fault, and who will make good on their injuries. Often, the answer is that no one is liable.

I have met with many clients who do not wish to spend the time, money, or energy making an estate plan to reduce estate taxes. That is their choice. Surely, the beneficiaries of the estate who have to pay more estate tax than might have been necessary do not have a cause of action against me because the estate plan does not provide tax savings that were possible.

But what if I didn't present the tax saving option to the client? What if it wasn't the client's choice, but simply the fact that the client wasn't informed of the alternatives available? Do the beneficiaries have a cause of action against me?

What if the client wanted to make bequests to five individuals and I left one of the names out of the will? Does the omitted person have a cause of action against me?

What if I prepared a plan for a married couple which required that the title to joint property be severed in order to obtain tax savings? They died without severing the title, and the tax savings was lost. Am I responsible?

Is the accountant who reviewed the estate plan and prepared income tax returns for the couple responsible? Is the financial planner who recommended the estate plan to the couple and sold them investments responsible? Is the trust company who holds the couple's assets and is named as executor and trustee in the couple's wills responsible?

Difficult questions, every one.

Until 1983 Pennsylvania was a "strict privity" state. An attorney-client relationship between the plaintiff and the lawyer was absolutely required before a suit could be brought for malpractice to claim an action in negligence for professional malpractice. For an error made by a lawyer in a will, this meant that *no one* could hold the lawyer accountable because the client was dead!

This ridiculous state of affairs was partially corrected in 1983 in the Pennsylvania Supreme Court case of *Guy v. Leiderbach*. Pennsylvania law still does not permit a negligence action, but some recourse is available to a beneficiary named in the will. Under the case of *Guy v. Leiderbach*, a named legatee of a will may bring suit as an intended third party beneficiary of the contract between the attorney and the testator for the drafting of a will which specifically names the legatee as a recipient of all or part of the estate. For that class of beneficiary, some relief is afforded. Others are still left without a remedy.

The problem is compounded by the fact that just about every lawyer thinks he can write a will. I wouldn't dream of taking on a criminal defense matter, a divorce, or a personal injury action. Yet for some reason, many of those lawyers write wills. Perhaps the fact that Pennsylvania was a strict privity state for so long gave lawyers a false sense of security. After all, if after your client died, no one could sue you for malpractice, what risk did you run? You could make all sorts of errors and not be accountable.

Another aspect to consider is that with the client dead, the best evidence of his intentions is dead with him. The client can't say what he asked for, what the lawyer recommended, what the client decided and why. How can we judge whether or not the client's intentions were carried out?

In most cases attorneys do not change title to assets, except for real estate which must be done by deed. For the most part, attorneys do not change beneficiary designations. Clients usually view these actions as things that they can do for themselves and that they do not have to pay attorney hourly rates to have accomplished. Perhaps so, if they do them, and if they are done correctly.

How many times have I recommended a beneficiary designation or account titling, only to hear from the client that an employee of an insurance company or a clerk advised them to do it a different way!

Who is responsible? Everyone and no one. Make sure you have good counsel and follow through with instructions.

LONG-TERM CARE

Planning For Home Care and Assisted Living

> *Our society must make it right and possible for old people not to fear the young or be deserted by them, for the test of a civilization is the way that it cares for its helpless members.*

Pearl S. Buck

A large segment of the population needs help, but not in a nursing home setting. Many folks do not need skilled nursing care, but need some help with errands, housekeeping, transportation, dressing and grooming, cooking, medication schedules, and things like that. These kinds of services are not covered by private medical insurance or Medicare. There may be some help available through Medicaid, but only after spending down all assets. This kind of help, which can be very expensive, must be paid for privately, or with long-term care insurance.

Most people want to "age in place," as AARP calls it. That is, they want to stay in their homes. (I do. Don't you?) Plus, more and more older people are choosing to stay in their homes after they lose physical skills as a result of an illness or accident. Relatives and friends often help out so people who wish to do so can remain in their homes. But often, more help is needed. Home care is available to help the person stay at home, rather than having to move the person into an institution. How do you pay for it?

To qualify for Medicare home health coverage, you must meet all four of the following conditions: (1) your doctor must say that you need medical care in your home, and your doctor must prepare a plan for your care at home, (2) the care you need must include intermittent (not full-time) skilled nursing care, or physical therapy or speech and language pathology services, (3) you must be homebound, and (4) the home health agency providing services to you must be approved by Medicare. If Medicare provides coverage, it covers visits, not shifts, and only those visits stated under the treatment plan.

Medicare does not cover 24-hour care at home, meals delivered to the home, homemaker services such as shopping, cleaning, and laundry (except that home health aides may do a small number of these chores when they are providing covered services), and personal care provided by home health aides, such as bathing, toileting, or providing help in getting dressed, if this is the only care you need. This latter type of care is called "custodial" care. Medicare does not pay for custodial care unless you are also getting skilled care such as nursing or therapy and the custodial care is related to the treatment of your illness or injury. Medigap policies do not pay for custodial care either.

Thus, these "custodial" services must be paid for privately, from income and savings, or by long-term care insurance. Since most care is outside of the skilled nursing center, much of the benefit used by long-term care policy holders covers such non-Medicare reimbursed expenses as aide care (shopping, cooking, cleaning), assisted living settings, and respite care.

When your savings are exhausted, then you are eligible for Medicaid. Medicaid is a federal program whose benefits and requirements vary from state to state depending on what options and limits the state's legislature has adopted. Each state's Medicaid program *must* pay for nursing home care for eligible persons age 21 and older. Medicaid is also required to pay for home health services for individuals who would qualify for nursing facility coverage, but cannot be placed in a nursing home. State Medicaid programs have the *option* of covering other long-term care services that can include personal care and home and community-based services under a "waiver" of federal Medicaid rules.

The Medicaid Act allows states to request waivers of certain federal laws in order to provide services to persons at home or in the community. Through these waiver programs, states can provide services that may not otherwise be available to recipients such as home modification, personal care, adult day care, and respite care. Some of these waiver programs have a limited number of slots, and many states do not provide programs for all the services you may need. All states, except Arizona, have at least one program. Pennsylvania has a number of waiver programs, including Attendant Care Waiver, Independence Waiver, Aging Waiver, to name a few.

For more information call the Long-Term Care Helpline toll-free at 1-866-286-3636 or visit *www.longtermcare.state.pa.us.*

Even if your state provides a waiver program for your home needs, none of these Medicaid services are available until you spend down your assets. This is even more of a reason to buy long-term care insurance. A good long-term care policy should cover the cost of (1) help in your home with daily activities like bathing and dressing, (2) community programs, such as adult day care, and (3) assisted living services that are provided in a special residential setting other than your own home. These services can include meals, health monitoring, and help with daily activities. Finally, it should cover care in a nursing home.

While you still have choices, it is important to evaluate the alternatives and make informed decisions about planning for the care of yourself and your loved ones.

What Is Medicaid and How Does It Work?

Medicaid is a program funded jointly by the federal government and the states, designed to aid those truly unable to pay for medical care. Not everyone is eligible to participate in the Medicaid program, as applicants and recipients of Medicaid must meet strict income and resource guidelines, among other criteria. Based upon an individual's eligibility category, covered services may include physician and clinic visits, inpatient hospital care, home health care, medical supplies and equipment, inpatient and outpatient psychiatric and drug and alcohol services, prescription drugs, dental, and other medically necessary services.

Medicaid also covers nursing facility care and other forms of long-term care. Long-term care is destined to become a hot button issue, as a greater percentage of the population grows older. The average cost of nursing home care in Pennsylvania for a semiprivate room is $248.00 per day, which is about $90,520 per year.

Many people assume Medicare, another federal program, which is available to persons who are 65 years of age and older and certain disabled persons, will cover the cost of living out their final years in a nursing home. Not so. Basically Medicare is the health insurance component of Social Security. Medicare Part A covers hospital care and a limited amount of "skilled" nursing care and home health care. Optional Medicare Part B covers part of physicians' costs and other medical services and supplies.

Medicare is the most cost-effective health insurance a senior citizen can buy. However, Medicare has certain deductibles, limited payment periods, and restrictions on the types of services covered. Two of the most severe restrictions are that it only covers nursing home care if it is "skilled" care rather than "custodial," and it covers only 100 days of nursing home care per spell of illness.

Because of the limited coverage of Medicare, even with Medigap insurance, the only alternative for many persons facing extensive health care needs either at home or in an institution is the Medicaid program.

Eligibility for Medicaid is determined by The Office of Income Maintenance's local county assistance offices and is based on the income you receive and the assets you own, including life insurance and retirement plans.

Qualification limits vary from state to state. In general, there are two tests for eligibility: an income test and an asset test. In Pennsylvania, you can have any amount of income and still qualify for benefits. You must spend your available income on your care, however, before qualifying for benefits for the balance of the cost of care.

Under the assets limitation test, almost all of an individual's assets must be used to pay for care before Medical Assistance (Medicaid) will pay any nursing home charges. In Pennsylvania, assets must be below $2,400 before Medical Assistance starts to pay. In addition to the just mentioned $2,400, a few specific items, defined as "exempt assets," are excluded from consideration. In Pennsylvania, these exempt assets include a primary residence, household goods and other personal items up to a total (equity) value of $2,400, one reasonably priced car, the value of a prepaid funeral which is either in a separate bank account or prepaid to a funeral director, and life insurance with a cash value under $1,500.

All your assets, (even those held jointly with your spouse or by your spouse alone, if you are married) will be considered in the eligibility determination process. Even assets that carry a penalty (for example, loss of interest, such as early liquidation of a CD, or payment of tax, such as withdrawal of an IRA) will be included as "asset."

The income and resources of married couples are treated differently than those for single persons so that the spouse who remains living at home (the "community spouse") will not be impoverished. The spouse who is or will be receiving skilled nursing care is referred to as the "institutionalized spouse." For married couples, the community spouse can keep all of his or her income, regardless of the amount.

According to current Medicaid law, the community spouse is allowed up to $2,898 in monthly income and one-half of the couple's available resources (excluding exempt assets) up to a maximum of $115,920.

While it is tempting to transfer your assets or make gifts to qualify for Medicaid, *beware*! When you apply for Medicaid, the local agency will analyze all financial transactions made by you and/or your spouse during a specified "look-back" period. The look-back period is 36 months for outright transfers and 60 months for transfers to certain trusts. Thus, if either you, or if you are married, your spouse, transfers assets for less than fair market value within the applicable look-back period, a penalty period, during which you will be ineligible to receive Medicaid benefits, will be imposed upon such transfers.

Medicaid Planning: The Debate

To date, the government has made no commitment to pay for everyone's health care. The current law and policy is that medical care is paid for by the recipient of the care. Medical care is a personal expense just like housing, clothing, food, and so forth. There is no entitlement to free medical care.

Medicaid is a program jointly funded by the federal and state governments to provide medical assistance to those "medically needy," further defined as low income persons who are aged, blind, or disabled. Our taxes support the Medicaid program to provide medical benefits on a needs-tested basis. That is, those who cannot afford medical care will be cared for. Those persons with the means to pay are expected to pay for their own care.

In part because there is no other publicly funded program covering long-term care, Medicaid has become a vehicle for the middle class to pay for nursing home care. "Medicaid Planning" means that a person gives away assets so that he can qualify for Medicaid, usually to cover the expensive long-term care costs. Other planning strategies include acquiring exempt assets and paying off debts. Advocates of Medicaid planning call it "preserving assets accumulated over a lifetime from dangers presented by the need for custodial care."

It is not as if a person can give everything away one day and qualify for Medicaid the next. Almost any gift or transfer of assets (money or property) by a Medical Assistance applicant or spouse will make the applicant ineligible for Medical Assistance for a period of time. This is known as the "period of ineligibility." The actual length of the ineligibility period will depend on the amount of the transfer.

In Pennsylvania, the ineligibility period is determined by dividing the value of the gift by the average monthly cost of nursing home care set by Pennsylvania. The ineligibility period will begin with the month of the first transfer of assets.

The state can look back only 36 months to see if any gifts or transfers were made by the Medical Assistance recipient or his or her spouse. (The look-back and ineligibility period is 60 months for transfers to trusts.) If no gifts or transfers were made within those 36 months, then there is no ineligibility period. The look-back and ineligibility periods apply only to gifts made by a Medicaid recipient or his or her spouse. Both spouses can still spend money on personal purchases and routine living expenses, such as clothes, debts, home repairs, or vacations, without worrying about triggering any penalty for transfers.

A spirited debate, however, rages over the ethics and morals of asset divestiture to qualify for Medicaid. Opponents call it "giving away your assets to avoid paying your own medical bills and imposing the burden on the taxpayers."

Others say that Medicaid planning is just like tax planning. They say that arranging your affairs to qualify for medical assistance is the same sort of thing as arranging your affairs to pay less tax through financial and estate planning. We must grant that either way, through reduced taxes or qualifying for Medicaid, there is a reduction of the public fisc.

Is there a qualitative difference between tax planning and Medicaid planning? Many people say there is. It is well established in our national consciousness that there is no need to pay more than your fair share of taxes. Revered justices of the Supreme Court have weighed in on the issue saying "Any one may so arrange his affairs that his taxes shall be as low as possible; he is not bound to choose the pattern which will best pay the Treasury; there is not even a patriotic duty to increase one's taxes." Learned Hand, *Helvering v. Gregory*, 69 F2d 809,810 (2nd Cir. 1934).

Paying less tax does reduce the governmental money available to fund all government programs and expenditures. Making asset transfers, in order to meet the tests needs to qualify for Medicaid, means that the individual is drawing from the public fisc. The public fisc is funded by other taxpayers, and thereby leaves less money available for other government programs and expenditures.

Medicaid is not the only option to pay for long-term care. Many have chosen to buy insurance as a way of covering their costs for medical care and long-term care. Insurance is a way of spreading the risk, or cost of the medical care. Unfortunately, most people do not think of insurance as something that they purchase — many folks have come to believe that medical insurance is somehow given or provided for us. Most insurance is provided through employment and the payment of the premiums by the employer is part of the employee's compensation. Even Medicare is insurance and is paid for with premiums paid from Social Security benefits.

Medicaid, however, is not an insurance program at all — it is a direct payment of personal medical expenses by the government. Is withdrawing funds from the public coffers the same as minimizing what you pay in taxes?

Filial Support Laws: Am I My Mother's Keeper?

> *A frail old man went to live with his son, daughter-in-law, and young grandson. The old man's hands trembled, and he often spilled his food. He dropped a good piece of china, breaking it. Exasperated, the son and daughter-in-law made wooden bowls and spoons for the old man and told him to eat in the kitchen while the rest of the family*

> *ate in the dining room. One day, the little boy was playing with wood scraps on the floor. 'What are you making'? his parents asked. The boy answered proudly, 'I am making wooden bowls and spoons for you, so that when you are old you can eat in the kitchen just like grandpa'. The words so struck the parents that they were speechless. That evening the husband took Grandfather's hand and gently led him back to the family table. For the remainder of his days Grandfather ate every meal with the family and no one seemed to care any longer when a fork was dropped or the tablecloth got soiled.*
>
> A parable

Filial responsibility is the personal obligation or duty that adult children have for protecting, caring for, and supporting their aging parents. Filial responsibility is recognized as a moral duty in most cultures and religions. Is it a legal duty? The duty of parental support is created by statute. Under ancient common law, an adult child had no duty or obligation to contribute to the support of his parents. In England, a statute changed this in the 17th century. The Elizabethan Act of 1601 for the Relief of the Poor, provided that "[T]he father and grandfather, and the mother and grandmother, and the children of every poor, old, blind, lame and incompetent person, or other poor person not able to work, being of a sufficient ability, shall, at their own charges, relieve and maintain every such poor person." These Elizabethan poor laws became the model for the United States legislation on the same subject.

In Pennsylvania, the first law imposing a duty of filial support is found in the Act of March 9, 1771, which required that children support their indigent parents if the children were of sufficient financial ability. This was obviously designed to relieve state and local authorities from the burden of supporting poor persons who had relatives of financial means who could care for them. The current formulation of the law has been on the books since 1937.

An example of its enforcement is the 1994 Pennsylvania Superior Court case, *Savoy v. Savoy* which involved an elderly parent whose reasonable care and maintenance expenses exceeded her monthly Social Security income. The Superior Court found that she was indigent and affirmed the lower court's order directing her son to pay $125 per month directly to her medical care providers.

In July 2005, the Pennsylvania legislature passed an Act which, among other things, moved the filial support provision in the Pennsylvania statutes to a central position in its Domestic Relations Code. The law reads: "all of the following individuals have the responsibility to care for and maintain or financially assist an indigent person: (i) the spouse of the indigent person, (ii) the child of the indigent person, (iii) the parent of the indigent person."

Historically, these filial responsibility laws have rarely been enforced. Some states that have these statutes on the books have never enforced them at all.

Why so little enforcement? One of the main reasons is that the government has taken over this traditionally familial responsibility. Since the 1960's, federal law (U.S. Code Title 42 §1396a(a)(17)(D)) has barred states from considering the financial responsibility of any individual (except a spouse) in determining the eligibility of an applicant or recipient of Medicaid or other poverty programs. In other words, even if family members have a legal duty to support a loved one, the federal government places the burden on taxpayers. In the words of Matthew Pakula, "The moral duty receded as society evolved, family life changed, and government created a variety of federal and state programs to meet the needs of the poor."

As the pending financial crisis of how to pay for the care of the nation's elderly looms, the issue of family responsibility is coming to the fore. Medicaid is the major funding source for long-term care. If a person consumes his financial assets and his income is low enough, he qualifies for Medicaid coverage. Medicaid paid $60 billion for long-term care in 2002. An increasing number of persons are transferring their assets in order to qualify for Medicaid. Their children receive their assets, and the taxpayers pay the bill for their care. Medicaid has become an inheritance protection plan. Enforcement of filial responsibility statutes could bring a stop to this.

Here is an idea that has been put forward: Allow states to consider an adult child able to pay toward care of an indigent parent unless the child files a public notice that they are not responsible for the debts of the parent, foreswears any inheritance rights and consents to the revocation of any trust set up for their benefit by the parent.

But maybe the carrot works better than the stick. Look at what South Korea has done: since 1999, children who live with and support their parents get more inheritance. A person who has supported his or her parent for a considerable time will get 50% more added to his or her share of inheritance. This is called the "filial piety inheritance system."

Honor thy father and mother. The Talmud teaches that 'honor' means the son must supply his father with food and drink, provide him with clothes and footwear, and assist his coming in and going out of the house.

Long-Term Care Insurance: An Alternative to Relying on Medicaid

When faced with long-term care, or planning for its possibility, many people, for many reasons, wish to avoid relying on Medicaid. Medicaid Planning, although a subject for ethical debate, typically consists of divesting one's assets to qualify for Medicaid coverage for nursing home care.

From a personal, rather than financial, perspective, Medicaid Planning may not bring the desired results. Transferring assets to a child may reduce the grandchildren's eligibility for college financial aid. Assets may also be lost due to the child's divorce, bankruptcy, or loss of a lawsuit. And, in the case of a married couple, while the community spouse may keep a certain level of assets and may keep the family house, liens are attached to the house to reimburse expenses paid by Medicaid on behalf of the institutionalized spouse.

In addition, Medicaid-participating nursing homes are not necessarily those in which the client will feel comfortable. For example, Medicaid patients don't get a private room. Medicaid beds are also sometimes in short supply, forcing a patient to move to a nursing home away from family and friends. In other words, is the patient willing to accept less than optimal living conditions in order to pass more along to his or her heirs?

For some people, simply being on Medicaid is undesirable. To qualify, an individual's assets must be reduced to the level where financial independence is extremely difficult. Consider the situation of a formerly independent woman who, after spending down her assets during nursing home rehabilitation following a hip replacement, must move in with her son and daughter-in-law.

The nursing home is no longer a place where the elderly go to wait until death. According to the National Health Care Associates, in 1997, more than 40% of nursing home patients stayed in the nursing home less than one year. This is primarily due to the use of nursing homes by hospitals for patients who need intensive or complex rehabilitation that can be completed at the nursing home rather than in the more expensive hospital setting.

According to the Health Care Financing Administration only one in four Americans can afford private nursing home care for one year. In addition, an AARP study states that only 15% of Americans, age 45 and older, are familiar with the cost of nursing home care and over half believe the costs are lower than they actually are.

Medicaid is not the only option to pay for long-term care. Many have chosen to buy insurance as a way of covering their costs for medical care and long-term care. Good long-term care insurance policies may cover all or most of nursing home care, assisted- living facility care, adult day care or home care. Some policies cover certain expenses to renovate an individual's home to make it possible for him or her to defer or avoid institutionalized care. Long-term care insurance also gives the individual options in choosing the facility and surroundings.

However, long-term care insurance can be costly. Premiums are based, in part, on the age of the applicant, so the insurance is most affordable when purchased at an early age. Health history is also important and certain medical conditions may increase the premiums or disqualify the applicant.

The average total cost, paid for 20 years through age 85, for a long-term care insurance policy purchased at age 65 was $20,000. If purchased at an earlier age, monthly costs are dramatically reduced, to the point of reducing the total lifetime costs. Employers are beginning to offer group long-term care insurance to employees, reducing the costs further while encouraging people to "sign up" at a younger age. Long-term care cost is also dependent on how long you want it to be in effect.

Compare the policies available from many insurance companies and then choose your policy wisely. Some things to look for are financial health of the insurance company, inflation protection, and coverage including assisted living care and home care in addition to nursing care. Information on how to shop for long-term care insurance can be found at the American Association of Retired Persons, *www.aarp.com*, and the American Health Care Association *www.ahca.org/info/what.htm*

While expensive, the cost of the premiums needs to be weighed against statistics that one-quarter of the U.S. population over the age of 85 lives in an institution (U.S. Census Bureau, 1995) and two out of five Americans will need long-term care at some point in their lives. (Health Care Financing Administration, 1996.) The expected lifetime cost of nursing home care, on average, for a man is $56,895 and for a woman is $124,370 (American Health Care Association).

Other avenues are available to manage long-term care expenses. One, self-funding, is an option that can be considered only by the wealthy. Care given by or paid for by family members, is preferred by some, although it may place a burden on the family. Reverse mortgages, using the equity in your home to provide an additional source of income, are used by some to pay nursing home costs while leaving the rest of their estates intact.

Interestingly, according to Lancaster attorney David Morrison, Japan requires people over age 40 to pay into a compulsory long-term care plan. The German version of Medicaid requires a ten-year look-back period for gifting, compared to our three-year period. In addition, Germans with incomes over a certain amount are required to pay for some, or all, of their parent's long-term care expenses.

ESTATE PLANNING FOR THE FAMILY BUSINESS

New PA Inheritance Exemption for Small Businesses

Pennsylvania's 2013-14 budget passed the legislature and was signed into law by the Governor on July 9, 2013. Tucked away in Section 34 on page 143 of the 165 page Act 52 is a new inheritance tax exemption for qualified family-owned businesses,

It states: "A transfer of a qualified family-owned business interest to one or more transferees is exempt from inheritance tax, if the qualified family-owned business interest . . . .continues to be owned by a qualified transferee for a minimum of seven years after the decedent's date of death."

The exemption will be available for decedent's dying after July 9, 2013.

Qualified Family-Owned Business Interest

A "qualified family-owned business interest" is an ownership interest in either: (1) a proprietorship that has been in existence for five years prior to the date of death, has fewer than fifty full-time equivalent employees as of the date of death, and has a net book value of assets of less than $5,000,000 as of the date of death; or (2) an interest in an entity carrying on a trade or business that has been in existence for five years prior to the date of death, has fewer than fifty full-time equivalent employees as of the date of death, has a net book value of assets of less than $5,000,000 as of the date of death, and, in either case, is wholly owned by the decedent or by the decedent and members of the decedent's family that meet the definition of a qualified transferee.

To qualify, the entity must be engaged in a trade or business the principal purpose of which is not the management of investments or income-producing assets owned by the entity. For example, if you put your stock portfolio in an LLC or partnership and call it a business - it's not really a business and doesn't qualify for this exemption.

Qualified Transferee

A "qualified transferee" is a decedent's husband or wife, lineal descendants, siblings and the sibling's lineal descendants, and ancestors and the ancestor's siblings.

"Lineal descendants" are all children of the natural parents and their descendants, whether or not they have been adopted by others, adopted descendants and their descendants and step-descendants.

"Sibling" is an individual who has at least one parent in common with the decedent, whether by blood or by adoption.

Additional requirements for the exemption include a requirement that the qualified family-owned business interest continue to be owned by a qualified transferee for a minimum of seven years after the decedent's date of death. Otherwise the and interest thereon from the date of death will be assessed. Also, the exemption will not be allowed for any property transferred by the decedent into the qualified family-owned business within one year of the date of death, unless the property was transferred for a legitimate business purpose.

Losing the Exemption

A qualified family-owned business interest that was exempted from inheritance tax will lose the exemption if it is no longer owned by a qualified transferee at any time within seven years after the decedent's date of death. In that event, the inheritance tax plus interest is due. Each year for seven years, owners of a qualified family-owned business interest exempted from inheritance tax are required to file a certification that the qualified family-owned business interest continues to be owned by a qualified transferee. A form is to be prepared by the Department of Revenue for this purpose. Owners must notify the Department within thirty days of any transaction or occurrence causing the qualified family-owned business interest to fail to qualify for the exemption. A failure to comply with the certification or notification requirements results in the loss of the exemption.

Legislative History

Last year, the legislature added a new exemption from the inheritance tax for farms that pass to family members, provided the property continues to be devoted to agriculture for a period of seven years. This year's new exemption for a business provision is very similar to the farm exemption. Also last year, there was a new inheritance tax exemption added for the transfer of an agricultural commodity, agricultural conservation easement, agricultural reserve, agricultural use property or a forest reserve to lineal descendants or siblings.

The persons who pushed for the new exemption for family-owned businesses claim that the Pennsylvania inheritance tax inflicts an especially disruptive and destructive burden on family-owned businesses. They say the transfer of productive business assets at death often results in the sudden need to liquidate essential business resources (or sometimes the entire business) to raise the cash necessary to pay the tax bill, all at a time when the business and its employees are most vulnerable, in the aftermath of the death of a principal owner.

I beg to differ. In 35 years of practice I have never seen a business or a farm required to be sold to pay the PA inheritance tax. Why are business owners and farmers singled out for special treatment?

Division of the Estate Among the Children

Experience shows that the biggest liquidity problem is not paying estate and inheritance taxes — it is equalizing the inheritance among the family members. Businesses are very difficult, if not impossible, to divide equitably. Many business owners ignore this problem. They leave behind them a legacy of hard feelings and bitterness.

Therefore, for the sake of family harmony and for the sake of the continuation of the business, a plan to equalize your inheritance among your heirs is vitally important. How important? If you are like most small business owners, almost all of your net worth is tied up in the business. The business gives you the best return on your investment so you are not interested in pulling cash out to sock away in a bank account or mutual fund.

Let=s say a business owner has three children. One of them is involved in the business and interested in continuing it. The business owner dies. Decedent=s daughter has been in the business for several years, works like crazy to keep the business going and is very successful. She wants to keep the business. The problem is, she has two brothers who aren't interested in the business. What do they get? There aren't any other assets that amount to anything. Shall each child receive a one-third ownership interest in the business? That leaves the daughter with all the responsibility for operating the ,business, but as a minority shareholder without control: responsibility without authority — not a wise management arrangement.

From the sons' point of view, what good is the one-third interest in a closely-held business? Closely-held businesses rarely pay dividends. The sons aren't doing any work in the business so they can't receive a salary. (Not to mention the daughter would be livid if her brothers got paid for doing nothing while she was working like crazy.) The sons cannot sell their interests. Even if sales were permitted, there is no market for a minority interest in a closely-held business. How can the sons receive an inheritance in this situation?

This is the really hard question, not how to pay estate tax. The business owner, in his or her estate plan, must recognize the realities of these concerns and discover the methods that work in his or her situation to provide equity to, and harmony among, his or her heirs.

Perhaps there are some business assets that can be separated. For example, the business real estate could be separated from the operating part of the business. The real estate could be given to the sons. It could generate rental income from the business, and could even be sold if that is what the sons decided to do.

Another option would be to give the ownership of the business in equal shares to the three children, but subject to a buy out agreement between the daughter and the two sons. The daughter could buyout her brothers over time out of the business cash flow. She would have the choice of borrowing money from a commercial source to end her obligation to her brothers or to remain obligated on a promissory note to them.

Appropriate arrangements would have to be made for control. As long as payments are current, it is usually appropriate to let the child who is in the business control the business without interference.

Another planning approach would be for the business owner to accumulate assets outside of the business to provide a source of funds to give an inheritance to the sons. This can be done by various investments including, but not limited to, the purchase of life insurance. An insurance death benefit can help equalize the inheritance for the sons.

Who Gets the Business? What Doest the Will Say?

Many business owners make no special provisions in their wills for the business. They have so-called "simple" wills that create a complicated mess when the business owner dies.

What if Number One Son has been running the carpentry business while Dad is ill? Dad dies and his will says that his estate goes to the four kids in equal shares. Does Number One Son only get one-fourth of the business? Yes. Is that what Dad intended? Probably not.

What if Dad's will says, "I leave my carpentry business to my son"? Dad has always operated as a sole proprietor. Does the "business" include the real estate on which the shop is located? Does it include the two trucks that were titled in Dad's name? Does it include the business checking account which has a $25,000 balance? This kind of situation creates a host of problems. Extremely careful drafting must be used to accomplish Dad's intentions and give the executor clear directions.

Many businesses are incorporated and, because of the favorable income tax treatment, are S-corporations. There are strict limitations on how long an estate can be a shareholder of an S-corporation. If the business interest is to be held in trust, the trusts must be specially drafted in order to qualify as shareholders, otherwise the corporation will lose its S election. These problems can be solved with appropriate planning and drafting. How are the beneficiaries of the trust to get any benefit? Must the corporation pay dividends?

For an executor, being responsible for an estate which owns a business can be very burdensome. The executor is responsible for safeguarding and preserving the value of the business. Often this means stepping in and taking an active role in management. Many persons are chosen as executors because of their family relationship to the deceased and are ill-equipped to handle these types of business and financial matters.

An executor also has substantial personal risk. Estate and inheritance taxes are imposed on the date of death value of the decedent's assets. At the moment of death, the value of the decedent's business might be $1 million. If the executor continues the business and cannot, or chooses not to, sell the business and the business runs into severe financial trouble, the business may be worth very little nine months from the date of death when taxes are due. The amount of the tax remains the same as the date of death amount (although some relief may be afforded by the six-month alternate valuation date) and the executor is personally liable for the amount of the tax even if the estate's assets have declined radically in value. (This is why most prudent executors want to liquidate or distribute assets as soon as possible — they do not want to take investment risk which can become their personal risk.) Business interests require special handling by executors and trustees.

A business is not well suited to being a trust investment. The law of trust investments directs a trustee to invest in "prudent" investments. Investing in a family business is much less prudent than investing in publicly traded large capitalization securities. Any small business venture has a high risk. Trustees are also required to diversify to eliminate unreasonable risk. A large concentration in the trust portfolio consisting of a closely held business is not good diversification. Further, trustees may not delegate their management responsibilities. When a trustee owns a controlling interest in the stock of a company, it has a duty, absent provisions in the governing instrument to the contrary, to exercise management responsibility over the business by placing one or more representatives on the board of directors. A trustee who owns a controlling interest in a business may find himself or herself caught between conflicting fiduciary duties to trust beneficiaries and the minority owners of the business. It may be in the best interest of the trust beneficiaries to sell the business, but this may hurt the minority shareholders.

Many professional fiduciaries will refuse to serve as executor and trustee when the estate includes a business, unless the documents are drafted to take care of all the problems and liabilities that might arise. Care must be taken in drafting to make sure that an executor or trustee has sufficient authority and power to deal with a business interest, but is also protected from the many liabilities that may arise. This requires more than boilerplate. If you are a business owner, make sure you get professional advice on planning your estate.

Keeping Continuity in Your Family's Business

What are the plans for continuing a family business after the death of the owner?

The answer to this question has many variables, only a few of which relate to tax and estate concerns. A family business is often dependent on the personal charm, talents, hard work, and intelligence of one person. Preserving the value of the family business after the death of such a person can be extremely difficult.

Aside from the issues of the owner's personal presence, any business's value is dependent on its continuing ability to generate income. If the business owner does not have a plan for the business to continue uninterrupted after his or her death, the beneficiaries will be lucky to end up with anything at all.

There are three possible solutions: (1) Transfer the business to family members, (2) Sell the business to co-owners, and (3) Sell the business to employees or outsiders.

Transferring the business to family members. If the owner wants to transfer the business to family members, are the family members interested? Do they have the proper training and education? Do they get along with each other? Do they want to run the business? Stories of dissension in families over these issues are legend. Many business owners want the business to stay in the family, but can't or won't turn over any responsibility to a child (even a 50-year-old man is still a child to his father). Some children view the family business as a monster that stole all their parents' time and want nothing to do with it.

What about the family members who are not involved in the business? How do they share in the inheritance? The children who are working in the business will get a salary and other perks, like company cars, benefits, retirement plans, vacations, etc. These family members will oppose paying dividends to family members who are not in the business. They will prefer to keep cash in the business (or in their own pockets) since they view themselves as the ones earning the money. Family members who are part owners of the business but don't work in it will feel that they have a worthless equity interest if they get no return on it. These family members will expect a return on their capital by way of dividends commensurate with the risk they are taking by leaving their capital in the business.

These problems are extremely difficult to resolve. Many estate planners recommend never giving a family member a minority interest in the family business if the family member is not going to be involved in the business. You can expect that some family members will want to remain active in the business and some will want to sell it. Some family members will want to derive income from the business and others will wish to reinvest the income to make the business grow.

The best gift the business owner can give his family is to make sure that a practical and effective plan is in place to handle these problems. Otherwise, the only inheritance provided for the family may be bitter dissension and no value from the business at all.

Selling the business to co-owners. If there are nonfamily co-owners, they may be interested in purchasing the deceased owner's interest. For a sale to co-owners, the biggest problem is agreeing on a method to value the deceased owner's interest in the company. What is the purchase price that will be paid to the estate? It is best to have an agreed-upon formula for valuing the company. The surviving owners may have a vastly different view of the value of the decedent's interest than the heirs of the deceased co-owner. The value of the business must be re-evaluated, at least annually, for the agreed upon valuation or valuation method to be effective. Busy owners often neglect this important part of their business. The press of daily operations and the natural reluctance to contemplate death often causes these considerations to be put permanently on the back burner. Business owners who would never neglect a customer frequently neglect to protect their families by maintaining an appropriate buy-sell agreement.

The source of funds for the buyout is the next problem for co-owners. Seldom does a business or business co-owner or employee have sufficient cash to buy out the deceased co-owner in a lump sum. Frequently life insurance on the deceased co-owner is used to fund this buyout obligation. Sometimes bank loans are the source of the payments. In other situations, installment payments are made over a period of years to the deceased co-owner's heirs or estate.

What if the co-owners decided to open a competing business instead of buying the decedent's share of the existing business? In a personal service business or a business dependent on a special process of confidential customer lists, this may be all too easy and leave the heirs with no value from the business at all. It is important for there to be agreements not to compete or use confidential information.

Selling the business to employees or outsiders. If family members and co-owners aren't able or willing to purchase the business, the only method left for the continuation of the business, is to become "under new management" and to sell the business, either to employees or to outsiders.

If the plan is to sell the business to outsiders when the owner dies, is there interim management? Someone has to be willing and able to step in to run the business while a buyer is found and a sale negotiated. This interim manager needs to be able to preserve and maximize the value of the business and prevent loss of employees and customers. This is a tough job to fill and will require substantial incentives because by definition it is a short-term job and requires exceptional skill and commitment. What plan is in place to retain customers and employees if the owner dies? All will be immediately concerned about the future stability and even existence of the business. How will they be retained? These concerns are not as significant when the buyers are employees of the business, as these buyers know the business and will work to maintain the business's value to protect their own interests.

Selling a business is not like selling shares in IBM. And selling the business without the key person is even more difficult. If the owner really thinks this is the best way to realize value for the family, the owner is much better off selling the business before he or she is called to his reward. This means facing up to exiting the business and selling — a big hurdle for some owners.

Whatever the chosen strategy, to preserve the value of the business for your beneficiaries; careful planning is absolutely necessary. Take the time to do it — it's the best gift you can give to your loved ones.

Continuing a Business if Family Doesn't Want it

To plan for the business to continue uninterrupted after his or her death, the business owner needs to choose among three possible scenarios: (1) Transfer the business to family members, (2) Sell the business to co-owners, and (3) Sell the business to employees or outsiders.

If the family isn't interested in being in the business, the owner should make plans for selling the business to co-owners, if any, or to employees or other outsiders. When family members don't wish to continue the business, the only way to realize the value of the business is for them to sell.

If there are nonfamily co-owners, they may be interested in purchasing the owner's interest following his or her death. Co-owners often prefer buying out a deceased owner, not wanting to be in business with the spouse or children of the deceased co-owner. For a sale to co-owners, the biggest problem is agreeing on a method to value each owner's interest in the company. What is the purchase price that will be paid to the deceased co-owner's estate? The surviving owners may have a vastly different view of the value of the decedent's interest than the heirs of the deceased co-owner. The method of valuation should be set in a buy-sell agreement with which all the owners enter. The buy-sell agreement is negotiated and signed as part of each owner's estate plan, hopefully long before death occurs. Maintaining the valuation part of the agreement is essential. The value of the business must be determined, at least annually, for the buy-sell agreement to be effective. Busy owners often neglect this important part of their business. Business owners who wouldn't neglect a customer frequently neglect to protect their families by maintaining an appropriate buy-sell agreement.

To give just one example of the inequity that can result, let's say two partners agree to buy each other out for $500,000. One partner dies. The surviving partner wants to sell the business. The estate of the deceased partner receives $500,000 pursuant to the buy-sell agreement. The next day the surviving partner sells the business for $2,000,000. Because the buy-sell agreement was not properly maintained, the heirs of the deceased partner don't get one-half of the real value of the business. They get the $500,000 buy-sell price instead of $1,000,000, which is half of the sales price of the company.

Reducing the Estate Taxes on a Closely Held Business

How much insurance is sold with the scare that the estate tax is due nine months from the date of death and you might have to sell the business in order to raise the cash?

True, the due date for the tax is nine months from the date of death. But what if you can't pay? First, if there are insufficient liquid funds to pay the tax when due, under Section 6161 of the Internal Revenue Code, the estate can apply for an extension of time to pay. The law authorizes an extension up to ten years. In practice, the extension is given only a year at a time. During the extension period, the executor is expected to be taking steps to raise the money by borrowing, liquidating assets, etc. In addition, whatever liquid funds are available should be applied to the tax. This is an obvious safety valve for the illiquid estate that is often overlooked. The unpaid tax accrues interest until it is paid, but if the extension is granted, there is no penalty. The availability of the extension is a godsend not only for closely held businesses, but also for estates with many real estate assets.

Even better is the tax relief, provided by Section 6166 of the Internal Revenue Code. If the estate qualifies, the estate is entitled to defer the estate taxes attributable to a closely held business for a period of four years, and then pay the tax in installments over a 10-year period. The closely held business must comprise at least 35% of the gross estate. Interest is payable on the unpaid tax, but the interest on tax on the first $1 million is just 2%. Some tax planners recommend that estates use this provision even if they have enough cash to pay the taxes just to get the benefit of the 2% money. Where else can you get a loan for 2% interest? This provision is not an extension granted at the discretion of the IRS. If the taxpaying estate qualifies, it is entitled to the relief as a matter of right. The IRS does have the discretion to require the posting of a bond or security which may make the technique more difficult to employ, but this has not been required in my limited experience.

Hand-in-hand with Section 6166, some estates use Section 303, which provides for favorable income tax treatment on the redemption of stock. In short, a corporation's redemption of stock from the estate is given capital gains treatment instead of dividend treatment. Since the shares received a step up in income tax basis because of the death, if the redemption price is at the date of death value, there is no gain and no loss. This is an excellent way to get cash or other property out of the corporation without paying income tax. Corporate tax lawyers are always trying to do this — and here is a perfect way. There is no tracing requirement, that is, the cash or property distributed by the corporation in the redemption transaction does not have to be used to pay taxes or expenses. The maximum amount of redemptions eligible for this very favorable treatment, are the amount of the estate taxes attributable to the stock plus expenses of administration of the estate.

Using the 14-year deferment and installments election of Section 6166 coupled with a program of serial redemptions under Section 303, it may be possible for the estate to pay the estate taxes attributable to the business out of the corporation's own cash flow. Before you buy more insurance to pay estate taxes, make sure you consider this option.

There are many ways to plan for the reduction of estate tax on a closely held business and many ways to plan for the liquidity to pay taxes.

How to Handle Buy-Sell Agreements Properly

If you are a partner or a shareholder in a closely held business, what happens to your interest in the business when you die? It depends.

For our purposes here, whether the form of organization of your business entity is a partnership, corporation, limited liability company, or limited liability partnership, we will refer to the co-owners as your partners.

Chances are, when you are dead, your partners don't want your spouse or your kids to be their new partners. Often, this issue is addressed in a written agreement among the co-owners of the business. Many of these agreements provide that on the death of an owner, the business entity or the other partners must purchase the deceased owner's interest from his or her estate. This is a very common approach that gives the beneficiaries of the deceased partner the right to realize the value of the business interest and for the remaining partner or partners to retain control of the business. It is usually impossible to sell an interest in a closely held business to anyone except the other owners, so unless the decedent's estate can sell to the surviving owners, there may be no market for the business interest.

The big question is: What is the purchase price? Some buy-sell agreements set a flat price. This is often inequitable because as time passes and the fortunes of the business wax and wane, the value of the owner's equity fluctuates as well.

Some buy-sell agreements provide that the partners should set a buyout price every year. While this is good in theory, the vast majority of partners neglect to do this. Then a partner dies and no price has been set for 15 years. In effect, this may mean that no price is set.

Some agreements provide a formula. Reference is made to the business's balance sheet and/or income statement, and a formula that includes numbers from these financial statements is used to derive the buyout price for the deceased partner's interest. Still other agreements provide that the value of the business or the deceased partner's interest in it will be determined by an appraiser. Sometimes the surviving partners choose an appraiser, the decedent's estate chooses an appraiser, and those two choose a third appraiser. The purchase price to be paid is then the average of all three appraisals.

What if there is no buy-sell agreement? If the decedent held a minority interest, 50% or less of the control of the business entity, then the decedent's beneficiaries may not be able to realize the value of the decedent's interest in the business. If the parties want, there could be a negotiation between the surviving owners of the business and the executor of the decedent's estate. But, if there is no buy-sell agreement, the surviving owners are not compelled to purchase the decedent's interest. This can be a nasty shock to the decedent's family, who finds they hold a minority interest in a closely held business that can't be sold and that isn't producing any income for them.

It is of crucial importance that anyone who has partners in a business has a buy-sell agreement. It is of the utmost importance that the buy-sell price is fair, appropriate, and updated as necessary.

It is not enough to just have the agreement. The next issue is a plan for the surviving owners to have the money available to meet the purchase price. Often business partners buy life insurance on each other to provide the cash necessary to meet the obligations of a buy-sell agreement. When partners own these policies on each other, the type of agreement is called a cross-purchase agreement, and the obligation to purchase the deceased partner's interest in the business is on the surviving partner or partners. Sometimes the insurance is held by the business entity itself, and the business entity has the obligation to buy or redeem the deceased partner's interest. This is called a redemption agreement. There are pros and cons to both types of agreements, and you should always seek the advice of qualified professionals when entering into one of these agreements.

When there is no insurance or when the insurance death benefit is less than the buy-sell price, the balance is often met with an installment obligation or note. The decedent's estate is paid in installments over a period of years instead of receiving a direct lump sum. Whether or not these installment obligations can be met often depends on the future viability and success of the business which is another risk that must be taken into account.

Some companies, instead of investing in insurance, establish a fund in which they accumulate cash and investments in order to have funds available in the case of a death and the resulting trigger of the buyout.

Business owners work hard and often have the biggest part of their assets tied up in the business. They need to make sure that their family can realize the value they have worked so hard to build.

ESTATE PLANNING FOR THE FAMILY FARM

Getting Started

Estate planning for the family farm should lay a framework for a smooth transition of both farm ownership and farm management. It should provide for all family members, even those who leave the farm. Good planning will reduce death taxes on land that is very valuable because of urbanization.

Making a will is not doing estate planning for your family farm. Every farmer or farm couple needs: (1) a retirement plan, (2) a plan for transfer of management, (3) a plan for transfer of ownership, which includes an up-to-date will, as well as business agreements, and (4) a contingency plan in case of disability.

Families who find themselves land rich but cash poor can be hurt if they fail to take steps to minimize the burden of estate tax. Planning will address liquidity — the farm is not a liquid asset. The tax laws are complex, and they keep changing. Planning for the farm may include trusts, partnerships, and lifetime gifts.

Any estate plan for the family farm must start with an examination of your goals and objectives. There are many questions to answer. Do you want to be in complete control of the whole farming operation as long as possible? Do you want to develop a successor? Do you want to maximize the sale value of the farm? Do you want to keep the farm in the family? Do you want to develop a retirement nest egg? Who will take over if you are disabled? What if one of the children wants to keep working the farm and the other children want to cash out?

Many farmers see the farm as part of the family heritage and identity — they want more than anything to keep the farm intact and in the family. Other farmers view the farm as an extremely valuable asset, the sale of which will take care of the children and grandchildren for their lifetimes.

For those who want to keep the farm in the family, one of the toughest problems is how to be equitable to both children on the farm and off the farm. An equitable division of your property doesn't necessarily mean giving equal shares of the farm to all of the children.

The children who are involved in working the farm have generally contributed a substantial amount of their time, energy, and resources to make the business succeed. These children may have substantial "sweat equity" in the farm they inherit. What has been given to children during lifetime will no doubt influence the decision about what should be given them at death.

The key to maintaining family good will is that no family member be surprised. Estate planning has many emotional implications and can often result in family disagreements and feelings of unfair treatment. Each family member should understand the plan and know where they fit in so they can make their own long-term plans. If John has stayed on the farm and is working for a low salary, he needs to be reassured that his efforts are going to be rewarded and he'll be able to continue farming after Mom and Dad die. If the farm is going equally to John and his four siblings, none of whom are even living in the state, he may realize that he will be forced into selling, and he won't have the wherewithal to buy.

An estate plan for the farm should transfer ownership and management of the farmland and the farm business, minimize federal and state death taxes, plan for retirement needs, and develop the next generation's management skills. Balancing the business goals of the farm and investment considerations can be difficult. All too often a farm worth more than $5 million generates only enough income to barely support a family, if that. How to have the farm support retirement and the next generation of farmers?

What about when you're gone? Must the land remain in farming? Is selling to the highest bidder acceptable? Can or will your spouse continue to run the farm? Who will decide what happens to the farm?

One of the very first steps to take in doing any planning is to provide for the minimization of estate and inheritance taxes. Many farms are jointly held between husband and wife. This means that only one $5 million exemption for the federal estate tax will be utilized, the one belonging to the surviving spouse. Dividing the title of the farm into tenants in common, with the wife owning one-half and the husband the other half plus the creation of a by-pass trust plan will double the federal exemption for this family.

Beginning a program of lifetime gifts can be important for building equity in children staying on the farm and reducing transfer taxes. Putting the farm into an entity, such as a trust or partnership, can facilitate these types of gifts and can generate valuation discounts. The transfer of a fractional interest in a farm is worth something less than the pro-rata fair market value of the farm because there is no market for these fractional interests. Using the $14,000 annual exclusion for all the descendants every year can very significantly whittle down the value subject to estate tax.

The cows will always need milking. The livestock will always need to be fed. The equipment will always need to be fixed. Planning ahead can always be put off until tomorrow. Tomorrow never comes. Before it is too late, give your family the gift of a workable and fair estate plan.

Your Options

A farm is a unique asset. For most farm families, the farm is the largest single investment of the family. It also represents a lifestyle and a way of life.

Owners of closely held businesses have similar situations — often the family business is the biggest, most valuable asset, and family life centers around the family business. It's the same with a farm, which is, after all, also a family business.

Farm life often gets painted as a romantic lifestyle. The farm landscape, the animals, the growing crops, the children running in the field — you get the picture. It used to be that anyone who could buy and hold any real estate had a great investment. There was no zoning, land was cheap. The land was viewed as a necessary part of the business — the source of income was the operation of the farm. Some had the vision (or perhaps luck) to buy any land they could and hold it.

Today, farmland is not the sure bet as an investment that it once was. There are more restrictions on land use than you can shake a stick at — from local zoning ordinances and urban growth boundaries, to federal regulations. And making a reasonable income from actual farming operations has become a dubious proposition.

There are those whose life-long dream is to have a successful, viable, family farm — buying the farm, the equipment, working around the clock, living spartanly, and getting by. These folks will probably never be out of debt without selling the farm. This is not the place for a debate on the public policy of farmland preservation. Suffice it to say that there are competing views and that there is some tension between farmers who view the farm as their retirement plan and family investment and those who want to maintain the rural landscape with open space and the quality of life enjoyed by the country residents.

To effectively plan an estate, you, the farm owner, have to be able to clearly identify your goals so that the right tools can be used to achieve your ends. Let's look at just two example situations of the many situations that present themselves.

For Farm Family One the farm is their biggest asset, by far. The Farmer wants to retire and looks at the farm as his retirement plan (especially since he hasn't had enough income from farming to make any other sort of retirement plan). This client might look at a sale of all or part of the farm, or at the generation of cash from the sale of a conservation easement, or at a combination of these approaches. The farmer then has the sale proceeds, cash for investment and the full panoply of estate planning alternatives available to any client with investments. When, and how to sell, is an important issue. Tremendous value can be lost due to local zoning decisions and government actions. This is something that is hard for the non-farmer to imagine. Can you imagine what it would be like to own an apartment building and to have the local government decide that it could not be used for residential purposes anymore? What does that do to the value of your building? It plummets. There is no compensation for this loss in value. So it is with the farm. The permitted use of the land is the most important factor in determining its value.

Farm Family Two has a farm that has been in the family for three generations and is the source of the family's identity and heritage. The Farmer's goal is to farm until he dies and to keep the farm in the family and the family on the farm. This client will look at ways to reduce and avoid estate tax, pay any estate tax due in installments, transfer equity to the next generation without paying transfer tax, and make a plan for the management of the farm and its continuation into the next generation and beyond. The techniques to address this situation are different and include things like special use valuation and installment payments.

Note that for Farm Family One, the best result is achieved with the highest possible fair market value for the farm. For Farm Family Two, the best result is achieved with the lowest possible fair market value for the farm. Both families need to plan for the incapacity and care of the older generation. Both families need to plan for the control and management of the process — whether it is liquidation or continued farm operation.

There are numerous variations and permutations on these themes. Sometimes what the older generation wants is not what the younger generation wants (a novel idea). There may be disagreement among the members of the younger generation. Not all family members may be equally capable of making decisions and assessing options. The first step is identifying the goal for the estate plan. The next step is consulting a qualified professional about the best way of achieving it.

Repeal of the PA Inheritance Tax on Family Farms

A new law ended the Pennsylvania inheritance tax on family farms as part of the 2012-13 state budget package. Governor Corbett signed the Act on July 2, 2012. The repeal of the inheritance tax on certain farms is effective for the estates of decedents dying after June 30, 2012.

Under previous Pennsylvania law, children who inherit farmland from their parents must pay a 4.5% inheritance tax. If the farmland is left to a sibling, the inheritor must pay a 12% inheritance tax in Pennsylvania. There already is a relief provision for farms - the special use valuation which allows a favorable value below fair market value for farms.

The new law provides that a transfer of real estate devoted to the business of agriculture between members of the same family will not be subject to the PA inheritance tax provided that 1) after the transfer the real estate continues to be devoted to the business of agriculture for a period of seven years beyond the transferor's death and 2) the real estate derives a yearly gross income of at least $2,000.

Also, the new law provides that a transfer of an agricultural commodity, agricultural conservation easement, agricultural reserve, agricultural use property or a forest reserve, as those terms are defined, to lineal descendants or siblings is exempt from inheritance tax.

For purposes of the law, a "member of the same family" can be the decedent's brothers, sisters, the brothers and sisters of the deceased's parents and grandparents, the ancestors and lineal descendants of any of the foregoing, or a spouse of any of the foregoing.

The "business of agriculture" is a defined term in the statute including leasing to members of the same family or leasing to a corporation or association owned by members of the same family. The business of agriculture does not include 1) recreational activities like hunting, fishing camping, show competition and racing, 2) the raising or breeding of game animals or game birds, fish, cats, dogs or pets intended for use in sporting or recreational activities (I assume that includes horses), 3) fur farming, 4) stockyard and slaughterhouse operations; or 5) manufacturing. Any farm that is no longer devoted to the business of agriculture within seven years beyond the transferor's date of death shall be subject to inheritance tax due the Commonwealth under section 2107, in the amount that would have been paid or payable on the basis of valuation authorized under section 2121 for nonexempt transfers of property, plus interest since the transferor's date of death.

Every owner of real estate that gets the benefit of this inheritance tax exemption must certify to the Department of Revenue annually that the land continues to qualify for the exemption. The owners must notify the department within 30 days of any transaction or occurrence causing the real estate to fail to qualify for the exemption.

Governor Corbett's press release said: "The death tax has forced too many families to sell their legacy, their land and their way of life. This tax has put too many farms out of business because it was too expensive for farmers to pass them down to their children. This will happen no more. We intend to save our farms." Giving special exemptions to one class of asset always raises the question of disparate treatment of owners of other classes of assets. For example, family businesses are frequently in the same position as family farms when it comes to inheritance tax? Is that fair? Here's an idea. Repeal the Pennsylvania inheritance tax all together.

A reader asked me to clarify a statement in last week's column about tax preparers. I said, "Persons who are certified public accountants (CPAs), attorneys or enrolled agents are required to register but are not required to take the exam or continuing education." They are not required to take the IRS mandated education and exam, but as part of their certifications or licensing as attorney, CPA or enrolled agent, they are subject to continuing education requirements.

New Realty Transfer Tax Exemption for Farms

On July 2, 2012 Governor Tom Corbett signed House Bill 761, Act 85, into law. This is the same new law that excludes family farms from Pennsylvania inheritance tax when the transfer is to family members and the property is kept in farming for seven years. But that's not all the good news for farmers in this law. Section 9 of the bill broadened the exemption from realty transfer tax for a family farm so that no realty transfer tax need be paid for the transfer of the family farm to additional types of legal entities.

Pennsylvania realty transfer tax is imposed at a rate of 1% on the value of real estate transferred by deed, instrument, long-term lease or other writing. The municipality and school district usually charge 1% between them for a total of 2%. Realty transfer tax in Lancaster County totals 2%.

Pennsylvania realty transfer tax is collected, often along with an additional local realty transfer tax, by the county Recorder of Deeds. The Recorder of Deeds remits the Commonwealth's 1% to the Department of Revenue, and the locals have the option to share their realty transfer tax among school districts and municipalities.

Some real estate transfers are exempt from realty transfer tax, including certain transfers among family members, to governmental units, between religious organizations, to shareholders or partners and to or from nonprofit industrial development agencies. Deeds to burial sites, certain transfers of ownership in real estate companies and certain farms and property passed by testate or intestate succession are also exempt from the tax.

The realty transfer tax of 2% has been a stumbling block for lots of estate planning techniques. In general, transfers of real estate to family members have been exempted from the realty transfer tax.

There was also an exemption for a transfer of a "family farm business" to a "family farm corporation" or to a general partnership. The exceptions were narrow and precluded a lot of planning techniques. What has not been exempt, however, is the transfer of farm real estate to many types of entities, even when the entity is wholly owned by family members. Many estate planning techniques that are desirable to reduce PA inheritance tax and federal estate tax, as well as providing for multiple family member ownership, require transferring interests in farm real estate to an entity such as a family limited partnership, LLC (limited liability company) or corporation. Many folks chose not to proceed with planning that otherwise made good sense because they didn't want to pay the transfer tax.

The new law, in section 9, first deleted the definition of a "family farm corporation," replacing it with a definition of a "family farm business." Now a transfer to a family farm business is exempt from the realty transfer tax. As defined, a "family farm business" is a corporation or association of which at least 75% of its assets are devoted to the business of agriculture and at least 75% of each class of stock of the corporation or the interests in the association is continuously owned by members of the same family. The business of agriculture shall include the leasing to members of the same family or the leasing to a corporation or association owned by members of the same family of property which is directly and principally used for agricultural purposes. The business of agriculture shall not be deemed to include:

(1) recreational activities such as, but not limited to, hunting, fishing, camping, skiing, show competition or racing;
(2) the raising, breeding or training of game animals or game birds, fish, cats, dogs or pets or animals intended for use in sporting or recreational activities;
(3) fur farming;
(4) stockyard and slaughterhouse operations; or
(5) manufacturing or processing operations of any kind.

The exemption applies to a transfer of real estate devoted to the business of agriculture to a family farm business by:

(1) a member of the same family which directly owns at least 75% of each class of the stock thereof or the interests in that family farm business;
(2) a family farm business, which family directly owns at least 75% of each class of stock thereof or the interests in that family farm business; or
(3) a transfer between members of the same family of an ownership interest in a real estate company or family farm business that owns real estate.

While the previous tax-free transfer transactions included only transfers to corporations and general partnerships, now any kind of entity, including limited partnerships and LLCs, can receive farm property free of transfer tax.

Family limited partnerships are a good entity to hold a family farm. Mom and Dad can put the farm in a family limited partnership without paying transfer tax and then transfer limited interests in the partnership to their children in portions low enough to minimize gift tax. Although the family farm can be exempted from Pennsylvania inheritance tax if the conditions of the exemptions are met, there is still the federal estate tax. Its exemption falls to $1 million as of January 1, 2013.

Special Use Valuation

Special Use Valuation is an election available to the executor of an estate to reduce the value of certain real estate included in the estate of a decedent. Property that qualifies for this approach are family farms and other real estate used in a family trade or business.

When property is included in the decedent's estate, it is included at its fair market value for its "highest and best use." Let's say the decedent used a gold bar as a door stop. Its value for estate tax purposes is as investment grade gold bouillon, not its value as a doorstop. Apply the concept to a farm. The farm as farmland is worth $250,000. As a location for Big Box Store, it is worth $1 million. What is the value to be included in the decedent's estate and subject to tax? $250,000 or $1 million? "The highest and best use" (an unfortunate legal term that means the use that brings the highest purchase price) is the Big Box Store site value of $1 million.

For the family of the decedent who wants to continue farming, paying the estate tax on a value of $1 million is a crippling debt that could ruin them. There is a relief provision for this situation in the tax code, called Special Use Valuation. The use value of the real estate, $250,000 in our example, is used for estate tax purposes if certain conditions are met, including the continuation of family farming, or business operation, for ten years. HERE??

The Special Use Value may be arrived at in a variety of ways. Here are some examples: the capitalization of expected income from farming, or from other closely held business; the capitalization of the fair rental value of the land for farming or business use; the assessed land value in a state that provides a differential or use value assessment law for farmland or closely held business; or comparable sales of other farm or closely held business property in the same geographical area, but far enough removed so that the development pressure for a nonagricultural use is not a significant factor.

The valuation most often used is the "farm method." This special use clause equals the average annual gross rental for comparable land, minus the average annual state and local real estate taxes on such land divided by the average annual effective interest rate for all new federal land bank loans.

In order to elect a Special Use Valuation, the property must meet seven qualifications. (1) The property must be in the United States. (2) The property must have been used by a member of the family in a trade or business. (3) The decedent must have been a citizen and resident of the U.S. (4) The property must be inherited by a qualified heir. (A qualified heir is a member of the decedent's family, including a spouse, parent, brother, sister, stepchild, and spouse or lineal descendant of these individuals, who acquires the property from the decedent.) (5) The adjusted value of the farm or business property (both *real* and *personal*) must be a minimum of 50% of the estate's adjusted gross value. (6) At least 25% of the adjusted gross estate must be qualified *real* property. (Qualified property can include residential buildings, related improvements, road and other structures functionally related to the qualified use.) (7) For at least five years out of the eight-year period ending with the decedent's retirement (attaining the age of 65), disability, or death, the decedent, *or a member of the decedent's family*, must have materially participated in the operation of the farm or business. (Material participation may include physical work, or participation in management decisions. The decedent, or a member of the decedent's family, must have been employed full time. Merely receiving a salary, or being listed as a partner, is not enough to qualify as material participation.)

The reduction in value by electing "special use" valuation over "highest and best use" appraisal cannot exceed $870,000 (for 2005). This limitation of reduction of value is allowed for each individual. With proper estate planning, a husband and wife could double the reduction in value to $1,680,000.

The election to use Special Use Valuation is made after death by the executor on the estate tax return. It must be made on the first return filed (even if late), but it can't be elected on an amended return. In addition to checking the box on the estate tax return, the return must be accompanied by a written agreement, signed by each person with an interest in the property.

The agreement is required because, if the real estate is sold within ten years of the death of the decedent, there is a recapture of the estate tax saved by making the election. If the qualified heir sells the property to Big Box Store within ten years, the estate tax that would have been due if the farm were valued at its highest value on the date of death must be paid. The policy here is that if the heir sells out at the highest value, there is no need for protection of the farm from the impact of estate tax. The relief provisions are only available if the qualified use continues. You can't have it both ways.

The agreement signed by all parties who hold an interest in the property is to ensure that all those persons are personally liable for this estate tax. The agreement also must designate an agent to act on behalf of all of the owners in dealings with the IRS.

In addition to a sale of the real estate to an unqualified heir, recapture tax is triggered if the real estate is no longer used as a farm or in a closely-held business within ten years of the decedent's date of death, or if the qualified heir ceases to materially participate for more than three years in any eight-year period following the date of death of the decedent.

Estate planning can be done to ensure qualification for the Special Use Valuation. To meet the 50% and 25% of adjusted gross estate value requirement (discussed in qualifiers (5) and (6) above), non-qualifying assets can be gifted during lifetime, so that the remaining qualifying farm or business property meets the percentage tests. Another way to meet the percentage tests is to purchase additional qualifying assets, perhaps in conjunction with the sale of non-qualifying assets. Advance planning can also make sure that the "material participation" requirement is met (discussed in qualifier (7) above) — not only before death, but also before retirement.

Conservation Easements

An easement is a restriction or burden on your land for the benefit of someone else. For example, you can grant an easement over your property to give a neighbor the right of access to their property by driving over yours. You still own your property, but the neighbor, by agreement, owns a right to pass over your land. This burden, or easement, "runs" with the land. That is, even if you sell your land or the neighbor sells his land, the easement that benefits his land and burdens your land remains in place for the new owners. Other examples of easements are the rights of way that utilities and municipalities obtain over private property for pipelines, electric power lines, and roads.

Conservation easements are legal agreements that restrict the type and amount of development that may take place on a particular parcel of land. Most easements are permanent. A landowner may donate an easement or may sell an easement. The name "conservation easement" is misleading. The owner is not required in any way to implement environmental conservation measures, pollution reduction, or anything else we usually associate with conservation of natural resources. The public receives no right to enter the agricultural property. You aren't creating a "nature preserve." Development rights are being affected. The landowner retains title and can farm, use the land as collateral for a loan, or sell the property. Conservation easements do not provide protection from eminent domain. If land under easement is taken, both the landowner and the holder of the easement must be compensated.

Landowners can sell or donate a conservation easement. In either case, it is important to determine the value of the easement. The value is the difference between the value of the land without the easement minus the value of the land with the easement, as determined by a qualified appraiser.

One of the factors to consider is that the sale of a conservation easement will generate a gain or loss for income tax purposes, just like the sale of any other asset. The basis of land is generally its cost, or if inherited, its date of death value. When the land contains improvements, often much of the basis is allocated to improvements and depreciated. Many times the income tax basis of farm land will be quite low, meaning that most of the sale proceeds for the easement will be subject to capital gains tax. A like kind exchange is a way of deferring the capital gain. The IRS has ruled that a conservation easement on a farm is "like kind" with ownership of other real estate used in a trade or business or for investment.

The sale of an easement can be attractive to those farmers who need cash for expanding farm operations, equipment purchase, or just retirement.

Gifts of conservation easements can provide a charitable income tax deduction. In general, the annual income deduction permitted is 30% of adjusted gross income. There is a five year carry-forward for unused deduction. This will be useful to some taxpayers, but to put it bluntly, you have to have income to use the deduction.

The gift of a conservation easement also qualifies for a charitable deduction on the estate tax return. Additional estate tax relief is available for the donation of a Qualified Conservation Easement (QCE). As much as 40% of the date of death value of the land may be subtracted from your federal gross estate, up to a maximum of $500,000 (in 2005). There used to be a geographic restriction on land that could use this benefit, but the Economic Growth and Tax Relief Reconciliation Act of 2001 eliminated this location restriction and now *all* lands in the United States are eligible for this tax relief.

Easements must be sold to or donated to qualifying organizations, either government entities or private land trusts authorized under state law to accept the easements and enforce their terms.

Accepting donated conservation easements is one of the major activities of private land trusts. Land trusts exist in all 50 states.

These trusts monitor and enforce the terms of the easements. Some also purchase conservation easements, or offer a "bargain sale," which is a part purchase, part gift. Their funding comes from the federal government under the Farmland Protection Program, state and local governments, membership dues, and private contributions, including corporate foundations and endowments. Whether or not an easement on your particular farm is attractive depends on the uniqueness of the property, its historical significance, or development pressure from surrounding areas — whether the restriction is acceptable to the potential receiving organization and if so what it is worth in dollars. Like any other real estate transaction, this is a sales negotiation.

For more information about a sale or donation to a private land trust, contact The Lancaster Farmland Trust, 128 East Marion Street, Lancaster, PA 17602, (717) 293-0707, *www.savelancasterfarms.org*. The local government entity involved in farmland preservation and the acquisition of development rights is The Lancaster County Agricultural Preserve Board. They can be reached at 50 N. Duke St., P.O. Box 83480, Lancaster, Pa. 17608-3480, (717) 299-8355, *www.co.lancaster.pa.us./lanco/cwp/view*.

Passing Down the Farm

> *Lottery agent to farmer: "What would you do if you won $1 million in the lottery?"*
>
> *Farmer to lottery agent: "I'd use the money to farm with and I'd keep farming until the money was gone."*
>
> Anonymous

The market value of a typical farm can be very high and yet the income generated may be very low, perhaps only a trickle. Cash difficulties are a common problem for farmers.

The death of the farm owner creates yet another cash problem. The problem is two-fold: (1) is there cash to pay any death taxes that are due, and (2) when the farm passes to the next generation, how can the heirs realize the value of the farm? The second problem is exacerbated when some heirs want to remain on the farm and others are off-farm and intending to stay that way.

As Donald Jonovic and Wayne Messick say in *Passing Down the Farm — The OTHER Farm Crisis* (Jamieson Press, 1996): "Farming, long valued as a way of life, is being forced by a changing world into a more economic focus. Today's financial realities have turned the farm into an investment, and new questions are arising. Is it a business? If so, how should it be managed? How will it survive, under whose direction and to whose benefit? There's an even more fundamental question: Can the *family* survive a serious investment in the family farm?"

We have looked at ways to reduce the value of the farm for estate taxes by using Special Use Valuation and by preserving the farm for agricultural use through the sale or donation of Conservation Easements. Now we will look at the farm as an investment — a very valuable, illiquid, unique asset that requires careful planning to preserve its value, minimize death taxes, and to ensure family harmony.

Solving the liquidity problem and reducing death taxes go hand in hand. There is no magic here — the standard estate planning techniques of making lifetime gifts, using all available exemptions and exclusions, using the marital deduction, creating valuation discounts, and using installment treatment for tax payments all apply.

If the farm owners are a married couple, the first step is to make sure that both spouses' \$1.5 million exclusions from the application of the federal estate tax are utilized. This is done by dividing the ownership of the farm between the two spouses — it should *not* be owned jointly. Each spouse signs an estate plan which creates a "bypass" trust for the benefit of the surviving spouse which uses the first spouse's exemption. Then, on the death of the survivor, the portion of the farm that is in the bypass trust is not subject to tax and the surviving spouse gets another exemption to apply to the remaining portion of the farm. This is basic estate planning for any married couple with assets greater than \$1.5 million — the family farm is no different.

For many farm families just doing that much will eliminate federal estate taxes. In 2004, the Federal exemption rose to \$1.5 million, meaning that \$3 million in value could pass free of federal estate tax. In 2006, with a \$2 million exemption, \$4 million can pass free of estate tax. As you can see, the problem of the federal estate tax for the family farm is fast disappearing. But proper estate planning and proper titling of the farm is absolutely essential if you need to double the value of the exemption.

With the estate tax problem solved, the focus moves to the second part of the problem: "When the farm passes to the next generation, how can the heirs realize the value of the farm?" As one of my favorite clients puts it, "How can we divide our estate without dividing our family?"

Let's say there are two children, who inherit equally. One child stays on the farm, does all the work, does all the worrying, and gets whatever income the farm produces. The other child lives across the country and gets nothing. Both of these children are unhappy — each one feels that he or she is being treated unfairly.

What about the family where one of the kids stayed and worked for Dad for 20 years, making much less than if employed elsewhere — only to find himself the owner of one-fifth of the farm with his other four off-farm siblings owning the other four-fifths — wanting him to buy their shares — which he feels he has already paid for with his sacrifices and underpaid labor.

What about the family where none of the heirs want to stay on the farm and are now co-owners of valuable real estate, each one with their own idea of how to maximize the value, each one with spouses to add to the mix, and each one with their own financial pressures, goals, and strategies. How can decisions be made? All of these situations need to be addressed. Equal treatment is not always fair treatment.

What needs to be done?

1. Decide how decisions are going to be made. Should there be a vote? Must there be unanimity? Can primary responsibility be given to one or two of the heirs?
2. Decide who gets what. Can the business of the farm be separated from the real estate and put under different ownership? Can the farm property be divided among heirs rather than passing it down in some form of joint ownership? Are there other assets that can be used to "equalize" distributions of real estate to some of the heirs?

3. Make an estate plan that provides financial security for Mom and Dad and the survivor of them, reduces death taxes, and plans for liquidity for the expenses of death.
4. Get competent professional help. Tax laws are very complex. Succession and governance issues are complicated. Family dynamics are difficult. None of these problems are new to professional advisors. All of these problems have solutions. Do it now. None of us knows how many days are in our allotted span.

The Family Farm Partnership

There are many factors to consider when determining how to transfer ownership of the farm: death taxes, gift tax, income tax issues, needs for retirement income, long-term care planning, management succession, and equity among children, to name a few. Don't forget the biggest one — the farmer's willingness to let go.

If, after careful consideration, it is part of your estate plan to begin transferring the farm to the next generation, how should you do it? Transferring the farm is a complex and serious business. If not done properly it can cause serious financial problems, as well as family relationship problems.

Farm partnerships have been used for many years — sometimes for family ownership and sometimes for two or more unrelated people who want to run a business together. A partnership can be a valuable transfer tool. Each partner holds partnership interest. These can be sold, given, or bequeathed in a will to others. For example, parents can gradually gift partnership interests to younger generation members using the $14,000 annual exclusion by transferring partnership interests to the kids. Gifts of partnership interests are especially attractive because the gift tax value of an interest in the partnership is worth less than a pro rata share of the underlying partnership asset. If you give a 1% interest in a $1 million farm to Junior, the 1% partnership interest represents a 1% share of the underlying $1 million asset, but for gift tax purposes, it is worth less than $10,000 because of the restrictions imposed on Junior's rights to sell or transfer the partnership interest, to liquidate it, or to borrow against it. This valuation discount allows much more to be transferred to the next generation by use of the partnership.

How do you form a partnership? Choose a name. Retain an attorney to prepare a partnership agreement that will fulfill your goals. The agreement should cover capital contribution: who does the work, makes the decisions; and what happens if a partner dies or withdraws. (Spencer's Rule #1 — Never enter into a partnership of any kind without a written partnership agreement.) Transfer assets to the partnership and you're in business.

A partnership pays no income taxes — the partnership "passes through" all items of income and deductions to the individual partners. The partnership does have to file a return, which is a Form 1065. The individual partners' shares of income and deductions are passed out to them on a K-1.

A *general* partner is liable for all the partnership debts and obligations. A *limited* partner is liable only to the extent of his or her investment in the partnership — a limited partner has no personal liability. Usually, when a family farm partnership is used to transfer portions of the ownership of the farm to the next generation, the next generation members are limited partners.

Farms have different sorts of assets. We usually think first of the actual farm land, but there are also growing and stored crops, livestock, machinery, and equipment. It may be desirable to transfer the machinery and equipment into one entity and the land into another. There are various ways to structure transfers to give the income benefits to some, and the equity benefits to others.

In Pennsylvania, there is a 2% realty transfer tax when real estate is transferred. There are exemptions for gifts to family members. A transfer of the farm to a family farm partnership may qualify for one of the exemptions of the realty transfer tax. The transfer of real estate devoted to agriculture to a family farm partnership by a member of the same family, if the family directly owns at least 75% of the interests in the partnership, is exempt from the application of the tax. Family members include brothers and sisters, the brothers and sisters of the transferor's parents and grandparents, and the ancestors and lineal descendants of all of these people and their respective spouses. In order to be devoted to agriculture, the farm could be leased to members of the family who use the property for farming.

A partnership provides an excellent management vehicle. Let's say you and your spouse have five children. If you want them all to share in the ownership of the farm, that makes seven owners, you, your spouse, and each of the five children. If you want to accelerate the transfer by using gift tax annual exclusions for gifts to the spouses of children, that's potentially 12 owners. Every time you want to do anything that involves the ownership of the farm, the signatures and consent of all owners, in this example, the consent and signature of all seven or 12 owners are required. Under the best of circumstances this is extremely unwieldy and under bad circumstances it is impossible. It makes sense for there to be one (or two, or three) person(s) in charge of managing the farm and handling the decisions. These people would be empowered to sell, lease, subdivide, mortgage, without getting consenting signatures from every single owner of a fraction of the farm. If you don't consolidate management and control in this way, the problem only gets worse. If one of the children who owns a one-seventh interest dies, his one-seventh may be divided up between his spouse and/or his own three children. To make matters worse, these children may be minors and unable to do anything at all with the property interest.

It really does not make sense to have ownership of anything, much less a farm, by a group of individuals. One solution is a trust, where the trustees can handle the property for the benefit of the beneficiaries. Another solution is a partnership where the general partners handle the property for the benefit of all of the partners. Other entities are also possibilities for part or all of the business. These are corporations, limited liability companies, and limited liability partnerships. All have their respective pros and cons — get good advice from estate planning counsel.

Yes, getting professional advice costs money. But remember, not getting advice can cost hundreds of thousands of dollars more. Making bad decisions, or making no decisions, can be very costly to you and to your family.

GIFTS

Gifts to Minors

One of the reasons people hold back in making $14,000 annual exclusion gifts is that they know it is a bad idea for minor children to have large amounts of money. Not only is there concern on prudential grounds that children should not have large amounts of money at their disposal without supervision, but there are significant practical difficulties as well. While property can be titled in the name of a minor, a minor cannot make binding contracts, cannot make changes in investments, and cannot utilize the assets during the period of minority.

Contrary to popular belief, a parent does not have legal authority to deal with a minor's property. The only way legal authority can be obtained is by the court appointment of a legal guardian. This is an expensive and cumbersome procedure; good planning will avoid it. Even if the route of seeking appointment of a legal guardian is taken, the age of majority in Pennsylvania is 18 and the child has full power over the assets upon attaining age 18.

An alternative is to make gifts to trusts for the benefit of minors. Where the gifts are of significant size this is often the best choice. But this route requires the services of a lawyer to draft the trust document and requires separate income tax reporting for the trust which is a separate entity. This is too expensive and too complex for most situations.

A very good solution to the problem is to register property that is given to a minor in the name of a custodian for the benefit of the minor under the Pennsylvania Uniform Transfers to Minors Act (PUTMA). It is sort of a trust created by statute that anyone can use.

To use the Pennsylvania Act, either the donor, the minor, the donor-named custodian, or the property must be in Pennsylvania at the time of the gift. The arrangement is created simply by titling the asset or account like this: "Jane Doe as Custodian under PUTMA for the benefit of John Jones." The custodian, who can be a parent or any other adult chosen by the person making the gift, manages the assets and controls the spending of the assets as he or she sees fit for the benefit of the minor. The law is very liberal as to what expenditures can be made so long as the expenditures are not made to fulfill the custodian's obligation to support his or her own children. Gifts can be made in cash, stocks, bonds, insurance policies, annuity contracts, tangible property, real property, virtually anything you can think of. The minor is entitled to distribution of the funds in most cases at age 21. Since many folks plan to use these funds for college, this is not a problem. Often the funds are used for college before the distribution age is reached.

The age 21 distribution for a PUTMA account compares very favorably with an account in the minor's name alone, over which he or she will have control at age 18. Distribution at age 21 as compared to age 18 may make the difference between the funds being spent on a Harley (or a Corvette) instead of college tuition.

The practical value of PUTMA is considerable. Parents can set up a stock or mutual fund account under PUTMA and then grandparents and uncles and aunts can make gifts to the account (or to the parent for deposit in the account). For tax purposes, the assets in a PUTMA account belong to the minor. Investing in low income growth investments is an attractive way to manage these funds.

Taxes would have to be paid on any income as it is earned if income exceeds the child's standard deduction plus another small sum. The income over this deduction amount of children under age 14 is taxed at the parent's rate. These days, the return on stock is heavily weighted on the side of growth; that is, the price per share increases, while cash dividends are low. The equity value compounds untaxed until the stock is sold. (Remember Albert Einstein's comment? Compound interest is a most amazing fact of math and science.)

PUTMA also provides a very useful tool for making bequests to minors. Grandmother can leave a bequest in her will to minor grandchildren, naming a custodian to hold the funds for them until age 21. This is a very efficient and economical way to carry out grandmother's intent. Wills should contain provisions authorizing the appointment of custodians whenever there is a possibility that a distribution could be made to a minor. If the will contains no authorizing language, a distribution up to $25,000 may be made to a custodian by the executor, but the executor cannot use PUTMA for larger amounts without seeking court approval, unless authorized in the will.

If insurance policies or retirement plans name minors as beneficiaries or contingent beneficiaries, the beneficiary designations should include the appointment of a custodian to receive the funds under PUTMA. Otherwise, a court-appointed guardian will be required to receive the funds on the minor's behalf.

Uniform Transfers to Minors Act Account

Contrary to popular belief, a parent does not have legal authority to deal with a minor's property. A minor is "legally incompetent," which means that a minor can't make enforceable contracts or otherwise engage in commercial activities on his or her own. The age of majority in most states is eighteen.

Minor children come by property in different ways. Some earn money working. Some receive gifts from grandparents and other family members. Some receive inheritances. Others are injured and have claims to make against others.

Money or property can be put in a minor's name. That is not a problem. The problem is that the minor then cannot do anything with it. Withdrawals can't be made. Investment changes can't be made. Money can't be used.

The only way legal authority can be obtained to use or manage the minor's assets is by the court appointment of a legal guardian. This is an expensive and cumbersome procedure. Good planning will avoid it. The court often appoints a parent — but not in every case. The court-appointed guardian must make frequent reports to the court, ask for permission to spend principal, and has limited authority to decide how the property should be managed. Even if the route of seeking appointment of a legal guardian is taken, the age of majority in Pennsylvania is eighteen (18), and the child has full power over the assets upon attaining that age.

Here is an alternative: The Uniform Transfers to Minors Act (UTMA) is a uniform act drafted and recommended by the National Conference of Commissioners on Uniform State Laws. Most states have adopted a version of the Act. Under this law a Custodian can hold property for a minor, invest it, and use it for the minor's benefit.

No court is involved. The person transferring money to the minor names the Custodian. The custodian's function is similar to a trustee for the minor. Under some states' statutes, the property can be held until the minor attains at least age twenty-one (three years longer than the age of majority).

Using UTMA is as simple as titling the asset appropriately. You don't have to go to a lawyer. There is no separate document. The asset is titled: "Jane Doe as Custodian under the Pennsylvania (name your state) UTMA for the benefit of John Jones." The Custodian then is the legal title holder and can deal with the asset. The law is very liberal as to what expenditures can be made so long as the expenditures are not made to fulfill the custodian's obligation to support his or her own children. The minor is entitled to distribution of the funds in most cases at age twenty-one (21).

The Uniform Act allows wills, trusts and beneficiary designations to include the deferral of the distribution age up to age 25. Check with counsel to see if your state adopted this provision. To specify an age later than the default age, you must change the wording of the custodianship language in the will, trust, or beneficiary designation form to: "Adult Smith as custodian for Minor Smith until age 25 under the (name your state) Uniform Transfers to Minors Act."

The delayed age (25) distribution date is not available for gifts. These transfers are still to be distributed at age 21. This is necessary in order for gifts to UTMA accounts for minors to qualify for the Internal Revenue Code's $14,000 annual exclusion for gifts of present interest.

The practical value of UTMA is considerable. Parents can set up a stock or mutual fund account under UTMA, and then grandparents and uncles and aunts can make gifts to the account (or to the parent for deposit in the account). For income tax purposes, the assets in a UTMA account belong to the minor.

UTMA also provides a very useful tool for making bequests to minors. Grandmother can leave a bequest in her will to minor grandchildren, naming a custodian to hold the funds for them until age 21. This is a very efficient and economical way to carry out grandmother's intent. Wills should contain provisions authorizing the appointment of custodians whenever there is a possibility that a distribution could be made to a minor. If the will contains no authorizing language, a distribution up to $14,000 may be made to a custodian by the executor, but the executor cannot use PUTMA for larger amounts without seeking court approval, unless authorized in the will. If insurance policies or retirement plans name minors as beneficiaries or contingent beneficiaries, the beneficiary designations should include the appointment of a custodian to receive the funds under UTMA. Otherwise, a court-appointed guardian will be required to receive the funds on the minor's behalf.

Giving Money Away May Be Trickier Than You Think

Are you shocked to find out that when you give money or property away, you may owe a tax? There is a federal gift tax. There is a lifetime exemption from the tax which in 2013 was raised to $5,250,000 — so unless you are giving away more than that amount, you won't have to pay a tax, although you may be required to file a gift tax return. This $5,250,000 exemption can be used during life to shelter gifts, or it can be used at death to shelter property from the estate tax.

There is also a $14,000 annual exclusion from the application of the gift tax. You can give $14,000 per calendar year to as many recipients as you wish. To get the $14,000 exclusion, the gifts must be gifts of present interests. That means the recipient has to receive the property now, not at some point in the future. If you have five children and they each have a spouse, and each child has produced two grandchildren; that gives you the potential of making 20 gifts of $14,000 each — removing $280,000 from your estate every year!

Some folks are under the impression that they are only "allowed" to give gifts up to $14,000 per year. Not so. You can give away anything that you want! However, if you give more than $14,000 to any individual, you must file a gift tax return. No tax will be due until you give more than $5,250,000, not counting $14,000 exclusion gifts. But a gift tax return must be filed because that is how the IRS and you keep track of how much of your $5,250,000 exemption you have used.

A husband and wife can give $28,000 per year to as many people as they want. If they each make $14,000 gifts, there is no return requirement. If only one of the spouses gives $28,000, then a gift tax return must be filed so that the spouses can "split" the gift, that is, each spouse will be considered to have made a gift of $14,000. A gift tax return is filed on Form 709 and is due at the same time as the personal income tax return, Form 1040.

Only when lifetime gifts (not counting $14,000 annual exclusion gifts) exceed $5,250,000 is there a gift tax actually due. It begins at a 40 percent rate for amounts over the $5,250,000. Gifts can be made with cash, securities, real estate, or any kind of property.

There is another very important exemption from the application of the gift tax. If a person pays another's tuition or medical expenses directly to the provider of the services, that is, directly to the college or directly to the hospital, these payments are not considered to be gifts. If Grandma wants to help pay for college, she may pay any amount directly to the college for tuition and this does not count against her $5270,000 exemption, nor does it count as an annual exclusion gift. With college costs where they are today, this is a very useful exemption.

Making gifts is good estate planning and very easy to accomplish. If you have an estate that will be subject to estate tax, say at the 40% rate, then, every time you make a gift of $14,000, you are saving $5,200 in estate tax. To the extent you can afford it, if you have a taxable estate, this is the simplest and most effective estate planning you can do. Make gifts.

Don't feel constrained to keep gifts under the $14,000 level. Making gifts to use up the $5,250,000 exemption during life is also excellent planning. Many people feel they have to "save" their exemption for use against their estate tax. Nothing is gained by doing this. Using the exemption sooner is advantageous. Anything that is given away during life through application of the exemption is out of the estate earlier. All subsequent appreciation is out of your estate. All income earned on the property subsequently is out of your estate. The earlier use of the exemption makes it more valuable.

Most folks are anxious to avoid estate taxes but are also loath to see their children and grandchildren "spoiled" by coming into too much wealth too soon. That is the most common objection to programs of gift giving. This is a problem that can be solved. Gifts can be made to trusts where the individual beneficiaries don't receive the benefit of the assets or ownership of them until they have attained more mature years.

All in the Family: Making Below-Market-Interest Loans

Can you make a loan to your child and charge them no interest or below-market interest? Yes, of course you can. Whether or not you can make a family loan without a family feud is another question. Suffice it to say that many family loans are never repaid and that this can cause much bitterness in the family. Let us examine the tax implications of a below-market loan to a family member or friend. There are two tax implications to consider: income tax and gift tax.

Even though the loan is interest free or carries a very low rate of interest, you may incur imputed interest income as a result of making the loan. What is imputed interest? It is interest considered by the IRS for tax purposes to have been received, even if no interest was actually paid. One example of imputed interest is the interest income you must report on zero-coupon bonds. These bonds pay no interest until they mature; nevertheless, you must report and pay tax on the interest as it accrues.

Imputed interest applies to below-market loans. A below-market loan is one that is interest free or one that carries stated interest below the applicable federal rate (AFR). The AFR is the minimum rate you can charge without creating tax side effects. Every month the IRS publishes AFRs. The AFR for a loan is the interest rate for loans of that duration in the month the loan is made. You can find the AFRs at the IRS website *www.irs.gov.*

Here is an example. Let's say you made a loan today. It was a short term loan (for less than 3 years); the AFR (with semiannual compounding) is .43% annually. If you charge at least that much interest, you don't have to worry about reading the rest of this section. (Note that the AFR is still quite a bit less than the rates charged by commercial lenders.)

If you charge no interest, or interest less than the .43%, then you are treated as if you made a gift to the borrower. This gift is the difference between the AFR and the interest you actually charged, if any. The borrower is then *deemed* to have paid that amount back to you as interest (this is the imputed interest). You must report the imputed interest as income on your income tax returns. The borrower may get a deduction depending on what the funds were used for.

If the loan is under $10,000, there is no problem. You can ignore the imputed gift and the imputed interest if the aggregate amount of loans between you and the individual is less than $10,000. Note that all loans outstanding between you and the individual when added up, must be less than $10,000.

If the loan is over $10,000, but less than $100,000, there is another exception to the application of the imputed interest rule which may save you. Taxable imputed interest income to you is zero as long as the borrower's net investment income for the year is no more than $1,000.

If the borrower's net investment income exceeds $1,000, your taxable imputed interest income is not more than his or her actual net investment income. In order to figure this out, the borrower must give you a signed statement disclosing his or her net investment income for the year which you will keep with your tax records.

To understand this rule it is helpful to understand why there is concern over below-market loans in the first place. Why does the IRS care about below-market loans? Before these rules, a family member could make a substantial loan to a lower-bracket family member (even a minor child). The child/borrower would invest the loan proceeds and receive and report the income. Thus the income was received by the child and was not treated as a gift, and the income was taxed at the child's income tax bracket, not the parent's. This was perceived as an abuse, and, in fact, it was for the very wealthy who would loan millions to family members.

To prevent this sort of income tax "gaming," we now have the below-market interest rules. The $100,000 exception was intended for loans that are below market but are used by the recipient for a purpose other than investment and generation of income. A perfect example is a loan that is used to buy a home. The parent who lends money to a child to help with the purchase of a home is not engaging in the income tax gaming that the imputed interest rule seeks to prevent.

Let's say you make a $100,000 interest-free loan to your daughter and she uses the money to buy a house. She has only $500 of net investment income for the year. Your taxable imputed interest income is zero — because her net investment income is less than $1,000. If your daughter's net investment income is $1,200, your taxable imputed interest income is the lesser of $1,200 or the actual imputed interest. For example, if the loan was a demand loan with .43% annual blended interest, the annual imputed interest would be $430. Your imputed interest income is $430. The interest is "imputed" — meaning that you have to pay income tax on it. The interest doesn't actually have to be *paid* to you by your daughter.

That takes care of the income tax, now for the gift tax. Unfortunately, there is no similar $100,000 exception for the gift tax. The best way to structure the loan for gift tax purposes is as a "demand loan," that is, a note that can be called for full payment by the lender at any time. With a demand loan, the imputed gift amount is computed every year and will fluctuate with the annual blended AFRs published each July. The annual imputed gift will be well under the $14,000 annual exclusion for gifts until the loan approaches $750,000 with the current rates. If the loan, rather than being a demand loan, is a term loan, the gift tax results are less favorable. When the loan is made, you are treated as making an immediate gift of the whole term's worth of below-market interest. This will likely exceed the $14,000 annual exclusion and require filing a gift tax return and use of part of your unified credit or actual payment of gift tax if your credit has already been used.

The best thing is to avoid all this complexity. If you make a loan of more than $10,000 to a friend or relative, charge the applicable federal rate of interest.

And get it in writing! If you make a below-market loan to a family member, and the loan is not repaid, the IRS may consider it a gift for tax purposes, whether you intended the money to be a gift or not. If this is the case, you may be required to file a federal gift tax return, depending upon the initial amount; and you will not be able to deduct it as a nonbusiness bad debt. If the loan is used by the family member to buy a home, make sure the note is secured by a mortgage. If it isn't, the borrower will not be able to deduct the interest that they do pay to you.

It is always possible to forgive payments on loans, converting a debt obligation to a gift. Since the annual exclusion is $14,000, you can forgive $14,000 of the debt obligation annually with no gift tax consequences.

Reviewing the Ins and Outs of Filing Gift Tax Returns

If the only gifts you made during the calendar year qualify for the annual exclusion you do not have to file a gift tax return. The annual exclusion is $14,000 per donee.

If a married couple made gifts in this year of more than $14,000, anywhere from $14,001 to $28,000, it is possible for the married couple to double the annual exclusion. There is a catch, however. If more than $14,000 came from either spouse, then in order to double the exclusion, a gift tax return, Form 709, must be filed and the spouses must elect gift-splitting.

Many taxpayers and tax preparers are unaware of this requirement. For example, let's say Mom and Dad gave Junior $28,000 for a down payment on a house. If Mom gave him $14,000 and Dad gave him $14,000, both gifts qualify for the annual exclusion and no gift tax return needs to be filed. If Dad gives the whole $28,000, then a gift tax return must be filed and Mom and Dad must elect gift-splitting in order to get two annual exclusions.

What if the gift is made from Mom and Dad's joint checking account and Mom writes a $28,000 check to Junior. Then do Mom and Dad have to file a gift tax return? The answer is "yes." Either Mom or Dad is permitted to make withdrawals from or write checks on a joint account. Whoever signed the check is the one making the gift. If the check signed by Mom was for more than $14,000, then Mom and Dad must file a gift tax return and elect gift-splitting in order to use both spouses' annual exclusions.

What happens if they don't file? The amount of the gift that exceeds the annual exclusion uses up part of the available exemption from gift and estate taxes. The current exemption is $5.25 million. If Dad writes a $28,000 check on a joint account, and Mom and Dad do not file gift tax return in order to elect gift-splitting, then only Dad's $14,000 annual exclusion is used. The rest of the gift uses $14,000 of the $5.25 million exemption, leaving $5,236,000 available.

If Mom and Dad make lots of annual exclusion gifts and do it every year, the reduction in exemption can add up to a large sum.

Usually no problem arises until Mom and Dad die. If a federal estate tax return must be filed, lifetime gifts in excess of the annual exclusion are required to be disclosed and reported. If they are not, and the return is examined and the taxable gifts are discovered, the amount of exemption available against the estate tax will be reduced and even more federal estate tax will be owed. The effective rate is about 40%. That means that for every $14,000 gift that should have been reported on a gift-splitting return, $5,600 of estate tax could be due. Not smart.

If total lifetime transfers plus transfers after death are less than $1 million, then there will not be a problem.

If a single person gives more than $14,000 per year per individual, or a couple gives more than $28,000, then a gift tax return is required. That is how taxpayers and the IRS keep track of what's been used of the $5.25 million lifetime exemption. Gifts over the annual exclusion amount are called taxable gifts. The taxpayer reports taxable gifts each year on the gift tax return. Each gift tax return is cumulative, and carries forward the amount of prior taxable gifts so that the lifetime usage of the exemption can be tracked. Actual payment of any tax doesn't begin until the total exemption has been gifted away.

The generation-skipping tax applies when property passes to grandchildren or great-grandchildren. There is a $5,250,000 exemption from this tax. The rules brought into effect in 2001, provide for an automatic allocation of exemption to gifts made to trusts. This reverses the prior rule. For example, in the past, if one made gifts to an irrevocable life insurance trust, in order to apply generation-skipping exemption to the gifts, one had to file a gift tax return and affirmatively elect the application of exemption.

Now, it will be necessary to file a gift tax return in order to elect *not* to have the exemption allocated to these gifts. This is going to be a bad result for many clients, especially when these trusts are holding term life insurance policies, which are intended to be in force for only a few years. Usually the generation-skipping exemption isn't allocated to these short-term policies. This means lots more gift tax returns will have to be prepared and filed. Tax preparers are cautioned to be on the look-out for this issue.

CHARITABLE GIVING

What Is Planned Giving?

> *You make a living by what you get, but you make a life by what you give.*
>
> Winston Churchill

A planned gift is a gift to charity that requires planning to make. Planned gifts can be made by the donor during life, or can be part of an estate plan effective at death. Through any of the several methods of planned giving to be discussed, donors can positively aide the work of their favorite charities. Less than 6% of American households have included nonprofits in their estate plans. Imagine the positive impact on our communities if everyone made a bequest — large or small — to favorite nonprofit organizations.

Charitable gifts carry with them a significant donor benefit — an income tax deduction. The higher the donor's income tax bracket, the more the deduction reduces the out-of-pocket cost of making a gift. The tax savings generated by the income tax charitable deduction allows a generous donor to give more than he or she initially thought possible.

A Planned Giving Primer

Some of the most common methods of planned giving are bequests, gifts of appreciated property, IRAs and qualified plans, gift annuities, pooled income funds, and charitable remainder trusts.

Bequests. Make a will. Make a bequest to charity. The simple act of making a gift to charity through a will makes it possible for everyone to leave a legacy of good work. A charitable gift from an estate is a way to express compassion and provide support for a cause beyond one's lifetime. It's an enduring expression of leadership to create a better community. Remember, when there is a will, there is a way — *your way*!

Many people are faithful annual contributors to charities whose missions draw their commitment. These annual gifts are usually made from the donor's income. Many donors, who need their income to support themselves and can only make relatively modest gifts during their lives, are often, when they die, in a position to make substantial charitable gifts from their assets.

Consider leaving a sum to charities you have supported annually to "endow" your annual gift. If you give $25 to a charity annually, consider leaving $500 to that charity in your will. At a 5% return, that means the charity will be able to have the benefit of your $25 annual gift long after you die.

Gifts to charity made in your will are completely exempt from federal estate taxes and state inheritance taxes. The exemption of charitable gifts from estate and gift tax is unlimited. Gifts and bequests of any size are completely free of death taxes. For a person with an estate in the 40% estate tax bracket, that means that 40% of every bequest to a charity is paid by Uncle Sam. This is a wonderful incentive to benefit charities in your will. A simple codicil can be added to your will to add charitable bequests.

Consider naming charities as the contingent beneficiaries of your estate. In the unfortunate event that all of your named beneficiaries predecease you, consider passing your estate to charity rather than letting state law determine where it will go.

Gifts of Appreciated Property. Gifts of securities and real estate held long term are deductible at the full present market value, with no tax on the appreciation. Gifts of long-term capital gain property are deductible up to 30% of adjusted gross income with a five-year carryover of any excess. A gift of appreciated capital gain property, for example, marketable securities, gives the donor an additional tax advantage that further reduces a gift's out-of-pocket cost. There is no income tax on the gift's appreciation.

If a donor wishes to contribute $1,000 to a charity, instead of writing a check for $1,000, he or she should consider transferring shares of stock equal to $1,000. If the donor sold the stock to generate the cash to make the gift, he or she would have to pay capital gains tax on any gain realized on the sale of the stock. He or she would have to sell considerably more than $1,000 of stock to have $1,000 after paying capital gains tax to make the charitable gift. If the stock had a zero cost basis for income tax purposes, the capital gain tax could be as high as $200, leaving only $800 net for the charitable gift. Instead of selling the stock, the donor could transfer the stock to charity, and get an income tax deduction for its $1,000 value and pay no capital gains tax. When the charity sells the stock, it pays no capital gains tax either.

IRAs and Qualified Plans. IRAs and qualified retirement plans such as 401(k) plans, profit sharing plans, and pension plans make wonderful charitable gifts. These plans are designed to provide incentives for retirement savings and have resulted in many Americans having very large plan balances. The income tax incentives are on the front end — contributions to the plans are tax deductible and the earnings inside the plans are income tax free. When money comes out of the plan, however, it is 100% taxable income. If the plan participant dies with a balance still in the plan, the balance is subject to estate tax and to income tax when the plan benefit is paid to the named beneficiary. Because of this double taxation, many beneficiaries receive only a small fraction of IRA and qualified plan benefits — most goes in taxes.

A charity can receive the plan benefit and pay no income tax and no estate tax. The tax incentive for giving IRAs and qualified plans to charity is enormous. These assets may be worth only 25 cents on the dollar to family beneficiaries but are worth the full $1 to a charity.

Anyone who is making a charitable gift in their estate plan and who has a qualified plan should consider using the qualified plan assets to make the charitable gift. This strategy results in both the family and the charity getting more. The U.S. Treasury is the only party who gets less.

Gift Annuities. A gift annuity is a combination of two things: (1) a charitable gift and (2) income for life for the donor. It is a form of charitable giving that gives the donor continued income but also assists the charity in a very important way.

A gift annuity achieves the same goals that a charitable remainder trust achieves. Appreciated property can be given to the charity; the donor gets an income tax deduction and an income stream for life, while the charity gets the balance of property on the donor's death. Charitable remainder trusts require the administration of a trust, and most advisors will tell you this is not cost effective unless you can put more than $500,000 in the trust.

Not many donors are in a position to give that much. For the same benefit, but with a smaller gift, consider a gift annuity. Gift annuities can be for any amount. Your favorite charity would be very happy to receive $10,000 in this form. Most will accept less and, of course, there is no upper limit.

The annuity rate is based on your age or, in the case of a deferred annuity, on the start date. All charitable organizations are free to set the rates that they offer as long as they comply with any applicable state regulation. Regulation of gift annuities varies from state to state. Many charities choose to follow the schedule of recommended maximum rates published by the American Council on Gift Annuities. The American Council on Gift Annuities publishes recommended rates (last changed January 1, 2012) that vary directly with age — the older you are, the higher the rate. At age 55, the return is 4%; at age 60, it's 4.4%; and so on. This means that if you are 55 and you put $10,000 in a gift annuity, you will get $400 per year for your lifetime. A portion of the $400 is tax free; it is a partial return of principal.

The gift annuity yields an immediate charitable deduction in the year of donation and provides a stream of income to the donor, some of which is tax-free return of capital. A donor can transfer cash or property in exchange for the annuity. If an appreciated asset, like stock, is transferred, a portion of the capital gains tax can be avoided.

The gift annuity is a contract between you and the charity. In exchange for the cash or property you give the charity, the charity promises to pay you (or your designated beneficiary) an annuity. The payment of the annuity by the charity depends on its financial soundness. The charity may not be obligated to set the annuity money aside; it may use the money for whatever purposes it chooses. If your charity is on shaky ground financially, it may not be able to make the annuity payments.

To address this concern, some charities insure the annuity obligations. That means that they buy an annuity from an insurance company to make sure that they will be able to fulfill their obligation to you. If the charity does this, you will be able to rely on the insurance company's assets as well as the charity's assets to make the payments. (Note that there is no guarantee like there is with an FDIC-insured bank account.)

Let's look at an example: Mrs. Contributor, who is 75, bought some stock several years ago for $2,500. Now the stock is worth $5,000, but is only paying a 2% dividend, $100 per year.

Mrs. Contributor would like additional income. She is also interested in supporting XYZ Charity. She gives the stock to XYZ Charity in exchange for a Gift Annuity. XYZ Charity agrees to pay an annuity to Mrs. Contributor of $385 per year (compare this to the $100 in stock dividends she received). She is getting more than three times the income she did before.

Mrs. Contributor also gets a current income tax deduction of $2,399. If she is in the 28% income tax bracket, this means that she reduces her income tax by $672. She must pay capital gains tax, but only on part of the gain. Compared to an outright sale of the stock, she would save up to $336 in capital gains tax.

Where do the numbers come from? Don't try this at home, but for the professionals out there, use the IRS Actuarial Tables, Book Aleph based on data from the 2000 U.S. census (not the Alpha Book for 1980 census numbers), and look for the annuity factor. In addition, in order to do the calculation, we need to know what the government says is the correct current interest rate to use. The IRS publishes interest rates every month. This calculation uses 120% of the midterm rate compounded semiannually. For September 2014, this rate is 2.27% (and rounded to the nearest two-tenths of one percent for the Section 7520 rate is 2.2%). Multiply the annuity amount by the annuity factor to get the commercial value of the annuity. The amount of the charitable deduction is the value transferred to the charity minus this commercial value. That is the value of the "gift" made to the charity and can be claimed as a deduction on our tax return next April.

When the donor receives the annuity payment, some of it is income and some of it is return of the original capital. The part that is return of capital is not taxable on the tax return. To determine how much is return of capital, divide the original investment by the donor's life expectancy according to IRS tables and that is how much of the annuity is considered return of capital.

If appreciated property is contributed to the charity in lieu of cash, then the transaction is treated as part sale and part gift. The donor's basis in the property is allocated between the gift element and the sale element. The donor will recognize some of the gain but not all of it.

Don't let the math scare you. If you are interested in this technique, the charity of your choice will be glad to provide all of the numbers and tax information; you won't have to do it. Charitable development professionals will be very familiar with charitable gift annuities and very happy to help you.

Pooled Income Funds. A pooled income fund is a fund maintained by a school, church, hospital, or other public charity that receives gifts of cash and securities from donors. The charity adds the donor's gift to a separately maintained pooled fund where it is invested with monies of other donors who make similar gifts. Each donor, or the donor's beneficiary, gets a *pro rata* share of the pooled income fund's earnings for each donor's life. When a donor dies, the charitable organization removes assets from the pooled income fund equal to that donor's share of the fund and uses the assets for its general charitable purposes.

Charitable Remainder Trusts. Do you have an asset that is not producing much income but which you can't sell because it would generate a huge taxable gain? Maybe a Charitable Remainder Trust can solve your problem.

Let's assume you have a farm, inherited or purchased years ago, that is now worth $1 million. You are 68, retired and need income. The farm produces none. In fact, even though you rent the land to the neighboring farmer, the rent doesn't cover the real estate taxes. You would like to sell the farm, but, if you do, you realize that almost all of the $1 million in proceeds will be taxable gain and you will owe the federal government $200,000 in capital gains tax. That would leave you with a net $800,000 to invest in income-producing assets. Perhaps you can invest in something that produces 5% income (although that is high if you invest part in equities) and you can generate $40,000 in income per year. When you die, if you still have the $800,000, it will be subject to estate tax (and may or may not be covered by the exemption). Your beneficiaries will receive the balance remaining after estate tax. If you have other assets and the estate tax is at 40%, they may receive only $480,000.

Now let's look at the Charitable Remainder Trust scenario. You transfer the farm to a Charitable Remainder Trust. This trust provides that you will be paid an annuity (or some other amount) for your life. Let's assume you choose an annuity equal to 8% of the initial value of the trust property. The Trustee of the Charitable Remainder Trust sells the farm and pays no capital gains tax. Thus, the trustee can invest the entire $1,000,000, unreduced by capital gains tax, in income-producing assets. An 8% annuity would generate a payout of $80,000 per year for life.

Furthermore, in the year the trust is created, you get a $358,000 income tax charitable deduction. The amount of the deduction is the present value of the charity's right to receive the remainder of the trust property after your death. This is an actuarial computation based on your life expectancy and the assumed rate of interest the IRS prescribes for these calculations. A $358,000 charitable deduction generates a $53,500 savings in income tax payable (assuming a 15% bracket). You can use this deduction over a five-year period. On your death, the charity gets whatever is left in the trust; this is how it gets its name — Charitable Remainder Trust. The charity gets what is remaining.

Some folks add another planning technique on top of this. With some of the extra cash generated by the income tax deduction, or with part of the extra income generated ($80,000 compared to $40,000), you purchase a life insurance policy on your life in the amount of $1,000,000. The life insurance policy is owned and payable to an Irrevocable Life Insurance Trust so that the value of the death benefit is not subject to estate tax in your estate. On your death, the insurance pays its $1 million death benefit which is distributed tax free to your beneficiaries. This replaces the value of the asset to your heirs and beneficiaries since the balance remaining in the Charitable Remainder Trust goes to charity. You have increased your income during life, and increased the amount passing to your beneficiaries while at the same time, giving a benefit to charity and paying no federal estate taxes on this property.

Using a Charitable Remainder Trust and an irrevocable life insurance trust is a favorite way of benefitting a charity while, at the same time, increasing your income, providing an inheritance for family members, and avoiding federal estate taxes. The Charitable Remainder Trust can be used alone to generate additional lifetime income if there is an intention to make a substantial charitable gift.

There are two types of Charitable Remainder Trusts. One is a Charitable Remainder *Annuity* Trust, and the other is a Charitable Remainder *Unitrust.* An annuity trust pays a fixed dollar amount annually. A unitrust pays a specified percentage of the market value of the trust assets. This will go up or down according to the investment performance of the trust assets. You, the creator of the Charitable Remainder Trust, can be the trustee. You can choose whatever charity or charities you wish to receive the remainder. Also, you can retain the right to change the charities.

If you have a large position in an appreciated stock with a low basis, the Charitable Remainder Trust can provide a means of diversifying that holding without paying capital gains tax. Rental real estate with a low depreciated basis can be used. You may be able to transfer part of or all of your business to a Charitable Remainder Trust. The trust can be made for any amount, but the costs of administration make it impractical to use this kind of planning technique if you are putting in less than $200,000. This is a technique that saves both income tax and estate tax.

Charitable Remainder Trusts Have All-or-Nothing Boundaries

> *Experience keeps a dear school, but fools will learn in no other.*
>
> Benjamin Franklin

We learn to avoid mistakes by experience. Experience comes from making mistakes. The trick is to gain experience from the mistakes of others.

One mistake that is made over and over again is creating trusts for charity that don't qualify for the estate tax charitable deduction. For example, a trust is set up for the benefit of a spouse or child for life, with the remainder to charity. The estate of the donor is entitled to a charitable deduction if, and only if, the trust is a charitable remainder unitrust or annuity trust. Both kinds of trusts have very specific technical requirements. There is little room for creativity in drafting these trusts. The statutory formula must be followed exactly. All too often the drafting attorney, perhaps at the insistence of the client, tries to add bells and whistles and loses the charitable deduction.

Mistakes in drafting these kinds of trusts are so common that the IRS has a special procedure to reform these trusts after the decedent's death. Even with faulty drafting there is still a chance to fix up the trust through a reformation proceeding in court and compliance with the IRS's guidelines. Not all faulty trusts will qualify for reformation, but many will. The fact that there exists an IRS approved procedure for reformation is very unusual. The IRS does not usually go out of its way to help taxpayers fix mistakes, especially when the fix means less tax revenue. The overriding public policy in favor of charitable giving is at work here.

A mistake in making one of these trusts comes from the ninth circuit (yes, that's California). A man included a trust in his will that gave an annual amount to his wife for her life if she survived him and the remainder went to charity. No problem there. Then he decided that she might outlive him long enough for inflation to eat away at the payment value, so he decided to adjust the payment annually for inflation. Seems harmless enough, doesn't it? But inflation adjustments are not permitted in charitable remainder trusts.

A trust can be written with inflation adjusted payouts, but don't look for a charitable deduction for the charitable remainder. In this case, *Sansone v. U.S.*, the executor filed a tax return taking the charitable deduction. The entire trust is shared by the surviving spouse and the charity. There are unlimited deductions for property passing to surviving spouse and to charities, but, in each case, only if the property interest qualifies for the deduction.

The charitable deduction was denied because the amount of future payments to the spouse was undeterminable because of the inflation adjustment. It did not meet the requirements for a charitable remainder trust. The estate, having lost the charitable deduction, reasoned then, that there would be no tax because the property would pass to the surviving spouse, also a fully deductible disposition.

Wrong again. The marital deduction was available only for the stated annuity amount. The inflation adjustment is undeterminable and thus, does not qualify for the marital deduction.

The taxpayer appealed to the Ninth Circuit Court of Appeals and the IRS prevailed again. The court said the regulations covering the marital deduction were fair, and that the remainder interest in the trust did not qualify for a charitable deduction because it was neither a charitable remainder annuity trust nor a charitable remainder unitrust.

What a weird result! Here is a trust going wholly to a surviving spouse and charity (both usually nontaxable dispositions) that is subject to estate tax. (Can you say malpractice?)

A charitable remainder trust requires that the payment to the non-charity be stated as a fixed annual amount (a CRAT) or a fixed percentage of the trust value as determined annually (a CRUT). Those are the only ways a charitable remainder trust will qualify for a charitable deduction. The only variance is that the payments may be limited to current income, either with or without a provision for shortfalls to be made up in following years when income becomes larger than the annual payment.

While it is permitted to include inflation adjustment for trust payments, such a provision cancels any charitable deduction, and the extra amounts paid in successive years do not qualify for the marital deduction.

The IRS has issued revised regulations on the applicable portions of the law and model CRAT and CRUT clauses are included. When a regulation is published saying, "look, you can save taxes this way, and here's how to do it," mistakes seem to drop dramatically.

Leaving Your IRA to Charity

If you want to leave something to charity when you pass away and you have a traditional IRA, naming a charity as an IRA beneficiary is an excellent strategy. Under current tax law, your IRA balance will be included in your estate for federal estate tax purposes. If you pass away with a taxable estate that exceeds the $5 million exemption from the federal estate tax, the balance in the IRA will be subject to tax to the extent your estate exceeds $5 million.

If the IRA is subject to estate tax, this will take about 40% of the balance. Assume a $8 million estate, that includes a $2 million IRA. The $ 2 million IRA is suddenly only a $1.2 million IRA. Remember, assets left to a spouse who is a U.S. citizen are not subject to estate tax, so this tax problem does not usually arise until the death of the survivor of the spouses.

Not only is the IRA subject to estate tax, but the IRA proceeds payable to beneficiaries are "income in respect of a decedent" for federal income tax purposes. Withdrawals taken from your IRA by your beneficiaries will be taxed as ordinary income to them, at rates that could run as high as 39.6%. These beneficiaries can get a deduction for estate tax paid, but it is a deduction, not a tax credit, so that the combined rate of taxation considering both estate and income tax is about 64%.

In Pennsylvania, IRA withdrawals are not subject to Pennsylvania income tax; however, the IRA balance is subject to inheritance tax when you die if you are over age 59½. If the IRA passes to your children and grandchildren, the inheritance tax rate is 4.5%. That brings the total tax rate up to 67.8%.Your $2 million IRA is worth only $644,400 to the beneficiaries.

The tax policy behind the tax advantages of an IRA during your lifetime is to encourage you to save for retirement. After you die, the income tax that was deferred must be paid, and if you have a large enough estate, your estate will pay estate tax. Tax policy is that IRAs are for retirement income, not for wealth transfer at death.

If you were already planning on leaving part of your estate to charity, consider using the IRA to make this gift. There is a charitable deduction for the federal estate tax so that 100% of any sum going to charity passes free of federal estate tax. Also, charities are income tax exempt. When the charity receives the IRA as a beneficiary, no income tax is payable. Neither is the IRA subject to Pennsylvania inheritance tax when paid to a charity. The charity, unlike your children and grandchildren, will receive 100% of the IRA. Then you can leave other assets that aren't taxed so brutally to your heirs — which means more after-tax cash for them. The charity and your family beneficiaries get more; the government gets less.

How Should You Leave Benefits to Charity?

The simplest and most effective way is to designate a charity as the primary beneficiary of your IRA. This technique also works if you want to leave the IRA to several charities. A group of charities can receive fractions or percentages of the benefit, all free of income tax and estate and inheritance tax.

What you shouldn't do, however, is name a person and a charity as co-beneficiaries within the same IRA. Keep the charity in a separate IRA. Why?

Generally, the Internal Revenue Code allows the beneficiaries of an IRA to withdraw the benefits in annual installments over the life expectancy of the designated beneficiaries. A charity does not qualify. Individual persons who are beneficiaries can use the life expectancy method but a charity may not. Furthermore, individual persons can only use the life expectancy method if ALL beneficiaries of the IRA are individuals. If a charity is one of a group of beneficiaries, then all beneficiaries must take a lump sum.

This can be a terrible tax result for individual beneficiaries, especially a young beneficiary who has a long life expectancy. Not only must the beneficiary pay all the income tax at once, but the tax advantage of tax free accumulation in the IRA is lost. There are two possible exceptions to mitigate the effect of this rule and allow a repair of this kind of designation.

1. If the beneficiaries' interests, as a group, are expressed as fractional or percentage shares; and the beneficiaries establish "separate" accounts for their respective shares in the IRA by December 31 of the year after the year of the IRA owner's death, then each separate account is treated as a separate IRA for distribution purposes. The obvious drawback of this approach is that the beneficiaries have to meet the deadline for establishing a separate account. (This, of course, assumes that the beneficiaries or the professional advisors know that a separate account is necessary and why.)
2. The other exception is that a beneficiary is "disregarded" if the beneficiary's interest in the IRA is completely distributed by September 30 of the year after the year of the participant's death. Thus, if the charity's share is paid out before the deadline, the remaining beneficiaries would be entitled to use the life expectancy method. Again the drawback is that time passes quickly and people miss deadlines, or people are unaware of the problem until it is too late.

If making sure that the beneficiaries can use the life expectancy payout method is an important goal, it is not recommended that you make a group designation including the charity for a portion. Instead, separate the IRA, and make a separate account that is wholly payable to charity. The individual beneficiaries can be beneficiaries of the other IRA. You can rebalance occasionally by moving funds from one IRA account to the other if the balances change or you change your mind about how much you want to give to charity.

One account you don't want to leave to charity, however, is your Roth IRA. Instead, you should leave Roth IRA balances to your individual beneficiaries by designating them as the account beneficiaries. All withdrawals taken by your beneficiaries are free of federal income tax. If you leave Roth IRA money to charity, this valuable tax break goes to waste.

Handling Charitable Gifts of Appreciated Property

A donor who makes a contribution to charity can take an income tax deduction for the value of the gift. The deduction is available only to taxpayers who itemize their deductions. It is not available if the taxpayer takes the standard deduction.

The effect of the charitable deduction is to reduce the donor's cost of giving $1.00 to charity to 85 cents, or maybe as little as 60 cents, depending on the taxpayer's income tax bracket. If a taxpayer in the 28% bracket gives $100 to charity, the taxpayer reduces his income tax bill by $28. The "cost" of giving the charity $100 is only $72. A taxpayer in the 39.6% bracket can give $100 to charity for a cost of $60.40.

A gift of appreciated capital gain property, such as marketable securities, gives the donor an additional tax advantage that further reduces a gift's out-of-pocket cost because there is no income tax on the gift's appreciation. Gifts of securities and real estate held long term are deductible at the *full* present market value, with no tax on the appreciation. The taxpayer gets to deduct the full value of the property and pays no capital gains tax. There are limitations on large deductions. Gifts of long-term capital gain property are deductible up to 30% of adjusted gross income with a five-year carryover of any excess. Alternatively, the gift of the long-term capital gain property can be deductible up to 50% of adjusted gross income with a five-year carryover but only if the deduction is limited to the donor's cost basis for the property, not its current fair market value.

If a donor wishes to contribute $1,000 to a charity, instead of writing a check for $1,000, he or she should consider transferring shares of stock equal to $1,000. If the donor sold the stock to generate the cash to make the gift, he or she would have to pay capital gains tax on any gain realized on the sale of the stock. The donor would have to sell considerably more than $1,000 of stock to have $1,000 after paying capital gains tax to make the charitable gift. If the stock had a zero cost basis for income tax purposes, the capital gains tax could be as high as $200, leaving only $800 net for the charitable gift. Instead of selling the stock, the donor could transfer the stock to charity, and get an income tax deduction for its $1,000 value and pay no capital gains tax. When the charity sells the stock, it pays no capital gains tax either.

Donating securities isn't just for wealthy people. You can give a small number of shares to your favorite charity every year. Most large charities, and even many smaller ones, are familiar with the handling of securities donations. If your securities are held in an account, directing transfer is very easy. If you hold the share certificates, you will have to deliver the shares with an executed stock power.

If the donor has investment property that has decreased in value, then the donor should sell the property and donate the proceeds. The donor can take a capital loss for the sale (subject to some restrictions) and use the proceeds for making the contribution that qualifies for the charitable deduction.

These rules apply to all property, not just stock. Appreciated real estate makes an ideal gift to charity. The donor can get a deduction for the fair market value of the real estate and pay no capital gains tax on the appreciation. Any capital asset is a candidate for this type of contribution.

Charitable gifts are 100% deductible for purposes of the gift tax and the estate tax. That means that a gift in any amount to a qualifying charity, during life or at death, results in no transfer tax. If you have bequests to charity in your will, it is wise tax planning to make the gifts to charity before you die. That way, you get an income tax deduction for making the gift, and the value of the gift is not subject to gift or estate tax.

Special rules apply if the taxpayer contributed (1) property subject to a debt, (2) a partial interest in property, (3) a future interest in tangible personal property, or (4) inventory from your business. Be sure to check with a qualified professional before making large donations.

Private Foundations Moving to Donor-Advised Funds

High net worth donors have traditionally used private foundations for their philanthropy. They can reduce taxes, leave a legacy to their communities, and retain significant control over the administration of investments and the grant-making process of the foundation. A private foundation can also provide high visibility for a donor's or a family's charitable gifts. Many families hope that the family foundation will be a way to instill philanthropy in succeeding generations by involving family members in the operation of the foundation.

After the foundation is established, things can change. There are over 40,0000 family foundations in the United States. About 60% of them have assets of less than $1 million. Many charitable donors find the costs of maintaining private foundations, as well as the time commitment required from family members, to be more burdensome than anticipated. The costs and time involved is out of proportion to the benefit for smaller foundations.

The time and costs involved in administering grant and scholarship programs from a private foundation mount up. There are accounting fees and attorney fees to pay. The time commitment can be huge. Family members must shoulder the burden or the foundation must hire staff to handle administration. Sometimes maintaining the foundation and making decisions about how it will be run, who will be trustees, and the grant making process may be much more work than the family realized. Over time, family members may lose interest or be unwilling to devote the necessary time and effort. The second and third generation may not have the enthusiasm of the founder. The time and effort required is often disproportionate to the charitable benefit. If a $1 million foundation makes $50,000 in grants per year, how much time and expense can truly be justified?

Liability of the trustees of a private foundation is also an issue and makes it difficult to find new trustees. Trustees can have personal liability if the private foundation does not comply with regulations, engages in self-dealing, has excess business holdings, doesn't distribute enough of its income, or doesn't administer grant or scholarship programs properly. With the transfer of the private foundation's assets to a donor-advised fund, all these problems go away. This realization is spurring an increasing number of donors to set up donor-advised funds instead of private foundations.

Many existing private foundations are closing and transferring all of their assets to donor-advised funds. Donor-advised funds invest the assets and make grants based on the donor's recommendations. They provide many of the same advantages as a private foundation but at a much lower cost.

As with a private foundation, by making contributions to a donor-advised fund a donor can accelerate tax deductions, involve family members, focus on grant making, and get visibility and recognition for giving if the donor wishes.

Donor-advised funds are available at institutional investment firms like Vanguard and Fidelity. They can also be found at universities and religious foundations. An important and popular option for a donor-advised fund is a community foundation.

The Lancaster County Community Foundation can accept assets transferred from a private foundation and set up a donor-advised fund. A donor-advised fund at the Lancaster County Community Foundation will get the benefit of a much lower cost, dedicated administration staff with expertise and experience in grant making, and an array of sophisticated investment options. Since the Lancaster County Community Foundation is a public charity, there are no excise taxes for the fund to pay and no expensive annual reports to file with the IRS. Fees are modest compared to the operating costs of a private foundation. This leaves more money to go to charities. The fund can continue in perpetuity and carry the family's name.

A donor-advised fund has many advantages over a private foundation. A private foundation must distribute 5% of its assets every year. Donor-advised funds don't have an annual distribution requirement. Contributions to a private foundation are limited to 30% of adjusted gross income (20% for appreciated property). Contributions to a donor-advised fund can be larger — limited by the 50% of adjusted gross income ceiling (30% for appreciated property). Private foundations are subject to an excise tax of 1 to 2% on net investment income. A donor-advised fund pays no excise tax. Donors can give all sorts of assets, cash, securities, artwork, real estate, all depending on the provisions of any particular fund. A gift of real estate or closely held stock to a private foundation can only be deducted to the extent of its cost basis (usually not an attractive option) while such a contribution to a donor-advised fund is eligible for the charitable deduction at its full fair market value.

There is also a privacy advantage. Private foundation tax forms (990s) which detail distributions and other information about the foundation are publicly available —they are easily found on the internet. The forms filed by donor-advised funds don't list individual accounts.

An IRS Ruling (2003-13) specifically approves the termination of a private foundation by distributing assets to a public charity such as a community foundation and the foundation's board members may be named as the advisors to the fund.

In this economy, with uncertain markets, and the fluctuation of value in investments, coupled with the high professional fees and excise taxes imposed on a private foundation, transferring assets to a donor-advised fund can be a win-win for the family and for the charities.

For information about Lancaster County Community Foundation, contact Sam Bressi, President & CEO, at (717) 397-1629, 53 W. James St., Lancaster PA 17603, or check out their web site at *www.lancastercountyfoundation.org*

Properly Substantiating Charitable Gifts Is Key

Don't be in such a hurry to file your income tax return. If you are claiming deductions for charitable deductions, filing your tax return early before you have all necessary information can cost you.

Congress encourages your philanthropy by allowing an income tax deduction for gifts to charities. However, the IRS has numerous reporting and substantiation requirements that must be followed in order for you to successfully claim the charitable deduction.

For noncash charitable contributions greater than $500 you have to include Form 8283 with your income tax return. For gifts under $5,000 only Section A of Form 8283 must be completed. This can be done by you or by your tax preparer. When the value of the noncash property you gave to charity is more than $5,000 then you have to have the property appraised. The $5,000 limit is not a per item amount — it applies to similar items of property. For example, if you have six paintings, each worth $1,000 and give them to 6 different charities, you need an appraisal since the total value of the similar items exceeds $5,000.

There is a special rule for publicly-traded securities. Even if the value exceeds $5,000, you do not need an appraisal. But the gifts or securities must be reported by completing Section A of Form 8283 and attaching it to your income tax return.

If you need an appraisal, the appraisal must be dated within 60 days of the date of the gift. The appraisal can be before or after the gift, so long as it is within 60 days. You must have the appraisal *in hand* by the due date of your income tax return. The appraisal summary goes on Schedule B of Form 8283. It must be signed by the appraiser *and* by the charity that received your gifts. It is essential that this be completed, signed and attached to your income tax return in order to claim the deduction.

The appraisal must be done by a "qualified appraiser." If the appraiser does not meet the definition of a "qualified appraiser," then you don't get the deduction. The appraiser must hold himself or herself out to the public as an appraiser and have credentials showing that he or she is qualified to appraise the type of property being valued. A qualified appraiser may not be related to or regularly employed by the charity who is the recipient of the gift. The appraisal fee can't be based on a percentage of the property's value. The fee for the appraisal is not a charitable gift, but is deductible as a miscellaneous deduction. The appraisal fee, together with any other miscellaneous deductions you might have, are only deductible to the extent they exceed 2% of adjusted gross income.

If you make a gift of artwork to a charity and the value exceeds $20,000 then your return has to include a copy of the appraisal itself, not just the appraisal summary. If any single artwork is worth $20,000 or more, you may be asked to produce an 8x10 color photo (or a 4x5 color slide) of the object.

When a charity receives a gift that is subject to these rules, the charity must report to the IRS if it sells or disposes of the item within two years. This is sometimes referred to as the "snitch rule." Let's say you donate a stamp collection to your alma mater and take a $10,000 deduction. Alma mater sells the collection one year later for $5,000. They are required to notify the IRS of the sale price. This is an invitation to the IRS to question the original deduction of $10,000.

For gifts of tangible personal property, for example, artwork, cars, collectibles, computers, the law imposes a restriction on the amount of the deduction allowable. If the use of such property by the charity is unrelated to its charitable purposes, the charitable deduction must be reduced by the amount of gain that would have been long-term capital gain had the property been sold at its fair market value. For example, an art collector purchased a painting for $2,000 in 1997. In 2000, when the fair market value of the painting was $5,000, the collector donated it to a charity. The organization's use of the painting is unrelated to its charitable purposes — the charity provides meals to the homeless and will sell the painting to raise cash. In that case, the collector's income tax deduction is limited to $2,000. It is the taxpayer's responsibility (in our example, the collector) to determine whether the charity will put the property to the required use.

The same rule applies to donations of tangible personal property to rummage sales or auctions. Although the proceeds of the sale of these items will be used to further the organization's charitable purposes, the items themselves are not used by the charity to further its exempt purposes. Accordingly, the donor's deduction must be reduced by the amount that would have been recognized as long-term gain had the donated property been sold at its fair market value. Many times this rule has no effect because the value of the property when donated is less than the purchase price.

For any gift of $250 or more, whether in cash or noncash, you must have a written receipt from the charity describing the gift. You must have the receipt *in hand* before your file your income tax return. This is crucial. Don't file your income tax return claiming charitable deductions until you have the receipts *in hand*. A cancelled check is not good enough which is just as well since many banks are not returning cancelled checks anymore. The charitable receipt must describe any goods and services that were given to you in exchange for the gift and give a good faith estimate of the value of the goods or services. If no goods or services were provided, the receipt must so state. Separate contributions are not usually aggregated for the $250 rule unless they are made on the same day.

If the charity received a gift of $75 or more from you and you received goods or services in exchange (other than an intangible religious benefit), the receipt must include a statement that the charitable deduction is limited to the excess of your contribution over the value of the goods or services received and provide you with a good faith estimate of the value of the goods and services. Token benefits can be ignored. Token is considered to be 2% of the contribution or $74, whichever is less. Or, if the donor gives the charity at least $47 and receives an item bearing the charity's name or logo costing no more than $7.40, such an item is considered a token benefit and is ignored.

Don't lose your charitable deductions by failing to meet substantiation requirements or missing the timing of those requirements.

Would Estate Tax Repeal Affect Charitable Giving?

The current estate and gift tax provides an unlimited deduction for amounts contributed to qualifying charities. If an estate is subject to the maximum 48% estate tax bracket, this means that a decedent can leave $1.00 to charity and have it "cost" his estate only 52¢.

It is widely thought that this charitable deduction from the estate and gift tax has provided an incentive to charitable giving. Charities are in a tough spot. They don't want to offend major donors by fighting repeal, but they want to keep collecting the contributions that the estate tax encourages.

Most charitable organizations will tell you the contributors do not give to charity solely because of the tax deductions. A donor doesn't make money by giving it to charity. To be a donor, you have to want to benefit the charity and its mission with a donation. The question is, does the charitable deduction affect how much these contributors will give?

Charitable giving increases with income and wealth. Without the necessity to pay taxes, more money is available for distribution to charities and the family. Repeal of the estate tax will certainly increase income and wealth — it may be that repeal increases giving.

Let's look at an example. Decedent has a $6 million estate, his children are his beneficiaries and he is interested in benefiting Favorite Charity. Under the 2014 law, the federal and Pennsylvania death taxes on a $6 million estate would be $290,100 (270,000 Pennsylvania + 156,000 federal) and a net of $5,574.,000 would pass to the children. If the estate tax were repealed, the children would get the whole $6,000,000 minus $270,000 PA inheritance tax, or $5,730,000.

Now let's include Favorite Charity for a $500,000 bequest. Under 2014 law, the $6 million estate would be distributed by $500,000 to Favorite Charity, $ 247,500 in Pennsylvania inheritance tax, no federal estate tax, and $5,253,000 to the children. If the estate tax were repealed, Favorite Charity would get $500,000 and the children would get $5,253,000 .

After repeal, on these facts there would be no change in the result. If the estate were larger so that a federal tax were due, then the after tax cost of the gift would be higher. However, there is much more money left for everyone (except the IRS) after repeal, so the tendency should be to at least maintain the present level of giving, or maybe even apportion the tax windfall between charity and family.

The theory that the estate tax provides an incentive to charitable giving is that when the estate tax applies, the "cost" of giving the $500,000 to charity is only $104,600, the rest being subsidized by the estate tax charitable deduction. However, with the repeal of the estate tax, the charity can get the contribution and the children get the balance, which is *more* than what the children would receive under the present system.

There is another tax incentive to charitable giving, which is the income tax charitable deduction. The policy of this deduction is the same, although this deduction is limited to an annual amount not exceeding 50% of the donor's adjusted gross income, or under some circumstances, 30% of adjusted gross income. This area won't be affected by the estate tax repeal.

Have You Planned Your Giving?

1. Decide to whom you'd like to leave a gift. Perhaps it's music you love or the work of a particular organization you admire. You may also want to leave a gift in memory of a loved one or for a specific use or purpose.
2. Contact your favorite charity for more information regarding what opportunities are open to you and how your gift helps their work.
3. Contact a professional such as an attorney, accountant, or financial advisor to tell you about the tax benefits of planned gifts.
4. Work with your advisor to make certain your planned giving is constructed properly — so it actually does what you want it to do. Sometimes, planned giving arrangements are complicated and the details are best left to a professional.
5. Review your estate plan — wills, trust, beneficiary designations, etc. — to make sure that your charitable wishes are accomplished.

Take steps today to include planned giving in your estate plan and thereby help assure that the important work of your favorite charity will continue.

INVESTMENTS

How Are Trust Investments Judged?

When we give money to a trustee to manage it for the benefit of our beneficiaries, to what standard is the trustee held? If the trustee manages $500,000 for our family, and buys XYZ stock a week before a disappointing quarterly report and the stock drops dramatically, is there legal recourse against the trustee? It depends.

The law of trusts used to provide that a trustee was held to the "prudent person standard." (Actually, the case establishing the rule refers to the "prudent man standard." With tongue in cheek, some of my friends say this is a lower standard than the "prudent person standard.") As applied, this standard looked at each investment the trustee made. Each investment holding in the trust was examined on its own, and the prudence of the trustee in acquiring or retaining a particular investment depended, in a large part, on the process of its evaluation and selection. A stock chosen with the appropriate level of care could be "prudent" even if it was a terrible performer. Conversely, if a trustee negligently selected one security and it declined in value, the trustee was liable for the loss even if the trust portfolio as a whole increased substantially in value. These rules forced trustees to invest trust money differently than an individual would.

Now we have a new standard. The new law is called the Prudent Investor Rule. The Prudent Investor Rule applies to the management of trusts and guardianships. It does not apply to custodianships under the Uniform Transfer to Minors Act, agencies created by a power of attorney, decedent's estates, municipal pensions, or retirement funds. If Husband's will gives $675,000 to a bypass trust for the benefit of Wife, the trustee's actions will be judged in accordance with the Prudent Investor Rule.

The new general rule is that "[a] fiduciary shall invest and manage property held in a trust as a prudent investor would, by considering the purposes, terms and other circumstances of the trust and by pursuing an overall investment strategy reasonably suited to the trust." All investments not precluded by the governing instrument are permissible investments. This change brings the law into sync with how individual investors look at the performance of their investment advisors. The trade-off between risk and return in all investing is identified as the fiduciary's central consideration. Trustees have now been brought into the world of Modern Portfolio Theory.

Considerations the fiduciary must take into account when making investments include (1) the size of the trust, (2) the nature and estimated duration of the fiduciary relationship, (3) liquidity and distribution requirements of the trust, (4) tax consequences of investments and distributions, (5) role each investment plays in the overall strategy, (6) the asset's special relationship or value to the trust or to the beneficiaries, (7) the needs of the beneficiaries, and (8) the resources of the beneficiaries.

A fiduciary shall reasonably diversify investments, unless logic dictates that the beneficiaries' best interest is reasonably determined to be best served otherwise. Using reasonable skill and care, the fiduciary may retain any asset received in kind, even though the asset constitutes a disproportionally large share of the portfolio. If Husband leaves $500,000 worth of Exxon in the bypass trust, it may be reasonable to leave the trust alone without diversifying.

A fiduciary may appoint an investment agent. As long as the agent is chosen in a reasonable manner and is periodically supervised, it is the agent, not the fiduciary, who is liable. An agent who represents that he has special investment skills shall exercise those skills. Out-of-town agents subject themselves to local courts by accepting responsibility. Co-fiduciaries may delegate to another co-fiduciary only if the first believes the second has greater investment skills and provided that the second is periodically reviewed by the first.

Investment in a mutual fund is not a delegation to the fund manager. The fiduciary retains responsibility, not the fund manager.

Un-invested cash may be held for near term distributions, debts, taxes, expenses of administration or reinvestment. Near term means within a quarter or ninety days. Also, if the amount available for investment does not justify the burden of investment, the cash may be held un-invested.

A trustee may acquire life insurance on the lives of the settlor, the settlor's spouse, or both. The trustee is not liable for losses due to his failure to determine that the life insurance contract remains a proper investment, that the insurance company is financially strong, that non-forfeiture provisions are exercised, or that the contract is diversified.

The fiduciary is judged by the conditions and knowledge available at the time of the decision. The fiduciary cannot be made liable based on eventual results, meaning hindsight cannot determine what was reasonable at the time. Decisions as to individual assets shall be considered in the context of the trust portfolio as a whole and as part of an overall investment strategy and not in isolation.

For example, Fiduciary Fred invests trust funds in A, B, C, D and E, all of which are in different segments of the investment universe. While A, B, C and D prosper, E fails. The portfolio as a whole performs at 80% of the S&P index. Fred is not liable for the failure of E. Had he invested entirely in E, or maybe entirely in A and E and the portfolio performed at 10% of the S&P index, he would be guilty of failure to diversify to protect against the failure of E.

The bottom line is that trustees are no longer held liable for performance, asset by asset, but rather by the entire portfolio. Judgment is based on conditions at the time of the decision, and whether any prudent investor might have done what the fiduciary did, considering the overall picture. In most instances this frees a trustee to make a broader range of investments to meet the trust beneficiary's needs. It also places a higher standard on the trustee. The trustee must consider all the factors listed above and demonstrate that these factors have been properly considered and taken into account in the investment of trust assets.

How to Make Trusts Better Market Performers

We do it that way because it's always been done that way!

That's about the best answer you can give to the question of why trusts are written so that different classes of beneficiaries are guaranteed to be at odds. Traditionally, and almost universally, trusts are written so that income, and possibly some principal under specified circumstances, is paid out to one person, or one group of people; and at some later point in time, the remaining principal is paid out or divided among another group of people.

The conflict is that income beneficiaries want the money invested in bonds to maximize income. Remaindermen understand the growth potential of stocks, and want equity growth to maximize their future benefit. When the market soars, the problem of conflicting interests intensifies. We live in an era of mounting stock returns and vanishing dividends. Lifetime income beneficiaries measure the performance of a trust in terms of the size of their monthly check, and they won't be satisfied with stock dividends. Remaindermen measure the performance of a trust against the current S&P performance plus inflation, and they don't want to hear about the stability of bonds.

One important aspect of the Prudent Investor Rule is a trustee's legal obligation to show impartiality among all beneficiaries, including remaindermen. Because of that rule, most corporate fiduciaries are reluctant to put less than one-half of the assets in equities because history shows that in the long run, stocks outperform bonds. That leaves the remaining one-half in bonds to benefit the income beneficiary. Simply by specifying income to lifetime beneficiaries and principal to remaindermen forces the trustee away from equities and toward fixed income assets, thus *lowering* the total return of the trust. The trust document, rather than sound investing principles, determines the trust's return. The tragedy is that none of the beneficiaries can be satisfied under such a structure.

Here's a hypothetical, but common example. Let's say your great-aunt passes away leaving a sizable estate but no children. Her will says that a trust is established at a trust company to pay the income to her niece and nephew, your aunt and father, for life. After the death of the survivor of your aunt and your father, you and your cousins divide what's left equally.

Your father retired a few years ago, so he is on a fixed income of social security and a meager pension and welcomes the income benefit. He remembers the depression era and still doesn't trust the stock market, though he might not admit it. Since he is the one receiving the money, he goes to the trust company and tells them to keep the money "safe" for you but to maximize his income by investing in Treasury Notes.

You receive statements and you are furious! This bank is supposed to be a professional money manager, and, yet, they are only providing a return of 11% after fees when your kid's college funds that you manage earned 20% last year. This trust has the potential to grow astronomically in one generation if they would only invest it in the surging market.

The problem was created when the will was written. Assuming that your great-aunt didn't want you and your father arguing with the bank over her legacy and that she would have wanted to maximize the benefits to both of you, what could have been done? Your great-aunt's attorney could have written a Total Return Unitrust.

In a Total Return Unitrust, a percentage of the entire trust balance is stipulated for payment to the lifetime beneficiary. The trust is invested for maximum total return, i.e., appreciation plus income, and it is diversified for safety. At specified intervals, a percentage of the trust market value is paid to the lifetime beneficiary, by selling some shares of stock as necessary.

Additional characteristics can be added to the provisions of the Unitrust. The percentage payout may be restricted to allow the corpus to grow with inflation or at a faster specified rate. The payout can also be based on a rolling average balance of the trust (let's say more than three years) to reduce the volatility of the annual payment to the lifetime beneficiary. The trustee could be given the power to change the rate of the payout to the lifetime beneficiary if circumstances change.

While the drafting becomes a bit more complicated, Total Return Unitrusts can be used in just about any situation, including Marital QTIP trusts, trusts with rights of withdrawal, discretionary trusts for children, perpetual trusts designed for use of the Generation-Skipping Tax Exemption, etc.

Simply put, the Total Return Unitrust is a modernization of the dispositive provisions of a trust. The trustee's difficulty of impartiality is removed, and the lifetime beneficiary's expectations can be met at no detriment to the long-term prospects of the remaindermen.

Figures Lie and Liars Figure: The Fallacy of Future Value

"One of the problems of technology is the implicit assumption that anything that *can* be calculated *should* be calculated. This often results in technological overkill, producing numbers, percentages, graphs, and other information that is meaningless at best and, even worse, potentially confusing and misleading." Daniel B. Evans, Timing of

Transfers: The Future Value Fallacy in Estate Tax Planning, *Probate and Property* Vol. 7, No. 1, p. 23.

You are reviewing your estate plan and looking at a bound volume full of numbers, pie charts, and graphs. You see illustrations of what your estate will be worth in 20 years if your assets grow at an annual rate of 8% (pick any number). If your estate grows at a rate of 8% for 20 years your current 2014 $5 million estate (which would not be subject to federal estate tax if you die now) will be worth $23 million in 2034 and the estate tax will be $7.3 million. How are your heirs going to pay it? Should you buy life insurance?

Don't be taken in. There is a fundamental fallacy here. What is this projected future value really telling you? In 20 years, at an 8% growth rate, all other things being equal, your estate will be worth $23 million. What are some of the other things that might not be equal? Spending, marriage, divorce, births, deaths, gifts, changes in the economic condition of the country and the world, illness, disability, changes in the tax law (at least one per year), inflation, natural disasters, war, and dare I say terrorism? All of these variables are unquantifiable. The assumed accumulation of assets given an 8% rate of return can be calculated. The ability to calculate the impact of one variable among many gives that variable an over-emphasized importance. It really is no more important than any of the other variables and to assume a steady 8% return unaffected by any other variables for 20 years is really pretty silly and meaningless.

As Daniel Evans points out "[W]hy should anyone pay premiums *now* for insurance that isn't needed *now* solely to provide liquidity that *might* be needed to pay taxes at a future date. . . . Future value calculations usually are speculative, confusing, and meaningless and generally should not be used in estate planning calculations or estate planning presentations to clients."

Another example of the future value fallacy is that advocates say it is always better to defer a tax than to pay it now. All other things being equal, it doesn't make sense to defer taxes. Let's say you have $100 and the tax rate is 50%. You can invest money and double it in 5 years. You have the choice of paying the 50% tax now, or at the end of the 5 years. Which is better? All other things being equal, it doesn't matter when you pay the tax. If you pay the tax now, you have $50 to invest and it doubles to $100 in 5 years. If you defer the tax and invest the $100, it doubles to $200. At the end of 5 years, you pay the 50% tax on $200 and you are left with the same $100.

The key to the example is "all other things being equal" — which they never are. In the real world we can't predict what tax rates will be next year, let alone 5 years from now. And in the real world, there are no investments guaranteed to double in 5 years (I don't care what anybody tells you). Then there's the psychological aspect. No one wants to pay a tax now that they can put off until later.

One of the biggest "unequal" things to consider is an intangible: owning $100 is much more prestigious than owning $50. I kid you not. In the course of doing estate planning for 25 years I have met many people who want very much to reduce the estate tax burden on their estates. However, when shown the techniques and transfers involved in reducing the tax bill, they can't bring themselves to do it because they won't have such a big net worth anymore. You can't have it both ways.

Financial planners and economists say that paying the tax later is better because of the "opportunity cost" of the money used to pay the tax. In our example, these folks would say that not paying the tax at the beginning and having the extra $50 to "work with" is better. Is it?

Opportunity cost is simply what you give up when you decide to do something. If you spend $1.00 on a soft drink, you can't use the dollar to buy popcorn. The inability to buy popcorn is the opportunity cost of buying the soft drink. What opportunity have you forgone by paying the 50% tax right now? The opportunity to spend the $50 (investing it doesn't get you farther ahead as we have already proven). If you want to spend the money, then of course, don't pay the tax early. But then what do you have at the end of 5 years? You spent $50, and invested $50 to double to $100 in 5 years. The $100 is subject to the 50% tax and you're left with $50. No magic here — you can't invest what you spend.

Others will look at this example and mutter something about the time value of money. That sounds very important and complicated, but it really isn't. It's a very simple concept. $1 today is worth more than $1.00 a year from now. Not because of inflation, but because if you have a dollar today and can invest it at 5%, a year from now you will have $1.05 — which is worth more than simply getting $1.00 a year from now. $1 a year from now (assuming an investment return of 5%) is really worth 95.23 cents today. 95.23 cents invested at 5% for one year equals $1.00.

While many future value computations can be misleading, there are some situations where a future value analysis is properly used. Future value *is* important in illustrating the value of lifetime gifts using the $14,000 annual exclusions and making gifts using the $5.26 million exemption. These gifts generate no tax. The advantage is shown by projecting growth only because this growth is not subjected to transfer tax and is the whole point of making gifts as part of an estate plan.

And remember:

> *In the long run we're all dead.*
>
> John Maynard Keynes

Understanding the Mysterious Things Called Annuities

The life expectancy of Americans has hit an all-time high. The Health and Human Services department says that overall life expectancy is at the record high of 77 years. Americans are living longer; they are healthier, and medical technology is improving. We're living longer and retiring earlier. But how do we plan for sufficient income for those retirement years? Employers aren't footing the bill in the same way as they used to.

With tax deferment and a regular savings habit, you should be all set for that long-awaited retirement. Right? Well, maybe. You will need enough money to supplement your social security and pension income so that you can withdraw funds annually and live comfortably, despite the erosion of inflation. Annuities are often touted as part of the solution to this problem.

What is an annuity? As the word is commonly used, it refers to an insurance product that comes in two basic forms: variable and fixed. The fixed version is a contract that can provide either a lump sum or a series of fixed lifetime payments to the annuitant. A variable annuity has a separate account attached to it — the value of the annuity and the payments paid from it depend on the investment made in the account. The total value of a variable annuity can fluctuate with the market. Annuities are sold by insurance companies and also by some mutual fund companies and brokerage houses.

To "annuitize" means to choose to receive payments at regular intervals over time instead of just letting funds accumulate. The annuitant is the person during whose life the annuity is payable, usually the person to receive the annuity.

An annuity with immediate payout begins payouts to the investor immediately. When the investor chooses a deferred annuity, the payout begins at a later date. In the meantime, the investment earnings inside the annuity accumulate.

A fixed annuity promises to pay a fixed monthly amount to the annuitant as long as he or she lives. The payment amount never changes. When the annuitant dies, nothing further is paid to his or her estate or heirs. The annuity terminates.

Variable annuities are usually deferred annuities and are really a combination of an insurance contract and an investment product. They use the insurance to provide tax deferral. The money inside the annuity wrapper is invested in stocks or bonds and the rate of return can vary, hence the name, variable annuity. The insurance portion of the annuity may guarantee that the full principal amount (what was initially contributed to the annuity) will be paid to beneficiaries if the annuitant dies before annuitization.

Annuities have some similarities to IRAs in that they both provide tax-deferred growth inside the IRA or annuity. Anyone can invest in an annuity in an unlimited amount. Only those with earned income can put money aside in an IRA, and the contributions to an IRA are limited.

Variable annuities are extremely profitable for the companies that sell them. Many investment advisors say that most people are better off in a low-cost equity index fund, which is extremely tax-efficient and provides an overall more favorable tax situation than an annuity. Annuities usually have a sales load, usually have very high expenses, and always have a mortality charge for insurance. A typical commission on an annuity sale would be 7% of the amount contributed to the annuity.

The theory is that with deferred taxation as in an IRA, the money grows faster; yes, and no. It should grow faster, but insurance plus management fees and surrender charges associated with the variable annuity are higher than management fees of an index fund alone. Experts have crunched these numbers for years, and can come out ahead or behind depending on which side, pro or con, hired the number cruncher. My own quick and dirty scenario showed the variable annuity falling slightly behind every year, with 1% fees for the mutual fund and 2% fees for the annuity. Other tax considerations can also put the annuity behind the mutual fund.

Almost all advisors agree that any individual should maximize contributions to IRAs, 401(k)s and other tax-deferred retirement plans before considering an annuity. Proponents of annuities suggest that you buy an annuity with all or part of your portfolio, whether it be certificates of deposit, stocks and bonds, or mutual funds.

The questions of whether to annuitize and when to annuitize comes down to whose number cruncher you believe. The answer depends in all cases on what financial assumptions are made for projected performance, what income tax rates will be, what investment performance will be, what fees and costs will be, and so on.

A word of caution: don't commit funds you can't afford to leave untouched. Annuitized funds are no longer liquid. Sometimes you can get to them in an emergency, but there are stiff penalties for early withdrawal and for contract termination.

Beware of Annuities' Taxation Shortcomings

Are you considering an annuity to save for your retirement? While often promoted as tax-advantaged investments, beware of annuities' pitfalls, which may outweigh any tax savings.

In a variable annuity (a combination of insurance contract and investment account often intended to provide retirement income) money grows tax-deferred. This means that interest earnings on your investment grow without being taxed until withdrawn or distributed. This is similar to how an IRA works.

Unlike an IRA, however, the money you put into the annuity is not deductible from your taxes. Also unlike an IRA, you can put as much money in an annuity as you wish; there is no maximum limitation.

Income deferral is completely irrelevant if the annuity is to be held in an IRA or other retirement account. The IRA or retirement plan already is tax-deferred. If anyone tries to convince you to buy an annuity inside your IRA or retirement plan, put your hand firmly on your wallet, turn, and run.

What if you need money before you annuitize? Like IRAs, there is a 10% federal tax penalty which applies to withdrawals before age 59½. When you make a withdrawal from your annuity, the withdrawal is considered to be interest first. Until you start withdrawing your original investment, all withdrawals are going to be taxable (note that this has the effect of turning capital gains into ordinary income). Further, if you make a withdrawal before 59½ you will probably have to pay a 10% penalty (the penalty can be avoided in a few narrowly defined instances such as disability).

If you are willing to pay the 10% penalty and pay the income tax, can you get money out? Most annuity contracts permit some withdrawal, perhaps 10%, free of charge (but not free of the 10% tax penalty for premature withdrawals).

Over the minimum allowed withdrawal, most annuities have a surrender charge in addition to the tax penalty. Some have a fixed surrender charge for a stated term of years or one that declines over a number of years. A few annuity contracts permit systematic withdrawals to provide a steady income without surrender charges. These withdrawals are subject to the same taxation as any other withdrawals.

Review fees and charges carefully. Find out what the annual administration fee is, the asset charges, the insurance and surrender charges and whether or not it costs to transfer your investment among portfolios. Morningstar says that the average costs on an annuity are 2.12% annually. It takes about 10 to 15 years, on average, for the tax deferral of an annuity with this high expense ratio to match the performance of a mutual fund.

A variable annuity has two "phases" — an accumulation phase and a payout phase. The accumulation phase begins as soon as you make the investments in the annuity whether you make one large payment to a single premium annuity or a series of payments of varying amounts to a flexible premium annuity.

Your investment purchases "accumulation units" in the insurance company's separate account for annuities. This separate account, in turn, is invested in various portfolios of securities. These underlying securities can earn interest, pay dividends, or produce capital gains that can be reinvested. Of course, the underlying securities can lose value also.

Most variable annuities permit you to make your own investment choices among these portfolios. These portfolios, also called variable annuity sub-accounts, have varying performances, just like mutual funds. The sub-accounts can be difficult to analyze and independent reports for them, like Morningstar, are not always available.

If you made the same investment in stocks and bonds or mutual funds outside of the annuity wrapper, any interest or dividends earned during the year are taxable income for that year. If you sell a security you may owe capital gains tax. If these transactions occur in an annuity, the income tax is deferred to a later time when you withdraw or take distributions.

The payout phase begins with annuitization. That means you exercise your election to stop the accumulation phase and begin the phase where you receive regular payments. Some annuitization options are for lifetime income and stop when you die. Another option, called "term certain", is for life, but with a minimum fixed term, say ten years. The term certain option, usually gives you a lower payout but provides something for your heirs if you die before the fixed term.

After you annuitize, each payment to you is treated as part return of principal and part interest. The part that is return of principal is not taxable. You can annuitize before 59½ and payments received before the 59½ will not be subject to the 10% penalty for premature withdrawals. After you annuitize, most companies do not allow any additional withdrawals, so your liquidity is gone.

What happens on death? Once you have annuitized, your heirs get nothing, unless you have elected a term certain option. Many retired people never annuitize for fear of not living long enough to recoup their investment.

If you die before you annuitize, the insurance piece of the contract guarantees that your beneficiary will receive at least the amount of your investment in the contract, even if your investment has declined in value. If you have not yet annuitized, the funds, when received by your heirs, are subject to estate tax as well as income tax. Annuities do not get a step-up in basis on death. If you are concerned about passing wealth to your beneficiaries, this is an important fact. This compares very unfavorably to investments in mutual funds without an annuity wrapper. Mutual funds *do* get a step-up in basis on the owner's death.

The ABCs of Mutual Funds

Mutual funds that have a "load," that is a charge associated with investing in the fund, are generally sold in three classes: A, B and C. They differ in the commission the broker is paid by the buyer for the sale, when it is paid, and the size and duration of annual fees taken by the fund company.

Class A funds are front-loaded. There is an up-front commission that is a percentage of the amount of the purchase. Annual fees, such as management fees and 12b-1 fees are charged for fund maintenance, sales and distribution. No commission is charged on redemption, although there may be redemption fees charged.

The front-load percent may start out around 5.75% but the percentage decreases in steps as the size of the purchase goes up, dropping to zero percent typically at one million dollars. Legally the front load can go as high as 8.5%.

Other ways to decrease the percentage of front-load fees are by owning other mutual funds offered by the same fund family, committing to regularly purchasing mutual fund shares, and having family members who hold funds in the same fund family.

The 12b-1 fees get their name from the SEC rule that governs them. Investors are not charged these fees directly, but fund managers are allowed to take these fees out of a mutual fund's assets to cover the annual costs of marketing and distribution. Since the fund assets are used to pay these costs, the value of a fund share is reduced and performance is adversely affected.

The current limit on 12b-1 fees is 0.75% per year, but there is no limit on how long a fund can pay these charges if it continues to make significant new sales to investors. As a result, shareholders may pay asset-based charges through the fund for as long as they own the fund.

Class B funds are back-end loaded. They charge higher expenses than Class A shares, usually for a period of four to eight years.

Class B shares normally impose a contingent deferred sales charge (CDSC), which is the back-end load. You pay the CDSC if you sell your shares within a certain number of years, normally before the end of six years. Some Class B shares convert to Class A shares after a certain number of years. Class A shares typically have lower management and 12b-1 fees than Class B shares, so it's significant that the back-end commission goes away years down the road and the fees drop.

Class B funds have fallen under scrutiny. Purchase of large amounts of Class B funds lose the benefit of the breakpoints inherent in Class A funds, not to mention the higher annual fees generated over the first six to eight years. Large purchases of Class B funds tend to benefit the broker at the expense of the buyer so some broker/dealers cap purchases at $50,000. Several fund families have announced that they are planning to drop their B shares altogether.

Class C funds are like Class B funds except that the back-end load is lower than found in Class B shares (typically around one percent) and is eliminated in a much shorter time, typically a year. However, their management and 12b-1 fees are higher than those of Class A shares. C shares tend to be used by investors who think they may need access to funds within three to four years.

No-load mutual funds charge no commission at purchase or at redemption, but are allowed to charge fees within limits. Financial Industry Regulatory Authority (FINRA) rules limit no-load funds to 12b-1 fees of no more than 0.25 percent and total fees of no more than 0.50 percent in order to call themselves no-load funds. By comparison, Class A funds typically charge 1.25 percent per year in fees and Class B and Class C funds typically charge two percent per year in fees.

FINRA also has a "fund analyzer" to let the user compute fund performance net of fees and loads for up to 20 years.

No-load funds can be purchased directly without advice, or with advice for an annual fee. This fee is in addition to the fund expenses. So why would managed portfolios hold funds with higher fees and loads? Because the advisors selling the funds get more commission for doing so.

You cannot deduct a commission you pay to a broker to buy investment property, so the loads you pay are not tax-deductible.

However, you can use the commission to figure gain or loss from the sale. A front-end load adds to the cost basis of the shares. A back-end load reduces the sale proceeds. 12b-1 fees are not deductible either, but they reduce the return of the investment, and in that way indirectly reduce taxable income.

On the other hand, investment manager and planner fees may be deductible (subject to the 2% floor for miscellaneous itemized deductions) to the extent they relate to taxable income. If the management fee is based on a percentage of assets, it is deductible. Since IRA management fees reduce the value of the IRA, they indirectly reduce the amount of income reportable by the beneficiary. If your IRA custodian permits, you can pay the management fee yourself (instead of having it deducted from the IRA), and then take it as an itemized deduction subject to the 2% floor.

Is Your 401(k) Advisor Buying Retail?

There is another class offered for many funds: Class I, which stands for institutional class. Class I shares are offered only to large investors, typically investment firms and minimum purchases are often more than $500,000. Class I shares' fees are typically 40% less than those of classes A, B and C.

What does this have to do with you and me? The connection is that our 401(k) managers can make Class I funds available as investment options for our retirement account. Since Class I funds have exactly the same underlying investment positions as the A, B and C class shares (ABCs), you would expect the fund manager would go with the better deal for us. Wouldn't you be upset if he were paying higher fees than he had to?

Think about it this way. You want to buy a car. There are two identical cars on the dealer's lot. One costs $5,000 more than the other. Which one would you buy?

Why would you pay $5,000 more for an identical car? Why would a fund dealer provide ABCs which carry a higher fee instead of Class I shares? Maybe carelessness. Or maybe because the additional fee charged benefits the fund manager or plan sponsor. That is exactly what happens when your 401(k) investment manager provides retail (ABCs) mutual funds for you. They call it "revenue sharing". The plan sponsor receives "offsets" from retail mutual funds, that is, the 12b-1 fees. They don't call it a kickback.

A recent court case should make 401(k) plan sponsors think twice before offering retail funds as investment options in the plan when investment class shares, Class I, are available with lower expenses. In a case in the middle district of California, *Tibble v. Edison International*, a group of plan participants went to federal court to complain about the plan buying non-institutional shares. Judge Stephen V. Wilson ruled that the company violated its duty of prudence by selecting retail shares instead of Class I shares for three of the funds held by the plan.

The Edison International Trust Investment Committee made retail share classes of three mutual funds available to participants in the Edison 401(k) Savings Plan. In deciding which funds to offer, the Committee did not consider, let alone evaluate, other share classes of the funds. However, it did solicit and rely upon the advice of Hewitt Financial Services, an affiliate of the plan's third-party record keeper. A class of plan participants sued the Edison International Committee, and others, seeking damages under ERISA for alleged financial losses suffered by the plan, in addition to injunctive and other equitable relief on account of breaches of fiduciary duty.

Judge Wilson stated, "In light of the fact that the institutional share classes offered the exact same investment at a lower fee, a prudent fiduciary acting in a like capacity would have invested in the institutional share classes."

Daniel Sonin reported this case on dailyfinance.com on July 28, 2010. He reported that Edison is not an isolated instance. He asserts that "over ninety percent of the funds he has examined have purchased retail class funds when institutional class funds of the same content were available."

If Class I shares' fees are typically 40% less than those of classes A, B and C, what would a 40% reduction in fees by offering Class I shares look like? Consider a fund of $200,000. For simplicity, assume no additions or withdrawals. Assume a rate of return of 8% minus annual fees of 2% for a net annual return of 6%. If the fees of 2% were forty percent lower, they would be just 1.2% per year, allowing the fund to grow at a net 6.8% per year. After ten years at 6%, it would grow to $358,170. At 6.8%, it would grow to $386,138, a difference of almost $28,000.

If Judge Wilson is correct and the company is liable for lost income; that would make many fund advisors think twice about recommending retail funds.

The Basics of Tax-Free Municipal Bonds

State and local governments and their agencies issue bonds in exchange for the use of the capital of individuals and corporations. The bonds obligate the state and local governments to make interest payments and to repay, at some stated time, the principal of the amount borrowed. Municipal bonds can be issued by cities, counties, redevelopment agencies, school districts, publicly owned airports, as well as other governmental entities.

Bonds are General Obligation Bonds (GOs) if they are to be paid from the general revenue and assets of the issuers. The repayment of GOs is generally supported by the issuer's taxing power; the issuer pledges its "full faith and credit." Bonds are Revenue Bonds if their repayment is restricted to certain types of revenue received by the issuer. Examples are repayment from bridge tolls or user fees at an airport.

If the bonds qualify as "tax-exempt," the interest income received by the individuals and corporations that hold the bonds is excluded from federal income taxation and usually from the income tax of the state in which they are issued. A bond that is free of federal, state and local taxes is called a "triple-tax-free." Usually, since the bonds enjoy this tax preference, they pay a lower interest rate than taxable debt instruments with a similar level of risk. They are most valuable to taxpayers with relatively high marginal income tax rates. However, in the current economic picture, the yield on tax-free municipal bonds is high relative to the yield on most taxable investments, so you should seriously take a look at tax-free bonds as an investment alternative — even if you pay very little income tax.

Not all municipal bonds are tax free, such as when they finance private activity. Also, bonds issued for some purposes are subject to the alternative minimum tax.

The tax policy behind the interest exemption was to encourage public capital facilities. Bond proceeds can be used for building schools, highways, sewage systems, and a variety of other projects. The tax exemption is limited to bonds that satisfy broadly defined "public" purposes. Generally, bonds are considered to have a public purpose if they meet one of two tests: (1) no more than 10% of the proceeds is used directly or indirectly in a trade or business, or (2) no more than 10% of the proceeds are secured directly or indirectly by property used in a trade or business. Bonds that can't pass the test are taxable and are referred to as private activity bonds.

Taxes reduce the net income produced by bonds so you cannot compare a municipal bond yield directly to a corporate bond yield. When evaluating tax-free municipal bond investments, you must first determine the "equivalent taxable yield" of the bond. This is done by subtracting your effective tax rate from 100% and dividing the tax-free yield by the result.

Here is an example: If you are a Pennsylvania resident in the 25% federal and 3.07% state tax brackets, your combined tax rate is 28.07%. A 3% yield on a PA municipal bond is equal to earning 4.17% on a taxable investment (3% divided by (1 - 28.07%)). A PA municipal bond paying 4% will pay the same (after tax) as a taxable bond or CD paying 5.56% (4% divided by (1 - 28.07%)). If you are looking at a bond from another state (e.g., you live in Pennsylvania, but the bond is issued by a New Jersey municipality), you would only take into consideration the federal tax bracket when calculating the taxable equivalent yield.

If you aren't comfortable with the math, you can go to the Securities Industry and Financial Markets Association (SIFRA) website called *www.investinginbonds.com*, click on calculators, and let the program do the math.

While it is true that interest on the obligations of state or local governments is exempt from federal income taxes under IRC Section 103(a), there can be some other tax consequences you should be aware of.

1. Tax-exempt interest from municipal bonds is included in the calculation of the taxable portion of Social Security and Railroad Retirement benefits. In some cases, each $1.00 in tax-free bond interest can result in an additional 85 cents of

taxable income, because the additional interest puts you over the limit and 85% of your social security becomes taxable.

2. Tax-exempt interest from "private activity bonds" is a tax preference for purposes of computing the Alternative Minimum Tax (AMT). If you are subject to AMT, then the interest from municipal bonds could be taxed at a rate of 26% or 28%.
3. The income tax exemption is only for the interest. If you sell a municipal bond and recognize a gain, that gain is subject to tax just like the gain on the sale of any other security.
4. If you buy tax-free bonds with money you have borrowed on "margin", the interest paid on the loan is not deductible as investment interest.

Some municipal bonds are insured, which means that a third-party insurer has assumed the risk of the issuer's default. The bond issuer must pay a premium for this insurance, which has the practical effect of reducing the investor's yield. The value of the insurance depends on the financial strength of the insurance company.

Mutual Fund Taxation

In general, a mutual fund itself is not taxed if it distributes substantially all of its income (at least 98%) to its shareholders. The shareholders must report mutual fund distributions as income. Dividends and interest from holdings inside the fund, as well as any capital gains from the sales inside the fund, are taxed to the shareholders.

There are two types of mutual fund distributions: (1) ordinary dividends and (2) capital gain distributions. Ordinary dividends are taken from the interest and dividends earned inside the mutual fund and are paid out to shareholders, often quarterly. Capital gain distributions are distributions made to fund shareholders when the gains from the fund's sales of securities exceed losses. Capital gain distributions are always treated as long term capital gain, no matter how long you owned the mutual fund shares.

Most funds offer their shareholders the option of having dividend and capital gain distributions automatically reinvested in the fund.

Reinvestment has no impact on the taxability of the distributions — you still pay income tax on them even if they are reinvested. The amount reinvested must be added to the cost basis of your mutual fund shares. This is crucial when calculating your gain or loss on the sale of shares.

Many mutual fund families permit a shareholder to exchange shares in one fund for shares of another fund in the family. These exchanges are not tax free. For tax purposes, an exchange is treated as a sale of shares in one fund for cash and then a purchase with cash of shares in the other. If the fund redeems your shares, this also is taxed as a sale.

Since mutual funds are required to distribute at least 98% of their income annually, and since net gains and losses cannot be determined with any accuracy until near year-end, many mutual funds make their largest distributions in December. Don't buy mutual fund shares right before a December capital gain distribution. This will result in you paying tax on the distribution, which represents earnings over the course of a year in which you did not participate.

Make sure that you keep your statements, especially the year-end statement. The statements show every transaction — every dividend, distribution, sale, purchase, and reinvestment. The fund will send you a 1099-B to report the proceeds of any sales, but you will need the statement information to help you calculate your cost basis.

If you sell less than all of your mutual fund shares, you need to determine the best way to allocate your basis among the shares. There are three approaches: (1) first-in, first-out (FIFO), (2) average cost, and (3) specific identification.

First-in, first-out assumes that the first shares you bought are the first shares you sold. Average cost is determined by adding up the total cost of all the shares you own and dividing by the number of shares. It can be done on all shares, or in two categories, the average cost of long-term shares and the average cost of short-term shares.

If you have a record of all the purchase dates and prices of all shares you own, including shares purchased with reinvested dividends, you can pick individual shares to be sold. If you use this third method, you can pick out the shares that have the highest basis to be the ones you sell, thus keeping your gain to a minimum. To use this method, you must indicate to the fund or your broker, which shares you are selling — you can't designate them after the fact.

Your mutual fund statement may calculate gain or loss for you. They usually use the average cost method. You are not required to calculate your gain or loss using the method shown on the statement. However, once you start reporting using average cost, you have to report all future sales using that method.

The New Tax Law Shifts Investment Strategy

Taxpayers got a major piece of tax legislation called the Jobs and Growth Tax Relief Reconciliation Act of 2003. In general, JAGTRRA brought more favorable income tax rates and reduced rates on qualified dividends and long-term capital gains. Some old strategies of investing with the tax effect in mind need to be reversed.

It used to be that equities were recommended for nontaxable accounts and interest-paying investments were recommended for taxable accounts. (By nontaxable accounts I mean retirement plan accounts and IRAs.) Now is the time to reverse that strategy — it's a good time for equities to be held in taxable accounts.

Since the maximum capital gains rate is 20%, you should consider holding capital gain investments in taxable accounts. Deferring tax on gains is not so attractive when the gains are taxed at this low rates. It can be a good choice to take gains at this rate before they rise again with changes in politics, the economy, and government spending. Plus, the low capital gains rates does you no good at all if the appreciated security is in an IRA or other nontaxable account. When distributed all IRA funds are taxed as ordinary income whether they were generated by capital gains or not. Invest for gains in taxable accounts. Beware: the maximum rate on gains from the sale of collectibles is 28%.

For those of you with high concentrations of wealth in a single stock or just a couple of stocks, consider diversifying. With maximum capital gains rate of 20%, you have a great opportunity to get out of that concentration which exposes your portfolio to too much risk. Then you can reinvest in higher income-producing investments. Consider using the additional income to buy long-term care insurance to protect your assets.

It's a great time to make gifts of appreciated stock with low tax basis to kids or custodians for kids in low brackets. They can sell the stock; and if they have no other income, pay only 5% in capital gains tax. This turns the conventional wisdom upside down. In prior years, it was recommended to give high basis stock as gifts because you didn't want to give capital gains liability. This 5% sale rate is hard to beat. (Beware the Kiddie tax for kids under 18 and in some circumstances up to age 23).

With dividend rates at 15% for qualifying dividends, this means dividends are going to be taxed at lower rates than interest on fixed income investments. Again, this points to stocks in taxable accounts and higher-yielding fixed income obligations in nontaxable accounts, the reversal of prior years' strategy.

Not all dividends qualify for the 15% rate. Money market distributions, while called dividends, are taxed as if they were interest. Almost all distribution from REITs (Real Estate Investment Trusts) are taxed as ordinary income, not at the 15% favorable dividend rate. Then there's the Draconian rule that in order to qualify for the 15% rate, you must hold the stock for more than 60 days during the 120-day period that begins 60 days before the ex-dividend date. (Who can we thank for that piece of gibberish?) Apparently this complex rule was put into the law to discourage people from buying a stock just to receive the dividend and then immediately selling the shares. You are required to own the stock for a minimum amount of time in order to qualify for the lower tax rate.

The IRS expects the number of people who pay the alternative minimum tax to more than double for 2003. Those most likely to be affected are those who live in states where there are high state taxes, and those taxpayers who have large families, who can claim numerous dependency exemptions. If you're going to get hit with AMT, the conventional tax plan of accelerating deductions into this tax year is the exact opposite of what you should do.

While overall tax rates have gone down, the "spread" between the top rate on ordinary income and the top rate on capital gains has widened. That means more folks are going to be engaging in strategies to convert ordinary income to capital gains. Update?

The 529 plans are somewhat less attractive. Withdrawals for education expenses of the beneficiary are still tax free but if you need to terminate the plan by withdrawing all money, you are essentially converting capital gains to ordinary income. Reconsider custodial accounts and Crummey trusts for gifts to children and grandchildren.

JAGTRAA makes tax-deferred annuities much less attractive (if you thought they were attractive in the first place). As Kaye Thomas in the *Tax Guide for Investors* says, "you now have to balance the tax benefit of deferral against the tax detriment of converting income that would otherwise be taxed at 15% into income taxed at ordinary rates. When you throw in other disadvantages — the up-front costs that often apply to these investments, the ongoing expenses and the possibility of surrender charges and early distribution tax penalty — TDAs have to overcome a great burden."

Looking ahead to the end of the year, beware of acquiring mutual funds before year-end just in time to receive a whole year's worth of the funds' dividend distributions. Don't unwittingly buy a tax liability when you buy a fund. While this was usually a warning heeded by buyers of equity funds when the stock market was soaring, since interest rates recently went down so dramatically, bond funds may have sold appreciated bonds. Municipal bond funds and other bond funds, especially long-term funds are likely to have high taxable distributions because of recognized capital gains.

Use Reverse Mortgage for More Lifetime Income

You're retired, you own your own home, but the funds don't stretch the way they used to and suddenly you need more income. Maybe you need to fix the roof. Or maybe your medical bills have increased. Or, simply, inflation has eroded your retirement fund.

Where's the money going to come from? You can sell your house for cash, but then, where do you live? A home equity loan may provide immediate cash, but that increases your monthly payments.

A reverse mortgage might be a solution. A reverse mortgage is a loan against the equity in the home that provides a tax-free lump sum or cash advances, but requires no payments during the term of the loan. You can get a stream of payments for a term or for life, or a lump sum payment, or a line of credit, or a combination of these.

A reverse mortgage, like any mortgage, involves interest, closing costs and fees. However, the debt you accumulate on the loan is not payable until you die, sell your house or move. The title to the home remains in your name and you are still responsible for home insurance and upkeep. If you die before the sum of payments plus interest equals the equity in the house, your estate gets the difference. If you sell the house, the proceeds are used to pay back the loan.

The loan is a "non-recourse" loan, which means that no matter how high the loan balance grows, you or your heirs never owe more than the home's market value. If you live a long time and the sum of the payments plus interest exceeds the equity in the house, the FHA or FNMA reimburses the bank, not the estate, for the excess. When the last co-owner dies, the institution gets the house as payment for the loan. Your estate is never subject to payments to the bank.

To qualify, you must be 62 years old, own your home or condominium or at least have a mortgage small enough to be paid off at closing, and agree to accept mortgage counseling from a HUD-approved counseling agency. If two owners are involved, the age of the younger owner will prevail.

In addition to the equity you have in your home, the funds you are able receive from a reverse mortgage are determined by the interest rate charged on the borrowed money and the age of the younger spouse. Lower interest rates yield larger payments. Older age yields larger payments.

The IRS currently treats monies received from a reverse mortgage to be loan advances and not taxable income. The interest that accrues is not deductible until the loan and interest is repaid, which only occurs if the owner sells the house before death of the last owner.

There are three types of reverse mortgages available. The least expensive, that is, with the lowest fees and typical interest rates, is the Single Purpose Reverse Mortgage. This type usually is available through state or local governments and is to be used for home repairs or property tax payments. With the exception of programs designed to defer yearly property tax payments, only a lump sum payment, designed to cover a specified expense, such as repairing the roof, is available.

The FHA offers the second type of reverse mortgage, the Home Equity Conversion Mortgage (HECM). You may choose a combination of a lump sum payment, periodic cash advances or regular, such as monthly, payments. You may borrow up to the value of the equity in your home or the home equity limit set for your county of residence by the Federal Housing Administration, whichever is lower. For Lancaster County, that limit is $144,336.

If your home is valued much higher than the home equity limit for your county, a third reverse mortgage option is available, a Proprietary Reverse Mortgage from a private lender, insured by Fannie Mae. Interest rates, closing costs, and fees for this type loan are much higher than the HECM and should be considered only if the need for funds is higher than the home equity limit.

How does a reverse mortgage affect Medicaid and Medicare? Medicare and Social Security do not care about assets. On the other hand, Medicaid does look at your assets, including your home. Payments from a reverse mortgage may be considered as income and may affect Medicaid eligibility. States run their programs differently, so you are encouraged to check with your local Office of Aging for more information.

There are some very good reasons for using a reverse mortgage. These include paying off your present mortgage, catching up on back taxes, preventing foreclosure due to debt on your home, paying for long-term care insurance, paying for in-home health care, updating a house to meet changing needs, and increasing monthly income to catch up with inflation.

However, there are also bad reasons for obtaining a reverse mortgage. These include getting a lump sum for reinvestment, getting money for a short term debt, helping a relative to start a new business, and helping a relative or friend get caught up on delinquent debts.

Reverse mortgages can be complicated. Before deciding to obtain one, do your homework. Visit the AARP website, *www.aarp.com/revmort/*, or write for their booklet on reverse mortgages.

Money for Nothing? Scams, Frauds, Cons

> *"A Con" is the slang phrase for "Confidence Game." The key is getting the victim to feel comfortable about trusting the perpetrator of the Con.*
>
> Unknown

Honest citizens lose about $40 billion in scams every year. As the old saying goes, "if it sounds too good to be true, it probably is." Anyone who tells you that you can make huge amounts of money, with very little investment, very little risk, and very little work, is almost certainly not telling you the truth. Participating in any pyramid scheme, Ponzi scheme, or any other scheme which promises that you will get rich quickly, with little effort, is foolish at best. True wealth is only gained through honest work, and honest investment, in enterprises that produce goods and services of value. There are no shortcuts, and anyone who tells you otherwise is almost certainly out to cheat you.

The SEC has a sample website designed to warn investors about stock market scams. The website offers a tremendous investment opportunity with lots of hype and time pressure. If you click on the icon to invest you get a warning "If you responded to an investment idea like this, you could get scammed!" Check it out at *www.mcwhortle.com*. The site was advertised by spoof press releases. It had 150,000 hits in 3 days — an astonishing number of people responded.

The North American Securities Administrators Association publishes a Top 10 List of Frauds. First on the list is Affinity Group Fraud. Affinity Group Frauds are investment scams targeting religious, ethnic, and professional groups, perpetrated by members of the groups or people claiming to want to help them. Remember New Era Philanthropy? In 1996 John G. Bennett, Jr. was indicted for defrauding hundreds of churches, charities, colleges, and philanthropists out of $135 million. Bennett was later sentenced to 12 years in federal prison after pleading "no contest." He promised to double the investment in six months from matching contributions made by a group of anonymous philanthropists. The Wall Street Journal, September 30, 1996: "New Era's lengthy list of participants included the American Red Cross, United Way, the Salvation Army and the University of Pennsylvania. In addition, scores of well-known philanthropists and Wall Street money managers, including Laurence S. Rockefeller and former Treasury Secretary William E. Simon, sent New Era millions." Lancaster County nonprofits and individuals were on the list too.

It's quite clear that the victims of scams are not just little old ladies. A recent AARP survey found that most victims of scams are well educated, have above average intelligence, and are socially active. Anyone can be a victim.

Next on the Top 10 List of Frauds are unlicensed individuals, often independent insurance agents, selling securities. Some sources say this is the biggest scam around. Scam artists use high commissions to entice insurance agents or financial planners to sell investments that the agents and planners know little about. What to do if you are approached? Call the Pennsylvania Securities Commission, (717) 787-8061, *www.psc.state.pa.us.* and ask if the salesperson is licensed and if the investment being offered is registered. If you get over those two hurdles, then review the product with extreme care.

In 2003 local newspapers carried news stories about accused scam artist Allen J. Perry, owner of the East Petersburg, Pennsylvania investment company, Senior Benefits Group, who was charged with more than 200 counts of securities fraud for allegedly selling more than $3.7 million in securities to Pennsylvania residents. The so-called securities were sold through Chemical Trust, and First Choice Management Services, both of which have been identified as Ponzi schemes.

How did he make the sales? By offering "insured" investments paying 11% interest, a "too-good-to-be-true" investment. Many of his victims were from Lancaster county. Perry was not registered with the Commonwealth to sell securities.

Many people are using the services of financial planners. Unfortunately, the financial planning industry is virtually unregulated and there are many opportunities for untrained, unlicensed, and unscrupulous con artists to offer financial planning advice. Sometimes money is never invested, the planner just absconds with it. Sometimes the fraud is recommending unsuitable investments with exorbitant fees and substantial losses for the client.

Investments and securities aren't the only area beset with con artists. Tax scams abound.

Every January, the IRS issues a nationwide alert, warning taxpayers to beware of the "Dirty Dozen" — twelve tax scams that usually surface each year in the beginning of the filing season. These range from false claims for slavery reparations, illegal schemes to avoid withholding taxes on wages, protesters who say that paying taxes is "voluntary" or "unconstitutional," to promoters of abusive trust schemes.

Beware of any tax gimmick that says you can deduct your personal living expenses. You can't create deductions by assigning assets or income to a trust, partnership, or other entity. Any scheme that claims to allow you to deduct your living expenses is highly suspect.

Stay far away from any scheme that depends on multiple trusts, partnerships, and other entities with no apparent business purpose other than reducing income taxes and making the money hard (but not impossible) to trace. The existence of multiple entities doesn't necessarily mean that anything is wrong, but multiple levels and multiple entities producing a zero tax result are probably fraudulent.

As the income tax filing season approaches, remember: (1) anyone who promises you a bigger refund without knowing your tax situation may well be misleading you, and (2) never sign a tax return without looking it over to make sure it's honest and correct. By signing the return you are affirming that it is correct.

The number and variety of tax, financial, and investment frauds is mind-boggling. Be aware. Defend yourself. Be skeptical. Getting something for nothing means just that — the scam artist gets your money and you get *nothing*.

Viatical Settlements: Making Life Insurance Pay Off

The term "viatical" is derived from the Latin *viaticum*, meaning "provisions for a journey." In ancient Rome a viaticum of money was given to a person before undertaking a journey of risk.

Life insurance is a misnomer. It should be called death insurance. It pays its benefit when the insured dies. Often the insured, especially if he or she is a victim of a major illness, could use the benefit before death. How to access the funds?

First, if the life insurance policy has any cash value, the owner of the policy may be able to borrow against the cash value. The borrowing rates are typically very modest but depending on the policy, the cash value may be a great deal less than the death benefit.

Second, either the policy by its terms, or more likely, the life insurance company, may have adopted practices that provide an accelerated benefits option. The accelerated death benefit allows the policy owner to receive a significant portion — often as much as 80% — of the death benefit that otherwise would be paid after death to the beneficiaries. It is usually available within the last year or two of the person's projected life. Many policies do not mention an accelerated death benefit option. Ask the company about it anyhow. While practices vary from company to company, this option may be available even though it is not part of the original policy contract.

Third, the policy owner may be able to borrow funds from friends or family using the life insurance policy as collateral to secure the loan.

Fourth, the policy could be cashed in for its cash value, if any. Often this is not desirable since the death benefit may be much more than the cash value and the insured may wish the beneficiaries to receive the entire death benefit if the policy is held for a year or two more.

Fifth, cash may be accessed by a "viatical settlement." A viatical settlement is the sale of a life insurance policy insuring a terminally ill individual to a third party. Usually a viatical settlement involves a person who has a life expectancy of less than two years. This assessment is based on the nature of the illness or condition and a review of the particular person's records by doctors. The owner of the policy (who is typically, but not necessarily, the individual with a life-threatening illness) receives cash for the policy, and the owner transfers the policy to the person buying the policy. In these transactions, the viatical settlement provider becomes the new owner and/or beneficiary of the life insurance policy and is responsible for paying all future premium payments and collecting the entire death benefit of the policy upon the death of the insured.

For tax purposes, amounts received by the insured (or the policy owner if different), if the insured is terminally or chronically ill, are considered to be like a life insurance death benefit and are tax-free to the insured. When the insured dies and the insurance company pays the death benefit to the purchaser of the policy, the receipt of the death benefit is now ordinary taxable income to the extent the death benefit exceeds the amount paid for the policy (including subsequent premiums) because the policy was transferred for valuable consideration.

Viatical settlements are based on a legitimate concept: allow investors to purchase the life insurance benefits from a terminally ill person, which allows the sick person to receive a partial payment on the policies while still alive, which can be a godsend to a terminally ill person and family. The investor pays about 60 to 70 cents on the dollar for the policy; then collects the full death benefit on the policy. Of course, you have to be able to handle the macabre aspect of hoping for the early death of a person whose insurance you buy.

Unfortunately, these programs are often run by cheats and frauds and can be disastrous for investors. Fraudulent schemes attract people who are desperately in need of more money from their small investment funds, by offering returns that are above market rates. This is a loosely-regulated industry where scam artists sell bogus policies and people feign illnesses.

Newly issued policies are referred to as "wet paper," which refers to life insurance policies less than two years old. Policies that are less than two years old are contestable — that is, the insurance company can challenge the contract based on things like misrepresentations in the application. "Wet paper" also sometimes refers to policies that are purchased with the intent of selling the contract to a third party. Often viaticals involving "wet paper" involve fraud during the policy application process.

Investments in viaticals involve very significant risks that are often not disclosed. What can go wrong? Lots. There may be significant expenses for you as the investor. Brokers' commissions are typically 10% of the face amount of the policy. You may have to pay various doctors who check out the medical records and maybe even examine the insured and report back to you. You may want to hire a lawyer to review the policy.

What else can go wrong for an investor? The insured person could live far longer than projected. Doctors can be wrong, and there are recoveries, remissions, and cures. New medical advances and drugs extend lives and cure previously untreatable diseases. Meanwhile, you have to continue to pay the premiums on the policies. Instead of collecting the death benefit, you could end up paying premiums for years.

What if the insured dies — then what can go wrong? The insurance company may refuse to pay the death benefit citing a material misrepresentation in the application. An imposter may have taken the medical exam in place of the proposed insured. The insurance company may go under. The policy could have expired having been only for a term. Perhaps you, as the investor, can't locate the insured and you can't get a death certificate. The insured may take the money he receives, go on a trip, and you'd not know when he dies, much less get a death certificate.

As with all investments — if you are promised a high rate of return with no risks — hold on to your wallet. If it sounds too good to be true, it is.

Stock Splits: Is 3/6 More Than 2/4?

What is a stock split? A stock split occurs when a corporation increases its number of outstanding shares by dividing each share. When a corporation declares a stock split and the new shares are issued, the stock price will decrease, but the number of shares increases proportionately. If you own 100 shares trading at $100 per share and the stock splits 2 for 1, you will receive an additional share for every share owned, making your new total of shares 200. The market price immediately becomes $50 per share. The dividend also would be reduced to half of what it otherwise would have been before the split. Splits can be in various proportions. The most common are 3-for-2, 2-for-1 and 3-for-1. You can even have reverse stock splits. A 1-for-5 stock split would give the investor 1 share for every 5 that he had owned.

A split decreases the market price of a share. However, the overall value of the corporation remains the same. If you had 100 shares that represent 1% of the corporation, after a 2-for-1 stock split you would own 200 shares that represent 1% of the corporation. Any finance professor will tell you that a stock split does absolutely nothing to change the value of the company. *Investopedia.com* gives this example to explain stock splits: "Let's say you have a $100 bill and someone offers you two $50 bills for it. Would you take the offer? This might sounds like a pointless question, but the action of a stock split puts you in a similar position." Putting it another way, a stock split is like cutting more slices from the same pie.

So why does a company split its stock? The answer: psychology. While the finance professor may say that the stock split has no effect on value, that's not what a lot of shareholders think. The average shareholder thinks, "Oh boy, now I have twice as many shares!"

Some investors think that when a stock's per share price gets too high it is "too expensive." Most American stocks trade between $10 and $100. (Not all, of course. Look at Berkshire Hathaway Class A — at the end of 2004 it was trading at $85,000 per share.) Some companies will have a split when the price gets near $100 to make the stock attractive to "smaller" investors who would be put-off by an "expensive" price. There is absolutely no difference between buying 100 shares at $50 per share or 25 shares at $200 per share. Since the stock splits usually occur when stock prices have risen to the high end of the range, it is easy to see how investors could think that the share price went up because the stock split instead of what really happened — the stock split because the price was going up.

The most important psychological effect of the stock split is giving investors the feeling that they own more shares than they did before. If you're paying commissions based on the number of shares you buy, buying a stock before it splits is an advantage. Most brokers offer flat fee commissions, so this isn't an advantage anymore.

A split is also considered to increase a corporation's liquidity. Stocks that trade at high prices sometimes have a large spread between the bid and ask prices. If you're a trader that can be important — for a long-term investor it makes little, if any, difference.

A stock dividend is payment of a corporate dividend in the form of stock rather than cash. The stock dividend may be additional shares in the company, or it may be shares in a subsidiary. Unlike a cash dividend which is taxable income when paid, stock dividends are not taxed until the shares are sold. For all practical purposes, a 100% stock dividend is the same thing as a 2-for-1 split. In either case the shareholder gets any additional share for every share owned.

After a split or a stock dividend, the cost basis of the shares is simply divided pro rata among the split shares. The shareholder's basis does not change — it is simply spread over a greater number of shares.

Let's say you own 99 shares, and there is a 3-for-2 split. You would now own 148.5 shares. Usually when this happens, the .5

fraction of a share is purchased by the company and you get a small check for its value. What is your cost basis in the fractional share? It gets a pro rata portion of the basis. If the basis of the 99 shares was $10 per share or a total of $990, then the basis of the 148.5 shares after the split is also $990, which works out to $6.66 per share or $3.33 for the .5 share. You report the sale of the fractional share on Schedule D of your 1040.

For holding period purposes, you are considered to have held the new shares for the same length of time you held your original shares. Even if you sell the split shares immediately, or sell a fractional share immediately, the gain is long term if the long-term holding period was met for the original owned shares.

Since a corporation has to undergo some significant expenses to undertake a stock split, the split may actually be a negative for the company's profitability and ultimate value.

Beware of a company that splits its stock as a promotional tool. Their stock is trading nowhere near the top of the range, and yet they have a stock split. Maybe the thinking is that they will entice the investors by generating excitement and hype about the company to drive the price up? Maybe even mask otherwise poor earnings' performance?

You still get half of the pie whether it's divided into two or twenty pieces.

What Is a Signature Guarantee?

A signature guarantee is not the same thing as notarization. A notary public cannot guarantee a signature. A signature guarantee, sometimes called a Medallion Guarantee, or a Green Medallion, is an authentication of a signature in the form of a stamp or seal by a bank, a stock exchange member or another acceptable guarantor. A guarantee of a person's signature is required by all Transfer Agents, under SEC Rule 17Ad-15, before a security transfer can take place.

The organization that guarantees the authenticity of the signature is liable for the financial value of the transaction. As this could be stock certificates worth millions of dollars, the financial institution must be very careful to establish the identity of the person whose signature they are guaranteeing. If the signature turns out to be a forgery, the guaranteeing institution will be expected to pay the loss. They may have a surety bond for this liability; but if there is willful negligence by their employees in guaranteeing the signature, the insurance company may not pay.

Transfer agents insist on signature guarantees because they limit their liability and losses if a signature turns out to be forged. One way to avoid having to get your signature guaranteed is to have your securities held in street name, meaning that your securities are held in the name of your brokerage firm instead of your name.

A commercial bank, savings bank, credit union, or broker dealer that participates in one of the Medallion signature guarantee programs can guarantee investors' signatures. The three Medallion signature guarantee programs are the Securities Transfer Agents Medallion Program (STAMP), the Stock Exchanges Medallion Program (SEMP), and the New York Stock Exchange Medallion Signature Program (MSP).

The financial institution must apply to the program, pay a fee, obtain a surety bond, and get special equipment. For example, the STAMP program requires a Medallion imprint that incorporates bar code technology. The stamp uses a special patented green ink which in addition to having a visible green pigment also contains an invisible security compound that is only detectable by special equipment. Transfer Agents who rely on a guarantee from a member of a Signature Guarantee Program are protected against loss from wrongful endorsements if the guaranteeing institution is unwilling to meet, or is incapable of meeting, its financial obligation to the transfer agent.

Because of the great liability undertaken by the guaranteeing institution, great care must be taken. Banks, for example, usually will not guarantee a signature unless the investor is a customer of the bank. An institution has no duty to provide the guarantee. They do it as a service to their customers. Banks and brokerage houses are careful in training employees who are permitted to give the guarantees and in safeguarding the special green medallion stamp.

The Uniform Commercial Code provides that a person guaranteeing a signature warrants that at the time of signing: (1) the signature was genuine, (2) the signer had legal capacity to sign, and (3) the signer was an appropriate person to endorse the security.

In general, you must appear in person to have your signature guaranteed, present appropriate identification, satisfy the guarantor that you are legally competent, and that you are the proper endorser. For example, to transfer a security held in joint names, both joint owners must have their signatures guaranteed. For securities of a decedent, the executor or administrator must produce a death certificate and a certificate evidencing their appointment to satisfy the guarantor that he or she is the appropriate endorser. If the securities are owned by a partnership or a trust, the document must be examined to determine who has the authority to endorse certificates.

You Can Transfer Securities on Death by Beneficiary Designation

The registration of a security determines who owns it. A stock certificate with your name on it means you own the shares. A brokerage account in the joint names of you and your spouse means you are joint owners, and on the death of one of you, the survivor becomes the sole owner. Usually, on the death of a sole owner, or on the death of the last surviving joint owner, the security becomes probate property and passes under the deceased owner's will, or under the intestacy statute.

There is an important exception. Since February 18, 1997, it has been possible to transfer securities on death by beneficiary designation. This is done by registering the securities in beneficiary form. Registration in beneficiary form is shown by the words "pay on death" or "transfer on death" or by the acronyms "POD" or "TOD" after the name of the owner and before the name of the beneficiary. A financial institute may offer this form of beneficiary designation, but is not required to.

This legislation was an attempt to avoid the perceived or imagined burdens of the probate process. The result is uncoordinated estate plans. By providing another avenue for the passage of property on death, the likelihood of uncoordinated estate plans is increased. Securities in beneficiary form do not pass under the will. If you wish to prepare a precise estate plan by means of a will and/or trust, you need to keep in mind the impact that the registration of securities in beneficiary form has on the overall plan. It is very important for these types of beneficiary designations to be closely coordinated with your estate plan. Make sure when consulting your attorney that you provide all information about securities registration.

The law permitting registration in beneficiary form applies to the registration of securities. A "security" is defined in the statute as a share, participation, or other interest in property, in a business or in an obligation of an enterprise or other issuer. The term "security" can mean a certificated security, an un-certificated security, or a securities account. Note that bank accounts are not included. A securities account includes a reinvestment account, a securities account with a securities dealer, broker or financial institution, and cash, interest, earnings or dividends earned or declared on a security in such an account, whether credited before or after the owner's death.

Solely owned accounts can have a beneficiary who takes after the death of the sole owner. Joint accounts can have a beneficiary who takes after the death of the surviving joint owner. There can be more than one beneficiary named so that an account could be divided among multiple beneficiaries. Here are some example registrations taken from the statute: "John S. Brown TOD (or POD) John S. Brown, Jr," or "John S. Brown TOD to Sally Smith, trustee under my trust (under will or deed) dated ______." Here is an example with multiple owners: "John S. Brown Mary B. Brown JT TEN TOD John S. Brown, Jr."

A named beneficiary's descendants can be substituted to take the place of the named beneficiary in the event of the beneficiary's death. This is done by appending the letters "LDPS" to the name of the beneficiary. LDPS stands for lineal descendants per stirpes. For example: John S. Brown Mary B Brown JT TEN TOD John S. Brown, Jr., LDPS. "Per stirpes" is a commonly used form of inheritance. A distribution per stirpes gives the issue of a deceased child the deceased child's share. Let's say the beneficiary had two children and each child, in turn, had three children. If the beneficiary is deceased and one child of the beneficiary is also deceased, a per stirpes distribution means that the surviving child gets one-half and the three surviving issue of the deceased child each take one-third of their parent's one-half share — that is one-sixth. So the surviving child gets one-half and each of the three grandchildren who take through the deceased child gets one-sixth.

Other substituted beneficiaries can be named as contingent beneficiaries. John S. Brown Mary B. Brown JT TEN TOD John S. Brown, Jr., SUB BENE Peter Q. Brown. Any beneficiary can be changed or canceled without notice.

Before the financial institution can transfer title or issuance of shares in the name of the beneficiary, proof of payment of the Pennsylvania inheritance tax or a waiver is presented to the registering entity. No inheritance taxes are saved and no income taxes are saved by using the beneficiary registration.

There are a host of unresolved issues. For example, it is unknown how these accounts will be treated in an insolvent estate, how they will affect a surviving spouse's elective share of the estate, and who is responsible for the inheritance and estate tax on these assets. These designations must be used with care and should be reviewed as part of your estate plan along with your will and beneficiary designations for life insurance and retirement plan benefits.

What Is Covered by FDIC Insurance?

The Federal Deposit Insurance Corporation (FDIC) is an independent government agency and was created in 1933 during the Great Depression. Its purpose is to protect depositors in insured banks against the loss of their deposits if the bank fails. The current limit is $250,000 which was made permanent in the Dodd Frank Wall Street Reform and Consumer Protection Act which was signed by President Obama on July 21, 2010. The $250,000 limit is per depositor, per bank, for each account ownership category.

1. Single Accounts. An account held in one person's name alone. This type of account is entitled to $250,000 of insurance per depositor per bank. Note that if a person has named a beneficiary for an account, the account is treated as a Revocable Trust Account, not a single account.
2. An estate account is a single account. An account held in the name of a business that is a sole proprietorship is a single account and is added to the owner's other single accounts in the same bank. A Uniform Transfers to Minors Act Account is a single account as is an escrow account.

3. Joint Accounts. An account owned by two or more people (living people, not entities) with no beneficiaries designated. If all co-owners have equal rights to withdraw from the account and all co-owners sign the signature cards (unless the account is a CD), then each co-owner's shares of every joint account that he or she owns at the same bank are added together and the total is insured up to $250,000. That is, each co-owner gets a maximum of $250,000 FDIC insurance, regardless of how many accounts are at that bank. For example, a husband and wife could have $500,000 in a joint account and the deposit would be fully insured. Using different social security numbers or reordering the order of names on joint accounts has no effect on how much insurance is available.
4. Certain Retirement Accounts. All insured retirement accounts owned by the same person at the same bank are insured up to $250,000. Insured retirement accounts include Traditional IRAs, Roth IRAs, SEP IRAs and SIMPLE IRAs, self-directed 401(k) plan accounts, self-directed Keogh accounts, Section 457 deferred compensation plan accounts.
5. Corporation/Partnership/Unincorporated Association Accounts. The entity must be involved in an independent activity. It can't be created just to multiply FDIC insurance. All deposits owned by a corporation, partnership or unincorporated association at the same bank are combined and insured up to $250,000. Both for-profit and not-for-profit organizations are included.
6. Revocable Trust Accounts. "Pay on death" accounts, Totten trusts, "in trust for" accounts, all created by the bank's deposit agreement, are called informal revocable trusts. Formal revocable trusts are written documents that create trusts, often for estate planning.

The owner of a revocable trust is insured up to $250,000 for each different beneficiary. A person who has the right to income for life is considered to be a beneficiary. The persons who receive the trust at the termination of the income interest are also counted as beneficiaries. When a trust has five or fewer beneficiaries, maximum coverage is $1,250,000 (5 x $250,000). Where a trust has six or more beneficiaries and all beneficiaries have equal interests, there is $250,000 insurance per beneficiary for an unlimited number of beneficiaries. When a trust with six or more beneficiaries has beneficiaries who do not receive equal amounts, then the maximum insurance is the greater of (1) the sum of each beneficiary's actual interest in the revocable trust up to $250,000 per beneficiary or (2) $1,250,000.

1. Irrevocable Trust Accounts. These accounts are held by trusts established by written trust documents. An irrevocable trust may also be created when the grantor of a revocable trust dies. The interests of a beneficiary in all accounts owned by an irrevocable trust at the same bank are added together and insured up to $250,000 but a beneficiary's interest must not be contingent. If the Trustee has the authority to invade principal, which would take principal away from the other beneficiaries (making their interests contingent on the trustee's non-exercise of the power), insurance coverage for an irrevocable trust is usually limited to $250,000 total.
2. Employee Benefit Plan Accounts. This insurance "passes through" the plan administrator to each participant's share up to $250,000 per participant.
3. Government Accounts. These are deposits of the United States, any state, county, municipality or political subdivision, or Indian tribe. Each official custodian of time and savings deposits of a public unit is insured up to $250,000. Demand deposits are separately insured up to another $250,000. Public deposits maintained in out-of-state banks are limited to a maximum of $250,000 in coverage per official custodian.

If an account owner dies, the insurance continues for six months as if the decedent were alive. When two or more banks merge, deposits are insured separately for six months after the merger. After the six-month period, the banks are treated as one bank. CDs are insured until the earliest maturity date after the end of the six-month period.

Confused? It is complicated. Try EDIE The Estimator at *www.fdic.gov/edie*. You can enter the bank, the category of account, the owner, beneficiary, etc. and EDIE will tell you how much FDIC insurance you have. It calculates one bank at a time.

Ladies, a Man Is Not a Financial Plan

According to the United States Bureau of the Census, at some point in their lives, an overwhelming majority of American women — fully 90% — will have to bear responsibility for their own financial security by virtue of widowhood, divorce, or choosing to remain single.

Women earn an average of 24% less than men doing the same jobs according to the U.S. Department of Labor. Seventy-five percent of all elderly Americans living below the poverty level are women. And these women are getting by on Social Security benefits of about $600 per month — 25% lower than the average benefit for a man. On average, women tend to live seven years longer than men according to the U.S. Census Bureau.

Let's see if I have this straight. Women live longer, make less, and have a 90% chance of being solely financially responsible for themselves at some point in their lives. Is it true that most women are "one man away from welfare?"

As a woman, you owe it to yourself, and your family, to make sure you are financially secure. This is not something you can let someone else take care of. Do not assume that your husband, father, or boyfriend has taken care of you. Imagine your shock when he passes away, and you find that you are destitute, or if not destitute, at least in strained financial circumstances. Imagine your position if he leaves, or divorces you, and you are left to support yourself on your own earnings or your own retirement income alone. Worse yet, would you be responsible for someone else's financial problems?

Take a look at Muriel Siebert's website, *http://www.wfn.com*. One section of the website, entitled The Women's Financial Network, notes that "when a marriage dissolves, women find themselves at a serious disadvantage financially. Fewer than one-fourth of divorced women age 62 and older receive any employer-sponsored pension income, whether from their own *or* their ex-husband's past work. An average woman's standard of living drops 45% in the year following divorce, while a man's rises 15%."

Do you know what you own? Do you know how your assets are titled? Do you own things jointly or are the accounts in his name alone? Do you know what his will says? Does he even have a will? Do you know what your income would be if he dropped dead tomorrow?

What are your debts? What are his debts? Are you liable for his debts? If his business fails, do you lose your house?

Who is the beneficiary of his life insurance? His IRA? His pension plan? Get copies. Don't sign any waivers of spousal rights without a sound understanding and financial reason to do so.

If your husband has to go to a nursing home, how will you pay for it? Can you afford to live at home and also pay for his care?

Do you have small children? If your husband died, how would you live? Is there enough insurance? If both of you die, who will take care of the children? How will the children be supported and educated?

You owe it to yourself, and your family, to make sure your financial affairs are in order. You, and no one else.

What about retirement? Ernst & Young's *Financial Planning for Women* points out that women take time off to raise families and care for elderly parents. Married women who are currently retired or nearing retirement are less likely to have worked throughout their adult lives than their husbands. Married women are more likely to have worked part time or seasonally. This is also true for single, divorced, and widowed women with children.

Women earn less money than men and work fewer years on average. Women also change jobs more often than men. As a result, they frequently don't qualify for pensions or retirement plans. Women who are currently retired or nearing retirement are less likely to have been eligible for defined-benefit pensions than are men in their age groups.

According to Dr. Nancy Dailey, a woman born during the baby boom will likely be widowed by age 67 and remain a widow for 15 years or longer. Also consider that 53% of women are not covered by a pension compared to only 22% of men.

Judith Briles points out in her book, *10 Smart Money Moves for Women*, that only 2 out of every 100 seniors 65 or older are financially independent. The other 98 depend on the government, friends, relatives, or by working until they die.

It's up to you. Take responsibility for yourself. Find out what you can do. Plan ahead. Don't be intimidated. Learn.

> *Remember, Ginger Rogers did everything Fred Astaire did, but backwards and in high heels.*
>
> Faith Whittlesey

MARRIAGE AND DIVORCE

Don't Tie the Knot 'Til You've Signed the Paperwork

Marriage creates property rights for the spouses. It has ever been so. Since time immemorial, there have been marriage contracts, dowries, Ketubot. The modern view is that contracts about money, property, and support are unromantic, and somehow show lack of faith and trust. Unromantic perhaps, but rather than lack of trust, they show a knowing prudence.

If a man and woman are married with no contract between them, the law makes provisions regarding their respective property rights and financial obligations. There is a duty for each to support the other. There is a duty to support children born of the marriage. The surviving spouse has a right to inherit a portion of the deceased spouse's estate. Each spouse has a right to an equitable distribution of property on divorce. The law provides for alimony and for child support. Marriage brings all of these financial obligations into being. By not contracting, the spouses are contenting themselves with the rights and duties provided by the law. I suppose this is unromantic too. But it is not any more unromantic for spouses to devise their own agreement, their own understanding of the property rights and financial obligations owed by each spouse to the other.

The law aims at the usual case. It provides one set of rules and one size must fit all. Legislatures, in passing statutes about such matters, hope to strike a balance, which will answer to most situations. Obviously, there are many differences and variations in the real world. That is why the law permits spouses to contract with each other, to modify the "usual" rule to suit their particular circumstances.

Premarital Agreements also go by the name of Prenuptial Agreements and Antenuptial Agreements. Note that "ante" means "before", not "against" like "anti". There is no "standard" form of agreement. Under Pennsylvania law, for a premarital agreement to be a binding contract, there must be a complete disclosure of assets by both parties, and each party should have independent counsel.

This cannot be emphasized enough. Start working on the contract *early*. Weddings create enough pressure without having to negotiate details of the contract within days (yes, even hours) of the wedding. Many couples fall into this trap thinking there is a standard form of agreement that simply requires signature. Nothing could be farther from the truth. A good premarital contract is the subject of negotiations and discussion, tailored to the particular circumstances of the couple.

There are some recognizable extremes. There's the "I have all the money, you have nothing, and it's going to stay that way" contract. I have only one word for that. Beware. On the other extreme, there are contracts which require one spouse to post a bond or security to ensure alimony and inheritance obligations. Most folks are in between, wanting to provide for the appropriate care and support of a spouse in the event of a termination of the marriage by divorce or by death, but something different than the amounts or proportions provided by the law. Sometimes the provisions are more generous than those provided by the law and sometimes less generous.

One of the most common situations where a premarital agreement is used is when one or both spouses have children from a prior marriage. Many folks in this situation want to make sure that the children from the prior marriage retain rights in property, rather than giving the new spouse rights that super-cede the children's. By the same token, these spouses want to provide for each other appropriately. The law is not designed to handle this situation. Under the law, the new spouse is given the same rights that the first spouse had, which may not be appropriate because the new spouse is not the parent of the children. Entering into a contract with regard to these issues should not be viewed as a lack of trust or commitment to the new spouse. Rather, it shows responsible concern for the welfare of the spouse and the children. No one is served by creating enmity between the children of the first marriage and the new spouse. A premarital agreement can go a long way to smoothing the foundation for this new pattern of relationships.

Premarital agreements can be, and often are, amended. After the marriage, in view of changed circumstances, the spouses are free to revise and amend the agreement made before the marriage. Premarital agreements often provide for increasing benefits to the new spouse depending on the length of the marriage. These contacts usually establish minimum requirements as a protection to the spouses; the husband and wife are *always* free to be more generous with each other.

Loving consideration may require the spouse to enter into a premarital agreement.

Marriage Contracts: Much Ado about Saying "I Do"

Should you have a marriage contract? It's a misleading question, as pointed out by the National Resource Center for Consumers of Legal Services. The fact is, if you're married, you already have a marriage contract. Your marriage contract consists of the obligations imposed on married couples by the inheritance and domestic relations laws of the state where you reside. Romantic or not, there is a marriage contract. The only question is whether you like the "one size fits all" marriage contract provided by the state or whether you want to substitute your own contract.

People routinely change the state law provisions for inheritance rights for married couples. They write wills, often giving the entire estate to the surviving spouse. This is common, socially acceptable, and even encouraged. Marriage contracts and prenuptial agreements settling other property rights, however, are still uncommon.

Not that marriage contracts haven't been around for thousands of years, mind you. Just imagine the tribal chief striking a deal with the neighboring chieftain over the dowry to be given with the bride.

My personal favorite is the Jewish marriage contract or Ketubah which has been in use for centuries B.C.E. to the present day. "Be my wife in accordance with the law of Moses and Israel. I will work for you; I will honor, support and maintain you, as it becomes Jewish husbands who work for their wives, honoring and supporting them faithfully. ..." Additionally, the Ketubah (1) outlines the obligations that a husband must fulfill in marriage — to honor his wife, to provide the necessities in life, such as food, clothing, and shelter, and to fulfill his wife's sexual needs; and (2) it specifies that he will pay his wife a particular sum of money in the event of death or divorce. Not bad.

The provisions regarding property division and financial obligations for married persons living in Pennsylvania include a duty for each spouse to support the other. There is a duty to support children born of the marriage. The surviving spouse has a right to inherit one-third of the deceased spouse's estate. Each spouse has a right to an equitable distribution of property on divorce. The law provides for alimony and for child support. There is no duty to provide an inheritance for children. Are you content with this deal? Personally, I have a problem with only getting one-third of my husband's estate. Do you think you should be entitled to more?

By making a prenuptial or postnuptial agreement (both of them are marriage contracts), the parties can modify the property rights granted to married people by the state. The contract can be more generous than state law, or more limiting than state law — all as negotiated by the parties.

Some public policy critics have proposed that several different "marriage contracts" should be defined and one selected when the marriage license is applied for. This would force the soon-to-be-married couple to focus on the contract they are making with regard to property and support. These proposals are criticized as being too burdensome and costly, imposing a need for counsel and negotiation just to apply for a marriage license. (Is that such a bad thing?)

The Marriage Penalty

What is the marriage penalty? It is an increase in federal individual income taxation solely as a result of marriage.

Let's compare the taxation of single people to the taxation of married people. If both spouses earn about the same amount of money, they end up in a higher tax bracket and are penalized for being married. On the other hand, if one spouse has income and the other doesn't, then they aren't penalized.

There are two reasons that our tax law generates a marriage penalty: (1) the income tax code treats the family as a taxable unit, as opposed to two or more individual taxpayers, and (2) the income tax is progressive, taxing higher amounts of income at higher rates.

Before 1948 there was no such thing as a joint return. Each taxpayer paid his or her own tax. However, an inequity was present because in community property states, wives had to report one-half of their husband's income. Thus, in community property states, a married couple often paid less tax since the income of the earning spouse was split in half and taxed at lower brackets.

In 1948, the law was changed so that spouses could put their income together on a joint tax return. In effect, each spouse paid tax on half of the joint income. This gave equal treatment to citizens in community property states and common law states.

Under this system single taxpayers paid much more tax than most married taxpayers. The pendulum swung in favor of single persons with the passage of The Tax Reform Act of 1969. A new rate schedule was enacted for single taxpayers. With the new rate schedule, when two people married, their tax often increased — hence the marriage penalty. They would pay lower taxes if they had remained single.

Not every married couple gets a penalty. If there is only one earner, often the couple receives a subsidy because the joint return of this couple produces a lower tax than if the earner had filed a single return.

It's true that a married couple can choose to file separate returns instead of a joint return. However, the standard deduction and tax rate table, applicable to a married-filing-separate return, results in a higher tax being paid than if the person were single.

The 2001 tax cut made a long-term commitment to eliminating the marriage penalty with relief being phased in over the years 2005 to 2009. The 2003 tax cut accelerated the planned relief and enacted it 100% for 2003 and 2004, but the current law reverts to the 2001 phase-in schedule after 2004.

Thanks to the tax cut passed in 2003, for 2003 and 2004, the standard deduction for married couples is twice the amount of the standard deduction for single taxpayers. This reduced the marriage penalty for married taxpayers who cannot itemize deductions.

The 2003 tax cut also increased the 15% bracket for married-filing-jointly taxpayers. This expansion of the lower bracket also removed some of the penalty for being married. While this is progress, for married couples who itemize, there still is a marriage penalty in the higher income brackets. The penalty can also surface when looking at the phase-out of itemized deductions, personal exemptions, and the amounts that can be contributed to IRAs

Making a tax system fair is possible if society doesn't change. But consider the social changes since 1969. There are many more single taxpayers, and many more families are dual income. The present system can be made fair for most, but not for long as U.S. society evolves.

Unconstitutionality of DOMA Raises Lots of Question

The Defense of Marriage Act (DOMA), signed into law by President Bill Clinton in 1996, prevented same-sex couples whose marriages were recognized by their home state from receiving benefits available to other married couples under federal law.

U.S. v. Windsor is the Supreme Court Case handed down July 29, 2013 holding that Section 3 of DOMA was unconstitutional. The case arose because the State of New York recognized the marriage of New York residents Edith Windsor and Thea Spyer, both female, who married in Ontario, Canada, in 2007. When Spyer died in 2009, she left her entire estate to Windsor. Windsor sought to claim the federal estate tax exemption for surviving spouses, which would have resulted in no federal estate tax being due in Spyer's estate. The marital deduction was barred by Section 3 of DOMA, which amended federal law to define "marriage" and "spouse" as excluding same-sex partners. Windsor paid $363,053 in federal estate taxes and filed for a refund, which the Internal Revenue Service denied. Windsor brought a refund suit on the ground that DOMA violates the principles of equal protection incorporated in the Fifth Amendment to the U.S. Constitution.

"The federal statute is invalid, for no legitimate purpose overcomes the purpose and effect to disparage and to injure those whom the State, by its marriage laws, sought to protect in personhood and dignity," Justice Anthony Kennedy wrote in the majority opinion. "By seeking to displace this protection and treating those persons as living in marriages less respected than others, the federal statute is in violation of the Fifth Amendment."

You might think that the decision by the Supreme Court answers the question. Well, it may answer one question, but it creates hundreds of others. How Windsor will affect the federal tax laws is a very murky matter.

Filing status.

After *Windsor*, if you live in a state where same-sex married is legal, then your filing status for federal purposes is now married. You can file as Married Filing Jointly or Married Filing Separately, if you're so inclined. If you live in a state that doesn't recognize same-sex marriage, your filing status for federal tax purposes does not change.

There are many unknowns:

1. Will same-sex married couples be able to amend prior year returns?
2. Will same-sex married couples be required to amend prior year returns?
3. If amendments are permitted or required, for which years?
4. What happens if a couple is married in a state or country that recognizes same-sex marriage but on 12/31, their residence is in a state that does not recognize their marriage? Do they file their 1040 as married or as single?
5. It is unclear what effect the Court's opinion will have in states that have domestic partnerships or civil unions. These may not be considered marriages.
6. What about 2012 for those taxpayers who are on extension? Will these questions be resolved in time for filing on or before October 15?

Credits, rates and taxation

The distinction between married and unmarried status comes into play in connection with income tax rates, the treatment of capital losses, credits for the elderly and disabled, taxation of Social Security benefits, and many other provisions.

Estate and Gift Tax

Marital status is also important in the estate and gift tax area where transfers to a spouse are not taxable. An unlimited amount of property can pass to a surviving spouse with no federal estate tax.

Gifts from one spouse to another are deductible for purposes of the gift tax, and gifts from one spouse to a third party are deemed to be from both spouses equally. Transfers of property from one spouse to another or to a former spouse if the transfer is incident to a divorce are permitted without any recognition of gain or loss. These provisions permit married couples to transfer substantial sums to one another, and to third parties, without tax liability in circumstances in which single taxpayers would not enjoy the same privilege.

Social Security

When one spouse dies, the survivor has the option of claiming either his or her own Social Security benefits or those of his or her spouse, whichever is higher. This will be an important change because often couples have a high-earning spouse and a low-earning spouse.

Similarly, a same-sex spouse should be able to collect a spouse's federal or military pension after the spouse dies.

Tax on Health Insurance

If you're straight and married, and your husband or wife gets health insurance through your job, that's a tax-free benefit to you. But people in a same-sex state-recognized marriage previously had to pay federal income tax on that employer contribution - called imputed income - to their partner's health insurance premium.

For spouses who had health-care coverage for their same-sex spouse, not only did they pay tax on the benefit, their employers paid FICA and withheld FICA on those benefits. Will amended 941 filings be required, optional, or not allowed? What will the process be for amending 941s and W-2s?

IRA and Qualified Plan Rollovers

Spouses get special privileges when it comes to rolling over IRAs or 401(k)s when they are named as beneficiaries. On death a spouse can rollover the IRA or qualified plan benefit to his or her own IRA. This permits additional deferral of income tax until the spouse attains age 70-1/2 and must begin withdrawing the minimum required distribution.

Tips on Estate Planning For Unmarried Couples

Absent the appropriate legal documents, an individual with whom you have spent your entire adult life has no legal entitlement to the house that you live in, the right to rear your children (natural or adopted), the ability to make life determining decisions in the event that you are incapacitated, or even the right to visit by your bedside. Without the appropriate legal documents, the interests of your biological family almost always prevail over the interests of those you consider to be your family. Blood relationships and the marriage contract "trump" other relationships.

Marriage creates lots of property rights and provides special tax treatment. Unmarried couples who are living together need to use legal and financial instruments such as wills, trusts, powers of attorney, adoption, and medical directives to secure their rights in child custody, medical decision making, income, gift and estate taxes, estate planning, and other areas.

If a person dies without a will, the Pennsylvania intestacy statute determines the descent and distribution of the decedent's property. State law provides for distribution to children and grandchildren, spouses, parents, brothers, sisters, nieces, and nephews, but not to any beneficiaries who are not "of the blood" or not married to the decedent. For unmarried couples, wills are absolutely essential.

Unfortunately, wills that pass property to persons who are not related by blood or marriage are challenged much more frequently than others. The "blood" relatives are quick to claim that the decedent was incompetent to make a will or under the "undue" influence of the person with whom the decedent lived. It is interesting to note that these arguments are seldom raised when a will passes property to a spouse or to blood relatives. Strange as it may seem, "blood" relatives who have had no contact with a decedent for years often feel very entitled to inherit the decedent's property. Parents who have refused to talk to their child for years find voice to challenge the child's will so that they can inherit. Estranged spouses who have had no contact for decades make claims for shares of the estate. Siblings who have not been heard from in 50 years appear to claim shares of their deceased brother's estate. There is an overwhelming prejudice in the collective unconscious in favor of blood.

This means that unmarried couples must exert extra care to make sure their wishes are carried out. Often, trusts are recommended for unmarried couples rather than wills. Title to property is transferred to a trust now. Because the transfer is made now, the decedent's state of mind and legal capacity are determined as of the current date, not the date of a later will. The trust, if it holds all of the decedent's property, avoids probate so there is no legal notice issued inviting objections by blood relatives and estranged spouses. The validity of the trust can be questioned, but the procedure is more difficult and most commentators agree that the likelihood of a successful challenge is much less with a funded inter vivos trust than with a will.

Transferring property to joint names can also be helpful although unmarried couples are subject to the same risks of termination of the relationship that married couples are. While unmarried couples are not given the benefits of the marriage contract, they also are not given the protection of the law upon divorce. The lawyer must take care to achieve both the client's objective to provide for a partner and, also, the protection of property rights in the event of an unexpected termination of the relationship. Some consider "living together" agreements that address the same sort of issue as prenuptial agreements.

Beneficiary designations on life insurance policies, IRAs, pensions, and other employee benefits must be reviewed, and care taken to make sure that the intended beneficiaries receive the benefits.

A power of attorney is essential. If you intend for your income and assets to support your partner in the event you are disabled or incapacitated, the power of attorney should specifically authorize this. Similarly, if you intend for your partner to continue to occupy your home, even if you cannot live there yourself, this also must be spelled out. Otherwise, your partner, who is acting as attorney-in-fact, could be accused of using your property illegally for his or her own benefit.

A medical directive should be made designating your partner as your surrogate. This will give him, or her, the authority to make decisions concerning your medical care, termination or beginning of treatment, and even, in combination with a power of attorney, control of your visitors.

For couples that can't get married as well as for couples who choose not to get married, the federal estate tax provides no marital deduction. That is, property in excess of $1,500,000 cannot pass to your partner without payment of the federal estate tax. Similarly, the Pennsylvania inheritance tax applies to transfers to persons other than spouses or certain "blood" relatives at the rate of 15%. Some of these taxes can be reduced by making lifetime transfers of property, either outright to your partner or in a trust.

Pennsylvania does recognize "common-law" marriages. Couples, who can otherwise, legally wed and who live together for long enough and hold themselves out as husband and wife may be considered to be legally married under the law. Never plan on this status to give you legal rights to property. The status is obviously subject to dispute.

Examining Community Property's Definition — And Impact

If you live in Pennsylvania and are thinking of moving to Arizona, have you considered the effect of community property? Pennsylvania is not a community property state; Arizona is.

Ten states have some form of community property: Louisiana, Texas, New Mexico, Arizona, Nevada, California, Washington, Wisconsin, Alaska, and Idaho. If you now or previously lived in one of these states, or are planning a move to one of these states, you need to be aware of the special rules that apply to community property. Any property you may have acquired while living in one of these states is probably community property today, regardless of where you live.

The other forty states are called common-law states or separate property states. These states derive the husband's and wife's property rights from the English common law. The spouses' ownership of property is determined by the title to the property. If all the property is titled in the husband's name, the husband is the owner of all of it. The wife is protected by statutes providing for equitable distribution in the event of divorce, or forced inheritance of a portion of the husband's assets in the event of his death. Many legal scholars believe that the community property system is fairer and easier to understand and administer.

In the community property states, property is generally divided into two categories: community (or marital) property and separate property. Property that was owned by either spouse before marriage or was acquired by one spouse after marriage as a gift or inheritance is considered to be separate property. Income from separate property is also separate property. If separate property is co-mingled with community property so as to make it impossible to identify, it is presumed to be community property.

If you have ever lived in a community property state, it is important to keep complete and accurate records of how separate property was obtained and used to overcome the presumption that it is community property. In a community property state, all property owned or acquired by a married person is considered to be community property unless the person can prove that it is separate property. For example, either spouse's earnings belong to the community. Each spouse owns one-half of the community property and has an equal right of management and control over the community property, but neither spouse may enter into any form of agreement to buy, sell, or mortgage the property without the other spouse's consent. Prenuptial and postnuptial agreements between the spouses can modify these rules.

How do you know what law applies to your property? Here are some guidelines: (1) the law of the state where real estate is located controls its ownership, (2) the law of the marital domicile at the time personal property is acquired controls the characterization of the property (separate or community), and (3) the law of the marital domicile at death of one spouse controls the survivor's rights to inheritance.

What happens if a couple acquires its wealth in a separate property state and moves to a community property state? At divorce, property accumulated during marriage is deemed quasi-community property and there is no problem. Each spouse gets one-half of the quasi-community property. At death, the same is true, except in Texas, Arizona, and Idaho. In those states there is no such thing as quasi-community property at death and the poorer spouse is left without a share of community property and without the right to elect against the estate, which would have been available in a common law state. The surviving spouse may get absolutely nothing from the deceased spouse's estate. This is the result which must be avoided by careful planning.

What happens if a community property couple moves to a separate property state? The property may be maintained as community property. It also may be converted to separate property if it is re-titled. Attorneys in common-law states are not usually familiar with community property laws, and this change in ownership may be suggested when its ramifications are not fully understood and have very costly results.

Suppose husband and wife acquire wealth in the form of stock with a basis of $200,000 in a community property state and move to a common-law property state (like Pennsylvania) to retire. It is worth $500,000 at the death of the first spouse.

If the stock was maintained as community property, then at the death of the first spouse, half the value of community property is subject to estate tax. It passes to the surviving spouse and qualifies for the marital deduction, so no federal estate tax is due. The entire value of the community property gets a step-up in basis, thus giving the surviving spouse an income tax basis of $500,000. If the surviving spouse later sells the stock for $525,000, she recognizes a capital gain of $25,000.

Now consider what happens if the property were converted to separate property in the common-law state. The estate tax consequences are the same, but the income tax consequence is quite different. Only half of the property gets a step-up in basis. The surviving spouse's basis is one-half of the original basis, $100,000, and one-half of the date of death value, $250,000, for a total basis of $350,000. If the survivor sells the stock later for $525,000, there is a gain of $175,000, compared to $25,000 if the community property had been maintained. The difference is $30,000 more in income tax due just because of failing to protect the identity of community property while residing in a separate property state.

Community property seems like a much fairer and more tax friendly approach to ownership of property by married couples. How can you get this treatment without moving? One way is to marry in Mexico, where you must make the election at marriage to treat property as separate or community. Another way is to place property in an Alaska Community Property Trust, which will convert separate property to community property. But remember, trusts cost money to prepare and maintain. You need to crunch the numbers to see if the advantages overcome the costs.

Estate Planning For Second Marriages: Remove the Risk

When Dad marries again, the children begin to wonder about their inheritances. It's a classic tension. Everyone has strong opinions in this situation. Some believe that Dad, having supported the children to adulthood, has no further obligation to them, and should arrange his estate as befits his responsibility as a husband. Some may want to make sure that the children from the prior marriage retain eventual rights to Dad's property. Others feel that the children's rights to the property need to be carefully balanced with caring for the new wife. And what about Step-Mom's children and any children Dad and Step-Mom have together? There are as many different plans and desires as there are families.

The law aims at what legislators believe is the average case. The legislature passes laws that it hopes will work in most situations. In the real world, obviously, there are many differences and variations. The basic inheritance laws are simply not designed to handle the second marriage. The law gives a new spouse the same rights that the first spouse had, which may not be appropriate because the new spouse is not the parent of the children from the first marriage.

Therefore, the law also permits couples to contract with each other, to modify the "usual" rule to suit their particular circumstances. Care must be taken to make sure that any contract between prospective spouses or current spouses is enforceable under applicable law.

Making such an agreement is strongly recommended to be sure that there is no misunderstanding and that the children (his, hers and theirs) and the surviving spouse receive what is intended.

A pre- or postnuptial agreement, which spells out the rights, duties, and obligations of the new couple, is the best way to plan for a couple's unique situation. Entering into a pre- or postnuptial contract, in order to care for multiple different sets of loved ones, shows responsible concern for the spouse's welfare and the welfare of the children. It should not be viewed as a lack of trust or commitment to the second spouse.

In a prenuptial agreement both the future husband and future wife disclose all of their assets and make agreements about the ownership and succession of their respective properties. It is common for each of them to make provisions for the other, but to require that property brought to the marriage ultimately goes to the children from the first marriage.

These contracts are made usually before the marriage takes place. Why? Under old common law, this was required. A husband and wife could not contract with each other, so any contract had to be solemnized before the marriage took place. Modern law has changed this and a husband and wife are free to make contracts between them. Postnuptial agreements are now common.

Again, making such a contract does not show lack of trust. Making the contract is taking good care of your new spouse and the rest of your family. It should be viewed just like making a will. After all, the law will distribute your property if you leave no will. By making a will you make sure your personal intentions are carried out. It is the same with a pre- or postnuptial agreement. You make sure your intentions are carried out instead of relying on the default provisions written by the state legislature.

Keep in mind that without an agreement between the spouses, the rights of children are determined in a lottery — whether they "win" depends on which spouse dies first. Make a plan. Something this important shouldn't be left to chance.

Trusts are another important part of this type of planning. By using trusts it is possible to benefit different classes of beneficiaries from the same property. This is often an ideal way to provide for income to a surviving spouse with the ultimate ownership of the principal going to the children. Multiple objectives can be attained with a trust, and its provisions can be hand-tailored to the situation. With this sort of split trust, the choice of trustee is a key element and a professional fiduciary can be invaluable. Neither the surviving spouse nor child will be well suited to making the distribution and investment decisions that will be necessary in this situation.

What Is an Annulment?

There is so little difference between husbands you might as well keep the first.

Adela Rogers St. Johns

Pop singer Britney Spears married her childhood sweetheart, Jason Alexander, at the Little White Wedding Chapel in Las Vegas Saturday morning, January 3, 2004 at 5:30 AM. She was escorted down the aisle by a hotel bellman. The bride wore jeans and a baseball hat. Fifty-five hours later, on Monday morning at about 10:00 AM, Britney's attorney filed a petition for annulment of the marriage. A few hours later it was granted. Britney married Kevin Federline nine months later on September 2004.

The petition for annulment said Britney "lacked understanding of her actions to the extent that she was incapable of agreeing to the marriage." Reasons given included: "Before entering into the marriage the plaintiff and defendant did not know each other's likes and dislikes, each other's desires to have or not have children, and each other's desires as to state of residency. . . Upon learning of each other's desires, they are so incompatible that there was a want of understanding of each other's actions in entering into this marriage."

An annulment is a ruling by the court that puts aside a marriage as though it never existed. Technically, an annulment refers only to making a voidable marriage null; if the marriage is void from the start, such as in the case of bigamy, then it is automatically null, although a legal declaration of nullity is required to establish this.

In Pennsylvania, invalid marriages include situations such as when either party had an existing spouse at the time of the marriage, when the parties are blood relatives within a certain degree, or when either party could not consent because of a mental defect or other related reason. These marriages are void without an annulment and their status can be established by a legal declaration of nullity.

Other marriages may be declared void by Pennsylvania courts and an annulment granted if (1) the spouses are less than 16 years of age and lack the consent of a parent or the court to marry, (2) where either party was under the influence of drugs or alcohol, (3) when either party was at the time of the marriage incurably impotent or (4) either party entered into the marriage as a result of fraud, duress, coercion, or force.

The rationale for granting an annulment is that marriage is a contract, and if either individual was unable to enter into the contract, the court may determine that no contract of marriage ever existed. After an annulment, the spouses have no right to inherit, one from the other, and no right to be supported.

Children born to or adopted within a marriage that is later annulled are legitimate children. They have the right to financial support from both parents and to get property at the death of either parent regardless of whether the parents' marriage was valid.

Many people mistakenly believe that annulments are common for short marriages, and that it is a proceeding that is easier and less expensive than divorce. Actually, an annulment is more complicated than divorce because it must be established that the marriage was entered into improperly; the parties can't just consent to an annulment. An annulment is sought in order to nullify the marriage and return the parties to their prior single status, as if they never married. Establishing the grounds for an annulment is difficult. Many Pennsylvania lawyers advise clients to file for divorce and avoid the difficulties.

There is a tax result, also, to be considered. If your marriage is annulled by court decree, and you are thus treated as if no marriage ever existed, then for federal income tax purposes you are considered unmarried even if you filed joint returns from earlier years. According to an IRS ruling, if an annulment is retroactive, you were never married and have no right to file joint returns. You must file amended returns claiming either single or head of household status for all tax years affected by the annulment that are not closed by the statute of limitations for filing a tax return. The statute of limitations generally does not expire until three years after your original return was filed.

An annulment granted through a church or other religious entity is not the same as a legal annulment. The courts consider marriage as a contract, not as a church sacrament. Only a legal annulment or divorce gives the parties the legal right to remarry according to the law in the United States. Religious annulment gives the parties the right to remarry through their religious organization.

While other denominations have annulments, one usually hears of them in the context of the Catholic Church where marriage is believed to be indissoluble. However, a person who is divorced may petition the Church to review the marriage and investigate whether a full, free-willed consent was exchanged at the time of the wedding. The Church uses the same rationale as the civil law. The annulment process is not a method to dissolve a marriage but rather to determine whether a marriage was valid. In the Jewish religion, marriages can be annulled but very rarely is it done.

A religious marriage or annulment has no effect on the civil status of the marriage. Similarly, a civil annulment has no effect in religious law.

Separation and Your Estate Plan

> *The difference between divorce and legal separation is that legal separation gives a husband time to hide his money.*
>
> Johnny Carson

In Pennsylvania, there is no such thing as legal separation for spouses. People are either married or single. Rights created by marriage can only be changed by divorce. This is not to say, of course, that spouses do not live separately. In fact, sometimes spouses live separately for many years. There can be religious or financial reasons for not dissolving the marriage even though the spouses live apart.

Separation simply means that two spouses no longer live together. Separation may occur by mutual consent or by one spouse leaving or being forced to leave the home. Under some circumstances, spouses may be considered separated even though they are still living together in the same residence. There is no legal requirement that a husband and wife be separated for a period of time in order to file for a divorce, and there is no legal requirement that a divorce be filed upon separation. In Pennsylvania, once parties have lived separate and apart for a period of two years, one party may seek a divorce without having to obtain the consent of the other party.

Living separately has no effect on the validity of your will, power of attorney or medical directive. After divorce, provisions in a will for a spouse are void. Also, upon filing for divorce, any power of attorney naming the spouse is revoked. Neither of these provisions applies to separation.

Some spouses change their wills when they separate and eliminate provisions in the will for the spouse. If you disinherit your spouse, the spouse has a right to elect against the will to claim a one-third (1/3) share. The surviving spouse is entitled to a one-third (1/3) share even if divorce proceedings are pending.

There are two exceptions to this right of election. A spouse who for one year or more before the death of the deceased spouse has "willfully neglected or refused to perform the duty to support the other spouse," or who for one year or more has "willfully and maliciously deserted the other spouse" shall have no right of election, or even of receiving an intestate share.

Another exception has been in the law since January of 2005: the right of election does not apply if the death of the spouse occurs during the divorce proceedings, a final decree of divorce has not been entered and grounds have been established. Grounds can be established, depending on the type of divorce action that is proceeding (1) if the court adopts a report of a master or makes its own findings that grounds for divorce exist, (2) if both parties have filed affidavits of consent, or (3) if an affidavit has been filed and no counter-affidavit has been filed or, if a counter-affidavit has been filed denying the affidavit's averments, the court determines that the marriage is irretrievably broken and the parties have lived separate and apart for at least two years at the time of the filing of the affidavit.

Sometimes when a husband and wife separate, they sign a Separation Agreement which is a legally binding contract. Typically, these agreements cover division of property, child support payments and spousal support payments during the period of separation. Custody arrangements can also be made in such an agreement.

Although spouses are separated, they still both remain fully liable for joint debts. Both may be responsible for 100% of the debt, not just one-half. A separated spouse may also be responsible for the necessities provided to the other spouse. For example, a husband or wife may be responsible for medical expenses for the other spouse even though they have lived apart for years.

If you file a joint return with your separated spouse, be aware that you are jointly liable for the tax. If your separated spouse doesn't pay or under reports income and gets interest and penalties, you are liable. Unless you are very sure your separated spouse is filing a correct joint return with you, refuse and file separately. You cannot be required to file a joint return. If you file a joint return there is no such thing as "my" refund. The refund is joint, just like the return.

Often as part of estate planning, spouses will execute general powers of attorney naming each other as agent. Usually, these powers of attorney grant the other spouse complete control over the assets of the individual granting the power. If a wife gives a husband a general power of attorney, the husband can use this power to close or make withdrawals from the wife's individual bank accounts, brokerage accounts, and other assets. Obviously, this can be ruinous. The only way to revoke a power of attorney is to locate all of the originals and destroy them and/or notify the agent that the power is revoked. Notifying the spouse that his power of attorney is revoked will do little good if the spouse is bent on taking your assets. Your only recourse is to give written notice to all the institutions which hold your assets to inform them that the power of attorney has been revoked. No doubt the wrong-doing of a spouse improperly using a power of attorney will be exposed during the divorce. The Court will try to remedy the situation and even impose sanctions. But if the money is gone, it's gone.

Property held jointly is not affected by separation — it automatically passes to the surviving joint owner. Separation has no effect on beneficiary designations on life insurance, annuities retirement plans or IRAs. Review the beneficiary designations that you have made. If you are not happy with the designations, make new ones. Remember that as long as you are married, your spouse is entitled to be the beneficiary of qualified retirement plans like 401(k) s and other ERISA plans unless he or she consents to be removed. The spouse does not have a right to be named as the beneficiary of an IRA.

What to Do With Your Inheritance if You Are Married

A little boy asked his father, "Daddy, how much does it cost to get married?" And the father replied, "I don't know, son, I'm still paying for it."

The statistics for termination of marriages in the United States are pretty grim. The latest statistics claim roughly 50% of first marriages end in divorce. Second or third marriages have only about 20% of couples remaining happily married.

On the dissolution of the marriage by divorce, there are a number of issues to be dealt with including child custody, support, and equitable distribution of assets.

In Pennsylvania, marital assets and debts of a divorcing couple are divided between them in a process called "equitable distribution." "Fault" or misconduct within a marriage that's ended is generally not a factor in determining the fair division of marital property during the equitable distribution decision.

Here are some of the factors that are considered by the court in making the division of marital property:

- The length of the marriage
- The existence of any prior marriages
- The age, health, station, income, vocational skills, employability, estate, liabilities and needs of each party
- Any contribution by one party to the education, training or increased earning power of the other
- Each party's opportunities for future acquisitions of capital assets and income
- Sources of income of both parties, including medical, retirement, insurance or other benefits
- Roles of each party in the acquisition, preservation, depreciation or appreciation of marital property, including contributions as homemaker
- Property values set apart to each party
- The parties' standard of living established during the marriage
- Your individual economic circumstances when the division of property becomes effective
- Tax ramifications associated with each asset to be divided

- Expenses related to a sale, transfer or liquidation associated with a particular asset
- Determination of which party will serve as the custodian of any dependent minor children

Generally, marital property means all property acquired by either party during the marriage, regardless of whose name it is in.

In Pennsylvania, separate or non-marital property is not subject to equitable distribution. Non-marital property includes property that a spouse brought into the marriage and kept separate during the marriage, inheritances received during the marriage and kept separate during the marriage, gifts received by just one spouse during the marriage and kept separate, and property excluded by a valid prenuptial agreement.

There is a very important distinction to be made here. While non-marital property remains the individual property of the spouse who owns it, the increase in value during the marriage of non-marital property is considered to be a marital asset and is subject to equitable distribution.

Here is an example: Let's say Husband inherited $100,000 from his grandmother and kept it in a separate account in his name only. The $100,000 was invested; and at the time of the couple's separation, was worth $150,000. The original $100,000 remains separate property, but the $50,000 increase in value is marital property subject to equitable distribution.

On the other hand, a different result is reached if the inherited $100,000 is co-mingled with marital property. If Husband deposits the $100,000 inheritance into a joint account with Wife or spends it on a joint asset, then the separate property loses its status as separate property and becomes marital property. If it is marital property, it's in the "pot" and will be divided like any other asset. In our example, if the $100,000 is in a joint account and grows to $150,000, then the whole $150,000 is marital property.

The Pennsylvania statute provides that the increase in value of non-marital property is measured from the date of marriage or later acquisition date to either the date of final separation or the date as close to the hearing on equitable distribution as possible, whichever date results in a lesser increase. Any decrease in value of the non-marital property of a party is offset against any increase in value of the non-marital property of that party. However, a decrease in value of the non-marital property of a party shall not be offset against any increase in value of the non-marital property of the other party or against any other marital property subject to equitable division.

If the marriage has deteriorated or may deteriorate, you should think carefully about what to do with a gift or inheritance. Since the future is always uncertain, the best course is to keep non-marital property separate.

Divorce and Your Estate Plan

> *So many persons think divorce a panacea for every ill, who find out, when they try it, that the remedy is worse than the disease.*
>
> Dorothy Dix

If you are considering divorce or beginning the process of divorcing, you must review your estate plan to make sure it is appropriate in light of the anticipated divorce. No matter how far along the divorce is or how long the action has been pending, the law considers you to be legally married until the judge signs the final decree ending the marriage.

If you die or become disabled prior to the final decree of divorce, your estranged spouse may have legal control over you and your estate, and may be entitled to most, if not all, of your estate. This is probably not what you intend. Through properly drafted estate planning documents, you can provide that someone other than your spouse will have control over you and your estate, and you can limit your estranged spouse's rights as a beneficiary of your estate.

If you made a will before you were divorced, the law provides that any provision in the will for the benefit of your former spouse is ineffective. The former spouse has no rights in your estate, either as a beneficiary or as an executor or administrator. The will is not revoked; it is interpreted as if your ex-spouse had predeceased you.

This rule of law applies only to the ex-spouse. If your will makes provisions for the ex-spouse's children or more remote issue, or other relatives of your ex-spouse, these provisions of the will stand. The divorce has no effect on them.

If you made a will before the divorce and indicated in the document itself that you intended the provisions for your soon-to-be ex-spouse to be still valid after the divorce, then your announced intention overcomes the law.

If you die during the divorce and before the final decree, the rule of law excluding your soon-to-be ex-spouse does not help you. If your will leaves everything to your soon-to-be ex-spouse, that's who will get your estate.

Any other estate planning document, such as a trust, will also be interpreted in the same way provided that it is revocable at the time of your death. If you have made a revocable inter vivos trust, sometimes called a living trust, any provision in this document for your ex-spouse will be invalid. The fact that the trust must be revocable for this rule to apply is an important one. If you made an irrevocable trust before your divorce, such as an (irrevocable life insurance trust or "ILIT"), and your ex-spouse is a beneficiary of that trust, the law will not save you. The transfer to the trust was made prior to the divorce and the ex-spouse's property rights were determined at that time since the trust, being irrevocable, cannot be changed by you in any manner. To avoid unintended results in this scenario, it is important in an irrevocable trust to specify that a divorce will remove the spouse from beneficiary status and that when used in the documents, "wife" or "husband" means whomever you are married to, not a specific individual who is now your ex-spouse.

If you have signed a power of attorney giving your spouse the authority to act as your agent, this grant of power is revoked when either spouse files an action for divorce. Until the action for divorce is filed, the spouse can act using the power of attorney — this can be a very dangerous power. Note that unlike the will, the provision naming the spouse in a power of attorney is revoked when the divorce action is filed, not at the final decree.

When a divorce action is filed, only the appointment of the spouse as agent in the power of attorney is revoked, the whole power of attorney is not revoked so the named successor agent can serve. If the power of attorney includes an appointment of the spouse as guardian, if a court appointed guardian is necessary, that appointment is not revoked by filing for divorce. Instead, a court would have to decide if filing for divorce is a good reason not to appoint a spouse as a guardian. When the divorce becomes final, however, the appointment of the ex-spouse as guardian is revoked.

Another issue to think about during a pending divorce is health care issues. Have you remembered to change your living will and medical directive? (If you don't, someone you might not want to make your decisions could be allowed to make decisions about your health.) It is unclear whether filing for divorce or even being granted a final divorce decree revokes the designation of a spouse as a surrogate under your medical directive. Arguably, the surrogate is the same as an agent under a power of attorney and under the law an agent's power is terminated when divorce is filed.

If an ex-spouse is designated as a beneficiary on a life insurance policy, annuity contract, pension, profit-sharing plan or other contractual arrangement providing for payments to the spouse, any designation which was revocable at the time of death is ineffective and the beneficiary designation is construed as if the ex-spouse had predeceased. If the designation or a separate contract (such as a property settlement agreement) provides that the designation is to remain in effect even after the divorce, then the designation remains effective.

Note that the financial institution involved will not know whether or not there has been a divorce. If the ex-spouse claims the benefit as named beneficiary, Pennsylvania law specifically provides that the paying company shall have no liability. The ex-spouse, of course, is liable but as is always the case with financial liability, one can only recover funds if the defendant still has the funds and has not spent them.

Joint Representation — Who Is the Client?

You're a married couple. If one of you needs a doctor, you go to your own appointment. You and your spouse may have different doctors. If you need a dentist, you go to your own dentist. But if you want to make an estate plan, you usually both go to the lawyer together.

Under the Rules for Professional Conduct, a lawyer may only represent multiple clients when the lawyer has disclosed the possible conflicts between the clients and the clients have consented to the dual representation. A husband and wife are two clients, not one. It cannot be assumed that it is appropriate for a single lawyer to represent both the husband and the wife. We are well beyond the days of the common-law adage that a husband and wife are considered one person (the husband.) On the other hand, the mere fact that two people are married does not inherently produce the potential for conflict contemplated by Rules.

There are lots of possibilities for conflict between spouses. There can be disagreements over rights to assets or the exercise of various rights, the selection of beneficiaries, and differing plans for remarriage. These conflicts don't necessarily bar a lawyer from representing both of the parties until the lawyer's quality of representation is altered. Joint representation assumes that spouses will agree on most points or each has independent property that does not require agreement.

If the possibility for conflict is disclosed and the parties agree to a single lawyer, then dual representation may be undertaken. If the joint representation is accepted, then the lawyer must not keep any confidences of one of the spouses from the other and if a conflict does arise between the husband and wife, the lawyer then cannot represent either one of them.

Additionally, clients need to realize that the client/lawyer relationships, for both husband and wife, do not end just because the will is signed and the lawyer's fees paid. If a husband comes back to the lawyer a few years after making reciprocal wills with his wife and tells the lawyer that he is planning to file for divorce and wants to change his will, what should the lawyer do? Does the lawyer have a duty to inform the wife (his other client) what the husband is planning? Can the lawyer change the will for the husband? Tough questions. Not all lawyers will agree on the answers. If both spouses are the lawyer's clients, how could the lawyer possibly keep such a secret? And how could the lawyer change a will on which his other client (the wife) was relying?

For many couples, the possibility of conflict is remote. In many situations dual representation is natural and appropriate, especially when the family finances are viewed as a unit. Also, since much of estate planning revolves around tax avoidance to maximize the inheritance for the children of the couple, there are common goals.

Just about any technique an estate planner can suggest to save estate taxes involves some loss of control. If a tax-savings technique is suggested and implemented that leaves the surviving spouse without control of the family assets, but rather beholden to a trustee, does the surviving spouse understand that? Agree to it? Are both spouses made aware of the disadvantages?

An unexpected loss of control is most keenly experienced by the surviving spouse. I can't tell you how many times after the first death, the surviving spouse is very unhappy to find that (she or he) does not have control of assets but instead must request funds from a trustee to get access to money. Sometimes the surviving spouse was not an active participant in the planning and is surprised to find out what the documents say after the first spouse is dead and it is too late to change the deceased spouse's plan.

Estate planning for a married couple often involves transferring the title of assets between spouses, making gifts, creating trusts, appointing agents. Are the costs and benefits of each move explained to both clients? Do both spouses understand that by taking property out of joint names and titling them separately that the survivor is no longer guaranteed the ownership of that property on the death of the owner spouse?

When there are prior marriages for both spouses and children from prior marriages, the possibility for conflict is much more obvious. Do both spouses understand what their respective rights are? Do they agree on the disposition? Does each spouse know that if he or she dies first, there may be nothing to stop the surviving spouse from changing the estate plan and cutting out the first spouse's children? Many situations like this require a postnuptial agreement between the husband and wife to make sure that inheritances for children are protected.

Do both spouses understand that the surviving spouse can remarry? And that upon remarriage, that new spouse acquires property rights in the surviving spouse's property, even property inherited from the first spouse? How many times have I seen children bitterly disappointed to see their expected inheritance in the hands of a stepparent?

Communication between husband and wife, the psychologists say, is the key to a successful marriage. Communication is also a key to a successful estate plan. All of these issues must be explored to make sure that your wishes are carried out.

PAYING FOR COLLEGE

Everything You Need to Know About Paying For College

Your fourteen-year-old, a long-time lover of dolphins and seashells, has just announced that she wants to attend the University of Miami to study marine biology. Gasp! Tuition and fees are $23,642 per year. But she's serious about the field, and if she keeps her grades up, she might get admitted.

How do you pay for college? There's no magic. Save, borrow, and try for scholarships, grants, and low interest loans. Here we look at college savings options, maximizing your chances for getting financial aid, and some of the tax incentives that can be a big boost to your college savings plans.

Paying for college is primarily managed in five different ways: savings (money set aside to pay higher education costs), scholarships (money for college awarded because of the student's ability or achievements and doesn't need to be repaid), grants (money for college that doesn't need to be repaid, and is based on financial need), loans (money borrowed that must be repaid with interest), and work-study arrangements (opportunities for a student's employment either on or off campus to help with college costs). Most students fund their college costs with a combination of these methods.

Popular wisdom has it that saving for college is counterproductive because having money in savings reduces the amount of financial aid. That's true to a degree. But, since most financial aid is awarded in the form of loans, not grants, saving for college allows you to keep borrowing to a minimum, thus avoiding quickly accumulating interest charges.

Congress has enacted a number of special provisions to provide incentives for educational savings and to give some very substantial tax breaks for college. One of these is the Coverdell Education Savings Account, a great tax-deferred vehicle.

The Coverdell Education Savings Account (also known as an Education Savings Account or ESA) works this way: non-deductible contributions are made to an account for the benefit of a child under age 18. The income on the money isn't taxed and money withdrawn to pay college bills is not taxed, either. A series of contributions to an ESA for a newborn can accumulate to a hefty sum by the time the baby reaches college age.

The limit for these contributions was $2,000. If you have several children, you can establish an account for each one and there will be a broader array of investment options for your contributions since the dollars are bigger

Permitted contributions begin to be phased out when the Adjusted Gross Income (AGI) hits $190,000 on a joint return and completely disappears at the $220,000 level. You can make the contribution any time up to April 15 of the following year. If Mom and Dad are over the income limits, Grandma and Grandpa can make contributions. Anyone can put in the money.

Through December 2001, the Education IRA was only for higher education costs. Now under the new 2002 law, withdrawals can be made for elementary and secondary school expenses including religious schooling, in addition to higher education expenses. The cost of computers, tutoring, and prep courses for standardized tests will also be permitted expenses.

Coverdell ESAs are self-directed. You can handle the investments. In 529 Plans (to be discussed later), you must turn your money over to the investments manager or managers selected by the state plan you choose to participate in. Also under the 2002 tax law you can have both a Coverdell ESA and a Section 529 Plan funded in the same year, every year.

Penalty-free withdrawals are permitted from regular IRAs to pay college tuition. This may be an option if you have adequate other retirement options and not enough in savings set aside for college.

Obviously, using savings as a means to pay for higher education, works best, if started years before your child starts school. So, if your child is already picking her courses (MSC360 — Behavior of Marine Organisms) or packing her bags (scuba gear), you'll need to investigate other forms of financial aid. These methods include tax credits and deductions, which can make paying your son or daughter's tuition bills more palatable, and Section 529 Plans, which offer not only a savings vehicle, but great tax relief as well.

Upromise Offers College Savings Through Everyday Spending

Of all the views of . . . education, none is more important, none more legitimate, than that of rendering the people safe as they are the ultimate guardians of their own liberty.

Thomas Jefferson, 1782

A college education can be the most important promise we make to our children. A new method is available to help parents fulfill this promise, supplementing the traditional methods of setting aside current income for college savings.

Upromise offers the ability to turn a small slice of your everyday purchases to a college savings program. The program allows families to "spend your way to college," in a similar fashion to accumulating frequent flyer miles.

How does it work? You buy goods and services from participating companies. Your family members and friends can join too in helping you save even more for college. The participating companies contribute a portion of your spending to your Upromise account, which is swept into section 529 plans, tax advantaged savings programs for college. The funds in the account can be withdrawn *tax free* for college costs.

Anyone can open a Upromise account for a future college student (or several students). It's easy and it's free. There is no special card, there is no special credit card, and you don't have to change the way you shop.

Here is an example Upromise has on its web site. "Let's say a grandfather who wants to help save for his five-year-old grandson spends about $25 a month on AT&T Long Distance and around $280 a month in credit card spending through Citibank. AT&T will contribute 4% to the grandfather's Upromise account. Citibank contributes 1%. These contributions alone could generate $1,283 in college savings. The projected cost for textbooks and supplies for one year at a public university in 15 years is $1,268. This grandfather's Upromise contributions can cover this cost."

Bill Bradley, former Senator and presidential candidate, is on the board of directors. When interviewed for the Wall Street Journal, he said that joining Upromise as a special advisor was "a perfect fit for me" because of his longtime interest in college affordability.

"It's a very innovative solution," he said. "I think it could become a movement."

Staples, Barnes & Noble, Toys 'R' Us, Kids 'R' Us, and Babies 'R' Us will contribute 2% of every purchase. Exxon and Mobil contribute 1 cent per gallon for regular and midgrade gas, 2 cents per gallon for Super or Supreme gas. Participating offices of Century 21, ERA and Coldwell Banker Real Estate companies will contribute ½% of a home's sale price. There are over 7,000 participating restaurants who will contribute 10% of your entire bill. McDonald's participates on a limited basis. Check the web site at *www.upromise.com* for other participating companies. Upromise has garnered instant credibility with its list of blue-chip participants.

You register your credit card with Upromise, and purchases at participating companies are automatically tracked. Also, loyalty cards, like CVS's ExtraCare Card can be used. Sometimes the tracking is from billing information, as with AT&T. There are also automatic contributions whenever you shop online at more than 70 sites. In addition, Upromise has added grocery stores to the list of participating companies.

Before you choose a 529 plan, either through Upromise or another 529 plan, make sure you understand how the funds will be invested, and what the fees will be. Review these plans carefully.

The Upromise program is free; however, you need to open a 529 plan through either Salomon Smith Barney or Fidelity Investments. These accounts have their own fees and minimum investments, which may be waived if account owners deposit a minimum amount into the account monthly. If you do not open such a 529 plan, the money in your Upromise account will not earn any interest. If you already have a 529 plan elsewhere, you cannot link it to Upromise.

Upromise contributions are held in a "non-interest-bearing cash account" until you open a section 529 plan through Salomon Smith Barney or Fidelity. Once the account is established, funds are swept quarterly from your Upromise account into your 529 plan.

Upromise is a private company. It will make money by collecting fees from participating companies on each transaction and from investing contributions in Upromise accounts until they are swept into the owner's 529 accounts. Upromise will also receive payments from Fidelity and Salomon Smith Barney.

Upromise is the brainchild of Michael Bronner. It's his idea to promote a socially worthy cause while building customer loyalty for the participating companies. As reported in Newsweek, "Once customers see 4% of their AT&T long-distance spending going into their college accounts, they won't change their carrier just to save a few pennies," says Howard McNealy, co-president of AT&T Consumer.

Upromise states that funds are secure in Upromise accounts, saying, "The money in your Upromise account is held in custody by Upromise Investments, a registered broker-dealer with the SEC and a member of the NASD and is insured by the Securities Investor Protection Corporation (SIPC), which protects securities customers of its members up to $500,000 (including $100,000 for claims for cash)." No one, including the companies participating in Upromise, receive "personally identifiable information" about any Upromise customer.

Section 529 Plans: The Best Gets Better

Your bright thirteen-year-old granddaughter, who has nursed every stray cat in the neighborhood, has been asking you about your alma mater, The University of Pennsylvania. Her science teacher told her it has one of the best pre-vet programs around. Wouldn't you love to be able to help her afford to wear the Penn Red & Blue?

Look into Section 529 plans. Officially known as Qualified Tuition Plans, they just can't be beat! Under the old law, these plans were very attractive — withdrawals were taxed at the student's bracket, a rate usually lower than that of the account owner, and the earnings inside the account were tax deferred.

Under the new tax law passed, these plans have moved to the head of the class. Qualified withdrawals, after January 1, 2002, from these popular state-sponsored plans will be completely *free of income tax* as long as the withdrawals are used for covered college costs.

529 plans are very, very flexible. Anyone can establish an account for any beneficiary. The account owner, that is, the contributor, retains control over the account, including when and for what purposes withdrawals are made. Anyone can contribute to a 529 plan regardless of how much he or she earns. Qualified expenses for which

tax free withdrawals can be made are tuition, fees, and, in most state plans, books, supplies, required equipment, and room and board. In most states, payouts are also free of state income tax.

If the money isn't used for your granddaughter's college it can be rolled into another plan for another child or relative. So if she gets a scholarship, the unused portion can be rolled over into a plan for her cousin or her brother. Unfortunately, (one of the few drawbacks) most plans can only be used for undergraduate study, so she will have to fund veterinary school another way.

The funds in the 529 plan can be used at any accredited institution of higher learning in the U.S., as well as at many foreign institutions. It's easy to start saving today with low minimum investments. Currently Pennsylvania's program, TAP (Tuition Assistance Program), waives the enrollment fee on accounts for newborns. You can contribute, until the total value of all accounts for a beneficiary, exceed $240,000. The earnings can continue to grow in excess of this limit.

There are many plans available with different investment options, each sponsored by a state. In most states, you need not be a resident of a state to use its plan, so you are free to choose the plan which you find most attractive. You can check out the various state plans at *www.savingforcollege.com*. Factors to consider when shopping for a plan are the available investment choices, the plan's contribution limit, enrollment restrictions, withdrawal restrictions, minimum contributions, costs and fees, and state income tax treatment.

Also under the new tax law, you can switch to another state's plan every 12 months without changing the beneficiary. The new law will permit shifting of beneficiaries among cousins as well as members of the immediate family. This is very attractive to grandparents who are given broad latitude to move funds around to help the grandchildren in need.

Contributions to 529 plans are considered to be completed gifts for gift tax purposes and qualify for the $14,000 annual gift tax exclusion. The account can be jump-started with a $140,000 contribution because a married couple can use five years' worth of annual exclusions at one time. Inside the 529 plan you get tax-free income and tax-free capital gains. Earnings not ultimately used for higher education purposes are subject to a 10% penalty when withdrawn.

You can have multiple 529 plans for a child and you can transfer existing UTMA/UGMA custodial accounts into a 529 plan. You can fund a 529 plan and an education IRA for the same beneficiary in the same year.

Don't overlook 529 plans as an estate planning tool. Money in 529 plans is not considered to be part of your estate for federal estate tax purposes. This is true even though you can revoke the plan, and take all the money back if you pay the 10% penalty. Just imagine — if you have 10 grandchildren, you could put as much as $2,240,000 in 529 plans, and no estate tax would be due on the total even though you have retained the power to get the money back! This is what savvy estate planners dream about: getting the assets out of your estate and still retaining control over them.

For more information I recommend Joseph F. Hurley's book, *The Best Way to Save for College, A Complete Guide to Section 529 Plans.*

Note: some financial advisors have been slow to embrace 529 plans and have not been recommending them to their financial planning clients. Some don't make the recommendation because they are unfamiliar with the plans or don't understand them. Some don't recommend them because they don't want to lose fees by transferring assets from their management to 529 plans. Others, like Doug Darmstetter of American Express, recommend the plans to clients as one of the absolute best ways to save for college. As Doug points out, the financial advisor is paid to give the best financial advice, and Section 529 plans offer advantages that shouldn't be missed.

Move UTMA Account to 529 Plan with Tax-Free Growth

Making gifts to your favorite minor children is good tax planning, allowing you to get assets out of your estate and into theirs. But, will any of these children be tempted to purchase a motorcycle instead of majoring in business management?

For years, parents and grandparents put money in Uniform Transfer to Minors Act (UTMA) accounts to save money for a child's college education. UTMA accounts, which give control of the assets to the child at his or her 21st birthday, are often used as the recipient of $14,000 annual exclusion gifts to minor children. The only available alternative used to be a trust, which was often perceived to be too costly to create and maintain.

In 1996, another option became available. Provisions creating Qualified State Tuition Plans were added to the Internal Revenue Code, Section 529. Qualified State Tuition Plans, also known as 529 plans, are more attractive than ever and they have become the vehicle of choice. In fact, many people are trying to find ways to get money out of UTMA accounts and into 529 plans.

In addition to earmarking the funds for post-secondary education, this option gives the opportunity for tax-free growth inside the 529 plan — something that is unavailable in a simple UTMA account. (In UTMA accounts, taxes on income or capital gains after a $1,500 exemption amount are paid at the parent's rate for children under age 14, and at the child's rate after age 14.) The investments in the 529 plan can grow completely tax free and the withdrawals for qualified expenses are not subject to tax when they are withdrawn. Funds in 529 plans may be used not only for traditional four-year colleges, but for a variety of qualified vocational, secretarial, and technical schools.

The custodian of an UTMA account has legal title to the minor's assets and is required to hold, invest, and distribute the funds in the UTMA account for the minor's benefit in accordance with the terms of the statute. The statute is very liberal and permits expenditures to benefit the minor, except that these funds should not be used to relieve a parent of basic support obligations. It is perfectly acceptable for the UTMA custodian to choose to invest the minor's assets in a 529 plan for the minor.

The custodian must be careful to choose a 529 plan where the minor's property interest in the UTMA account will be safeguarded. For example, in a regular 529 plan, the beneficiary of the plan can be changed. This would not be permitted in an UTMA 529. The minor for whom the account is opened is the owner and only permissible beneficiary. Also, the minor must have unrestricted access to the account at age 21. You need to check the state's plan you are interested in to see if such registration is permitted. The Illinois 529 plan is one that does. See *www.brightstartsavings.com*. Remember, you don't have to be a resident of a state to use its 529 plan.

The custodian of the UTMA account can open a 529 plan and transfer the UTMA funds to it. The funds are still owned by the minor. The owner of the 529 plan is the UTMA custodian for the benefit of the minor.

When the minor reaches age 21, the custodian is out of the picture and the minor is in control of the 529 plan. In other words, a child who prefers a Harley over Harvard at age 21 has control of the funds. To withdraw the funds, however, he or she would be required to pay a ten percent penalty and income tax on the interest. This may be enough to convince him or her to keep the funds in the 529 plan for future, yet unknown, education expenses. If he or she opts never to attend college, the account may be transferred to a 529 account for a spouse, child, or another qualified relative with plans for higher education.

One negative aspect of this approach is that any investments in the UTMA account must be liquidated before the transfer. 529 plans can accept only cash, so this may cause some unwelcome gain recognition. In addition, ownership of a 529 plan by the child will affect the availability of financial aid. Of course, since we are talking about moving an UTMA to a 529 plan this problem already existed.

For future gifts, consider a 529 owned by the parent instead of adding to the UTMA 529. This 529 plan can be the recipient of contributions from anyone. Parents can contribute, as well as aunts, uncles, and grandparents. The minor can also contribute his or her earnings from paper routes and babysitting. Save-while-you-shop plans, such as Upromise, can grow 529 plans with cash contributions from vendors like Toys 'R' Us and McDonalds.

Some of the states permit trusts to have 529 accounts. If you have set up a trust and now wish that those funds could be in a 529 plan, the trustee can invest the trust funds in a 529 fund.

The Problem

According to The College Board, the 2013-2014 average annual tuition and fees for a four-year public college (in-state students) are $8,655. For a four-year public college (out-of-state students) it is $21,706. . The average tuition and fees for a four-year private college are $29,056. This is repeated from the beginning?

Coverdell ESA

Congress has enacted a number of special provisions to provide incentives for educational savings and to give some very substantial tax breaks for college. One of these is the Coverdell Education Savings Account (ESA), a great tax-deferred vehicle.

The Coverdell ESA works this way: non-deductible contributions are made to an account for the benefit of a child before they reach age 18. Contributions can continue past age 17 if the child has special needs. The income on the savings is tax free.

If you have several children, you can establish an account for each one. Contributions for a calendar year can be made up until April 15 of the following year.

Limits

Repeated from beginning

Anyone, even Grandma and Grandpa, can make contributions each year, but total contributions from all donors cannot exceed $2,000 per account per year. If they do, a six percent penalty is applied. The account must be depleted by age 30 or be subject to income tax and a 10% excise tax. It can, however, be rolled over tax-free into an ESA for another younger family member.

Other Features

Withdrawals can be made for elementary and secondary school expenses including religious schooling, in addition to higher education expenses. The cost of computers, tutoring, and prep courses for standardized tests are considered permitted expenses.

Coverdell ESAs are self-directed. You can handle the investments, in contrast to institution-managed 529 plans. You can have both an ESA and a Section 529 Plan funded in the same year, every year.

IRA Alternative

Penalty-free withdrawals are permitted from regular IRAs to pay college tuition. This may be an option if you have adequate other retirement options and not enough in savings set aside for college.

If your child is already picking her courses (Biology of Marine Mammals) or packing her bags (scuba gear), you'll need to investigate other forms of financial aid.

Income Tax Breaks for Education?

This September, your son and your money will be going to Franklin and Marshall College.

You've saved some money for his tuition, but you were thinking about a state university at the time. Is there a tuition fairy godmother out there?

Yes! A virtual scholarship is waiting to be claimed on your income tax form in your choice of one of three possible methods: The American Opportunity Tax Credit, The Lifetime Learning Tax Credit or the Tuition and Fees tax deduction.

American Opportunity Tax Credit

The American Opportunity Tax Credit is a credit of up to $2,500 per eligible student for qualified tuition expenses for each of the first 4 years of undergraduate study. You can claim the credit if you pay qualified tuition for yourself, a spouse or a dependent. Up to 40% of the credit (up to $1,000) is refundable.

The taxpayer can claim a tax credit per return based on 100% of the first $2,000, plus 25 percent of the next $2,000.

Lifetime Learning Credit

The Lifetime Learning Credit can be claimed for an unlimited number of years for both undergraduate and graduate study, but cannot be used the same year as other education tax credits or deductions. This credit does not have to be used for degree work. It can be used for tuition for a drawing class or cooking school.

Both the American Opportunity Tax Credit and the Lifetime Learning Credit phase out for taxpayers with Modified Adjusted Gross Income (MAGI) from $53,000 to $63,000 for single filers and from $107,000 to $127,000 for joint filers.

These credits only apply to tuition and certain related fees and cannot be used if you pay the tuition with certain tax-free funds, such as Pell Grants and scholarships. No double benefits are allowed. If you are paying the tuition from the proceeds of a loan, however, you claim the American Opportunity Tax Credit in the year in which the expenses are paid, not the year you repay the loan.

Tuition and Fees Tax Deduction

If your MAGI is more than the phase-out limits for these credits, the law permits an income tax deduction for college costs: The Tuition and Fees tax deduction. Taxpayers are able to deduct up to $4,000 in college costs, whether or not they itemize.

A $4,000 deduction is available. Above MAGI of $80,000 ($160,000 if filing jointly) there is no deduction available.

Interest Deduction

If you are using student loans to pay your son's tuition bills, you can also deduct the interest. The student loan interest can only be deducted if it can't be claimed elsewhere on your tax forms, for example, as interest on a home-equity loan. It also doesn't count if parents, siblings, or a qualified employer plan loaned you the money. This deduction phases out for individual taxpayers with MAGI of $75,000 and for joint filers $155,000.

Tax Free Employer-Paid Tuition

If your employer has a tuition program, the limit is $5,250 that can be given tax-free.

When you fill out your tax forms, you'll need to do the math to determine which tax-reducing method helps you most. You generally cannot claim more than one tax benefit for the same dollar spent on education. Tread carefully, and get a copy of the IRS publication 970, "Tax Benefits for Education."

Financial Aid Overview

Who would have believed that the years would sail by so fast? That little bundle with booties is now mailing his or her applications for college. How can you afford that Chemical Engineering degree that would send your son or daughter into self-sufficient adulthood?

The help you need can come from a couple of sources: either scholarships, or financial aid. Financial aid is the broad term encompassing grants, loans and work-study programs. Students may fund their college costs with a combination of these methods.

Scholarships

Scholarship aid is usually awarded by the schools themselves and from philanthropic groups. Pennsylvania also administers a few scholarship programs in exchange for agreeing to work in Pennsylvania after graduation. Guidance offices have more information.

Financial Aid

But what if your son or daughter isn't the center on the basketball team or the class valedictorian? Most aid is awarded on the basis of the family's ability to pay. The federal government is responsible for 72% of financial aid, mostly through loans. State governments, colleges and universities offer the remaining percentage in the form of grants and loans.

Forms

To determine eligibility for aid, every college requires students to complete yearly the Free Application for Federal Student Aid (FAFSA).

In addition to the FAFSA, some schools require a second financial aid form, College Scholarship Service's Financial Aid PROFILE. The PROFILE asks additional questions that some colleges and programs use in awarding their own funds. Check with your school to determine which forms it requires and the deadlines.

Both the FAFSA and the PROFILE use the parents' income and assets and the student's income and assets to determine the expected family contribution (EFC). A financial aid package, a combination of grants, loans and work-study, is then offered through the school to help fill the gap between the EFC and the total cost.

Grants

Federal Grant Programs have been put into place to help those with a major financial need to have an opportunity for college. Pell Grants offer a maximum of $5,550 to students whose family's income is under $50,000. Supplemental Educational Opportunity Grants, averaging under $1,000, are distributed through the school to low-income students as well.

The Pennsylvania State Grant Program may offer a full-time student up to $4,363 yearly if studying at a Pennsylvania institution or $557 ($743 for veterans) for out-of-state schools.

Loans

The Federal Loan Program supplements the Grant Program and has options for those whose financial need doesn't meet grant requirements. The Federal Loan Program includes Subsidized Stafford Loans, Unsubsidized Stafford Loans, and PLUS (Parent Loans for Undergraduate Students).

Subsidized Stafford Loans (for students) are low-rate, currently 3.86%, loans based on financial need. The federal government pays the interest while the student is in school. Repayment of the principal is deferred until six months after the student graduates or is no longer attending school. The standard repayment plan requires a fixed payment, at least $50 per month, for up to ten years.

Unsubsidized Stafford Loans differ only in that the federal government does not pay the interest while in school. The student pays all the (deferred) interest and principal.

PLUS Loans (for parents) are not based on financial need and are available to parents of dependent students at 6.41% currently. Interest and principal payments are due from the date the loan is disbursed.

Perkins Loans are low-interest (5%) loans to students who demonstrate financial need, and are distributed through the schools.

Work-Study

Financial Aid packages often contain an amount for work-study, allowing students to earn as they learn. These part-time jobs are often arranged to correspond to the student's academic or career interests.

Section 529 Plans: Two Ways to Save

Look into Section 529 plans (Qualified Tuition Plans). There are two kinds: prepaid tuition plans and college savings plans.

Prepaid Tuition Plans

The prepaid tuition plan locks in tuition prices at eligible schools. The savings are often guaranteed. Inflation will not affect the units that are purchased. All state plans cover tuition and mandatory fees. Some allow the purchase of a room and board option or use of excess tuition for other qualified expenses. Most plans set lump sum or installment payments based on beneficiary age and number of years of tuition purchased. There may be an age or grade limit for the beneficiary. Residency requirements may apply. Enrollment periods are limited.

College Savings Plans

College savings plans do not lock in prices of tuition and are not guaranteed. Funds may be spent on any qualified educational expense, not just tuition and mandatory fees. There are no age limits for the beneficiary. There are no residency requirements. Enrollment is open at all times.

Income Taxes

Qualified withdrawals are free of federal tax and, in most states, are free of state income tax.

Flexibility

Anyone can establish an account for any beneficiary. The contributor retains control over the account, including when and for what purposes withdrawals are made. There are no income limits for contributing.

If the money isn't used for your granddaughter's college, it can be rolled into another plan for another child or relative. So if she gets a scholarship, the unused portion can be rolled over into a plan for her cousin or her brother. Unfortunately, most plans can only be used for undergraduate study, so she will have to fund veterinary school another way.

You can switch to another state's plan every 12 months without changing the beneficiary.

Funding

Anyone can contribute until the total value of all accounts for a beneficiary reach a limit ($452,210 in Pennsylvania). The earnings can continue to grow in excess of this limit.

You can have multiple 529 plans for a child and you can transfer existing UTMA/UGMA custodial accounts into a 529 plan.

Every state sponsors at least one plan. You can compare various state plans at *www.savingforcollege.com*. Factors to consider are the available investment choices, the plan's contribution limit, enrollment restrictions, withdrawal restrictions, minimum contributions, costs and fees, and state income tax treatment.

INCOME TAX

Watch Out for the 3.8% Medicare Surtax

In 2010, as part of the health care legislation often referred to as 'Obamacare', Congress passed a new tax provision, the Unearned Income Medicare Contribution. This is a 3.8% surtax, which became effective January 1, 2013, for investment income for individuals, trusts, and estates.

It is referred to variously as the "3.8% surtax," the "3.8% investment tax", and the "3.8% Medicare tax". The 3.8% surtax is found in Section 1411 of the Internal Revenue Code. The IRS issued proposed regulations in December 2012 intended to "help" taxpayers understand the new tax. The "help" is over 100 pages long. The IRS hopes to have final regulations in place by the end of 2013. In the meantime taxpayers can refer to the proposed regulations.

For individuals, the calculation of the 3.8% Medicare Surtax is dependent on two numbers defined as follows: 1) the taxpayer's net investment income (NII) and 2) the taxpayer's modified adjusted gross income (MAGI). For each taxable year, the MAGI, after being reduced by a fixed threshold, is compared to the NII. The 3.8% Medicare Surtax is applied on the lessor of the two. This means that for individuals who have little or no net investment income, their 3.8% Medicare Surtax will be minimal if not zero. The three thresholds mentioned above are:

- 250,000 for married couples filing jointly
- $125,000 for married couples filing separately
- $200,000 for everyone else

Here is an example. Mary Smith, who is single, made $150,000 in salary for 2013. In addition, Mary Smith earned $75,000 of net investment income. Mary's modified adjusted gross income would be the sum of her salary and net investment income, which is $225,000. Her threshold is $200,000. MAGI after being reduced by a fixed threshold is $25,000 ($225,000 – $200,000). When compared to her $75,000 of NII, the 3.8% Medicare Surtax is applied to the $25,000 because it is the lesser of the two numbers. On Mary's 2013 form 1040 she will owe additional taxes of $25,000 x 3.8% or $950. For Mary, the effect of the new surtax is $950 in additional tax.

Estates and trusts get hit harder. The calculation of the 3.8% Medicare Surtax is also dependent on two numbers: an estate or trust's undistributed net investment income ('UNII') and the estate or trust's adjusted gross income (AGI). Similar to the calculation for individuals, the AGI for the taxable year is first reduced by a fixed threshold amount and then compared to UNII. The lessor of the two is multiplied by 3.8% to determine the 3.8% Medicare Surtax for that taxable year. However, the threshold is adjusted each year based on the dollar amount that starts the highest tax bracket. For the fiscal year of 2013, that amount is only $11,950. Compare this to $250,000 for married couple filing jointly.

In order to determine if the surtax applies, it is important to understand what qualifies as net investment income. Net investment income includes the following items, reduced by any deductions allocable to such income:

- Interest, dividends, royalties, annuities, rents
- Income derived from passive activities
- Income from trading financial instruments and commodities
- Net capital gains derived from the disposition of property (other than property held in an active trade or business)

Net investment income does not include the following:

- Active trade or business income
- Gain on sale of an active interest in a partnership or S corporation
- Distributions from IRAs or qualified retirement plans
- Income from tax-exempt municipal bonds
- Tax deferred non-qualified annuities
- Income taken into account for self-employment tax purposes
- Capital gain excluded on the disposition of a personal residence

Retirees could be surprised to find that they are victims of the surtax. Although income received from a pension, traditional IRA or company-sponsored retirement plan is not subject to the surtax itself, it can push your other income above the threshold, exposing it to the surtax.

Planning strategies to avoid or reduce the 3.8% surtax are aimed at managing the income threshold limits, as well as the amount of net investment income incurred by the taxpayer. Making deductible contributions ($5,000 max, $6,000 max for those over age 50) to an IRA will lower one's MAGI. Traditional IRA owners are required to take minimum distributions upon reaching age 70 ½. While such distributions are not considered net investment income, they will count toward the surtax's income thresholds.

Income from municipal bonds is not considered net investment income, nor is it considered for purposes of the surtax's income thresholds. It may make sense to consider rebalancing an investment portfolio to increase its municipal bonds.

Family Limited Partnerships (FLP) can serve as vehicles to shelter a portion of an individual's net investment income. Parents can employ the FLP structure to gift partnership interests to younger generations so as to reduce their own net investment income that may be subject to the surtax, as well as distribute such interests to a group of individuals who may be below the MAGI thresholds. The planning strategy can also help the parents reduce the size of their gross estate for estate tax purposes.

Death and Capital Gains Tax: (And you thought there was only the estate tax to worry about.)

> *There are two systems of taxation in our country: One for the informed and one for the uninformed.*
>
> Judge Learned Hand (1872-1961)

Everyone knows that when you sell a capital asset at a profit, you must pay a capital gains tax. Conversely, if you sell a capital asset at a loss you recognize a capital loss that may offset capital gains or in limited circumstances, other income.

A common example of a capital asset that may generate a capital gain or loss is a marketable security held for investment. It is easy to figure out the gain or loss for stock that you, yourself, bought. The "basis" for computing the gain or loss is what you paid for the stock. The difference between the basis and sale proceeds determines your gain or loss.

What if you received the stock as a gift? Let's say your grandmother gave you 100 shares of IBM when it was worth $50 a share. You sold it for $70 a share. What is your capital gain? We can't tell. Your basis in the IBM stock is not what it was worth when Grandmother gave it to you. Your basis is equal to what Grandmother's basis was. Gifted property gets a "carry-over" basis in the hands of the recipient. If Grandmother paid $10 a share for the stock, gave it to you when it was worth $50 and you later sold it for $70, your capital gain is $60. $70 is the sales proceeds; the basis is $10, making the gain $60.

If the gift you receive is so large that donor of the gift has to pay gift tax on the gift, then you get to add the gift tax attributable to the appreciation in the property to the basis. Let's say Grandmother had to pay a gift tax of 50% of the value of the IBM stock she gave you. If the stock was worth $50 when she gave it to you, a 50% gift tax would be $25. The amount of the gift tax attributable to the appreciation in the property is 4/5ths. (The appreciation is $40 — the difference between the original purchase price of $10 to the value on the date of the gift of $50.) Thus, 4/5ths of the $25 gift tax can be added to the recipient's basis. Four-fifths of $25 is $20 which makes the basis of the stock in the hands of the recipient $30 (the $10 basis of the donor plus the $20 gift tax attributable to the appreciation). Simple, don't you think?

What if you inherit the stock? Under current federal law, if Grandmother leaves the IBM stock to you in her will, then you get a new basis. The new basis is the date of death value. Thus, if the IBM stock was purchased by Grandmother for $10 and was worth $50 of the day she died, you get a $50 basis for the stock. When you sell it later for $70, you have a $20 gain. No one — not you, not the estate, not Grandmother — ever pays any capital gains tax on the $40 of gain that is the difference between Grandmother's purchase price and the value on her date of death.

This rule which provides a new basis for inherited property has for years been called a "step-up" in basis. It was called a "step-up" because most of the time, the date of death value of capital assets, especially marketable securities, was *higher* than the decedent's purchase price.

What happens if the date of death value is *lower* than the decedent's purchase price? You guessed it — it's a "step-down." The beneficiary's new basis is the lower date of death value. These days with the financial markets way down, all too often beneficiaries are facing step-downs in basis. You have no choice. The date of death value becomes the basis.

There is one exception to date of death value as basis. Executors can elect to make an alternate valuation of the estate's assets on the date that is exactly six months after the date of the decedent's death. This is called the alternate valuation date. The alternate valuation date can be used only if it results in less estate tax being payable. In other words, it can only be used if values go down. If the value of estate assets declines during the six months after the decedent's death, and if the executor elects the alternate valuation date, it would be possible to reduce the amount of estate tax payable. If alternate valuation is elected it applies to all assets; you can't pick and choose. For basis purposes, the value on the alternate valuation date then becomes the beneficiary's basis. This would result in lower basis — another step-down. But the advantage of paying less estate tax is often worth the reduction in basis.

Qualified Dividends Taxed at 15% — Or Are They?

Congress wants to encourage long-term holding of securities and leave short-term traders out of the dividend tax break. The tax break is a lowering of the rate of taxation on qualified dividends from the taxpayer's top bracket (possibly 35%) to just 15% (5% for the very low income earners).

For a mutual fund investor it's not enough that the fund itself meets the holding-period requirements for the stock it owns in dividend-paying companies. The fund shareholder individually must also meet the holding-period requirement for her mutual fund stock — and it's up to the individual shareholder to figure that out.

Partnerships, S corporations, estates, and revocable trusts treated as part of an, can pass through dividends received to their partners, shareholders, and beneficiaries as dividends qualifying for the lower tax rates, to the extent that the dividends are otherwise qualified.

In general, the 15% rate is available for "qualified dividends" which means the payout has to be truly a "dividend," and it has to be "qualified." Dividends from common stocks are most likely eligible for the new low rate. Most distributions from preferred stocks won't qualify because the preferred stocks are more like debt. Distributions from Real Estate Investment Trusts (REITs) generally aren't true dividends, nor are money-market distributions. Mutual funds distributions retain their original character as received by the fund — payouts from bond funds, for example, are still interest income.

"Qualified" refers to the holding period — which is the cause of all the confusion described above. If you just hold onto your stock and never sell — you don't have a problem. Your dividends will meet the holding-period test without a problem. If you bought and sold during the year, it's up to you to figure out if you can claim the 15% rate. If you bought a stock on July 15 and the ex-dividend date was August 1, then you'll only qualify for the 15% rate if you're still holding that stock in the middle of September.

Shares bought in a dividend reinvestment program (DRIP) are also subject to these rules. You have to track each share purchase separately to see if the holding period is met.

This tax break is a record-keeping nightmare. Save all of your documentation, in case you are audited. Don't be surprised if you get corrected 1099s. You might want to hold off filing your return, even if it's completed. That way you can avoid filing an amended return.

Does it make enough difference for you to spend time worrying about it? If you're already in the 15% tax bracket, obviously not. But otherwise, at the highest bracket, on a $1,000 dividend it can be the difference between paying $350 or $150 in tax. That's a big difference!

If Life Gives You Losses, Make Tax Benefits

After crosses and losses, men grow humbler and wiser.

Benjamin Franklin

More than a few have become acquainted with losses over the last few years, thanks to the general trend of the stock market. Tax benefits from your losses can take out at least some of the sting.

A capital loss is recognized when you sell an investment for less than the purchase price (or other cost basis). Expenses of the sale are deducted from the proceeds, thus adding to the loss.

Holding onto stock that has fallen below the price at which you bought it does not generate a loss. There is no loss for tax purposes until you sell.

You can recover part of a capital loss from the government; a capital loss directly reduces your taxable income so that you pay less tax.

Losses are categorized as short term or long term, just like capital gains. Long-term losses are losses on sales of assets held for more than one year. The losses are applied in a special order. (1) Short-term losses reduce short-term gains, (2) long-term losses reduce long-term gains, (3) short- and long-term net gains or losses are combined. A net short-term loss could offset net long-term gain, or a net long-term loss could offset net short-term gain. If there is still a loss, you can apply up to $3,000 of it against ordinary income. If there is still a loss left after that, you can carry-forward the remaining loss to the next year's tax return. A capital loss can be carried forward indefinitely.

Capital losses are most valuable when used against high bracket income. Being able to deduct a capital loss against ordinary income (up to $3,000), or against short-term capital gains, which are taxed at ordinary income rates, is most beneficial. Long-term capital gains are taxed at a low maximum of 20% so the deduction of losses there, while still good, is not as good as the deduction against short-term gains or ordinary income.

If you have a loss security that you want to use for a charitable contribution, the usual rule is reversed. In this situation you should sell the stock first to recognize the capital loss and then donate the sale proceeds to charity. (If it were a gain security you would want to give the stock to the charity in kind and let the charity sell it. That way you recognize no capital gain.)

If you are making gifts to family members, give them gain securities first, that is, securities that have current values above your cost basis. Why? If you give your son a security that you hold at a loss, for example, its current fair market value is $1,000 but you paid

$2,000. The basis your son receives for the computation of his losses is the fair market value, that is, $1,000. If son sells the security for $1,000 he recognizes no gain and no loss. The reduction in basis from $2,000 to $1,000 gives no tax benefit to anyone and is lost. If the son holds on to the security and it recovers and appreciates, and then if he sells it for $2,500, for purposes of computing gain his basis is $2,000. The loss of tax benefit only occurs if the security is given to the son and then the son sells it at a loss. In other words, you can't "give" losses to someone. For purposes of determining loss, the tax basis in the hands of the donee is the lesser of the donor's cost basis or the fair market value on the date of gift. For purposes of determining gain, the tax basis in the hands of the donee is the donor's basis. (If gift tax is paid on the gift there is a further adjustment.)

If you have a security that is in a loss position now, but you think will eventually recover and want to hold on to it you can sell it, recognize the loss, and then buy it back. The catch here is that you must avoid the IRS's wash sale rule. This rule says you can't claim a loss from sale of a security (such as stock) if you buy the identical security as a replacement within the period beginning 30 days before the sale and ending 30 days after the sale.

Remember, none of this makes sense with investment in an IRA or qualified plan. Retirement plans are tax-exempt. Buys and sells can be made inside the retirement plan without regard to gains and losses for tax purposes. Some advisors say you can buy stock immediately without waiting the 30 days for the wash sale rule if you sell it in your personal portfolio and buy it in your IRA (or vice versa). Don't do this. The IRS's position is that the simultaneous sale and purchase is an indirect sale of the security to the IRA which is a related party.

For estate planning purposes, if death is imminent, sell stocks that are at a loss. There is no point in dying with unrecognized losses. The securities will get a new basis on death (the date of death value) so the new basis may be a step-down basis, that is lower than what was paid for the stock. Then nobody gets the chance to take advantage of the loss. Sell the loss stocks and try to recognize gain to soak up the losses. An individual's losses don't get carried forward to an estate. Conversely, don't sell gain stocks before death because the stocks will get a step-up in basis to date of death value and tax on the gain can be completely avoided.

Health Savings Accounts: The Medical IRA

Health Savings Accounts (HSA) are tax-free savings accounts that can be used to pay for medical expenses.

Anyone under age 65 can participate in an HSA if they buy or participate in a high-deductible health insurance policy. For a plan that insures just one individual, the deductible must be at least $1,000 and there must be a $5,000 cap on out-of-pocket expenses. For family policies, the deductible must be at least $2,000 with a $10,000 cap on out-of pocket expenses.

Instead of buying high-priced health insurance with low co-pays and low deductibles, the idea of the HSA is to buy a low-cost health insurance policy with a high deductible and save the difference to cover smaller medical costs. Commentators predict that insurance premiums will be lowered 20% to 40% when you change from a low-deductible to a high-deductible plan.

You can contribute to the HSA up to the amount of the deductible but no more than $2600 for individuals and $5,150 for families. You can add an extra $500 per year if you were born before 1950 to help "catch-up" for retirement expenses. If both spouses are over age 55, two catch-up contributions can be made in one year. The contribution is tax deductible even if you don't itemize your deductions — just like an IRA. Withdrawals for medical expenses are tax-free. Permissible withdrawals include payment for prescription drugs, deductibles, co-pays, chronic care, health insurance premiums for the unemployed, Medicare expenses, and retiree health plans (but not Medigap). Over-the-counter drugs and long-term care insurance premiums are also permissible expenditures.

Money withdrawn for non-medical expenses before age 65 will be subject to income tax and a 10% early withdrawal penalty. After age 65, non-medical withdrawals will be subject to income tax but not penalty — it can supplement retirement income just like an IRA for those over age 65.

The tax benefits are significant. Contributions, withdrawals for medical expenses, and account earnings are all tax-free. Since withdrawals for medical expenses are tax-free, that makes the tax shelter provided by these vehicles even better than IRAs. Of course, you don't get an accumulation in the account unless you don't spend it all on medical expenses.

HSAs can be set up by individuals or by employers, and contributions can be made by the individual, family members, and employers. Employer contributions are not subject to FICA taxes. Amounts in the plan belong to the individuals and are completely portable. The custodian of the plan is not required to monitor the appropriateness of withdrawals — that is up to the individual.

On death, the HSA can pass to a spouse's HSA on a tax-free basis.

Proponents point out that the HSA gives consumers of medical services more freedom of choice because what they pay for out of the HSA allows them to choose any provider without the restrictions imposed by HMOs.

From a public policy viewpoint, when people have higher deductibles, that means they are paying from their own pockets and are more likely to shop competitively for medical services and pay more attention to spending. On the other hand, the argument is made that healthy, affluent workers will opt out of traditional health plans in favor of the HSAs and high deductible policies. If large numbers of healthy workers pull out of traditional plans, the remaining members of the pool will be older and sicker, and their premiums will rise significantly.

These plans offer a tremendous advantage over flexible spending accounts. Those plans, sometimes provided as an employee benefit, provide that any money in the plan not spent by year-end is lost to the employee and reverts to the employer. Plus, money in the flexible spending account earns no interest to the employee. With the HSA, any money not spent is saved, invested, and is tax deferred. Flexible spending accounts probably won't disappear completely because they allow coverage of some health care items not covered by HSAs.

Various providers will offer the HSA plans. Some are accessed by check and some by debit card. Like IRAs, different companies tout different investments inside these plans.

Residence Gains

If you have not sold a house in a while, you may not be current on your understanding of the income tax implications.

If you sell your principal residence for more than you paid for it, the difference is a capital gain. In general, capital gains are subject to tax, but there are some special rules for gains on the sale of a personal residence which can make the gain nontaxable.

Your "principal residence" is the one you own and use. Using means living there. Prior to the change in the law on April 6, 1997, you had to own and use the residence for three out of the previous five years to take advantage of the tax relief. Under the old pre-April 1997 rules, if you bought a new principal residence and invested the entire sale proceeds within two years before or after the sale of the old one, the capital gain could be rolled over into the new house and no tax paid until the new house was sold. This rollover approach to gains on the sale of personal residences is now history.

Also, under the old law, there was a special relief provision if you wanted to sell a principal residence and not buy another bigger, better house. For example, if you wanted to downsize to an empty-nest-sized home you could buy a less expensive house and still be able to avoid tax on some of the gain. If you were over the age of 55, the old law forgave you up to $125,000 of capital gain once in your lifetime. This provision is also no longer part of the law.

Things changed dramatically in 1997. Section 121 of the Internal Revenue Code became much more friendly to the new, younger retiring generation (which includes our representatives in Congress). Three years of owning and using shrank to two years. The exemption rose from $125,000 to $250,000. Married couples can exempt $500,000. Also, for married couples, if one spouse owns the residence, both spouses are deemed to be owners of the property. You don't have to be 55 or over, and you can own and sell your house every two years!

If the own-and-use times aren't met, or if the two-year interval since the last sale isn't met, there is still a way to get a prorated part of the exemption. If such sale or exchange is because of a change in place of employment, health, or unforeseen circumstances, to the extent provided in regulations, then a prorated exemption is allowed. "Unforeseen circumstances" have included divorce or separation in some court cases. Involuntary conversion (fire, earthquakes, condemnation) also triggers the prorated clause.

Let's look at an example. Jane buys a house for $100,000, then sells it 18 months later for $150,000 because she's gotten a new job in York. She fails the two-year own-and-use test, but, because her sale was due to changing jobs, she can get a prorated exemption of 18/24 (18 months out of 24) of $250,000 or $187,500, well under the $50,000 gain she realized.

The exemption can be disclaimed if desired. Suppose a couple owns a home in Pennsylvania and has lived there three years. Suppose they retire, move to Florida, and owns the Florida house for two years. The house in Pennsylvania is small, and has only a $10,000 gain and they intend to sell it. They intend to sell their Florida home to a professional athlete at a large gain this year. They might want to disclaim any tax forgiveness on the Pennsylvania house so they can use the exemption on the Florida sale. Both houses would qualify, and the first sale would disqualify the second sale for two years. To sell the Pennsylvania home and preserve the exemption for the Florida sale, merely list the capital gain on the first sale in Schedule D and take no exemption.

Pennsylvania changed its personal residence capital gains treatment as of January 1, 1998, so that it would be similar to the federal law. Formerly, there were ownership and use rules and recent prior sale prohibitions, and there was a limit on how much could be exempted. The current law is contained in Title 72 of Pennsylvania Statutes at Section 7303(1)(3)(vii)(A-C). It starts by saying net gains don't include gains from the sale, exchange, or other disposition of a personal residence. There is no limit on the dollar amount!

Pennsylvania requires ownership and use for two of the previous five years. It requires no previous sales for two years. There is proration of gain exclusion that is word-for-word identical to the IRS "job, health, and unforeseen circumstances" exceptions. If the property sold consists of part residence and part non-residence (like a home office), the part of the gain attributable to the home may be exempted. If the property sold includes a portion that has been depreciated, the part of the gain attributable to the non-depreciated property is excluded.

Now, not only is selling a home usually a tax-free event, a person could actually make a nice living from buying highly appreciable personal residences every two years. As long as your elected representatives have to move to and from Washington expect this law to survive.

Vacation Homes — What Can You Deduct?

According to the National Association of Realtors, the market for vacation homes is thriving. Mortgage rates are low, unemployment is coming down, and the aging baby boomer population is looking forward to retirement. There have been changes in the capital gain tax law, and many people have looked for alternative investments to stocks.

A vacation home is referred to as a "second residence" under the tax code. It must have sleeping, cooking, and toilet facilities to be eligible for the mortgage interest deduction. Any type of home can qualify: a house, a condominium, cooperative unit, houseboat, mobile home, or house trailer.

The income tax treatment of income and deductions attributable to your vacation home depends on the amount of personal use compared to the amount of rental use. Personal use includes all days you used the home, other than those days spent making repairs or preparing the property for rental. It also includes time spent in the home by family members or friends. Rental to anyone for less than fair market value is considered as personal use. Personal use also includes time when the owner donates use of the house for a charitable fund-raising event — no charitable deduction is available for a contribution of a part interest in property like this.

Depending on the amount of personal use, there are four categories of taxation your vacation home could fall into.

1. The Free Ride. This is for the person who just makes a few extra dollars renting the home for a short period. If a home is rented less than 15 days of the year, you don't have to report the rent received as income. Consistent with this, you can't deduct expenses incurred in the production of this rental income although you do not lose any of your interest or tax expenses that you can take on the home. This classification

can be used to great advantage if you rent out your principal residence or your vacation home for a major sporting event or festival.

2. Primary Personal Vacation Home. This category includes vacation homes that are rented more than 15 days during the year, and the taxpayer's personal use exceeds 14 days or 10 percent of the rented days. This kind of vacation home is considered to be a personal residence. You can deduct the interest on up to $1 million of mortgage debt on two personal residences (and up to an additional $100,000 for home equity loans). Property taxes are generally deductible, no matter how many homes you own. If you own more than two homes, you can pick the two with the biggest mortgage interest deduction.

   You must divide your other expenses and apportion them between rental and personal use. Expenses allocated to personal use are not deductible. If your rental portion generates a loss, you do not get to offset your other income with the tax losses. You can only take deductions to the extent of rental income. In general, expenses are allocated to rental use by a fraction, the numerator of which is the number of days the home is rented and the denominator is usually 365.

3. Primary Rental Vacation Home. This category applies if you rent the vacation home more than 15 days of the year and your personal use does not exceed 14 days or 10 percent of the rented days of the year. Expenses must be allocated between personal and rental use. The most important impact of this classification is that, subject to the passive activity rules, if you have a loss generated by the rental, you can use the loss to offset other income such as salary.

   Passive activity loss rules apply to rental real estate activities unless the owner is a real estate professional. Non-deductible passive activity losses can be carried forward and become fully deductible when the vacation home is sold. Many owners of vacation homes find that this passive activity loss limitation means they can't deduct losses. You can deduct up to $25,000 if you actively participate in the activity and meet an income limitation. Active participation means making contributions in the decision making concerning the property, such as setting rents. However, the $25,000 deduction phases out as income rises above $100,000 until it is fully phased out at $150,000.

4. Straight Rental Vacation Homes. If the home is rented more than 15 days of the year, and you have no personal use at all, the property is taxed as a straight rental property. The taxation is the same as if it were a Primary Rental Vacation Home except that there is no allocation of expenses since there is no personal use.

There is a major tax break for the exclusion of gain on the sale of a personal residence. This break does not apply to a vacation home. Otherwise, tax treatment varies in the four stages listed above.

Beware the Alternative Minimum Tax

Many taxpayers are under the mistaken impression that there is only one system of federal income taxation in this country. There are in fact two distinct but parallel systems; the regular tax system that most people are familiar with and the Alternative Minimum Tax (AMT) system.

When first enacted, the AMT was intended to apply to high-income taxpayers who took advantage of too many loopholes. The idea was to stop people with very large incomes from getting away with paying little or no tax. Congress said that taxpayers shouldn't get too big a tax break from tax advantaged investments or benefit too much from otherwise deductible items such as state taxes or job related expenses.

How can you know if it applies to you? If you use a computer program to prepare your 1040, it may do the AMT calculations for you. If preparing your return by hand, or if your computer program doesn't calculate it, you must fill out form 6251 to determine if you are subject to the AMT. There is, however, no substitute for getting professional tax advice.

Every taxpayer is legally obligated to compute his or her tax liability under both the regular and AMT tax systems and to pay whichever tax is higher. If your regular tax is higher than your alternative minimum tax, you pay the regular tax and there is no AMT. If your alternative minimum tax is higher than your regular tax, you must pay the regular tax plus the difference between the two amounts as additional alternative minimum tax.

For "ordinary" taxpayers, there are tax attributes that might put you at risk for the AMT. If you have any of these on your 1040 you may be subject to the AMT.

1. Do you have a large family? Personal exemptions are allowed to reduce your regular tax, but not the AMT. Let's say Husband and Wife have 6 kids. The family as a whole gets 8 personal exemptions at $ 2,900 each. They can reduce their regular taxable income by $23,200. For AMT purposes these exemptions are ignored, so if there are other AMT issues on the return, this family may well find that they are subject to the AMT.
2. Are your state and local taxes high? State and local taxes can be claimed as itemized deductions against the regular tax, but not so for AMT purposes. If possible, pay these taxes in years when you are not subject to the AMT. You might find that paying some penalty and interest to defer payment of state and local taxes may be less than the AMT. Similarly, if you think you'll be subject to the AMT next year, accelerate the deduction of state and local taxes to this year by paying early.
3. Do you have a second mortgage? You can deduct the interest on a mortgage under the AMT only if the mortgage proceeds were used to buy, build, or improve your home. If you took out a home equity loan to buy a boat or car or to pay for college, that interest, while deductible against the regular tax, it is not deductible for AMT purposes.
4. Has this been a year of high medical expenses? To deduct medical expenses for the regular income tax, the expenses must exceed 7.5% of adjusted gross income. When calculating

the AMT, the medical expenses must exceed 10% of adjusted gross income to be deducted.

5. Miscellaneous itemized deductions subject to the 2% floor, such as unreimbursed employee business expenses, tax return preparer's fees, and investment expenses, are deductible in calculating the regular tax. They aren't deductible in calculating the AMT.
6. Exercising a large Incentive Stock Option is almost certain to cause you to pay the AMT. Usually you don't have to report any income when you exercise an ISO. No such luck for AMT purposes. With careful planning, you can exercise your stock options in such a way that it won't create an AMT liability.
7. Large capital gains can be a problem. There is an AMT exemption which is designed to make sure that the AMT doesn't apply until income goes above a certain level. Capital gains are taxed at the same top rate of 20% for both AMT and regular tax, but a large capital gain can cause you to lose the exemption built into the AMT system. Carefully timing your capital gains may help.

There is one piece of good news. All or part of any AMT you pay may be able to be used to reduce the regular tax you owe on subsequent years' returns. Congress recognized that in some cases the AMT creates inequities in tax results. Therefore, if you pay AMT in one year, you might be eligible for a tax credit against your regular tax liability in the following year.

Are You Paying Employment Taxes for Your Housekeeper and Babysitter?

Remember Zoe Baird? Kimba Wood? In 1994 attorney general candidates, Zoe Baird and Kimba Wood, and defense secretary designate, Bobby Ray Inman, had their nominations derailed because they ran afoul of long-standing rules that require quarterly tax payments for household help if payments were as little as $50 per quarter. The rules were revised and thanks to Zoe and Kimba, the taxes now frequently are referred to as the "Nanny Tax."

The nanny tax is employment taxes on wages of domestic workers such as gardeners, nurses, babysitters, nannies, and housekeepers. If you paid such a worker more than $1,700 in 2010 or 2011, you may be required to pay social security and Medicare tax on the wages.

You owe the nanny tax if the household worker is your employee. The household worker is your employee if you control the work that is done and how it is done. It doesn't matter whether or not the work is full or part-time, or whether or not you hired the worker through an agency. If the household worker controls the work and how it is done, then the worker is not your employee but a self-employed independent contractor. Self-employed household workers usually provide their own tools and equipment and offer their services to the public. These self-employed workers are responsible for paying their own taxes.

There are some important exceptions to the requirement to pay nanny taxes. If your household worker is your parent, spouse, child under age 21, or another person under age 18, whose principal occupation is not household employment, then you do not have to pay the nanny tax. (Note that that does not mean that these workers don't have to report the income.)

There are actually three separate federal employment taxes: (1) Social Security, (2) Medicare tax (together known as "FICA," Federal Insurance Contributions Act), and (3) Federal Unemployment Tax Act (FUTA). You are not required to withhold federal income taxes from a household employee's wages, but may if the employee requests. You must withhold FICA from your household employee's wages, 7.65%, and you must remit the withheld amount plus a matching contribution (another 7.65%) to the IRS. You also must pay FUTA taxes on the household employee's wages. The FUTA rate is 0.8%.

Under the old, pre-Zoe Baird rules, employers had to file quarterly returns and pay taxes just like a business. Now Congress has tried to simplify matters and allow you, the employer, to file annually along with your 1040. How to report and pay? File Schedule H, Household Employment Taxes with your 1040. You will need another tax identification number. You must apply for an Employer Identification Number (EIN) on a Form SS-4. Even though you don't have to file employment taxes annually, the taxes are part of your regular income tax liability. Therefore, you may have to make quarterly estimated tax payments (or increase your estimated payments) to cover the new combined tax liability.

To simplify reporting these taxes, Schedule H, Household Employment Taxes, was added to your Form 1040. While this simplifies filing and paying the tax, now taxpayers have a new dilemma. If they fail to pay the nanny tax they are filing an incorrect and fraudulent income tax return. Getting caught could result in charges of perjury or even tax evasion, not to mention huge penalties and interest.

Adding Schedule H to the Form 1040 had an unexpected effect. Approximately 500,000 taxpayers paid the tax in 1994, but only about 290,000 paid such taxes in 1999. Is this more noncompliance? Are we overrun with tax cheats? Or are household employees earning less, or working through agencies?

Failing to report and pay required nanny taxes is tax fraud. If your employer increased profits by not paying payroll taxes on your salary, I'm sure you'd be among the first to condemn him. Of course, your employer could save money by not paying payroll taxes, or not reporting workers' wages so that they could pay lower salaries. It is no different with employers of household workers except that in this situation the law is broken far more often. Sometimes employers of household help pay "under the table" so they can pay lower salaries to a worker who is evading income taxes.

Not only is this against the law, but it is also very detrimental to the employee. Being legal means your employment can be proven and shown on job applications, credit card applications, student loan applications — many things that are critical to daily life. Is it a good thing for a worker to be unable to collect unemployment compensation, to be unable to prove her income when applying for a car loan or a mortgage? Will the worker need social security at some time in the future when what should have been paid by you as the employer on her behalf becomes of crucial importance?

Neither the IRS nor state tax authorities are aggressive in pursuing nanny tax evaders. The issue usually comes up when complaints are brought by disgruntled workers, perhaps a worker who is presented with a 1099 at the end of the year, or maybe when a former worker applies for unemployment.

Admittedly, compliance is not easy. Not one of the 50 states has followed the federal lead to make reporting nanny taxes easier. Even if you can just add your federal household employee taxes to your 1040, you can't do that for state taxes. This leaves the employer with a quarterly filing responsibility for the state. Also, writing paychecks is a problem. When workers are paid hourly or by other varying amounts, each paycheck requires the calculations of varying amounts of withholding (some by percentages or reference to tables or charts.)

Check out Publication 15-A, Employer's Supplemental Tax Guide, available from the IRS and for more information get IRS Publication 926, Household Employer's Tax Guide. There are many companies who provide nanny tax services who will sell you software to help you do-it-yourself or provide payroll and tax services for you to relieve you of the burden.

Home Sweet Office: Taking a Deduction for a Home Office

According to CNN/Money nearly a third of the U.S. workforce, or about 44 million people, regularly worked at home in 2004. Of these, only 2.5 million claimed the office in home deduction. Many do not meet these strict requirements for the deduction, but many are afraid to take the deduction, thinking it is equivalent to writing "Please Audit Me" across the top of their income tax return.

If you are an employee, you can only deduct the home office if it is for the convenience of your employer. If your employer wants you to work at home to save the employer money on office space, you can claim the home office deduction. It's not enough that the home office is helpful, it must actually be required by the employer. If you are permitted to work at home because you begged or pleaded to, that is not for the convenience of the employer. That is for your convenience and you don't qualify for the deduction.

If you are self-employed, in order to qualify to deduct a portion of home-connected expenses such as utilities, rent, depreciation, homeowner's insurance, mortgage interest, real estate taxes, maintenance and repairs, you must be able to prove: (1) that you regularly use part of your home exclusively for a trade or business, and (2) you must also be able to prove at least one of the following:

1. You use your home as your principal place of business,

2. You meet patients, clients, or customers at home, or
3. You use a separate structure on your property exclusively for business purposes.

The requirement that part of your home be used exclusively for a trade or business is a tough one. Exclusive use means that you use a portion of your home only for business. If you use a room or part of your home for business and for personal use, you don't qualify for the deduction. If your home office doubles as a guest room, that's not exclusive use for business.

If you balance your personal checkbook at the desk in your home office does that mean you fail the exclusive use test? Turbo-tax reports that one tax–payer lost the home office deduction because a picture of her desk showed that the dog's water bowl was under her desk. Don't push the envelope — if you take this deduction make sure the space for which you take deductions is used only for your business.

There are two exceptions to the exclusive use test. One is that the taxpayer uses part of his home to store inventory or product samples for the trade or business of selling products at retail or wholesale in which he is engaged, and the residence is the sole fixed location of that business. The other exception is if you run a qualified daycare facility at your home.

For sole proprietors, if you qualify for the home office deduction, you must figure the amount of your deduction on IRS Form 8829, Expenses for Business Use of Your Home. Deduct 100% of expenses that are directly related to the home office. This can include painting, cleaning and the premium for a home office rider on your homeowner's insurance policy. Ditto for your office telephone line and utilities, if you have separate hookups.

You are also allowed to deduct a percentage of indirect expenses that relate to your entire residence. These include mortgage interest, real estate taxes, condo fees, rent, depreciation (over 39 years), utilities, security, garbage pickup, maintenance, repairs, insurance, snow removal, and so on.

What percentage of these expenses can you deduct? If you follow the instructions for Form 8829, it will lead you through a square footage analysis. Count only living space in figuring the percentage (not your garage, unfinished basement or covered patio). Also, if you have a bathroom adjoining your office that's never used otherwise, treat the square footage as part of your office.

Despite what the instructions for Form 8829 say, you can also use any other "reasonable method" to compute the business portion for indirect expenses. For example, you can count the number of rooms in your house and divide. If you have 10 rooms that are generally the same size and use one for the business, you can deduct 10% of your indirect expenses. The office doesn't have to be a whole separate room. It may be just a defined space that is used for business.

You can't take more deductions for a home office than you have income generated by the business. Thus, you cannot use the home office deduction to generate a tax loss. Any unused losses can be carried over to the next year.

Be prepared to prove to the IRS that you are entitled to take the home office deduction. Here are some ideas:

1. Photograph your home office and draw a diagram showing the location of the office in your home. Keep this information in your tax folder.
2. Have your business mail sent to your home.
3. Use your home address on your business cards and stationery and in all business ads.
4. Get a separate phone line for the business.
5. Have clients or customers visit your home office — and keep a log of those visits.
6. Keep track of the time you spend working at home.

As long as you live in your house for two out of the last five years and the proceeds of the sale are less than $250,000 for single filers and $500,000 for couples filing jointly, you don't have to pay capital gains taxes on any part of your house. However, if you depreciated your home office, you'll need to add up the total amount you depreciated and claim that as ordinary income.

Ordinary business expenses are deductible even if you don't qualify for the home office deduction. You can still deduct ordinary and necessary business expenses that arise at your home such as, a separate business telephone line and office supplies and equipment.

Income Tax Deduction for Medical Insurance Premiums

Our life is frittered away by detail.... Simplify, simplify.

Henry David Thoreau

Can you deduct the cost of medical insurance? Sounds like a simple question. Humph. You can get lost in the labyrinthine twists of the answer to that question.

If your employer pays for your medical insurance, the employer gets a full deduction and you, as the employee, incur no taxable income from the benefit you receive from the insurance. In this case, the full cost of the medical insurance is tax deductible by the employer.

What if you pay for your own medical insurance through your employer's plan? If you pay the premiums yourself, you can only deduct the cost of the premiums if you itemize your deductions instead of taking the standard deduction. However, (ouch) you can only deduct medical expenses (including premiums) that exceed 7.5% of adjusted gross income.

What if your employer pays for part of the premium and you have to pay the rest? Well, then the employer can deduct 100% of the portion of the premium he or she paid. Your portion can, in effect, only be deducted by you if your employer has a special type of plan, called a cafeteria plan, that allows your portion to be treated as pre-tax. If your employer offers a cafeteria plan, you can allocate pre-tax dollars to be spent on your choice of a series of qualified benefits. Rather than deducting your portion of the premium, your taxable income is adjusted.

If your employer does not have a cafeteria plan, then your portion can only be deducted if you itemize and to the extent your medical expenses exceed 7.5% of your adjusted gross income (double ouch). Your employer still can deduct 100% of the portion of the premium he or she pays.

What about deductible or co-pay amounts? If your employer has a cafeteria plan, insurance deductibles can be pre-tax but only to the extent you elected, at the beginning of the year, to contribute to a flexible spending account, if available. These accounts have a "use it or lose it" feature, and do not come with a crystal ball. Without a cafeteria plan's flexible spending account, your deductibles are itemized deductions subject to exceeding that 7.5% of your adjusted gross income.

What if you have your own business, and are self-employed, filing a Schedule C to report your income? Can you deduct medical insurance premium? It depends. If you are self-employed and you had a profit for the year, then you can deduct up to 100% of the amount paid for health insurance on behalf of yourself, your spouse, and dependents. This includes dental and long-term care coverage. To qualify you must have no other health insurance coverage and you must have business income. If your business incurs a loss you get no deduction.

A self-employed person cannot participate in a cafeteria plan so there is no opportunity to treat premium that are non-deductible under the above rules. You may be able to deduct them as itemized deductions subject to the 7.5% of adjusted gross income limit.

So, can you deduct the cost of medical insurance? Maybe . . . well, partly . . . if you've had medical expenses exceeding 7.5% of your income . . . or if you are employed by the right kind of employer, offering the right kind of healthcare plan . . . or if you're a self-employed owner of a profitable business.

It is worth it, however, to track what you spend on medical insurance and expenses. If you find yourself in a year with high medical expenses, research if scheduling elective laser eye surgery, enrolling in a smoking cessation program, or removing the lead paint in your home may boost your total qualified medical expenses over your 7.5%. Also, if you have high medical bills near the end of a year, consider paying for them the next year. That may boost next year's medical expenses to the deductible 7.5%.

You Need ESP to Figure Out Your ESPP

Does your employer give you the opportunity to buy its stock at a discount? Millions of employees have become shareholders in the company where they work through these Employee Stock Purchase Plans (ESPPs). These plans are usually only available in public companies. They are a great way to encourage saving and investing.

There are two kinds of ESPPs: (1) "Qualified ESPPs," meaning the plan meets the requirements of Section 423 of the Internal Revenue Code, and (2) "Nonqualified ESSPs." A Qualified Employee Stock Purchase Plan under Section 423 offers special tax treatment for shares held for the requisite holding period — no taxes on the discount are owed at the time of purchase.

To qualify under Section 423 the plan must meet the following requirements: (1) only employees of the company may participate in the plan, (2) the plan must be approved by a vote of the shareholders of the company before it is adopted by the board of directors, (3) any employee owning more the 5% of the company's stock may not participate, (4) all employees must get the same rights and privileges on a nondiscriminatory basis except that the amount of stock you can purchase may be based on compensation and two years of service may be required before participation, (5) the purchase price may not be less than the lesser of 85% of the fair market value of the stock at the beginning of the offering period or on the purchase date, (6) an employee may not purchase more than $25,000 worth of stock for each calendar year of the offering period, and (7) the maximum offering period cannot exceed 27 months. (The offering period can be five years if the purchase price is based solely on the fair market value at the time of purchase. The offering period is the period during which payroll deductions are accumulated. Usually the offering period is 3 months.)

Without special tax treatment, the employee would be required to pay income tax on the 15% discount when the stock is purchased. This difference between the purchase price and the fair market value of the stock is called the "spread." In a qualified ESPP, the spread is not taxed until the stock is sold if the stock is held for the required period. The employee must hold the stock for at least two years after the start of the purchasing period and for at least one year after the shares are purchased. Any difference between the purchase price and the ultimate sales price of the stock is treated as capital gain or loss.

If the employee makes a sale not in compliance with these rules, it is a disqualifying event and the spread is taxable when the shares are purchased, just like in a nonqualified ESPP. The spread when the shares are purchased is not computed on the lower of the price at the beginning of the offering period or when the shares are purchased, it is simply the difference between the price paid and the market value of the shares when purchased.

That can create a *big* problem. Holding onto the stock to get the tax break may cause you to incur a tax bill greater than your gain! Many high-tech company employees found themselves in this position when the stock of their employer sank. Here is an example from CBS Market Watch: "Say times are good and your company's shares double to $20 from $10 over a six-month offering period. You buy 1,000 shares of stock at $8.50 and sell immediately, capturing a $11,500 gain. Investors in a 25% income tax bracket would bank a cool $8,624. . . . But consider what could happen if you hold that stock for tax reasons (to get long-term capital gains treatment) and the shares tumble back to $10 six months later. Stock costing $8,500 is now worth $10,000, so you hurry to salvage a quick $1,500 profit. Now the tax treatment gets more complicated, as you don't report a $1,500 gain. You sold the shares before two years passed since the initial date of the grant or one year from purchase. To the IRS, the stock was purchased when the market price was $20. This leaves you owing ordinary income taxes on the difference between your purchase price of $8.50 and the $20 market price — a numbing $11,500 phantom gain. The only consolation: You do have a $20 a share cost basis, which translates to a $10,000 short-term capital loss on the sale."

In the above example, Joe employee exercised the option to buy for $8.50 per share after the price had climbed to $20 a share, then sold hastily at $10 a share before the holding period ended. By selling early, he had to declare ordinary income. It was calculated by subtracting the discount price when offered from the share price when purchased, not from the market price when originally offered.

With the stock price plummeting you are stuck because if you sell before the 2-year period is up you may have phantom income and if you hold on, the price may sink even lower.

That is why many sophisticated investment advisors advise selling ESPP shares quickly and not holding on for two years from the date of the offering to employees for the favorable tax treatment. Sell as soon as you can and get the gain promised by the 15% discount even if it's taxed as ordinary income. Selling stock you bought at a

15% discount immediately is a guaranteed immediate 17.6% gain ($1,500/$8,500). Where can you beat that?

Can it be worth it to hold for two years to get capital gain treatment instead of ordinary income when holding for the two years includes the risk of phantom income discussed above?

A sale before the holding period is up is a disqualifying transfer and the employer must report the spread income to you on your W-2.

Do income taxes and social security taxes have to be withheld on the spread? In 1971 the IRS issued a ruling that said the spread did not constitute wages for withholding purposes. Controversy erupted because some IRS offices have asserted tax deficiencies against employers for not withholding taxes and social security from the spread. Now the IRS has declared an indefinite moratorium on this issue and employers do not have to withhold taxes on the spread. If you are an employer and withheld taxes in the past, you may be entitled to a refund.

Nonqualified Employee Stock Purchase Plans are payroll deduction plans that allow the purchase of employer stock at a discount. There is no special tax treatment. In a plan like this, the spread is taxed as ordinary income when the shares are purchased. Any additional gain of the sale above the market price on the purchase date is capital gain — short or long-term depending on the taxpayer's holding period for the shares. The appeal of these plans is that they provide an easy and convenient way to invest in your employer's stock and commissions are picked up by the employer. Every one of your dollars goes to purchase stock at the 15% discount.

While ESPPs can be great ways of investing keep in mind the need for diversification. Remember Enron and WorldCom (not to mention Armstrong)? Don't invest all of your savings in stock of your employer.

Can Employer-Reimbursed Tuition Be Excluded from Income? Maybe.

Education costs money, but then so does ignorance.

Sir Moser Claus, Daily Telegraph
(London, August 21, 1990).

Does your employer reimburse you for tuition you spend on your education? If so, that reimbursement, up to $5,250, might be excludable from your gross wages.

Section 127 of the Internal Revenue Code allows such exclusion from gross wages reported by an employer. However, there are a number of hoops that the employer's program must jump through to exclude such payments.

First, the plan must be a written plan. Oral agreements with employees do not suffice.

Second, it must be for the exclusive benefit of employees. That means the employer can't develop a plan to take care of his children and then include his employees as well.

Third, the program must identify the class of employees eligible for the benefit, and the IRS must not find that it discriminates in favor of highly compensated employees, within the meaning of section 414(q). This section defines highly compensated employees as those who either (1) own more than five percent of the company or (2) both earned more than $80,000 the previous year (adjusted for inflation from 1996) and were in the top twenty percent compensation-wise in the company the previous year. New hires, minors, and part-timers are excluded when figuring the twenty percent limit, unless they are union members.

Fourth, no more than five percent of the education reimbursement may be paid to people who own five percent of the company (either in stock of the capital or profits) or are spouses or children of such five-percent owners.

Fifth, the program cannot offer a choice in benefits of either the tuition reimbursement or some other remuneration includable in gross income. For example, if the employer plan states that either education reimbursement or first home purchase will be assisted by the employer, the plan does not qualify.

Sixth, notification of the availability and terms of the program must be provided to eligible employees.

If your employer has such a plan, then reimbursed tuition might not be added to income until such reimbursement exceeds $5,250 for a given year. Suppose your employer doesn't exclude it from income. What can you do to recoup the withheld taxes?

First, you need to be sure the plan qualifies in the year you want to recoup the taxes. The employer may have included such payments for a variety of reasons. One may be that the payroll software doesn't handle exclusion of payments, or if it does, the paymaster doesn't know how to use that function. Or, it may be the employer knows that for some reason the plan won't qualify in that year.

If disqualification is the reason, stop. The exclusion is not available to you.

If your employer says it qualifies, ask him to amend your W-2 or at least sign a statement saying your wages should be reduced by X amount. Then you can enter a number for wages paid that doesn't match the employer-reported wages, the difference being the tuition reimbursement that the employer included in wages.

If you do this, you will have to prove your right to reduce this amount and include the proof with your return. That would include at a minimum the employer's signed statement, a copy of the written plan, a pay stub showing that tuition was reimbursed as stated on the pay stub, and that the pay stub shows tuition was included in figuring withholding, plus your explanation.

Alternatively, you could claim the reimbursements as a tuition deduction on line 26 of your 1040, but that requires an earnings limit of $65,000 for single taxpayers, $135,000 for married taxpayers filing jointly. See the current year's instructions for details.

You could forget the line 26 deduction and try to claim a lifetime learning credit or Hope credit. Such credits are subject to earnings limitations. If you are single and earn more than $51,000, you can't qualify. If you are married and earn more than $102,000, you can't qualify.

Note that you cannot use both the $5,250 exclusion and the lifetime learning credit. It's one or the other. The best part of the tuition reimbursement exclusion is that not only is income tax not withheld, but neither is Social Security.

Are You Engaged in a Business for Profit? Or Is It a Hobby?

> *Hobby: a pursuit outside one's regular occupation engaged in especially for relaxation*
>
> Merriam Webster

Beware the hobby loss rules. If the IRS considers your business a hobby, you may not be able to deduct your losses.

If the taxpayer's activity is considered a business, the deduction of expenses and the claiming of losses are subject to the normal business expense and business loss rules. In general, taxpayers may deduct all the ordinary and necessary expenses attributable to a trade or business or an activity engaged in for the production of income or for profit. Where expenses exceed the income from an activity, the deduction of the expenses creates a loss that may offset the taxpayer's income from other sources.

Losses incurred in connection with a hobby are deductible only to the extent of the income produced by the hobby. You can't use a loss generated by a hobby to offset other taxable income.

Hobby income is reported on line 23 of your 1040 as "other income," and the expenses associated with the hobby are deductible only if you itemize deductions. Even then, they are miscellaneous itemized deductions and are deductible only to the extent they exceed the floor of 2% of adjusted gross income.

What kinds of businesses are challenged on this ground? All kinds, but you can expect special scrutiny on "gentleman farming," craft businesses run from the home, horse breeding operations, and day-trading.

A typical example is Dr. Bones, highly compensated employee of ABC medical practice, who buys a farm. He goes to the farm on the weekends, plants some corn, builds a new barn, and repairs the fence. Of course, the expenses far exceed the income generated by the sale of the corn. Are these expenses deductible as business expenses for his "farming business" or are they just personal expenditures to prepare a country home for his retirement years? If Dr. Bones' operation of the farm does not look like, walk like, or quack like a real business, the IRS may disallow the losses.

Here's another one. Mrs. Gates raises and shows horses. She boards her horses at the stable of a neighbor and expects to make a profit from winning prize money at horse shows and from breeder fees. Considering the expense of the horses' board, feed (horses eat money), training, equipment, and travel, Mrs. Gates never makes a profit. Can she deduct her losses as a business loss against her other earned income?

Internal Revenue Code Section 183 addresses this issue. When there is no profit motive, you can only deduct expenses up to the amount of income; losses cannot be taken against other income. If the taxpayer can show a profit from the activity in three out of the most recent five consecutive years including the current year, the activity will be considered as engaged in for profit. There is a special rule for breeding, training, showing, or racing horses. If these horse activities show a profit in two of the last seven tax years, including the current year, the activity is considered to be engaged in for profit.

If you can't pass the three-year (or two-year) test, then the IRS presumes that the activity is a hobby. This presumption can be overcome by the taxpayer if the taxpayer can prove by the facts and circumstances that the activity really is a business intended to make a profit.

The best way to demonstrate that your business is profit-motivated is to make it profitable. If the activity is not, in fact, profitable, how can you prove that you intend to make a profit? Here are some things the IRS may look at:

> Do you maintain a separate bank account for business?
> Do you have a name for your business?
> Do you keep a set of books?
> Do you have a business license?
> Do you have a separate area in your house where you conduct your business?
> Do you have a separate phone and fax line for business?
> Do you have stationery and business cards?
> Do you have a business plan?
> Do you advertise, market or promote your business?
> Do you spend time each day or week on your business?
> Are you trying new ways to advertise and market your business?
> Are you meeting with customers and clients each week?
> Are you making a reasonable effort to make a profit the way other people do in this business?
> Are your losses due to circumstances beyond your control?

Some tax advisors advise taxpayers in start-up businesses, especially farms, that may be questioned as hobbies, to file Form 5213. If you file this form, the IRS will not immediately question whether your activity is a business or just a hobby. The activity will not be evaluated until the end of five (or seven for horse activities) years.

Quite simply, it buys you time. In exchange, filing Form 5213 automatically extends the statute of limitations for disallowance of deductions related to the activity on any year in the five-year (or seven-year) period to two years after the due date of the return for the last year of the period. So, if you do not deduct losses greater than income, and the activity becomes profitable, you can go back and amend the returns and take the deductions. This can be a substantial advantage.

It's a Business Trip, so I'm Deducting it

Travel expenses are the ordinary and necessary expenses that you pay while temporarily traveling away from home on business. If you go on a business trip and add on some vacation days, you know you can deduct some of your expenses. The only question is how much.

Domestic Travel. For travel within the United States, transportation expenses, the cost of getting there and back including fares, cabs, and tips, are 100% deductible as long as the primary reason for the trip is business rather than pleasure. If vacation is the primary reason for your travel, none of your transportation expenses are deductible. How does one determine what is the primary reason for the trip? No regulatory guidelines are determined but one can look at the foreign travel rules for some help. Look at the number of business days compared to the number of pleasure days. Travel days are counted as business days. Weekends and holidays count as business days if they fall between days devoted to business and it would be impractical to return home. "Standby days" also count as business days. These are days when you need to be available but aren't actually called upon to work.

Expenses for lodging, 50% of meals, and fees for business days are fully deductible. Expenses for personal days are not deductible.

An exception to this rule is the "Saturday Night Stay-over." If you can show that staying over Saturday night costs less (or no more) than coming back home immediately after the business meeting is over, the IRS allows you to deduct your additional meal and lodging expenses (subject to the 50% rule for meals) for the extra days. Of course, the primary purpose of the trip still has to be for business. Make sure that you document that your airfare savings due to the Saturday night stay equaled or exceeded the out-of-pocket costs of staying the extra days.

No matter what, you can't deduct extra cost of a trip for your spouse or companion, and you can't deduct the costs of personal entertainment, of course, for you or your traveling companion.

Foreign Travel

The general rule for foreign travel is that you must allocate all of the costs of travel, including the cost of getting there and back, between personal non-deductible costs and deductible business expenses. The non-deductible portion is computed on a time basis, usually the proportion of non-business days to all travel days. As is often the case in tax law, the exceptions to the rule are where it gets interesting.

The first exception is that you can deduct 100% of your transportation expenses if you meet either of the following rules:

The One-week Rule. If your business trip is a week or less, not counting the day you leave, but counting the day you return, you can deduct 100% of your transportation costs and 100% of your other out-of-pocket expenses for business days (subject to the 50% rule for meals). Weekends and holidays between business days count as business days. Days between two business meeting days count as business days. "Standby days" when you have to be there but aren't called upon to work also count as business days.

The 25% Rule. If your trip lasts over a week but you spend less than 25% of your time in vacation you can also deduct 100% of your transportation expenses. Both the day you leave and the day you return count as business days.

If you don't meet the one week rule or the 25% rule, you can still deduct 100% of your transportation costs if you're traveling under a reimbursement or travel allowance arrangement and you're not a managing executive of the company or related to your employer.

And then there are these fuzzy catchalls: If you can prove a personal vacation was not a consideration in choosing to make the trip you can still deduct 100% of transportation expenses. Also, if you did not have substantial control over arranging the business trip, 100% of transportation expense are deductible. If 100% of your transportation expenses aren't deductible, the business proportion of your transportation costs are still deductible if the trip is primarily for business.

Foreign Conventions

If you are traveling outside of North America in order to attend a business convention you must follow all of the above foreign travel rules plus show it was just as reasonable for the meeting to be held on foreign soil as in North America and that the time spent in business meetings or activities was substantial when compared to that spent sight-seeing and engaging in other personal activities. If not, you can only deduct the registration fees and other fees directly-related to business while on your trip.

You will note that the key words were "outside of North America." For this purpose North America includes Canada, Mexico, Puerto Rico, the U.S. Virgin Islands, American Samoa, the Northern Mariana Islands, Guam, the Marshall Islands, Micronesia, Palau, Barbados, Bermuda, Costa Rica, Dominica, Dominican Republic, Grenada, Guyana, Honduras, Jamaica, Saint Lucia, Trinidad and Tobago, Midway Islands, Palmyra, Baker Island, Howland Island, Jarvis Island, Johnston Island, Kingman Reef, and Wake Island.

If your convention is in "North America" then the more liberal domestic travel rules apply.

If a convention is held on a cruise ship, the deduction for business expense is limited to $2,000 per person per year no matter what your story is. Plus, the ship must be a U.S. registered vessel, and all of its ports-of-call must be in the U.S. or its possessions.

If your employer reimburses you for expenses of a business trip, this is not income as long as the employer requires an adequate accounting. If your employer does not reimburse you, your allowable travel expenses are figured on Form 2106, Employee Business Expenses, or 2106-EZ, Unreimbursed Employee Business Expenses. Unreimbursed expenses are carried from Form 2106 or 2106-EZ to Schedule A, Form 1040, subject to the 2% of adjusted gross income deduction floor. If you are self-employed, travel expenses are deductible on Schedule C, C-EZ, or F, Form 1040. See IRS Publication 463 for a detailed treatment of this subject.

Tax Relief for Our Soldiers: Defending Our Defenders

How about all those servicemen and servicewomen who were overseas on April 15? Do they have to file income tax returns?

For federal tax purposes, United States Armed Forces include officers and enlisted personnel in all regular and reserve units controlled by the Secretaries of Defense, of the Army, Navy, and Air Force. The Coast Guard is included, but not the U.S. Merchant Marine or the American Red Cross.

Combat Pay Exclusion

Soldiers deployed to Kuwait, Afghanistan, Iraq, and other countries in that theater or otherwise considered to be in a combat zone, along with those countries in the Balkans, are allowed extra time to file and pay their income taxes. Soldiers will have at least 180 days after they redeploy home to file their federal tax returns, and no penalty or interest will accrue during this period.

U.S. Armed Forces civilian employees and contractors deployed to a combat zone in direct support of the military are also eligible for these tax extensions.

Soldiers also do not pay any income taxes on the wages they earn while deployed in a combat zone, nor do they pay taxes on hazardous duty pay. For enlisted troops and warrant officers, if any part of a month is spent in a combat zone, then that entire month's wages are exempt. For officers, the exclusion is limited to the highest rate of enlisted pay.

Afghanistan has been considered a combat zone since Sept. 19, 2001. Jordan, Pakistan, Tajikistan, Kyrgyzstan, and Uzbekistan have also been designated as areas in direct support of the military operation for Enduring Freedom. Kuwait was declared a combat zone in 1991 along with the Persian Gulf, the Red Sea, Gulf of Oman, Gulf of Aden, Iraq, Saudi Arabia, Oman, Bahrain, Qatar, and the United Arab Emirates. That designation has never been lifted. Bosnia and Herzegovina, Croatia, Macedonia, and Kosovo are considered hazardous duty areas and soldiers serving there receive the same deferral on their taxes as those in combat zones.

If you're serving in a designated combat zone or hazardous duty area, much of your military pay and reimbursements will be exempt from federal tax.

To determine exactly what compensation or benefits are taxable and what are exempt, see IRS Publication 3, Armed Forces Tax Guide (see http://www.unclefed.com/IRS-Forms or call 1-800-829-3676).

For enlisted troops and warrant officers, if any part of a month is spent in a combat zone, then that entire month's wages are exempt. For officers, the exclusion is limited to the highest rate of enlisted pay. There are also automatically later deadlines for filing tax returns, paying taxes, submitting refund claims or taking other actions with the IRS. The basic extension period is 180 days, but it might be lengthened depending upon when in the tax season you were shipped to a combat zone.

You don't have to be in a combat zone for IRS relief rules to apply. If you are deployed to a region in support of but not directly involved in combat, you also receive the 180-day (or more) extension. In addition, the deadline for the IRS to take certain actions, such as tax collection and examination of your returns, is extended and no penalties or interest will be imposed for not filing or paying taxes during this time.

The extension of time to file also applies to spouses of military members deployed to combat zones. On the other hand, if a family is owed tax refunds and wants to get money back immediately, the spouse back home can file tax returns on behalf of the deployed soldier.

Earned Income Tax Credit

For 2002 and subsequent tax years the definition of "earned income" no longer includes nontaxable income such as military pay for housing, subsistence allowances, or combat. This change expands the number of military personnel who may be eligible for the Earned Income Tax credit, according to IRS officials. Both the income limits and the maximum credit have increased for the 2004 tax year with the automatic cost of living calculations. To qualify for the credit, both the earned income and the adjusted gross income for 2004 must be less than $30,338 for a taxpayer with one qualifying child ($31,338 for married filing jointly), $34,458 for a taxpayer with more than one qualifying child ($35,458 for married filing jointly), and $11,490 for a taxpayer with no qualifying children ($12,490 for married filing jointly).

What about Pennsylvania?

Military pay earned by Pennsylvania residents is fully taxable unless received while on federal active duty or federal active duty for training outside Pennsylvania. Income received by a Pennsylvania resident for military service performed inside Pennsylvania, even if on federal active duty or federal active duty for training, is fully taxable as compensation.

Income received for military service outside Pennsylvania while on active duty as a member of the Armed Forces of the United States is not taxable as compensation. You may deduct such income if included in your W-2 form. Therefore, when completing your Pennsylvania income tax return, do not include military pay earned outside of Pennsylvania on Line 1a of your Pennsylvania return. Attach a copy of your orders to the copy of your W-2 along with an explanation of the amount of income excluded from Line 1a.

Pennsylvania reservists and National Guard members ordered to active duty for training pursuant to Title 10 or Title 32 of the U.S. Code are on federal active duty. When performing active duty service outside Pennsylvania, such military pay received is not taxable. For more information see https://revenue-pa.custhelp.com.

Soldiers and Sailors Civil Relief Act

This federal statute can help servicemen and servicewomen stop a civil legal action (not a criminal action) and avoid default judgments if they cannot attend court due to military obligations. Civil actions that can be stopped include (but are not limited to) bankruptcy, foreclosure, and divorce proceedings. It also provides some other relief provisions including protection from lease termination in certain circumstances, limiting the interest rate on certain debts, and protection from some state taxes.

Federal soldiers relief acts date back to the Civil War. The policy behind Congressional passage of these acts is two-fold: (1) it wanted service members to fight the war without worrying about problems that might arise at home, and (2) most of the soldiers and sailors were not well paid, so it was difficult for them to honor pre-service debts such as mortgages or other credit. Our current Soldiers and Sailors Civil Relief Act is circa 1940 and has been effective since then. It is a very powerful protection for servicemen and servicewomen.

Like Kind Exchanges

Like kind exchanges are a very important tax deferral technique for real estate owners. If you own real property and wish to sell it, you can expect to pay capital gains tax on the sale if you recognize gain. With the proceeds you may wish to acquire a different piece of property. You will not have the entire proceeds to reinvest — you will have to pay capital gains tax first.

There is a way to escape paying the capital gains tax at this point — it is by doing a like kind exchange, trading one property for another. A trade of like kind property is not a gain recognition event and you can defer the payment of the capital gains tax that would otherwise be payable.

It is rare that a straight exchange can be arranged — that would require two owners willing to swap with each other. Instead, Section 1031 of the Internal Revenue Code allows a deferred exchange. You sell your property, put the proceeds in escrow with an intermediary, identify a replacement property, the intermediary acquires the property with the cash proceeds from the first sale and then conveys the replacement property to you and you pay no capital gains tax!

Here's an example of how it works: Farmer Brown owns Blackacre. He wants to sell it and buy Big Office Building. City Slicker wants to buy Blackacre. Tom Landlord wants to sell Big Office Building to Farmer Brown.

Farmer Brown sells Blackacre to City Slicker, but as part of the sales agreement the sales proceeds are not received by Farmer Brown; instead they are paid to a qualified intermediary. The qualified intermediary buys Big Office Building from Tom Landlord using the proceeds from the sale of Blackacre and then transfers Big Office Building to Farmer Brown. Farmer Brown has completed a like kind exchange, receiving Big Office Building in exchange for Blackacre and pays no tax on the gain on the sale of Blackacre. The gain is deferred until a subsequent sale of Big Office Building.

Determine what your tax would be if you do not do an exchange. If you would like to defer the payment of that tax, a like kind exchange may be for you. A tax-free exchange is only available for exchange of "like kind" property. In general, any real estate is "like kind" with any other real estate. Thus, a farm can be like kind to residential rental property. A shopping center can be like kind with a warehouse. The property must be either held for productive use in a trade or business or for investment. You cannot do a like kind exchange with personal use property — like your home (although other non-recognition may be available there).

You must identify the replacement property which you wish to receive in exchange within 45 days of closing on the first property. The identification must be made in writing. You can identify three properties. Within the 45-day period you can revoke an identification and identify three other properties. You must close on one of them (or more) within 180 days of the first property's closing. Alternatively, instead of identifying three properties, you can identify any number of properties as long as their total value does not exceed 200% of the value of the property that was sold. Or you can acquire any number of properties worth any amount of money as long as you acquire them all. If you acquire enough of the identified properties to make up 95% of the aggregate value of the identified properties, your identification will qualify.

The person making the exchange must not have actual or constructive receipt of the sale proceeds. To prevent constructive receipt, the sale proceeds can be held in escrow or held by a qualified intermediary. It is very important that the funds are not held by a related party. The holder of the funds cannot be your relative, an employee, your attorney, or your broker.

If the exchange is between family members, the replacement property must be held for at least two years. When the exchange is between nonfamily members, the important factor is the taxpayer's intent at the time of the exchange. The replacement property must be investment property at the time it is acquired and intended to be held as such. Some advisors say that at least a year should pass before converting an investment property to personal use or before selling the replacement property.

It is also possible to acquire the replacement property first and then sell the old property. This is called a "reverse" exchange.

The like kind exchange provisions of the Internal Revenue Code are highly technical and complicated. The exchange must be correctly structured right from the start. You must retain expert legal counsel. When done correctly, this is one of the most effective tax planning tools available to real estate owners.

How Does the IRS Tax Social Security Benefits?

Since many baby boomers will soon be eligible for Social Security benefits, the question, "what fraction of those benefits will be taxed," is becoming a popular question. The answer, as you might guess, is, "it depends."

Social Security Disability Income (SSI) payments are never taxable. Monthly Social Security benefits and Survivor's benefits are sometimes subject to tax. Tier 1 railroad retirement benefits are taxed the same way as Social Security benefits.

Social Security benefits are never 100 percent included in income for taxation. They are sometimes not included at all. The amount includable varies from zero to 85 percent. The more other income you have, the higher amount of your Social Security benefit that gets taxed. The public policy of taxing higher income earners more than lower income workers is well established. But we're not talking about simple graduated tables here. (Nothing about taxes is simple.)

For those who like to read the law directly, the applicable section is IRC Section 86. It contains some definitions that we need to address. "Modified adjusted gross income" means the sum of adjusted gross income plus tax-free interest. So when you think you have your gross income for figuring Social Security inclusion, remember to add in any tax-exempt interest too.

Defined terms also include "base amount" and "adjusted base amount." These are dollar figures that are essentially cutoff points for computations. The base amount is the point below which none of your Social Security benefits are taxable, and beyond which you start towards including 50 percent of your benefits.

The "base amount" is to be compared to the sum of your "modified adjusted gross income" plus one-half of your Social Security benefits.

If you are $100 over the base amount, then $50 is included in income. If you are $5,000 over the base amount, $2,500 is included in income. This continues until half the amount you are over the base amount exceeds half of your Social Security benefits. Until your "modified adjusted gross income" reaches the second cutoff point, the "adjusted base amount," you include no more than half of your benefits.

The "adjusted base amount" is the point above which you begin approaching the 85 percent inclusion of benefits.

Generally, the "base amount," the first cutoff point, is $25,000 of modified adjusted gross income for singles and $32,000 for married people filing a joint return. The base amount is $0 for people who are married at the end of the year, and file anything other than a joint return, and who fail to live apart for the entire year. This is a severe result.

Generally, the "adjusted base amount," the second cutoff point, is $34,000 for singles and $44,000 for married people filing a joint return. Again, the base amount is $0 for people who are married at the end of the year, and file anything other than a joint return, and who fail to live apart for the entire year.

The effect of having $0 as both cutoff points is that 85 percent of Social Security is taxable, starting with dollar one. Why the draconian treatment? It appears that the IRS takes a dim view of people who are married, spend any time at all living together as man and wife, and still try to escape the marriage penalty by filing anything other than a joint return.

What does "living apart" mean? It has been addressed in cases other than Social Security cases. In Costa v. Commissioner, T.C. Memo 1990-572, the court held that intermittent visits to the taxpayer's home by the taxpayer's spouse were sufficient to find that the spouse and the taxpayer did not live apart. In a Social Security case of first impression, the same was held in McAdams v. Commissioner, 118 T.C. No. 24 (5/15/02).

In the McAdams case, the taxpayer lived apart from his wife, to whom he was still married, for all but about 30 days of the year in question. During those thirty days, he and his wife lived at her address but in separate bedrooms. He claimed that by using separate bedrooms, that counted as continuing to live apart.

Needless to say, the Court is not going to impose on anyone the burden of proving who slept where. Living in the same house means they did not live apart for the entire year, period.

It seems that thirty days was no magic number, and that if both resided even one day at either spouse's residence, that would be enough to invoke the $0 base limit, $0 adjusted base limit, and the resulting 85 percent fraction.

All of this involved small money but the IRS pursued it to tax court anyway. His Social Security benefits came to $11,182. He claimed no inclusion, and the IRS claimed 85% inclusion, or $9,504.70. Taxation at a nominal 28% meant a deficiency of $2,662.32 plus penalty and interest from 1998.

The thing to remember is that Social Security benefits taxation is tricky. The worksheet (of 1040 instructions, or at the appropriate place in your tax software) walks you through the numbers and cutoff points listed above. When asked about **living apart** for the entire year, notice that "living apart" is in bold face type. They mean that not even one day was spent together at one of the spouse's addresses, regardless of the bunking arrangements.

I Won the Lottery! And So Did Uncle Sam.

Congratulations! You bought the winning ticket. How much of the prize do you get to keep?

Yes, Virginia, lottery winnings are taxable income.

In fact, all gambling winnings are taxable income for federal income tax. Gambling losses are deductible, but only to the extent of gambling winnings. You cannot deduct gambling losses against other types of income. As for Pennsylvania income tax, no tax is due on winnings from the Pennsylvania State Lottery, whether the winner is a resident or not.

If you are holding that winning Power Ball ticket that will pay either $110 million in an annuity or $60 million if you take the lump sum, which should you take? It depends. First, there are the nontax considerations. Do you need the $60 million to spend right now? (After tax, of course, it's more like $36 million.) Does your money manager want to get the fee for managing the lump sum instead of receiving the installments? (Higher fees and commissions for him or her.) Have you already quit your job and signed the contract for the villa, the yacht, and the jet? (In other words, did you spend it already?)

Maybe you would take a lump sum, and maybe you would take it in an annuity. What should you do? Are there tax benefits to either method? The answer is yes, but the benefits might be small, especially if you're the one holding that recent big Power Ball winning ticket.

The advantage to taking a prize as an annuity is that you get more of the advantage of the bracketing in income tax rates. The effective tax (tax due divided by gross income) on $60 million is 34.95 percent, while for $3.6 million, it is 34.20 percent. Generally, when money is won and the recipient has an option to take it all or take it in segments, the IRS treats it as if received all at once.

Any time you see the word "constructive" in a legal phrase, you know you're about to encounter a legal fiction. That means the law will treat one situation as if it were another in order to reach a certain result. In the case of an annuity option, the person receiving an annuity by choice is treated as if he received a lump sum all in the first tax year. This is constructive receipt. Payment of the tax on the entire amount is generally expected in the first tax year.

When you see the word "generally," that means there's an exception. The Internal Revenue Code, section 452(h), makes an exception for "qualified prizes." These are prizes or awards from contests, lotteries, jackpots, games, or similar arrangements that provide a series of payments over a period of at least ten years, provided that the prize or award does not relate to any past services performed by the recipient and does not require the recipient to perform any substantial future service.

The choice of annuity instead of lump sum must be made within 60 days of constructive receipt of the winnings. That is no problem in Pennsylvania's Super Six Lotto, since the option is assumed to be an annuity unless the lump sum is chosen and that option must be chosen at the point of sale, even before a prize is won. You only have ten minutes from the time of sale to change your option about lump sum or annuity, so the sixty-day limit is not a problem.

Getting past the tax issue, how do you decide what makes financial sense? Our Power Ball winner in Pennsylvania has a choice of taking $110,750,000 in annuity payments over 30 years, or taking a lump sum of $60,149,751. (That is a result of an assumed interest rate of 2.0556 percent, guaranteed.) What to do?

From a financial viewpoint, you should compare the lump sum to the "present value" of the stream of annuity payments. Present value of a future payment refers to the time value of money. If someone gives me $100 today, the worth is $100. If they promise to pay it to me one year from now and the interest rate is 10 percent, it is only worth $90.91 to me today because that amount at that interest will yield $100 a year from now. Similarly, $100 two years from now has a present value of $82.64.

From an income tax standpoint, it would save 16 percent on federal taxes to take the annuity. This results from many assumptions, including the current federal interest rate of 4.23 percent, personal investment return of 6 percent, inflation rate of 2.5 percent, married filing jointly, $60,000 annual income, $60,000 spending of the prize each year, taking all income taxes from the prize each year, and increasing wages and prize spending with inflation each year. With different assumptions you will get a different answer.

Plus, there are so many factors in deciding which to take, such as current needs, charitable intentions, needs of dependents in future years, etc. that competent financial advice should be obtained.

What if you want to assign some or all of the winnings to someone else? If you wait until you win, you will be treated as the owner who then makes a gift. You will be taxed on all of the income even though you don't receive all of the payments. If you make the assignment before the winning numbers are determined, then you will not be treated as being the owner of the assigned portion and the assignee will be liable for the tax on the assigned share.

The IRS usually challenges assignment of winnings, especially to family members. The reason is obvious. People might want to assign interests to low income members of the family to save income tax. But if the assignment is documented, the taxpayer usually wins that fight.

What about the estate tax on winnings not collected before death? The IRS will include the present value of the future stream of payments in the decedent's estate. A decreasing term life insurance policy to pay the estate tax on any winnings remaining after death might be prudent.

Amended Tax Returns

The United States is the only country where it takes more brains to figure your tax than to earn the money to pay it.

Edward J. Gurney, U.S. Senator from Florida
1969-1974

Isn't it appropriate that the month of the tax begins with April Fool's Day and ends with cries of "May Day!"

Robert Knauerhase

Taxes. Didn't pay enough? Paid too much? Can't pay at all? Feel like you've got to choose between the frying pan and the fire? You're not alone and there are ways to settle up with the IRS for common income tax mistakes — without jail time. Here are some solutions to the most common problems with the IRS.

Did you omit an item of income on your income tax return? Amend it. It's simple and easy. File Form 1040X and report the income and pay the additional tax. It also works the other way. Did you forget to include a deduction? Amend the return and get your refund.

You can amend your last three years' returns. These are called the open years. The general rule is that a refund or credit can be claimed within three years from the date the return was filed or two years after the date the tax was paid, whichever is later. It's an old wives' tale that amending your return increases your chances for an audit.

What if you have completed your return and it shows a tax due but you don't have the money to pay the tax? Whatever you do, file the tax return anyhow, even if you can't pay the balance due. At least there will not be penalties for late filing. And you will have avoided the criminal charge of non-filing. Non-filers can be fined up to $25,000 and imprisoned for up to one year.

You may be able to get more time to pay. If the amount you owe is less than $10,000, you may automatically qualify for an installment agreement if you don't owe any other back taxes. This is an agreement with the IRS whereby you agree to pay the tax in installments plus interest and penalties. Form 9465, Installment Agreement Request, is used to apply. If you owe more than $10,000 you may still apply but the acceptance of the application is not automatic.

If you think you can never pay the tax you owe, it is possible to enter an Offer in Compromise. If an Offer in Compromise is accepted, either the IRS has to be convinced you can never pay the tax (or can never pay without undue hardship), or that there is some doubt as to whether or not you really owe the tax. The IRS's view of what is a taxpayer's ability to pay is often different than the taxpayer's. An Offer in Compromise is made on Form 656. You must disclose all of your assets and all of your income, and list all of your living expenses. Obviously, you will not be allowed lavish living expenses. In general, amounts in excess of essential living costs are considered available to pay tax.

Some folks' IRS problems go back awhile. They have fallen into the trap of not filing tax returns for year after year. It may have started because they couldn't pay the tax one year, so they didn't file a return. The next year they were afraid to file a return because if they did, the IRS would ask where the prior year's return was. I have seen people caught in this circular fallacy for years. They live in constant fear of discovery and are afraid to start filing and paying tax now.

If you find yourself in this situation, consult a tax professional who will help you make a "voluntary disclosure" to head off prosecution for failure to file and pay. Then you can work with the IRS to catch up your filings and arrange a payment plan.

It is the IRS's policy to use prosecution for deterrent purposes. Where a taxpayer makes a voluntary disclosure before the IRS takes any action, the IRS usually opts not to prosecute. By not prosecuting taxpayers who make voluntary disclosures, the IRS hopes to encourage voluntary compliance with the laws, as opposed to encouraging other guilty taxpayers to continue evading their tax obligations.

Mere failure to pay tax is not a crime. To be a criminal offense, the failure to pay must be willful, meaning that the taxpayer had the ability to pay but intentionally and deliberately refused to do so.

Tax evasion is a felony and is very broadly defined. It is aimed not only at persons who try to evade liability for tax, but also at persons who try to defeat the collection of the tax; for example, by moving assets beyond the reach of the IRS. Evasion is punishable by imprisonment for up to five years and a fine up to $100,000. A convicted tax evader will lose his or her right to vote and to hold public office, perhaps lose professional licenses, not be able to obtain employment — not to mention the devastating effect it can have on family relations.

One of the factors the IRS will consider when determining whether or not to recommend criminal prosecution to the Department of Justice is whether or not the taxpayer voluntarily disclosed the violation. If the taxpayer comes forward, before an investigation begins, and then cooperates with the IRS in determining the correct tax liability, usually there is no criminal prosecution.

So fess up, get professional assistance and you'll be able to get out of the frying pan without landing in the fire!

Tax Protesters

There is a debt of service due from every man to his country, proportioned to the bounties which nature and fortune have measured to him.

Thomas Jefferson

No one enjoys paying taxes. Most of us, however, pay our fair share if not out of a sense of civic duty, then because we are aware of the very real penalties we incur if we don't pay our taxes.

However, tax protesters and tax protest movements have been around for years, believing that Jefferson's words and the laws of the United States somehow don't apply to them. These groups deprive the government of substantial tax revenue. In 1999 a study found that 47,000 illegal tax protesters owed more than $540 million in income taxes.

These tax protests are illegal and, beyond that, immoral, because they cloak lies in the cloth of truth. Tax protesters frequently lure innocent taxpayers into their schemes to pay little or no taxes. They claim to know the real truth while the rest of us honest citizens have been duped. Don't be taken in by these protestors and their arguments. They are not hurting some amorphous and impersonal "government" — they are hurting you — the law-abiding taxpayer.

Here is a sampling of typical illegal tax protester arguments:

1. Filing an income tax return is voluntary. These protesters say they choose not to volunteer. The IRS instruction book for filling out a 1040 says the tax system is voluntary. The U.S. Supreme Court has said "our system of taxation is based upon voluntary assessment and payment not upon distraint." The word "voluntary" in this context means that taxpayers determine the correct amount of tax by preparing their own returns. You do not have to go to a government office where a government functionary calculates and assesses the tax you are to pay.
2. The First Amendment protects them. Some illegal protesters use the Freedom of Religion clause of the First Amendment to the Constitution to reduce income tax liability. Scheming taxpayers obtain minister's credentials and a church charter through the mail for a fee. They set up a new organization on paper that they call a "church." Then they take a vow of poverty, and transfer all their assets to the new organization. The "church" owns their home, cars, bank accounts, stock portfolio, etc. This is nothing more than a sham.
3. Wages and other compensation for work are not income. These illegal protesters say that when labor is exchanged for money there is no taxable gain. The courts have consistently held that all compensation, no matter what the form of the payment, must be included in gross income.
4. Federal reserve notes are not income. Since federal reserve notes can't be exchanged for gold or silver, some protesters say these notes are not valid currency and can't be taxed. (Note that tax protesters make this argument notwithstanding the

fact that the federal reserve notes are accepted as payment for groceries, utilities, mortgage payments, etc.) This argument is clearly frivolous.

5. Tax protesters sometimes claim they are not Untied States citizens. They claim they are only citizens of the state in which they live and have renounced their federal citizenship. Thus, they say, since only U.S. citizens have to pay income tax, they are exempt. The Fourteenth Amendment to the Constitution, however, clearly established simultaneous state and federal citizenship.
6. Collecting taxes is a "taking" of property without due process. The Fifth Amendment provides that a person shall not be "deprived of life, liberty, or property, without due process of law; . . ." These protestors say that collecting taxes is an unconstitutional "taking," despite the fact that the U.S. Supreme Court has repeatedly affirmed that the Fifth Amendment is not a limitation on taxing authority.
7. Filing a tax return would be in violation of the Fifth Amendment's protection against self-incrimination. As the Supreme Court so deftly puts it: a taxpayer "could not draw a conjurer's circle around the whole matter by his own declaration that to write any word upon the government blank would bring him into danger of the law."
8. The Sixteenth Amendment to the Constitution was not properly ratified and thus the federal income tax is unconstitutional. The courts have consistently upheld the validity and proper ratification of the Sixteenth Amendment, which provides that Congress shall have the power to lay and collect taxes on income.
9. The IRS is not an agency of the United States but is a private corporation. Illegal tax protestors say that Congress did not create the IRS. However, Congress mandated that the Secretary of the Treasury has full authority to administer and enforce the law and has the power to create an agency to enforce such laws.

The list goes on. The ways people attempt to justify their criminal decision not to pay tax are legion. Keep in mind that failure to file a tax return could result in criminal penalties, including fines and imprisonment, as well as civil penalties. People who wish to express displeasure with taxes must choose other forums, and there are many available.

As the Seventh Court of Appeals noted, "Like moths to a flame, some people find themselves irresistibly drawn to the tax protestor movement's illusory claim that there is no legal requirement to pay federal income tax. And, like moths, these people sometimes get burned.

Is the Parsonage Allowance Constitutional?

Supreme Court Justice Antonin Scalia, spoke at an event celebrating Religious Freedom Day. The Constitution says the government cannot "establish" or promote religion, but Scalia said the framers did not intend for God to be stripped from public life. "That is contrary to our whole tradition, to 'in God we trust' on the coins, to (presidential) Thanksgiving proclamations, to (congressional) chaplains, to tax exemption for places of worship, which has always existed in America."

Tell that to Federal Appeals Court judges in California. In 2001 the Ninth Circuit Court of Appeals in San Francisco, ruled that reciting the Pledge of Allegiance in public schools is an unconstitutional "endorsement of religion" because of the phrase "under God." Those words, "under God", were added to the pledge 1954 by Congress. An 11-member panel of the Ninth Circuit reconsidered the decision, which was denounced by President Bush and both houses of Congress. The 11-member panel upheld the ruling but the Supreme Court reversed it in June 2004 permitting the recitation of the pledge. That's not all. The California Ninth Circuit judges also challenged the constitutionality of an income tax provision that benefits clergy by providing an income tax free parsonage allowance.

Many churches and synagogues own homes called parsonages which are given to religious leaders to use as residences free of charge. This tradition dates back many centuries. No doubt you remember reading in your Jane Austen about the parson with "a living" on the manor. Not all religious bodies own parsonages. Some congregations provide their clergy with a rental or housing allowance to put them on an even keel with their fellow clerics who get to live in a parsonage.

In Richard D. Warren, 282 F3d 1119, the Ninth Circuit Appeals Court reviewed a Tax Court decision allowing Warren, a minister, and his wife to exclude up to $80,000 of parsonage allowance. The Tax Court appealed to the Ninth Circuit because they thought the $80,000 number was too high and should be limited to fair rental value. The Ninth Circuit took the ball and ran with it — right off the field! The Ninth Circuit judges, acting on their own, sidestepped the technical tax issue and ordered lawyers for the government and the minister to address the constitutional question. (In fairness, only two of the judges ruled this way, the third wrote an angry dissent.) The judges then asked a law professor to write a brief as an "amicus curiae" (friend of the court) on the constitutionality of the allowance.

Since 1921, Section 107 of the Internal Revenue Code has permitted a "minister of the gospel" to exclude from income the rental value (including utilities) of a home the religious institution furnishes to him or her, or to exclude from income a cash rental or housing allowance to the extent the minister uses the allowance to rent or provide a home. A designated housing allowance was not included in the minister's taxable income to the extent that it was used for qualified expenses, although the allowance is subject to social security tax.

The law professor's amicus curiae brief filed in the Warren appeal takes the position that the purpose of the parsonage allowance is to advance religion Because the provision applied only to clergy, it didn't appear to have a secular legislative purpose since only clergy had the advantage of receiving part of their income free of tax. Thus, the law professor concludes that it is unconstitutional as an impermissible establishment of religion.

A group of church-related organizations and the Department of Justice also submitted amicus briefs. Both said the Ninth Circuit lacked jurisdiction to question the parsonage allowance's constitutionality. But if the court did, in fact, have such jurisdiction, both parties argued the allowance was constitutional — pointing out that this was just one of many tax code provisions that allow employers to provide tax-free housing to employees, with no group getting preferential treatment.

While all this was going on, the IRS and the taxpayer, Warren, came to a settlement and both motioned for the dismissal of the case. The Ninth Circuit dismissed. Thus, there is no ruling on the issue at this time.

Congress, appalled at the possibility that the parsonage allowance might be declared unconstitutional, passed the Clergy Housing Allowance Clarification Act of 2002 in May 2002. The new law limits the allowance to fair rental value and was intended to support the constitutionality of the parsonage allowance. (Although there is nothing to stop a court from declaring this new legislation unconstitutional as well.)

If the parsonage allowance is unconstitutional, then what about the exemption from income tax enjoyed by churches, synagogues, mosques, and other religious organizations? Is that unconstitutional, too? If so, then maybe all nonprofit organizations and educational institutions that have religious precepts in their mission statements are receiving unconstitutional tax favors as well. Where will it end?

The United States has a long-standing history of exempting religious organizations from tax. As the Church Alliance, a coalition of religious organizations, wrote in an amicus brief, "[t]he American constitutional tradition holds that while religion is not entitled to a public subsidy, it may be exempted from taxation so long as none was favored over others and none suffered interference."

I agree. The First Amendment prohibits Congress from playing favorites among religions, and it was drafted primarily to protect religion from government interference. A tax break that neutrally benefits all clergy of all religions is not "an establishment of religion."

Year-End Tax Planning

How can you accelerate deductions? Prepay your state income tax instead of waiting for April 15. Make an extra mortgage payment to get the additional interest deduction. Make donations to charity. Clean out your closet and donate clothes and household goods — make sure you get receipts for contributions of $250 or more. If you conducted a job search this year, even if you didn't get a job, don't forget to deduct the expenses. In order to take advantage of these deductions you must itemize instead of taking the standard deduction.

Beware of the Alternative Minimum Tax (AMT). Many people whose incomes have grown over the past decade with the economy have been pushed into paying the AMT, a "privilege" once reserved for the very rich. In addition, new tax rules have expanded the sweep of the AMT, ensnaring even more taxpayers in its net. All taxpayers must figure their tax both ways, under the regular tax and under the alternative minimum tax, and pay whichever one is more. The AMT rate is lower than the top regular tax rates but it applies to more income. For example, when calculating the AMT you have to add back in state and local taxes and personal exemptions. The Tax Policy Center estimates that 4 million Americans will pay AMT in 2015. If it looks like you but don't owe AMT in the current year, but will in the coming year, definitely accelerate as many deductions as you can into this year.

To delay income, you may be able to delay commission income or year-end bonuses until next year.

When there is a dramatic decline in the stock market, you may be sitting on some valuable losses. If you make the investment decision to sell a stock at a loss, use the loss to offset capital gains. You must match long-term losses against long-term gains, most of which are taxed at 20%. Short-term losses (on securities held for less than 1 year) are netted against short-term gains. Remaining losses are then set off against remaining gains.

If you don't have net gains, up to $3,000 of remaining losses can be deducted against ordinary income. Unused capital losses can be carried forward to subsequent years. If you want to recognize a loss but maintain the investment, you can't repurchase the investment within 30 days. This wash-sale rule applies even if you buy new shares before you sell the losing ones.

Consider selling mutual fund shares well before December 31. Most funds distribute dividends and capital gains some time in December. You could be taxed on significant gains recognized inside the fund even though the value of the fund has declined. The only way to avoid this is to not own the fund on the distribution date.

If you converted your traditional IRA to a Roth IRA earlier this year and the value has now declined significantly, you may be kicking yourself. You owe income tax on the whole amount of the conversion even though the value is now significantly less. You can switch your Roth IRA back to a regular IRA. You can reverse the original conversion to a Roth anytime, before your tax return is due. If you do it in one year, you must wait 30 days, and into the next year, to convert the account to a Roth again.

Check to see if you've maxed out your contributions to retirement plans — IRAs, 401(k)s. Make sure that you have made the maximum permissible contribution and get it taken from your paychecks before year-end.

Consider delaying the exercise of stock options until after year-end, providing that does not put you past the expiration date. (Remember: beware the AMT.)

If you use a flexible spending account for childcare or medical expenses, make sure you incur enough expense and have receipts to collect the balance in your account before year-end. You will lose any unused funds in the account. The costs must be incurred in one year but you can wait until the next year to submit the receipts for reimbursement.

If you are self-employed, consider sending bills in January next year instead of December this year. Buy any equipment like computers, phone systems, copiers, and furniture this year. Business owners can deduct up to $24,000 in one lump sum. (This is called "expensing" instead of deducting just a portion of the cost each year over a period of time.) Open a retirement plan that will allow a contribution up to 20% of your business income before year-end. The plan must be in existence before year-end but you can get the deduction for the current year as long as you make the contribution before the due date for the current year's tax return.

IRS Updates the Dirty Dozen

No, not the WWII movie with Lee Marvin, Ernest Borgnine, Telly Savallas, and Charles Bronson. This Dirty Dozen is a list of the 12 most common tax scams. Every year during tax season the IRS releases an alert warning taxpayers not to fall prey of one of the "Dirty Dozen" tax scams. Scam victims end up losing the cash they pay to the promoters of these scans. But even worse, they find themselves in deeper debt to the IRS. Federal law requires you pay your rightful taxes plus any penalty charges and back interest that accrued because of your use of questionable tax-relief techniques. Here are the Dirty Dozen.

1. African-Americans get a special tax refund. Thousands of African-Americans have been misled by people offering to file for tax credits or refunds related to reparations for slavery. Promoters charge as much as $150 to help people prepare a return claiming a credit of as much as $40,000. As despicable as slavery was, there is no provision in tax law that allows for African-Americans to get a special tax refund as a reparation. Promoters of reparations tax schemes have been convicted and imprisoned.
2. No taxes being withheld from your wages. Illegal schemes are being promoted that instruct employers not to withhold federal income tax or employment taxes from wages paid to their employees. The promoters assert the so-called Section 861 argument — that only income from foreign sources is subject to U.S. tax, and not amounts U.S. employers pay to U.S. citizens. Recent court cases have resulted in criminal convictions of promoters. Employer participants could also be held responsible for back payments of employment taxes, plus penalties and interest. Employees who have no withholdings are still responsible for payment of their personal taxes. In the years 2001 through 2003, 127 individuals have been sentenced to confinement in either federal prison, a halfway house, home detention or some combination thereof on employment tax issues.
3. "I don't pay taxes — Why should you?" Con artists may talk about how they don't file or pay taxes and then charge people a fee to share their "secret." The real secret that these people don't reveal is that many of them actually do file and pay taxes — they just won't publicly admit it. Again, the IRS reminds people that failure to file or pay taxes is subject to civil and/or criminal tax penalties.
4. Pay the tax, then get the prize. The caller says you've won a prize and all you have to do to get it is pay the income tax due. Don't believe it. If you really won a prize, you may need

to make an estimated tax payment to cover the taxes that will be due at the end of the year. Any tax due always goes to the IRS — not the caller.

5. Untax yourself for $49.95. This one's as old as snake oil, but people continue to be taken in. And now it's on the Internet. The ads may say that paying taxes is "voluntary," but it is absolutely wrong. The U.S. courts have continuously rejected this and other similar arguments that the income tax is unconstitutional. Unfortunately, hundreds of people across the country have paid for the "secret" of not paying taxes or have bought "untax packages" before finding out that following the advice contained in them can result in civil and/or criminal tax penalties being assessed. Numerous sellers of these bogus packages have been convicted on criminal tax charges.
6. Social Security tax scheme. Taxpayers shouldn't fall victim to a scam offering them refunds of the Social Security taxes they have paid during their lifetimes. The scam works by the victim paying a "paperwork" fee of $100, plus a percentage of any refund received, to file a refund claim with the IRS. This hoax fleeces the victims for the up-front fee. The law does not allow such a refund of Social Security taxes paid. The IRS processing centers are alert to this hoax and have been stopping the false claims.
7. "I can get you a big refund ... for a fee!" Refund scheme operators may approach you wanting to "borrow" your Social Security number or give you a phony W-2 so it appears that you qualify for a big refund. They may promise to split the refund with you, but the IRS catches most of these false refund claims before they go out. And when one does go out, the participant usually ends up paying back the refund along with stiff penalties and interest. Two lessons to remember: (1) Anyone who promises you a bigger refund without knowing your tax situation could be misleading you, and (2) Never sign a tax return without looking it over to make sure it's honest and correct.
8. Share/borrow EITC dependents. Unscrupulous tax preparers "share" one client's qualifying children with another client in

order to allow both clients to claim the Earned Income Tax Credit (EITC). For example, if one client has four children, she only needs to list two for EITC purposes to get the maximum credit. The preparer will list two children on the first client's return and list the other two on another client's tax return. The preparer and the client "selling" the dependents split a fee.

9. IRS "agent" comes to your house to collect. First, do not let anyone into your home unless they identify themselves to your satisfaction. IRS special agents, field auditors, and collection officers carry picture IDs and will normally try to contact you before they visit. If you think the person on your doorstep is an impostor, lock your door and call the local police.
10. "Put your money in a trust and never pay taxes again." There are professional trust-pushers out there who promise to show people (for a price, of course) how to use trusts to illegally hide the true ownership of assets and income. Promoters of abusive trust schemes may charge $5,000 to $70,000 for "trust" packages. The promoters claim the trusts can be used to reduce income that is subject to tax and take deductions for personal expenses paid by the trust. Certainly, setting up a trust for estate planning purposes is not illegal. Establishing one to hide taxable income is.
11. Improper home-based business. This scheme purports to offer tax "relief" but in reality is illegal tax avoidance. The promoters of these schemes claim that individual taxpayers can deduct most, or all, of their personal expenses as business expenses by setting up a bogus home-based business. But, the tax code firmly establishes that a clear business purpose and profit motive must exist in order to generate and claim allowable business expenses.
12. Claim disabled access credit for pay phones. Con artists sell expensive coin-operated pay telephones to individuals, contending they can claim a $5,000 Disabled Access Credit on their tax return because the telephones have volume controls. Buyers think they are getting a low-risk investment with a guaranteed annual return. (Sometimes they never

even get the telephones.) In reality, the Disabled Access Credit is limited to bona fide businesses that are coming into compliance with the Americans with Disabilities Act.

Federal law requires you pay your rightful taxes. If your spouse is engaging in one of these scams, do not sign a joint return with him or her. Don't fall prey to these scams which can result not only in your paying the owed tax, penalties and interest but also in criminal charges and possible imprisonment. This Dirty Dozen is not a remake you want to have a starring role in.

Pennsylvania's Income Tax — a Different Animal

Pennsylvania has imposed an income tax since 1971. The Pennsylvania income tax is not based on the federal system — it is quite a different animal. Why? Because of a particular provision in the Commonwealth's Constitution called the uniformity clause.

The Uniformity Clause of the Pennsylvania Constitution as found in Article VIII Section 1 provides: "All taxes shall be uniform, upon the same class of subjects, within the territorial limits of the authority levying the tax, and shall be levied and collected under general laws." The Supreme Court of Pennsylvania has interpreted the uniformity clause as prohibiting graduated rates, exemptions, and deductions. Thus, the Pennsylvania income tax is a flat rate; and exemptions and deductions like those permitted for the federal income tax are not permitted.

The Pennsylvania personal income tax rate has been 3.07% since January 1, 2004. If you received more than $33 of income in 2001, you are required to file a Pennsylvania income tax return even if no tax is due with the return.

Pennsylvania residents are taxed on worldwide income. Pennsylvania nonresidents are taxed only on Pennsylvania source income. Pennsylvania source income is income earned by reason of ownership or disposition of real or tangible property located in Pennsylvania, in connection with a trade or business in Pennsylvania (including employee compensation) as a share of the income of an unincorporated business, Pennsylvania S corporation, or profession, or from intangible personal property used in a trade or business carried on in Pennsylvania. Pennsylvania residents are allowed a credit for taxes paid to other states or countries. Pennsylvania has reciprocity agreements with Indiana, Maryland, New Jersey, Ohio, Virginia, and West Virginia. Under these agreements employee compensation (but not other types of income) earned in Pennsylvania by a resident of one of these states will not be taxed in Pennsylvania.

Special provisions for low income taxpayers are permitted because of a 1986 amendment to the Pennsylvania Constitution which permits treatment of low income taxpayers as a separate class. Low income taxpayers get an exemption from state income tax depending on the number of persons in their family. For example, a family of four would be exempt from Pennsylvania income tax if their income is less than $31,000.

The Pennsylvania flat rate tax is imposed on eight different classes of income. Income that doesn't fall into one of the eight classes is exempt. The biggest and most dramatic example is retirement income — it does not fall into any of the eight classes. Income from pension plans, social security, SSI, railroad retirement, veterans pensions, IRAs and 401(k)s are not subject to Pennsylvania income tax. Another example of income exempt from Pennsylvania income tax is alimony — which is taxable income federally but is not subject to Pennsylvania income tax.

This is a dramatically different approach than the federal income tax. Under the federal tax everything is income unless it is specifically exempted, excluded, or deducted. For Pennsylvania an item is income only if it fits into one of the eight enumerated categories.

The eight income classes are:

1. Compensation. This includes wages, salaries, commissions, bonuses, and tips. Military pay received while on active duty outside of Pennsylvania is specifically excluded from compensation income.
2. Interest. This category includes bank account interest, bond interest, interest on promissory notes and mortgages, interest on tax refunds, and so forth. Interest on federal obligations like treasury bills and notes is exempt from Pennsylvania taxation. You can't assume that interest that is exempt from federal income tax is also exempt from Pennsylvania

income tax. Pennsylvania municipal bonds are exempt from Pennsylvania taxation.

3. Dividends. This includes any distribution from a corporation or business trust made out of earnings and profits. Distribution from money market funds, mutual funds and real estate investment trusts are taxed as dividends, including capital gains distributions.
4. Net profits from businesses, professions, or farms. Net profits from a business are included in this category. The business must be a commercial enterprise — handling your own personal investment is not a business. If you have two businesses and one has a profit and the other a loss, the loss can be used to offset the income from the other business. This offset happens only within this category — losses in one category cannot be used to offset income in other categories.
5. Net gain from sale or disposition of property. These are normally referred to as capital gains and losses. Unlike the federal income tax, there is no special rate for these gains — they are subject to the same Pennsylvania tax rate as other classes of income. Capital gains distributions from mutual funds are classified as dividends. For computing gains or loss, property acquired from a decedent gets a cost basis of the value on the date of death. The basis for other items is cost (as adjusted). For property acquired before June 1, 1971, the basis is its value on June 1, 1971. Gains on tangible personal property or real property can be reported on the installment basis. There is a special exemption for the gain on sale of a personal residence if ownership and use requirements are met.
6. Net income from rents, royalties, patents, and copyrights.
7. Gambling and lottery winnings (except Pennsylvania state lottery prizes). In calculating winnings, you may deduct gambling losses.
8. Net gains or income derived from estates or trusts. If you have this kind of income, you should receive a reporting document from the executor or trustee. All of the distribution you receive from a trust or estate is not subject to income tax. Only the amount reported on the K-1 is taxable.

You cannot use a loss in one class of income to offset income in another class. Also, gains and losses cannot be carried forward or backward from year to year.

Even though the uniformity clause is interpreted as prohibiting deductions, two classes of income are defined as net of expense: (1) net profits from a business or profession and (2) net gain from the sale or disposition of property. Also, employee business expenses are excludable from income.

Local governments in Pennsylvania may also levy an income tax. Municipalities and school districts can impose taxes on earned income. These taxes are sometimes referred to as "wage" taxes, but they also apply to net profits from the operation of a business. Lancaster's rate is 1.0%. Scranton's is 2.5%. Philadelphia's is 4.3310% for residents and 3.8197% for nonresidents.

Like any flat tax, the Pennsylvania income tax is sometimes criticized as being regressive. The only solution would be either an amendment to the Constitution or repeal of the tax!

Sales and Use Tax

Don't tax you, don't tax me, tax the fellow behind the tree.

Russell B. Long

Thirty-five percent of Pennsylvania's general fund revenue is derived from the Sales and Use Tax. The Commonwealth imposes a 6% Sales Tax on the retail sale of taxable goods and services within the Commonwealth. The Sales Tax is collected by retailers and remitted to the Commonwealth. The Sales Tax is not levied on either groceries or clothing, with some exceptions. Also exempt are drugs, textbooks, sales for resale, and residential heating fuels.

Purchases of taxable goods and services outside of Pennsylvania are also taxable. A person who purchases taxable personal property or services outside this Commonwealth, that are used in the Commonwealth, incurs a Use Tax liability at the rate of 6% of the purchase price. The 6% also applies to shipping and handling charges. If the Sales Tax paid to another jurisdiction and collected by an out-of-state vendor equals or exceeds the Pennsylvania Use Tax, then no Use Tax is due to the Commonwealth of Pennsylvania. The tax is imposed on the use of items purchased outside the Commonwealth, but used within the Commonwealth. Also, items bought at garage sales, through classified ads, from a catalog, or over the internet are subject to the Use Tax. The Use Tax is the same 6% rate and has the same exemptions as the Sales Tax. In addition, a local Sales and Use Tax of 1% is imposed in Philadelphia and Allegheny counties.

Why is there a Use Tax? Vendors in the Commonwealth have to charge the 6% Sales Tax. If you can go across the state line and buy the same merchandise with no Sales Tax, that gives the out-of-state vendor an obvious advantage. To make the playing field level, Pennsylvania imposes a Use Tax, in an amount equal to the Sales Tax, on that property you bought in the other state. The only problem is, it's up to you, the taxpayer, to report and pay the Use Tax. No vendor is collecting it. Does anybody pay Use Tax? Are we all just scofflaws? Did you pay the Use Tax on those books you got from Amazon.com last week?

Don't be confused by the Internet Tax Freedom Act. This law prohibits the taxation of internet access, and prohibits various other discriminatory taxes and tax collection practices. It does not prohibit the collection of Use Taxes on property sold over the Internet.

The Pennsylvania Department of Revenue publishes a brochure called "Pennsylvania Use Tax and You" (available on their web page at http://www.revenue.state.pa.us/revenue/lib/revenue/rev-1748.pdf). Here is the first example given in the pamphlet: "Example 1 — A resident of Reading orders $50 worth of flower bulbs from an out-of-state catalog company on February 1. The company charges $3 shipping and handling. A Use Tax payment in the amount of $3.18 ($53 x 6%) would be due by March 20." The tax is to be reported on the Sales and Use Tax Return (PA-3) for licensed accounts or an Individual Use Tax Return (PA-1).

Some people are paying Use Tax. In order to register a motor craft, aircraft, or water craft in Pennsylvania, you have to provide proof of the payment of either the Sales Tax or the Use Tax. So, if you buy a car out of state, you have to pay Pennsylvania Use Tax on it before it can be registered.

Many small business owners will face Use Tax problems in the future. One reason for this is that many owners believe they can avoid paying Sales Taxes if inventory or equipment is purchased from companies not located in Pennsylvania. Many owners turn to the Internet to make purchases from companies in other states. Contrary to popular opinion, such sales are not exempt from tax. A purchaser located in Pennsylvania, who uses or consumes a product in Pennsylvania, purchased outside of Pennsylvania, is liable for a Use Tax equal to the amount of any Sales Tax not collected by the out-of-state seller at the time of purchase. Such out-of-state sales will become subject to growing audit scrutiny. If the state finds your business has not reported Use Taxes, it will likely attempt to assess stringent penalty amounts.

The Department of Revenue can identify people who owe Use Tax during routine audits, from complaints, investigations, and by obtaining lists of out-of-state purchases through the cooperation of vendors and other states. Just imagine — Big City Discount Store gives to the Pennsylvania Department of Revenue a complete list of everyone who bought office equipment, computers, furniture, and appliances. All the Department of Revenue has to do is send out assessments, plus penalties and interest, of course. Believe me, this has happened.

Catalog and Internet sales have been proliferating at a staggering pace. All the states have become concerned that they are losing Sales Tax revenue to catalog and Internet sales, and that collecting the Use Tax is too impractical to be a counterweight. The General Accounting Office estimates that state and local Sales Tax losses due to Internet sales will be in the billions of dollars.

In response to the growing problem, the Streamlined Sales Tax Project (SSTP) was organized by the National Governors Association and the National Conference of States Legislatures. The goal of the project is to simplify and modernize sales and Use Tax collection through a multi-state agreement. The project is greatly supported by so-called "bricks and mortar" businesses who feel the unfair competition of Internet sellers who don't have to charge Sales Tax. Part of the program is the need to pass federal legislation that will permit states to collect taxes for other states on remote sales.

New legislation is needed because the U.S. Supreme Court has held that a state cannot compel an out-of-state vendor to collect the state's Sales and Use Taxes, unless that vendor has a physical presence in the state. This was viewed as an undue burden on interstate commerce — and perhaps it would be, as experts estimate that there are 6,000 different Sales and Use Taxes to deal with in the United States.

The SSTP has approved a Uniform Sales and Use Tax Administration Act for enactment in the various states. If a state passes this legislation, it is authorized to join in a multi-state agreement for the collection of Sales and Use Tax. So far, 34 states and the District of Columbia have enacted the legislation. Pennsylvania is not one of them. Sellers would only have to file and remit taxes to their own state. That state is responsible for the distribution of those taxes to the appropriate tax jurisdictions.

With the decline in revenue being experienced by all of the states, we can expect efforts to collect Sales and Use Tax to be stepped up. Noncompliance with the tax laws is not how you should save money.

AFTER DEATH

PROBATE

What Is Probate?

"Probate" is much maligned. To hear some folks talk, having your estate subject to probate is worse than dying. What is all the fuss about?

Probate is a title proceeding. If a person dies owning property, the question arises "Who is the next rightful owner?". Probate is the procedure by which the ownership is determined.

If the decedent left a will, the will is filed with the Register of Wills, the executor (who is the person in charge of the estate) is sworn in, and notice is given to all persons who have an interest in the estate, including creditors. Anyone who wishes to contest the will, which means to object to the will, may do so within a prescribed time period. Grounds for contesting a will might be that the decedent did not know what he was doing when he signed the will. The law calls this lack of "testamentary capacity." A will can be contested on the grounds that the decedent was under "undue influence" at the time she signed the will. For example, someone was pressuring and pushing her, and the decedent was susceptible to the influence. An improperly executed will can be contested also. For example, a will may not have enough witnesses, or the witnesses may be disqualified persons. In Pennsylvania, the forum for all these sorts of "contests" or objections is the county Orphan's Court.

If the decedent left no will, or if the decedent's will is found to be invalid, then the next rightful owner(s) of the decedent's property are determined by state statute. This statute determines the decedent's heirs. The heirs of a decedent are first, children or more remote issue, then parents, and then siblings and their issue. Also, a surviving spouse is entitled to a share, usually about one-third (1/3) of the estate.

There is a common misconception that a surviving spouse inherits all of the deceased spouse's property. If there are children in the marriage, the spouse's share of the estate is one-third. If there are no children, the spouse takes the first $30,000 plus one-third; the decedent's parents or other relatives take the remaining two-thirds.

This is the distribution for property that was in the decedent's name alone. If property was held jointly with the surviving spouse, it passes immediately on death to the surviving joint owner. A will or the intestacy statute only operates on property that was solely owned by the decedent.

Contrary to popular belief, if you die without a will, your property does not go to the state. The probate proceeding is still necessary to determine who are the heirs, and in what proportion they take the decedent's property. Creditors are also given the opportunity to come forward with their claims.

The court appoints an executor or an administrator. An executor is a person or bank or trust company named in the will to be responsible for the settlement of the estate. An administrator is someone appointed by the court to administer the will if the named executor is unavailable or unwilling, or to administer the estate if there is an intestacy. When the decedent dies without a will, that is called dying intestate.

So what's so terrible about probate? Nothing. It is a fairly simple and logical process. Probate gets its bad reputation from the professional fees that are charged. The executor or administrator and any professionals such as attorneys and accountants who are engaged to assist with the estate settlement process are to be compensated. The duties of the executor and her advisors go far beyond the probate process, including the filing and payment of federal estate taxes, Pennsylvania inheritance tax, and so on. The executor or administrator and attorney are, of course, entitled to be compensated for their work on behalf of the estate. It is common in this area for executors and administrators and for attorneys to compute their fee for services as a percentage of the assets included in the estate, say five percent, or perhaps less. The problem with this approach to fees is that it does not always bear a reasonable relationship to the work and responsibility involved.

High fees are the source of most of the horror stories one hears about probate. The procedure itself is not expensive; it is the professional fees charged that are sometimes excessive. The answer to this is to be an educated consumer. When planning your estate and if you are the executor or administrator or an estate, you need to make sure that the compensation arrangements that you enter into with professionals are fair and reasonable. There is no question that the services are valuable and deserve to be compensated. The question is, how much? The leading case on attorneys' fees in Pennsylvania says that reasonable compensation takes into account the amount of work, the time involved, the results obtained, the amount of money or value of property in question, and the professional skill and standing of the attorney.

Big Bad Probate

Probate has the undeserved reputation of causing delays and being expensive, among other concerns. Usually avoiding probate means creating a living trust and transferring title of your assets to the trust. There is nothing wrong with this and there can be good reasons to do so. However, just avoiding the probate process is not a sufficient reason to go this route.

Whether a decedent dies with a will or a trust, whether the estate is subject to probate or not subject to probate, much of the same work must be done. All assets must be valued and appraised. Debts and expenses must be determined and settled. State and possibly federal death tax returns must be prepared and filed. The decedent's final income tax return must be filed. Consideration must be given to the various tax elections that are available to the Executor or Trustee. The income tax returns for the estate or for the trust must be prepared and filed. Bequests and specific dispositions directed in the will or trust must be carried out. The executor or the trustee must account to the beneficiaries for all activity and transactions. Finally, the directions for distribution of the property given in the will or the trust must be carried out.

Most executors and trustees need help. The legal, tax and accounting issues can be complex - even in what you might think is a simple estate. The executor or trustee must understand and be able to compute and file state inheritance tax returns, state estate tax returns, federal estate tax returns, and fiduciary income tax returns. They must know the due dates and time table, how to interpret the words of the governing documents, how to notify beneficiaries, how to value assets for tax purposes, what items are permissible deductions, the list goes on and on. Usually the executor hires an attorney to help, sometimes an accountant as well.

Most of the cost for estate settlement comes from these activities, which are required whether or not the estate is subject to probate. The actual probate procedure itself does not add much to the cost. In fact, probate fees, themselves, are quite modest. Each county has a schedule of fees which vary according to the action requested and the value of the estate. For example, in Lancaster County, a will for a decedent with a $ 1 million probate estate can be admitted to probate for less than $1000. Notice must be published in two newspapers, each costing cost about $60.

Avoiding probate will not cause the estate to be settled faster. Most of the time involved has to do with tax filings, waiting for acceptance letters from the IRS and the Department of Revenue, and perhaps going through tax audits (which are quite common in estates). The time-frame is the same for a probate estate or a trust.

Avoiding probate does offer some privacy. A will when probated becomes a public record which can be viewed by anyone. Similarly, the inventory of the estate assets and the accounting, if any, are matters of public record. However, even where there is no probate property, the inheritance tax return is filed with the Register of Wills, so much of the financial information may be available to the public. County practices differ on how these returns are handled. In Lancaster County, inheritance tax returns are available for public inspection, whether or not the estate was probated.

Some lawyers think that a trust is less likely to be contested than a will. This may be so, although both can be challenged on the grounds that the decedent did not have sufficient capacity when the document was executed, or that the decedent was under undue influence. In the probate process beneficiaries are notified and asked to come forward with objections, if any. Trust beneficiaries receive no such invitation, but are free to contest the trust in the same way.

Avoiding probate in multiple states can also be a good idea. A decedent's will must be probated in every state in which the decedent owned real estate. It is often wise to avoid these multiple proceedings by transferring the real estate to a form of title that will avoid probate.

In large part, probate gets its bad reputation from the professional fees that are charged. The procedure itself is not expensive; but the professional fees charged are sometimes out of kilter with the amount of work involved.

The problem is that, with probate, executors and attorneys for estates may charge fees based on the value of the estate's assets. This often results in an excessive fee. Charging five percent of an estate that consists entirely of $800,000 in easily-probated Certificates of Deposit is obviously not in proportion to the amount of work involved. In a case like this it is possible for the executor and the attorney to each demand $40,000. But the same value of rental properties that must be vacated and sold, or maybe a former gas station to be sold would make a five percent fee look like a bargain.

It is up to the executor or trustee to be an educated consumer. Interview several lawyers and several accountants. Determine their experience level. Ask what their fees will be. How are they computed? Are they on a percentage basis or will they charge by the hour? If you want to do some of the work yourself, will they accommodate you?

What Do Those Legal Estate Notices In the Newspaper Mean?

You have probably seen estate advertisements in the legal notice section of the newspaper. What are they for? The publication is intended to be a notice to creditors and debtors of the decedent's death. If the decedent owed a creditor any money, this is notification to the creditor to come forward. A short statute of limitations applies to claims against the estate. A debt that normally would have a couple of years for collection has the collection period cut short when the debtor dies, provided that creditors are given notice of the death through the newspaper publication. On the other hand, the publication is also notice to those debtors who owe money to the decedent to come forward and make payment without delay.

Who else gets notice? Pennsylvania Supreme Court Orphan's Court Rule 5.6 requires that within three months after the executor or administrator takes office, a written notice of the probate must be given to various interested parties. Every person or entity named in the decedent's will, and the decedent's spouse and children, whether or not they are named in the will as beneficiaries, are to receive a formal written notice in the mail. Also, notices must be sent to the parent or legal guardian of any beneficiary under 18, the guardian of any incapacitated person who is a beneficiary, the attorney general if a charitable beneficiary receives more than $25,000 or if the charitable bequest will not be paid in full, and the trustee of any trust that is a beneficiary. If there is no will, notice goes to the heirs. That is, to those persons who are entitled to inherit the decedent's property under the Pennsylvania Intestacy Statute.

The form of the written notice to be delivered is prescribed in the court's rules. Receiving a notice does not necessarily mean you will receive anything from the estate. It means that you have an interest and may receive something. A copy of the will is not required to be included with the notice, but I have always considered it good practice and a courtesy to include a copy. If you receive a notice without a copy of the will you can either call the legal representative named in the notice to request a copy or go to the Register of Wills to view the original probated will.

The most notable thing about these requirements is who doesn't get notice. If Uncle Fred, who has no living spouse or children, left a will leaving everything to his housekeeper, then no family members get notice. In some states, intestate heirs (those people who would take a decedent's property if they left no will) are given notice. This makes sense because the intestate heirs are the so-called "natural objects of the decedent's bounty" and may well have objections to an instrument which excludes them. If that rule applied in Pennsylvania (but it does not), Uncle Fred's brothers and sisters or nieces and nephews would get notice and would be able to evaluate the situation.

Similarly, if Uncle Fred made three prior wills naming various beneficiaries, none of these beneficiaries of prior wills would get notice. Since wills are ambulatory; that is, they are not proven or take effect until probated after death, prior wills have no legal status. So we can understand that no notice to prior beneficiaries is required. It is troubling, however, because if the last will leaving all to Uncle Fred's housekeeper was procured by undue influence, or made while Uncle Fred lacked testamentary capacity, aren't the beneficiaries of his prior will the ones with the interests to be protected?

Many wills set up trusts. They direct property to a trustee to hold for the benefit of named beneficiaries. There are many kinds of trusts, created for many different reasons. Sometimes a trust is created because a beneficiary is a minor. Sometimes it is because the beneficiary is deemed by the testator to be incapable of handling money. Sometimes there are tax-planning techniques involving trusts used as part of the estate plan.

In the case of a will which creates a trust, notice is required to be given to the trustee, but not to the beneficiaries of the trust. This has always troubled me. Often the executor and the trustee are one and the same person or institution. When that is the case, the people and organizations who are named as beneficiaries of the trust get no notice at all. There is no check on the executor's actions by any beneficiaries. The laws of the 50 states vary on this point. Some states require notice to trust beneficiaries and some only require notice when the executor and the trustee are identical. The theory is that if the trustee is someone other than the executor, the trustee can be counted on to review the executor's actions on behalf of trust beneficiaries. But, if the trustee is the same person as the executor, then no one is reviewing the executor's actions on behalf of the trust beneficiaries, and in that case notice to the trust beneficiaries is required.

Notice and an opportunity to be heard is the very foundation for the protection of property rights and due process. It is an oddity of Pennsylvania trust practice that trust beneficiaries, in general, are not given notice of their interests. You could be a beneficiary of a trust and have no idea that you are named in a trust. Trusts often have different classes of beneficiaries. For example, one person may be entitled to income, and another person, called the remainderman, may be entitled to the balance of the trust property when the income beneficiary dies. In many cases, the remainder beneficiary does not know of his or her interest in the trust. If beneficiaries don't know of their interest, how can they enforce their rights and monitor the trustee's actions? A trust can only be enforced by its beneficiaries and if the beneficiaries don't know who they are, how can the trust be enforced? Many professional trustees inform all trust beneficiaries of their interests, but many don't. In fact, some professional trustees when asked for information by remainder beneficiaries don't realize that they are required to make disclosure.

An honest trustee, on the death of the income beneficiary, will contact the remainder beneficiary and give a full accounting of the administration of the trust during the income beneficiary's lifetime.

That's nice, but the income beneficiary received income for 30 years, and if the trustee's investment of the trust funds favored the production of income instead of equally balancing the interests of the remainder beneficiary for preserving the purchasing power of the fund, what can be done? Errors like that compounded over 30 years reach an astronomical number, and courts have not seen fit to make these remaindermen whole. The only practical approach is to be able to monitor the trustee's investments and actions during the income beneficiary's life. In many states, accountings are required to be given annually to all trust beneficiaries. Doesn't that make more sense? Pennsylvania trust law needs an overhaul.

Amateur Efforts to Avoid Probate Can Be Disastrous

Since 1997 Pennsylvania law has permitted the registration of securities in "POD" or "TOD" form. POD means "pay on death" and TOD means "transfer on death." Titling accounts POD or TOD permits the naming of a beneficiary on all sorts of investments. In the past only life insurance and pension plans had this option available.

Unfortunately, all sorts of tellers, clerks, customer service representatives, brokers, account managers, and other employees of financial institutions are giving customers advice about how to title accounts. This wreaks havoc with many estate plans and causes untold problems. You wouldn't think of letting one of these people write your will — why would you let them prepare beneficiary designations?

Here is an example, provided by one of my colleagues, of what can go wrong. Son, who is the Co-executor of Mom's will, comes to me for help. A so-called "expert" told Mom that she could avoid probate by changing the title on her brokerage account to read POD (pay on death) to Son, Baby Brother, Sister One, and three nephews (sons of deceased Sister Two). Count 'em — that's six beneficiaries. The only asset in the account is one large bond. Mom passed away.

The broker says he cannot divide the large bond six ways and he needs everyone to agree that it should be sold so that he can give cash to the beneficiaries. He can't distribute pieces of the bond. Son is not on good terms with Baby Brother who wants Son to pay for the lost value in the bond (interest rates went up since Mom died) and blames Son that nothing has been done in the three months since Mom passed away. Son is executor but since this account is not probate property, the Executor has no authority over it, so it really is not Son's responsibility. (But tell that to Baby Brother.) Sister One is not speaking to any of her co-owners because she says the three nephews (who are getting half of the account, one-sixth each) are getting more than their share. Sister One says that the nephews should only receive the one-fourth share that would have been Sister Two's if she lived. After all, that's what Mom's will says. Of course, the will doesn't operate on the POD account thanks to the advice of the "expert."

The accountant says that since Mom died last year, the sale proceeds should not be reported to Mom's social security number. That makes sense, but not one of the six named beneficiaries is willing to have the entire sale proceeds reported to them on a 1099-B; and the broker can only use one social security number for the transaction. Mom's lawyer, who is the other Co-Executor, is angry because the plan he designed is messed up, and it looks like the six beneficiaries of the brokerage account are going to have to be treated as a partnership comprised of the six beneficiaries for income tax purposes. The partnership's tax ID number then can be used for the 1099 instead of any one of the six beneficiaries. That will require a tax I.D. number, a partnership agreement, and federal and state partnership income tax returns — all very costly, time-consuming and unnecessary. Since some of the beneficiaries are unhappy and hostile to each other, getting them to understand and cooperate looks like many hours of legal work.

The three nephews are begging for money. Since their mother died, they are in need of money to pay college tuition. They can't get financial aid because they have an asset that they must spend first. Each owns one-sixth of the brokerage account. One of them is under 18, and the brokerage house will not pay out anything to the minor nephew unless a legal guardian is appointed for them. Ironically, the probate proceeding required for guardianship is much more onerous and expensive than probate of a will.

Mom's will was so simple; she gave everything to her issue per stirpes. If the brokerage account had not been POD or TOD, it would have passed under Mom's will. The three nephews would have shared their deceased mother's one-fourth share. The Executors would have authority to sell the bond. Any income tax consequence would be reported and paid handled by the estate. The nephew could have received distribution for tuition. The payment could have been made to the college or to a custodian for the benefit of the minor. No partnership would have to be created, and no partnership income tax returns filed.

The will would have worked beautifully. All of the decedents' and the beneficiaries' goals and needs would have been met. Yes, the POD registration avoided probate, but it created a host of other problems.

When you register an account or an investment in POD or TOD form, you are making your will irrelevant to the disposition of that asset. A dispositive scheme that is carefully thought out and designed is abandoned so that you can "avoid probate."

Probate is the proceeding used to determine the next owner of property titled in the decedent's name alone. The will becomes the document that governs who gets what and an executor is appointed to administer the estate. The evils of probate are largely imaginary. Seminar hucksters try to drum up business for living trust mills by painting probate as worse than death. Sometimes it is beneficial to use trusts, and there can be good reasons to avoid probate, but for most people, it is not a concern.

Certainly, for Mom in our example, avoiding probate caused many, many problems. The so-called "expert" who advised her really did not have any knowledge, training, or experience in estate settlement and the various property law and tax issues involved.

New Account Forms at investment institutions now routinely ask you to name a beneficiary. Do not feel that you have to name a beneficiary. In most cases you're better off leaving that section of the form blank. When the clerk wants you to fill it in, say, "No, thank you. I have a carefully thought out will and estate plan which I intend to use to dispose of my assets."

Remember that how your assets are titled is an important part of your estate plan. The will and any trust you have are designed to work with your assets as they are titled when you made the plan. If you change the title to assets, you are changing the estate plan and often bringing about unintended and inequitable results. Don't change titles or name beneficiaries without having a qualified professional review your estate plan. You could be changing more than you think.

Safe Deposit Boxes: They're Safe, But Not Sealed

I want to debunk a myth. I have heard many times that a safe deposit box is "sealed" when the owner dies. This is not true in Pennsylvania. Safe deposit boxes are not sealed. In fact, the box is the safest place for your will, life insurance policies, stock certificates, and other valuables.

I always recommend that clients keep their wills in the safe deposit box. Wills kept at home often get lost, misplaced, or accidentally destroyed. It is not easy to probate a copy — a lost will is presumed to have been destroyed with the intention of revoking it. In this age of photocopies, a will is one document where the original is the only one that counts.

Sometimes wills "disappear" when they are found by a beneficiary who doesn't like what they find. Sometimes they are hidden in a "safe place" and are never found. Don't place all your trust in "fireproof" boxes either. Most of these are fire-rated for only one or two hours — and the embers of a doused fire are hot long after that.

The lawyer who wrote the will sometimes offers to keep the will. Sometimes the lawyer's motivation for keeping the will is to make sure that the family has to come to that lawyer to retrieve it — thus giving that lawyer first crack at the business of settling the estate. Despite this motivation, this could provide needed safety and is a good option so long as the executor and family understand that the will is being held for safekeeping and the executor is free to interview other firms and compare fees before hiring an attorney for the estate.

There *are* some restrictions on entry into a safe deposit box in the decedent's name. The purpose of these restrictions is to prevent inheritance tax evasion. If unreported cash, jewelry, bearer bonds, or other valuables are stored in the box, the Commonwealth wants to make sure that these items are reported and that inheritance tax is paid on them. Nevertheless, banks recognize the right of the family, next of kin or executor (if known), to search the contents of a decedent's safe deposit box for wills, codicils, trusts, life insurance policies, and cemetery deeds. If the key cannot be found, the box can be drilled. The law permits removal of such documents provided a bank employee certifies that no other assets have been removed. It is worth noting that the bank is entitled to demand that wills or other documents remain in their custody until lodged with the Register of Wills, though they seldom insist on this.

Far from being sealed, the box is opened to search for documents that are needed at the time of death.

The restrictions on entry apply to a safe deposit box that is "in the decedent's name." A safe deposit box is considered to be "in the decedent's name" if it is (1) registered in the decedent's name alone, (2) registered jointly in name of decedent and one or more others (except husband and wife), or (3) registered in a partnership or trade name where decedent had access to the box, as principal agent or deputy. For example, a box held jointly with the decedent and the decedent's son is a box "in the decedent's name." A box held in the name of the XYZ partnership where the decedent had the right of entry to the box is also "in the decedent's name." It is important to note that a box held jointly by the decedent and the decedent's surviving spouse is *not* "in the decedent's name."

"In the decedent's name" is a term defined in the Pennsylvania state statute. It seems odd but a box in the joint names of the decedent and a spouse is *not* "in the decedent's name," while a joint box in the names of the decedent and any other person *is* "in the decedent's name."

None of the restrictions on access are applicable to boxes registered in the name of decedent and spouse. In that case, decedent's surviving spouse, or the surviving spouse's deputy, may enter the box and remove anything with no restriction whatsoever.

After the swearing in of an executor, it is the executor's responsibility to enter the box to collect assets. The executor must arrange with the estate's attorney for the Pennsylvania Department of Revenue to issue a commission for the opening and inventorying of the box. It is the duty of the person commissioned to list the contents of the box or to certify that only the will or cemetery deed has been removed. This is called "inventorying" the box.

If the safe deposit box was rented jointly by decedent and another surviving party, the right of entry is probably limited to the surviving joint owner, although the restrictions about inventory still apply, even to this joint owner.

Subsequent entries by the executor or surviving joint owner are free of restriction.

Taking inventory of the safe deposit box is always part of the estate settlement process. Complying with the requirements is not difficult. Since the safe deposit box is probably the "safest" place, please consider keeping your will and other valuable papers there. Although this discussion may suggest a complicated procedure to lay persons, in actuality, bank personnel are accustomed to handling this in the ordinary course of their business.

FEDERAL ESTATE TAX

A Little History: Death Taxes Are Nothing New

Taxes due at death have been in existence since civilization began, going back to the Romans, the Greeks, and even the Egyptians. Consider that when a person dies, his belongings suddenly have no owner at least temporarily. Everyone wants part of the bounty, and the government is no exception. Our Supreme Court has held that while there is a right to life, liberty, and the pursuit of happiness, there is no right to inheritance. In the United States, a decedent's property is inheritable by heirs and beneficiaries only because this privilege is granted by the state legislatures. Thus, the state legislatures could pass laws that abolish inheritance and provide that the decedent's property passes to the government. In a like manner, the states and the federal governments are free to enact death taxes to take a portion of the decedent's property.

Death taxes come in two varieties: estate taxes and inheritance taxes. An estate tax is an excise tax on the value of the property transferred by the decedent. An inheritance tax is an excise tax levied on the value of the property received by a beneficiary. The federal government levies an estate tax, as do about a dozen states; other states levy an inheritance tax. Most of the states also have a "sponge tax" (more on that later).

The U.S. Congress first imposed a stamp tax on legacies in 1797 when relations with France deteriorated. (It didn't take them long, did it?) These levies disappeared in five years, then re-emerged during the Civil War, after which they disappeared again. Congress imposed an inheritance tax to fund the hostility with Spain in the 1890s, also discarded after victory.

Developing in the 1890s were disparities of riches and the emergence of the great wealthy families of John D. Rockefeller, J. P. Morgan, and the rest. People pressured Congress to use taxes to level these great fortunes, but Congress was reluctant to act. (Imagine that!) Finally, in 1916, military expenditures were rising, and it was time to enact a death tax again. Congress had a legitimate reason now to enact an estate tax to raise funds for the military and appease the cry to put a stop to our growing aristocracy. It was because of this leveling of wealth that the tax was not repealed at the end of World War I. As a response to pressure from the rich, Congress did, however, reduce the wartime rates.

The great loophole in the estate tax was to give money away before death. The estate tax could be avoided if the decedent gave away his property and died with no assets. It took ten years to correct, but, in 1926, the gift tax was established to fix the leak. The gift tax applied to lifetime transfers of property. To soften the blow, the gift tax came with an annual exclusion. Congress recognized that most people made gifts for birthdays, weddings, graduations, and other occasions. These types of gifts were not meant to be taxed, so there is an annual exclusion from the gift tax to cover these relatively small gifts. This exclusion amount is $14,000 in 2014. Any person can make gifts of $14,000 each to an unlimited number of beneficiaries each calendar year.

The states demanded that they share in the estate tax. In 1926, Congress allowed the states to claim up to 80 percent of the federal estate tax levied on their residents for themselves. This was accomplished by allowing a credit for state death taxes against the federal estate tax. The states enacted their own estate taxes in the amount of the maximum permissible credit. These state estate taxes go by various names: the sponge tax, the slack tax, or the pick-up tax. Congress has since gnawed away at this form of revenue sharing with the states until the amount that can be claimed by the states is a sliding scale of only 1 to 16 percent of the taxable estate. Pennsylvania uses an inheritance tax and the slack tax. For Trivial Pursuit players, only Nevada has no state death tax.

The Great Depression, in 1931, caused the need for more taxes, so the Hoover Administration doubled the top estate tax rate to 45 percent. Franklin Roosevelt saw a greater need for leveling the playing field for the very wealthy and raised the rates again. World War II raised them even more. The peak rate was reached in 1954, when the exemption was $60,000, and the top rate was 77 percent. Gift tax rates were at 75 percent of estate tax rates.

As wartime rates rose, the advantage of community property states swelled. Their advantage was that while only half of a couple's property was taxed at the first death, it all received a step-up in basis.

Several states initiated legislation to help their taxpayers out, but the Government stepped in, leveling the playing field with the separate property states by allowing a tax exemption on 50 percent of the property if it was left to the spouse either directly or in a life estate with a general power of appointment.

The Tax Reform Act of 1976 unified the gift and estate taxes, making them all one system. The only difference is in the base of the tax — gift taxes being based on the gift alone; and estate taxes being based on the amount transferred plus the tax. This leads to about a 25 to 35 percent tax savings for taxable gifts over bequests. Also, the exemption was phased in until it became $600,000.

The Economic Recovery Act of 1981 made a sweeping change to the marital deduction. Congress was concerned that the 50 percent limit on marital deductions was determining how much was being left to a surviving spouse. The remedy was to raise the marital deduction limit to 100 percent of the estate. Additionally, all inter vivos transfers between spouses became tax free.

The Tax Reform Act of 1986 struck the worst blow yet to the rich. Formerly, the rich could put money into trusts for a century at a time (limited only by the statute against perpetuities) and have wealth passed on for generations, tax free after the first transfer tax occasion. The IRS wanted a tax levied at each generation, and, thus, the Generation Skipping Transfer Tax (GSTT) was born. If money is given, distributed, or transferred to someone two generations below the transferor, an extra tax, at the highest transfer tax rate then existing, is levied. That's an extra 48 percent these days. To soften the blow, a once in a lifetime million dollar exclusion was included, now up to $5,000,000.

In 1997, Congress decided that existing credits and exemptions were becoming outdated. The exemption from the federal estate tax was put on a schedule to rise to $3.5 million by 2009, infinity in 2010, and $5,000,000 in 2011. The gift tax annual exclusion and the GSTT exclusions, as well as other credits and exclusions, were pegged to inflation. The gift tax is now nailed at $1 million and the GSST exclusion is now the same as the unified credit amount. Talk is rampant of repealing the estate tax. Just remember, no estate tax does not mean no generation skipping transfer tax. More importantly, no estate tax also means, no step-up in basis at death. Beneficiaries would be getting inherited assets at the decedent's cost basis. On liquidation of the decedent's assets, capital gains tax would be due. For many situations where the value of the estate is near or below the exemption level, this means beneficiaries are going to pay more in taxes, not less. They will be paying more in capital gains taxes than ever before. Is repeal such a good deal?

Overview of the Federal Estate and Gift Taxes

The federal estate tax is an excise tax on the transfer of property at death. There is much academic dispute as to whether such a tax is constitutional. Critics claim it is an infringement of the right to private property. But it is well-settled law that the estate and gift taxes are not taxes *on the property*, but rather *on the right to transfer the property*. A review of the history of the common law will show that the right to transmit property on death is not part of the right to private property as that right was originally understood. In fact, in early English days, on death, a lord's property reverted to the crown. It became the custom for the crown to return the property to the eldest son of the lord.

When Franklin Roosevelt was president, the highest estate tax rate was 70 percent (it is now 48 percent). The tax policy is that in a democracy there should not be a moneyed class. The theory is that the estate tax breaks up large fortunes, preventing the development of an aristocracy or an oligarchy.

The federal estate and gift taxes are excise taxes on the right to transfer property at death. The measurement of the tax is the fair market value of the assets that pass at the time of the gift or at the time of death. The tax has a much more dramatic effect than the income tax, which taxes only the income produced on assets. The estate and gift taxes apply to the fair market value of the underlying assets — a much larger tax base.

The federal estate tax was enacted by Congress in 1916. It applied to property that passed on account of the death of a decedent. It did not take people long to figure out that if a person gave away all his property before he died, nothing would be left to be taxed by the estate tax. Enter the gift tax. In 1924, Congress enacted the first gift tax which taxed lifetime transfers so that the excise tax on property transfers could not be avoided.

Ever since there has been a gift tax, there has been an exception for gifts that are considered to be part of everyday life. There has been a dollar amount of gifts which, on an annual basis, are not subject to the gift tax. Today, in 2014, this amount is $14,000. The policy behind the exclusion is to permit birthday gifts, wedding gifts, graduation gifts, and the like, from being taxable and requiring the filing of a gift tax return. Any individual can give $14,000 to as many persons as he or she wishes every year. This is called the $14,000 annual exclusion and has come to be used as a planning technique.

The estate and gift tax are two separate taxes, but they are designed to fit together in some respects. For example, they both have the same rates. Also, each person has a tax credit which will currently shelter $5,340,000 in assets from the estate tax and $5,340,000 from the gift tax. I sometimes refer to this amount as the "free pass". Each person can transfer assets, either during life or at death, valued up to $5,340,000 with no gift tax and $5,340,000 with estate tax payable. The free passes are used first during life to shelter assets from the application of the gift tax. Any amount of the free pass remaining at death is available to shelter assets from the application of the estate tax.

One Fiscal Cliff-hanger is Over

They call it the American Taxpayer Relief Act. Funny, that overall it produces tax increases—that's relief?

Early January 1, 2013, the Senate, by a vote of 89-8, passed the "American Taxpayer Relief Act". Late on that same day, after the government had technically gone over the "fiscal cliff", the House of Representatives, by a vote of 257 to 167, also passed the bill. The Act, which we expect the President to gain imminently, prevents many tax increases from going into effect, but it increases income taxes for some high-income individuals and slightly increases estate and gift taxes.

Other fiscal cliffs remain in our future. The debt ceiling cliff is coming in a month or two and the sequester cliff comes in March (since the Act put off the automatic sequester cuts for two months).

Here are the highlights from the new Act:

Estate and Gift Taxes. The estate tax exemption slated to fall to $1 million has been retained at the 2013 level of about $5.27 million. The top rate was slated to go from 35% to 55%. The Act provides an increase in the top rate to 40%.

For those taxpayers who made large gifts in 2012 to use your exemption before it fell to $1 million, for most of you this was still good planning. Future income and growth on those assets has been removed from your future taxable estates. Plus, who knows how long this law will be with us? There is no "sunset" with this law, but Congress can always create an instant "sunset".

The Act also includes the extension of "portability" which allows the estate of the first spouse to die to transfer his or her unused estate tax exemption to the surviving spouse.

Dividends and Capital Gains. The maximum rate on dividends and capital gains will be 23.8%, up from 15 % in 2012. The 23.8% rate includes the new 20% maximum capital gains tax plus the 3.8% surtax from the Affordable Care Act. (The surtax applies only to individuals with over $200,000, and married couples filing jointly with over $250,000, in modified adjusted gross income.)

Individual Tax Rates. Individual rates have been retained at 10%, 15%, 25%, 28%, 33% and 35% . A new 39.6% rate applies to income of $450,000 for joint filers, $425,000 for heads of household, and $400,000 for single filers. There is a marriage penalty here. Two single people living together could each make up to $400,000 before the 39.6% rate applies. A married couple filing jointly pays the 39.6% when combined income exceeds $450,000.

Alternative Minimum Tax. The Act has made permanent an increase in exemption amounts, and the index of those amounts with inflation. No more year-end panic waiting for an AMT patch. Before the Act, the individual AMT exemption amounts for 2012 were to have been $33,750 for unmarried taxpayers, $45,000 for joint filers and $22,500 for married persons filing separately. Retroactively effective for tax years beginning after 2011, the Act permanently increases these exemption amounts to $50,600 for unmarried taxpayers, $78,750 for joint filers and $39,375 for married persons filing separately. Beginning in 2013, these exemption amounts are indexed for inflation.

Personal Exemption Phase out. Personal exemptions begin to phase out for those making $300,000 for joint filers, $275,000 for heads of household, $250,000 for single filers and $150,000 for married taxpayers filing separately.

Itemized Deduction Phase out. Itemized deductions are reduced by 3% of the amount by which the taxpayer's adjusted gross income (AGI) exceeds the threshold amount, with the reduction not to exceed 80% of the otherwise allowable itemized deductions. The starting thresholds are $300,000 for joint filers and a surviving spouse, $275,000 for heads of household, $250,000 for single filers and $150,000 for married taxpayers filing separately.

The effect of these phase-outs is to raise the top bracket from 35% to 41%.

Charitable Contributions from IRAs. The ability to make tax-free distributions from individual retirement plans directly to qualifying charities has been extended through 2013 and made retroactive for 2012.

Payroll Tax Cut Allowed to Expire. An extension of the 2% payroll tax cut that expires at the end of 2012 was not included in the Act. These taxes go back up to 12.4% from last year's 10.4%.

5-year Extensions. The following credits slated to expire at the end of 2012 have been extended for 5 years: Child Tax Credit, Earned Income Tax Credit, and the American Opportunity Tax Credit.

Federal Estate Tax and Portability

The American Taxpayer Relief Act of 2012 (ATRA), which tried to keep us from going over the "fiscal cliff," raised the federal estate tax exemption to $5.25 million and made permanent an estate tax concept called "portability." How long the exemption will stay at $5.25 million (ignoring annual inflation adjustments) is anybody's guess.

"Portable" means easily carried or transferred, like a portable typewriter (remember those?). In this case, "portable" means easily transferred to a surviving spouse.

The federal estate and gift tax gives one exemption per person, so with planning, a married couple can potentially use two exemptions. For years, the classic estate plan for a married couple with assets over the exemption amount has been to divide assets between the spouses and for each spouse to have an estate plan which creates a trust on the first spouse's death, or at least the possibility of funding a trust with a disclaimer. The first spouse to die's exemption is applied to the trust, by-passing the tax. The surviving spouse is the beneficiary of the trust during his or her period of survivorship. When the surviving spouse dies, he or she gets another exemption, and the assets in the by-pass trust are not taxed again. Thus, the couple has used two exemptions.

Critics of the estate tax point out that the practical effect of this is to create two systems of estate tax: one for those who consult lawyers and make estate plans with by-pass trusts, and a second system of taxation for those who don't.

The idea for portability of the exemption is that it is a way for both spouses' exemptions to be used without separating title to assets and creating a by-pass trust.

In order to "port" a deceased spouse's exemption to the surviving spouse, the executor of the first deceased spouse's estate must file a federal estate tax return and make an election to allocate the unused exemption to the surviving spouse. That means that for estates of decedents for which a federal estate tax return would normally not be filed, a federal estate tax return will now have to be filed just to "port" the exemption. Where there are separate families because of second marriages, there will be situations where the fiduciary who is responsible for the first dying spouse's estate will not cooperate to make the election. Some commentators have suggested that wills (or codicils) include language to permit the surviving spouse to require the filing of an estate tax return and the filing of the election, and may require the surviving spouse to pay expenses attributable thereto.

The deceased spouse's unused exemption amount is the "DSUEA." Only the last deceased spouse counts. A surviving spouse does not lose the first deceased spouse's DSUEA by remarrying (or remarrying and divorcing). Only when the subsequent spouse predeceases the survivor during marriage does he or she replace the prior spouse for purposes of determining the DSUEA available to the surviving spouse.

Even with portability, we recommend that married couples continue to structure their estate plans to take full advantage of their estate and gift tax exemptions by using by-pass trusts and splitting up ownership of their assets. There are several reasons for this:

- There is no guarantee that there will be a DSUEA in the future.
- Appreciation of assets placed in the by-pass trust will escape estate taxation in the survivor's estate.
- Creditor protection for by-pass trust beneficiaries is achieved.
- Funding of the trust helps ensure that the children of the first dying spouse have a good chance to receive an inheritance, especially if the surviving spouse remarries and is inclined to share assets with the next spouse and his or her family.
- The generation-skipping transfer (GST) tax exemption is not portable so without a by-pass trust to which the first dying spouse's GST tax exemption could be allocated, the first spouse's GST tax exemption could be lost.

The disadvantages of a by-pass trust are:

- There would be no further stepped-up basis on death of surviving spouse (although perhaps an unrelated trust protector could dissolve the trust for distribution to surviving spouse).
- The first estate may consist in large part of property that it is desirable to leave to the surviving spouse rather than to be put in a by-pass trust (for example, an IRA, which can be rolled over by the spouse but not by the trustee of a by-pass trust).
- If the estate tax is repealed (for real), then administrative costs are wasted (accounting, income tax returns, etc.).
- Some clients think it's too complicated to have a trust.

Property Owned by the Decedent

The first category of assets subject to estate tax is property that the decedent owned at death. This is the easiest and most obvious property interest to identify. It includes anything owned by the decedent. Real estate, bank accounts, marketable securities, collections, jewelry, all these things are subject to the tax. They are valued at the fair market value on the date of death. Fair market value is the price a willing buyer would pay a willing seller, both knowing all relevant facts, and neither being under a compulsion to buy or sell. The fair market value of real estate is determined by appraisal. Assessed value is not the value that is taxed. The fair market value of bank accounts and certificates of deposit are the balances in the accounts, plus accrued interest on the date of death. The fair market value of marketable securities is the mean of the high and low prices, on the date of death, or the mean of the bid and ask.

For the estate tax, there is an alternate valuation date. The assets may be valued at the date which is six months after the date of death if, and only if, there is an estate tax due and if the use of the alternate valuation date results in a lower tax. The alternate value is an election that is made by the executor. If the alternate value is elected, it must be used for all property interests included in the estate. The date is six months from the date of death unless the property is sold or disposed of before the six month date, in which case the sale or disposition date is the date for alternate value for that particular asset.

If the decedent was a sole proprietor of a business, the value of the business is subject to tax. This value is also determined by appraisal. Shares of stock in a closely held business are also valued by appraisal, as is a partnership interest. Appraisals are obtained by the executor and submitted along with the tax return to the IRS. The IRS may accept the appraisal, or challenge the values. Sometimes they hire their own appraisers. The valuation for estate and gift tax purposes of closely held businesses, real estate, and other hard to value assets is a challenging area which requires expert attention. Much of estate planning is aimed at establishing low values for hard to value assets included in the estate.

Joint Property

Jointly-owned property is property that has two or more concurrent owners. All kinds of property — real estate, securities, bank accounts . . . (you name it), can be jointly owned.

There are three types: (1) Tenancy in Common, (2) Joint Tenancy and (3) Tenancy by the Entirety. "Tenancy" is the mode or way that property is owned. In ordinary English usage we have come to think of a "tenant" as someone who pays rent for the right to occupy real estate. Indeed, that is a kind of "Tenancy." But "Tenancy" has a much broader meaning in the law and includes any mode of ownership, use or occupancy.

(1) Tenancy in Common is co-ownership among two or more persons where each co-owner has an interest in the property that can be passed to their heirs.
(2) Joint Tenancy is co-ownership among two or more persons where the property interest of a deceased co-owner passes to the surviving joint owners. A person who is a holder of joint property cannot dispose of his interest by will. However, he can convey his interest to a third party. Also, his interest as a joint tenant can be partitioned by the court or it can be seized by a creditor. The new owner becomes a Tenant in Common with the remaining joint owners if one of these events happens. Thus, any joint owner has the power to convert a Joint Tenancy to a Tenancy in Common.
(3) Tenancy by the Entirety is co-ownership of property by a husband and wife where the surviving spouse becomes the owner of the entire property. Neither spouse can transfer his or her interest in the property without the consent of the other. A creditor of one spouse cannot reach property held by that spouse as a tenant by the entireties.

Title to joint property has important consequences. The type of tenancy determines "who gets what" and also determines what proportion of the property is subject to estate and inheritance tax when a co-owner dies.

Tenancy in Common is sometimes referred to as ownership by co-tenants. If Mary and Jane own a house as tenants in common, then each of them has a half interest in the house. They don't draw a line down the middle of the house, through the dining room, living room, and down the middle of the stairs. There is no physical division of the house; Mary and Jane each own half of the whole. The law calls the portion owned by each an undivided one-half interest. If Mary dies, her half passes under her will — perhaps to her husband, perhaps to her children, perhaps to another beneficiary, who then becomes a co-tenant or co-owner with Jane. For Pennsylvania inheritance tax purposes *and* for federal estate tax purposes, one-half of the value of the whole property on Mary's date of death is included in her estate and subject to tax.

Joint Tenancy is sometimes called Joint Tenants With Right Of Survivorship, which is redundant, because Joint Tenancy by definition includes the survivorship feature. But I suppose adding "WROS" makes it abundantly clear. (WROS is the acronym for "with right of survivorship.") If one of the owners dies, the account or property belongs to the surviving joint owner or owners, and ultimately in its totality to the last survivor.

How can you tell what you have? For accounts with banks, brokers, and other financial institutions, you need to look at the account title *and* the account agreement with the institution. The form of ownership and the rights accruing to each co-owner will be spelled out in the account agreement or under state law. For real estate, often the deed will specify the form of tenancy. If the deed does not specify the type of tenancy, you may need to consult an attorney. There are various presumptions For example, a deed to a husband and wife, without any words specifying the form of tenancy, creates a Tenancy by the Entirety.

For Pennsylvania inheritance tax, for both Tenants in Common and Joint Tenancies, on the death of a co-owner, the taxable estate of the co-owner includes a fraction of the value of the property. The fraction is one over the number of co-tenants. For example, if three brothers own a farm, whether as tenants in common or as joint tenants, on the death of one of them, one-third of the value of the farm is subject to Pennsylvania inheritance tax.

For the federal estate tax, for property held as Tenants in Common, the same treatment applies. A fraction of the property is subject to estate tax, the fraction being one over the number of co-tenants.

However, the federal estate tax applies to property owned in Joint Tenancy by a contribution rule. Only a fraction of the date-of-death value of jointly owned property is taxable. The fraction is the decedent's contribution divided by the total original cost. Who contributed funds for acquisition determines what portion is taxed. For example, if Dad uses his funds to open a joint bank account with Daughter and Dad subsequently dies, since he contributed 100 percent of the initial funds to the account, then 100 percent of the date-of-death value of the joint account is subject to federal estate tax in his estate. Conversely, if Daughter dies after the creation of the joint bank account with Dad's funds, none of the joint account is included in her estate for federal estate tax purposes because she contributed nothing to the account.

How is contribution determined? The tax law takes the view that whoever dies first contributed 100 percent. It figures, doesn't it? Whenever a joint owner dies, it is *presumed* that the full value of the property is subject to federal estate tax unless the deceased's executor can prove otherwise. The burden is on the executor to come up with proof of contribution by the surviving joint owner(s). If the asset was acquired many years ago, this may be simply impossible So here is what can happen: A and B own property jointly. "A" dies. One hundred percent of the value of the property is taxed in A's estate. The property passes to B as the surviving joint owner. Later, B dies. One hundred percent of the value of the property is taxed in B's estate.

Property held as Tenants by the Entirety is not subject to Pennsylvania inheritance tax on the death of either spouse. For federal estate tax purposes, one-half of the value (regardless of each spouse's contribution) is included in the deceased spouse's estate. However, this property passes to the surviving spouse and qualifies for the marital deduction so there is also no federal taxation on property held as tenants by the entirety.

Titling assets in joint names can wreak havoc with an estate plan. Let's assume you title an asset in joint names with one of your three children. Your will provides that each child gets one-third of your estate. What happens? A will doesn't operate on jointly owned assets. They pass outside of the will. One child will get the jointly owned asset *plus* one-third of your other assets. The other two kids will each get one-third of the other assets and they will not share in the joint asset.

To make matters worse, most wills tell the executor to pay all estate and inheritance taxes out of the residue of the estate. If that happens, then the other two kids will have their shares reduced by taxes due on the joint account — an asset they do not share in. If you want to give a child access to your funds to pay bills if you are incapacitated or unavailable, the better way is by giving the child a Power of Attorney.

Changing the title to property is an important part of estate planning. Title and how it is held is obviously important in planning for the future ownership of the property and the state and federal death taxes applicable to it.

Life Insurance

The death benefits paid on life insurance policies are subject to estate tax in two situations. First, if the death benefit is paid to the estate of the insured, then the whole amount of the death benefit is included in the estate and subject to estate tax. Second, if the deceased insured was the owner of the policy on the date of death, the whole amount of the death benefit is included in the estate and subject to estate tax.

Most people name individuals as beneficiaries, so the death benefit is not payable to an estate. The estate taxation of the insurance is usually governed by the second consideration, that is, who is the owner of the policy. Do you know the owner of your insurance policies?

An insurance policy is a contract between the owner of the policy and the insurance company. The terms of the contract provide that in exchange for the payment of premiums, the insurance company will pay a death benefit to a beneficiary designated by the owner. The time for the payment of the death benefit is the date of death of the insured.

The owner has all the lifetime rights to the contract. The owner can borrow against the policy, cancel the policy and receive the cash surrender value, designate a beneficiary and exercise any policy options for the application of dividends or conversion features. The owner is the person who applies for the insurance coverage. Most of the time, the question of who should be the owner of the policy is not even discussed when the application for insurance is completed. Very often the insured is the owner. For example, if Husband wants to buy insurance on Husband's life, usually Husband is the applicant/owner. Husband's life is insured, and Wife is named as the primary beneficiary with the kids as contingent beneficiaries.

If Husband dies first, the death benefit is paid to Wife. The full value of the death benefit is included in the estate, but is not taxed if it is paid to Wife, because it qualifies for the marital deduction and no estate tax is payable. Wife then has the cash and unless it is spent, it will be subject to estate tax in her estate. If Wife dies first, then on Husband's death, the death benefit is payable to the children and since Husband was the owner of the policy the death benefit is included in the estate and is subject to estate tax.

Under current estate tax law, most assets that pass to a surviving spouse are not subject to estate tax. This is because there is a deduction available, called the marital deduction, for the value of all property passing to the surviving spouse. For couples who utilize this approach to their estate planning, there is no tax payable until the death of the survivor.

Let's assume that there is no surviving spouse, either because the spouse predeceased, or the decedent was not married at the time of death. If the decedent was the owner of insurance policies insuring his or her life, the full value of the death benefit is subject to estate tax. Let's assume the beneficiary is the decedent's child. What if, instead of the decedent having been the owner of the policy, the child was the owner?

Child, as the owner, is the party to the contract with the insurance company. Parent is the insured. The death benefit on Parent's death is paid to the child or to any beneficiary the child designates. How much of the death benefit is included in Parent's estate and subject to estate tax? Zero. That's right — zero. The death benefit is received by Child (or Child's designated beneficiary) estate, tax free.

Obviously the ownership of life insurance policies is an important factor in how much estate tax is due. If the policy was for $500,000 and the estate is in the 40 percent bracket, we're talking about saving $200,000 in tax.

Changing the ownership of life insurance policies is an important estate planning technique. A change in ownership is a transfer of the policy and is a gift. The value of the gift is something called the "interpolated terminal reserve value" of the policy. The interpolated terminal reserve value is a complex calculation the insurance company will provide to you, and which, in my experience, always works out to something very close to the cash value of the policy.

For the transfer technique to succeed in removing the death benefit from the taxable estate, the original owner must survive the transfer by three years. If death occurs within three years of the transfer, the decedent is deemed to be the owner of the policy and the full value of the death benefit is includable. The moral of the story is: Don't wait; make the transfer as soon as you can.

Many people transfer their policies to a trust rather than to children or other individuals. This trust is called an Irrevocable Life Insurance Trust or "ILIT." If this technique is used, the ILIT becomes the owner and beneficiary of the policies. The death benefit, when paid to the trust, is not subject to estate tax, assuming the insured survives the transfer by three years.

If the ILIT acquires a new policy insuring the decedent's life, rather than receiving the insurance policy by transfer, then the three year rule does not apply. The death benefit is out of the estate from the start. This is a very important distinction. The reason the three year rule is inapplicable is that the insurance policy was not transferred; the insurance policy was purchased by the Trustee of the ILIT.

Planning for insurance is an important part of estate planning. You should make sure your beneficiary designation coordinates with the rest of your estate plan and you should get advice on whether or not you should consider transferring the ownership of policies.

Annuities and Qualified Plans

Annuity benefits, retirement plans, and IRAs are among the assets that are subject to estate tax. These assets are often tax-favored during the accumulation period, the tax policy being to encourage accumulation of assets to provide retirement income. On death, these assets are often subjected to two taxes — both the estate tax and the income tax — reducing their value in the hands of the beneficiaries to a fraction of their date-of-death value.

Annuity contracts take a variety of forms. A "simple" annuity is a single-life annuity with no refund feature. The annuity is paid in equal amounts over the term of the annuitant's life. On the annuitant's death, no further payments are due. If a decedent purchases this kind of annuity, nothing is included in his estate for federal estate tax purposes. The rights to payments end on decedent's death. There is no value that passes to anyone.

Other annuity contracts provide definitely or contingently for something to be paid to beneficiaries on the annuitant's death. For example, an annuity contract may provide that if the payments the annuitant received during life do not exceed his investment in the contract, the difference will be paid to the annuitant's estate or to a beneficiary named by the annuitant. This kind of annuity is said to include a "refund feature."

Under other contracts, the annuity that had been paid to the deceased annuitant is paid to some other person for that person's lifetime — sometimes called a self and survivor annuity. A similar type of annuity is a joint and survivor annuity where the annuity amount is paid to two annuitants jointly during their lives and then continues to the survivor, sometimes in a reduced amount, during the period of survivorship.

In general, the value of the annuity that is paid to the annuitant's estate, a named beneficiary, or a continuing annuitant is included in the deceased annuitant's estate for estate tax purposes. If the benefit is payable in a lump sum, the lump sum value is the amount included in the estate and subject to tax. If the benefits are payable in periodic payments, an actuarial computation of the present value of this stream of payments is calculated and this is the value that is subject to tax.

Employee retirement benefits are subjected to estate tax under the rules that require the inclusion of annuities. The full value of pension, profit sharing, and 401(k) plans is included in the estate, as well as the full value of ESOPs, IRAs, Keoghs, SEPs, and any other retirement plans. The amount includable is the value of the survivor's benefits on the date of death of the participant. The full value is subject to estate tax, including the parts attributable to employee contributions and employer contributions. (There are two minor exceptions to this rule that may apply to plans where the participant retired before 1985 and made certain elections.)

Retirement plans, including IRAs, are substantial assets in the estates of many clients. These plans are still recognized as the "quintessential tax-shelter" because income taxes are deferred on both contributions to the plans and to the earnings on the assets inside the plans. The accounts can grow at a phenomenal rate. For many individuals, these plans have far exceeded the growth of other estate assets and constitute the principal asset in the estate.

There is a maze of complicated income and estate rules governing these plans. The practitioner must navigate through this maze of rules and penalties for distributions Too Soon, Too Much, Too Little, Too Late. Even minor deviations from the rules can result in severe penalties. Overlay these rules with the estate tax and one has a very complicated tax situation.

Although retirement plan benefits have a tax-favored status during the participant's life, the taxation of these benefits on the participant's death can be devastating. The full value of the benefits is subject to estate tax, *and* the benefits are also subject to income tax when received by the beneficiary. Let's assume decedent had a $1 million IRA and decedent's estate is in the 40 percent federal estate tax bracket, subject to a 4.5 percent Pennsylvania inheritance tax, and the named beneficiary of the IRA, who received the benefit in a lump sum, is in the 39.6 percent income tax bracket. The combined estate, inheritance, and income tax on a $1 million IRA would be $682,600. The decedent thought she was leaving a $1 million IRA to her beneficiary when in fact, the beneficiary will receive only $317,400. For this reason, retirement plans and IRAs are often "illusory" assets.

Large qualified plans and IRAs require special planning and attention to maximize their value and minimize taxes. Much of this planning is aimed at deferring payment of the estate and income taxes. For example, estate taxes can be deferred if the benefits can be directed to a surviving spouse, either outright to the surviving spouse or in a trust for the surviving spouse. Income taxes can be deferred by taking advantage of a surviving spouse being able to roll over the benefit to his or her own IRA, or by planning for a payout of the plan benefits over time to the spouse or to children or other named beneficiaries so that the tax-free buildup inside the plan can be maintained as long as possible.

Transfers with Retained Interests

Many transfers of property during life are pulled back into the estate to be taxed on the death of the decedent. This can be quite a surprise. Many assume that property transferred during life is out of the taxable estate.

Transferred property is brought back into the gross estate for tax purposes when the person who transferred the property keeps a "string". The most obvious example of a string is the right to revoke the transfer. If the decedent can get the transferred property back, then this is enough control to subject the value of the property to estate tax in the deceased transferor's estate. Any transfer of property that can be revoked is subject to the estate tax.

Many people have created revocable trusts, sometimes called "living trusts," to hold their assets. Because the person who creates this trust can revoke it and demand the return of the trust assets at any time, this is tantamount to outright ownership. The assets in these trusts are fully taxable for estate tax purposes and for Pennsylvania inheritance tax.

What if the trust couldn't be revoked, but could be amended? The assets of the trust would still be subject to estate tax because of the retained control in the hands of the person who created the trust to change its terms.

An "in trust for" bank account is another type of revocable transfer. For example, a bank account is titled in Grandfather's name *in trust for* Grandson. This means that on Grandfather's death, the account becomes the property of Grandson. However, as long as Grandfather lives, Grandson has no rights to make withdrawals and Grandfather can withdraw the whole amount. This kind of a bank account is sometimes called a "Totten Trust." Since Grandfather can revoke the transfer by closing the account, the full value of the account is included for estate tax purposes in Grandfather's estate.

Another kind of lifetime transfer that is brought back into the estate for tax purposes because of a retained string is a transfer with a retained right to receive the income from or the use or occupancy of the transferred property. An example of this is a life estate in real estate. If Mother transfers her house to Son retaining a life estate, she has retained the legal right to use and occupy the property for her life. On her death, the house becomes the sole property of Son. Because Mother retained this right of occupancy, she has retained a string which pulls the whole value of the house into her estate for federal estate tax purposes as well as for Pennsylvania inheritance tax purposes. Similarly, if Mother transfers the whole deed to Son but by mutual agreement retains the right to occupy the premises; the full value of the house is still brought back into her estate for tax purposes.

Another example would be the transfer of property to an irrevocable trust but retaining the right to receive the income from the trust. The retained right to receive the trust income is a string that causes the full value of the trust assets to be brought back into the estate for tax purposes. Many would assume that since the trust is irrevocable, meaning that the person who created the trust cannot get the property back, that the trust assets would not be subject to estate tax. This is a trap for the unwary. The irrevocable transfer of the property with the retained right to receive the income is enough to keep the property included in the estate for tax purposes. From a tax policy viewpoint, this makes sense. The transferor is keeping important benefits from the property and has not made a complete transfer of all of the interest in the property. It's a case of trying to have your cake and eat it too.

Let's look at another example. Father makes a trust that is irrevocable. Father names himself as Trustee and the Trustee may distribute income and principal to Daughter. The trust is not revocable, so it is not drawn into Father's estate for that reason. Father has no right to receive the income from the transferred property. But, Father, as Trustee, has full control over how much income and principal is distributed, when, and to whom. This retained power, even though held as a Trustee, is a string that causes the full value of the trust property to be pulled back into the Father's estate for estate tax purposes.

Another example is an account under the Uniform Transfers to Minors Act. If a parent transfers money to an account for a minor child, if the parent dies before the child comes of age, the full value of the account is included in the parent's estate. This is because the Custodian's powers to use the property for the child's benefit are very broad. This retained power of the parent as Custodian is the string that pulls the account back into the parent's estate.

Many people assume that they can prepare estate and inheritance tax returns, by themselves. In fact, the returns themselves can be quite simple, requiring just a listing of assets, values, and computation of the tax. The hard part is determining what assets, and what lifetime transfers are includable and are subject to tax. Identifying the assets that are taxable takes professional advice.

Powers of Appointment

There is a famous analogy that property is like a bundle of sticks. The whole property is the bundle, but there are various property interests, each of which is a stick in the bundle.

For example, if you own a parcel of real estate, you own a whole bundle of sticks — the leasehold interest, the life estate, the remainder interest, and easement rights to cross the property. You can give some of the sticks away or sell some of the sticks while keeping others. Different people can hold sticks from the same bundle. You can give your mother a life estate in the house, lease the acreage to a farmer, give an easement to the adjoining landowner to cross the land, sell the mineral rights underneath the land, and give the bank a mortgage. All of these interests in the real estate are property interests of one sort or another.

You don't have to hold all the sticks in the bundle in order to have the property value included in your estate. For example, transferring all of the sticks but retaining a life estate, the right to use and occupy the real estate, is enough to cause the whole value of the real estate to be included in your estate for tax purposes.

A power of appointment is a power to determine who is to be the owner of property. Here is an example: Father creates a trust for the benefit of Daughter. Under the terms of the trust, the Trustee is directed to pay the income to Daughter for her life. On Daughter's death she has the "power to appoint" the trust property in her will. That is, in her will she can direct whom the Trustee should distribute the trust property to on her death. If Daughter does not exercise her power of appointment, the trust property goes to the contingent remaindermen specified in the trust document, perhaps to Daughter's children.

The power to appoint the property is obviously a valuable right. It gives Daughter control over who will be the next owner of the property even though Daughter herself was not the owner. All Daughter was entitled to, was the income generated by the property. Daughter held two sticks from the bundle. She had the right to receive income and she had the power of appointment in her will.

This control over who should be the next owner of the property is enough to make the whole value of the property included in Daughter's estate for estate tax purposes. The Internal Revenue Code provides that property that is subject to a *general* power of appointment is included in the power-holder's estate and subject to estate tax.

In our example, Daughter is the "holder" of the power, and those persons she names in her will to receive the trust property on her death are the "objects" of the power. According to the Internal Revenue Code, only *general* powers of appointment are subject to estate tax. A general power is one which included among its objects either, Daughter, Daughter's estate, Daughter's creditors, or the creditors of Daughter's estate.

If Daughter could appoint the trust property only to those in the group consisting of her children and grandchildren, then her power of appointment would not be "big" enough to cause it to be subject to estate tax. If on the other hand, Daughter could appoint the property to her creditors, then the property is included in her estate for tax purposes.

A power of appointment that has a limited class of objects in order to avoid being subject to the estate tax is called a "special power" or a "limited power."

If the power of appointment is given to the holder in a trust document, it is pretty easy to recognize. The document will state "I give my daughter the power to appoint the trust property in her will."

The problem is that the Internal Revenue Code definition of a power of appointment is broad enough to pull in other property that you wouldn't think of as being subject to a power of appointment.

Let's suppose Mother makes a gift of stock to Son and registers it in her name as Custodian for the benefit of Son under the Uniform Transfers to Minors Act. When Son is age 16, Mother dies. The full value of the stock that had been given to Son is included in Mother's estate. Why? She had a general power of appointment. Under the Uniform Transfers to Minors Act the Custodian has broad powers to use the custodial property for the benefit of the minor. The Custodian is empowered to use the custodial property to pay for the minor's care. Since Mother could have (even if she never did) spent the custodial property to discharge her support obligation, she has a general power of appointment because as Custodian she could appoint the custodial property to her creditors.

Powers of appointment are a tricky business. There are many traps for the unwary. Care must be taken in arranging the title to property and drafting wills and trusts to avoid unintended estate tax because of the grant of a power of appointment.

Estate Tax Deduction for Funeral Expenses

The federal estate tax is an excise tax on the value of property transferred by a decedent. The Pennsylvania inheritance tax is an excise tax on the value of property received by beneficiaries. In both cases, funeral expenses are permitted as deductions in determining the value of property that is subject to tax.

The Pennsylvania inheritance tax allows a deduction for the funeral expenses, the cost of a burial lot, and bequests or amounts expended for the care of the lot in which the decedent is buried. Bequests for masses or other religious observances are allowed as deductions. Reasonable and customary expenses for the purchase and erection of a monument, gravestone, or marker on the decedent's burial lot or final resting place are also deductible. The cost of a funeral meal is usually allowed as a deduction.

All such expenses are deductible only to the extent they are *reasonable*. Whether the expense is reasonable or customary depends on the decedent's station in life and the size of the decedent's estate. In a 1950 case where the decedent included in his will an authorization to spend $12,000 on the funeral, and the estate actually spent $26,000, the deduction was limited to $5,000. According to the National Association of Funeral Directors, the average cost of a funeral is about $5,000, not including burial costs.

Amounts for embalming, cremation, casket, hearse, limousines, and other amounts paid to the undertaker and for floral and other decorations have consistently been recognized as reasonable expenditures. The cost of transporting the body for funeral is a funeral expense and so is the cost of transportation of the person accompanying the body. Travel expenses for members of the family to attend the funeral are *not* deductible as funeral expenses. These are the personal expenses of the family members.

The federal estate tax permits deductions for funeral expenses to the extent they are allowable under state law. Since the IRS is only bound by decisions of a state's highest court, it is possible to have amounts permitted as payable funeral expenses by the county Orphan's Court and have the deduction denied by the IRS for the federal estate tax.

The duty of the executor with regard to funeral arrangements is primarily one of payment rather than of selection of the burial site or employment of the undertaker. The person who expects to be the executor should consider advising those ordering the funeral that their right to reimbursement from the estate is limited to what will be considered reasonable. If the funeral is too elaborate, the person ordering it takes the risk of personal liability for the excessive costs. If there is any likelihood that the estate will be insolvent, that is, that the debts of the decedent will exceed his assets, special care must be taken as only a nominal sum may be allowed for the funeral.

Historically, the common law has taken the position that the decedent's remains are not "owned" by the estate. "Ownership" of the body belongs to the next of kin. The decedent's wishes expressed in a will, while good evidence of decedent's wishes, are not necessarily binding.

The wishes of the decedent with regard to disposition of the body are given a lot of weight. If a dispute arises, this is the general order of preferences recognized in Pennsylvania case law: (1) the wishes of a surviving spouse if a normal marriage relationship existed at death, (2) the wishes of the decedent, especially if strongly and recently expressed, (3) the wishes of the next of kin according to their relationship or association with the decedent. There is no hard and fast rule that will apply to all situations and each situation has to be considered on its own. If a dispute arises about the disposition of the decedent's remains that cannot be resolved, the Orphan's Court Division has exclusive jurisdiction of the control of the decedent's burial. Extravagant burial directions are not honored as a matter of public policy. The movie star who wants to be buried in her Ferrari is a good example. Directions for interment in a solid silver or solid gold casket are in the same category. Directions to bury jewelry and other valuables with the decedent are also not enforceable under the law. Such directions are considered to be contrary to public policy — the theory being that such practices will result in grave robbing. You really can't take it with you.

Estate Tax Deductions for Debts

The federal estate tax is an excise tax on the value of property transferred by a decedent. The Pennsylvania inheritance tax is an excise tax on the value of property received by beneficiaries. In both cases, the first step is to determine the value of property interests that are included in the estate and subject to tax. The next step is to determine what deductions are available.

The value of the property is reduced by funeral expenses, expenses of administration of the estate, and debts of the decedent. Since the tax is on the value of the property that is either transferred or received, if property is subject to debts and claims, the property value is reduced. If the decedent owned a home, the full fair market value of the home is included in the estate. If the home was subject to a mortgage, then a deduction is available for the amount of the outstanding debt on the date of the decedent's death, plus interest accrued since the last payment date. Thus, after the completion of the computation, only the equity in the house is subject to the federal estate tax and the Pennsylvania inheritance tax.

Other debts are also deductible. Any balances due on credit cards are deductible because the estate is liable for all of the decedent's debts. (Always check to see if the unpaid balances on a decedent's cards are covered by life insurance from the card issuer.) Unpaid bills of all sorts are deductible. Utility bills unpaid when the decedent died for services before the date of death are debts. Real estate taxes that are due and unpaid, or have become a lien on the property, are deductible.

Income tax is a deductible debt. If the decedent dies in September, even though the income tax return and payment of the tax is not due until the following April 15, the liability for the tax is present at the decedent's death. The income tax that will be paid later is a deductible debt. Note that if the decedent is due a refund, that is an asset of the estate and subject to tax.

Expenses of the last illness are the debts of the decedent and deductible. Any medical insurance reimbursements received are assets. Checks that are outstanding on the date of death and subsequently clear the bank are treated as debts of the decedent. Charitable pledges, if they are legally enforceable, are deductible debts.

In general, for debts to be deductible, they must be actually paid from the estate. Remember that the policy for allowance of the deduction is that the debt item reduces the value of the property that passes to beneficiaries. If the debt is never paid, then there is no reduction in value. This rule is not followed for mortgages and liens. The principal debt of a mortgage is deductible even though the mortgage is not paid off from the estate. The promissory note of the decedent was secured by a mortgage of the real estate. The beneficiary who received the real estate received it subject to that mortgage.

No deduction is permitted for estate or inheritance taxes paid from the estate.

What about joint property? If the decedent died owning property jointly with another, the portion of the value of the property that is included in the estate and subject to tax depends on a couple of factors. First, if the joint owner is a spouse, half of the value is included in decedent's estate. If both spouses are liable on the mortgage note, how much of the mortgage is deductible? One-half is deductible — the same proportion of the value of the property that is includible. If the jointly held property was owned by the decedent and sister, and both the decedent and sister were liable on the mortgage note, then if the whole property value was included in the decedent's estate because the decedent furnished all the consideration for the acquisition of the joint property, the whole value of the unpaid mortgage is permitted as a deduction.

Many wills contain a "boilerplate" direction to the executor to pay all the decedent's debts. This is actually unnecessary because the executor or administrator is required by law to pay the decedent's debts. Often it is included just as a guidepost for an unsophisticated executor. A general direction in the will to pay debts does not mean that the executor has to pay off mortgages. Care should be taken if one wishes different beneficiaries to receive different parcels of real estate. The decedent's intentions about the debt on the real estate should be clarified in the will.

Creditors usually have several years to make their claims. When a person dies, notice to creditors is made by publication in newspapers as ordered by the Register of Wills. Creditors have one year to make a claim against the estate; after that, they must pursue their claim against the beneficiaries. Executors are very reluctant to distribute estate assets before the expiration of one year because creditors could come forward after distribution and then the executor would be personally liable to the creditor.

Generation Skipping Transfer Tax

There is a federal estate tax which applies to transfers of property on death. There is a federal gift tax which applies to lifetime transfers of property.

But that isn't enough. There is yet another federal transfer tax — the Generation Skipping Transfer Tax. This tax applies in addition to the estate tax and/or gift tax and has an exemption after 2003 equal to the Estate Tax Exclusion Amount. Since the exemption is so high, most people will not have to worry about this tax. However, for those with assets over the exemption amount, the tax must be reckoned with as it can wipe out your estate.

Here is an example: Let's assume our decedent has assets well in excess of the $5.34 million exemption amount and he leaves them all to grandchildren. His children are well taken care of and he wants to pass property to the next generation instead of giving it to his children. If he gave it to his children, it would be subjected to estate tax again in their estates before reaching the grandchildren. If the decedent's estate is $8,000,000 and death occurred in the year 2014, there was $3,001,800 in federal estate tax, $360,000 in Pennsylvania inheritance tax, and $1,064,000 for the generation skipping transfer tax. That's a combined tax bill of $4,425,800 on the $8 million. Decedent died with $8 million and the beneficiaries got $3,574,200. Ouch!

Want to hear something worse? Let's assume the $8 million was in an IRA payable to a grandchild. Now the grandchild owes income tax, too, on the whole $8 million! The grandchild could end up literally with nothing, or worse, be in a negative position. Sounds crazy doesn't it? But it is true.

The policy behind the generation skipping tax is to make sure that the government gets a transfer tax at each generation level. In the ordinary course, people usually leave their assets to their children. When the property passes to the decedent's children, it is subject to estate tax (or if it is transferred to them during life, it is subject to gift tax). The children, in turn, leave it to their issue, and on a child's death, the estate tax is paid again, and so forth and so on.

For hundreds of years, the very wealthy have avoided this tax at each generation level by making trusts. Instead of giving property to children, the decedent had created a trust. This pays income to children for their lifetimes, then to grandchildren, and then to great-grandchildren. You've heard of "trust fund kids?" Those are the children and grandchildren who are the beneficiaries of these arrangements. As each generation died off there were no federal transfer taxes. Congress decided to close this "loophole" by enactment of the generation skipping tax. Now, if such a trust is created, to the extent the amount of property exceeds the $5,340,000 exemption, when each generation dies off, a 48 percent tax is payable to make up for the fact that the government isn't getting estate tax.

Unfortunately, the tax has broad applicability, and lots of ordinary estate planning dispositions can fall into the generation skipping tax trap. Most planners try to take advantage of the $5,340,000 exemption by planning for its use and then avoiding any generation skipping taxable event in the rest of the plan. A common recommendation is for the funding of a $5,340,000 generation skipping trust, either during life or at death, in order to use the exemption and take advantage of the ability to "skip" taxes for generations on the exemption amount.

This technique is often referred to as a "Dynasty Trust." The exemption amount is set aside in a trust for the maximum permissible time period. The trust benefits successive generations. The first beneficiaries are the donor's or decedent's children who can receive the income and principal at the trustee's discretion. Next would be grandchildren, great-grandchildren, and so on. The terms of the trust can be very flexible and can be custom designed to fit any individual family's needs and desires.

The maximum permissible existence for such a trust used to be governed in Pennsylvania by an arcane common law rule called the Rule Against Perpetuities. The Pennsylvania legislature has repealed the rule (in most instances) and now your Dynasty Trust can last literally forever! Many people create trust in Delaware to take advantage of other favorable laws. All that is needed to take advantage of Delaware's rule is to have a Delaware Trustee. Delaware's professional trustees have been marketing this idea — and it's a good one.

Gate's Book Offers a Different Perspective on the Estate Tax

> *What is most important for democracy is not that great fortunes should not exist, but that great fortunes should not remain in the same hands.*
>
> Alexis de Tocqueville

I bring to your attention this book: *Wealth and Our Commonwealth: Why America Should Tax Accumulated Fortunes* by William H. Gates, Sr. and Chuck Collins, Foreword by Paul Volcker, 193 pp., Beacon Press: 2003, $25.00, ISBN 080704718x.

William H. Gates, Sr., father of the richest man in the world and one of the founding members of an organization called Responsible Wealth, is a co-chairman of the Bill and Melinda Gates Foundation in Seattle.

Chuck Collins is a co-founder and program director of United for a Fair Economy and Responsible Wealth (*http://www.responsiblewealth.org*) and the great-grandson of meat packer Oscar Mayer. Collins gave away his inheritance at the age of 26. On Valentine's Day 2001, The New York Times published a front page article about Responsible Wealth's campaign to oppose the Bush administration's push for wholesale repeal of the estate tax. The paper called it the "billionaire backlash." There is something weird about the billionaires begging to be taxed. Seems like a simple solution would be for billionaires just to bequeath as much of their estate as they wanted to the federal government — that's what Oliver Wendell Holmes did. Why impose a tax?

Gates and Collins take the position that repeal of the estate tax is an economically and morally bankrupt idea. The Gates name alone will probably assure book sales. Fear not, all of the authors' proceeds from the sale of this book go to supporting efforts to preserve the estate tax.

Keep in mind that only 2% of estates pay any estate tax at all; and only 1/10 of 1% (.001%) of the total estates are responsible for generating 50% of the total estate tax revenue collected. It really is only a tax on the very wealthy. Because of the upcoming huge intergenerational wealth transfer, the authors estimate that the repeal of the estate tax will cost $850 billion in tax revenue over the next 20 years.

So where does the pressure for repeal come from if the billionaires want to be taxed? According to Gates and Collins, the Gallo Wine family, the Mars Candy family, and the Association of Independent Newspapers.

While the book does a good job of reviewing the history and policy arguments for the estate tax, its polemical style leads it to overstate the case. Nowhere is it mentioned that along with the administration's repeal of the estate tax comes the return of "carry-over basis," a monster first enacted in 1976. Congress came to its senses and repealed it before its 1980 implementation date. This time, carry-over basis is slated to become law in 2010. Assets in the hands of the beneficiary will have the same basis they had in the hands of the decedent, as opposed to a step-up in cost basis to date of death value. Thus, appreciation will be subject to capital gains tax, instead of estate tax. I wonder why Gates and Collins don't mention this? And they fail to take into account the extra capital gains tax that would be generated by carry-over basis when they project the loss of revenue occasioned by the repeal of the estate tax.

The authors repeatedly refer to insurance as prepaying estate tax. They have obviously been taken in by the insurance industry's sales pitch. Insurance, like any other investment, is an asset. Using insurance to pay tax means your assets are reduced. There is no magic to it.

The book debunks the myth that the estate tax hurts "family farmers." The authors claim that when reporters searched for these alleged victims, that is, families who were forced to sell the farm to pay estate tax, not a *single one* could be found. The American Farm Bureau Federation, when asked, could not point to a single case in the entire United States of a family farm lost due to the estate tax. Ironically, politicians who cry foul over the estate tax on behalf of farmers have opposed other legislation that would actually have helped the family farm. Farmers face many inequities and injustices, but the estate tax is not one of them.

What about family businesses? Gates and Collins point out that a very wide range of companies call themselves family businesses such as Gallo Wine, Blethen Newspapers, Mars Candy, L.L. Bean, the Dorrances of Campbell's Soup, and the Johnsons of Johnson Wax. These "family businesses" employ thousands of people and are worth hundreds of millions of dollars. The heirs of these families are not poor souls whose livelihood is being taxed away.

A lot of small family businesses do fail in subsequent generations, but it's not because of the estate tax. The estate tax is the scapegoat for a multitude of reasons why their businesses fail. According to Gates and Collins, studies have found that 77% of business owners could pay estate tax without borrowing or having it affect their business. The estate tax is planned for. Most pay liabilities out of insurance and other liquid assets. There are already relief provisions for the payment of the estate tax over a 14-year period, with interest only paid in the first four years.

While individual effort is indispensable for building wealth, there are no "self-made" millionaires. Financial success for the millionaires in our midst is a product of being born in the United States, where education and research are subsidized, where there is an orderly market, where property rights are given protection, and where the private sector gets tremendous benefits from public investment. The authors ask: "What's wrong with people who accumulate $20 million or $100 million or $500 million putting a third of that back into the place that made possible the enormous accumulation of wealth for them? What is it worth to be an American?"

The Saga of the Pennsylvania Sponge Tax

> *The art of taxation consists in so plucking the goose as to obtain the largest amount of feathers with the least possible amount of hissing.*
>
> Jean-Baptiste Colbert

In June 2002, President George W. Bush signed tax legislation passed by Congress that claimed to cut the federal estate tax. I say claimed, because while it is true the nominal estate tax rates were cut, it was accomplished by phasing out the state death tax credit and thus reducing the amount of tax going to the states in revenue sharing. This resulted in actually increasing the estate tax collections of the federal government. Combined federal and state death taxes are reduced, not because the federal tax is less, but because the states are given less through federally allowed state tax credits. It is not true that the IRS will collect estate tax at a lower rate. It just seemed that way.

The plucking of this goose occurred when the exemption from the application of the federal estate tax was raised, plus the top tax bracket was put on a long-term reduction. Nobody hissed because they didn't understand it. The various state departments of revenue figured it out, and the hissing began.

Pennsylvania has joined a long list of states that have changed their own death tax systems to restore the revenue taken away by the fed's actions. The states have been passing legislation to keep their death taxes at the same level regardless of the state death tax credit actually allowed on the federal estate tax.

For large estates, the IRS taxed at 55 cents on the dollar. But, Congress used to say that it wasn't fair for an estate to have to pay federal tax on money used to pay state death taxes. In order to give some equity, Congress allowed a credit against the federal tax for the death tax payable to the state. The upper limit of the credit was determined by a bracketed table, rising from zero up to sixteen percent so that the states couldn't say that their death tax was equal to the federal tax and scoop up all of the revenue. The states were no dummies, and seeing this as the ultimate in revenue sharing, all passed estate tax laws that insured that the state's share of the death taxes would equal the maximum credit allowed against the federal estate tax. In general, the IRS got 39 cents and the states 16 cents of every dollar.

When the federal estate tax "cut" was passed, the state death tax credit was scheduled to be phased out by 2005. I guess Congress changed their minds about the fairness of paying federal tax on money you use to pay state tax. Now, apparently, that is OK. In 2003 the IRS got 38 cents on the dollar, and the states 12 cents on the dollar, a total drop of one percent from the IRS point of view, but a four percent drop from the state point of view. The following years will see the IRS actually getting more than before the tax cut, ignoring the raising of the tax free floor, a reasonable assumption for very large estates.

The states ended up paying for the tax cut. One by one, the states are rewriting their death tax laws so that they will continue to levy the old amount. The estate, not the state, will end up funding the IRS tax "cut." So now it is clear, there will be an overall increase in death taxes, not a cut at all. Who didn't know that would happen?

Pennsylvania's legislature has passed House Bill 1848 which became Act 89 of 2002. The very skillful artistry of the General Assembly's plucking of the goose is to be at once admired and despised. Section 9117 of Title 73 of the Pennsylvania Code is the section that levies the state estate tax, or sponge tax. That section was not changed in Act 89. What was changed was section 2102 which lists the definitions for the affected section. An addition was made as follows: "... unless specifically provided otherwise, any reference in this article to the Internal Revenue Code of 1986 shall mean the Internal Revenue Code of 1986 (Public Law 99-514, 26 U.S.C. Section 1 et.seq.) as amended to June 1, 2001."

That's it. That's the change. And that is what causes the tax increase. Very sneaky. I wonder how many legislators who voted for this knew what it did?

Those last few words, "as amended to June 1, 2001", mean that Pennsylvania would assess the Pennsylvania estate tax at the rates that the IRS said was fair before the last tax cut legislation went into effect.

What effect does this have? An estate of ten million dollars will see increases in taxes over the next four years of 5.5, 11, 13, and 4 percent. If a billionaire dies here in 2004, he would be looking at a 21 percent bigger tax bill than if Pennsylvania had done nothing.

One thing the five magic words didn't change is the trigger that starts the sponge tax. Pennsylvania law still says that a sponge tax is triggered by payment of estate taxes to the IRS. That means no Pennsylvania sponge tax will be due until a federal estate tax is paid. Right now, the threshold amount for paying federal estate is $5 million. But it's only 2005, so that might still change. Hisssssssssss. The sponge tax change has been undone, meaning the five magic words were removed. The State Constitution made graduated taxes illegal. Until the IRS changes tax law again, there will be no sponge tax in Pennsylvania.

Why the States Really Don't Like the Current Federal Estate Tax Law

The states are not happy with the current federal estate tax law. While the new law gives income and death tax relief to many, the states are footing the bill for death tax cutbacks for the first three years. The reduction in the states' revenue is an unintended, but costly, consequence of the federal tax reform.

The result is unintended because the legislators didn't understand how the federal estate tax and state death taxes are intertwined.

The federal tax is an estate tax, based on the net value of an estate which was owned by the decedent. Every state also has an estate tax. A few states, like Pennsylvania and New York, also have an inheritance tax, an excise tax based on both the amount received as an inheritance and the degree of relationship the inheritor bears to the decedent.

The state-level estate tax is sometimes called the slack tax, or the sponge tax, or the pick-up tax. Whatever you call it, the state estate tax is a revenue sharing device. This tax has been a painless way for states to get tax revenue because the sponge tax doesn't cost the grieving family one extra dime — it simply shifts tax revenue from the federal government's estate tax collections to the states' coffers.

This has been, until the current law was passed, quite a deal for the states. A large estate would pay 55 cents on the dollar in federal tax, but get a credit of 16 cents on the dollar for the tax it had to pay to the state. The federal government took the heat for having a 55% top tax rate, but, in fact, at the top bracket the federal government got 39% and the state got 16%.

Now the current federal legislation changes things. The credit for state death taxes allowed on federal estate tax returns was phased out over three years, with the credit being 75% of the table value (the value for 2001) in 2002. The credit was 50% in 2003, and 25% in 2004.

In 2005 there was a huge change. Everything a state charges in death taxes is deducted from the federal gross estate instead of being a credit against the federal estate tax. What this means is that federal estate tax rate actually is increasing.

In 2002, even though the official federal maximum rate dropped from 55% to 50%, the split at the top bracket was 38% to the feds and 12% to the states. In 2003, the split was 41% to the feds and 8% to the states. In 2004, 44% to the feds and 4% to the states. Remember, under the old law the split was 39% to the feds and 16% to the states.

Haven't they been telling us the federal estate tax rate is going down? Over the three years (2002, 2003, 2004), the federal estate tax effective rate actually climbed, at the expense of the states' revenues. The states are footing that bill.

What happened in 2005? The amount paid to the states became a deduction on the federal estate tax return. Now, there is no dollar for dollar reduction in federal taxes for estate taxes paid as there was with the credit. The revenue sharing aspect is much diminished with a deduction instead of a credit.

How much does this hurt the states?

In Pennsylvania, for the fiscal year ending July 1999, according to the Governor's Budget Office, the sponge tax produced .2% of the general fund revenue, $40 million. Pennsylvania's inheritance tax produces about 4% of the state's revenue. (Pennsylvania's inheritance tax levies a zero percent tax for a spouse's inheritance. Lineal relatives like children pay 4.5% and siblings pay 12%. Other beneficiaries pay 15%.)

However, many states have adopted the sponge tax as their only death tax. These states are going to get hit harder, as a major source of revenue dramatically decreases.

How are the states going to make up the shortfall? Increase state death taxes? That would be my guess. In fact, some states, like New

York and New Jersey, passed legislation requiring executors to pay an estate tax as if it were 2001. Some states, like Pennsylvania, tried that, but then state constitution level tax clause struck it down.

> *It will be of little avail to the people that the laws are made by men of their own choice, if the laws be so voluminous that they cannot be read, or so incoherent that they cannot be understood; if they be repealed or revised before they are promulgated, or undergo such incessant changes that no man who knows what the law is today can guess what it will be tomorrow.*

The Federalist Papers No. 62, at 2:190 (1788)

PENNSYLVANIA VS. THE FEDS

Life Insurance Death Benefits

Many of you have probably heard that life insurance death benefits are completely tax free. While it is true that the death benefit will escape many taxes, it does not escape them all. The death benefit paid on a life insurance policy is not subject to federal or state income tax. Except in very rare circumstances, there will not be any income tax due on the death benefit. The death benefit also is not subject to Pennsylvania inheritance tax. For Pennsylvania inheritance tax purposes, the proceeds of life insurance policies are exempt.

Prior to 1982, if life insurance was payable to the estate, it was subject to Pennsylvania inheritance tax. If the insurance was payable to a named beneficiary, it was exempt from Pennsylvania inheritance tax. For this reason it was very common for a pre-1982 estate plan to set up a separate life insurance trust just to receive the death benefit from life insurance policies. If you have one of these trusts, it is well past time to review your plan. Since 1982 life insurance death benefits have been exempt from Pennsylvania inheritance tax regardless of whether or not the estate is a beneficiary.

The catch is the federal estate tax. There are two circumstances under which the death benefit may be subject to federal estate tax. First, if the death benefit is paid to the estate of the insured, then the whole amount of the death benefit is included in the estate and subject to estate tax. (Note that Pennsylvania abandoned this position in 1982.) Second, if the deceased insured owned the policy on the date of death, the whole amount of the death benefit is included in the estate and subject to estate tax.

Most people name individuals as beneficiaries, so the death benefit is not payable to an estate. The federal estate taxation of the insurance is usually governed by the second consideration, that is, who is the owner of the policy. Do you know the owner of your insurance policies?

The owner is the person who can cancel the policy, name the beneficiary, borrow against the cash value, and exercise any policy options for the application of dividends or conversion features. Very often the insured is the owner. If the insured is the owner, then when the insured dies, the value of the death benefit is subject to estate taxation in the insured's estate.

Whether any federal estate tax is due depends on the size of the total estate (the current exemption amount is $5.34 million) and to whom the death benefit is payable. If the death benefit is paid to the surviving spouse, it will qualify for the marital deduction and no federal estate tax will be due, although of course, the proceeds become part of the surviving spouse's estate.

Obviously the ownership of life insurance policies is an important factor in how much estate tax is due. Changing the ownership of life insurance policies is an important estate planning technique. If your estate is over the $5.34 million exemption amount and there is no surviving spouse, you can expect roughly one-half of the death benefit to be paid to the federal government in estate tax. It is easy to avoid this, so make sure you get competent advise if you are in this situation.

Many policy owners decided to transfer the ownership of policies to their children. Another popular alternative is the transfer of the ownership of the policies to an Irrevocable Life Insurance Trust or "ILIT." If this technique is used, the ILIT becomes the owner and beneficiary of the policies. The death benefit, when paid to the trust, is not subject to estate tax, assuming the insured survives the transfer by three years.

For the change in ownership of the life insurance policy to succeed in removing the death benefit from the federal taxable estate, the transferring owner must survive the transfer by three years. If death occurs within three years of the transfer, the decedent is deemed to be the owner of the policy and the full value of the death benefit is includable.

This so-called three year rule is not applicable in Pennsylvania since life insurance death benefits are exempt from Pennsylvania inheritance tax in any event.

If the children or the ILIT acquires a new policy insuring the decedent's life, rather than receiving the insurance policy by transfer, then the three year rule does not apply. The death benefit is out of the estate from the start. This is a very important distinction. The reason the three year rule is inapplicable is that the ownership of the insurance policy was not transferred; the insurance policy was purchased by the children or by the Trustee of the ILIT.

Joint Property

Jointly held property is very common, but its taxation is commonly misunderstood. There are many aspects to consider. First, let's look at the property interest itself. When a joint owner dies, the joint property does not go through probate. The title to jointly owned property passes to the surviving joint owners at the moment of death. A will has no effect on joint property. If the decedent left a will leaving his estate equally to his three children, but had all of his accounts and investments titled in joint names with only one of the children, the will is of no effect. The joint property all passes to the single child who is the surviving joint owner.

Maybe an account is made joint merely so that one of the children can write checks for the contributor. This is sometimes called a convenience account. If that is the case, then the account is made part of the residuary estate, and follows distribution according to the residuary clause in the will. If there is no will and no surviving spouse, a convenience account would be distributed equally among the surviving children.

Property owned by a decedent jointly with others is subject to both federal estate tax and Pennsylvania inheritance tax. For federal estate tax purposes what portion of the joint property is subject to federal estate tax? If the joint property is held jointly by a husband and wife, including property held by the spouses as tenants by the entirety; then one-half the value of the property is included in the first deceased owner's estate.

If the property is jointly held with someone other than a spouse, a contribution rule is followed for the federal estate tax. If the decedent contributed all of the funds for acquisition of the asset, the whole value of the asset is included in the decedent's estate. Here is an example. Dad had CDs at Local Bank in which he had invested his savings. He puts the account in joint names with daughter. Dad dies. Even though daughter was a joint owner, she contributed nothing to the acquisition so 100% of the value of the CDs is included in Dad's estate.

Now let's reverse the situation. Suppose daughter predeceased Dad. Since she had contributed nothing to the acquisition of the joint CDs no part of the value of the joint CDs is subject to federal estate tax in her estate.

What is the effect on income tax basis? Property that is included in the decedent's federal gross estate gets a step-up in basis to the date of death value. (Actually it could be a step-down in basis. Regardless of the decedent's actual basis, the new basis is the date of death value, or perhaps the alternate valuation date value which is six months later.) When the federal income tax basis of property gets stepped up on death, there is a great income tax benefit. No one ever pays income tax on that gain.

For spousal joint tenancies created before 1977, there is a special rule which may be applicable. There have been a series of cases, beginning with the Gallenstein case (975 F.2d 286), which have provided a different result for spousal joint tenancies created before 1977. Gallenstein (and its progeny) holds that the full value of jointly held spousal property is includable in the estate of the spouse who contributed to the purchase of the property. This means that a surviving spouse and holder of such an interest, who did not contribute toward the purchase of the property, is entitled to a full step-up in basis for the property upon the death of the contributing spouse. This can be a very important benefit. Since there is an unlimited marital deduction, no federal estate tax will be payable no matter how much of the jointly held assets value is included in the decedent's estate. The result of applying Gallenstein is still no federal estate tax, but double the step-up in basis. Without Gallenstein, the surviving spouse gets a step-up in only half of the property. Gallenstein gives a full step-up. If you are a surviving spouse you may be able to take advantage of Gallenstein. Consult your tax advisor.

For Pennsylvania inheritance tax purposes, only the proportionate ownership of jointly held property is subject to tax. Let's say Mom owns the house jointly with daughter and son. Mom dies. Only one-third of the value of the house is subject to Pennsylvania inheritance tax. Since the house passes by right of survivorship to daughter and son, this one-third share of the house's value is taxed at the rate of 4½%.

There is an important exception to this rule. If the property was put into joint names within one year of the decedent's death, it is taxed as if it were titled the way it was before the transfer to joint names. In our last example, if Dad owned a house and put the house in joint names with daughter and son six months before he died, the whole value of the house would be subject to the Pennsylvania inheritance tax at the 4½% rate. The house still passes to daughter and son by right of survivorship; it's just that the whole value is taxed instead of one-third since Dad died within a year of making the transfer.

Who pays the estate and inheritance tax? It depends. If there is a will it may have a provision that specifies whether or not the tax on joint property is paid from the estate or whether or not the surviving joint owner must pay the tax. If there is no will, or if the will is silent on the subject, Pennsylvania law requires that the surviving joint owner pay the tax.

What happens to your Pennsylvania basis when you are the surviving joint owner? Nothing. There is no step-up because Pennsylvania does not view this as inherited property, and only inherited property is entitled to a step-up in Pennsylvania basis.

Retirement Plans and IRAs

The federal estate tax applies to almost all retirement plans and IRAs. In general, the balance in your account or the value of your benefit is subject to federal estate tax. If your spouse is your beneficiary, the retirement plan or IRA may also qualify for the marital deduction and no tax will be due. However, the full value of the benefits is included in the estate and is potentially subject to the federal estate tax. If your spouse is not your beneficiary and your taxable estate is less than the federal exemption, $5.34 million in 2024, there is still no estate tax.

There are two very limited circumstances where a decedent's retirement benefits (other than IRAs) are not subject to federal estate tax at all. Many moons ago, before 1982, all retirement benefits were 100% exempted from the estate tax. From 1982 to 1984 the first $100,000 of retirement benefits were exempt from estate tax. Post 1984, all such benefits are taxable unless one of two grandfather rules applies. A decedent who separated from service before 1983 and died after 1984 without having changed the form of benefit before his death is entitled to have the entire value of the retirement benefit exempt from federal estate tax in his estate. A decedent who separated from service after 1982 but before 1985 and did not change the form of benefit is entitled to a $100,000 exclusion. Changing a beneficiary is permitted. It is the change of the form of benefits that causes loss of the grandfathered exclusions. If you might qualify for one of these grandfathered exclusions you should be very cautious about making any changes to your benefit selection.

If the retirement benefit is exempt from the federal estate tax, then it is also exempt from Pennsylvania inheritance tax.

For Pennsylvania inheritance tax purposes, whether or not a traditional IRA is taxable depends on the age of the decedent at the date of death and whether or not the decedent was disabled. If the decedent was over age 59½ or disabled at any age, then the full amount of the IRA could be withdrawn by the decedent and is not subject to the 10% penalty. Since the full amount can be withdrawn with no penalty, it is deemed "available" to the owner and is fully subject to Pennsylvania inheritance tax. If the decedent was under 59½ at death and not disabled; then the IRA is not subject to inheritance tax because the state interprets the 10% penalty as making the IRA proceeds "not available" to the decedent.

For a Roth IRA, there are additional considerations for determining whether or not it is subject to Pennsylvania inheritance tax. A Roth IRA is one to which contributions are not deductible and distributions from the Roth IRA are income tax free if certain conditions are met. The contributions are always able to be withdrawn without tax and without penalty. For earnings on contributions, there is no 10% penalty after the assets are held by the Roth for five years and if withdrawals are made after the owner attained age 59½ or is disabled. (There are a couple of other minor exceptions such as funds for a home purchase under certain conditions.) For the contributions to the Roth, Pennsylvania inheritance tax is payable because these can be withdrawn at any time without tax and without penalty — they are fully available and thus subject to Pennsylvania inheritance tax. For earnings, if the five-year mark is not passed, then if the owner is under 59½ and not disabled, the accumulated earnings are subject to the 10% penalty upon withdrawal and thus the accumulated earnings are not subject to Pennsylvania inheritance tax. If the owner of the Roth IRA is over 59½ or is disabled, then the accumulated earnings are subject to Pennsylvania inheritance tax because they can be withdrawn without penalty and are thus "available" to the owner.

There are special exemption provisions that apply to public school employee's retirement benefits and state employee's retirement benefits so that these types of benefits are not subject to the Pennsylvania inheritance tax. (Note that these plans are not exempted from the federal estate tax.)

For other retirement plans, including pension plans, stock bonus plans, profit sharing plans, 401(k) plans, and HR 10 (Keogh) plans, Pennsylvania looks at a number of criteria. Retirement benefits are subject to Pennsylvania inheritance tax if the decedent had any one or more of the following rights or powers: (1) the right to withdraw benefits, including the right to withdraw only upon payment of a penalty (providing the penalty is less than 10% of the withdrawal), (2) the right to borrow from the plan, (3) the right to assign the benefits of the plan to another, (4) the right to pledge the plan and/or its benefits, (5) the right to anticipate the benefits (other than in regular monthly installments), or (6) the right, by contract or otherwise, to materially alter the provisions of the plans.

A decedent whose only rights under the plan were to designate a beneficiary and to receive monthly payment is not considered as having the right to possess, enjoy, or anticipate. The instructions for filling out the inheritance form state that "[t]herefore, the possession of either the right to designate a beneficiary or the right to receive regular monthly payments under the plan, either alone or together, will not subject the plan to Inheritance Tax, as long as no other rights exist."

When Are Life Time Gifts Subject to Death Taxes?

Ever since there has been an estate tax people have tried to avoid it by making gifts during life. The logic is clear. If the estate tax applies to what you own when you die, then give everything away before you die, just as advised in the title of a currently popular book, *"Die Broke."* Congress caught on to that planning technique soon after the enactment of the estate tax and enacted a gift tax, too. On the federal level, we have what is called a "unified transfer tax system." That is, a federal estate tax and a federal gift tax that fit together and have the same rates and exemption amount. The estate tax and gift tax are designed to fit together. The estate tax takes over where the gift tax leaves off.

If you make gifts during life that exceed the $14,000 annual exclusion, then you begin using up your exemption. Any exemption left when you die is available against the estate tax. It is often good planning to use up the exemption during life since assets may be passed through the transfer tax system at a lower value.

For example, if you make a $50,000 gift to your daughter, then you have used $37,000 of your $5.34 million exemption.

Pennsylvania has an inheritance tax that applies to property passing at death, but Pennsylvania does not have a gift tax. In order to catch transfers made before death, the inheritance tax has a one-year look back. If the decedent made gifts within one year of death, part of the value of the gifts is added back to the estate for determining the amount of the inheritance tax. Gifts within one year of death are included to the extent that they exceed $3,000 per recipient. The year is calculated by counting back 12 months before the date of death; it is not the calendar year.

For example, if the decedent gave $10,000 to each of his 6 grandchildren and then passed away six months later, $7,000 of each of the six gifts would be subject to inheritance tax at the 4½% rate.

Pennsylvania also applies the one-year rule to property placed in joint names. In general, for Pennsylvania inheritance tax purposes, when property is jointly held by the decedent and one or more others, the amount subject to inheritance tax is only the decedent's proportionate share. For example, if a bank account is held jointly with a child, then only one-half of the value of the account is subject to inheritance tax in the decedent's estate. The full value of the account is subject to inheritance tax if the account was put into joint names within one year of death. The rule applies to all jointly held property including real estate that is transferred into joint names.

Before 1981, the federal estate tax had a similar look-back for gifts except that the look-back period was three years. Gifts made within three years of death used to be deemed made in contemplation of death and brought back into the estate for federal estate tax purposes. That is no longer the case; however, there are a few instances where the three year rule applies. The most well-known instance where it applies is in gifts of life insurance policies. If you transfer the ownership of a life insurance policy on your life within three years of death, then the full value of the death benefit is subject to estate tax. The theory behind this is that the gift tax value of the policy and the estate tax value of the policy are very different. The gift tax value is something called the interpolated terminal reserve value which is very close to the cash value, or in the case of term insurance, the replacement cost. The estate tax value, on the other hand, is the full value of the death benefit. In order for the gift tax and the estate tax to "fit" together, it would not be fair if the transfer tax value of a life insurance policy before death was $2,000, and the day after death, $200,000. Because of this broad disparity in gift tax value compared to death tax value, any transfer of a life insurance policy within three years of the decedent's death is brought back into the estate for federal estate tax purposes so that the estate tax applies to the full value of the death benefit of the policy. This is why it is so important when setting up an irrevocable insurance trust that the trustee of the trust apply for and acquire the policy instead of the insured.

Except for a few very arcane exceptions, gifts other than life insurance within three years of death (or any time before death) are not subject to federal estate tax.

When Must a Surviving Spouse Pay Death Taxes?

When I first studied the federal estate tax in law school I was shocked to find, at that time, that a surviving spouse had to pay estate tax on 50% of the assets inherited from a deceased spouse. It was almost unbelievable that a surviving spouse would have to pay a significant amount of tax just because her husband had died. Apparently enough people were shocked because in 1981 the law was changed and now any amount of property can pass from a decedent to a surviving spouse completely free of federal estate tax.

Today, all property that passes to a surviving spouse is free of federal estate tax. Of course, there is a catch. (Isn't there always?) The law arrives at this result by including all of the decedent's property in his gross estate, and then giving the estate an unlimited deduction for all property passing to the surviving spouse. This is called the "marital deduction."

There are numerous qualification requirements for the marital deduction including that the surviving spouse be a U.S. citizen. If the property passes from the decedent to a trust for the benefit of the surviving spouse, it may qualify for the marital deduction even though it doesn't pass outright to the spouse if the trusts meet certain requirements. Professional assistance is definitely required for creating these types of trusts.

In addition to a marital deduction, all decedent's estates can pass the first $5 million in assets to beneficiaries free of the federal estate tax. It is a very common estate planning technique for a married couple to create a trust to use the first spouse's $5 million exemption from tax and then dispose of the balance of the estate assets by passing them to the surviving spouse in a way that qualifies for the marital deduction.

Pennsylvania Inheritance Tax

In Pennsylvania, up until 1995 there has been a tax on property passing to the surviving spouse. From 1967 to June 1994 the rate was 6%. For a six-month period from June 1994 to January 1995 the rate was 3%. Since January 1995 the rate has been 0%. When property passing to a surviving spouse was taxable, joint property was exempt so that spouses who held everything jointly could escape the tax. Pennsylvania was the last state in the union to abolish the death tax on property passing to a spouse. The tax used to be called the "widow's tax" and was very unpopular indeed.

Since 1995 property passing to a surviving spouse in Pennsylvania is taxed at the zero rate. For outright transfers, this is clear. Then the property passes from the decedent to a trust for the benefit of the surviving spouse, the situation is different. Property in a trust is held for several beneficiaries. Typically the trust will continue for the life of the surviving spouse and then distribute to children and/or grandchildren. Transfers to children are subject to inheritance tax at the 4½% rate. Thus the Pennsylvania Department of Revenue must collect a tax on the property that ultimately passes to the children.

The question is, though, how much will the surviving spouse receive and how much will the children receive? Sometimes the amounts can be determined by actuarial calculation. For example, if the spouse is to receive all income and the children receive the remainder, an actuarial factor based on the surviving spouse's age will determine what portion of the trust is taxed at the spouse's zero rate and what portion is taxed at the children's 4½% rate.

Other trusts, however, may contain various contingencies. For example, trusts may provide that the trustee may invade principal for the spouse, or for the children. In these cases, the actuarial calculation is not sufficient and subjective factors come into play such as whether or not there are anticipated principal needs of the spouse and children, what other assets are available, what is the health and lifestyle of the surviving spouse and of the children.

If a contingency makes it impossible on the day of death to determine the rate of tax which will apply to future interests the estate may seek a "Future Interest Compromise." If the taxpayer does not seek a compromise, the Department of Revenue will assess tax at the highest rate at all points of uncertainty.

Another approach is available if the trust of the spouse is a "Sole Use Trust." If the trust is for the sole use of the spouse during his or her period of survivorship, then no inheritance tax is due on the first spouse's death and the whole value of the trust remaining on the surviving spouse's death is subject to inheritance tax on the death of the surviving spouse as if the surviving spouse transferred the trust at that time. The rate is the lesser of the rate that would apply on the first spouse's death or the surviving spouse's death.

The executor can elect to pay the inheritance tax at the time of the first spouse's death. This election to pay the inheritance tax on the remainder interest at the time of the first spouse's death may be advantageous from a tax planning point of view. The tax is paid on the present market value with a deduction for the actuarial value of the surviving spouse's interest rather than on a hopefully appreciated value at the time of the surviving spouse's death with no deduction for the surviving spouse's interest.

The Pennsylvania Legislature recently changed the definition of a sole use trust. House Bill 1848 which was approved by the governor on June 29, 2002 provides that for a trust to be a sole use trust, no person, including the transferee, may possess a power of appointment over the property. Trusts that give surviving spouses general or limited powers of appointment, and general or limited withdrawal powers, must be reviewed. The pay early election will not be available and the tax will have to be compromised.

Pennsylvania Inheritance Tax: Pay Now Or Pay Later?

When a person's assets pass to heirs at death, the IRS may or may not tax the transfer, depending on the size of the estate. This year, below $5.34 million, a federal return need not even be filed except for portability of exemption cases. The State is a different matter altogether. Pennsylvania has three tax brackets, but they depend not on the size of the estate but on the relationship of the heir to the decedent. Assets going to a spouse pay a zero percent tax, those to family members pay six percent, and those to anyone else pay a fifteen percent tax.

The zero percent tax paid on assets going to a spouse is really a deferral. The State correctly believes they'll get the six or fifteen percent tax when the surviving spouse dies; and the assets will be unspent, converted to other taxable assets, or even grown to a larger amount. Tax is deferred for surviving spouses because legislators get nervous thinking about a widow being forced out of her home by taxes with a film crew from 60 Minutes on her doorstep.

An option available for planning for the Pennsylvania Inheritance Tax is a spousal sole use trust. This is a trust created by a decedent solely for the benefit of a surviving spouse. With this kind of a trust, the executor can elect to pay taxes at the death of the first spouse so none will have to be paid later when the survivor dies. If it were a toss-up, few would do it, preferring to have more capital working to pay the surviving spouse more income during the rest of her life. But there's a benefit in paying early, enough of one so that many who can afford to pay early do so. Often, people learn of this option by exploring the topic with counsel.

The theory is that if the survivor kept the tax money, all income from the account would be drawn off by the survivor and spent, leaving only the original principal at the survivor's death. That's a generous assumption since hardly ever does a person spend every cent of income without accumulating something of value for their own estate years down the road. Cars, houses, books, art, investments all would increase the survivor's estate at death.

Then the time value of money is considered. If a surviving spouse is at an age where the life expectancy is twenty years, then the question becomes "What is the present value of this future $500,000 estate?" In other words, how much would a person have to put in the bank today earning interest at current rates to have $500,000 twenty years from now? Without delving into fancy mathematics, the answer is a little under $120,000. This assumes a rate of return of 7.4 percent. The twenty year life expectancy comes from the person's age and actuarial tables.

If the executor chooses to pay the tax now, then, instead of paying six percent tax on $500,000 when the surviving spouse dies, just six percent of $120,000 is paid now. All of you sharp readers are probably saying, so what — you could invest the tax on $120,000 and it would grow, if it earned 7.4 percent, to what the tax on $500,000 would be in twenty years. True. But this is a guaranteed 7.4 percent over twenty years. T-bills and municipal bonds don't pay nearly that much, plus, if the principal earns more than 7.4 percent, the excess will be free of state inheritance tax. The S&P 500 grows at about ten percent a year (on a long-term average) so it likely will produce more than the assumed rate.

But wait, there's more. There's paying now, and then there's paying early. If the estate pays taxes in three months rather than in the allowed nine months, there's a bonus. You get to deduct five percent off the tax bill. That's five percent for six months or ten percent on an annualized basis. This is a rare opportunity to get a guaranteed ten percent interest on a short-term investment.

If you have to pay the state anyway, why not pay the inheritance tax now instead of in the estate of the surviving spouse? And if you pay now, why not take advantage of the discount by paying within three months?

POSTMORTEM PLANNING

Electing Against the Will; You Can't Disinherit Your Spouse

What if your husband dies leaving a will that gives you very little? What can you do? In Pennsylvania a spouse cannot be disinherited. The surviving spouse is entitled to a certain portion of the deceased spouse's estate. If she does not receive it under the will, the surviving spouse has a right to "elect against the will."

It is the policy of the law to make sure that a surviving spouse does not become impoverished because of the loss of the support of the deceased spouse. It is also the policy of the law to reward the spouse's contribution to the financial success of the marriage. In a community property state, like California, the surviving spouse automatically owns half of the community property at the death of the spouse. In common law states, like Pennsylvania, the surviving spouse is entitled to whatever the state legislature has determined is a reasonable share. In most states this share is one-third or one-half. In Pennsylvania, the surviving spouse is entitled to one-third.

Marriage creates property rights. The right of the surviving spouse to inherit is one of them. While you can do lots of things in a will, you can't disinherit your spouse. If this is what you want to do, you and your prospective spouse or current spouse need to get a prenuptial agreement or a postnuptial agreement in which this right of inheritance is waived.

Whether the marriage lasts for one day or 50 years, the elective share is one-third. The one-third share is not limited to property acquired after the marriage, but applies to all of the deceased spouse's property interests, including assets brought into the marriage and gifts and inheritances from his side of the family. Whether the current spouse is the first, second, third, or later spouse, the current spouse is still entitled to the one-third share. (Earlier spouses lose their inheritance right upon divorce, even if they are named in a pre-divorce will.)

The surviving spouse is entitled to the one-third share even if divorce proceedings are pending. However, a spouse who for one year or more before the death of the deceased spouse has "willfully neglected or refused to perform the duty to support the other spouse," or who for one year or more has "willfully and maliciously deserted the other spouse" shall have no right of election, or even of receiving an intestate share.

The share is not paid automatically. There are specific procedural requirements. To claim the share, the surviving spouse must "elect" to take the share. Presumably a spouse will not make the election if he or she is satisfied with what she receives under the will. The spouse has six months from the date of probate of the deceased spouse's will to make this election. (If there is no probate, other procedures and time limits apply.) The election is made by filing a claim with the Clerk of the Orphan's Court in the county of the decedent's domicile.

How is the one-third share computed? If the election is made, the surviving spouse is entitled to one-third of the following items: (1) the decedent's probate property, that is, property that passes under the decedent's will (2) property from which the decedent was entitled to receive the income if that property was transferred by the decedent during the marriage, (3) property transferred by the decedent during life where the decedent could revoke the transfer and get the property back, or could withdraw or invade the principal of the property for the decedent's own benefit (for example, property in a revocable trust), (4) joint property owned with another to the extent the decedent could have conveyed or revoked the joint account, (5) annuity payments to the extent the annuity was purchased during the marriage and the decedent was receiving payments, and (6) gifts made within one year of death to the extent they exceed $3,000 per beneficiary.

The following property interests are not subject to the election: (1) any transfer made with the consent of the surviving spouse, (2) life insurance on the decedent's life, and (3) retirement plans (although many retirement plans other than IRAs must be paid to the surviving spouse unless the surviving spouse consented to a different beneficiary designation.)

The surviving spouse cannot have her cake and eat it too. If she makes this election for a one-third share, she is treated as if she disclaims everything that comes to her under the will and some property interests that pass to her outside of the will. For example, if she receives a house pursuant to the terms of the will, she can't elect a one-third share of the other assets and get the house. She must choose whether to take what comes to her under the will or what comes from the election. That is the choice: keep what you get, or give up what you get and elect a one-third share. If the deceased spouse purchased a life insurance policy with a death benefit payable to the surviving spouse, the value of this life insurance death benefit is set off against the surviving spouse's elective share. The surviving spouse can't collect both the life insurance and receive a one-third elective share. Similarly, joint property passing to the surviving spouse by operation of law, to the extent its value is from the decedent's contributions, is set off against the one-third elective share.

If you think you may be entitled to more from your deceased spouse's estate, it is essential to get prompt and competent legal advice. If you have agreed with your spouse not to make provisions for each other in your wills — you need a postnuptial agreement. The law of a spouse's elective share aims at equitable treatment — but it is always better to make your own plans rather than to rely on the rough justice of this statute.

Disclaimers

It's never too late to do estate planning. Even if the decedent did little or no estate planning, or worse, did bad estate planning, it may not be too late.

An important tool in postmortem estate planning is the disclaimer. A disclaimer is a beneficiary's written refusal to accept property he or she would receive due to the death of the decedent.

"Why would anyone refuse to accept a gift or inheritance?" you might ask. Refusal would be wise when the person receiving the property does not need it and there is a tax advantage to passing it to the person or persons who are next in line.

Here is an example: Let's say grandmother, who has lived until age 95, leaves a will dividing her estate equally among her children. Her children are now all in their 70s and have more than sufficient assets of their own. If grandmother's 70-year old son disclaims his inheritance it passes to that son's own children. The advantage of the son's making the disclaimer instead of accepting the inheritance from grandmother is that the son's own issue receive the inheritance and only one death tax is encountered, that is, the estate tax on the grandmother's estate. If the son accepts the inheritance and then it passes through the son's estate or son makes a gift of it, it passes through the transfer tax system twice — once in grandmother's estate and once in the son's.

Property that is disclaimed passes as if the person making the disclaimer had predeceased the decedent. For example, suppose decedent's will provides that everything passes to the spouse if living, but if not, then in equal shares to the children. If the surviving spouse disclaims, the property disclaimed will pass in equal shares to the children, as it would if the spouse had not survived the decedent.

Ordinarily, if the surviving spouse accepted the property and then gave it to the children, this transfer would be a gift and subject to the gift tax. If the disclaimer is "qualified," however, the property passes directly from the decedent to the children and there is no additional tax ramification.

For the disclaimer to be "qualified" it must meet the requirements of Internal Revenue Code Section 2518. A qualified disclaimer is one that is not treated as a gift. For the disclaimer to be qualified, the refusal to accept an interest in property must be in writing and must occur within nine months of the day the interest is transferred, in most cases, the date of death. For inherited property, the date of death generally begins the nine-month period. If the intended recipient has not accepted the interest or any benefit of the property, the disclaimed property passes to an alternate beneficiary under the decedent's will or trust.

In order for the disclaimer to be qualified, the disclaimer must be irrevocable, in writing, and delivered to the transferor of the interest, the executor or administrator, or the person in possession of the property no later than nine months after the date of death (no extensions). The person making the disclaimer must not have accepted any benefits (such as receiving the income) from the disclaimed property, the disclaimant must not direct the disposition of the disclaimed property and the disclaimant must have no benefit from the disclaimed property unless the disclaimant is the surviving spouse.

All too often people act in too much haste after a death and do not give due consideration to the tax planning opportunities available. Do not act hastily. By trying to deposit every uncashed check and claiming every bit of property you may be "accepting" a benefit and unwittingly forgoing your opportunity to make a disclaimer.

For jointly held property, in general, a qualified disclaimer must be made no later than nine months after the creation of the tenancy — not from the date of death of the first joint tenant. A special rule applies to joint bank, brokerage, and other investment accounts. In the case of the death of a joint owner of such an account, if the decedent could have unilaterally regained his own contributions from the account without the consent of the other cotenant, the transfer creating the survivor's interest in the decedent's share of the account occurs on the date of death of the deceased cotenant. Accordingly, if a surviving joint tenant desires to make a qualified disclaimer with respect to funds contributed by the deceased cotenant, the disclaimer must be made within nine months of the cotenant's death.

There are many situations where a disclaimer can be helpful. If the will or trust contains appropriate provisions, it is even possible for a surviving spouse to disclaim an interest in property even if it passes to a trust for her benefit. Disclaimers can be especially useful for IRAs and qualified plan benefits and the lineup of contingent beneficiaries. Trusts with drafting errors can sometimes be corrected using disclaimers.

Disclaimers are not for amateurs and there is no substitute for a careful consideration of all the advantages and disadvantages of a disclaimer in the particular circumstances. Before making a disclaimer, get professional advice.

Tax Elections

So you think you can do the estate and inheritance tax returns for Mother's estate by yourself? Maybe.

The forms for filing death tax returns look deceptively simple. They consist of a series of schedules for different types of property and deductions. Each schedule has a title at the top and then the rest of the page is left blank for you to list the property, deductions, and values. It's your basic *tabula rasa* (for the Latin-challenged, a blank slate).

What goes on the schedules and how the value is determined is the important part. To know this you have to have a clear and detailed understanding of both the federal estate tax and the Pennsylvania inheritance tax regulations. In addition, there are lots of tax elections that can be made that will change the tax effect for estate tax, inheritance tax, and income tax.

Making a plan to minimize estate, inheritance, and income taxes for the estate is a complex matter. Let's look at some of the elections just to give you an idea of the issues.

If the value of the estate declines, the executor may elect to value all assets as of the date six months after the date of death (or if disposed of at an earlier date, valued at the disposition date). This is called alternate valuation. It is available for the federal estate tax return but not the Pennsylvania inheritance tax return. This means the same assets could be reported at different values on the two returns.

The executor may choose a fiscal year for the estate and may make an election to have the decedent's estate and revocable trust taxed together as if they were one entity instead of two.

The executor chooses whether to take expenses of administration as deductions on the estate tax return or on the estate's income tax return. Yes, Virginia, the estate has to file an income tax return, too. While the assets are held in the estate, the income is taxable to the estate — which makes sense. The decedent is certainly not paying income tax anymore, and the beneficiaries don't have the money yet. The estate files a Form 1041 for federal income tax and Form PA-41 for Pennsylvania income tax.

The income tax rates that apply to the estate are the same as individual income tax rates except that the brackets are very compressed. An estate reaches the top bracket of 35% at just $9,950 of income while an individual doesn't get to the highest 35% bracket until there is $319,100 of income. This difference in income tax rates often makes it desirable to distribute income from the estate to the beneficiaries during the course of administration. Then the income can be taxed at beneficiaries' lower brackets. Planning for these distributions must take into account the estate's fiscal year, liquidity, and the tax situations of the beneficiaries.

Similarly, when to close the estate and when to pay the administration expenses, requires planning. This is an area where haste often causes more tax to be paid earlier.

Another choice for the executor to decide is whether to deduct payments for medical expenses on the decedent's final 1040 or on the estate tax return.

For Series E bonds the executor can elect to have accumulated interest taxed on the decedent's final return or on the estate's income tax return.

An election is available to qualify certain types of trusts for the marital deduction. This is called a "QTIP" election, not for the cotton swab, but for a "qualified terminable interest in property."

The executor is responsible for filing the decedent's final income tax return and the decedent's final gift tax return, if one is due. There are elections available here, too. One of them is whether or not to "split" gifts with the surviving spouse.

For Pennsylvania inheritance tax there is an election for certain trusts called spousal sole use trusts, whether to pay the inheritance tax on the first spouse's death or on the second spouse's death. This election involves an actuarial computation based on the survivor's life expectancy.

Then there is the family farm. The estate may qualify for special use valuation which allows the farm to be valued, under certain conditions, as working farmland instead of at its highest and best use which may be for development. To elect the farm value, the beneficiaries must continue to use it as a farm for 10 years and meet other technical requirements.

It is quite a challenge for the executor and his attorney to figure out which combination of elections and options will produce the best overall tax result for the estate. Obviously, paying less in tax increases what the beneficiaries receive.

This list of elections is not exhaustive and is not intended to teach you how to do this on your own. Thanks to our Senators and Representatives, we have an extremely complex system of tax laws governing estates. Don't try this at home — get professional help.

IRAs and Retirement Plans: S-T-R-E-T-C-H-I-N-G Out the Payments

IRA and qualified retirement plan distribution rules are maddeningly complex. Making the wrong choice can cost the beneficiary huge amounts of tax. Navigating the shoals between choices for distributions requires a skilled pilot.

IRAs and/or qualified retirement plans like 401(k)s are terrific tax shelters. They allow the deferral of income tax on the employee/owner's earnings that are contributed, and they also allow tax-free accumulation and reinvestment of investment earnings inside the plan until the amounts are withdrawn by the owner or a beneficiary.

Because of these valuable income tax advantages, it is usually the best plan for a beneficiary to stretch out the IRA payments over time to keep the tax-free, inside build-up going as long as possible and to spread the income tax out over a number of years, hopefully at lower brackets. This is what is referred to as a "stretch IRA."

Qualified retirement plans and 401(k) plans theoretically can be "stretch" plans, but usually the plan documents do not include payment stretch-outs for beneficiaries as an option. Much more flexibility in payout options for beneficiaries is obtained by rolling over these benefits into an IRA.

When the IRA or plan owner is deceased, the benefits pass to whoever is named as a beneficiary. The benefit is paid by contract. The owner's will does not effect who gets the benefit unless he has named no beneficiary at all. If no beneficiaries are named, or if all named beneficiaries have predeceased the owner, then the will governs its disposition. Having it payable to the estate is usually a bad choice because the estate beneficiaries lose the opportunity to "stretch out" the benefit. For small plans, an estate as beneficiary may be suitable.

If the IRA or qualified retirement plan is payable to a single individual, that person has a couple of choices. If the beneficiary is the surviving spouse, the decedent's IRA can be rolled over into the survivor's own IRA. No estate tax or inheritance tax would be payable and the surviving spouse can delay taking out distributions until he or she attains age 70½.

Alternatively, the surviving spouse can keep the IRA in the deceased spouse's name and treat it as an inherited IRA. Then the survivor can withdraw following the decedent's withdrawal schedule. A young spouse who wants to make more than the minimum withdrawals is better off with an inherited IRA than a rollover IRA.

If the surviving spouse is under 59½ the 10% excise tax on premature withdrawals applies to the rollover IRA but not to an inherited IRA.

If the beneficiary is an individual other than the surviving spouse, then he or she may choose to withdraw the whole amount, or make it a stretch IRA, taking the benefits in installments over his or her life expectancy. If multiple individuals are named as beneficiaries, in a group; then, if the IRA is separated into separate accounts by December 31 of the year following the year of the decedent's death, each beneficiary can make withdrawals over his or her life expectancy — each having his or her own stretch IRA. If separate accounts are not set up, then all beneficiaries must use the life expectancy of the oldest member of the group (which will be the shortest possible time period, shortening the "stretch".)

Beware of naming a charity as a beneficiary if it is one member of a group. A charity is considered to have a zero life expectancy so no stretch-out is permitted.

If a charity is the sole beneficiary of the IRA, there is no problem. In fact, that is an excellent way to benefit your favorite charity because the charity, unlike any other beneficiary, can receive the IRA estate tax *and* income tax free.

The designated beneficiary (designated beneficiary is a term of art in this arm of the tax law and has a special definition) is not determined until September 30 of the year after the year in which the decedent dies. That means that you have until then to fix up bad designations. For example, if a charity is named as a member of a group beneficiary designation, the charity could be paid its share so that it is no longer a beneficiary on September 30 and thus won't foul up the ability of the remaining individual beneficiaries to get stretch IRA treatment.

This period of time until September 30 of the year following the date of death (known as the "gap" period) is also a time when disclaimers can be made. If the primary beneficiary disclaims, then the next contingent beneficiary takes his place. Similarly, if the first contingent beneficiary also disclaims, the second contingent beneficiary takes his place. It is very important that the IRA designation be planned with the possibility of disclaimers in mind.

As you can see, the beneficiary designation is very important. Most plan custodians give you a tiny space on their forms to name a beneficiary. Any custodian worth its salt will allow a custom designation to be attached that will ensure that the best tax treatment is available for the beneficiaries. If your custodian won't allow this, move your account. If the custodian won't permit a custom designation, it is only interested in collecting a fee, not in helping you and your beneficiaries get the best financial result.

For many people, their IRA or 401(k) is their largest asset. Making sure that it is not consumed excessively with estate and income taxes should be a high priority. It is always best to plan before death, but there are ways to reduce taxes with postmortem actions.

IRAs with Trusts as Beneficiaries Are Very Tricky

Done properly, the tax shelter provided by the IRA payouts to individual beneficiaries can be continued for many years. Things get more complicated if the beneficiary is a trust. Often it is desirable to name a trust to exert more control over the disposition of the benefit. For example, you might want a trust to be a beneficiary if a beneficiary is a minor. A 10-year-old can't exercise any rights over the IRA and no one wants to have to get a court appointed guardian just to receive an IRA payout.

You might want to provide benefits for your spouse, but after her death, have the remainder of the IRA go to your children from your first marriage — another situation where a trust is what you need.

You may have a combined net worth over the federal exemption amount (currently $5.34 million) so that you need to create a by-pass trust and if the only asset available to fund the by-pass trust is your IRA, you may need to name a trust as beneficiary of the IRA in order to avoid federal estate taxes.

The challenge is to name a trust and at the same time retain the ability to get a stretch-out of IRA payments over the lifetime of the trust beneficiary. How do you do this? The trust must qualify as a "designated beneficiary." There is one requirement that can be a trap for the unwary: a copy of the trust (or a form giving information about the trust) must be delivered to the IRA custodian no later than October 31 of the year following the year in which the decedent died. This gives 10 to 22 months to get the trust document into the hands of the IRA administrator. Don't be late. If this is not done, no stretch-out is possible. Make sure that if a trust is named as beneficiary, that a copy of the trust is in the hands of the IRA custodian before that date — and make sure you can prove that you gave it to them in case they lose it! This can be done during your lifetime if you want to make sure.

If the trust qualifies, then a stretch-out over the life expectancy of the oldest beneficiary is possible. Beware, though of contingent beneficiaries in the trust. The IRS looks at all possible trust beneficiaries (the beneficiary club, as Ed Slott, named "the best" source for IRA advice by *The Wall Street Journal*, refers to it) and determines the stretch period based on the oldest member. If the primary beneficiaries are children, and a contingent beneficiary is a brother, about 20 to 30 years of stretch will be lost. In other words, if your trust provides that your property passes to your children, but if they do not survive you, to your brother; then the beneficiary club consists of your children and your brother and the stretch period will be determined by reference to the life expectancy of the oldest beneficiary. So your brother's life expectancy would determine the IRA stretch-out period even though he would only inherit if your children were deceased. To determine the stretch period, you use the life expectancy of the oldest beneficiary. If your brother is 55, the stretch is 29.6 years. If your oldest child is 25 and you could use his life expectancy, the stretch would be 58.2 years. That's a big difference.

If the trust provides that if all beneficiaries are deceased, the remainder is paid to a charity, then the charity in the beneficiary group will prevent the IRA from being able to be stretched out at all. The life expectancy of a charity is assumed to be zero. If a charity is a member of the beneficiary club, no stretch out is possible. This can be a truly bad result because all of the IRA will have to be withdrawn and taxed either within five years (if the decedent died before reaching age 70½) or over the remaining life expectancy of the decedent (if he died after attaining age 70½).

The worst mistake that can be made when a trust is named as a beneficiary is by transferring to the trust the whole IRA or more money than is needed to make the annual required minimum distribution (RMD). If you mistakenly transfer all of the IRA to the trust, then all of that transfer is subject to income tax, and once done, cannot be undone. Worse, the top tax bracket (39.6%) is reached at just $12,150 for trusts, compared to the top tax bracket for married filing jointly being reached at $457,600 (2014 numbers).

The way to transfer money from an IRA to a trust beneficiary and keep the benefit of the stretch-out is for the Trustee to only withdraw the annual RMD amount and leave the rest in the IRA. Do not close the IRA and pay the balance to the trust. As the trust receives the annual RMD distributions, they will become part of the trust property to be accumulated or paid out to beneficiaries as the trust directs. If the trustee distributes all or part of the RMD, the trust gets a distribution deduction and the individual beneficiary receiving the distribution from the trust reports the portion of the RMD received by him or her on his or her personal 1040.

A trust that passes out the entire RMD it receives is called a conduit trust. Then the trust pays no income tax on the RMD, which is good, especially considering the compressed trust income tax table.

A trust that passes through some but not all of the money it withdraws from the IRA is called an accumulation trust. The part that goes to beneficiaries is taxed to the beneficiaries, and the amount kept (accumulated) in the trust, is taxed to the trust. Accumulation trusts are used for more control by the original plan owner to be sure the trust beneficiary isn't given more money all at once than the deceased thought was wise. It does end up being more costly in taxes, but that's often the trade-off for more control.

The best plan of all is to convert to a Roth IRA before death. Of course, you have to meet the qualification requirements to convert to a Roth in order to do this. Then the income taxes are prepaid, thus lowering the value of the assets for estate tax, and there is no income tax consequence to withdrawals. The beneficiaries can withdraw and pay no income tax at all. But conversion to a Roth is not postmortem planning. After death it's too late for a Roth conversion.

ESTATE PLANNING GLOSSARY

There is no such thing as "legalese." Legal documents are written in English. Okay, okay, maybe an occasional word or two in Latin, *de minimis* only. But for the most part, it is the good old Queen's English that you are reading. Now your vocabulary, that's another issue. Many terms come from English common law, property law concepts, and the Internal Revenue Code, which is not familiar bedtime reading for many. While in English, it is unfamiliar. Here is a glossary to help you out.

529 plan. This is a Qualified State Tuition Plan under Internal Revenue Code Section 529. It is a popular option for families saving for a child's college education. A 529 plan is exempt from federal income tax on earnings, and withdrawals are tax-exempt as long as they are used to pay for college. There are two types: college savings plans and prepaid tuition plans. College savings plans let parents use their plan funds for college expenses at any college. Prepaid tuition plans let parents' lock-in future tuition at in-state public colleges at present prices. They are a great vehicle for grandparents to make gifts: 529 contributions are considered completed gifts and are excluded from the grandparents' estate. Grandparents can also switch beneficiaries to other grandchildren. As a special benefit, five years' worth of annual exclusions can be used at once so any person can make a $55,000 gift to as many 529 plans for different beneficiaries as they choose.

Abatement. With respect to estates, an abatement is a proportional diminution or reduction of the monetary legacies, or bequests when the funds or assets out of which such legacies or bequests are payable are insufficient to pay them in full. The intention of the testator, when expressed in the will, governs the order in which property will abate. Where the will is silent, abatement occurs in the following order: intestate property, gifts that pass by the residuary clause in the will, general legacies, and specific legacies.

Accumulation Trust. An arrangement whereby property is transferred by its owner—the settlor—with the intention that it be administered by someone else—a trustee—for another person's benefit. It would also be with the direction that the trustee gather, rather than distribute, the income of the trust and any profits made from the sale of any of the property making up the trust, until the time specified in the document that created the trust. Many states have laws governing the time over which accumulations may be made.

Ademption. From the Latin meaning "to take away." This refers to a legacy that is extinguished by the testator by disposal of the property before his death. Property not in the possession of the testator at the time of death cannot be willed away. For example, if testator's will includes a bequest of his pink Cadillac to Martha, but he sold the pink Cadillac before he died, Martha gets nothing.

Age of Majority. The age at which a person is granted by law the rights and responsibilities of an adult. The age of majority is now set by statute and may differ from state to state. In Pennsylvania it is eighteen.

Alternative Minimum Tax (AMT). The alternative minimum tax (AMT) is an income tax imposed by the United States federal government on individuals, corporations, estates, and trusts. AMT is imposed at a nearly flat rate on an adjusted amount of taxable income above a certain threshold (also known as exemption). This exemption is substantially higher than the exemption from regular income tax.

Regular taxable income is adjusted for certain items computed differently for AMT, such as depreciation and medical expenses. No deduction is allowed for state taxes or miscellaneous itemized deductions in computing AMT income. Taxpayers with incomes above the exemption whose regular Federal income tax is below the amount of AMT must pay the higher AMT amount.

Ancillary Probate. Ancillary probate refers to a probate proceeding that is required in addition to the primary probate proceeding in the decedent's domiciliary state. An Ancillary probate is required in another state is the decedent owned real estate or tangible personal property located in another state. A state can only control the ownership of property located within its own borders.

Annual exclusion gifts. Any person can make an unlimited number of gifts up to $14,000 per recipient per year with no gift tax payable and no gift tax return filing requirement. These are called annual exclusion gifts because they can be made every year, and they are excluded from any reporting requirement. The amount of $14,000 is not the amount of gift you are "allowed" to make. You may make gifts of any amount you want. If the gift exceeds $14,000 to any given individual in a calendar year, the fact that you made the gift must be reported on a gift tax return. When lifetime gifts in excess of the annual exclusion exceed $5.34 million, then there will be gift tax due.

Annuitize. Annuitize means to "flip the switch" and start taking income from an annuity. Instead of continuing to accumulate, the annuity contract requires the payment of a monthly amount for a term of years or for the life of the annuitant, or some combination.

Antenuptial Agreement (prenuptial agreement). A written contract between two people who are about to marry, setting out the terms of possession of assets, treatment of future earnings, control of the property of each, and potential division if the marriage if later dissolved by death or divorce. These agreements are fairly common if either -- or both -- parties have substantial assets, children from a prior marriage, potential inheritances, high incomes, or have been "taken" by a prior spouse.

Arbiter. One who controls and makes a decision in an arbitration proceeding, or, informally, anyone who settles a dispute or argument.

Beneficiary. The recipient of funds, property, or other benefits, as from an insurance policy, will, trust or other instrument providing for successor ownership on death.

Bequest. A gift of a specific item of personal property or a specified sum of money made in a will, e.g., "I give my red corvette and $10,000 to my good friend, Wayne."

By-Pass Trust. The first step in estate planning for a married couple when their combined assets exceed the $5.34 million federal estate tax exemption from the application of the federal estate tax, is to double the exemption so each spouse can use an exemption effectively (sheltering $3 million from the estate tax). This is done by the use of a By-Pass Trust. When the first spouse dies, the exemption amount goes into a trust for the benefit of the surviving spouse. This $5.34 million "by-passes" the estate tax in both spouses' estates. When the surviving spouse dies, he or she gets another $ 5.34 exemption to apply to their separately owned assets. For this plan to work, each spouse must have separately titled assets. It is common to divide jointly held property for this purpose. This kind of trust plan is sometimes called an A-B Trust or Credit Shelter Trust.

Charitable Deduction (Estate and Gift Tax). You can give an unlimited amount to charity either during your life or at death. The charitable gift is 100% deductible for the gift tax and the estate tax . But for income tax see below..

Charitable Deduction (Income Tax). Gifts to charity are deductible for income tax purposes, but only to the extent they do not exceed 50% of your adjusted gross income. For gifts of appreciated property, the limitation is 30% of adjusted gross income. Deductions that are barred by the percentage limitation can be carried forward to future tax years.

Charitable Remainder Trust. A type of trust which pays an annual dollar or percentage amount to the donor (or other individual beneficiaries) and on their death pays the remainder of the trust property to charity. It is often used to own appreciated property such as real estate because the trust can sell the property and pay no capital gains tax. The gross proceeds can be invested to generate the annuity or percentage payments to the individuals. Many charities prefer to be their own trustee so they can manage the money. The donor gets a deduction (actuarially computed) for income tax purposes.

Codicil. An amendment to a will, that is, a change to a part or parts of the will without revoking the will.

Common Law Marriage. A marriage not solemnized in the usual fashion but created by cohabitation. There is a common misconception that the cohabitation has to continue for a certain number of years. There is no time limit. In Pennsylvania, CL Marriage is no longer in effect as of January 1, 2005. Common law marriages entered into before January 1, 2005 in PA, however, are still recognized.

Common Law State. A state whose rules governing the ownership, division and inheritance of income and property acquired by a husband or wife during the course of their marriage holds that, subject to various qualifications, each spouse owns and has complete control over his or her own income and property. These states are also referred to as common law property states and separate property states. This system is contrasted to community property.

Community Property. Community property is a marital property regime that originated in civil law jurisdictions. In a community property jurisdiction, most property acquired during the marriage (except for gifts or inheritances) is owned jointly by both spouses and is divided upon divorce, annulment, or death. Joint ownership is automatically presumed by law in the absence of specific evidence that would point to a contrary conclusion for a particular piece of property. Property that is owned by one spouse before the marriage is the separate property of that spouse, unless the property is "transmuted" into community property. The rules for this vary from jurisdiction to jurisdiction. There are nine community property states: Arizona, California, Idaho, Louisiana, Nevada, New Mexico, Texas, Washington, and Wisconsin.

Community Spouse. One who has the free will to be a part of the society they live in; to participate in the neighborhood where they reside. This term is used in contrast to a spouse who is in a nursing home or other facility.

Consanguinity. Kinship or blood relation from the same ancestry.

Conservation Easement. A conservation easement is an interest in real property established by agreement between a landowner and land trust or unit of government which restricts the use of the subject real property for conservation purposes.

Contingent Deferred Sales Charge (CDSC). A fee that mutual fund investors pay when selling Class-B fund shares within a specified number of years of the date on which they were originally purchased.

Cotenant. One of two or more owners sharing undivided fractional interests in property.

CRAT (Charitable Remainder Annuity Trust). A Planned Giving vehicle that entails a donor placing a major gift of cash or property into a trust. The trust then pays a fixed amount of income each year to the donor or the donor's specified beneficiary. When the donor dies, the remainder of the trust is transferred to the charity. See Charitable Remainder Trust.

Crummey Power. A man named Mr. Crummey won a case in Tax Court in the 1960's. His idea was that a gift to a trust could qualify for the annual exclusion *if* a beneficiary had the right to withdraw the sum he contributed to the trust, for a limited time. However, even if the beneficiary did not make the withdrawal, the transfer to the trust would be treated as a gift to that beneficiary (for gift tax purposes). In addition, it would qualify for the gift tax annual exclusion.

CRUT (A Charitable Remainder Unitrust). An irrevocable trust created under the authority of Internal Revenue Code 664. This special, irrevocable trust (known as a "CRUT") has two primary characteristics: (1) Once established, the CRUT distributes a fixed percentage of the value of its assets (on an annual or more frequent basis) to a non-charitable beneficiary (which is considered the <u>settlor</u> of the trust); and (2) at the expiration of a specified time (usually the death of the settlor), the remaining balance of the CRUTs assets are distributed to charity. See Charitable Remainder Trust.

Custodian. Two unrelated definitions: (1) a person who holds property for the benefit of a minor under the Uniform Transfer to Minors Act. The custodian can invest, reinvest, and use the custodial property for the minor's benefit. The property held by the custodian must be turned over to the minor beneficiary at age twenty-one (the age may differ from state to state or under different circumstances). (2) A bank or other institution that holds the title to investments but is not responsible for investing them.

Decedent. A deceased person.

Declarant. Someone who makes a declaration or statement.

Demand Loan. A loan with no specified maturity date that must be paid at the time of the creditor's request.

Dependent Relative Revocation. The doctrine that regards as mutually related the acts of a testator destroying a will and executing a second will. In such cases, if the second will is either never made or improperly executed, there is a rebuttable presumption that the testator would have preferred the former will to no will at all, which allows the possibility of probate of the destroyed will.

Disclaimer. A refusal to accept property. For example a beneficiary under a will or trust may disclaim or refuse to accept the benefit left to him or her. For tax purpose, a disclaimer by a beneficiary is treated as a gift unless the disclaimer is qualified under IRC §2518 which requires that the disclaimer be made within 9 months of the date of the creation of the interest and that the disclaimant had accepted no benefits from the disclaimed property.

Domicile. Where a person has legal residence and plans on staying or returning.

Donee. A gift recipient. One to whom a gift or bequest is given.

Dynasty Trust. Usually refers to a trust that lasts for many years, possibly forever and benefits the succeeding generations of a family.

Often the trust is exempt from the generation-skipping tax and escapes both estate and gift tax at every generation after the first. These trusts are marketed heavily in states like Delaware and Alaska where the rule against perpetuities has been repealed, that is, these states have made it possible for trust to exist for an unlimited period of time, in other words, be perpetual.

Election Against the Will. If a person dies and leaves a will which disinherits the surviving spouse, or gives the spouse less than his or her minimum share, the surviving spouse has a right to "elect against the will" and take his or her statutory share. The surviving spouse's share is generally one-third. Some property that passes outside the will is included in the computation. The surviving spouse can't have it both ways. Either he or she gets the elective share, or keeps the joint property and beneficiary designated assets, not both. No one other than a spouse can "elect against the will."

"En Ventre Sa Mere". A Latin phrase meaning "in the womb" or gestation. A child in the womb on a decedent's date of death is considered to be living issue if later born alive.

Enumerated. To specify each item, to name one by one.

Equitable Distribution. In some states, as part of divorce the courts are granted the power to distribute equitably the estate of husband and wife or either, whether legal title lies in their individual or joint names.

Estate Administration. The process by which a decedent's estate is settled including collection and valuing of assets, notification of creditors, determination of debts and liabilities, filing and payment of all inheritance, estate taxes, preparation of decedent's final income tax return and fiduciary income tax returns for the estate, selling assets as appropriate, and in general, carrying out the terms of the will.

Estate Tax. A transfer tax payable on the value of a decedent's property that passes by reason of his or her death. There is a federal estate tax with a current exemption of $5,340,000. Some states have estate taxes. Pennsylvania used to have an estate tax; however, it was phased out at the end of 2004. Pennsylvania continues to have an inheritance tax. The inheritance tax is based on the amount received by a beneficiary on account of the decedent's death.

Executor. The person, persons, bank, or trust company named in a will to be in charge of settling the estate. The executor is responsible for carrying out all duties of estate administration and is personally liable to the beneficiaries for the proper performance of the executor's duties. It is not a position to be undertaken lightly and without professional advice. An administrator is a person appointed by the court to settle the estate of someone who left no will, or of someone who's named executor cannot, or will not, serve.

Exemption. That amount of money or value that may pass free of tax.

Family Limited Partnership. A partnership with at least one general partner and usually several limited partners where all partners are family members. The partnership may hold a variety of assets and the general partner(s) is in control of the partnership, its investments, its distributions, its liquidation, etc. Often gifts of limited partnership interest are made to younger generation family members as part of the older generation's estate plan. The valuation of the limited interest is usually claimed by taxpayers to be at discount from the value of the underlying partnership assets because of the retained control by the general partner and the limited partners' inability to sell or otherwise realize the benefit of the assets. The amount and existence of this discount is a favorite topic for IRS audits and the issue is being litigated in the federal courts, so far mainly in the taxpayers' favor.

(FICA) Federal Insurance Contributions Act. Tax for the social security and Medicare programs imposed by the federal government on employees, employers, and the self-employed. Under F.I.C.A. employers match the tax paid by the employee.

(FUTA) Federal Unemployment Tax Act. A United States federal law that imposes a federal employer tax used to help fund state workforce agencies. Employers report this tax by filing an annual Form 940 with the Internal Revenue Service.

Fiduciary. From the Latin term, *fiducia*. A fiduciary is a person who holds and/or administers property for the benefit of another. Examples of fiduciaries are Executors, Administrators, Trustees, Guardians, Agents under a Powers of Attorney, and Custodians. Attorneys are also fiduciaries for their clients and Boards of Directors are fiduciaries for the corporation. All fiduciaries have a duty to preserve and protect the property in their care for the benefit of the person on whose behalf they act and to always act in the best interests of the beneficiary. A person acting in a fiduciary capacity is required to make complete disclosures of his or her actions and is forbidden from taking personal advantage (other than reasonable compensation) from his or her position. It is said to be the highest duty known to the law.

Filial Responsibility. The obligation of a child.

Fraud. A false representation in order to gain some unfair or dishonest advantage.

Generation-Skipping Transfer Tax. It has long been a technique for the wealthy to make trusts that endure for several generations. That's how we get "trust fund kids" — spoiled scions of the wealthy who excel in conspicuous consumption and never do a lick of work. Most folks pass their assets to their children and pay a tax and, in turn, those children pass the assets on to the next generation and pay a tax. The very wealthy, by creating long bomb trusts, can skip the transfer tax at several generation levels, by having the assets stay in trust where they are not taxed while still providing Jaguars, mansions, and jewels to the succeeding generations. In 1976, Congress enacted the generation-skipping transfer tax, a very complex and intricate system of taxation aimed at exacting a transfer tax at each generation level in these long-term trusts. The tax has an exemption but only applies if there is a generation-skipping taxable event. Unfortunately, the tax includes many traps for the unwary, and many people who do not intend to skip generations unwittingly fall into the tax. It is another reason why estate planning is so intricate and expensive.

Gift Tax. Primordial estate planners figured out that if you give everything away before you die, there is nothing left on which to pay an estate tax. Congress responded within 10 years to this rudimentary estate planning by enacting the gift tax. Lifetime transfers are also subject to tax. The gift and estate tax systems work together and exemption amounts change frequently. It's important to discuss your options with you estate attorney.

Grantor. A Grantor is a person who creates a trust. Different lawyers use different words for this. Some call the person who creates a trust the Settlor, some the Trustor, some the Donor. All of these terms refer to the person who makes the transfer of property to the trust, either during life, or at death, that starts the trust.

Grantor Trust. A Grantor Trust is a trust in which the Grantor is treated as the owner for income tax purposes. That means that all of the trust's items of income and deduction pass through onto the Grantor's personal 1040. The trust is not recognized as a separate taxable entity. The most common example of a Grantor Trust is any revocable trust while the grantor is still alive and can revoke it. A Grantor trust may or may not be included in the grantor's estate. The fact that it is a Grantor Trust for income tax purposes does not control its treatment for estate tax purposes.

Gross Estate. No, not a disgusting estate. Gross in this context means whole, as in total before subtracting deductions like administration expenses. For federal estate tax purposes, the gross estate includes all the property the decedent owned in his name alone, all property over which the decedent had control, all property which had been transferred by the decedent and in which he retained the right to receive income, jointly held property, IRA's and annuities, the value of life insurance death benefit if the benefit is payable to the estate or the decedent insured was the owner of the policy. Note that only a small portion of this property passes under the decedent's will. Some passes to surviving joint owners and some to designated beneficiaries. Nevertheless, all of these assets are included in the gross estate for purposes of determining the federal estate tax. For Pennsylvania inheritance tax purposes, the gross taxable estate includes these items with a few exceptions; most notably, the exclusion of life insurance proceeds.

Guardian. A guardian is a person or bank appointed to care for the assets and income of a person and/or to have physical custody of the person. There are two kinds: (1) Guardian of a Minor is for a person under age 18. A court-appointed guardian of the minor's property will have control of the minor's finances and a court-appointed guardian of the minor's person will have physical custody. A parent, just by virtue of being a parent, does not have the authority to deal with the property and assets of a minor. Only a court appointed guardian can do this. That is why it is very inadvisable to put property in a child's name. It is very important to appoint a guardian for your minor children in your will. Guardian of an incapacitated Person is for a person of any age who is unable to care for him or herself or his or her financial affairs. Again, these guardians must be appointed by the court. It is advisable to avoid the necessity of a court proceeding by having in place a Power of Attorney naming an agent to handle your affairs in the event of your incapacity.

Heir Apparent. Someone who is expected to inherit based on their order of ancestry. For instance, the king's heir apparent is his eldest son.

Heirs. A decedent's heirs are those persons who would inherit his or her property if he or she died without a will. A living person has no heirs. Heirs presumptive are those who would inherit if a living person were to die immediately.

Holographic Will. A will written wholly in the handwriting of the person making it and signed at the end. In Pennsylvania, such a will is valid even if it is not witnessed.

ILIT (Irrevocable Life Insurance Trust). An irrevocable life insurance trust is one in which the grantor completely gives up all rights in the property transferred to the trust, and retains no rights to revoke, terminate or modify the trust in any material way.

Illiquid Assets. Real estate, closely-held stock or any other asset that cannot easily be sold or exchanged for cash without a substantial loss in value. Illiquid assets also cannot be sold quickly because of a lack of ready and willing buyers to purchase the asset.

Imputed Interest Income. For some long-term sales on property the IRS will convert an amount of gain into interest income if there is no minimum rate of interest paid by the purchaser.

Incapacity. Lack of ability or control, physical or mental.

Incentive Trust. A trust designed to encourage or discourage certain behaviors by using distributions of trust income, or principal, as an incentive. A typical incentive trust might encourage a beneficiary to complete a degree, enter a profession, or abstain from harmful conduct such as substance abuse. The beneficiary might be paid a certain amount of money from the trust upon graduating from college, or the trust might pay a dollar of income from the trust for every dollar the beneficiary earns.

Inheritance Tax. A tax on the receipt of property by a beneficiary as a result of the death of the decedent. Pennsylvania has an inheritance tax. There is no exemption; the first $1.00 is taxable. For property received by a surviving spouse the rate is zero, thus no tax. For property passing to Children, grandchildren, mother, father, grandmother, grandfather, wife or widow of a child, husband or widower of a child, the rate is 4.5%. Lineal descendants include children and more remote descendants. Children include stepchildren and adopted children. For property passing to siblings the rate is 12%. For property passing to all others, the rate is 15%. The inheritance tax does not apply to the proceeds of life insurance (in any amount) on the life of the decedent. Property passing to a qualifying charity is exempt from the application of the inheritance tax. The tax must be paid within nine (9) months of the decedent's death. If the tax is paid within three months of the date of death, there is a five percent discount available for early payment.

Insolvent Estate. An insolvent estate is an estate with more debts than assets – similar to bankruptcy.

Institutionalized Spouse. One who resides in a public place such as a hospital or nursing home.

Interpolated Terminal Reserve Value. Interpolated terminal reserve is the method by which the reserve on any life insurance policy is valued between anniversaries. This value is used as a value for insurance policies for gift and estate tax purposes.

In *Terrorem* Clause. Latin for "in fear," a provision in a will which threatens that if anyone challenges the legality of the will or any part of it, then that person will be cut off or given only a dollar, instead of getting the full gift provided in the will.

Inter vivos Trust. A trust created during the life of the Settlor. When revocable, sometimes called a "living trust." The property is then placed in trust with a trustee (often the Settlor during his/her lifetime) and distribution will take place according to the terms of the trust, both during the Settlor's lifetime and then upon the Settlor's death.

Intestate. A person dies intestate if he or she dies without a will. In that case, the state intestacy statute specifies who inherits.

IRA (Individual Retirement Arrangement). A form of retirement plan provided by many financial institutions that provides tax advantages for retirement savings in the United States, as described in IRS Publication 590, Individual Retirement Arrangement (IRAs). The term IRA encompasses an individual retirement account; a trust or custodial account set up for the exclusive benefit of taxpayers or their beneficiaries; and an individual retirement annuity, by which the taxpayers purchase an annuity contract or an endowment contract from a life insurance company.

IRD (Income in Respect of a Decedent). Those amounts to which a decedent was entitled as gross income, but which were not properly includable in computing his taxable income (for the taxable year) ending with the date of his death. IRD is both an asset of the estate for estate tax purposes and is taxable income when received by the ultimate recipient..

Irrevocable Life Insurance Trust (ILIT). An irrevocable trust which is the owner and beneficiary of one or more life insurance policies.

Irrevocable Trust. A trust that can't be modified or terminated. The grantor, having transferred assets into the trust, effectively gives up all of his or her rights of ownership to the assets and the trust.

Issue. Descendants of all generations — children, grandchildren, great-grandchildren, etc. In Pennsylvania an adopted child is considered the issue of his adopting parent or parents. An adopted child may also be considered to be the issue of natural kin (other than a natural parent) if a relationship has been maintained. A child born out of wedlock is considered an issue of the mother. A child born out of wedlock is considered an issue of the father if the mother and father marry each other, the father openly holds out the child to be his and receives the child into his home or provides support for the child, or there is clear and convincing evidence that the man was the father, which may include a court determination of paternity.

Legacy. A bequest. A general legacy comes from the overall assets of the estates. A specific legacy refers to a legacy payable specifically from an asset of the estate.

Legatee. A person who is bequeathed a legacy.

Life Tenant. Someone who holds an estate of land for his lifetime or for the life of another person (life estate *pur autre vie*).

Lineal Descendant. An individual who is in a direct line of kinship such as a daughter or granddaughter, as opposed to a niece or nephew who would be considered a collateral descendant.

Living Issue. Living descendants of all generations.

Living Trust. A revocable trust created by the Settlor during his or her lifetime, as opposed to in his or her will. Sometimes called a revocable inter-vivos trust.

Living Will. A legal document in which a person expresses his or her wishes about medical treatment in the event of terminal illness or permanent unconsciousness. It is often accompanied by a Medical Directive and/or Medical Power of Attorney.

Marital Deduction. While all of a decedent's property is subject to federal estate tax, property that passes to a surviving spouse qualifies for a special deduction called the marital deduction, and is therefore not taxed. It is the policy of the federal government to only tax property when it moves to the next generation, not between spouses.

Materially Participated. You materially participated in a trade or business activity for a tax year if you satisfy any of seven descriptors. The full list can be seen at: http://www.taxslayer.com/support/854/What-does-materially-participate-mean?page=28

Medical Directive. A legal document which appoints a surrogate to make medical decisions for you and may, or may not, include a living will.

Medicaid. Also known as Medical Assistance, Medicaid is a program funded jointly by the Federal government and the states. Not everyone is eligible to participate in the Medicaid program, as applicants and recipients of Medicaid must meet strict income and resource guidelines, among other criteria. For those individuals eligible for Medicaid benefits, Medicaid covers physicians' services, hospital care, medications, supplies, and other reasonable and necessary services. Perhaps, most importantly, Medicaid covers the costs of long-term care in either your home or a skilled nursing facility. In Pennsylvania it is administered by the Department of Public Welfare.

Medicare. The federal health insurance program for the elderly (65 and over) was first implemented in 1965. It also is available to those collecting Social Security Disability Income for 2 years and over, and persons with end stage renal disease. Part A, or hospital insurance, is financed by payroll deductions from working people. Part B, Supplemental Medical Insurance, is financed by monthly premiums and general revenues (the premiums you pay are roughly 25% of the cost of this insurance). Medicare Part B is optional and covers part of physicians' costs and other medical services and supplies. Medicare has certain deductibles, limited payment periods, and restrictions on the types of services covered. Two of the most severe restrictions are that it only covers nursing home care if it is "skilled" care rather than "custodial," and it covers up to 100 days of nursing home care per spell of illness.

Minimum Required Distribution (MRD). Minimum Required Distributions (MRDs) generally are minimum amounts that a retirement plan account owner must withdraw annually starting with the year that he or she reaches 70 ½ years of age or, if later, the year in which he or she retires. However, if the retirement plan account is an IRA or the account owner is a 5% owner of the business sponsoring the retirement plan, the RMDs must begin once the account holder is age 70 ½, regardless of whether he or she is retired.

Minor's Trust. A trust for a minor transfers to which qualify for the $14,000 annual gift exclusion even though the transfer is a future interest. The trust must provide for distribution to the minor at age 21. This is not used very much anymore since a Uniform Transfers to Minor's Act Account can accomplish similar objectives at a fraction of the cost.

(MAGI) Modified Adjusted Gross Income. Generally, your modified adjusted gross income is the total of your adjusted gross income and tax-exempt interest income you may have.

Nanny Tax. The portion of Social Security and Medicare taxes paid by the employer of a nanny, gardener, or other household worker.

(NASD) National Association of Stock Dealers. The NASD watched over the Nasdaq to make sure the market operates correctly. In 2007, the NASD merged with the New York Stock Exchange's regulation committee to form the Financial Industry Regulatory Authority or FINRA.

Natural Objects of Your Bounty. The phrase "the natural objects of one's bounty" means the closest surviving members of one's family. It usually describes those to whom property of a dead person will go if the dead person did not make and leave a will.

Non-countable Asset. In relation to Medicaid: Something that doesn't count as a resource available to pay for your care.

Notary. Also called a notary public. A public officer whose function it is to administer oaths; to attest and certify, by his hand and official seal, certain classes of documents, in order to give them credit and authenticity. Someone who is authorized by state or federal government to attest to the authority of signature authenticity and to administer oaths.

Passive Activity Loss Rules. According to tax law, it is a loss from any activity which a taxpayer is not a participant and is generally not deductible.

Pecuniary Bequest. A gift of money in a will, as opposed to some other asset. For example, if a man's will gives his son $100,000 cash, rather than ownership of his home, the man has made a pecuniary bequest.

Per Capita. A method of dividing an estate. *Per capita* means by the head or by the polls, according to the number of individuals, share and share alike. Example: Grandmother had two sons; one of them had one child, and the other had three. Both of the sons predeceased Grandmother. A *per capita* distribution of her estate would be that each of the four grandchildren would receive equal one-fourth (1/4) shares of her estate — equally near, equally dear. Division is not calculated until reaching a generation that has at least one surviving member.

Perpetuity. Continuing indefinitely. The Rule against Perpetuities pertains to real property and conditions or restrictions extending beyond a lifetime plus twenty-one years.

Per Stirpes. *Per stirpes* means by the stocks or by the roots. The method of dividing an estate where a group of beneficiaries take the share which their deceased ancestor would have been entitled to, had he or she lived. The group of beneficiaries take by their right of representing the ancestor and not because they are owed anything as individuals. Example: Grandmother had two sons; one of them had one child, and the other had three. Both of the sons predeceased Grandmother. A *per stirpes* distribution of her estate would be that the grandchild who is the only child of a deceased son gets one-half of the estate and the other three grandchildren share the other deceased son's one-half share, each receiving one-sixth. Division is calculated at the first generation regardless of whether there is a surviving member of that generation.

POD. (Payable on Death). An arrangement between a bank or credit union and a client that designates beneficiaries to receive all the client's assets.

Ponzi Scheme. A fraudulent investment operation that pays returns to its investors from their own money or the money paid by subsequent investors, rather than from profit earned by the individual or organization running the operation.

Postnuptial Agreement. A contract made between a man and a woman after they marry which may also contain provisions regarding the termination of marriage by divorce or by death of one of the spouses.

Power of Attorney. A document which appoints an agent to act on behalf of a principal. Powers of attorney were originally used in commercial contexts and at common law the authority of the agent only continued so long as the principal was competent and could review the actions of the agent. They have become an important part of personal estate planning since the agent's authority is needed most when the principal does become incapacitated. We now have durable powers of attorney — durable because the authority granted by them last even though the principal who granted the power becomes incompetent. A general power of attorney is one that grants full and complete authority to do everything that the principal could do. A limited power of attorney is for a particular purpose - for example, a limited power of attorney may grant the agent the authority to sell a piece of real estate, but nothing else.

Precatory Language. A decedents prayer or request that something either be fulfilled or not (but not a demand) and not legally enforceable.

Prenuptial Agreement. A contract made between a man and a woman before they marry. The contract may make provision for what will happen if the parties become divorced or what rights of inheritance a surviving spouse will have in the event of death of one of the spouses. To be enforceable the contract must be reasonable, there must be a complete disclosure of each party's assets and liabilities to the other and it is highly recommended that each spouse have separate counsel. Previously, these contracts had to be made before marriage because the common law provided that a married woman was incompetent to make contracts by herself. See Antenuptial Agreement.

Present Interest Gifts. A gift which can be immediately possessed.

Primogeniture. Inheritance by the first born male among other siblings from the same parents.

Principal. The amount borrowed or the amount still owed on a loan, separate from interest. Or the assets of a trust or estate as opposed to the income generated by the assets.

Principle Residence. Your primary home, where you live.

Privity. A connection of two parties with a mutual interest.

Probate. A title proceeding. If a person dies owning property, the question arises "Who is the next rightful owner?" Probate is the procedure by which the ownership is determined. If the decedent left a will, the will is filed with the Register of Wills, the executor (who is the person in charge of the estate) is sworn in, and notice is given to all persons who have an interest in the estate, including creditors. Anyone who wishes to contest the will, which means to object to the will, may do so within a prescribed time period. Grounds for contesting a will might be that the decedent did not know what he was doing when he signed the will. The law calls this lack of "testamentary capacity." A will can be contested on the grounds that the decedent was under "undue influence" at the time she signed the will. For example, someone was pressuring and pushing her, and the decedent was susceptible to the influence. An improperly executed will can be contested also. For example, a will may not have enough witnesses, or the witnesses may be disqualified persons. In Pennsylvania, the forum for all these sorts of "contests" or objections is the county Orphan's Court. If the decedent left no will, or if the decedent's will is found to be invalid, then the next rightful owner(s) of the decedent's property are determined by the state intestacy statute. This statute determines the decedent's heirs. The heirs of a decedent are first, children or more remote issue, then parents, and then siblings and their issue. Also, a surviving spouse is entitled to a share, usually about one-third (1/3) of the estate.

Property — real, personal, tangible. Real property is land and anything that is erected or growing upon or affixed to the land. Personal property is everything that is subject to ownership other than real property, for example, stocks and bonds, and bank accounts. Tangible personal property is a subset of personal property and consists of movables such as animals, furniture, jewelry, vehicles, china, etc.

PUTMA (PA Uniform Transfer to Minors Act). Provides an inexpensive easy mechanism for giving property to minors by delivery to a custodian and the custodian's registration of the property in his or her name as custodian under the Pennsylvania Uniform Transfers to Minors Act.

QTIP (Qualified terminable interest in property). A type of trust that enables the grantor to provide for a surviving spouse and also to maintain control of how the trust's assets are distributed once the surviving spouse has also died, while still qualifying for the estate tax marital deduction. Income, and sometimes principal, generated from the trust is given to the surviving spouse to ensure that he or she is taken care of for the rest of his or her life

QPRT (Qualified Personal Residence Trust). Residence trusts are used to transfer a grantor's residence out of the grantor's estate at a low gift tax value. Once the trust is funded with the grantor's residence, the residence and any future appreciation of the residence is excluded from grantor's estate, provided the grantor survives the term of retained occupancy.

Qualified Plan. A retirement plan that meets Internal Revenue Code rules and regulations that allows employers to receive certain deductions and other tax benefits. These plans also meet the requirements of the Employee Retirement Income Security Act ("ERISA"). Qualified plans allow employees to defer income tax on employer's contributions and all earnings until distributed. Examples of qualified plans are: defined benefit pension plans, profit-sharing plans, 401(k) plans, and Employee Stock Ownership Plans ("ESOP's"). An IRA is not a qualified plan.

Remainderman. One who is entitled to receive the balance of an estate or trust after a particular time period has expired or after a named beneficiary dies.

RMD (Required Minimum Distribution). Required Minimum Distributions, often referred to as RMDs, are amounts that the federal government requires you to withdraw annually from traditional IRAs and employer-sponsored retirement plans.

Residuary. Pertaining to the surplus of the estate after all taxes, debts, bills, bequests and legacies have been paid.

Residue. In everyday English usage, we think of residue as a small amount leftover, the dregs, or a remnant. As used in the context of wills or trust, it means the remainder of a testator's estate after all claims, debts, and bequests are satisfied. In most estates, the "residue" is the biggest part of the estate. Let's say you have $500,000 estate, with $10,000 in debts and claims and a bequest of $1,000 to a nephew. The residue is $489,000 - hardly a small amount leftover.

Revocable Trust. A trust that can be revoked by the person who made it. The power of revocation includes the power to amend.

Rule Against Perpetuities. The Rule Against Perpetuities puts a limit on how long a trust can tie up property. Only a purely charitable trust can exist in perpetuity. Private trusts, that is, trusts with individuals as beneficiaries, must come to an end. The classic statement of the Rule is "No interest [in real or personal property] is good unless it must vest, if at all, not later than 21 years after some life in being at the creation of the interest." All trusts must comply with the rule to be valid. Most well-drafted trusts will include a Savings Clause, to make sure that the Rule Against Perpetuities is complied with. The Savings Clause provides that, notwithstanding any other provisions in the trust, the trust will end no later than 21 years after the death of the last survivor of a described group of people. Several states have eliminated the Rule Against Perpetuities, among them Delaware and Alaska. Trustees in these states are marketing their services as providing an opportunity for trusts that last forever. They call them Dynasty Trusts. (Maybe the dead hand *can* rule from the grave.)

Securities and Exchange Commission (SEC). A government agency which regulates such laws as the Securities Act of 1933, the Securities Exchange Act of 1934, the Public Utility Holding Company Act of 1935, the Trust Indenture Act of 1939, the Investment Adviser's Act, and the Investment Company Act of 1940.

Second-to-Die/Survivorship Life Insurance. A policy that insures two lives — usually a husband and wife. The death benefit isn't paid out until the second insured person dies. Usually, the death benefit from a second-to-die life insurance policy is intended to pay taxes owed after both spouses pass away.

Self-proving. Many wills are "self-proving" by the addition of an affidavit as prescribed by a state statute signed by the testator, the witnesses and notarized. If a will is self-proving, it can be probated without the testimony of witnesses.

Signatory. A person who becomes a party to a contract signed either personally or through their agent.

Signature Guarantee. A medallion signature guarantee is a special signature guarantee for the transfer of securities. It is a guarantee by the issuing financial institution that the signature is genuine and the financial institution accepts liability for any forgery. Signature guarantees protect shareholders by preventing unauthorized transfers and possible investor losses. They also limit the liability of the transfer agent who accepts the certificates.

Simple or Complex Trust. A simple trust is one that is required to distribute all income. A complex trust is one that does not require that all income be distributed and may have discretion for the distribution of income and principal

Special Needs Trust. If a person is receiving needs-tested government benefits, inheriting assets may disqualify them from receiving the benefits. Many parents and grandparents who wish to leave money for the benefit of a disabled child do so using a Special Needs Trust. Government benefits will not be terminated, and the trustee can use the trust funds for supplemental needs, things like vacations, social events, and sporting goods.

Sponge Tax. The sponge tax was a state death tax computed by reference to the amount of state death tax credit allowed on the federal estate tax. States with this tax collected the amount allowable as a tax credit to the federal estate tax. Now that the federal estate tax has a deduction for state death taxes instead of a credit, sponge taxes are no more.

Spousal Sole Use Trust. For the Pennsylvania Inheritance Tax, if a trust is for the sole use of the decedent's surviving spouse for his or her lifetime, the inheritance tax on the remainder interest is not due until the death of the surviving spouse, at which time the entire property passing to the remaindermen is taxed at the appropriate rate. The executor may elect to pay this tax early, that is, nine months from the decedent's death. If the "pay early" election is made, the amount of the trust subject to tax is the actuarial value of the remainder based on the surviving spouse's age and the current interest rate. The decision of whether or not to pay the tax early should be made with the advice of competent counsel. Once made, it cannot be changed.

Springing Power of Attorney. A power of attorney which becomes legally effective on the occurrence of an event (such as incapacity). The occurrence of the triggering event must be proved.

Stepped-up Basis. When an asset is sold, the sale proceeds are compared to the basis to determine the amount of gain or loss for income tax purposes. Usually basis is the acquisition price adjusted for improvements and depreciation, if any. Under current law, when a person dies, while the value of his or her assets will be subject to death taxes, the assets also get a changed basis for income tax purposes. The new basis is equal to the value for estate tax purposes — usually the fair market value on the date of death. This is commonly referred to as a "step-up" in basis because for the last 50 years or so the general trend in asset values of all classes has been appreciation. However, it is possible for there to be a step-down in basis.

"Sui juris". Latin, meaning having the right to or legal possession of.in his own right; adult and under no disability.

Tabula rasa. Means a blank slate in Latin; it is the epistemological theory that individuals are born without built-in mental content and that their knowledge comes from experience and perception.

Tangible Personal Property. Things. Property that can be touched, felt in its physical form, moved, etc.; not intangible.

Tenancy. "Tenancy" is the mode or way that property is owned. Tenancy in Common is co-ownership among two or more persons where each co-owner has an interest in the property that she can pass to her heirs. Joint Tenancy is co-ownership among two or more persons where the property interest of a deceased co-owner passes to the surviving joint owners. Tenancy by the Entirety is joint ownership of property by a husband and wife where the surviving spouse becomes the owner of the entire property. Neither spouse can transfer his or her interest in the property without the consent of the other. A creditor of one spouse cannot reach property held by that spouse as a tenant by the entireties.

Terminal Condition. An irreversible, incurable and untreatable condition caused by disease, illness or injury.

Testamentary Capacity. Sufficient mental capacity measured by the law as sufficient to make a will.

Testamentary Trust. A trust contained within a will that takes effect upon the testator's death.

Testator. One who dies and leaves a will.

TOD. Transfer on death registration allows you to pass the securities you own directly to another person or entity upon your death without having to go through probate.

Totten Trust. A Totten trust (also referred to as a "Payable on Death" account) is a form of trust in the United States in which one party (the settlor of the trust) places money in a bank account or security with instructions that upon the settlor's death, whatever is in that account will pass to a named beneficiary. For example, a Totten trust arises when a bank account is titled in the form "[depositor], in trust for [beneficiary]".

Trust. A trust is a creation of English common law, originally devised to avoid the reversion of lands to the crown and the strictures of primogeniture. A trust is a relationship with respect to property. The grantor (or settlor) creates the trust either by declaring himself trustee or making a transfer to a trustee. Legal title to the property is held by the trustee, but the property is held by the trustee for the benefit of the beneficiaries on the terms specified by the grantor.

Trust Mill. Trust mills are organizations which promote the indiscriminate marketing of *inter vivos* trusts by non-lawyers; often with the assistance of local counsel. Typically trust mill organizations consist of insurance agents, financial planners, stockbrokers, and other individuals who are not lawyers, but who prepare estate planning documents from various forms.

Undue Influence. Controlling another person's decisions or taking away his initial intentions and replacing them with yours using pressure or persuasion other than physical power.

UTMA (Uniform Transfer to Minors). Most people are wary of giving money to minor children. Enter the Uniform Transfer to Minors Act (UTMA). The minor's property is given to a custodian for the benefit of the minor. The custodian manages the assets and may use the assets for the benefit of the minor, as long as they aren't spent to fulfill the custodian's support obligations if the custodian is the parent. In general, the assets must be turned over to the minor at age 21. It is possible for wills, trusts and beneficiary designations to include the deferral of the distribution age up to age 25. To specify an age older than 21, you must change the wording of the custodianship language in the will or trust to Adult Smith "as custodian for Minor Smith *until age 25* under the Pennsylvania Uniform Transfers to Minors Act."

Viatical Settlement. A viatical settlement (from the Latin "*Viaticum*") is the sale of a policy owner's existing <u>life insurance</u> policy to a third party for more than its <u>cash surrender value</u>, but less than its net death benefit. Such a sale provides the policy owner with an lump sum. The third party becomes the new owner of the policy, pays the monthly premiums, and receives the full benefit of the policy when the insured dies.

Ward. A person, referring to a child or incompetent, who needs the care of the court and the supervision of a guardian.

Wash Sale Rule. The equal exchange through sale and purchasing of a same or similar asset within a short time period.

WROS (With Right of Survivorships). To increase the ease and speed of the transfer of certain assets, it may be helpful to have them designated as jointly owned with rights of survivorship.

INDEX

Symbols

A

B

C

F

G

H

I

J

K

L

Q

R

S

Z

Made in the USA
San Bernardino, CA
27 December 2015